A HISTORY
OF THE LABOUR PARTY
FROM 1914

A HISTORY
OF THE LABOUR PARTY
FROM 1914

by

G. D. H. COLE

*Chichele Professor of Social
and Political Theory
Oxford University*

ROUTLEDGE & KEGAN PAUL
LONDON, HENLEY AND BOSTON

First published in 1948
by Routledge & Kegan Paul Ltd
39 Store Street,
London WC1E 7DD,
Broadway House,
Newtown Road,
Henley-on-Thames,
Oxon RG9 1EN and
9 Park Street,
Boston, Mass. 02108, USA
Reprinted 1950, 1969, 1978
Printed in Great Britain by
Weatherby Woolnough, Wellingborough, Northants

ISBN 0 7100 6628 7

TABLE OF CONTENTS

LIST OF TABLES

PREFACE

I published in 1941 a volume entitled *British Working-Class Politics, 1832-1914*, in which I dealt both with earlier ventures in Labour politics and with the history of the Labour Representation Committee and the Labour Party up to the outbreak of the first World War. The present volume is a sequel to this earlier work. The Great War of 1914-18 brought with it a sharp break in the history of the Labour Party, which had been up to 1914 only a small fourth Party in a Parliament still dominated by Liberals and Conservatives, as well as complicated by the presence of a large Nationalist Party from Ireland. Only during the war years did the Labour Party reorganise itself on a truly national basis, with the aim of taking over from the divided Liberals the position which they had forfeited and of becoming a claimant to power. Accordingly, the present volume tells the complete story from the emergence of the Labour Party as a national parliamentary force. I have stopped the historical record at 1945, because the time has not yet come for passing historical judgment on the work of the first Labour Government to take office in Great Britain with a clear majority behind it. It may be possible for me to carry the story further in a future edition when the achievement of the Labour Government during the whole life of the Parliament elected in 1945 can be better assessed.

In writing this book I have relied mainly on the published records of the Party, on the newspapers, and on my own recollections and researches into the records of the earlier movements. I have neither sought nor obtained any access to confidential information. I have, however, particularly to thank Mr. Michael Young and Miss Rose Davy, of the Labour Party Head Office, for a number of valuable suggestions, and Mr. John McNair, General Secretary of the Independent Labour Party, for help in obtaining access to documents which I do not myself possess. I have also to thank Alderman D. H. Daines, Secretary of the London Labour Party, for information used in the chapter on Local Government, and Mr. John Taylor, Secretary of the Labour Party Scottish Council, for information concerning the Labour Party's activities in Scottish local government, as well as a number of good Socialists who were kind enough to help me in filling up the gaps in my file of Labour Party Reports.

Hendon, December, 1947.   G.D.H.C.

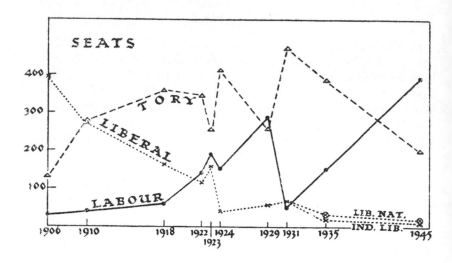

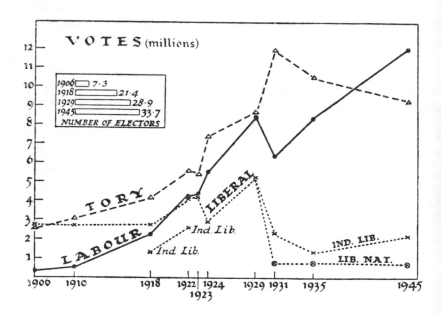

SEATS AND VOTES AT GENERAL ELECTIONS 1906–45
Main Parties only

x

CHAPTER I

THE LABOUR PARTY IN 1914

(a) Introductory

General Elections of 1906 and 1910—The Osborne Judgment—The National Insurance Act—Wages and Prices and Industrial Unrest—By-elections from 1910–14—The Labour Party's fortunes on the ebb—Labour and Liberalism in the pre-war Parliaments—How far was the Labour Party Socialist?—The position of the I.L.P.—Analysis of the Election of December, 1910—Labour as a Minority Party—The absence of Local Party Organisation—Woolwich and Barnard Castle—The I.L.P. and the Trade Unions—The Labour Party and the Second International—The Second International's policy on war and peace—The Stuttgart resolution—The events leading to the war of 1914—Liberal diplomacy and Labour reactions.

(b) Organisation

Labour Party membership in 1914—Membership of the I.L.P. and the British Socialist Party—Local Labour Parties and Labour Associations—Trades Councils and Trades and Labour Councils—Analysis of local organisation—I.L.P. Branches and Federations—The position in Lancashire and Cheshire—in Yorkshire—in Wales—in the Northern Counties—in the Midlands—in the Eastern Counties—in the South—in the West and South-west—in Scotland—in Greater London—The Second International and Socialist Unity—The I.L.P., the Fabian Society and the British Socialist Party—Attempts to form a United Socialist Council—The question of Labour and Socialist candidates and that of " Progressive " candidates—The position of the Miners' Federation—The I.L.P. and the Trade Unions.

(a) Introductory

In 1914, when the first World War began, the Labour Party had been in effective existence for only eight years. It had been created, as a party, in the General Election of 1906, which sent the Liberals back to power with an overwhelming majority ; and the great majority of its seats had been won with the aid of Liberal votes. For the first four years, from 1906 to 1909, it had been in a position, when and if it wished, to act pretty much in independence of the Liberals, whose majority was too big to be endangered by anything it did ; but in practice it had usually found itself supporting Liberal measures of social reform. Its chief success, as a party, had come right at the beginning, when it forced the Liberals, tied by their own election pledges, to accept the complete reversal of the Taff Vale Judgment by passing the Trade Disputes Act of 1906.

After 1909, the situation had been different. The General Elections of 1910, fought mainly on the issues raised by Lloyd George's Land Tax Budget of 1909 and by the Lords' rejection of it, had cost the Liberals enough seats to leave the Government dependent on Labour and Irish votes ; and the Labour Party,

with its very existence menaced by the Osborne Judgment*
and in view of its agreement with the Liberals over the Budget,
the Lords, and Irish Home Rule, could not afford to risk the
Government's fall. It was thus tied, as a very junior partner, to
the fortunes of the Liberal Party ; and its position was complicated by the sharp differences of opinion within its own ranks over
the social insurance legislation of 1911. A section of the party,
headed by Philip Snowden, denounced the contributory principle
and regarded the National Insurance Bill as an anti-Socialist
measure designed to make the poor pay for the poor ; whereas
most of the Trade Unionists in the party saw in it a means of
strengthening the bargaining position of the Trade Unions as well
as of reducing the hardships of sickness and unemployment. There
were thus divided voices inside the party at a time when, in any
event, its hands were largely tied ; and in relation to the section
of the electorate to which it had to look for support—the Trade
Unionists in the main centres of industry—its influence was
waning because it seemed able to do so little to focus parliamentary attention on working-class grievances. Rising prices, with
wages lagging behind, were leading to a growth of industrial
militancy and to a preaching of " direct action " doctrines which
denied the effectiveness of parliamentary proceedings and denounced the Labour parliamentarians as " collaborationists "
whose compromising tactics blurred the realities of the class-war.
Syndicalism and Industrial Unionism were in the air, and owed
their vogue not only to the lag in real wages but also to the
catchingness of the militancy of the women suffragists and of the
Ulster diehards and their English Conservative allies.

Between the General Election of December, 1910, and the
outbreak of war the Labour Party fought fourteen by-elections,
without a single success. Indeed, it actually lost four seats, three
through the death of ex-Liberal-Labour miners and one when

---

*The Osborne Judgment, given in the House of Lords on a case brought by a
certain W. V. Osborne against his Trade Union, the Amalgamated Society of Railway
Servants, declared all political action by Trade Unions to be *ultra vires*. It thus
prevented Trade Unions from either putting forward their own candidates at national
or local elections or subscribing out of their funds to any political party. This judgment struck away the main foundation of the Labour Party finances, and caused it to
contest the two General Elections of 1910 under a serious handicap. The effect of the
judgment was reversed in 1913, when the Trade Union Act legalised political expenditure by Trade Unions on condition (a) that such expenditure was to be met only
from a separate Political Fund ; (b) that such a fund should be set up only after a
ballot vote of the members had given a favourable decision ; and (c) that any member
of the Union concerned who objected to contributing to the Political Fund should be
allowed to sign a form " contracting-out " of payment of the Political Levy, without
thereby forfeiting any of his other rights as a member of the Union.

George Lansbury, disagreeing with his party's attitude on the issue of Women's Suffrage, resigned and fought a by-election as an independent champion of the women's cause. In addition, seven by-elections were fought by Socialist Independents, where official Labour failed to produce a candidate ; but they were all heavily beaten. Labour's political fortunes in 1914 were on the ebb, and the hopes aroused by the advent of the party in 1906 had suffered a sad reverse.

No doubt, to a great extent this setback was not the Labour Party's fault. It could not help playing second fiddle to the Liberals, first in the struggle over the Land Tax Budget and then over Irish Home Rule. It was badly handicapped by the Osborne Judgment, which had upset its financial basis ; and it was in a real difficulty over Women's Suffrage, because it was not pre-pared to give the women's claims priority over everything else. But, when all this has been admitted, the Labour Party's own shortcomings still appear serious enough ; for, in sober truth, it had no clearly conceived policy of its own and was made up of elements which were too discrepant to provide the basis for an effective fighting party.

Right up to 1914 the Labour Party neither stood, nor pro-fessed to stand, for Socialism. There were, of course, Socialists in its ranks and Socialist Societies affiliated to it and playing a large part in its work : indeed, most of its leaders were Socialists and so, probably, were a majority of its members. But in its ranks were quite a number who neither were, nor called themselves Socialists ; and behind these men were Trade Unions, as yet precariously attached to the Labour Party, and by no means ready to insist that their candidates must profess the Socialist faith. The Fabian leaders, intent on their policy of " permea-tion " and sceptical of the Labour Party's prospects, were hardly more than lukewarm supporters right up to 1914. The I.L.P., its largest affiliated Socialist Society, and in effect its creator, of course stood for Socialism, but the I.L.P. leaders inside the Labour Party were in no mind to jeopardise its unity by pressing too hard upon the Trade Union section The L.R.C. had been based on a compromise whereby Trade Unionists and Socialists had agreed to work together under the banner of " Labour " without raising awkward questions about who were Socialists and who were not ; and Ramsay MacDonald, of the I.L.P., was as set as Arthur Henderson, of the Friendly Society of Ironfounders, who was then barely a Socialist, or as other

Trade Union leaders who were not Socialists in any sense of the term, on keeping strictly to the terms of the compact. The Trade Union leaders who sat in the Parliaments of 1906 to 1914 included some who had fought side by side with Keir Hardie to make the Independent Labour Party a success—men such as G. N. Barnes, John Hodge, and J. R. Clynes. It included at any rate one old stalwart of the Social Democratic Federation—Will Thorne, of the Gasworkers' Union. But it was heavily weighed down on the right by men who had changed their party at the behest of their Trade Union without therewith changing their opinions ; and this right wing of the party was the stronger in influence because most of the rest were well aware that they held their seats upon Liberal sufferance, and with the support of Liberal votes.

Of the forty-two Labour M.P.s elected in December, 1910, twenty-seven had been elected in straight fights against Conservatives, and one (in Scotland) against a Liberal with no Conservative in the field. Three had been returned unopposed ; and eleven had been elected in two-member constituencies in which only one Labour candidate had been put forward. All these eleven had Liberal colleagues in the representation ; and among the eleven were Keir Hardie, MacDonald, Snowden, Thomas, and G. H. Roberts. Not one Labour M.P. had been elected in the eleven three-cornered contests, and only one, a Scottish miner, against a Liberal opponent. Any serious clash with the Liberal Government might have endangered every Labour seat, except perhaps a very few which were " pocket boroughs " of the Miners' Federation. Of course, a clash would also have endangered many Liberal seats, where the M.P.s were dependent upon Labour votes. The Liberals had good cause for keeping on friendly terms with the Labour Party, as well as the Labour Party for keeping in with the Liberals. Nevertheless, the effect was that the party could not easily assert itself or show a bold front ; and it was in fact in continual difficulties with its own Left Wing, which denounced it for not fighting by-elections except where the Liberals could be persuaded to stand down, and in particular for refusing to allow a second Labour candidate to enter the lists in any double-barrelled constituency where there was an informal pact between Liberals and Labour to share the seats.

It needs to be emphasised that right up to 1914 the Labour Party was making no real claim to be more than a minority party, with a mission to press working-class claims in Parliament, but with no immediate prospect of challenging the predominance of the two great traditional parties. In 1906 the Labour Party fought only fifty-one seats (*plus* five fought by the separate Scottish Workers' Representation Committee). It fought eighty-one seats in January, 1910. when it had been reinforced by the accession of most of the miners, and had absorbed the S.W.R.C. ; but in December 1910, it fought only fifty-seven, in an election which caught it seriously short of funds, as well as reluctant to jeopardise the Parliament Bill by three-cornered contests. Even if all its candidates had been elected, it would have been smaller than the Irish Nationalist Party. In the great majority of constituencies, including almost all the county areas outside the coalfields, there was no sort of Labour electoral organisation—not even a struggling I.L.P. branch. Except in Woolwich and in Barnard Castle, where Will Crooks and Arthur Henderson had built up their own independent local organisations, the Labour Party had no individual members. In most places where it was organised, it worked through a local Trades and Labour Council or a group of Miners' Lodges, or depended almost entirely on the local branch of the I.L.P. Two-thirds of all the seats fought by Labour in December, 1910, were in the North or in South Wales : over a large part of the country not a single Labour candidate took the field. How localised Labour political activity still was can be seen from the accompanying Table.

Thus, in 1914, the political Labour movement was still at a rudimentary stage of development, and, except at election times,

DISTRIBUTION OF LABOUR SEATS IN PARLIAMENT, 1914 AND OF SEATS CONTESTED IN JANUARY OR DECEMBER, 1910

	M.P.s in 1914	Seats contested in either Election, 1910	Additional seats contested by Independent Socialists
Scotland	3	12	1
North-east	4	7	—
North-west	1	2	1
Lancs and Cheshire	10	21	3
Yorkshire	6	13	3
Midlands	6	11	2
Eastern Counties	1	1	—
Greater London	3	5	3
South	0	3	—
Wales and Monmouth	5	9	—
N. Ireland	0	1	—
	39	85	13

the I.L.P. still counted for a good deal more over most of the country than the Labour Party of which it was nominally a part. The outstanding leaders of the Labour Party in Parliament, except Arthur Henderson and J. H. Thomas, were much more closely associated in their everyday work with the I.L.P. than with the Labour Party ; and in effect the work of framing Labour policy and of gaining adherents was left mainly to the I.L.P., though its views were always liable to be over-ridden either at the Labour Party Conference, where the Trade Unions had the decisive voice if they chose to use it, or at party meetings, where most of the Miners' members and some of the other Trade Union representatives were still inclined to put a brake on any action that might be liable to cause a breach with the Liberals.

No doubt the Labour Party had been since 1904 affiliated to the Socialist International, to which the leading British Socialist bodies—the I.L.P., the Fabian Society, and the British Socialist Party—also independently belonged.   There had been many hesitations on both sides over the admission of the Labour Party to the International, which included the " class war " among its tenets and rested on professedly Marxian foundations.   The difficulty had been overcome, on Karl Kautsky's motion, by admitting the Labour Party as a party which practised the class war, even though it refused to preach it ; but the Party had not in fact taken its affiliation very seriously, though it had participated in the discussions in which, during the pre-war decade, the International had been attempting to define its attitude to war and to devise means of preventing it by the united action of the working class.   There had been much discussion of the project of an international general strike to stop any war between the nations ; and this very question was down for consideration at the Vienna Conference which was due to meet in August, 1914. In the meantime, the action of the affiliated parties towards any threat of war, and in face of its outbreak should their efforts fail to prevent it, had been laid down at the Stuttgart Conference of 1907, and reaffirmed three years later at Copenhagen. The declaration of the International on this issue was worded as follows :—

If war threatens to break out, it is the duty of the working class in the countries concerned and of their parliamentary representatives, with the help of the International Socialist Bureau as a means of coordinating their action, to use every effort to prevent war by all the means which seem to them most appropriate, having regard to the sharpness of the class war and to the general political situation ;

Should war none the less break out, their duty is to intervene to bring it promptly to an end, and with all their energies to use the political and economic crisis created by the war to rouse the populace from its slumbers, and to hasten the fall of capitalist domination.

This resolution, which was the result of a compromise unanimously endorsed after long debate, obviously failed to face up to essential considerations. At the back of it was the assumption, made consciously by some of the delegates but by no means by all, that from the standpoint of the working classes in any war between the nations the question of who was in the right or wrong simply would not arise. It was assumed that in the first instance the Socialists of all countries, including those of the prospective belligerents, would feel able to act together in an attempt to stop the war, without being inhibited by any conflicts of opinion concerning the responsibility for provoking it. Still larger was the assumption that, should war actually break out, the workers of the belligerent countries would be indifferent about its military outcome and would be prepared to take united anti-war action and to concentrate their efforts on " hastening the fall of capitalist domination "—a phrase which, if seriously meant, implied revolutionary action against their own Governments. In fact, it even appeared, in 1914, that, though nearly all the Socialist Parties in the International were prepared to demonstrate against war prior to its outbreak, most of them were not prepared, even at this stage, to attempt any action designed to make war impossible by hampering the military preparations of their own States. Even less were most of them prepared, when war had actually broken out, to do anything that would prejudice their own country's aims, or play into the hands of its enemies. Nor, had the leaders of the various parties been prepared to act up to the terms of the International's resolution, would the majority of the workers in most countries have been prepared to follow them.

Great wars happen neither without cause, nor for causes which are plain and simple, so that everyone can agree about them. The first link in the chain of events which led up *immediately* to the Great War of 1914 was the Austro-Hungarian ultimatum to Serbia, following upon the murder of the Archduke Charles at Serajevo. This ultimatum brought in Russia on the side of Serbia ; and the Russian move promptly brought in Germany to support Austria-Hungary. The action of Germany involved France, which was allied to Russia ; and as soon as France became involved, the question of British participation was bound to arise, because Great Britain was closely linked to France by an *Entente* openly directed against German expansion. Actually the Germans, in deciding to violate Belgium's guaranteed neutrality in order to find a quick way of overcoming France, made the entry of Great Britain into the war certain, by bringing over a great mass of public opinion that might have been reluctant to sanction participation in a struggle with which Great Britain appeared to have no direct concern. But even when the violation of Belgium has been added to the chain of immediate causes, it remains clear that these causes mean nothing except in relation to a sequence of earlier events which had led the European Powers to group themselves in a certain way. War had nearly broken out several times in the twentieth century before 1914 ; and on each occasion the potential line-up of the Great Powers (including Italy's ambiguous attitude) had been much the same. The underlying cause of the first World War is to be sought in this system of Great Power relations and rivalries : the Austro-Serbian dispute was no more than the match that finally set the train alight.

This, of course, does not necessarily mean that there were no rights and wrongs about the matter, either in its immediate aspects or in relation to the underlying factors. In a sense, it is clear enough that in the Great War of 1914–18, the Germans and their allies were the aggressors ; for in relation to the existing set-up of European affairs they were the discontented parties, whereas their opponents would have been well content to let things stay as they were. There were, however, many who held this to be much too simplified an explanation of the causes of the war, and laid a large part of the blame on the diplomacy of Sir Edward Grey and of the Liberal Imperialists inside the Cabinet. These men, they held, had been responsible for the fatal line-up of the great Powers of Europe into two contending groups, for the alliance with reactionary Russia, and for the commitment to support France's manœuvres for the leadership of a continental coalition directed against Germany. Such critics had, of course, for the most part no wish to exonerate the German leaders from at least an equal share of the blame : they put the onus of bringing the war about either on " power politics and secret diplomacy "— the Liberal bugbears—or, if they were Socialists, on " the capitalist-imperialist system," as the factor underlying great power rivalries and leading the nations on to war.

This book is not the place for any attempt at evaluation of these opinions. What the present writer thought about them at the time can be found in his *Labour in War-time*, published in 1915. What concerns us here is the reaction of the war situation on the British Labour movement and more particularly on the Labour Party, with its federal structure as an alliance of Socialists and Trade Unionists on the basis of a programme and a policy not definitely Socialist, but Socialist enough to have led the party to become and to be accepted as an affiliated section of the Second International.

(b) Organisation

When war broke out in 1914, the Labour Party had approximately 1,600,000 affiliated members connected with it through Trade Unions, and 33,000 on whom affiliation fees were paid by the two Socialist Societies. The I.L.P. paid dues on 30,000 members, and the Fabian Society on 3,304. In the case of the I.L.P. the actual membership was doubtless considerably greater, as many of its branches paid dues to its own head office on much less than their full membership, and the head office itself paid at most only in accordance with what it received. When the British Socialist Party was accepted as an additional affiliated body, it paid on 10,000 members ; but its application to join, though made before the outbreak of war, was not accepted until January, 1916, no Conference being held in 1915 owing to the war situation. If we count the B.S.P., there were perhaps as many as 65,000 individual members enrolled in the three Socialist Societies.

In 1914, as we have seen, the Labour Party itself had no individual members, though in a very few constituencies—notably Woolwich and Barnard Castle—there were local Labour Parties or Associations which enrolled individuals as members. Elsewhere the local organisation was in the hands of a variety of federal bodies, which were in many cases simply the local Trades Councils formed for mainly industrial purposes, in others the Trades Councils with representatives of the local Socialist Societies added, and in yet others specially formed Local Labour Parties. In all, the local constituents of the Labour Party in 1914 were made up as follows :

LABOUR PARTY LOCAL ORGANISATION IN 1914

Mainly Industrial			Mainly Political		
Trades Councils	. . .	74	Local Labour Parties	. .	34
Trades and Labour Councils	.	11	Labour Representation Committees	. . .	25
Trades Councils and Labour Representation Committees or Labour Parties (combined)		5	Labour Associations	. .	6
Labour Councils or Leagues	.	3			
		93			65

Thus the Labour Party had some sort of local organisation in only 158 areas, except where it was in effect represented by a branch of the I.L.P. It had an organisation designed mainly for political, as distinct from industrial, purposes in only sixty-five places. A number of these places were big towns, where a single organisation covered more than one constituency ; but even when allowance has been made for this factor, it remains true that in the great majority of constituencies the Labour Party had, in 1914, no organisation at all of its own, and in the majority not even a Trades Council acting as its agent. As against this, the Independent Labour Patry had in 1914 no fewer than 672 branches, covering a much wider field. The figures are not comparable, because in a number of large towns the I.L.P. had several branches, linked up in a Federation of their own. Moreover, many of the I.L.P.'s branches were very small : only 244 of them were actually represented at the I.L.P.'s "Coming-of-Age" Conference held at Bradford in 1914. Even so, it is plain that a very large part of the Labour Party's local organisation was still in the hands of the I.L.P., which was in effect in most places both the natural organisation for active Labour propagandists to join and the only body which kept up any sort of continuous political activity between elections.

Let us look rather more closely into the situation in the various parts of Great Britain. In Lancashire and Cheshire there were eighteen Local Labour Parties and twenty-four areas in which the local Trades Councils or Trades and Labour Councils acted as local agencies for the Labour Party. Liverpool, Manchester and Salford, Blackburn, Rochdale and Wigan had Local Labour Parties ; but in Birkenhead, Oldham, Preston, Stockport and Warrington the Trades Councils were the bodies affiliated to the central Labour Party. Barrow-in-Furness and St. Helens had combined Trades and Labour Councils. In the case of Manchester and Salford, though there was a Local Labour Party, the Trades Council also was affiliated to the Labour Party nationally. All these areas had also I.L.P. branches, one or more ; and the British Socialist Party also had a number of branches in the area. There were four local Fabian Societies, in Liverpool, Manchester, Blackburn and Darwen.

Or take Yorkshire. There were only four Local Labour Parties in all—at York, Holmfirth, Normanton and Sowerby, as against fifteen affiliated Trades Councils, including Leeds, Sheffield, Bradford, Huddersfield and Hull, and one Trades and Labour Council, at Halifax. The I.L.P., however, was strong in all the large towns, and had branches throughout the textile and engineering area, though not many in the coalfield. There were a number of B.S.P. branches, and three Fabian Societies—at Sheffield, York and Hull.

In Wales there were five Local Labour Parties, and two Local Labour Associations (Llanelly and Swansea) ; but there were only four affiliated Trades Councils. In North and Central Wales there was hardly any organisation at all, and over most of South Wales nothing except the Lodges and Districts of the South Wales Miners' Federation, the branches of the Steel Smelters, and the fairly numerous I.L.P. branches, together with a few belonging to the B.S.P. There was one small Fabian Group, at Swansea.

In the four Northern Counties, or rather in the coalfields and the bigger towns in them, organisation was comparatively good. There were nine Local Labour Parties and three Labour Associations, as compared with three Trades Councils affiliated to the national Party. There were Local Labour Parties at Newcastle, Gateshead, South Shields, Jarrow, and Sunderland, and also in the mining constituencies of Wansbeck and North-West Durham, and in Whitehaven and Egremont, in Cumberland. Barnard Castle, Bishop Auckland, and the Hartlepools had Local Labour Associations. Darlington, Carlisle and Workington operated through Trades Councils. The I.L.P. had branches in most of the towns and in a good number of colliery villages ; and the B.S.P. was also strong in Newcastle-on-Tyne. Newcastle and Sunderland had local Fabian Societies.

In the Midlands, East and West, there were in all only seven Local Labour Parties, three Trades and Labour Councils, and thirteen Trades Councils doing political work. Birmingham, Nottingham, Stoke-on-Trent, Coventry and Leicester had Local

Labour Parties ; but Derby, Lincoln and most of the smaller towns had only Trades Councils, or even no organisation at all. The I.L.P. was strong in Birmingham and Leicester, and had a good many scattered branches ; and Northampton was an old centre of both I.L.P. and B.S.P. activity. But the coalfields were still largely under Liberal control, a number of the Miners' leaders having refused to give up their Liberal allegiance when the Miners' Federation joined the Labour Party in 1909. There were only two Fabian Societies—Leicester and Chesterfield—in the entire Midland region.

In the Eastern Counties there were Local Labour Parties at Cambridge and Ipswich, and a Trades and Labour Council at Yarmouth. Norwich had a Trades Council. Norwich and Ipswich were I.L.P. strongholds, but elsewhere even the I.L.P. had only a few struggling branches. Ipswich and Chelmsford had Fabian Societies. So had Luton, with a Trades and Labour Council. That was all.

The South, apart from London, was mainly a Labour desert, There were Local Labour Parties at Gravesend and at Eastleigh. and a Trades and Labour Council at Guildford. Chatham, Hastings, Portsmouth and Southampton had affiliated Trades Councils. I.L.P. branches were few—Portsmouth, Southampton, Bournemouth, Eastleigh, Gillingham, and a few more. Dover had a Fabian Society.

In the West and South-west there were only patches of organisation—four Local Labour Parties, at Bristol, Cheltenham, Gloucester and Devonport ; one affiliated Trades Council, at Swindon ; I.L.P. branches at Bristol, Gloucester, Exeter, Stroud and a few other places ; a very few B.S.P. branches ; and a Fabian Society at Bristol. Bristol, indeed, was almost the only well-organised district.

In Scotland there were five Local Labour Parties, at Glasgow, Edinburgh, Aberdeen, Dundee and Montrose, three Trades Councils, at Glasgow (a second case of double affiliation), Greenock and Coatbridge, and two Trades and Labour Councils, at Leith and Paisley. In the coalfields, organisation was left largely to the Scottish Miners' Federation ; but the I.L.P. had more branches in Scotland than in any other of its Divisions, the B.S.P. had quite a number, and, well outside the Labour Party, the extreme Marxist Socialist Labour Party had a substantial following on Clydeside. Glasgow, Edinburgh, Perth and Dundee had local Fabian Societies.

Finally, in Greater London there were five Local Labour Parties, three of them outside the L.C.C. area, and also local Labour Associations at Deptford and at Woolwich. Four areas had combined Trades and Labour Councils, and six had Trades Councils affiliated to the Labour Party, in addition to the London Trades Council, covering the inner London area. The I.L.P. and the B.S.P. were both fairly widespread ; and the Fabian Society had its main membership in London. The Metropolitan district was, however, on the whole rather weakly organised. At the General Election of December, 1910, the Labour Party had won only three London seats—Deptford, Woolwich, and Bow and Bromley—and had fought only one other seat.

Of course, there were other Trades Councils, not mentioned in this analysis, because they were not affiliated to the Labour Party. On the other hand, many of the Councils that were affiliated took their allegiance very lightly and engaged in very little political work, even in local government affairs. The I.L.P. estimated that in the local government elections of 1913 there were in all fewer than 500 Labour and Socialist candidates, of whom 228 were put forward by the I.L.P. Just under 200, including 109 I.L.P. candidates, were elected—a net gain of eighty-five seats.

Just before 1914 the Second International had been engaged in a campaign for Socialist Unity in each country. The British Section of the International then included, besides the Labour Party, which appointed representatives of the Trades Union Congress as members of its delegation, the three leading Socialist Societies—the I.L.P., the Fabian Society, and the B.S.P. Each of these was separately affiliated to the International, had its own members in the British Section, and sent its own delegations to International Socialist Congresses. The International wanted the British Societies to come together into a united body. The I.L.P. and the Fabian Society already had a joint Committee, mainly for educational and lecturing work, but felt no need to carry unity further, as they worked along essentially different and complementary lines. The position of the British Socialist Party was another matter. It had been formed only in 1911, by the fusion of the Social Democratic Party (formerly the S.D.F.) with a number of left-wing groups, largely seceders from the I L.P. The B.S.P. was not affiliated to the Labour Party, which indeed it was accustomed fiercely to denounce for its compromises with capitalist Liberalism and for its refusal to wage, or to preach, the class war. The B.S.P. was Marxist, and had gathered most of the

left-wing malcontents into its ranks—except the still more extreme
adherents of the Socialist Labour Party (in Scotland) and the
Socialist Party of Great Britain (mainly in London), both of which
had left the S.D.F. because it did not go far enough. These two,
not being connected with the International, were not invited to
the Unity negotiations. A Committee representing the other
three, under pressure from the International Socialist Bureau,
agreed, not to fusion, which was rejected as impracticable, but
to the formation of a United Socialist Council, on condition
that it should be open only to bodies affiliated to the Labour Party.
When, however, the representatives met again, after reporting to
their respective Societies, a fresh issue arose, out of a demand from
the B.S.P. that candidates standing under Labour Party auspices
should be allowed to describe themselves as not merely " Labour,"
but, if they wished, " Labour and Socialist." The joint committee agreed that a proposal to allow this should be laid before
the next Labour Party Conference ; but when the proposal was
reported to the I.L.P. Conference of 1914, the delegates rejected
it, mainly on the ground that it would open the door to other
proposals from bodies which might wish to put forward candidates as " Labour and Progressive," or even " Labour and
Liberal." Several of the County Miners' Associations had been
insisting on putting forward candidates in association with the
Liberals, and their exclusion had cost the Labour Party several
coalfield seats. The I.L.P. was not prepared, in the interests of
unity with the B.S.P., whose leaders it much disliked, to risk
encouraging further " Lib-Lab " activities ; and accordingly it
rejected the B.S.P. plan. It did, however, agree to support the
B.S.P.'s application for affiliation to the Labour Party ; and this,
as we have seen, was ultimately accepted in 1916, after a long
delay due to the postponement of the 1915 Labour Party Conference.

Meanwhile, a Socialist Unity Demonstration Committee,
formed at the end of 1913, had held a series of demonstrations in
favour of unity, addressed by leading speakers from the three
Socialist Societies, including Keir Hardie, H. M. Hyndman,
Sidney Webb, and Bernard Shaw. But the Fabian Annual
Conference of 1914, after hearing addresses by Hardie and
Hyndman, voted to proceed to the next business, mainly because,
like the I.L.P., it was not prepared to run the risks involved in the
proposal to allow candidates to run on a " Labour and Socialist "
ticket. Then came the war, and despite further attempts by the

B.S.P. to stir the other bodies into action, the project of Socialist Unity was quietly shelved. Indeed, the B.S.P. itself was in process of splitting into pro-war and anti-war factions. Hyndman and Robert Blatchford were strongly in favour of the war, whereas the majority of the members took up an anti-war line. In 1916, the B.S.P. having voted down the followers of Hyndman, a number of the old stalwarts of the Social Democratic Federation seceded and set up the National Socialist Party, which joined the Labour Party, and, a few years later, resumed the old name, and became the S.D.F.

The " Unity " plan had, in fact, never stood any real chance of success. The Fabians were throughout quite unwilling to merge their identity, as a society concerned mainly with research and education and with the conversion of the " intellectuals," in a general propagandist body, and especially in one in which they would become utterly eclipsed. The I.L.P. leaders, even when they were critical of the Labour Party, were determined to do nothing that might risk breaking their alliance with the Trade Unions—the more so because most of them were bitterly opposed to Hyndman's doctrinaire Marxism, and scornful of the mixed assembly of malcontents that had joined forces under the B.S.P. banner. The B.S.P., for its part, wanted Unity, but only on terms which would preserve its full freedom to attack the Labour Party from within and to denounce the compromising policies of MacDonald and other I.L.P. leaders as well as of Henderson and the Labour Party head office. The conditions of acute labour unrest of the years just before 1914 had put the Socialist rank and file into a mood to wish for unity ; and the I.L.P. leaders did not venture to attack it openly. But most of them were glad when the outbreak of war, by creating a new situation, enabled them to drop negotiations for which they had never felt any enthusiasm. Even a common opposition to the war did not suffice to unite the I.L.P. and the B.S.P., though, as we shall see, it did presently lead to a renewal of negotiations on a somewhat different basis.

CHAPTER II

LABOUR IN WAR-TIME

(a) The First Phase

The outbreak of war in 1914—International Socialist action—The British Section of the Second International—MacDonald resigns the Leadership : Arthur Henderson becomes Leader—The Labour Party's attitude to the war—The War Emergency Workers' National Committee—The I.L.P. Manifesto of August, 1914—Labour and the recruiting campaign—The Vienna International Socialist Conference abandoned—The anti-war group in the House of Commons—The Labour War Manifesto of October, 1914—The Labour Party Conference postponed—The I.L.P. Conference of Easter, 1915—The International Socialist Bureau in war-time—Attempts to secure an international Socialist meeting—Allied Labour and Socialist Conference of February, 1915—French refusal to meet the Germans—The Allied Socialist Manifesto—Effects of the war on employment—War-time dilution of labour—The Treasury Agreements of 1915—The Government sets up a National Labour Advisory Committee—The Industrial Truce—The Munitions of War Act of 1915—The First Coalition Government, May, 1915—Henderson joins the Government—The I.L.P. opposes the Coalition—John Hodge becomes Acting Leader of the Labour Party—The South Wales mining crisis of 1915—The conscription issue and the Derby Scheme—Labour's attitude to conscription—The Bristol Conference of January, 1916—Labour and the extension of conscription—Troubles over dilution—The Clyde Workers' Committee and the Clyde deportations—Keir Hardie's death and its effects—Police raids on the Socialist bodies—The Zimmerwald Conference of December, 1915—The I.L.P. and the Zimmerwald Conference—Henderson becomes Labour Adviser to the Government—Fall of the Asquith Coalition : Lloyd George Prime Minister—Labour in the Lloyd George Coalition.

(b) The Second Phase

President Wilson's Peace Note and the Allied answer—The Labour Party on post-war problems—Lloyd George advises " audacity "—The May Strikes of 1917 and the Shop Stewards' Movement—The first Russian Revolution—The Leeds Conference of June, 1917—The Stockholm Conference proposal—Labour's attitude to the Stockholm Conference—The Kerensky Government in Russia—Henderson's Russian Mission—Henderson's return from Russia—His advocacy of the Stockholm Conference—The Labour Conferences on Stockholm—Composition of the British delegation—Henderson resigns from the Government and gives up the Party Leadership—Further negotiations about Stockholm—The Stockholm Conference abandoned—The Statement of Allied War Aims—The Trades Union Congress on international policy—The Shop Stewards and the Commissions on Labour Unrest—The second Russian Revolution and its effects—President Wilson's Fourteen Points—The Allied Labour and Socialist Conference on War Aims—Reorganisation of the Labour Party—The Representation of the People Act, 1918—The Bolsheviks dissolve the Constituent Assembly—The Brest-Litovsk Treaty—Development of Left-wing Movements in Great Britain—The I.L.P. and the Bolsheviks—The Manpower Crisis in Great Britain—The Trade Unions formulate their post-war programmes—Guild Socialism and Workers' Control—Preparations for International Socialist action—American Labour and the Peace Conference—Collapse of the Central Powers—The Sailors' and Firemen's Union and the International—The Labour Party leaves the Coalition—Bernard Shaw's speech—Action of Coalition Labour Ministers.

(c) The New Labour Party of 1918

The New Labour Party Constitution of 1918—The development of local organisation and of individual membership—The Trade Unions and the Party—The new Constitution and the I.L.P.—The I.L.P.'s Leicester Conference of 1918—I.L.P.

reactions to the new Labour Party—The attitude of Ramsay MacDonald—The
question of Trade Union domination—The National Executive under the new
Constitution—The Labour Party and the International Socialist Bureau—Attempts
to form a separate Trade Union Party—Local Labour Parties and women's representation on the National Executive—Elimination of the Trades Councils from the
Party—The Trades Councils and the T.U.C.—The growth of Local Labour Party
organisation—The position of the Co-operative Movement—The Trade Unions
accept the new Constitution—Composition of the new Executive—Relations between the Executive and the Parliamentary Party—Rights of candidates at Elections and in Parliament—The formulation of a new programme—The Labour
Party declares for Socialism—*Labour and the New Social Order*—Sidney Webb—State
Socialism and Industrial Democracy—" The Democratic Control of Industry "—
The discussions on *Labour and the New Social Order*—*Labour and the New Social Order*
analysed—Evolutionary Socialism—" The Four Pillars of the House of To-
morrow "—The employment problem and the Right to Work—Public Ownership
—The revolution in national finance—The National Minimum and the Capital
Levy—Services proposed for Nationalisation—Bulk purchase and control of essen-
tial industries—Costing and price-fixing—Fabianism and the Labour Party—
Arthur Henderson's policy—Trade Union and I.L.P. attitudes to *Labour and the New
Social Order*—Its reception in the world as a whole—Foundation of the Co-operative
Party—History of earlier attempts at Co-operative politics—The Co-operative
Representation Committee and the Co-operative Party—Relations between the
Co-operative Movement, the Trade Unions and the Labour Party—The first
Co-operative candidate—Divided opinion among Co-operators.

Appendix I : Resolution of the Labour Party Conference of June, 1918

Appendix II : The Labour Party Constitutions of 1914 and 1918

Membership—Party objects (*a*) National (*b*) Inter-Dominion (*c*) International—
Party Programme—The Party Conference—The National Executive—Parliamentary Candidates—Affiliation fees and delegates—Standing Orders.

(a) The First Phase

Austria-Hungary declared war on Serbia on July 25, 1914 :
British mobilisation began officially on August 3, and Great
Britain declared war on Germany on August 4. Into the ten
days between the first of these events and the British mobilisation
were crowded the attempts of the British Labour movement and
of the International Socialist Bureau to act on the policy laid
down at Stuttgart in 1907. The Austrian declaration of war was
met by prompt protests from the various Socialist bodies, and on
July 29 the International Socialist Bureau met at Brussels and
agreed that the Socialist bodies in every country should organise
demonstrations and take every possible action for the preservation
of peace in Europe. On the same day, at an international demonstration held in Brussels, Keir Hardie for Great Britain, Haase
for Germany, Jaurès for France, Vandervelde for Belgium,
Morgari for Italy, and Rabinovitch for Russia, joined in the
demand that the war should be stopped. On July 30, the
British Labour Members of Parliament met and passed a resolution in favour of Great Britain staying out of the war, even if it
could not be prevented altogether. On August 1, the British

Section of the International, including the Labour Party as well as the Socialist bodies, drew up a manifesto against war ; and on the following day the British Section held a great meeting in Trafalgar Square, at which Keir Hardie and Arthur Henderson joined in the demand for peace. On that same day Germany declared war on France and Russia and delivered its ultimatum to Belgium. The next day Sir Edward Grey made his famous speech in the House of Commons, in effect bringing Great Britain into the war. Ramsay MacDonald, speaking on behalf of the Labour Party and with its authority, urged that every possible step should be taken to keep Great Britain out of the war ; but on August 4, the British Government declared war on Germany, and the Labour Party, after several meetings, decided to give its support. Thereupon, Ramsay MacDonald resigned from the leadership of the Labour Party, and Arthur Henderson was elected in his place. Meanwhile, the German Social Democratic Party had decided to vote for the war credits demanded by the German Government, and in France the Socialist Party had rallied by a majority to the support of the war.

The Labour Party's support of the war was not unqualified. In a circular issued on August 7 it attributed the outbreak to the action of " Foreign Ministers pursuing diplomatic politics for the purpose of maintaining a balance of power," and argued that the British " national policy of understandings with France and Russia only was bound to increase the power of Russia both in Europe and Asia, and to endanger good relations with Germany." It went on to argue that Sir Edward Grey " committed, without the knowledge of the people, the honour of the country to supporting France in the event of any war in which she was seriously involved, and gave definite assurances of support before the House of Commons had any chance of considering the matter." The circular went on to say that " the Labour movement reiterates the fact that it has opposed the policy which has produced the war, and that its duty is now to secure peace at the earliest possible moment on such conditions as will provide the best opportunities for the re-establishment of amicable feelings between the workers of Europe." Then it was added that the Labour Party Executive, " without in any way receding from the position that the Labour movement has taken up in opposition to our engaging in a European War, advises that, while watching for the earliest opportunity of taking effective action in the interests of peace . . . all Labour and Socialist organisations should concentrate their energies meantime upon the task of carrying out the resolutions passed at the Conference of Labour organisations held at the House of Commons on August 5, detailing measures to mitigate the destitution which will inevitably overtake our working people while the state of war lasts."

The reference here made is to an emergency conference, to which all important Labour and Socialist bodies were summoned while war and peace were still in the balance. This Conference actually met after war had broken out and, instead of discussing the peace issue, decided to set up an all-inclusive Labour body—called the "War Emergency Workers' National Committee"—to deal with the serious problems of economic dislocation and distress that were expected to arise. On this body, which continued in active existence throughout the war, pro-war and anti-war Socialists acted for the most part amicably together on economic and social issues, carefully keeping off the political questions which divided them. The emphasis soon shifted from unemployment and distress to rising prices and rents, profiteering, and the problems arising out of a shortage, instead of a surplus, of man-power ; but throughout the war the War Emergency Workers' Committee was able to do a great deal of useful work, and was an important factor in preventing a serious split in the British Labour movement such as occurred in most other countries.

At the stage when the W.E.W.N.C. was formed and when the Labour Party Executive sent out the circular from which I have quoted, the Labour movement's attitude to the war was still equivocal. The Parliamentary Labour Party had voted for war credits, and had changed its leader, and the Trades Union Congress's Parliamentary Committee had also given its support to the war ; but the Labour Party Executive, on which the I.L.P. was influential, was moving more cautiously. Its Chairman, W. C. Anderson, was a leading member of the I.L.P. ; and the I.L.P. was already making clear its determination to take a line of its own. On August 13, it issued a manifesto in the cause of International Socialism, in the course of which it declared :

Out of the darkness and the depth we hail our working-class comrades of every land. Across the roar of guns, we send sympathy and greeting to the German Socialists. They have laboured unceasingly to promote good relations with Britain, as we with Germany. They are no enemies of ours, but faithful friends.

In forcing this appalling crime upon the nations, it is the rulers, the diplomats, the militarists who have sealed their doom. In tears of blood and bitterness the greater democracy will be born. . . . Long live Freedom and Fraternity ! Long live International Socialism !

Despite this manifesto, the differences inside the Labour Party did not come to a head until August 29, 1914, when the Labour Party Executive was called upon to pronounce upon the question of the Labour movement taking part in a recruiting campaign for voluntary enlistment in the armed forces. The Parliamentary Labour Party had already voted in favour of this course, and the Executive by a majority endorsed its decision and agreed to place the party machinery at the service of the campaign. At the same time, the political parties agreed upon an Electoral Truce for the duration of the war, an Industrial Truce having been already declared on August 24.

In the meantime the International Socialist Conference originally due to meet in Vienna towards the end of August, 1914, had been definitely abandoned, after an attempt on July 29 to summon it to Paris instead for August 9. The British Trades Union Congress, due to meet early in September, was also called off, the Congress's Parliamentary Committee issuing instead a Manifesto in which it gave strong support to the war, and endorsed participation in the recruiting campaign. By September 11, even Ramsay MacDonald, responding to an invitation to take part in a recruiting effort in his own constituency, Leicester, expressed the view that " we are in it : it will work itself out now . . . Victory, therefore, must be ours . . . We cannot go back, nor can we turn to the right or to the left. We must go straight through."* Even Keir Hardie, who was heartbroken by the collapse of International Socialism, and died in 1915, largely because he no longer felt the will to live, was of much the same opinion, and felt it impossible to refuse support to the workers who had responded to the call for war service.

Nevertheless, the rift was wide. The majority of the British Socialist Party was uncompromisingly anti-war, and hardly less so was the rank and file of the I.L.P. Of the seven M.P.s who sat in the House of Commons under I.L.P. auspices, five were against the war, or at any rate in favour of the earliest possible peace by negotiation. These were Hardie, MacDonald, Snowden, Jowett, and Thomas Richardson, who were soon joined by W. C. Anderson, returned unopposed for Attercliffe under the Electoral

*For the full text of MacDonald's letter, see my *Labour in War-time*, p. 31.

Truce. Only two, J. R. Clynes and James Parker, went with the majority of the Labour Party. But most of the Members of Parliament who belonged to the I.L.P., but had been elected under Trade Union auspices, took the pro-war view, or soon rallied to it : so that the I.L.P. group in the House of Commons was reduced to a very few.

On October 15, 1914, the majority of the Labour M.P.s, in conjunction with the Parliamentary Committee of the Trades Union Congress and with other Labour leaders, came out with a Manifesto that was plainly meant as a counterblast to the I.L.P.'s Manifesto of August 15. Putting the entire blame for the outbreak of war on the German Government, it in effect repudiated not only the I.L.P. view, but also that which had been stated on August 7 by the Executive of the Labour Party itself. The Manifesto was in part a defence of the fullest partici- pation of Labour in the recruiting campaign and in any other national effort that might be needed for winning the war, which it represented simply as a struggle of democracy against military despotism. The change of tone from the earlier Manifesto of the Labour Party was striking : those who signed were no longer in a mood to consider any pre-war faults in British diplomacy, or to take account of any pre-war struggle for power : they had caught the war mood, and did not stop to argue. All that remained of the earlier attitude was an insistence that " when the time comes to discuss the terms of peace the Labour Party will stand, as it has always stood, for an international agreement among all civilised nations that disputes and misunderstandings in the future shall be settled not by machine guns but by arbitration."

The Labour Party's Annual Conference was due to meet, at the usual time, in January, 1915. It was postponed, after a postal ballot of the affiliated Societies had been taken. No Party Conference met till January, 1916, and before then a good deal more had happened. The I.L.P., however, held its Annual Conference at Easter, 1915, in spite of war conditions. The I.L.P. had opposed Labour participation in the recuiting cam- paign, and had urged that, if the Labour Party did decide to help recruiting, this ought to be done from its own platforms and not at meetings organised jointly with the capitalist parties. When a number of I.L.P. members ignored this view, branches began sending resolutions of protest to the I.L.P. National Council, which replied that " while recognising that such matters as enlistment and the urging of recruiting are matters for the individual conscience," the Council felt it desirable " to draw attention to our recommendation that no part in the recruiting campaign should be taken by branches of the Party " (i.e., of the I.L.P.). On the other hand, the I.L.P. played an active part in the work of the War Emergency Workers' National Committee and in the organisation of relief work, including work for Belgian refugees. After the abandonment of the Vienna International Socialist Congress it pressed strongly for the maintenance of the International during the war, supported the removal of the office of the International Socialist Bureau from Brussels to neutral territory at the Hague, and pressed for a meeting of the Bureau to be attended by delegates from both belligerent and neutral countries. The removal to the Hague was soon effected, Camille Huysmans, the Belgian Secretary, taking up residence there ; and in January, 1915, the Socialists of the four northern countries—Sweden, Norway, Denmark and Holland—held a joint Conference and set up, under Hjalmar Branting, the Swedish leader, a Committee of Neutrals to help in holding International Socialism together and to watch for an opportunity of intervention in the interest of peace.

The attempts of the I.L.P. and of the Bureau officials at the Hague to bring about an international meeting did not for the time succeed. They did, however, provoke, in February, 1915, a first Conference of the Socialist and Labour Parties of the Allied Countries only, called largely to consider what attitude to adopt to the efforts of the neutrals. The British Section appears to have been, at one point, not unfavourable to a full international meeting ; but the majority of the French Socialist Party refused to be represented at any Conference attended by German delegates as long as any part of France remained under German occupation. The British Section then took the initiative in convening the London Allied Socialist Conference of February, 1915, over which Keir Hardie presided. The resolutions approved by this meeting, while they were unequivocal in their support of the Allied cause, were very different in tone from the British Manifesto of October, 1914. They described the war as " a monstrous product of the antagonisms which tear asunder capitalist society and of the policy of colonial dependencies and aggressive imperialism . . . in which every Government has its share of responsibility." They expressed the intention " to resist any attempt to transform this defensive war into a war of conquest, which would only prepare fresh conflicts, create new grievances, and subject

the various peoples more than ever to the double plague of armaments and war." The Allied Socialists asserted that " they are
not at war with the peoples of Germany and Austria, but only
with the Governments of those countries, by which they are
oppressed." Finally, they asserted the need, on the conclusion
of the war, to "establish some international authority to settle
points of difference among the nations by compulsory conciliation and arbitration, and to compel all nations to maintain
peace." In the meantime, however, the war had to be won.

After this Conference, the neutral Executive of the International Socialist Bureau, as part of its procedure of holding
meetings with the Socialists of all the belligerent nations, invited
the British Section to meet it at the Hague, and the Section
appointed Henderson and MacDonald to go, as representing the
rival views. In the event, however, the meeting was not held,
owing to objections from the more extreme pro-war group ; but
the British Section kept up its connection with the International
Bureau and advanced money to help it in meeting its expenses
during the emergency.

By this time it was becoming apparent that the anticipation of
the war causing widespread unemployment and distress as long
as it lasted had been very much beside the mark. The first great
munitions crisis was beginning, as the armed forces ran short of
shells and other equipment, and as the enormous expenditure of
munitions involved in modern warfare began to be understood.
Unemployment and distress there had been, at the very outset,
with peace-time industries closing down. But by February, 1915,
many of the closed factories had been re-opened, and the cry was
going up for more men to work in more and bigger war factories—
and for women as well, to supplement the men's labours and to
replace those who enlisted—still voluntarily—in the armed forces.
Except in the light metal trades in and around Birmingham and
in a few heavier trades in the Black Country, women, up to 1914,
had been but little employed in metal-working ; and there were
strong prejudices against their employment, as well as fears of
its effects in cutting the men's wages. But now an imperative
demand arose for the use of women to make and fill shells and
cartridge cases and to undertake other processes simplified by the
sub-division of jobs ; and the Amalgamated Society of Engineers
found itself under the necessity of sanctioning women's employment, first at the Vickers works at Crayford and then, more
generally, under the Shells and Fuses Agreement of March 5,

1915. Such sectional concessions were not, however, deemed nearly enough ; and on March 17, Lloyd George summoned the Trade Unions to the first Treasury Conference, at which the Government asked for a suspension for the duration of the war of all Trade Union practices and customs that might impede war production, on a promise that no obstacles would be put in the way of the restoration of the suspended practices when the war was over. It required a further Conference, a week later, at which the Government promised a limitation of profits on munitions work, to induce the powerful Amalgamated Society of Engineers to accept the Treasury Agreement ; but the other Unions concerned, except the Miners' Federation, accepted at once, and as soon as the A.S.E. had come in the Government set up a National Labour Advisory Committee, under Arthur Henderson's chairmanship, to advise it on labour problems arising under the Agreement. The terms included compulsory arbitration of wartime disputes as well as the suspension of Trade Union practices as a means to what soon came to be known as " dilution " of labour.

Thus, the Industrial Truce, which had been at the outset a unilateral act of the Trade Unions, became embodied in a formal agreement with the Government (but with the Miners standing out). A few months later, in July, 1915, the Treasury Agreement was given statutory force by embodiment in the Munitions of War Act, under which both compulsory arbitration and dilution of labour acquired legal sanctions. The formal co-operation of the Labour movement in the industrial conduct of the war began, however, with the Treasury Agreement and the setting up of the National Labour Advisory Committee under Henderson. Henderson from that point was attempting to double the parts of Leader of the Labour Party in the House of Commons and *de facto* Industrial Adviser to a Government in which Labour was not represented—to say nothing of his further offices as Secretary both of the Labour Party and of the British Section of the International Socialist movement. So difficult and anomalous a situation could not last. It was ended in May, 1915, by the formation of the first war-time Coalition Government. This was in the main a Coalition of Liberals and Conservatives ; for the Irish Party did not come in, and the Labour Party was still too small to be offered more than a scanty share. The Prime Minister, Asquith, invited Henderson to accept the office of President of the Board of Education, but to regard it as a war-time sinecure and to devote his main attention, as before, to acting as the Government's Adviser on Labour questions. Henderson was to be the only Labour representative in the Cabinet ; but two other Labour M.P.s were given minor office—the South Wales miner, William Brace, as Under Secretary at the Home Office, and the printer, G. H. Roberts, as a Government Whip.

This invitation to enter a Coalition Government dominated by the capitalist parties caused much searching of hearts. The I.L.P. opposed acceptance, and on this occasion J.. R. Clynes was in agreement with the I.L.P. colleagues from whom he had broken on the general war issue. Arthur Henderson himself was uncomfortable about it. Besides his unwillingness to become President of the Board of Education—an office for which he did not feel fit and which he objected to regarding as a sinecure—there was the difficult question whether he would not forfeit his hold on the Labour Party by joining a Government which he could have but little power to influence. He realised that, if he took office, the Government would use him to put across the Labour Party and the Trade Union measures which were certain to arouse resentment, and that the effect might be to antagonise Labour from the war effort instead of strengthening its participation. Nevertheless, pressed by Asquith, he did not see how, as a supporter of the war, he could refuse, unless the Labour Party would refuse for him. He at once consulted both the Labour Party Executive and the Labour M.P.s ; and, despite considerable opposition, both gave majorities in favour of participation—an attitude which was subsequently endorsed both by the Trades Union Congress in September, 1915, and by the Labour Party Conference in January, 1916.

It was, however, clear that Henderson, as a Cabinet Minister, could continue to act neither as Secretary to the Labour Party nor as its Parliamentary Leader. The decision was that he should substantively retain both posts ; but that an Acting Secretary and an Acting Leader should be appointed for as long as he continued in the Government. Consequently, the Assistant Secretary, J. S. Middleton, became Acting Secretary of the party organisation, and John Hodge, of the Steel Smelters, was elected as Acting Leader of the Party in the House of Commons.

Henderson had not long to wait for the expected difficulties. In July, immediately after the enactment of the Munitions Act, came the strike of the South Wales Miners and its " proclamation " by the Government as unlawful under the terms of the Act.

But coal—South Wales steam coal above all—was urgently needed ; and it would have been useless, even if it had been possible, to clap 200,000 striking miners into gaol. The Government had to give way, and to grant the miners their terms ; and though Lloyd George played the main part in the proceedings, Henderson had to take his share, and can hardly have helped feeling it as somewhat ignominious. There was, however, worse to come. Pledges had been given, when the Coalition was formed, that there would be no conscription for the armed forces ; but it soon became evident to many people that the vast numbers of men who would be needed if the war went on for long could not easily be got under the voluntary system. National Registration was enforced in August, 1915, under the asseveration that it had nothing to do with the matter. In September the Trades Union Congress recorded its unqualified opposition to compulsory military service, which was by this time the subject of an intensive newspaper campaign and was finding strong support in the Cabinet. Later in the month, Henderson had to preside over a special conference of Labour organisations, before which Lord Kitchener, the War Secretary, laid a statement of the Government's demand for recruits. The conference, under pressure, agreed, in the hope of saving the voluntary system, to launch a Labour Recruiting Campaign of its own ; and in October the Government inaugurated the " Derby Scheme " of attestation, under which all men of military age were called upon to " attest " for service, whether or not they were engaged on essential work, leaving it to the authorities to judge whether they should be called up for military service or not. This scheme involved strong pressure, though not full compulsion ; and no sooner had it and the Labour Recruiting Campaign been set on foot than the clamour for conscription was re-doubled. The Prime Minister, in order to induce married men to attest, gave a pledge that single men would be called up first, thus in effect making conscription unavoidable. The Labour organisations protested in vain : the Government, despite its earlier pledges, decided to introduce a Bill for Compulsory Military Service, applicable to single men only, and represented as necessary in order to give effect to the promise made to the married men ; for 600,000 single men, it was reported, had failed to attest.

In these circumstances, the Labour organisations, which had been negotiating with Lord Derby and with the Government mainly through Henderson, decided to call a special Congress

representing the entire Labour movement in order to decide
what to do. At this meeting, on January 6th, 1915, a resolution
in favour of accepting conscription of single men was
defeated by 2,121,000 votes to 541,000, and a resolution of
uncompromising opposition, put forward by the National Union
of Railwaymen and the Amalgamated Society of Engineers, was
carried by 1,715,000 to 934,000, and then, on a second vote, by
1,998,000 to 783,000. This resolution called on the Parliamentary
Labour Party to oppose the Conscription Bill in all its stages.

Upon this, the Labour Party and the Parliamentary Party
met and decided to call the Labour Ministers out of the Coalition.
This ultimatum was followed by a meeting of both bodies with
the Prime Minister, who well understood the difficulty of enforcing conscription in face of organised Labour opposition. Asquith
was lavish with his promises—there should be no conscription of
married men, the firmest safeguards should be provided against
any form of industrial conscription, the tribunals to adjudicate on
calling-up should be civilian, and not military, the position of
conscientious objectors should be amply secured. Under these
inducements, the Labour Party was persuaded to withdraw the
resignations from the Government, and to refer the whole matter
for decision at the impending Party Conference.

The Conference met at Bristol during the last week of January,
1916. A general resolution expressing hostility to " Conscription
in any form " was carried by an overwhelming majority. Then
the Women's Labour League and the N.U.R. moved and seconded
a resolution in the following terms :

That this Conference declares its opposition to the Military Service
(No. 2) Bill [the Conscription Bill] and, in the event of it becoming law,
decides to agitate for its repeal.

These words were carefully chosen. They did not commit
Labour to positive resistance to conscription ; but if they had
been accepted the Labour Ministers could hardly have remained
in the Government. What the Conference did, on the motion of
Will Thorne, was to delete the second half, thus limiting the
resolution to a recording of opposition, but by implication
agreeing to accept the Bill if it became an Act. The discussion
was confused, and many of those who voted against the second
part of the resolution, as the speeches show, did not understand
what the real issue was. The effect, however, was to allow the
Labour Ministers to remain in the Government, and to leave the

opponents of the Military Service Act protesting but powerless :
so that when, despite the pledges that had been given, Parliament
went on in May, 1916, to pass a further Act applying conscription
to married men, the Labour forces had become sharply divided.
In April, 1916, Asquith, Kitchener and Bonar Law again conferred with representatives of the Labour Party and the Trade
Unions ; and, after hearing their statements, the Parliamentary
Committee of the Trades Union Congress agreed to accept the
new Bill. At the meeting of the Labour Party Executive—to quote
the reticent language of the Annual Report—" a resolution emphatically protesting against the extension of compulsory military
service was not carried." A proposal that a National Conference
of the whole Labour movement should be summoned was put
forward, but " was not pressed."

Thus Labour came, albeit under protest, to accept conscription
for both single and married men. It was in fact a war necessity,
on the assumption of a fight to the finish on which the war was
being fought. Labour speakers might argue, with truth, that the
voluntary system had not been given a fair trial, and that they
had been tricked into accepting, first attestation, then compulsory
service for single men only, and then all-round conscription,
largely by men who had intended all the time, despite promises
in which they tacitly acquiesced, to go the whole way. All this
was the case ; but it was also the case that the claims of total
war had to be met, if victory were the object, and that the devious
course actually followed by the Government was probably the
only, and certainly the easiest, way of reaching the required
end.

While the conscription issue was being thus handled, serious
labour troubles were developing on other issues as well. In
January, 1916, a special body of Dilution Commissioners had
begun work on the Clyde, largely with a view to securing more
men for the forces by more extensive substitution of women on
war work. Over their activities and over other factors of discontent arose the Parkhead strike of March 17, 1916, and the
spreading unrest which the Government attempted to quell by
deporting the leaders of the Clyde Workers' Committee, an
unofficial, militant movement based on the shop stewards in the
munition works and shipyards of Clydeside, and led by Socialists
of the Marxist Socialist Labour Party and the British Socialist
Party as well as of the I.L.P. Henderson was not consulted about
these deportations, and knew nothing about them until they had

been made ; but as the Labour member of the Cabinet (though not of the inner War Council, on which the Labour Party had no seat) he got a good deal of the odium arising out of the Government's high-handed proceedings. Hard upon the Clyde deportations followed the Easter Rebellion in Ireland, which cost James Connolly, Sheehy Skeffington and other Socialists their lives, and then the Second Conscription Act.

Meanwhile, the I.L.P. and the anti-war opposition as a whole had been passing through difficult times. Keir Hardie's death in September, 1915, had involved a by-election at Merthyr. Under the Electoral Truce this would ordinarily have meant an unopposed return ; but when the South Wales Miners, who claimed the seat, put forward one of their own officials, James Winstone, who took the I.L.P. view, his violently pro-war defeated rival, C. B. Stanton, also an official of the Miners' Federation, resigned his Trade Union office in order to fight the seat, and was elected in November, 1915, by 10,286 to 6,080.

Before this, in August, 1915, there had been extensive raids on the I.L.P., B.S.P., and other anti-war bodies by the police, who seized and confiscated pamphlets and other documents putting the anti-war view. The following month a leading Italian Socialist, Odelino Morgari, came to England on behalf of the Italian and Swiss Socialist Parties in order to urge British participation in an international conference of parties or sections of parties favouring a vigorous peace propaganda. The I.L.P. appointed two of its leaders, F. W. Jowett and J. Bruce Glasier, to attend this conference, which was held at Zimmerwald in September, 1915. The Government, however, refused passports both to the I.L.P. delegates and to the delegate chosen by the B.S.P. ; and the famous Zimmerwald Conference, at which Lenin took a leading part, passed off without British participation. The Zimmerwald Manifesto, however, with its vigorous denunciation of the Socialist war-supporters in all countries, reached the I.L.P. with a request for its endorsement. The I.L.P., in its reply, declared its support of the aspirations of working-class action for peace, but expressed its disapproval " of those passages condemning other Socialist groups for the action they have taken in connection with the war." Despite this qualification on its approval, it expressed its wish to be represented at the further Conference that was being called, if passports could be obtained. Even at this stage, however, it was clear enough that in Great Britain, as in other countries, there were really two anti-war

oppositions, the one, headed internationally by Lenin, revolutionary and entirely unconcerned with the merits of the case
advanced by any capitalist Government, and the other either
out-and-out pacifist or working for peace by negotiation, but
opposed to any attempt to invoke revolutionary violence as a
means of ending the war by international working-class revolution.   The I.L.P., though it had revolutionaries in its ranks,
belonged essentially to the second of these groups ; the British
Socialist Party, having shed its pro-war section, was moving
rapidly towards the first. At the I.L.P. Conference of April, 1916,
a resolution calling upon the party to " reconsider its affiliation
with the Labour Party " on account of the latter's war attitude
was heavily defeated, and a resolution urging Socialists of all
nations to " refuse support to every war entered into by any
Government, whatever the ostensible object of the war," moved
by a leading pacifist, Dr. Alfred Salter, was carried by 235 votes
to 3.

In August, 1916, Arthur Henderson was at length allowed to
resign his nominal position as President of the Board of Education,
in order to become full-time Labour Adviser to the Government
in name as well as in fact. The pressure for further enlistments and
for further dilution and substitution of labour—no longer only on
munitions work—was more severe than ever ; and many discontents were accumulating over the conduct of the war on both
the military and the economic side.   The Asquith Coalition
staggered on for a few months more ; but behind the scenes
Lloyd George was intriguing hard against his political leader,
and by the end of November he had won over both the Tories
and a section of the Liberal Party.   On December 5, Asquith
was forced to resign, and Lloyd George was invited to form a new
Coalition Government, in which he was the more anxious to
secure the support of Labour because of the increasing factory
unrest and the need for further unpopular measures if the war
was to be fought through to the bitter end.

Henderson remained loyal to Asquith up to the moment of his
resignation, and resisted blandishments to join Lloyd George's
intrigue. When, however, the Asquith Government had actually
fallen, it had to be decided afresh what line the Labour Party
should take.   Lloyd George was offering attractive terms—a seat
for Henderson in the inner War Cabinet, the establishment of a
Ministry of Labour under a Labour Minister, state control of
mines and shipping, an improved policy of food distribution, and

various other things for which, in face of Asquith's strong *laissez-faire* tendency, Labour had hitherto been pressing in vain. Under these inducements the Labour Party agreed without much difficulty to join the new Coalition, with Henderson in the War Cabinet, John Hodge as Minister of Labour, G. N. Barnes of the Engineers as Minister of Pensions, and William Brace, G. H. Roberts, and James Parker in minor posts. J. H. Thomas, of the N.U.R., refused office. J. R. Clynes, who had opposed Labour's entry into the first Coalition, was now in favour. At the Labour Party Conference, held in January, 1917, the Party's entry into the Coalition was approved by a vote of 1,849,000 to 307,000.

(b) The Second Phase

A new phase of the first World War began in December, 1916, with the formation of the Lloyd George Coalition. On November 19, President Wilson had addressed a Peace Note to the warring Powers ; and on December 18, soon after the change of Government in Great Britain, German Peace Proposals were received from the American Ambassador in London. Two days later, an American Note to the British Government suggested that it should formulate its war aims with a view to a negotiated peace. The Allied answer was sent on 30th December, banging the door ; but in effect the decision had been made, as far as Great Britain was concerned, when Lloyd George overthrew the Asquith Coalition. The very basis of the new Government's policy was that the war should be fought out to the bitter end, even if some of those who supported Labour's entry into the new Coalition were far from realising the truth. Little more than three months after the sending of the Allied answer, the pursuance of the campaign of " unrestricted " submarine warfare by Germany brought the United States into the war.

In the meantime, while peace talk, however unreal, was in the air, the Labour movement had begun thinking seriously about post-war problems. On March 6, 1917, a Labour Party deputation visited Lloyd George to present to him the resolutions on domestic reconstruction passed by the Party Conference in January. These resolutions, drafted by Sidney Webb, were largely based on a series of reports prepared during 1916 by the War Emergency Workers' National Committee. It was in reply to

these resolutions, which dealt with the post-war use of war factories, the prevention of unemployment, the nationalisation of
mines and railways, the assurance of a living wage, and a number
of other economic questions, that Lloyd George uttered his
characteristic, but hollow, incitement to the Labour deputation
to be " audacious." " I am not afraid," he said, " of the audacity
of these proposals. I believe the settlement after the war will
succeed in proportion to its audacity. . . . If I could have
presumed to be the adviser of the working classes . . . I should
say to them, Audacity is the thing for you."

That, of course, was said before the Revolution in Russia ;
and Lloyd George was careful to give no specific approval to the
Labour deputation's individual proposals. There was nothing
that he could be held to afterwards, when the issues actually arose.
He was simply bidding for Labour support for the measures which
he regarded as necessary for military victory, in the knowledge
that there would be no victory if the Labour front were to
crack.

Within a month or two further combing out of the war factories for the armed forces and the extension of dilution, coupled
with grievances especially among skilled workers who, tied to
their skilled jobs, saw unskilled " dilutees " earning higher wages
than they were allowed to receive, led to a sequence of strikes,
culminating in the widespread " May Strikes " under the leadership of the now nation-wide Shop Stewards' Movement. This
agitation was at an early stage when, on March 12, 1917, the
first Russian Revolution broke out, leading to the enforced abdication of the Czar and to the attempt to carry on with a moderate
Liberal Government under the leadership of Prince Lvov. This
Revolution had an immense effect on Labour opinion. Most
Labour men had been uneasy at the war alliance with the
reactionary Czarist Government ; and the Revolution was hailed
as a grand liberation for the consciences of Allied Socialists as well
as for the Russian peoples. Moreover, the Russian workers,
feeling for the most part no sort of obligation to carry on the
Czarist war policy and aware besides that the whole country was
on the verge of military as well as of economic collapse, at once
began to demand a negotiated peace, and to urge the Socialists
of the belligerent countries to force a peace policy upon their
several Governments. These sentiments added to the enthusiasm
of the elements in the British Labour movement that were hostile
to Lloyd George's war policy ; and there went up from the Labour

left wing a demand that the British workers should form Workers'
and Soldiers' Councils on the Russian model and should take the
task of making peace and re-making Great Britain into their own
hands.   At the unofficial Leeds Conference of June 3, 1917,
organised by George Lansbury's *Herald* followers in conjunction
with nearly all the left-wing groups, delegates saw the incon-
gruous spectacle of Ramsay MacDonald, Snowden, and other
I.L.P. leaders making flamboyant speeches to the cheers of
revolutionary shop stewards and other left-wing Socialists of
whose behaviour they at bottom thoroughly disapproved.   The
Conference decided in favour of the formation of local Workers'
and Soldiers' Councils throughout the country, with purposes
that were but vaguely defined.   But when the shouting was over,
nothing much happened.   Neither the Labour Party nor the
Trades Union Congress would have anything to say to the doings
at Leeds.   The Labour Party kept its place in the Coalition
Government ;   and when the Government had appointed, in
June, a number of Commissions on Industrial Unrest, to report
upon the causes of the May strikes and the troubled state of the
country, there was a pause, during which the Whitley Committee
issued its first Report on the Relations between Employers and
Employed, recommending the establishment of Joint Industrial
Councils, and the Government announced the setting up of a
Ministry of Reconstruction to prepare the way for the post-war
settlement of home affairs.

The pause was short.   Early in 1917 the Scandinavian-Dutch
Committee of neutral Socialists under Branting's chairmanship
had begun to make tentative preparations for the calling at
Stockholm of an International Socialist Conference, to include
the Socialists of the belligerent countries, with the object of laying
down peace terms which the workers' organisations would then
proceed to force upon their respective Governments.   After the
first Russian Revolution, the Russian Workers' and Soldiers'
Councils took up the cry, and demanded a Conference at Stockholm to reach decisions which should become binding upon all
the Socialist and Labour Parties throughout the world.   In May
the Labour Party, sharply divided on the Stockholm issue,
decided to send a delegation—G. H. Roberts, William Carter of
the Miners' Federation, and Ramsay MacDonald—to Russia to
explore the situation with the Russian Socialists and to report
back on the line which the Party should take.   At this point the
Russian Government fell, and was replaced by a semi-Socialist

Government under Kerensky's leadership, which proceeded to ask for an Allied Conference for the discussion of war aims, while maintaining an ambiguous attitude to the proposal of the Workers' and Soldiers' Councils for an all-in Socialist Conference. The British Government thereupon decided to send Arthur Henderson on a special mission to Russia, to report on the situation and to suggest the steps necessary to keep the Russians from making a separate peace. Henderson, from Petrograd, cabled advising that MacDonald should be allowed to go to Russia ; and the Government at length issued passports to the Labour delegation—which was, however stopped at Aberdeen by the refusal of Havelock Wilson's Sailors' and Firemen's Union to allow MacDonald to proceed.

In June, while Henderson was in Russia, the Kerensky Government, under strong pressure from London and Paris, launched its ill-fated offensive against the Germans, only to be faced almost at once with the collapse of its forces owing to lack of transport, munitions, and other supplies—to say nothing of the sheer war-weariness of most of the Russian soldiers. The collapse came while Henderson was on his way home, fully convinced that the Russians were in no mood or condition to follow Lloyd George's " fight-to-a-finish " exhortations, and that, in order to prevent a separate peace, it was essential for the Allied Governments to allow the Stockholm Conference to be held, and to use it as a means of fostering the peace movement inside Germany and of bringing pressure from within upon the German Government.

An extraordinary series of confusions, cross-purposes, and mutual recriminations followed Arthur Henderson's return from Russia. In his absence, the leaders of the Labour Party had been debating the Stockholm invitation without reaching any decision, but with a tendency for those who supported war to the bitter end to be hostile. Henderson, on his way back, had met a group of Russian delegates who were on their way to England ; and these delegates now joined their voices to his in pressing that the invitation should be accepted. Indeed, they wanted the Stockholm Conference, in accordance with the terms of the original invitation, to be authorised to arrive at binding decisions, whereas Henderson (and Albert Thomas in France) favoured only a consultative conference. Henderson, even with this reinforcement, found difficulty with his own Executive ; and it was decided that he, MacDonald and G. J. Wardle, the Acting Chairman of the Parliamentary Party, should go to Paris to talk matters over with the French Socialists before any decision was taken, and that the question of going or not going to Stockholm should be decided by a specially summoned Labour Conference in the light of the results of this visit.

Henderson, however, had to reckon not only with the Labour Party and the Trade Unions, but also with his colleagues in the War Cabinet. When he got back from Russia, Lloyd George was absent in France ; and when he reported to the other members that he proposed to support the Stockholm project he found them solidly hostile—so much so that he proffered his resignation, which, with Lloyd George away, they were not in a position to accept. Lloyd George, who had at an earlier point been converted to the Stockholm proposal, had now changed his mind and, on his return, had high words with Henderson. This was partly because Henderson's visit to Paris in company with MacDonald had been widely denounced in the press as a pacifist manœuvre ; but it was even more because Lloyd George had come back from his consultations with the French in a new mood, and was dallying with the idea of allowing Germany to do what it pleased with Russia, provided that the other Allies got all they wanted. The last thing the Prime Minister desired just then was to be faced with a set of War Aims accepted by the Russian, French and British Socialists—and perhaps by the German Socialists as well—and to be forced to define the Government's attitude to these aims.

Henderson, however, had fully made up his mind. At Paris, he had secured, with a good deal of difficulty, agreement that the Stockholm Conference should be regarded only as consultative, and not as mandatory ; and on these terms he was determined to proceed, whether the War Cabinet approved or disapproved, if only he could get his own party to agree. When the emergency Labour Conference met, on August 10, 1917, to decide the issue, Henderson argued strongly for Stockholm, and was able to secure a large majority vote in its favour—1,846,000 to 550,000—which means that most of the big Trade Unions voted on his side. There was, however, an important and even destructive rider ; for the Labour Conference also voted, on the motion of the Miners' Federation, that the British delegation to Stockholm should consist entirely of nominees of the Labour Party and the Trades Union Congress, and that the other bodies affiliated to the International Socialist Bureau—the I.L.P., B.S.P. and Fabian Society—should not be allowed to send independent delegates, though it was of course open to the Labour Party to include some of their members among its own delegation. This resolution ran directly counter to the terms of the Stockholm invitation, which had insisted on the representation of minority as well as majority groups from each country invited ; and it drew emphatic pro-tests both from the I.L.P. and from the Russian delegates in England.

For the moment, however, this awkward problem was pushed into the background by the news that Henderson had resigned—or rather had been forced to resign—from the War Cabinet. This was a sequel to the celebrated " doormat " incident of August 1, 1917, when Henderson, on his return from Paris, was kept waiting outside the Cabinet room while that body, with G. N. Barnes taking his place (as he had done during Henderson's Russian visit) discussed his iniquity in persisting with the Stockholm project and in going to Paris to discuss it with the French Socialists in MacDonald's company. The public—and even Henderson's Labour colleagues—knew nothing of this incident at the time ; nor did they know that during the ten days between the incident and the Labour Conference there had been pressure on Henderson from more than one quarter, or that the Government had at least half made up its mind to refuse pass-ports to any British delegates who might be sent to Stockholm by the Labour Conference. All this came out only later : the delegates who voted for Stockholm on August 10 had no idea that their representatives would be refused permission to go or that Henderson's position in the Cabinet was at stake. And it appears that, up to the very last moment, Lloyd George himself had hoped, or even expected, both that Henderson would with-draw his proposal and that, if he did not, the Labour Conference would turn it down.

The Labour Conference's decision, procured largely by Henderson's advocacy, made his position in the Cabinet un-tenable ; and he resigned in justifiable anger at his colleagues' treatment of him, and particularly at Lloyd George's tergiversa-tions. This, however, did not mean that the Labour Party came out of the Coalition, or that Henderson tried to bring it out. On the contrary, G. N. Barnes was allowed to take his place in the War Cabinet without protest, and outwardly Labour's place in the Coalition remained unaffected by the withdrawal of its leader, who automatically resumed his position both as Secretary to the Party and as Leader in the House of Commons. He soon, however,

asked for release from the parliamentary leadership, on the plea
that he wanted to devote all his energies to reorganising the party
machine with a view to the post-war struggle, but also because,
in his new position as leader of an anti-government group working
for the resumption of international Socialist relations, he found
the position of parliamentary leader difficult and hampering.
Wardle, the previous Acting Leader, had joined the Government
on Henderson's resignation, and the Parliamentary Party chose
the innocuous William Adamson, of the Scottish Miners, as
Chairman and Leader in Henderson's place.

The decisions of August 11 had not in fact settled the
Stockholm issue. The Miners' resolution concerning the choice of
delegates had led to an impasse, as the Conference had no power
to exclude the Socialist Societies from appointing delegates to
Stockholm if they wished. The Conference had therefore decided
to adjourn until August 21, in order to give time for the Executive to deal with the situation, and to meet again on that date for
the purpose of choosing its delegates. The Russians and the
Branting Committee in Stockholm were strongly opposed to the
exclusion of minority representation ; whereas a strong Trade
Union group in Great Britain was determined to wreck the
Conference rather than allow the I.L.P. and the B.S.P. to be
represented at it. Between August 10 and August 21 a furious
controversy raged both in the Labour movement and in the Press
over the whole Stockholm issue ; and it became plain that when
the Conference reassembled the basic decision to send delegates
would be again challenged.

It was challenged, to such effect that the resumed Conference,
while agreeing to protest against the Government's decision to
refuse passports, carried the proposal to send delegates only by the
tiny margin of 1,234,000 votes to 1,231,000, and, in spite of the
Executive's pleadings, reaffirmed by a large majority its ban on
delegates attending on behalf of the Socialist bodies. This was
carried by 2,124,000 against a mere 175,000.

These votes were in effect the end of Stockholm—for they had
their parallel in France. The Inter-Allied Socialist Conference
which met in London on August 28, and had been intended to
carry an agreed policy for presentation at Stockholm, in effect
broke down in face of keen disagreements. A majority there
insisted on minority representation as a *sine qua non* ; and there
was a babel of voices for and against every possible attitude. The
British delegation had prepared a statement of Allied War Aims,

which had been approved by the Conference of August 11 ;
but even this failed to secure endorsement, though it was agreed
by a narrow majority to set up an Inter-Allied Committee to
draft an amended statement for presentation to a further Allied
Conference. Thus, what came out of it all was not a Socialist
Conference, to be attended by neutrals and by belligerents on
both sides, but only a prospect of a further Allied Socialist Conference, at a date still to be settled, at which Allied Socialist
differences would be further debated and, if possible, reconciled.
The Stockholm proposal was dead, though it still stood as formally approved, some months before the Bolshevik Revolution
altered the entire face of International Socialist relations.

It is easy enough to see now that there was never much real
chance of success for the Stockholm project. The Trades Union
Congress in September, 1917, wrote its epitaph by declaring that
the Conference, however desirable, " at the present moment could
not be successful." The T.U.C.'s Parliamentary Committee
expressed the view that " general agreement of aim amongst the
working classes of the Allied Nations " was " a fundamental
condition of a successful International Congress "—and such
agreement clearly did not exist. At the same time the Trades
Union Congress declared emphatically in favour of an International Congress as " a necessary preliminary to the conclusion
of a lasting and democratic peace," and instructed its Committee
to work with this object in view. But it also re-affirmed that " the
voting shall be by nationalities, sectional bodies within nationalities to be governed by the majority of the nationality," or that,if
minority delegations were allowed, " each section should be given
voting power according to the number of persons actually
represented "—i.e., that the I.L.P. and B.S.P. should have only
their 40,000 or so votes as against the millions of the Labour Party
and the T.U.C.

For a month or two after the burial of the Stockholm project
the main centre of interest shifted back to home affairs, which had
been temporarily overshadowed. Unrest was still widespread
among the munition workers ; and in September the local Shop
Stewards' Committees came definitely together into a Shop
Stewards' National Committee. The Reports of the Commissions on Labour Unrest were followed, in October, by the
abolition of the Leaving Certificates which had been so acute a
source of grievance, and by the concession of a wage bonus of
$12\frac{1}{2}$ per cent to skilled time-workers in the munitions industries,

in order to bring their earnings up to a better relative level. Unfortunately for the success of this concession, the problem of defining a " skilled wörker " gave rise to so much difficulty that presently the bonus had to be granted to unskilled men as well, where they were on time-work ; and this in turn upset the piece-workers, who had to be given 7½ per cent to keep them quiet. The entire purpose of the original grant was thus defeated ; but for a little while the hubbub over the bonus took the attention of the shop stewards—the most militant section of the Trade Unions—off political issues.

Their attention was sharply recalled in November—by the Bolshevik Revolution, which was speedily followed by the announcement that peace negotiations were to be opened between Russia and Germany. On the heels of this announcement came Lord Lansdowne's letter, proposing a negotiated peace, and the publication by the Bolsheviks (and the re-publication in the *Manchester Guardian* in December) of the hitherto unknown, though not unsuspected, secret treaties made among the Allies in 1915. Before this, early in December, President Wilson had addressed to the United States Congress the first of his famous Messages on War Aims. Despite the failure of the Stockholm project, peace talk was in the air. The German Reichstag had passed its peace resolution in July, and though the new German Government under Michaelis was in effect controlled by the High Command and not by the Reichstag, it began to seem possible that the advocates of a fight to a finish on both sides might be overborne. Then, in the middle of December, came the news that the negotiations between the Germans and the Russians at Brest-Litovsk had broken down. On January 2, 1918, the new Russian Government made proposals to the Allies for a general peace : on January 8, President Wilson produced his famous Fourteen Points as a basis for a peace without annexations or indemnities.

Just before, on December 28, 1917, a further Labour Con-ference in London had approved a revised Statement of War Aims for presentation to an Allied Labour and Socialist Conference which was to meet in February, 1918. Henderson, baulked of Stockholm, was endeavouring to weld together the Socialists of the Allied countries in a demand for a reasonable peace, and was now acting as closely as he dared with MacDonald and the I.L.P. group against the extreme anti-German section of his own party. He was also pressing ahead with his promised plans for the reconstruction of the party with a view to the coming political struggle. At the Annual Labour Party Conference held at Nottingham in January, 1918, a comprehensive new statement of policy, *Labour and the New Social Order*, was presented and a new Party Constitution was put forward, designed to transform the Party into a nation-wide organisation capable of offering a real challenge to the Tories and Liberals at the next General Election. This new Constitution, which was adopted at an adjourned Party Conference in February, 1918, will be described and discussed, together with the new statement of policy, in the next chapter. It has to be mentioned here, because it represented the real break with the Lloyd George Coalition, even though the Labour Ministers retained their seats in the Government right up to the conclusion of the war. The enactment of the Representation of the People Act, enfranchising practically all men and many women, on February 6, 1918, defined the greatly enlarged electorate to which the new Labour Party would be able to appeal.

Meanwhile, in Russia, the Bolsheviks had convened the Constituent Assembly for which they had been calling before the Second Revolution, only to dissolve it at once, and to replace it on January 27, 1918, by a Congress of Soviets which declared itself the supreme governing authority of the new State. The Soviet system had begun, and the Soviet leaders, realising the impracticability of either resisting the Germans or securing a general peace, were making the best of a bad bargain at the resumed negotiations at Brest-Litovsk. The Brest-Litovsk Treaty, which took Russia definitely out of the war, was signed on March 3, 1918, and ratified twelve days later. In Germany, the widespread strikes which had broken out at the end of January had been repressed. At the beginning of March, the great new German offensive in the West was launched.

Even before this, in January, the man-power position in Great Britain had become acute, and an extensive new comb-out had begun. This accentuated the unrest, especially among the munition workers, and helped to give the Shop Stewards' Movement a more definitely political twist. This movement, concerned at first primarily with industrial grievances, grew more and more political as the emphasis shifted from dilution designed to increase output to the combing-out of more reluctant workers for military service ; and the Second Russian Revolution gave the more left-wing leaders a more coherent revolutionary purpose than the first Revolution had imparted. There was as yet no Communist

Party in Great Britain and no Communist International to proclaim a policy of World Revolution. But Bolshevik Russia was already becoming a focus of loyalty for the extreme left in all countries—and at the same time, of course, a focus of opposition for the right, whose friends among the Russian Socialists had been driven from power and in many cases were fleeing into exile and uttering fierce denunciations of Lenin and his associates as betrayers of democracy, both in Russia and in world affairs.

In Great Britain, whatever the shop stewards might feel, the leaders of the Trade Unions, of the Labour Party, and of the I.L.P. were at one in their dislike of the Bolsheviks. MacDonald and Snowden loved Lenin and Trotsky no better than did Henderson or Sidney Webb—the two chief architects of the new Labour Party. The Russian Revolution was still acclaimed ; but the phrase meant one Revolution to the established leaders, and another to the left wing. The British Socialist Party, having already shed its old Social Democratic leaders, was ready to acclaim the Bolshevik Revolution, though not, as appeared later, to accept without an internal struggle the Bolshevik doctrine of " democratic centralism." The I.L.P. was sharply divided, its best-known leaders more and more anti-Bolshevik as the character of the second Revolution became more plain, its rank and file somewhat bewildered and for the most part wishful to go leftwards without ceasing to be a parliamentary party working within the Labour Party on constitutional lines. Even the small, militant Socialist Labour Party was divided, between an " old guard " which was not prepared to let anything—even World Revolution —impair the purity of its cherished doctrine, and a shop steward group which eagerly embraced the new Leninist gospel.

In March and April, in face of the German offensive, the man-power crisis became more acute than ever. The Government forced through an Act raising the age of military service to fifty and even attempted to impose conscription on the Irish people. This measure undoubtedly did much to increase the strength of anti-war feeling. The Labour Party's further Conference, held in June, 1918, voted by 1,704,000 against 951,000 in favour of putting a formal end to the Electoral Truce and resuming its freedom to fight by-elections against Government candidates of the other parties. This Conference also passed a series of resolutions covering the main ground of home reconstruction policy, as the complement to the declaration of international policy already embodied in its Memorandum on War Aims. Individual

Trade Unions were also by this time formulating their post-war demands. The National Union of Railwaymen had done this as early as November, 1917, when it put forward a plan for the nationalisation of the railways, with workers' representation on the public boards to which control was to be entrusted on behalf of the people. Now, in July, 1918, the Miners' Federation, at its Southport Conference, scrapped its older nationalisation plan, in which it had proposed a simple taking over of the mines by the State, and put forward instead a complete plan of public owner-ship combined with workers' control. Guild Socialism was rapidly gaining adherents in the Trade Unions ; workers' control was being demanded by more and more Trade Unionists—though those who made the demand meant different things by it, as was to appear presently when British Communism emerged as an or-ganised movement.

Early in August, 1918, a delegation from the Trades Union Congress and the Labour Party, headed by Arthur Henderson and C.W. Bowerman, proposed to attend a meeting in Switzer-land, convened by the International Socialist Bureau, for the purpose of hearing and considering the replies of the Socialists of the enemy countries to the Allied Labour Memorandum on War Aims, which had been transmitted to them through the Bureau. The Government, however, refused passports, and the delegates were unable to go. Strong protests were made at the Jubilee Trades Union Congress, held early in September, and at a further Allied Labour and Socialist Conference, which met in London on September 17. This meeting, from which the Socialist Societies were again excluded, was notable for the attendance of a delegation from the American Federation of Labor, including Samuel Gompers. The Americans put forward their alternative draft of War Aims, based mainly on President Wilson's Fourteen Points ; and they abstained from voting on the composite Statement which was finally adopted by the Conference. They agreed, however, that an International Labour Conference, representing all nations, ought to meet simultaneously with the Peace Conference when the war was over. In the meantime, they put forward a resolution, which was heavily defeated, " urging that we [i.e., the Allied Labour movements] will meet in Confer-ence only those of the Central Powers who are in open revolt against their autocratic governors." The Americans agreed, however, to appoint a representative [Gompers] to serve on a Joint International Committee which was to approach the various

Allied Governments in order to ensure that Labour representatives should be included in the official delegations attending the Peace Conference, and was also to organise the World Labour Conference that was to meet at the same time.

This September Conference met the day after the reception of the Peace Note from Austria-Hungary, which heralded the collapse of the Central Powers. Little more than a fortnight later, Prince Max of Baden became German Chancellor, and it became plain that the end was near. In mid-October the German Government announced its preparedness to accept President Wilson's terms. Peace was evidently imminent when Henderson, in company with Camille Huysmans, the Secretary of the International Socialist Bureau, left London to attend a meeting of the Joint International Committee, which had been called to meet in Paris on October 26. They were stopped at Folkestone under orders from the National Sailors' and Firemen's Union, which refused to let its members sail with them on board. This, as we have seen, was not the first occasion on which such action had been taken. Havelock Wilson, the Sailors' leader, summoned before the Congress Parliamentary Committee, said that his objection was to Huysmans, who had been meeting the German Socialists, and not to Henderson ; but he refused to give any pledge against a repetition of the incident. It was in fact repeated, against Huysmans, later in the year ; but no further interference was attempted with the movements of British Labour delegates.

On November 1 came the Austrian Revolution, and on November 6 the German naval revolt at Kiel. A Republic was proclaimed in Bavaria on November 7, and two days later the Kaiser abdicated, and the majority Socialist, Ebert, became the first Chancellor of the German Republic, which was formally proclaimed on November 11, the day that the Armistice was signed. On November 14 a specially summoned Labour Party Conference in London, at which Bernard Shaw made a memorable speech, decided by a vote of 2,117,000 against 810,000 to leave the Coalition at once and to resume complete independence as a party.

The majority in favour of this decision was large ; but the minority was considerable. The latter had, moreover, the support of the Parliamentary Labour Party ; and it was on that body's behalf that Clynes moved an amendment to the Party Executive's resolution in favour of resuming independence. Clynes and those who supported him—including James Sexton, Tom Shaw, and Will Thorne—argued that Labour should remain in the Coalition

Government in order to have a share in making the peace. The Coalition, they said, was popular ; and Labour, in leaving it, would be inviting disaster at the polls. Hardly anyone doubted that Lloyd George would rush on an election and do his best to fight it on the prestige of victory ; and probably few Labour men expected that, under such circumstances, the Labour Party could poll well. Nevertheless, though a few of the big Trade Unions were on Clynes's side, there was no doubt about the views of the great majority of the delegates. Shaw twitted Clynes with coming empty-handed to ask Labour to surrender its freedom. Lloyd George, he said, had made large concessions to the Tories, but was offering Labour nothing except a promise to " consider " its claims. " Sympathetic consideration " was what the governing classes always offered the workers. " Mr. Clynes has come from Mr. Lloyd George and done the best he can. I ask you to send Mr. Clynes back to him with the message ' Nothing doing ! ' "

The Conference, having made its main decision, proceeded, on MacDonald's motion, to demand Labour representation at the Peace Conference and to vote for a World Labour Conference to meet at the same time and place. Robert Smillie seconded. The leaders who had been in eclipse were already stepping back into their places. But the next hurdle before them was the General Election.

The Labour Ministers did not all obey the Conference's orders. Clynes loyally resigned at once from his office as Food Controller, which he was loath to leave. Four, however, fought the General Election as Coalition Labour candidates, and stayed on to be gradually discarded. These were G. N. Barnes, who attended the Paris Peace Conference as the Government's Labour nominee ; G. H. Roberts, who succeeded Clynes as Food Controller ; James Parker ; and G. J. Wardle. The rest, including John Hodge, rejoined their Labour colleagues in opposition.

(c) *The New Labour Party of 1918*

The new Labour Party Constitution, to which reference was made in the preceding chapter, was drafted, mainly by Arthur Henderson and Sidney Webb, in 1917, and, after approval by the Party Executive, was widely circulated in readiness for presentation to the Annual Conference in January, 1918. Its essential purpose was to transform the Labour Party from a Federation, able to act only through its affiliated societies, into a nationally organised Party, with a Local Party of its own in every parliamentary constituency. In order to achieve this, at least three things were necessary. In the first place, the local Trades Councils, which were primarily federations of Trade Union branches for industrial purposes, had to be pushed out of their established position as the Party's local agents in many areas, in favour of Local Parties which would be not so much affiliated societies with a separate life of their own, as subordinate branches of the Labour Party itself. This also meant bringing the existing Local Labour Parties, Labour Representation Committees, and Labour Associations under closer central regulation, so as to convert them too into branches ; and accordingly the draft of the new Constitution was accompanied by a draft set of rules to be adopted by Local Labour Parties, or rather by several sets designed to meet varying local conditions.

Secondly, the Labour Party, as now to be re-born, had to be equipped with its own individual members, instead of depending mainly on the individual members of the I.L.P. In the few areas in which local Labour Associations enrolling individual members existed already, the very loose contact (or in some cases no contact at all) that had previously existed between the members of these Associations and the national Labour Party had to be changed into a recognised membership of the Party. Special provision had also to be made for the enrolment of women members ; for it was intended, though nothing was specifically said on the point, to convert the branches of the hitherto independent Women's Labour League into Women's Sections of the reorganised Local Labour Parties.

Thirdly, it was necessary to persuade the Trade Unions to pay substantially increased affiliation fees to the Party, in order to finance the much more extensive functions which, as a nationally organised body, as against a mere federation, it would need to undertake.

In relation to all these matters, there were obstacles to be overcome. Most obviously, the I.L.P. was not going to like a change that would deprive it of its key position as the principal organisation with branches which local supporters of the Labour Party could join, and would present it with a rival (and cheaper) organisation—which, moreover, its members would be called upon, as loyal Labour Party adherents, to help get on its feet.

This, emphatically, was not what Keir Hardie had meant by the
" Labour Alliance " he had spent his life in bringing to birth.
True, the pill was gilded by the fact that the new Constitution was
accompanied by a new Statement of Policy—*Labour and the New
Social Order*—which for the first time definitely committed the
Labour Party to Socialism ; but this, from the standpoint of the
I.L.P., only made the projected new Local Labour Parties, with
their individual members as well as their affiliated bodies, more
formidable rivals. From the standpoint of getting the new Constitution through the Party Conference, any opposition the I.L.P.
might offer, so far from mattering, would make things easier ;
for the I.L.P., owing to its anti-war attitude, was unpopular with
most of the leaders of the Trade Unions, and they would certainly
hold up their card votes with gusto for any proposal that promised
to supersede the I.L.P.'s influence. Henderson and Webb, however, were well aware, if many of the Trade Union leaders were
not, that the new Labour Party could by no means afford to do
without the I.L.P.'s help, because its members were the tried
experts in local organisation and had the enthusiasm as well as
the skill needed to make the new system work. If the I.L.P. had
gone into united opposition to working the new Labour Party
Constitution after its adoption, Henderson would not have found
it at all easy to replace its members as the builders of the new local
machine.

The I.L.P., however, did not oppose, though its leaders had
some doubts, which were reflected in the Report of its National
Administrative Council to its Conference held at Leicester in 1918
a month or two after the Labour Party had endorsed the new
plan. This Report drew attention to the danger of the new Local
Labour Parties, with their lower fees, competing with the I.L.P.
branches, but reached the comforting conclusion that, on the
whole, the organisation of a mass of lukewarm Socialists or half-
Socialists in the Local Labour Parties would stimulate rather than
injure I.L.P. branches, by providing them with a ready-made
recruiting ground. The N.A.C. expressed the hope that Local
Labour Parties would be formed in all constituencies, but indicated its uneasiness by adding the hope that they would not be
formed by existing members of the I.L.P. diverting their energies
to the new organisation. In fact, as we shall see, the attitude of
the I.L.P. branches varied from place to place. Some I.L.Pers
transferred their activities to the Labour Party : some became
active in the Local Labour Parties for the purpose of capturing

them ; some refused to help them on to their feet or even tried to
prevent them from setting out at all to enrol individual members.
The I.L.Pers who had dropped out of the I.L.P. through dislike
of its anti-war policy mostly rallied to the Local Labour Parties ;
and, besides these, there was a considerable group round Ramsay
MacDonald, who wanted to keep the I.L.P. as a foundation for
his own position, but at the same time wanted, like Henderson,
to build up a powerful and nation-wide Labour Party machine,
capable of helping the Labour Party before long to make a real
bid for power and office. MacDonald, never anti-war to anything
like the same extent as Snowden or Jowett, and always on the
right of the Socialist movement in matters of general policy, was
already beginning that straddle between the I.L.P. and the
Labour Party which was to end in his final breach with the
former on the issue of " Socialism in Our Time." MacDonald,
as Treasurer of the Labour Party, and displaced Parliamentary
Leader with the hope of getting back his old position when the
war was over, was not at all minded to oppose Henderson's new
Constitution, about which Henderson was careful to consult him
fully at every stage. And, if MacDonald favoured the plan, the
I.L.P. could hardly oppose it, even though Snowden and others
indicated that they received it with mixed feelings.

In fact, the I.L.P.'s criticism of the new Labour Party Constitution turned mainly, not on the proposal to open the doors
wide to individual members, but on what it regarded as the
strengthening of Trade Union domination over the Party. Under
the constitution in force up to 1918, the National Executive of the
Labour Party consisted of sixteen members (including the
Treasurer), of whom eleven represented the Trade Unions, one
the Trades Councils, Local Labour Parties, and Women's
Organisations combined, and three the affiliated Socialist
Societies ; and each of these three sections elected its own
representatives, so that the Socialists were always sure of three
seats, and the I.L.P. of at least one, even if it conceded parity to
the B.S.P. as well as to the Fabian Society. Under the new
Constitution, on the other hand, there was to be an Executive of
twenty-one members (raised to twenty-three by the Labour Party
Conference in amending the draft), and of these, eleven (raised to
thirteen) were to represent the national affiliated organisations
as a single group, including Socialist Societies as well as Trade
Unions ; five were to represent the Local Labour Parties ; and
there were to be four seats reserved for women. The Treasurer,

as before, was to be elected separately. But, whereas previously each section had elected its own representatives, now only nominations were to be made separately for each section, and the entire Conference was to vote for all the groups of which the Executive was to be composed.

The I.L.P. objected strongly to the Socialist Societies losing their separate position as a group, and to being deprived of the right to choose their own representatives for the Executive. Nor is this surprising ; for the change was obviously proposed in order to get the support of the big Trade Unions which had insisted on excluding the Socialist Societies from separate representation at war-time Allied and International Labour Conferences, and had reaffirmed their point of view by an overwhelming majority when it was opposed by both the Labour Party Executive and the International Socialist Bureau in connection with the Stockholm Conference. Henderson was convinced that he could not get the new Constitution adopted, whatever his personal views, without giving up the claim of the Socialist Societies either to choose their own representatives, or to be represented at all as of right, on the Labour Party Executive ; and MacDonald was no less aware of this. Moreover, both of them, and the I.L.P. itself, had to reckon with the danger that, if the Socialist representation were maintained, there might be a Trade Union secession to form a separate Trade Union Party. A substantial group of jingo fire-eaters, including a number of Trade Union leaders, had already taken steps to form a National Democratic Party in strong opposition to the Labour Party ; and some of this group, reinforced by other Trade Unionists, were already putting forward plans for a purely Trade Union Party from which the Socialist Societies were to be entirely shut out. This movement was not prevented by the changes made in the new Labour Party Constitution ; but its teeth were drawn. When its sponsors, led by J. B. Williams, the Secretary of the Musicians' Union, attempted to found their Trade Union Party in June, 1918, they found almost no support. They would certainly have found more had it not been for the change in the Labour Party's Constitution, which gave the Trade Unions power, if they chose to use it, to elect every single member of the Party Executive, as well as the power, which they had possessed from the outset, to determine all Conference decisions by the weight of the block vote.

The new method of electing the Executive was, indeed, the way chosen by Henderson and Webb of ensuring that the Trade

Unions would support the new Constitution and would be prepared to pay the increased affiliation fees without which it could not be worked. The disappearance of the Socialist reserved seats on the Executive also made room for the increased representation assigned to the Local Labour Parties and for the new element to which Henderson, with his eye on the enfranchised women in the constituencies, was determined to assign a place. These elements could not have been brought in without either making the Executive too big, or reducing the proportion of direct Trade Union representation below what the Trade Unions would ever have agreed to accept, unless the Socialists had been ruthlessly cleared out of the way. Even as it was, the Trade Unions, when it came to the issue, insisted on being given two more seats than had been proposed in the draft, so as to have thirteen members as against nine, *plus* the Treasurer, from all other sources. They insisted on this, though, as we have seen, the changed method of voting enabled them, if they chose to act together, to choose the whole twenty-three.

The Trade Unions were determined to keep their control over the Labour Party machine—the more so because of the war-begotten unpopularity of the largest Socialist body—but they felt no disposition to come to the rescue of the local Trades Councils, which Henderson and Webb were proposing to demote from their established position in the Party. The Trades Councils had, indeed, few influential friends. They had been expelled in 1895 from the Trades Union Congress, of which they had been the principal founders : they had played an important part in the Labour Representation Committee and in the Labour Party during its formative years. But this did not save them when the Labour Party had at length decided to create a nation-wide local organisation of its own. Henderson and Webb had no compunction in proposing that, wherever possible, they should be simply swallowed up in the new Local Labour Parties, surviving, if at all, merely as subordinate Industrial Sections of these primarily political bodies. The Trades Councils had in fact increased greatly in numbers during the war, many new ones having been founded mainly for the purpose of providing local Labour representatives on various official Committees connected with war services. They had, however, but little power, except in a few areas ; and they were nearly all badly short of funds. The Trade Union leaders were apt to regard them as potential points of focus for left-wing discontents ; and many Unions gave their branches no encouragement to join them. They seemed, in 1918, to be ripe in many cases to be swallowed up by the new Labour Party, which was ready to offer them, transformed into Local Labour Parties, a recognition and a helping hand which the Trades Union Congress was still not prepared to give. Not until some time later did the Trades Union Congress, after being itself reorganised, begin to pay some attention to the Trades Councils, and to attempt to bring them under its own leadership as a means of preventing their capture by the left wing.

In 1918, a good many Trades Councils obediently converted themselves into Local Labour Parties, though many did not, and though, in many places where the conversion was temporarily achieved, separate Trades Councils were re-founded later on. The success of the Labour Party in this respect can be measured by the fall in the course of 1919 of the number of affiliated Trades Councils from 132 to 50, as against a rise from 85 to 292 in the number of Local Labour Parties and Labour Representation Committees. The full story, both of the growth of local Labour political organisations during the war years and of Henderson's success in converting much of it into the form which was favoured under the new Constitution, is told in the Table on this page. In 1913, out of a total of 145 affiliated local bodies, eighty-five were primarily industrial, and only seventy exclusively or largely political. By 1917, with the war-time growth of Trades Councils, out of a total of 260 bodies, 153 were mainly industrial, as against

LOCAL LABOUR PARTY ORGANISATION IN 1913, 1917 AND 1918
Local Bodies Affiliated to the Labour Party

	1913	1917	1918
Trades Councils	74	132	50
Trades and Labour Councils . . .	11	21	23
Trades Councils and Labour Parties (or L.R.C.s) combined	5	12	25
Labour Parties	34	57	276
Labour Representation Committees . .	25	28	16
Labour and Co-operative R.C.s . . .	—	1	2
Labour Associations or Leagues . .	6	9	6
TOTALS	145	260	398

107 of the other types. But a year later, out of 398 local bodies, the mainly industrial numbered only seventy-three, whereas the largely or exclusively political groups had risen to 325. Of course, there were many Trades Councils that were not affiliated to the national Labour Party, including a fair number that had become affiliated to the Local Labour Parties in their areas, as well as many more that were without political affiliations. In general, however, the new Constitution, in this aspect, had achieved a remarkable success.

It will be observed that among the bodies affiliated to the Labour Party in 1918 were two which bore the name of " Labour and Co-operative." There were a few other areas in which the local Co-operative Societies became affiliated to the Local Labour Parties without the word " Co-operative " appearing in their names. In general, however, the Co-operators held aloof. As we shall see, they had just, in 1917, set about creating a Co-operative Party of their own ; and most of the leaders of the movement frowned on affiliation to the Labour Party, either nationally or locally, though they soon showed a readiness to bargain with it over the putting forward of candidates and over arrangements for constituency organisation.

When the draft of the new Constitution, after some months' consideration by the affiliated bodies, was brought forward for discussion at the Nottingham Labour Party Conference in January, 1918, it did not get a perfectly smooth passage. The Miners' Federation and the United Textile Factory Workers' Association joined forces to move the reference back, though their spokesmen, Robert Smillie and J. W. Ogden, both made it clear that their action was not to be taken as indicating opposition. Both were, in fact, broadly favourable, though Smillie at any rate shared some of the I.L.P.'s doubts. The reference back was moved, and carried without challenge, mainly in order to give the Trade Union leaders who were favourable to the change a further opportunity of persuading their colleagues and of squelching the attempt to create a separate Trade Union Party. When the adjournment had been agreed upon, George Lansbury at once rose and moved that it should be for no more than a single month ; and this was carried almost without demur. On February 26, 1918, the Labour Conference reassembled and carried the new Constitution with only secondary amendments, including the concession of two additional seats on the Executive to the representatives of the national affiliated bodies. Moreover, when, in

June, 1919, the Conference proceeded to elect its first Executive under the new Constitution, the Socialist Societies actually secured four seats, two for the National Societies Group and two for the Women's Group, in addition to Ramsay MacDonald, as Treasurer, and Ben Spoor, an I.L.P. Member of Parliament, who won a seat as a Local Labour Party representative. Despite the abolition of their separate representation, the Socialist Societies had certainly nothing to complain of in what was actually accorded to them.

Of these seats, two went to Fabians—Sidney Webb and Susan Lawrence—and the rest to the I.L.P.—F. W. Jowett and Mrs. Snowden, besides MacDonald and Spoor ; and there were several others on the Executive who were I.L.P. members, though less actively associated with its work. The " Labour Alliance " had been in effect preserved, after the careful nursing which Henderson had given to it during the danger-time of war.

The other main amendment which was made in the draft of the Constitution turned on an important point of principle. It had been proposed in the draft that it should be " the duty of the National Executive, prior to every General Election, to define the principal issues for that Election " : that is to say, the formulation of the Election Programme had been made the exclusive province of the National Executive, within the limits defined by the General Policy Statement of the Party, expressing its long-term objectives. In the draft, the Parliamentary Labour Party had been left out ; and it was prompt to protest against its exclusion. The Constitution as adopted read that " it shall be the duty of the National Executive *and the Parliamentary Labour Party* " to define the issues prior to each election, but was silent about what was to happen if they disagreed. They did in fact almost at once proceed to disagree, not directly about an election programme, but on the vital question whether Labour should leave the Coalition immediately after the Armistice ; and the issue between them was decided, in favour of the National Executive, by a Special Party Conference. In effect, that was left as the only way in which a disagreement between the National Executive and the Parliamentary Party could be resolved.

The remaining change of substance was that, whereas the draft, though binding all Labour Party candidates to give prominence in their election addresses and campaigns to the issues selected for the Party's election manifesto, explicitly laid down that they should " remain free to include, in addition, any other proposals not inconsistent therewith, and to discuss any other subjects at their own discretion," these phrases were left out of the new Constitution in its final form. Both draft and adopted Constitution, however, laid down that " every Parliamentary representative of the Party " should " be guided by the decision of the meetings of such Parliamentary representatives, with a view to giving effect to the decisions of the Party Conference as to the General Programme of the Party."

Thus, in February, 1918, Arthur Henderson got what he wanted—an instrument which could be used for the building up of an effective Labour Party election machine all over the country—and thus fulfilled the first part of the purpose he had set before himself when he retired from the Parliamentary leadership in order to devote himself to the re-organisation of the Party. Or rather, he did not get quite all he wanted ; for he had hoped to bring in the Co-operators as well, and had even toyed with the notion of a change of name—to " People's Party "—or some such thing, in the hope of securing their adhesion.

The re-building of the machine, however, was only one aspect of what Henderson and Sidney Webb set out to do. They also wanted a new programme, on which the Party could appeal to the enlarged electorate, and also on the basis of which it could itself acquire strength and coherent purpose. The old Labour Party Constitution was remarkable in that it contained no word at all to indicate what the Party stood for in terms of concrete policy. Its sole reference to objects was contained in the words " To organise and maintain in Parliament and in the country a political Labour Party." What this Party was for—what it stood for, or what policy it was to promote—the old Constitution simply did not say. This was, of course, a legacy from the circumstances under which its progenitor, the Labour Representation Committee, had been established in 1900. Nothing had been said then about policy, because the attempt to define the Party's objects would have led to a head-on collision between the Socialists, who would have wished to commit it to Socialism, and the majority of the Trade Union leaders, who would have repudiated any such commitment and were in fact still largely Liberals in their general political creed. Right up to 1914, any attempt to commit the Labour Party to Socialism would have endangered Trade Union support. It would probably have prevented the Miners' Federation from joining the Party after the Osborne Judgment and would have made it much more difficult to get the effects of that

Judgment cancelled by the Trade Union Act of 1913. The war, however, had made an immense difference to Trade Union opinion. Hostile as many of the Trade Union leaders were to the I.L.P., most of them were no longer hostile to Socialism of a kind—the kind which Webb skilfully embodied in his draft of *Labour and the New Social Order.* The old Lib-Lab. stalwarts had in many cases died or retired : the new generation of Trade Unionists was at any rate much more Socialist than the old.

Accordingly, Henderson and Webb were able without difficulty to get a plainly Socialist declaration embodied in the new Constitution itself. The Labour Party, from February, 1918, stood explicitly for the following objects :

To secure for the producers by hand and by brain the full fruits of their industry, and the most equitable distribution thereof that may be possible, *upon the basis of the common ownership of the means of production* and the best obtainable system of popular administration and control of each industry and service.

The adoption of this socialist objective—though the word " Socialism " was still avoided—provided the basis for the fuller statement of socialist policy embodied in Webb's draft of *Labour and the New Social Order,* which, circulated to the affiliated bodies together with the new draft Constitution, and widely accepted at once as a statement of the Party's objects, was officially adopted only at the Labour Party Conference—the first under the new Constitution—held in June, 1918.

The phrasing of the new clause in the Constitution, to be sure, was guarded ; for Sidney Webb, himself a strong opponent of Guild Socialism and of " workers' control " in all its forms, had to be careful in expressing himself on the issue of " control," in face of the tide which was then setting strongly in its favour in the Trade Unions. The Miners' Federation and the National Union of Railwaymen, as well as the Post Officers Workers, had come out strongly in favour of " workers' control," or at any rate a large element of it, in nationalised undertakings ; and the " control " movement was also strong in the engineering and in a good many other industries. A considerable struggle was in progress over the same issue inside the I.L.P., where Snowden and other old-time advocates of State Socialism were showing themselves strongly hostile to the new notion of "industrial democracy." The National Guilds League, small but active, was carrying on a lively workers' control propaganda ; and the shop stewards' movement was also actively pressing the demand.

When, however, the demand for " workers' control " had been met to the extent of including in the draft new Constitution the words quoted concerning " the best obtainable system of popular administration and control of each industry and service," the Party Executive appears to have considered that it had gone quite far enough ; and in the fuller statement of policy embodied in its " Reconstruction Manifesto," *Labour and the New Social Order*, though it included a section under the title " The Democratic Control of Industry," most of this section was not about this subject at all, but dealt with the restoration of personal freedom, the abolition of conscription, and the reform of Parliament and of the electoral law. Only at the end did it deal with the problems of industry, and then mainly for the purpose of affirming the need for the abolition of capitalist control and the establishment of " common ownership of the means of production " ; and its only reference to the future system of control and administration of industrial enterprises was contained in a phrase demanding " the adoption, in particular services and occupations, of those systems and methods of administration and control that may be found, in practice, best to promote, not profiteering, but the general interest." This was evidently not only an evasion of the problem, but a statement of it in terms which implied, though they did not positively profess, hostility to the claims of the advocates of " workers' control." Webb, who was the main author of the document, would in fact have no truck with what he regarded as " Syndicalist " follies, and had repeatedly denounced them when they had been put forward from any quarter. Webb and those who thought with him were, moreover, able to get away without challenge on this issue by the simple device of submitting no resolution at all upon the subject among the twenty-six Resolutions voted upon by the Party Conference which adopted the new programme : so that the matter was not discussed, and the evasive statement which has just been quoted was allowed to stand.

Labour and the New Social Order, as we have seen, was circulated in draft form in 1917 together with the draft of the new Constitution, and at once attracted widespread notice. It was laid before the Party Conference which met to consider the Constitution in January, 1918, but was not discussed either then or at the adjourned Conference in February, when the Constitution was actually adopted. Instead, the affiliated Societies and Local Parties were asked to give full consideration to it in time for it to be debated in full at the next Conference, which was provisionally fixed for June, 1918. At this June Conference the National Executive, instead of submitting the document itself, put forward twenty-six Policy Resolutions mainly based upon it, but including a considerable number of additional points, while omitting, as we have seen, the disputed question of democratic industrial control. The original draft had been incomplete at many points, and it was amplified by new sections dealing with women's industrial rights (including equal pay), the rights of demobilised members of the armed forces, the representation of minorities in Parliament, the right of Ireland to self-government, the re-organisation of the British Empire as a Free Commonwealth, the establishment of separate Legislatures for Scotland and Wales, " and even for England," the development of local government services and of a comprehensive public system of Free Education, an extensive Housing policy, a generous provision of Health Services, the re-modelling of agricultural production and distribution, and several other matters which had been touched upon but lightly, or not at all, in the original draft. The twenty-six Resolutions, which went through the Conference with very little substantial amendment, took up all the available time, and left no room for the discussion of such topics as they failed to cover. International policy, except for a very general reference or two to peace and the spirit of Internationalism, was left out, as having been sufficiently covered in the War Aims Memorandum which the Party had adopted at an earlier stage.

Labour and the New Social Order, looked at in retrospect nearly thirty years later, is seen to contain in substance by far the greater part of what has been put forward in respect of home policy in subsequent Labour Programmes, and of the actual policy which the Labour Government of 1945 began vigorously to carry into effect. It is an historic document of the greatest significance, not only because it unequivocally committed the Labour Party to Socialist objectives in the sense in which Socialism had been advocated by the Fabian Society and by other " evolutionary " Socialists, but also because of the form and proportions in which the new objectives were set out. The key objectives—called in the language of Sidney Webb " the Four Pillars of the House of Tomorrow "—were set out in these words :

(a) The Universal Enforcement of the National Minimum ;
(b) The Democratic Control of Industry ;
(c) The Revolution in National Finance ; and
(d) The Surplus Wealth for the Common Good.

This way of stating the fundamental principles does not, however, fully square with the content of the document, or at all events fails to bring out some of its salient points. It begins in fact with a statement in favour of a national policy designed to assure to every citizen a minimum standard of civilised life ; and it treats as an essential part of such a policy not only the general enforcement of a living wage (to which the Conference itself added a maximum working week of forty-eight hours), but also what would be called nowadays a comprehensive policy of " Full Employment." The recognition of the obligation to ensure employment for the whole labour force as resting upon the State and the Government, and the assertion of this as being well within the Government's power by means of public works and con-trolled investment, are often regarded as derivatives of the new " Keynesian " economics which found widespread acceptance in the 1930's ; but, though the phraseology was different, the essentials of the " full employment " doctrine were contained in *Labour and the New Social Order* and were in fact put right in the forefront of the Labour programme. With this insistence on the keeping of employment at a high level went the demand for the maintenance at a satisfactory standard of life of such workers as still remained unemployed. I am not suggesting that these ideas were new, even in 1918 : they were in effect a re-statement of the old doctrine of the " Right to Work or Maintenance " which had been one of the chief slogans of Keir Hardie's I.L.P. in the 1890's and of the more realistic section of the Social Democratic Federation in the 1880's. In *Labour and the New Social Order*, however, they were already more definitely related to the pheno-menon of cyclical fluctuation in the demand for labour than they had been in earlier versions, and were also connected explicitly with the notion of " public works " as a balancing factor to be used in steadying the demand by keeping investment at a con-sistently high level.

By the second " Pillar of the House," Democratic Control of Industry, the draftsman of *Labour and the New Social Order* meant mainly public ownership under the control of a democratic Parliament, *plus* the safeguarding of personal industrial freedoms and of Trade Union bargaining rights. The draft, probably of set intention, had avoided the words " socialisation " and " national-isation," using " common ownership " instead. The Conference insisted on putting in an explicit demand for " the socialisation of industry " in the opening statement of the principles on which the document was based.

By " The Revolution in National Finance " was meant mainly a drastic overhauling of the system of taxation, designed both to prevent taxes from being levied in such a way as to trench on the National Minimum Standard of Life and to ensure progressive taxation of large incomes and the redistribution of the proceeds by way of a comprehensive system of social services—or, as we should say nowadays, Social Security.   The specific proposals included both an immediate Capital Levy for the purposes of paying off at any rate a large fraction of the War Debt and a permanent system of inheritance taxation designed to limit the amounts of money which those dying could transmit to their heirs and to appropriate more and more of the national wealth by this method for the public advantage.

Finally, " The Surplus for the Common Good " meant the application of the resources held by the public or appropriated to its use by taxation for the purpose of ensuring the largest practicable equality of opportunity for all, by means of a generous system of education, fuller provision for scientific and social research, and the development of a civilisation based on the co-operative efforts of common men and women.

It would take far too much space to summarise in this chapter the specific proposals contained in *Labour and the New Social Order*, which covered an immense amount of ground. It has seemed preferable to give, in an Appendix, a summary of the twenty-six Resolutions on which, in its final form, it was mainly based, and to round off the discussion of it here with no more than a brief comment on its general significance, elucidated by some reference to a very few particular points.

The new programme demanded in general terms " the socialisation of industry so as to secure the elimination of every kind of inefficiency and waste."   More specifically, it proposed " the Common Ownership of the nation's land, to be applied as suitable opportunities occur," and " the immediate Nationalisation of Railways, Mines, and the production of Electrical Power." It went on to demand, but without the same immediacy, the public ownership of canals, harbours and steamships—the public ownership of roads, posts and telegraphs being referred to as an accomplished fact.   These latter services, from railways to posts and telegraphs, were to be brought together " in a united national service of Communication and Transport " ;   and in this case it was laid down that there was to be " a steadily increasing participation of the organised workers in the management, both central and local." These were the only industries specifically marked down for nationalisation, though stress was laid on the need for an extension of municipal ownership in other fields. The remaining nationalisation proposal dealt with the service of Insurance, with particular reference to Industrial Life Assurance. It was further proposed that " the entire manufacture and retailing of alcoholic drink " should be taken out of private hands ; but it was not made clear how far the production was to be nationalised or municipalised, though " local option " to prohibit the sale of alcoholic drink was insisted on, and it was laid down that, where such drink continued to be sold, the sale should be under public auspices of one sort or another.

Thus land, on the one hand, and fuel, power and transport on the other occupied the key positions in the Labour Party's socialisation programme. There was no reference to steel ; but it has to be remembered that the Party's War Aims already included nationalisation of the manufacture of weapons of war. As for other industries, *Labour and the New Social Order* declared for the continuance of bulk purchase by the State of essential imports of foodstuffs and materials, and of the war-time controls over essential industries producing food and other consumers' goods. It declared for the continued " rationing " of supplies to factories in accordance with estimated national needs, and for the maintenance of the systems of " costing " for purposes of price-control that had been built up during the latter stages of the war. It demanded, on the basis of this " costing," the " fixing, for standardised products, of maximum prices at the factory, at the warehouse of the wholesale trader, and in the retail shop." This, it was said, should be " just as much the function of Government, and just as necessary a part of the Democratic Regulation of Industry, to safeguard the interests of the community as a whole, and those of all grades and sections of private consumers, in the matter of prices, as it is, by the Factory and Trade Boards Acts, to protect the rights of the wage-earning producers in the matter of wages, hours of labour, and sanitation, or, by the organised police force, the householder from the burglar."

I have stressed the point that *Labour and the New Social Order*, though it appeared under the aegis of the Labour Party Executive and was nominally drafted by a Committee of the Executive, was essentially the work of Sidney Webb and an expression of the Fabian philosophy and of Fabian policy. The Fabian Society itself was by this time ceasing to make a large contribution to the work of the Party : its energy passed over to its offspring, the Fabian Research Department. This body, after setting on foot valuable contributions to Socialist policy in its Reports on *International Government* (written by Leonard Woolf) and *How to Pay for the War*, came under Guild Socialist influence, broke away to become the Labour Research Department, and established for a time close links with the Labour Party and the Trades Union Congress, acting as their agency for purposes of research and information until they decided by stages to set up a separate organisation of their own. When the war ended, the present writer went to the Labour Party as Officer for Advisory Committees on Policy, retaining at the same time his position as Honorary Secretary of the Labour Research Department ; and for several years the connections remained very close. But Sidney Webb, who had taken a leading part in the earlier work of the Fabian Research Department (which he and Beatrice Webb had in effect founded) was now acting, not mainly through the Labour Research Department or the Fabian Society, but directly as a member of the Labour Party Executive, and in very close personal connection with Arthur Henderson.

Now Henderson, right up to 1912, when he joined the Fabian Society, had had no connections with any Socialist body. Even thereafter he took no active part in Fabian work. He had been a Trade Unionist, who had passed from his earlier Liberalism to the Labour Party ; and he had taken a particular interest in matters of labour legislation and of the living wage. He had been a keen supporter of the British and International Associations for Labour Legislation, of Trade Boards and of Anti-Sweating Crusades, but not of Socialism in any explicit sense. His study of the position had, however, convinced him, by 1917, that some sort of Socialist faith was the necessary basis for the consolidation of the Labour Party into an effective national force ; and he turned naturally to the moderate, evolutionary, social-reform Socialism of Webb and of the Fabian Society for the new gospel which he needed to give substance to the new Constitution that he had in mind.

This kind of Socialism also appealed, or at any rate appeared preferable to any more extreme or more obviously dogmatic Socialist gospel, to most of the Trade Union leaders whom Henderson had to carry with him. A good many of the professing Socialists in the Labour Party would have preferred much stronger meat. The B.S.P. wanted a full adhesion to the gospel according to Karl Marx ; and there was a substantial revolutionary, or half-revolutionary, faction in the I.L.P. as well. But the I.L.P. leaders were themselves divided, and were in a difficult position. The Fabian gospel just suited Ramsay MacDonald. It did not wholly suit Snowden, who was then a good deal further to the left ; but it suited Snowden much better than the Marxist alternative, or than any Guild Socialist gospel—to both of which he was utterly opposed by both conviction and temperament. Accordingly, the I.L.P. leaders were for the most part on Henderson's side ; and with their consent the new programme went through the Party Conference with hardly any opposition. The B.S.P. was far too weak to fight it ; and the Guild Socialists were not a political but primarily an industrial group and had no place as a body in the Labour Party.

Both at home and abroad, the Labour Party's new gospel achieved a very favourable reception, except from the extreme left. Its rival in world appeal was the new *Communist Manifesto* put forward in March, 1919, by the first Congress of the Third, or Communist, International. This proclaimed the advent of the World Revolution, and provided the basis for the foundation of Communist parties in the various countries, including Great Britain. But in 1917 and 1918, when the Labour Party's new projects were under discussion, Communism did not exist as an organised power outside the Soviet Union, and neither in Great Britain nor in most other countries had the extreme left any common leadership or programme. The traditional " reformed " Marxism of the German and other Social Democratic Parties had fallen into considerable discredit as a result of the Second International's collapse in 1914 ; and there was in Socialist thinking of the right and centre a void which *Labour and the New Social Order* appeared opportunely to fill. These conditions help to explain its enthusiastic reception in many countries—not least by progressives in the United States. In Great Britain, for both good and ill, it charted the course on which the Labour Party has been set ever since.

It remains in this chapter to record briefly the advent of a new political force which was to become the Labour Party's steady, though not always fully contented, ally during the period which culminated in the election victory of 1945. In 1917 the Annual Co-operative Congress, irritated by the subjection of Co-operative Societies to the Excess Profits Tax, by unfair treatment in the allocation of food supplies, and by the passing over of Co-operators in the appointment of Government committees dealing with food and related questions, voted, by an overwhelming majority, in favour of establishing a Co-operative Representation Committee to " secure direct representation in Parliament and on all local administrative bodies." This was a sharp reversal of policy. The Co-operative Movement had long professed its " political neutrality," which had indeed come to be regarded as one of the essential " Rochdale Principles." The Congress had once before, in 1897, on the initiative of its Scottish leader, William Maxwell, voted in favour of direct representation in Parliament ; but the following year, faced with the unwillingness of the local Societies to take any action, it had resolved to do nothing. The matter had been further considered during the next two years ; but in 1900 a Scottish resolution in favour of political action had been decisively rejected. This was the year in which the Labour Representation Committee was formed ; and from that time on a minority of Co-operators continually urged the movement to join forces with it. In 1905 the Joint Parliamentary Committee of the Co-operative Congress had again recommended political action, and a vaguely worded resolution had been carried at Congress ; but an amendment in favour of joining forces with the L.R.C. had been rejected by a large majority. In 1906 and in 1908 the advocates of Co-operative political action had met with further defeats. In 1912, however, on Maxwell's insistence, a joint committee had been set up to consider how best the Co-operative, Trade Union, and political Labour movements could work together for the purpose of " raising the economic status of the people " ; but the Co-operative Congress of 1913 rejected the committee's report, and resolved that " this Congress, while approving of concerted action with Trade Unions and other organised bodies for raising the status of labour, cannot sanction union with the political Labour Party ; and that the Central Board be instructed strictly to maintain the neutrality of the Movement in respect of party politics, so that political dissension in our ranks may be avoided." An attempt to reopen the question was met by the Congress of 1915 with a decision against any further action for " co-operation with other forces."*

War-time resentment rapidly altered the Co-operators' attitude, but not to the extent of making them ready to join forces with the Labour Party. At an emergency Conference in October, 1917, the

*For a fuller account, see my *A Century of Co-operation*, Chapter XIX.

Co-operators set up a National Co-operative Representation Committee and authorised the establishment of Local Co-operative Political Councils. They were thus already in the field as a separate political party at the time when the Labour Party adopted its new Constitution and its new Socialist statement of policy.

There was, however, obviously no room in practice for two separate mainly working-class parties, with pretty much the same immediate objectives and appealing to much the same sections of the electorate—for Trade Union and Co-operative households largely overlapped, and the new Women's Sections of the Labour Party were bound to be appealing largely to women Co-operators. Joint action began with the establishment of a Joint Committee in January, 1918, between the Parliamentary Committees of the Co-operative and Trades Union Congresses and the Labour Party Executive for the purpose of avoiding electoral clashes and of considering other forms of joint action ; and the three bodies acted together in a Manifesto welcoming President Wilson's Fourteen Points. Early in 1918 the Co-operative Representation Committee fought its first parliamentary by-election at Prestwich, in Lancashire, with H. J. May, then Secretary of the Co-operative Parliamentary Committee, as candidate. He was beaten by a Coalition Liberal by 8,520 votes to 2,832, despite local Labour support. The Co-operative Congress of 1918 decided that its candidates must run under the exclusive designation of " Co-operative," and not as " Co-operative and Labour " ; and the ten candidates whom it put into the field at the General Election of 1918 were labelled simply " Co-operative," though in fact there were informal local arrangements in the chosen constituencies to ensure Labour support. The one Co-operative candidate who secured election, A. E. Waterson at Kettering, Northamptonshire—an old Co-operative stronghold—joined the Labour Party after his election ; and the situation which then arose led to renewed negotiations in 1919 for " an electoral federation, with the ultimate aim of a united People's or Democratic Party." These resulted in 1920, not in fusion of the two parties, but in a formal draft for a " Labour and Co-operative Political Alliance." The Labour Party Executive was willing to recommend the plan ; but the Co-operative Congress of 1921 rejected it by a narrow majority, after a heated debate in which Liberal Co-operators took a prominent part. It was, indeed, rejected, not by the adherents of the Co-operative Party, but mainly by Co-operators who were hostile to Co-operative intervention in politics in any form. This was possible because the Co-operative Representation Committee had been set up, not, like the L.R.C. of 1900, as an independent body, but as a Committee of the Co-operative Parliamentary Committee, which was itself responsible to the Co-operative Congress representing the whole Co-operative movement. The further story of Co-operative-Labour political relations and of the Co-operative Party which developed out of the C.R.C. must be reserved for a subsequent chapter. Here it need only be observed that the Co-operative political enthusiasm of 1917 soon showed signs of cooling off, and that for some years the majority of Co-operative Societies gave either no support, or but lukewarm support, to the new venture.

(c) APPENDIX I

SUMMARY OF RESOLUTIONS PASSED AT THE LABOUR PARTY CONFERENCE IN LONDON, JUNE, 1918, IN CONNECTION WITH THE ENDORSEMENT OF

Labour and the New Social Order

Resolution I.—THE TASK OF SOCIAL RECONSTRUCTION, laid down that this task " ought to be regarded as involving, not any patchwork jerrymandering of the anarchic individualism and profiteering of the competitive capitalism of pre-war time . . . but the gradual building up of a new social order based, not on internecine conflict, inequality of riches, and dominion over subject classes, subject races, or a subject sex, but on the deliberately planned co-operation in production and distribution, the sympathetic approach to a healthy equality, the widest possible participation in power, both economic and political, and the general consciousness of consent which characterise a true democracy."

Resolution II.—THE NEED FOR INCREASED PRODUCTION, began by taking note of the inefficiency of capitalism and of the structure of private profit, and " its evil shadow of wages driven down by competition often below subsistence level." The resolution recognised the need for increased aggregate production of useful commodities and services, to be sought neither " in reducing the means of subsistence of the workers, whether by hand or by brain, nor yet in lengthening their hours of work . . . but in (a) the socialisation of industry in order to secure the elimination of every kind of inefficiency and waste ; (b) the application both of more honest determination to produce the very best, and of more science and intelligence to every branch of the nation's work ; together with (c) an improvement in social, political and industrial organisation ; and (d) the indispensable marshalling of the nation's resources so that each need is met in the order of, and in proportion to, its real national importance."

Resolution III.—THE MAINTENANCE AND PROTECTION OF THE STANDARD OF LIFE, advocated (i) . . . " That the standard rates of wages in all trades should, relatively to the cost of living, be fully maintained." (ii) That it should be made clear to employers that any attempt to reduce wages or worsen conditions would lead to bitter industrial strife, and that the Government should take all possible steps to avert such a calamity. (iii) That the Government, as the greatest employer of labour, should both set a good example and endeavour to influence employers, especially by insisting " on the most rigorous observance of the Fair Wages Clause in public contracts, and by recommending every local authority to adopt the

same policy." (iv) That existing industrial legislation needed amendment at many points in order to secure to every worker by hand or
brain at least the prescribed minimum of health, education, leisure
and subsistence, and that the system of a legal basic wage should be
" extended and developed so as to ensure to every adult worker of
either sex a statutory base line of wages (to be revised with every
substantial rise in prices) not less than enough to provide all the
requirements of a full development of body, mind, and character
. . ."

Resolution IV.—The Provision for the Soldiers and Sailors,
dealt with the treatment of men demobilised from the armed forces
in respect of gratuities, unemployment benefit, and the Government's duty of placing the demobilised soldier within reach of a
suitable situation at the Trade Union standard rate.

Resolution V.—The Discharge of Civilian War Workers, demanded careful advance preparation for replacing in situations the
workers discharged from the war trades.

Resolution VI.—The Restoration of Trade Union Conditions,
dealt with the implementation of Government pledges to restore all
Trade Union rules and customs suspended during the war, both in
munition factories and in other factories in which war-time substitution and dilution had been applied.

Resolution VII.—The Prevention of Unemployment, anticipating
post-war dislocation of employment, laid down that " it is the duty of
the Ministry, before demobilisation is actually begun, so to arrange
the next ten years' programme of national and local government
works and services—including housing, schools, roads, railways,
canals, harbours, afforestation, reclamation, etc.—as to be able to
put this programme in hand, at such a rate and in such districts,
as any temporary congestion of the labour market may require."
The resolution proceeded to lay upon the Government the obligation for ensuring " that the aggregate total demand for labour shall
be maintained, year in and year out, at an approximately even
level," and held that this could be secured " by nothing more
difficult or more revolutionary than a sensible distribution of the
public orders for works and services."

Resolution VIII.—Unemployment Insurance, declared that " the
best provision is the out-of-work pay of a strong Trade Union, duly
supplemented by the Government subvention guaranteed by Part
II of the Insurance Act," and thus favoured a system of State subventions to Trade Union benefits as against a general system of State
contributory unemployment insurance.

Resolution IX.—The Complete Emancipation of Women, began
by drawing attention to the changes in the position of women during
the war and went on to urge that work or maintenance should be
provided for all women displaced from employment to make way for

men returning from war service, that the principle of "equal pay for equal work" should be everywhere adopted, that Trade Unions should accept women as members in all trades in which they were employed, and that women in such trades should be employed only at Trade Union rates. It further urged (i) "That all legal restrictions on the entry of women to the professions on the same conditions as men should be abrogated. (ii) That women should have all franchises, and be eligible for election to all public bodies (including Parliament), on the same conditions as men." It also urged the inclusion of women on Committees or Commissions dealing with subjects "that are not of exclusively masculine interest," and that married women, for purposes of income tax, should be treated as "independent human beings."

Resolution X.—THE RESTORATION OF PERSONAL LIBERTY, ran as follows : "That this Conference regards as fundamental the immediate repeal and abrogation as soon as the war ends of the whole system of the Military Service Acts, and of all the provisions of the Defence of the Realm Acts restricting freedom of speech freedom of publication, freedom of the Press, freedom of travel, and freedom of choice of residence or of occupation."

Resolution XI.—POLITICAL REFORMS, urged the adoption of complete adult suffrage with absolutely equal rights for both sexes, with effective provision for absent voters and the best practicable arrangements for ensuring that every minority should have its proportionate and no more than its proportionate representation ; civic rights for soldiers and sailors, shorter Parliaments, and the "complete abandonment of any attempt to control the people's representatives by a House of Lords." The resolution also protested against the defects of the Representation of the People Act of 1918 and against the denial of political rights to Civil Servants, and recorded its opposition to any plan for a new Second Chamber, whether elected or not, embodying "any element of heredity or privilege ; any ex-officio members, such as Royal Dukes, Bishops or Law Lords ; . . . any power of veto on the decisions of the House of Commons" ; and to "any Constitution by which the Labour Party, or any other party, will find itself proportionately less strongly represented in the Second Chamber than it may be, for the time being, in the House of Commons itself."

Resolution XII.—IRELAND, unhesitatingly recognised the claim of the people of Ireland to Home Rule and to "self-determination in all exclusively Irish affairs."

Resolution XIII.—CONSTITUTIONAL DEVOLUTION, asserted that "some early devolution from Westminster of both legislation and administration is imperatively called for." It advocated that, "along with the grant of Home Rule to Ireland, there should be constituted separate statutory legislative assemblies for Scotland, Wales and even England, with autonomous administration in matters of local concern." It advocated the retention of Parliament at Westminster as a "federal assembly for the United Kingdom," and that the Ministers responsible for the Federal Departments should form, "together with Ministers representing the Dominions and India, whenever these can be brought in, the Cabinet for Commonwealth affairs for the Britannic Commonwealth as a whole."

Resolution XIV.—LOCAL GOVERNMENT, urged that in order to avoid the evils of centralisation and the drawbacks of bureaucracy the largest possible powers "should be given to the democratically elected local governing bodies," which "should be given a free hand to develop their own services, over and above the prescribed national minimum, in whatever way they choose." It urged that the local authorities should be given powers to acquire land cheaply and expeditiously and to obtain capital from the Government at cost price, and that local Councils, in addition to the "necessarily costly services of education, sanitation, and police, and the functions to be taken over from the Boards of Guardians," and to the acquisition of local public utility services, "should greatly extend their enterprises in housing and town planning, parks, and public libraries, the provision of music and the organisation of popular recreation, and also that they should be empowered to undertake, not only the retailing of coal, but also other services of common utility, particularly the local supply of milk, where this is not already fully and satisfactorily organised by a Co-operative Society." Finally, the resolution urged that new elections for the whole of each Council should be held at once and that "all Councillors should be provided with payment for any necessary travelling expenses, and for the time spent on the public service."

Resolution XV.—EDUCATION, called for . . . "a genuine nationalisation of education, which shall get rid of all class distinctions and privileges, and bring effectively within the reach, not only of every boy and girl, but also of every adult citizen, all the training, physical, mental and moral, literary, technical and artistic, of which he is capable." The resolution went on to express dissatisfaction with the recent proposals of the Government and to ask for "a systematic reorganisation of the whole educational system, from the nursery school to the university, on the basis of (a) social equality ; (b) the provision for each age, for child, youth and adult, of the best and most varied education of which it is capable, and with due regard to its physical welfare and development, but without any form of military training ; (c) the educational institutions, irrespective of social class or wealth, to be planned, equipped, and staffed according to their several functions up to the same high level for elementary, secondary, or university teaching, with regard solely to the greatest possible educational efficiency, and free maintenance of such a kind as to enable the child to derive the full benefit of the education given ; and (d) the recognition of the teaching profession, without distinction of grade, as one of the most valuable to the community."

Resolution XVI.—HOUSING, called for "a national campaign of cottage building at the public expense, in town and country alike, as the most urgent of social requirements." It demanded the building of a million new cottages during the first two or three years of peace "with capital supplied by the National Government, free of interest, and a grant-in-aid . . . at least sufficient to prevent the schemes involving any charge on the rates " ; these cottages, to be designed to fit in with local circumstances, to include "four or five rooms, larder, scullery, cupboards, and fitted bath," and to be built not more than ten or twelve to the acre with sufficient garden ground.

Resolution XVII.—THE ABOLITION OF THE POOR LAW AND THE DEVELOPMENT OF THE MUNICIPAL HEALTH SERVICE, called for "the immediate reorganisation, in town and country alike, of the public provision for the prevention and treatment of disease, and the care of the orphans, the infirm, the incapacitated, and the aged needing institutional care." It called for the abolition of the Poor Law and for the merging of the Poor Law functions in those of directly elected general local authorities "without either the stigma of pauperism or the hampering limitations of the Poor Law system."

Resolution XVIII.—TEMPERANCE REFORM, advocated taking "the entire manufacture and retailing of alcoholic drink out of the hands of those who find profit in promoting the utmost possible consumption." The resolution went on to advocate local option, either to prohibit the sale of alcoholic drink or to regulate the conditions of sale and the number of public houses, and also to lay down "the manner in which the public places of refreshment and social intercourse in their own districts should be organised and controlled."

Resolution XIX.—RAILWAYS AND CANALS, insisted on the retention in public hands of the railways and canals, with "expropriation of the present stockholders on equitable terms," with the purpose of establishing, "in conjunction with harbours, docks, ports and telegraphs " "a united national public service of communications and transport, to be worked, unhampered by any private interest (and with a steadily increasing participation of the organised workers in the management, both central and local) exclusively for the common good."

Resolution XX.—THE NEW ELECTRICITY SUPPLY, advocated "the provision, by the Government itself, of the score of gigantic superpower stations by which the whole kingdom could be supplied," and "the linking up of the present municipal and joint stock services for distribution to factories and dwelling-houses at the lowest possible rates."

Resolution XXI.—COAL AND IRON MINES, opposed the handing back of the coal mines to private ownership, and advocated the complete expropriation of private interests in coal and iron resources and their development. It demanded that "the supply of these minerals should henceforth be conducted as a public service (with steadily increasing participation in the management, both central and local, of the workers concerned) ", and called for the retail distribution of household coal at a fixed price " identical at all railway stations throughout the kingdom " by the elected local authorities of the areas concerned.

Resolution XXII.—LIFE ASSURANCE, declared for the nationalisation, with compensation, of " the whole function of assurance." It further proposed that the State should develop the insurance business in conjunction with the Friendly Societies and should organise in conjunction with them " a safe and remunerative investment of popular savings."

Resolution XXIII.—AGRICULTURE AND RURAL LIFE, demanded that " the Government should resume control of the nation's agricultural land and ensure its utilisation, not for rent, not for game, not for the social amenity of a small social class, not even for obtaining the largest percentage on the capital employed, but solely with a view to the production of the largest possible proportion of the foodstuffs required by the population of these islands under conditions allowing of a good life to the rural population and at a price not exceeding that for which foodstuffs can be brought from other lands." The resolution proposed a combination of Government farms, small holdings, municipal agricultural enterprise, and " farms let to co-operative societies and other tenants, under covenants requiring the kind of cultivation desired." It further urged the provision of healthy and commodious cottages with allotments and small holdings for agricultural labourers, and of an adequate agricultural minimum wage ; and it proposed that the distribution of foodstuffs in the towns " should be taken out of the hands of the present multiplicity of dealers and shopkeepers, and organised by consumers' Co-operative Societies and the local authorities working in conjunction."

Resolution XXIV.—CONTROL OF CAPITALIST INDUSTRY, insisted on the need for maintaining the system of war controls and audits over processes, profits and prices in capitalist industry, for retaining "the economies of centralised purchasing of raw materials, foodstuffs and other imports," and, " therefore, the ' rationing ' of all establishments under a collective control."

Resolution XXV.—NATIONAL FINANCE, demanded that . . ." an equitable system of conscription of accumulated wealth should be put into operation forthwith, with exemption for fortunes below £1,000, and a graduated scale or rate for larger totals." The resolution went on to urge that necessary national revenue should be derived " mainly from direct taxation alike of land and accumulated wealth, and of income and profits, together with suitable imposts upon luxuries, and that the death duties and the taxation upon unearned incomes should be substantially increased and equitably regraded." It demanded that the system of land taxation should be revised so as to give effect to the principle that the land of the nation belongs to the nation and should be used for the nation's benefit. The resolution further protested against the unfair taxation of Co-operative Societies, and urged that the Post Office Savings Bank "should be developed into a national banking system for the common service of the whole community."

Resolution XXVI.—THE NEED FOR A "PEACE BOOK," demanded that the Government should formulate and publish for public criticism in a "Peace Book" the main outlines of its reconstruction policy before it finally adopted such policy.

Resolution XXVII.—"LABOUR AND THE NEW SOCIAL ORDER," ordered that the draft Report on Reconstruction entitled *Labour and the New Social Order* should be revised in accordance with the resolutions carried by the Conference.

(c) APPENDIX 2

THE LABOUR PARTY CONSTITUTIONS OF 1914 AND 1918

1918

1. NAME
The Labour Party.

2. MEMBERSHIP
The Labour Party shall consist of all its affiliated organisations,* together with those men and women who are individual members of a Local Labour Party and who subscribe to the Constitution and Programme of the Party.

*Trade Unions, Socialist Societies, Co-operative Societies, Trades Councils and Local Labour Parties. (Footnote in original.)

3. PARTY OBJECTS
National
(a) To organise and maintain in Parliament and in the country a Political Labour Party, and to

1914

1. The Labour Party is a Federation consisting of Trade Unions, Trades Councils, Socialist Societies, and Local Labour Parties.

2. (See below).

3. Co-operative Societies are also eligible.

4. A National Organisation of Women, accepting the basis of this Constitution and the policy of the Party, and formed for the purpose of assisting the Party, shall be eligible for affiliation as though it were a Trades Council.

2. OBJECT
To organise and maintain in Parliament and the country a political Labour Party.

ensure the establishment of a Local Labour Party in every County Constituency and in every Parliamentary Borough, with suitable divisional organisation in the separate constituencies of Divided Boroughs ;

(*b*) To co-operate with the Parliamentary Committee of the Trades Union Congress, or other kindred organisations, in joint political or other action in harmony with the Party Constitution and Standing Orders ;

(*c*) To give effect as far as may be practicable to the principles from time to time approved by the Party Conference ;

(*d*) To secure for the producers by hand or by brain the full fruits of their industry, and the most equitable distribution thereof that may be possible, upon the basis of the common ownership of the means of production and the best obtainable system of popular administration and control of each industry and service ;

(*e*) Generally to promote the Political, Social, and Economic Emancipation of the People, and more particularly of those who depend directly upon their own exertions by hand or by brain for the means of life.

Inter-Dominion

(*f*) To co-operate with the Labour and Socialist organisations in the Dominions and the Dependencies with a view to promoting the purposes of the Party, and to take common action for the promotion of a higher standard of social and economic life for the working population of the respective countries.

1918   1914

International

(g) To co-operate with the Labour and Socialist organisations in other countries, and to assist in organising a Federation of Nations for the maintenance of Freedom and Peace, for the establishment of suitable machinery for the adjustment and settlement of International Disputes by Conciliation or Judicial Arbitration, and for such International Legislation as may be practicable.

4. PARTY PROGRAMME

(a) It shall be the duty of the Party Conference to decide, from time to time, what specific proposals of legislative, financial, or administrative reform shall receive the general support of the Party, and be promoted, as occasion may present itself, by the National Executive and the Parliamentary Labour Party : provided that no such proposal shall be made definitely part of the General Programme of the Party unless it has been adopted by the Conference by a majority of not less than two-thirds of the votes recorded on a card vote.

(b) It shall be the duty of the National Executive and the Parliamentary Labour Party, prior to every General Election, to define the principal issues for that Election which in their judgment should be made the Special Party Programme for that particular Election Campaign, which shall be issued as a manifesto by the Executive to all constituencies where a Labour Candidate is standing.

(c) It shall be the duty of every Parliamentary representative of the Party

1918   1914

to be guided by the decision of the meetings of such Parliamentary representatives, with a view to giving effect to the decisions of the Party Conference as to the General Programme of the Party.

5. THE PARTY CONFERENCE

1. The work of the Party shall be under the direction and control of the Party Conference, which shall itself be subject to the Constitution and Standing Orders of the Party. ⸱ The Party Conference shall meet regularly once in each year, and also at such other times as it may be convened by the National Executive.

2. The Party Conference shall be constituted as follows :—

(a) Trade Unions and other societies affiliated to the Party may send one delegate for each thousand members on which fees are paid.

(b) Local Labour Party delegates may be either men or women resident or having a place of business in the constituency they represent, and shall be appointed as follows :

In Borough and County Constituencies returning one Member to Parliament, the Local Labour Party may appoint one delegate.

In undivided Boroughs returning two Members, two delegates may be appointed.

In Divided Boroughs one delegate may be appointed for each separate constituency within the area. The Local Labour Party within the constituency shall nominate and the Central Labour Party of the Divided Borough shall appoint the delegates. In addition to such delegates, the Central Labour Party in each

9.* ANNUAL CONFERENCE

The National Executive shall convene a Conference of its affiliated Societies in the month of January each year.

Notice of resolutions for the Conference and all amendments to the Constitution shall be sent to the Secretary by November 1st and shall be forthwith forwarded to all affiliated organisations.

Notice of amendments and nominations for Executive Committee, Treasurer, Secretary, two Auditors, and Annual Conference Arrangements Committee of five members, shall be sent to the Secretary by December 15th, and shall be printed on the Agenda.

*The matters covered in this Rule were transferred in 1918 to Standing Orders, the material change being the transference of the Conference from January to June.

1918

Divided Borough may appoint one delegate.

An additional woman delegate may be appointed for each constituency in which the number of affiliated and individual woman members exceeds 500.

(c) Trades Councils under Section 8, clause c, shall be entitled to one delegate.

(d) The members of the National Executive, including the Treasurer, the members of the Parliamentary Labour Party, and the duly sanctioned Parliamentary Candidates shall be *ex officio* members of the Party Conference, but shall, unless delegates, have no right to vote.

6. THE NATIONAL EXECUTIVE

(a) There shall be a National Executive of the Party consisting of twenty-three members (including the Treasurer) elected by the Party Conference at its regular Annual Meeting, in such proportion and under such conditions as may be set out in the Standing Orders for the time being in force, and this National Executive shall, subject to the control and directions of the Party Conference, be the Administrative Authority of the Party.

(b) The National Executive shall be responsible for the conduct of the general work of the Party. The National Executive shall take steps to ensure that the Party is represented by a properly constituted organisation in each constituency in which this is found practicable ; it shall give effect to the decisions of the Party Conference ; and it shall interpret the Constitution and Standing Orders and Rules of the

5.* THE NATIONAL EXECUTIVE

The National Executive shall consist of 16 members, 11 representing the Trade Unions, 1 the Trades Councils, Women's Organisations, and Local Labour Parties, and 3 the Socialist Societies, who shall be elected by ballot at the Annual Conference by their respective sections, and the Treasurer, who shall also be elected by the Conference.

*A part of the matter covered by this Rule was transferred to Standing Orders in 1918.

6. The National Executive Committee shall :

1. Appoint a Chairman and Vice-Chairman, and shall transact the general business of the Party ;

1918

Party in all cases of dispute, subject to an appeal to the next regular Annual Meeting of the Party Conference by the organisation or persons concerned.

(c) The National Executive shall confer with the Parliamentary Labour Party at the opening of each Parliamentary session, and also at any other time when the National Executive or the Parliamentary Party may desire such conference, on any matters relating to the work and progress of the Party, or to the efforts necessary to give effect to the General Programme of the Party.

7. PARLIAMENTARY CANDIDATES

(a) The National Executive shall co-operate with the Local Labour Party in any constituency with a view to nominating a Labour Candidate at any Parliamentary General or By-Election. Before any Parliamentary Candidate can be regarded as finally adopted for a constituency as a Candidate of the Labour Party, his candidature must be sanctioned by the National Executive.

1914

2. Issue a list of its Candidates from time to time, and recommend them for the support of the electors ;

3. Take all necessary steps to maintain this Constitution.

4. All its members shall abstain strictly from identifying themselves with or promoting the interests of any other Party.

(4) 1. A Candidate must be promoted by one or more affiliated Societies which make themselves responsible for his election expenses.

2. A Candidate must be selected for a constituency by a regularly convened Labour Party Conference in the constituency.

3. Before a Candidate can be regarded as adopted for a constituency, his candidature must be sanctioned by the National Executive ; and when at the time of a by-election no candidate has been so sanctioned, the National Executive shall have power to withhold its sanction.

1918

(*b*) Candidates approved by the National Executive shall appear before their constituencies under the designation of " Labour Candidate " only. At any General Election they shall include in their Election Addresses and give prominence in their campaigns to the issues for that Election as defined by the National Executive for the General Party Programme. If they are elected, they shall act in harmony with the Constitution and Standing Orders of the Party in seeking to discharge the responsibilities established by Parliamentary practice.

(*c*) Party Candidates shall receive financial assistance for election expenditure from the Party funds on the following basis :

Borough Constituencies, £1 per 1,000 electors.

County Divisions, £1 15s. per 1,000 electors.

8. AFFILIATION FEES

1. Trade Unions, Socialist Societies, Co-operative Societies, and other organisations directly affiliated to the Party (but not being affiliated Local Labour Parties or Trades Councils) shall pay 2d. per member per annum to the Central Party Funds with a minimum of 30s. od.

The membership of a Trade Union for the purpose of this clause shall be those members contributing to the political fund of the Union established under the Trade Union Act, 1913.

1914

3. Candidates and Members must maintain this constitution ; appear before their constituencies under the title of Labour candidates only ; abstain strictly from identifying themselves with or promoting the interests of any other Party ; and accept the responsibilities established by Parliamentary practice.

(4) 4. 25 per cent of the Returning Officer's net expenses shall be paid in respect of Candidates, but no such payment shall be made to a Candidate of any Society which is in arrears in its contributions to the Party.

8. AFFILIATION FEES AND DELEGATES

1. Trade Unions and Socialist Societies shall pay 1d. per member per annum, with a minimum of 10s., and may send to the Annual Conference one delegate for each thousand members.

The membership of a Trade Union for the purpose of this clause shall be those members contributing to the political fund of the Union established under the Trade Union Act, 1913.

1918

1914

2. The affiliation of Trades Councils will be subject to the following conditions :

(a) Where Local Labour Parties and Trades Councils at present exist in the same area every effort must be made to amalgamate these bodies, retaining in one organisation the industrial and political functions, and incorporating the constitution and rules for Local Labour Parties in the orders of the amalgamated body.

(b) Where no Local Labour Party is in existence and the Trades Council is discharging the political functions, such Trades Council shall be eligible for affiliation as a Local Labour Party, providing that its rules and title be extended so as to include Local Labour Party functions.

(c) Where a Local Labour Party and a Trades Council exist in the same area, the Trades Council shall be eligible to be affiliated to the Local Labour Party, but not to the National Party, except in such cases where the Trades Council was affiliated to the National Party prior to November 1, 1917. In these cases the Executive Committee shall have power to continue affiliation on such conditions as may be deemed necessary.

(d) Trades Councils included under Section (c) shall pay an annual affiliation fee of 30s. od.

Local Labour Parties must charge individually enrolled members, male, a minimum of 1s. od. per annum, female 6d. per annum ; and 2d. per member so collected must be remitted to the Central Office with a minimum of 30s. od., as the affiliation fee of such Local Labour Party.

(1) 2. A Local Labour Party in any constituency is eligible for affiliation, provided it accepts the Constitution and policy of the Party, and that there is no affiliated Trades Council covering the constituency, or that, if there be such a Council, it has been consulted in the first instance.

2. Trades Councils and Local Labour Parties with 5,000 members or under shall be affiliated on an annual payment of 15s. ; similar organisations with a membership of over 5,000 shall pay £1 10s., the former Councils to be entitled to send one delegate with one vote to the Annual

1918   1914

Conference, the latter to be
entitled to send two delegates and have two votes.

In addition to these payments, a
delegation fee of 5s. 0d. to the Party
Conference or to any Special Conference may be charged.

In addition to these pay-
ments, a delegate's fee to
the Annual Conference may
be charged.

EXTRACTS FROM THE STANDING ORDERS.

RULES continued*

3. VOTING

Voting at the Party Conference shall
be by Cards issued as follows :
Trade Unions and other affiliated
Societies shall receive one Voting Card
for each 1,000 members or fraction
thereof paid for.
Trades Councils affiliated under
Section 8, clause c, shall receive one
Voting Card.
Every Local Labour Party shall
receive one Voting Card for each
delegate sent in respect of each Parlia-
mentary Constituency within its area.
Central Labour Parties in Divided
Boroughs shall receive one Voting Card.

10†. VOTING AT ANNUAL
    CONFERENCE

There shall be issued to
affiliated Societies represented at the Annual Con-
ference voting cards as
follows :
1. Trade Unions and
Socialist Societies shall receive one voting card for
each thousand members, or
fraction thereof, paid for.
2. Trades Councils, Local
Labour Parties, and Wo-
men's Organisations shall
receive one card for each
delegate they are entitled to
send.
Any delegate may claim
to have a vote taken by card.

*These points were included in
the Rules in 1918.

†A part of the matter covered
by this Rule was transferred to
Standing Orders in 1914.

4. NATIONAL EXECUTIVE

See Rule 5, on page 75.

1. The National Executive shall be
elected by the Annual Conference,
as a whole, and shall consist, apart
from the Treasurer, of (a) 13 representatives of the affiliated organisations ; (b) 5 representatives of the
Local Labour Parties ; and (c) 4
women. The Executive shall be elected

by ballot vote on the card basis from three lists of nominations.

2. Each affiliated national organisation shall be entitled to nominate one candidate for List A ; and two candidates if the membership exceeds 500,000. Each candidate must be a *bona fide* member of the organisation by which he or she is nominated.

3. Each Parliamentary Constituency organisation, through its Local Labour Party or Trades Council, may nominate one candidate for List B, and the candidate so nominated must be resident or have his or her place of business within the area of the nominating Local Labour Party.

4. Each affiliated organisation shall be entitled to nominate one woman candidate for List C, and two candidates if the membership exceeds 500,000 ; whether such nominees are or are not members of the nominating organisation.

5. The National Executive shall elect its own Chairman and Vice-Chairman at its first meeting each year, and shall see that all its officers and members conform to the Constitution and Standing Orders of the Party. The National Executive shall present to the Annual Conference a Report covering the work and progress of the Party during its year of office, together with the Financial Statement and Accounts duly audited.

6. No member of the Parliamentary Committee of the Trades Union Congress is eligible for nomination to the National Executive.

5. TREASURER

The Treasurer shall be elected separately at the Annual Conference.

See Rule 5, on page 75.

1918   1914

Each affiliated organisation may nominate a candidate for the Treasurership
independent of any other nomination
it makes for the National Executive.

6. Secretary	7. The Secretary
The Secretary shall be elected by the Annual Party Conference, and be *ex officio* a member of the Conference ; he shall devote his whole time to the work of the Party, but this shall not prevent him being a Candidate for or a Member of Parliament. He shall remain in office so long as his work gives satisfaction to the National Executive and Party Conference. Should a vacancy in the office occur between two Annual Conferences, the Executive shall have full power to fill the vacancy, subject to the approval of the Annual Conference next following.	The Secretary shall be elected by the Annual Conference, and shall be under the direction of the National Executive.

Nominations for the office shall be
on the same conditions as for the
Treasurership.

CHAPTER III

POST-WAR

(a) The General Election of 1918

The results of the elections—Composition of the Parliamentary Labour Party—Defeat of the I.L.P. leaders and of Arthur Henderson—Labour representation by regions—How Lloyd George won the Election—" Hanging the Kaiser " and " Making Germany Pay "—The fate of Coalition Labour.

(b) The Transition to Peace

The main events of 1919—The Berne International Conference—The International Federation of Trade Unions and the International Co-operative Alliance rebuilt—Demobilisation and Inflation—Labour Unrest—Control of wages and prices in the Miners' Southport Programme—The Coal Commission—The Clyde and Belfast Strikes—The National Industrial Conference—The Coal Commission's Interim Report—Labour's gains at Local Elections—The International Labour Charter and the I.L.O.—Workers' Control—Labour and the Peace Treaties—The Coal Commission's Final Reports—The Government and the Miners—The Miners appeal to the whole Trade Union movement—The Railway Strike of September, 1919—The T.U.C., the Miners and the Triple Alliance—The " Mines for the Nation " Campaign—The change in the Trade Unions—The I.L.P. in Transition—The question of " Socialist Unity "—The I.L.P. and the International —The Second International at Berne—" War Responsibility "—" Democracy and Dictatorship "—The " Branting " and the " Adler-Longuet " Resolutions—The Second International after Berne—"Direct Action "—Secessions from the Second International—The foundation of the Third International—The beginnings of the Communist Party—Lenin on Communist policy—The Communist Party applies for affiliation to the Labour Party.

(c) Direct Action

The question of " political " strikes—The T.U.C. rejects a general strike for Mines Nationalisation—The Soviet-Polish War—The *Jolly George* incident—Labour and intervention in Russia—The Hands Off Russia Committee—Lloyd George's Russian policy—Labour sets up the Council of Action—A General Strike threatened—War with Russia averted—A further Mining Crisis—The Miners call on the Triple Alliance—The T.U.C. promises support—The Miners strike alone—The Emergency Powers Act—The " Datum Line " settlement—The centre of disturbance shifts to Ireland—The " Black and Tans "—The post-war boom ends—Rising unemployment—Unemployed demonstrations begin—The Labour Commission to Ireland—Labour's Irish Policy—Labour Conference on Unemployment—*Unemployment : a Labour Policy*—The decline of revolutionary feeling—The Labour Party rejects Communist affiliation.

(d) Black Friday and After

The growth of unemployment—The East Woolwich by-election—Decontrol of the coal mines—A new mining crisis develops—The mining lock-out of 1921—Labour support for the Miners—Frank Hodges at the House of Commons—The Triple Alliance and the Miners' claims—" Black Friday "—The Miners fight on—Their defeat—More than 2 millions out of work—The Labour movement and the unemployed—The rise of Local Unemployed Committees—Hunger Marches—The National Unemployed Workers' Committee Movement—Calls for " Direct Action " rejected—The Poplar Guardians sent to prison—" Poplarism " and the Government's relief policy—The burden of local relief.

(a) The General Election of 1918

Until 1918 the words " Khaki Election " meant the General
Election of 1900, held in the heat of the South African War. From
1918 they were used also, as an alternative to " Coupon Election,"
in referring to the General Election which was rushed on after
the Armistice—a contest which returned Lloyd George's
Coalition with an enormous majority. The new House
of Commons which met at the beginning of 1919 consisted of 359
Coalition Unionists and Conservatives, including a few who
called themselves " National," 127 Coalition Liberals, and
fifteen Coalition Labour or " National Democratic " M.P.s, as
against fifty-seven official Labour M.P.s, a single Co-operator,
and three unofficial Labour men, of whom two became regular
members of the Parliamentary Labour Party after the Election.
The remainder of the new House consisted of thirty-four
Asquithite Liberals, seven Irish Nationalists, seventy-three Sinn
Feiners (who refused to take their seats), and a few " Independents." The Conservatives, in the absence of the Sinn Feiners,
had a clear majority of the whole House : the Liberals, both
wings together, were down from nearly 387 in 1905 and 272 in
December, 1910, to 161, and the vast majority of these for the
time being followed Lloyd George. The Labour Party was
numerically a little stronger than in 1910, when it had numbered
only forty-two ; but in relation to the vastly increased number of
its candidates it suffered a very severe defeat, in which most of its
best known leaders were involved. Out of 363 endorsed candidates it returned only fifty-seven, and out of another thirty-one
unendorsed Labour candidates who were more or less in sympathy
with its policy only three were elected—of whom one later rejoined
the Liberal Party. Of the Co-operative candidates only one was
elected ; and five left-wing Socialists, mostly soon to join the
Communist Party, were all beaten. So were the two candidates
of the Highland Land League ; whereas the four sitting Labour
M.P.s who fought on the Coalition ticket all retained their seats
and were reinforced by ten (out of twenty-eight candidates)
elected as representatives of the jingo National Democratic Party
and by one Seamen's candidate of a similar complexion.
Of the sixty—including the Co-operator and two of the " unendorsed " Labour M.P.s—who made up the Labour Party in
the new House of Commons—no fewer than twenty-five were
candidates put forward by the Miners' Federation, and another

twenty-four represented other Trade Unions. Out of fifty candidates put forward by the I.L.P., only three secured election ;
and the B.S.P. did not secure the return of a single candidate.
The Local Labour Parties were not much more fortunate, only
seven of their 140 nominees being successful. The new Labour
Party, during the first Parliament after the war, was overwhelmingly a Trade Union Party, and half of the Trade Union representation was drawn from a single Union.

Among those who met defeat were all the members of the small
I.L.P. group that had sat in the war-time Parliament. Ramsay
MacDonald, at Leicester, and F. W. Jowett, at Bradford, were
beaten by Coalition N.D.P. candidates. Snowden, standing alone
for the double-barrelled constituency of Blackburn, was beaten
by a Coalition Liberal and a Coalition Unionist running in
double harness. W. C. Anderson, in the Attercliffe division of
Sheffield, regarded as a Labour stronghold, was heavily beaten
by a Trade Unionist who stood as a Coalition Liberal. Finally,
Tom Richardson, not re-adopted for his old constituency,
Workington, was defeated in the Bosworth division of Leicester-
shire by a Coalition Liberal. The three I.L.P. men who won
seats were newcomers—Ben Spoor, at Bishop Auckland, Neil
Maclean, at Govan, in Glasgow, and William Graham, at
Edinburgh. In addition to the fifty candidates who stood directly
under I.L.P. auspices, many others were members of the I.L.P.—
in fact, nearly half the total number of Labour candidates—but
the great majority of them were beaten. Even George Lansbury
lost at Bow and Bromley to a Coalition Unionist. On the other
hand, J. R. Clynes, who had parted company with the I.L.P.
on the war issue, was returned unopposed for the Platting division
of Manchester—his old seat.

The losses were not limited to the anti-war Labour men. Arthur
Henderson, who moved from Barnard Castle, which had been cut
in two by the re-distribution under the Representation of the
People Act, to East Ham South, was also heavily defeated by a
representative of the National Democratic Party. Among the
beaten candidates who had not been members of the old Parliament were Ernest Bevin at Bristol, Walter Citrine, at Wallasey,
and Sidney Webb, who put up a good fight for London University.

The election results left the Labour Party badly short of leaders
in the new Parliament. Besides Clynes, the ex-members of the
war-time Government who had obeyed the call to leave the

Coalition and had kept their seats included John Hodge and William Brace. William Adamson, who had led the Party since Henderson's withdrawal, was also returned ; and other leading figures included J. H. Thomas, of the N.U.R., Will Crooks, Tom Shaw of the Textile Workers, and Ben Tillett. These formed but a weak parliamentary team, to face the difficult problems of the transition from war to peace ; and the weakness of the Parliamentary Labour Party was one factor in shifting the centre of Labour activity from the House of Commons to the industrial field. Henderson got back for Widnes, at a by-election held in August, 1919 ; but he did not resume the leadership of the Party, and continued to devote himself mainly to the work of organisation outside Parliament.

As for the Election itself, Lloyd George swept the board with the aid of his war prestige and a most unscrupulous exploitation of an excited but bewildered public. The Coalition candidates fought largely on the issues—as far as there were any issues—of " hanging the Kaiser " and " making Germany pay " the full costs of the war—pay " till the pips squeaked," as one Coalition leader eloquently declaimed. I was not a candidate ; but I spoke at a good many places, and in all save one large and attentive audiences seemed to take well my demonstrations of the absurdity and unreality of these popular slogans. But when it came to the polling, not one of the candidates I had spoken for was elected. Many better-known figures must have had the same experience. Almost everywhere, there were enough Labour supporters of a decent peace and a reconstructed social order to fill a good-sized hall ; but on polling day these voters were overwhelmed, except in some of the mining areas and in a few other working-class districts. Of the sixty-one who formed the Labour Party at the beginning of 1919, no fewer than twenty-six represented the Northern Counties, ten Wales and Monmouthshire, and thirteen the industrial Midlands. Seven were from Scotland ; whereas Greater London had but four, and the whole of the rest of Southern and Western England only one—from the Forest of Dean coalfield. The total Labour vote was about 2,250,000, out of nearly 11,000,000 votes cast. The electorate numbered over 21,000,000 ; but this total included about 4,000,000 service voters, of whom fewer than 1,000,000 actually voted.

The results were not, or at any rate are not in retrospect, at all surprising. Omitting Ireland, the total British electorate was 7,000,000 in 1910, and 19,500,000, or thereabouts, in 1918. Most

LABOUR AND SO-CALLED LABOUR CANDIDATES AT THE GENERAL ELECTION OF 1918

	Endorsed Labour		Co-operative		Un-endorsed Labour		Socialist		Highland Land League		Coalition Labour		N.D.P.		Seamen's	
	E	D	E	D	E	D	E	D	E	D	E	D	E	D	E	D
London	2	28	—	—	—	4	—	—	—	—	—	—	—	—	—	—
English Boroughs	18	112	—	5	1	5	—	4	—	—	2	1	7	8	1	1
English Counties	22	110	1	1	—	8	—	1	—	—	1	—	1	7	—	—
Welsh Boroughs	2	8	—	—	—	—	—	—	—	—	—	—	1	—	—	—
Welsh Counties	7	8	—	—	1	1	—	—	—	—	—	—	—	—	—	—
Scottish Burghs	3	19	—	1	1	3	—	—	—	—	1	—	1	2	—	—
Scottish Counties	3	15	—	2	—	2	—	—	—	2	—	—	—	1	—	—
Northern Ireland	—	—	—	—	—	5	—	—	—	—	—	—	—	—	—	—
Universities	—	6	—	—	—	—	—	—	—	—	—	—	—	—	—	—
TOTAL ELECTED	57	—	1	—	3*	—	—	—	—	—	4†	—	10	—	1	—
Defeated Candidates	—	306	—	9	—	28	—	5	—	2	—	1	—	18	—	1
	363		10		31		5		2		5		28		2	

Total Labour (endorsed and unendorsed), Co-operative and Socialist candidates numbered 409.
*Jack Jones, F. H. Rose and Sir Owen Thomas.
†In addition, Colonel Wedgwood was elected as a Coalition Radical.
E—Elected.   D—Defeated.

LABOUR PARTY : BODIES SPONSORING ENDORSED CANDIDATES, 1918

	Elected	Defeated	Total
I.L.P.	3	47	50
B.S.P.	—	4	4
Local Parties	5	135	140
Miners' Federation	25	26	51
U. Textile Factory Workers . .	4	6	10
General Workers	4	3	7
Dockers	2	2	4
Steel Smelters	2	2	4
Engineers	1	16	17
N.U.R.	1	5	6
R.C.A.	—	6	6
Other Trade Unions . . .	10	48	58
Total Socialist Societies . . .	3	51	54
Total Local Parties . . .	5	135	140
Total Trade Unions	49	114	163
	57	300	357
	Universities . .		6
			363

of the electors, including all the women, were voting for the first time, under conditions which allowed hardly any opportunity for political education. The Liberal Party had been shattered by the war, and was divided into two bitterly warring factions. The Labour Party had only just been reorganised, and was hampered by the sharp divisions in its ranks over the war issue. Most of its candidates were newcomers in the parliamentary field, and had little electoral organisation behind them. With the Tory machine in good working order, and Tories and Coalition Liberals working closely together and reinforced by enough Labour dissidents to create confusion in the electors' minds, it was no wonder that Arthur Henderson's hastily improvised machine was unable to stand the heavy strain that was put upon it. The position in 1945 was entirely different ; for by then Labour was well established as one of the two great claimants to political power, and the Labour election machine all over the country was at least as good as anything that its opponents could set against it.

It is convenient at this point to write the epitaph of " Coalition Labour " and of the National Democratic Party. Of the four " Labour " Ministers who remained in the Coalition, G. J. Wardle resigned for health reasons in 1920, and G. N. Barnes retired and James Parker was defeated in 1922, leaving only G. H. Roberts to sit in the Parliament of 1922 and to go down to defeat the following year. In addition to these four, Stephen Walsh, who had been elected as a Labour M.P. under the auspices of the Miners' Federation, accepted an invitation after the General Election to join the Coalition Government ; but after a narrow division of the Lancashire and Cheshire Miners on a motion to demand his resignation, he left the Government a few days after joining it, and remained to become a Cabinet Minister in the Labour Government of 1924. Of the ten N.D.P. Members in the 1918 Parliament, one, Eldred Hallas, joined the Labour Party, but did not stand again in 1922 ; and the other nine were all defeated by Labour candidates at the 1922 Election. Thus passed away the predecessor of the " National Labour Party " of 1931, which was to perish hardly less ingloriously in its turn.

LABOUR REPRESENTATION BY REGIONS, 1918
(Including Co-op and Unendorsed)

Greater London	4
Southern England	—
Western England	1
West Midlands	6
East Midlands	7
Lancashire and Cheshire	14
Yorkshire	6
Northern Counties	6
Wales and Monmouthshire	10
Scotland	7
Northern Ireland	—
Universities	—
	61

(b) The Transition to Peace

The year 1919, the first of the transition from war to peace, was crowded with a confusion of events at home and abroad. In international affairs, it was the year of the Peace Conference in Paris, of the signing of the Peace Treaty (in June) and of the setting up of the League of Nations and of the International Labour Organisation. In Germany it began with the suppression of the Spartacists, and ended with the Weimar Constitution in operation. In Italy it saw the foundation of the Fascist Party by Mussolini and the occupation of Fiume by D'Annunzio. In

Ireland it was a year of premonitory disturbances, leading up in November to the Government's attempt to suppress Dail Eirann and the Sinn Fein movement and to formulate compromise proposals for an Irish settlement. It saw Soviet Governments come and go in Bavaria and in Hungary. In the Soviet Union it was a period of civil war and foreign intervention on the side of various " White Hopes " ; but it ended with Kharkov and Kiev in the hands of the Red Army. In India the year was one of increasingly serious disturbances, following upon the announcement of the Rowlatt Bills endowing the Government with drastic police powers : it was the year of the Amritsar Massacre ; and it ended with the enactment of the Montagu-Chelmsford Reforms vitiated by the alienation of the Indian national leaders.

In the world of international Socialism, 1919 began with the meeting of the Berne International Socialist Conference, and was filled with arguments about the respective merits of the Second and Third Internationals and the possibilities of International Socialist unity. It also saw the reconstitution of the International Federation of Trade Unions at Amsterdam in June, and of the International Co-operative Alliance. It saw Socialists of almost all complexions protesting vigorously against the terms of the Peace Treaty with Germany, and against Allied intervention in Russia.

Economically, 1919 was a year of confusion, with demobilisation proceeding fast in the belligerent countries and with endless troubles over the building of new States with new frontiers and the adjustment of currency problems. Inflation was continuing and increasing its momentum over a large part of the world ; and labour troubles were everywhere, as Trade Unions attempted to negotiate new terms of employment or joined with consumers to protest against the rising cost of living. Many of the year's problems did not come to a head until later, as Governments played for time in the hope that revolutionary feelings would die down and a return to " normalcy "—in the current phrase—become possible if only the emergency of demobilisation could be successfully got over.

Great Britain shared in the troubled confusions of the time, but felt them much less than most of the European countries. War had left the British economic structure almost intact ; and there were no troubles over frontiers or the settlement of new constitutional régimes. Nor was the currency, though inflated, as yet seriously out of hand. The Government's main problems were those of demobilisation and of widespread labour unrest, ready at any moment to take form in large strikes and outpourings of half-revolutionary phrases, but never to go seriously to the length of really revolutionary action.

In these circumstances, the Government's main objects were, first, to get demobilisation over as quickly as possible, and to ensure at the same time that the demobilised soldiers should have no hardships or grievances sufficient to turn their thoughts in a revolutionary direction ; and secondly, to play for time in handling the unrest in industry, so as to avoid having too many industrial disputes simultaneously on its hands. On the whole, Lloyd George handled these problems with much adroitness, though not without making a good many promises which he repudiated when the immediate danger was over.

Demobilisation had to be speeded up beyond the planned rate, because it proved impossible to maintain discipline in many of the camps in which soldiers were kept hanging about with nothing to do. In order to speed it up without serious repercussions, the Government adopted the " donation " plan, which assured the discharged soldier or sailor (and also, for a shorter period, the discharged munition worker) a weekly benefit until he could find employment. Meanwhile, in industry, wages were pegged at the existing levels, as a minimum, by the Wages Temporary Regulation Act ; and the war-time control machinery was preserved just enough to check for a time the rise in prices. This did not become really sharp until the following year, when decontrol took full effect and there was an orgy of speculation and profiteering in every field.

At the beginning of 1919 there were two special danger points. The Miners' Federation, at its Southport Conference in January, threatened to strike at once on a programme which included not only higher wages and reduced hours of labour but also nationalisation of the mines, with control by a Mining Council of which the Miners' Federation claimed the right to nominate half the members. Behind this was the further threat of combined action by the Triple Industrial Alliance of Miners, Railwaymen and Transport Workers—of which the completion was announced on February 25. Before this, on February 12, the Miners had decided on a strike ballot, and the Government had endeavoured to buy them off with the offer of a Coal Commission to report both upon their wages and hours' demands and upon the issue of nationalisation. The Miners' Federation would not agree, unless it were allowed to nominate half the members of the Commission ; and after long argument the Federation got a good deal of its way, being allowed three direct representatives, *plus* three non-miners appointed with its approval, as against three colliery owners and three other representatives of employer interests. These twelve, with the Chairman, were to constitute the Commission, and the Government gave an explicit promise to abide by its recommendations. The Commission was set up by Act of Parliament, under Mr. Justice Sankey, and began its sessions on March 3, pledged to report on wages and hours in little more than a fortnight, and on nationalisation with the very minimum of delay.

Meanwhile important sections of the engineers and shipyard workers had taken action upon their own, without waiting for the sanction of the national Trade Unions concerned. In January, 1919, strikes broke out in Belfast for a working week of forty-four hours, and on the Clyde for one of forty hours. On the Clyde especially, there were serious disturbances arising out of the strike ; and the Riot Act was read on January 31. Unsupported by the national Trade Unions, which denounced their unconstitutional precipitancy, these local movements could not succeed unless rank and file action spread to other areas. In these circumstances Lloyd George decided to summon a National Industrial Conference of employers and Trade Unions and Whitley Councils to meet on February 27, in the hope of stemming the unrest by persuading the two sides to enter into negotiations for a new charter of industrial relations ; and most of the Trade Unions were persuaded to accept this invitation, though the Miners, Railwaymen and Transport Workers, united in the Triple Alliance, and also the Engineers refused. Thus seriously weakened, the Conference began to bargain about a post-war charter covering hours of labour, minimum wage legislation, and the establishment of permanent negotiating machinery for the adjustment of general relations in industry ; and while the delegates talked, and the employers made large concessions on which they were to go back as soon as the crisis was over, the moment for successful action passed.

It was, however, not enough to keep the lesser Unions talking, unless the Miners' Federation could be prevented from calling a strike ; for such a strike, very likely to be supported by the Railwaymen and Transport Workers, might easily have been the signal for a general industrial upheaval. Accordingly the Sankey Commission, dividing its task into two, rushed out on March 20 with an Interim Report granting the miners' demands for higher wages, conceding a seven hours' day and holding out the prospect of a six hours' day to come, and thus endeavouring to split the Miners' programme into two halves, in the hope that the meeting of the purely economic claims would cause the strike threat to be given up. That indeed is what did immediately happen : the Miners' Federation accepted the concessions offered, and agreed to await the Coal Commission's further report ; and on March 26 an Interim Report from the National Industrial Conference held forth pleasing prospects of a universal maximum working week of forty-eight hours, of minimum wage legislation, and of other significant industrial reforms.

In the course of the following month, April, the Labour Party made large gains at the local elections for County and District Councils—the first since the war—and a few days later the Peace Conference adopted a high-sounding Labour Charter, to serve as a basis for the work of the projected International Labour Organisation, which was to be set up in conjunction with the League of Nations. Then, in May, came the publication of the Peace Terms, followed promptly by a repudiation by the Labour Party. A few days later the Government, pretending to be eager to meet the demand for " workers' control," offered to sell the National Shipyards built during the war to the Trade Unions—well aware that they were unfitted to compete under peace conditions with the private shipyards and that the offer would, if accepted, involve the Unions in certain economic disaster. The offer was refused ; and thereafter the Unions could be taunted with a reluctance to face up to the responsibilities of control when the chance was given them.

Early in June the Labour Party issued a full-length Manifesto, decisively condemning the Allied Government's Peace Proposals, and this protest was endorsed by the Party Conference held at Southport later in the month. On June 23 appeared the further Reports of the Coal Commission, dealing with the questions of nationalisation and control. On these issues, the members had very naturally failed to reach agreement ; and there were four rival reports, signed respectively by the Chairman, by the six Labour representatives, by five out of the six employers, including the three colliery owners, and by a leading technical engineer, Sir Arthur Duckham. Both the Chairman, Sir John Sankey, and the Labour representatives advocated nationalisation of the mines, which the minority of six opposed. The five employers favoured a continuance of the existing form of ownership, whereas Duckham advocated the establishment of district amalgamations of collieries, with a minority of workers' representatives on their boards of directors, but under private ownership and majority shareholder control. As against this, all four Reports were in favour of the nationalisation of the ownership of the coal measures themselves.

There was thus a bare majority for mines nationalisation, as well as a unanimous approval of the public ownership of coal, but, unfortunately, Sir John Sankey and the six Labour representatives differed on the question of control. Sir John recommended a system of management by District Councils, loosely co-ordinated by a National Mining Council, but mainly autonomous, with a minority of their members appointed by the workers and the majority nationally. The Labour Report insisted on a larger representation of the workers on the lines of the Miners' Federation plan of joint control. Furthermore, the three Miners' Federation representatives opposed giving compensation to landowners, while approving of it in the case of colliery concerns, whereas the three other Labour representatives, who included Sidney Webb, were in favour of compensation for all property taken over by the State.

These secondary differences were soon to be used by the Government as an excuse for refusal to carry out the terms of the Reports. There was, Lloyd George argued, no majority in favour of anything, or why had no report signed by a majority of the Commission been produced? The Miners' Federation at its Keswick Conference in mid-July agreed to accept the Sankey proposals, though it expressed its dissatisfaction with them. A local strike in Yorkshire enabled the Government to defer until mid-August any public announcement of its policy ; but rumours that nationalisation was to be rejected were in circulation almost from the moment when the Reports were issued. They proved to have been correct : Lloyd George, on the plea that the Commission had failed to agree, rejected nationalisation outright, and put forward instead a diluted version of Sir Arthur Duckham's scheme, which was at once nicknamed " Duckham and water." It was hardly meant to be taken seriously : nobody supported it, and the Government took advantage of its cold reception to recede from it, putting nothing at all in its place.

The Miners, confronted with the Government's refusal to nationalise the industry, though a majority of the Coal Commission had recommended nationalisation and the Government had promised to act on its Report, had to consider whether to carry out the strike threat which had been suspended by the Commission's appointment. After consulting their partners in the Triple Industrial Alliance, they decided against calling a strike by themselves and in favour of an appeal to the entire Trade Union movement to take action to compel the Government to carry out its promise. A few days later the Trades Union Congress, in full session, pledged its support to the Miners' Federation, and resolved to call a Special Congress "for the purpose of deciding the form of action to be taken to compel the Government to accept the Majority Report of the Commission" should persuasion prove to be of no avail.

At this point the mining problem was pushed temporarily into the background by the national railway dispute of September, 1919. The railway Trade Unions had been negotiating with the Railway Executive Committee (the railways being still under Government control) for a new post-war agreement. In September, when the Unions rejected what Sir Eric Geddes, the Minister of Transport, called his "definitive offer," the negotiations broke down ; and on September 27 the railway Trade Unions called a national strike. Instead of acting through either the Trades Union Congress or the Triple Alliance, the Trade Unions, in consultation with the Railwaymen, formed a special Trade Union Mediation Committee to negotiate with the Government, and with the help of this body a compromise was reached, and the strike ended on October 3. A few days later, the Trade Union leaders met Lloyd George and pressed him to agree to nationalise the mines, only to be faced with an unequivocal refusal.

In accordance with the decision taken in September, it therefore became necessary to summon a Special Trades Union Congress to settle what action to take. This Congress, however, did not meet until December ; and in the meantime there had been a considerable cooling off. In particular, awkward questions had been asked about the control of policy in any sympathetic strike in which one Union received the support of others. If the Triple Alliance, or the Trades Union Congress, called a strike on behalf of the Miners' claims, would it be for the supporting body or for the Miners to decide on what terms the strike should be brought to an end ? This was to prove a difficult question to settle, both in 1921 and in 1926. Moreover, events were not working out in accordance with the neat ideas on which the Triple Alliance had been founded. The Alliance plan had been that all the Unions included in it should formulate their separate programmes and should put them all forward simultaneously, with the united support of all sections, and further that no section should settle, or order a return to work, until the claims of all the others had been met. It was not, however, proving easy in practice to adhere to this arrangement. The crises in the mining and railway industries came to a head, not simultaneously, but at different times ; and the Transport Workers had not reached their own point of crisis, or of readiness for action on their own demands, when their partners in the Alliance in turn arrived at the point of proposing to strike. The Miners, after calling for the support of the Triple Alliance in July, had agreed to go with their partners to the Trades Union Congress and to call for the help of the whole Trade Union movement, rather than rely on the Railwaymen and the Transport Workers alone to come out in their support. The Railwaymen, when their own crisis arrived, did not want the Miners or Transport Workers to strike with them : they preferred a limited strike, backed by mediation under the auspices of as many other Unions as possible ; and thereafter they were inclined to argue that, as they had not called on the Miners to strike for them, the Miners had no claim to call on them for strike action on an issue affecting only themselves.

Accordingly, when the Special Trades Union Congress met in December, 1919, nobody was much surprised when it was decided, instead of declaring a strike in favour of nationalisation of the mines, to resort to " political action " in the form of a " Mines for the Nation " propaganda campaign, to which all sections of the Labour movement were invited to give the fullest support. This campaign was designed to educate public opinion, which had been found to be somewhat apathetic about the nationalisation issue. Accordingly, meetings on " The Mines for the Nation " were held all over the country during the following months ; but the practical effect was that the Miners' Federation's bluff appeared to have been called, and Lloyd George to have got away with his repudiation of the Government's promise to carry the Coal Commission's recommendations into effect. Even the agreed recommendation that the ownership of the coal itself should be socialised was dropped ; and it was made plain that the Government's policy was to have no truck with nationalisation in any field, and to terminate as quickly as possible such of the war-time controls as had not been given up already.

In effect, between the beginning and the end of 1919 the atmosphere of the Labour movement had greatly changed. Even among the miners, the meeting of the wages and hours claims had done much to lessen the pressure for strike action ; and in most Unions, as the unsettlements due to the cessation of war work and the general post back to peace-time employments became less, the orthodox leaders regained control and the rank and file rebel leaders lost much of their power. This applied especially in engineering and shipbulding, for there employers took advantage of the cessation of war contracts and of the consequent scaling down to dismiss the more militant shop stewards. The Shop Stewards' Committees, which had been the most aggressive element in the Trade Union movement, rapidly melted away ; and, although much militant feeling remained, it found for the time no point of focus or of common leadership.

The Socialists, even if they wished, were in no position at this stage to give a lead. The I.L.P. in particular, was in the thick of an internal argument which covered the whole field of future policy, including the function which it ought to take in the Labour movement now that the Labour Party had adopted a broadly Socialist programme and had decided to become a mass-party based on individual as well as on affiliated membership. Ramsay MacDonald, now out of Parliament, had agreed early in 1919 to take charge of the task of reorganising the I.L.P. to fulfil its new functions ; but at the same time the left wing inside it was pressing for Socialist Unity in support of the Russian Revolution and for a new programme of a more revolutionary cast, including much more explicit provision for " workers' control " than the Labour Party had written into its new programme, or than either MacDonald or Snowden was able to stomach. At the same time the British Socialist Party, inspired by the Russian Revolution and by the *Communist Manifesto* of the Third International, was pressing for Socialist Unity, and above all for common Socialist action to stop the continuing Allied intervention in Russia ; and the I.L.P. was induced to join with the B.S.P. and the still more militant Socialist Labour Party first in a joint Manifesto on the question of intervention, and then in negotiations for permanent joint action over a wider field. These negotiations soon broke down on a rift between the I.L.P. and B.S.P. on the one hand and the S.L.P. on the other over the question of using parliamentary action for constructive purposes, and not merely for propaganda, and on the question of affiliation to the Labour Party, to which the S.L.P. was then irreconcilably opposed. But the differences inside the I.L.P. itself continued to give trouble. The I.L.P. Conference, held at Easter, 1919, passed, on Neil Maclean's motion, a resolution in favour of workers' control in industry, defeating a hostile amendment ; and differences also arose between F. W. Jowett on the one hand and Snowden and MacDonald on the other over the question of parliamentary procedure. Jowett and his Bradford followers wanted a drastic reform of Parliament, involving the introduction of a Standing Committee procedure based on that of the local authorities and the virtual abolition of Cabinet responsibility. Their resolution was met by the carrying of the Previous Question, but only on the understanding that the matter would be further considered in the branches during the coming year and brought up again for decision at the next I.L.P. Conference.

At this stage the I.L.P., far from losing members as a result of the new Labour Party Constitution, was growing fast. One hundred and thirty-nine new branches were established during the year 1918–19 ; and the Council estimated the total membership at Easter, 1919, at 80,000—a figure which had to be drastically reduced a year later, when it was put at 45,000. Even this lower estimate, however, meant a big increase over the war-time figures. In fact, the membership was highly fluid, new members flocking in fast only to drop out as the immediate excitement of the early months of 1919 declined.

Not the least difficult of the problems facing the I.L.P. was that of its relation to the International Socialist movement. As we have seen, it had been excluded from independent representation at the Allied Labour and Socialist Conferences held during the war, and also from the Labour delegation to the proposed Stockholm Conference ; but it had continued, together with the B.S.P. and the Fabian Society, to be represented on the British Section of the International Socialist Bureau. As soon as the Armistice was signed, the Labour Party Executive authorised Henderson, who was still secretary to the British Section of the Bureau, to take steps to co-operate with the Socialists of other countries in convening an International Labour Conference to meet simultaneously with the Peace Conference in accordance with the decisions taken by the Allied Labour Conference in 1918. This gathering was finally fixed, not for Paris, but for Berne, in Switzerland, the date of assembly being January 26, 1919. But the Labour Party Executive felt its hands to be tied by the earlier decisions in the matter of representation at Berne ; and accordingly the British delegation was made up entirely of Labour Party and Trades Union Congress representatives, the Socialist Societies being again excluded from separate representation. Henderson, however, anxious to placate the I.L.P., secured that MacDonald and Mrs. Snowden, as members of the Labour Party Executive, should be included in the delegation.

The Berne Conference, owing to delays over passports and other formalities, was not able to open its official sessions until February 3 ; when all the delegates had arrived, there were eighty, representing twenty-one countries. The American Federation of Labor, which had been represented in London in 1918, refused to send delegates. So did the Swiss Socialist Party, which had been active in the Zimmerwald and Kienthal Conferences and was hostile to the Second International. The Italian Socialists attended only with a watching brief. Russia was represented only by delegates of the exiled groups of Mensheviks and Social Revolutionaries, by two delegates from Georgia, and by two Ukrainian separatists, who put in an appearance at the last moment. The German delegation represented both the Majority and the Independent Social Democratic Parties ; and both Majority and Minority wings of the French Socialists were in attendance. Huysmans, the Belgian secretary of the International Socialist Bureau, acted as Secretary to the Conference.

The Berne Conference, which was designed both to bring immediate pressure on the peace negotiators at Paris and to take the first steps towards the reconstruction of the Second International, travelled over a great deal of ground. It was confronted at the outset with a demand from some of the delegates—notably some of the French—for priority on the agenda for a discussion of " war reponsibility," in effect an arraignment of the German Majority Socialists. This issue was referred to a special Commission, which secured from the German Majority a declaration, not admitting war guilt, but affirming that " by the Revolution the German proletariat has overthrown and destroyed the old system that was responsible for the war," and pledging the German Socialists " to fight in the spirit and service of the International, side by side with the Socialists of all countries, for the realisation of Socialism within the League of Nations." This did not satisfy everybody, but it afforded a means of shelving the question and of getting down to business.

The other question for which priority was demanded was the

problem of " Democracy and Dictatorship "—in other words,
that of the issues between the adherents of Bolshevism and orthodox Social Democracy or evolutionary Socialism of the British
type. On this set of issues the Conference was of course heavily
weighted on the anti-Bolshevik side ; but it was unable to reach
agreement. The resolution adopted by a large majority—called
the " Branting " resolution after the Swedish Socialist leader—
was unequivocally hostile to Bolshevism and all its works. It
laid down that

A reorganised society more and more permeated with Socialism
cannot be realised, much less permanently established, unless it rests
upon triumphs of Democracy and is rooted in the principles of liberty.

Those institutions which constitute Democracy—freedom of speech
and of the Press, the right of assembly, universal suffrage, a Government responsible to Parliament, with arrangements guaranteeing
popular co-operation and respect for the wishes of the people, the
right of association, etc.,—these also provide the working classes with
the means of carrying on the class struggle.

The resolution, after dealing at some length with the immediate
situation, went on to call upon Socialists throughout the world to
close their ranks, and " to do their utmost to ensure that Socialism
and Democracy, which are inseparable, shall triumph everywhere." Its terms make plain that its authors were postulating
parliamentary institutions of a West European type as the means
of achieving Socialism by gradualist means, the pace of advance
being limited by the necessity of securing popular consent at
every stage. It is further to be observed that the resolution
defined Democracy in purely political and non-economic terms,
and treated Socialism and Democracy as " inseparable," but also
as two quite distinct things—a point of view wholly at variance
with that of Bolshevism.

The rival resolution, known as the " Adler-Longuet Resolution," after its Austrian and French sponsors, proceeded from the
anti-war Socialists, and began by denouncing the " patriots "
who had paralysed international Socialist action during the war
and by " warning the working classes against any kind of stigma
which may be applied to the Russian Soviet Republic." It went
on to affirm that no sufficient materials existed for a judgment on
the Russian system, and to warn against " any decision which
would make the meeting of the working classes of all countries
more difficult in the future." " We desire," it declared, " to
reserve free entry into the International for the Socialist and

Revolutionary Parties of all countries conscious of their class interests." This resolution was supported by the Dutch, Norwegian, Irish, and Spanish delegates, by the French majority, by half the Austrian delegation, and by one Greek. The Branting resolution was carried by the votes of the British, both the German parties, the Swedes and Danes, the Finns, the Hungarians, the Canadians and a number of other delegations, as well as by minorities from France and Italy (the Italian majority not taking part in the division) and by the various Russian, Ukrainian and Georgian delegations.

Thus the stage was set for the long battle between "Democracy" and " Dictatorship," between the rival Internationals, and between Communist and Social Democratic doctrines in many countries. Not that the Berne minority stood for Communism, in any form. Far from it. The Adler-Longuet group wanted a single International, within which all tendencies would be represented, and the lion and the lamb would lie down together in the name of Socialist Unity.

This is not the place for any account of the rest of the labours of the Berne Conference—of the high hopes based upon the League of Nations, the long resolutions dealing with the terms of peace, the welcome given to the proposal to set up the International Labour Organisation, the draft Labour Charter drawn up for presentation to the Paris negotiators, and the demand for the speedy release of prisoners of war. All that need be said further is that the Conference set up an Executive of three—Branting, Henderson and Huysmans—to carry out its decisions and to take further action in conjunction with a Commission of two representatives from each country. This Commission sent delegates to interview Clemenceau as President of the Peace Conference (and got little out of him), prepared a long series of resolutions dealing mainly with particular territorial issues and with the organisation of the League of Nations, and decided to convene a further International Labour and Socialist Conference to meet in Geneva in February, 1920, at which further steps were to be taken towards reconstituting the International on a permanent basis. At this Conference, the question of " Democracy and Dictatorship " was to be further discussed. In the event, its meeting was postponed until July, 1920.

Meanwhile the Commission, meeting at Lucerne in August, 1919, had decided to set up a special Commission to study the problem of " Democracy and Dictatorship " ; and in October

Huysmans sent out a letter to all the Labour and Socialist bodies asking for a report on " The Political System of Socialism," to be submitted to this Commission. The I.L.P. prepared in response to this request a report which, after recognising certain shortcomings of the existing parliamentary system, went on to reject the Soviet system as " not the best form for an industrial democracy, though it may be a very efficient revolutionary form," and to declare in favour of an amended parliamentary régime and against " direct action " for political purposes, of which it stated that " the risks of failure are so great that its political practicability is slight." The I.L.P. report made, however, some concession to the revolutionary point of view when it declared that :

A revolutionary dictatorship of the proletariat need not be necessary for the transition from Capitalism to Socialism, but whether it has to be resorted to or not depends solely upon the policy of the capitalists themselves, and not upon the political necessities of Socialism.

This concession, however, was promptly discounted in the next two sentences.

Socialists ought not to allow capitalist interests and designs to direct Socialist propaganda and methods. That, in most politically democratic countries, will only strengthen the hands of the reaction, and in countries well equipped with modern military weapons will only lead to massacre, not to revolution.

The I.L.P., though it found itself on the Adler-Longuet side in the controversy over dictatorship, was not in any real disagreement on this question—or at any rate its leaders were not —with the Labour Party. There was, however, enough pressure upon it from its own left wing, and it was enough in sympathy with the opposition to the " social patriots," not to wish to cut connections with the Bolsheviks. It therefore attempted to stand for a United Socialist International, though there was no real prospect that its attitude and that of the adherents of the Third International could be reconciled. For the time being, however, the middle point of view to which it adhered was gaining strength. At Berne, the German Independent Socialists had voted with the majority ; but their party Conference in December, 1919, decided to leave the Second International and to open up negotiations for unity with the Third. The I.L.P. gave its support to this move, in which the Swiss Socialist Party assumed the lead. A few months later, in March, 1920, the French Socialist Party also seceded from the Second International.

Meanwhile, the foundation of the Third International at the World Conference called by the Bolsheviks in March, 1919, was followed by an attempt to create a Communist Party in Great Britain under the directions laid down by the Conference. When the I.L.P. had dropped out of the negotiations for " Socialist Unity," there remained as possible elements for incorporation the British Socialist Party, the Socialist Labour Party, and a few localised bodies, of which the most important were the South Wales Socialist Society and Sylvia Pankhurst's Workers' Socialist Federation, which had developed out of a left-wing women's organisation in East London that had broken away from the militant suffragists. When these bodies met to discuss unity, serious differences at once appeared. The B.S.F. was affiliated to the Labour Party and wished to retain its affiliation ; but the other three bodies were all hostile. Indeed, the South Wales Socialist Society and the Workers' Socialist Federation were both against parliamentary action of any kind, holding Syndicalist or Anarchist rather than political Communist views. The Socialist Labour Party was not against political action, but insisted that Parliament must be used only as a means of revolutionary propaganda, and opposed affiliation to the Labour Party, which it regarded as a " tool of Capitalism." Actually, before long the S.L.P. Executive withdrew from the Unity negotiations, only to find that the majority of the members, impressed by the need for obedience to the decrees of the Third International, did not agree with it. The result was that a number of members of the S.L.P. called in April, 1920, an unofficial Conference of their own, to which most of the branches sent delegates. This Conference threw the Executive over, and resumed negotiations under a new Committee. The outcome was the formation of a body called the Communist Party Unity Group, which joined hands with the B.S.P. in a Provisional Joint Committee for the Communist Party, and decided to summon a Communist Unity Conference to meet in July, 1920.

Before the Conference met, a magistral voice intervened in the dispute. Answering a request for guidance from the Joint Provisional Committee, Lenin wrote as follows :

DEAR COMRADES,

Having received the letter of the Joint Provisional Committee of the Communist Party of Britain, dated 20 June, I hasten to reply, in accordance with their request, that I am in complete sympathy with their plans for the immediate organisation of the party in England.

I consider the policy of Comrade Sylvia Pankhurst and of the Workers' Socialist Federation in refusing to collaborate in the amalgamation of the British Socialist Party, Socialist Labour Party and others into a Communist Party to be wrong.

I personally am in favour of participation in parliament, and adhesion to the Labour Party on condition of free and independent Communist activity. This policy I am going to defend at the Second Congress of the Third International on 15 July at Moscow. I consider it most desirable that a Communist Party be speedily organised on the basis of the decisions and principles of the Third International, and that the Party be brought into close touch with the Industrial Workers of the World and the Shop Stewards' Movement in order to bring about their complete union.

LENIN.

Moscow, 8 July.

This letter, of course, achieved the desired result. At the Communist Unity Conference of July, 1920, a resolution in favour of affiliation to the Labour Party was carried by 115 votes to 85 ; and early in August the Executive of the newly formed Communist Party of Great Britain made the first of its many applications for affiliation. The number of dissentients, however, was large ; and the Party suffered from severe growing pains, though Lenin's letter was followed by the endorsement of his policy at the Moscow Congress and by the publication of his book *Left Wing Communism : an Infantile Disorder*, in which he amplified and rammed home his arguments against the " deviationists."

(c) Direct Action

Hardly had the I.L.P. issued its report condemning the use of the General Strike for political purposes when the question came again dramatically to the front. In the course of 1920 a political use of the strike weapon was mooted on three separate occasions— on the issue of mines nationalisation, as a move designed to stop British intervention on the Polish side in the Russo-Polish War, and as a protest against the Government's policy of repression in Ireland. The first of these occasions arose out of Lloyd George's final refusal to nationalise the coal mines, and out of the evident inefficacy of the Mines for the Nation campaign in inducing him to change his attitude. In March, 1920, in accordance with the decision of the Trades Union Congress when the campaign was launched, a Special Congress was held for the purpose of deciding what further action to take. The Miners' Federation, meeting on the previous day, had voted by 524,000 to 346,000 in favour of a general strike to enforce nationalisation ; but at the Special Trades Union Congress only 1,050,000 votes were cast in support of this course, whereas 3,732,000 voted in preference for further political action—which meant in effect no action for the time being.

No sooner had the Trade Unions resolved against industrial action on the question of nationalising the mines than a fresh issue involving direct action for a political purpose began to develop. In April, 1920, the Poles launched their offensive against the Ukraine and, to the accompaniment of loud plaudits from the reactionaries in the West, advanced upon Kiev, which was captured on May 8. Two days later, the London dockers who were called upon to load a vessel named the *Jolly George* with munitions of war destined for Poland, having made sure of the support of their Union, refused to coal the ship until the munitions were removed.

Ever since the Bolshevik Revolution the British Labour Movement had been protesting against British and Allied intervention in Russian affairs. Direct action to stop British intervention had been mooted at the Labour Party Conference of 1919, at which both Robert Smillie and Herbert Morrison had strongly criticised the inaction of the Parliamentary Party, and had demanded that, in Morrison's words, intervention " should be resisted with the full political and industrial power of the whole Trade Union movement " ; and the Conference by a two-to-one majority had endorsed their attitude. In November, 1919, mainly under left-wing pressure, but supported by the main groups of all tendencies except the extreme right, a national Hands Off Russia Committee had been set up. By the beginning of 1920, direct British intervention seemed to have collapsed with the defeat one after another of the " White Hopes " to whom aid and countenance had been given. But now came a still more dangerous onslaught ; for the Poles had an organised army, and it was regarded as doubtful whether the Red Army would be strong enough to resist the attack. Very speedily, however, the tide turned. Kiev was re-taken on June 13, and it soon became clear that Poland was threatened with defeat. The British Government thereupon intervened with proposals for an armistice on terms most disadvantageous to the Russians, who at first rejected them but subsequently agreed to enter into negotiations with the Polish Government. On August 1 the negotiations for an armistice broke down ; and the British Government thereupon addressed to the Soviet Union a note threatening intervention on the Polish side unless the Russians halted their advance. On August 6 what was practically a British ultimatum was sent to Moscow. The Poles, meantime, had agreed to re-open direct negotiations ; but the British and French Governments agreed nevertheless to act together against the Russians.

These were the circumstances under which the British Labour movement felt impelled to take action to stop further British intervention against the Soviet Union. On August 4, Henderson, on behalf of the Labour Party, sent telegrams to all the local affiliated bodies, calling for immediate " Citizen Demonstrations" to protest against war with Russia. The response was widespread and enthusiastic ; but in face of the combined threat of the British and French Governments it was evident that more drastic measures were needed. On August 9, a joint meeting of the Trades Union Congress Parliamentary Committee, the Labour Party Executive, and the Parliamentary Labour Party unanimously passed the following resolution :

> That this Joint Conference, representing the Trades Union Congress, the Labour Party, and the Parliamentary Labour Party, feel certain that war is being engineered between the Allied Powers and Soviet Russia on the issue of Poland, and declares that such a war would be an intolerable crime against humanity ; it therefore warns the Government that the whole industrial power of the organised workers will be used to defeat this war ; that the Executive Committees of affiliated organisations throughout the country be summoned to hold themselves ready to proceed immediately to London for a National Conference ; that they be advised to instruct their members to "down tools" on instructions from that National Conference ; and that a Council of Action be immediately constituted to take such steps as may be necessary to carry the above decisions into effect.

The Conference then proceeded to appoint the Council of Action and to send a delegation to interview Lloyd George on the following day. The interviewers found Lloyd George defiant. Asserting that Polish independence was at stake, he appealed to Labour's resolutions in favour of an independent Poland, and gave every sign, both on this occasion and in the House of Commons later the same day, of his intention to persist with intervention. The same evening, the publication of the Russian peace terms made it clear that the Soviet Union, so far from threatening

Polish independence, was offering the Poles a frontier more favourable than had been proposed by the Allies in the " Curzon Line." Meanwhile the French Government poured oil upon the flames by not only offering the Poles the fullest military assistance, but also recognising the " White " Government set up by General Wrangel in South Russia.

On August 13, the Special Labour Conference summoned by the Council of Action met in London and endorsed the action taken by the meeting of August 9, and the decision to form the Council. It instructed the Council of Action " to remain in being until they had secured ..

(1) An absolute guarantee that the armed forces of Great Britain shall not be used in support of Poland, Baron Wrangel, or any other military or naval effort against the Soviet Government.

(2) The withdrawal of all British naval forces operating directly or indirectly as a blockading influence against Russia.

(3) The recognition of the Russian Soviet Government and the establishment of unrestricted trading and commercial relationships between Great Britain and Russia.

In a further resolution, the Conference authorised " the Council of Action to call for any and every form of withdrawal of labour which circumstances may require to give effect to the fore-going policy," and called " upon every Trade Union official, Executive Committee, Local Council of Action, and the membership in general to act swiftly, loyally, and courageously in order to sweep away secret bargaining and diplomacy and to ensure that the foreign policy of Great Britain may be in accord with the well-known desires of the people for an end to war and the interminable threats of war." The Council of Action was empowered to take all necessary steps to implement this policy ; and the Trades Union Congress was called upon to raise a general levy to meet the costs of any measures that might be required.

This was drastic enough. The Labour delegates were conscious that the great mass of public opinion was with them in opposing the war. Earlier in the year, German Labour had demonstrated the effectiveness of a General Strike backed by wide popular support in defeating the Kupp Putsch of January, 1920. This success undoubtedly helped to stiffen the British Labour attitude in the Polish crisis.

The crisis, however, was by no means at an end ; for the French persisted in their intervention and, under their influence, the Russo-Polish negotiations which had begun at Minsk were broken off. The British Government, in conjunction with the Italians, issued a further note threatening a refusal to have any dealings with the Soviet Government. The Council of Action sought a further interview with the British Government ; but Balfour, who was acting in Lloyd George's absence, refused to receive them. Meanwhile, negotiations were resumed at Riga ; and the Council decided to send a delegation to attend, only to be met by a refusal to issue passports. The Government thus continued to flout the Council ; but there can be no doubt that Lloyd George was in fact frightened by its threats into abandoning his policy of intervention, or that it did succeed in preventing Great Britain from giving further assistance either to the Poles or to General Wrangel. The British Labour movement was not in a position to stop French intervention ; but it did greatly weaken the French Government's position, and make possible the conclusion of the Riga Treaty of October between the Poles and the Soviet Union.

A prominent feature of the Labour action during the Polish crisis was the rapid establishment by the Trades Councils and Local Labour Parties of Local Councils of Action in all the important centres. The Labour movement showed an excellent capacity for improvising local organisation to meet the emergency, as it did again in 1926. If it had been necessary to call a General Strike, there can be no doubt that there would have been a practically universal response from Trade Unionists, backed by a very large amount of sympathy from the rest of the public.

As matters turned out, the resumption of peace negotiations and Lloyd George's change of policy under Labour pressure made strike action unnecessary on the Polish issue. The Polish crisis, however, was still in being when attention was sharply diverted to other matters. The Miners' Federation was no longer pressing for a strike to enforce nationalisation ; but it had reached a deadlock with the Coal Controller on its demand for higher wages to meet the rapidly rising cost of living, coupled with a reduction in the price of coal, which had been raised so as to yield a very high profit-margin ; and on August 31 the Miners' delegates voted in favour of strike action and called upon their partners in the Triple Alliance for support. The Railwaymen and Transport Workers met and agreed to give backing to the Miners' demands ; and on September 2 it was announced that a mining strike would be called on September 25 unless the Government gave way. On September 8 the Trades Union Congress endorsed the Miners' claims. Further negotiations followed, the Government refusing any advance in wages except in return for an increased output of coal. Strike action was postponed ; but on the failure of the discussions the Miners' Federation again appealed to the Triple Alliance for support. At the ensuing meeting of the Alliance, J. H. Thomas, on behalf of the Railwaymen, stated that, if they were called upon to strike on the Miners' behalf, they would insist on full power to settle the dispute being placed in the Alliance's hands ; and the meeting ended without any definite promise of combined strike action, with a decision that a deputation from the Alliance should visit the Prime Minister and urge him to concede the Miners' claims. The deputation was fruitless : it was already clear that a combined strike of the three big industries in the Alliance was improbable, and the Government felt able to take a stiff line. Some of the Miners' leaders, including Robert Smillie, thereupon urged that the Miners should agree to arbitration on the wages issue, which had been offered by the Government ; but the Miners' Conference rejected this advice. The Railwaymen's leaders then announced that their Conference had decided against a sympathetic strike, and the Transport Workers that they had reached no decision, but favoured a renewed attempt at mediation. The Miners, after a further deputation to Lloyd George, thereupon postponed their strike notices and reopened negotiations ; but these again broke down, and on October 16 the Miners struck alone, without any further attempt to secure sympathetic action by the Triple Alliance. This body, however, reappeared on the scene a few days later, and on October 21 the National Union of Railwaymen announced that it would strike three days later unless a settlement were reached.

The Government met this threat by introducing into Parliament on the following day the Emergency Powers Bill, arming it with wide powers to maintain public services in face of a strike. The same day, the Parliamentary Committee of the Trades Union Congress summoned a special Conference of all Trade Union Executives to deal with the critical situation that appeared to be in prospect. But before this Conference could meet, Lloyd George had reopened negotiations with the Miners' leaders ; and these negotiations were still in progress when it did meet, on October 27, the day on which the Emergency Powers Bill became an Act. On the following day, the Miners' Executive reached a provisional settlement with the Government, and agreed to refer it to a ballot vote ; and upon this the Trade Union Conference dispersed without taking any further action. The ballot vote of the Miners actually resulted in a very small majority in favour of rejecting the proposed settlement ; but the majority was too small for the Miners' Executive to feel justified in continuing the strike, which was accordingly ended on November 3, on the basis of a wage-compromise relating the miners' future earnings to the amount of coal produced. The threatened sympathetic strike of the railway workers was called off : the Trade Unions in general were not called upon to take any action. Nevertheless, once again the nation had come to the very verge of a strike which, if not general, would have gone far to paralyse industry and to dislocate the entire system of supply to the consuming public. On this occasion the issue had been purely industrial, and no question of striking for a political object had been involved.

No sooner was the coal problem temporarily out of the way than the centre of interest shifted to Ireland, where an irregular war had been for some time proceeding between the Sinn Feiners and the British army of occupation. The British, through the notorious " Black and Tans," were pursuing a policy of violent and brutal reprisals in an attempt to suppress the Irish Rebellion. Already in July, a special Trade Union Conference had declared in favour of a ballot on the question of strike action to enforce the withdrawal of the British forces from Ireland and the conclusion of a settlement with Sinn Fein ; but the question had been for a time submerged, first by the Polish crisis and then by the mining dispute. Now it came back, complicated by the accumulating evidence that the post-war boom was drawing to an end, and that unemployment, which had already become substantial, was likely to grow rapidly unless measures were taken to counteract it. The absence of any general system of Unemployment Insurance, which involved many unemployed workers in the necessity of appealing to the Poor Law for help, was already aggravating the discontent ; and there was a foretaste of troubles to come when, on October 18, during the coal dispute, a body of the unemployed organised a protest march to Downing Street. On the following day, the Government announced plans for remedial action against unemployment, including large road schemes, increased employment of ex-service men on housing, and, to the anger of the Trade Unions, the adoption of new measures of labour dilution to encourage the absorption of unskilled workers who were out of jobs.

The Irish question, however, held the centre of the stage from

October onwards. On October 23, in the House of Commons, Henderson made an impassioned speech attacking the Government's Irish policy and calling for " an independent investigation . . . into the causes, nature and extent of reprisals on the part of those whose duty is the maintenance of law and order." On the refusal of this demand, the Labour Party decided to send its own Commission to Ireland to investigate and report, under Henderson as Chairman ; and this Commission visited Ireland in December and reported to a special Party Conference in London on December 29. The Report revealed a terrible situation : outrages on the Irish side had been met by appalling reprisals by the Black and Tans upon the people of Ireland, and it was clear that the Government was giving its full support to these acts of violence, and that the state of affairs was going steadily from bad to worse.

In these circumstances, the Labour Conference, on Henderson's motion, called for a withdrawal of the British armed forces, and for the convocation of an Irish Constituent Assembly " charged to work out, at the earliest possible moment, without limitations or fetters, whatever Constitution for Ireland the Irish people desire, subject only to two conditions, that it affords protection to minorities, and that the Constitution should prevent Ireland from becoming a military or naval menace to Great Britain." The Labour Conference was followed in the early months of 1921 by a National Campaign on the Irish question, in the course of which there was evidence of strong public backing for the Labour Party's policy. This helped to prepare the way for the Government's change of front later in the year, and for the settlement which led to the recognition of the Irish Free State.

Meanwhile, opportunity had been taken, at the instance of the Council of Action, which was still in being, to bring an emergency resolution on unemployment before the December Conference on the Irish question. This resolution began by blaming the growth of unemployment largely on the failure to promote a reasonable settlement in Europe, on the iniquities of the Peace Treaty, and above all on " the unwarrantable delay in securing peace and opening trade relationships with the Russian Government." It went on to demand that the Government should provide credits for the restoration of European trade ; should undertake and support schemes of public works ; and should guarantee reasonable maintenance to all who were unable to find work. Finally, it warned the Government that " both the unemployed and the employed workers are not prepared to remain the victims of the pernicious economic system which exposes them and their families to hardship and demoralisation as a consequence of unemployment."

The Government met this demand by setting up two committees, with very restricted terms of reference, to study the unemployment problem. Labour was invited to be represented on one of these committees, but not at first upon the other, though subsequently the invitation was extended to cover both. A joint meeting of the Labour Party and the Trades Union Congress, regarding the terms of appointment as unsatisfactory, refused to accept the invitation, and decided that the Labour movement should set up its own independent committee to formulate practical schemes and proposals for consideration by a special Conference of both bodies to be held in January, 1921. This Committee duly drew up a scheme, largely based on a Report which had been prepared in 1917 by the War Emergency Workers' National Committee ; and this scheme, which was issued as a pamphlet under the title *Unemployment—A Labour Policy* early in 1921, was accepted by the special Conference, which, after instructing the two bodies to press the Government to adopt it, adjourned for a month in order to give the Trade Unions time " to take the opinion of their members in order to decide on any further steps that may be necessary in order to secure the adoption of the recommendation." Thus, yet again, the Labour movement issued what was in effect a threat of concerted direct action designed to coerce the Government into the adoption of the policy which it put forward.

When, however, the Conference reassembled in February, 1921, there were clear signs of a lower temperature of Trade Union feeling. A proposal by the National Union of Boot and Shoe Operatives for a one-day protest general strike was decisively beaten ; and no union proposed any more drastic action. Instead, as in the case of the coal mines a year earlier, it was decided to take only " political action," by conducting a campaign in preparation for the next General Election with Labour's unemployment policy as its central feature. There were protests from the unemployed and from the extreme left against this decision ; and the Conference itself denounced the inadequacy of the Government's measures, which included the announced intention to extend Unemployment Insurance to cover the great majority of the employed population. But the very evil against which the Labour movement was protesting was of such a nature as to make the Trade Unions reluctant to commit themselves to any kind of strike action ; for the growth of unemployment carried with it a weakening of Trade Union strength, and a reduced effectiveness of the strike weapon—unless indeed it was intended that strike action should take a positively revolutionary form.

In effect, the militancy which, after declining in the latter months of 1919, had surged up again in 1920 under the influence of the Russian and Irish crises, was again receding as the post-war boom passed into recession and as the threat of a serious slump began to appear. A further crisis was soon to come, under these less propitious conditions ; and the far-seeing could already descry it. But for the time being there was a feeling of anti-climax about the February Labour Conference ; and the more constitutionally minded and right-wing Labour leaders began to hope that the wave of half-revolutionary feeling among the workers had spent its force.

In the midst of the excitements of 1920, as we have seen, the newly unified Communist Party of Great Britain, under Lenin's persuasion, had made its first application for admission to the Labour Party as an affiliated Socialist society. The letter of application was couched in by no means conciliatory terms. It declared the Communist Party's support of the Soviet system " as a means whereby the working class shall achieve power and take control of the forces of production " : it pronounced in favour of " the dictatorship of the proletariat as a necessary means for combating the counter-revolution during the transition period between Capitalism and Communism " : it announced its adherence to the Third International ; and it was unequivocal in its condemnation of the view that " a Social Revolution can be achieved by the ordinary methods of Parliamentary Democracy," or by parliamentary action except " as providing a means of propaganda and agitation towards the Revolution." It announced that in all cases parliamentary or municipal representatives " must be considered as holding a mandate from the Party " [i.e., the Communist Party], and not from the particular constituency for which they happened to sit ; and it laid down that any representative violating the decisions of the Party would be called upon to resign his seat.

To these unequivocal declarations of policy the Labour Party replied, through Henderson, that " the basis of affiliation to the

Labour Party is the acceptance of its constitution, principles and programme, with which the objects of the Communist Party do not appear to be in accord." The application for affiliation was therefore rejected. The Communist Party replied with a long argumentative letter in which it asked whether the Labour Party decisively rejected the Soviet system and the dictatorship of the proletariat, and demanded for the adherents of Communism the same wide latitude within the Labour Party as had been accorded to the I.L.P. during the war. Henderson, on the Labour Party's behalf, retorted by quoting Arthur MacManus, the Chairman of the Communist Party, who had written in *The Communist*, its official paper, that " those urging for affiliation to the Labour Party did not urge for, nor contemplate, working with the Labour Party. The antagonism to the Labour Party [at the Conference which formed the C.P.G.B.] was general, but those for affiliation held the opinion that such antagonism would be best urged within their own camp." A further long letter from the Communist Party followed, reiterating the questions previously asked ; but the Labour Party Executive answered only that it had " nothing further to add."

Despite the uncompromising tone of the Communist Party's application, the Labour Party Executive was not unanimous in voting for its rejection. When the matter came up on report to the Labour Party's Annual Conference in June, 1921, a resolution was moved urging that the application should be accepted " on the condition that the constitution of the Labour Party is accepted and the rules of the Communist Party are in conformity with the same." This resolution, moved by a delegate from Norwood, was supported, first by Duncan Carmichael, the Secretary of the London Trades Council, who made the startling statement that, " if the Conference turned down the resolution, there was not a single seat in London that was going to be held by the Labour Movement " [cries of " Nonsense "], and then by Arthur Cook and Herbert Smith on behalf of the Miners' Federation of Great Britain. Cook spoke as a Communist Party member, whereas Herbert Smith, the Miners' President, disclaimed the Miners' support of Communism, but favoured their admission because " we are not frightened of these people " and he " wanted them to have an opportunity to put themselves in order." In effect, the Miners were supporting, not unconditional affiliation, but acceptance of the Communists only if they would agree to conform to the Labour Party's constitution and policy—which, however, the Miners desired to see amended and strengthened. Against these advocates of qualified acceptance were ranged Fred Bramley, Emanuel Shinwell, and Henderson himself, besides other speakers ; and the debate ended with the carrying of the Previous Question by 4,115,000 votes to 224,000, and with the endorsement without a further division of the Executive's rejection of the Communist Party's application.

(d) Black Friday and After

By February, 1921, the numbers out of work were above 1,000,000—a figure which seemed enormous at the time, though before long it was to come to be regarded as normal, or even as low. In that month, J. R. Clynes succeeded William Adamson as Leader of the Labour Party in Parliament ; and at the beginning of March the result of the East Woolwich by-election was announced. East Woolwich had been Will Crooks's seat, which he had held unopposed even in the General Election of 1918. On his death the Local Labour Party selected Ramsay MacDonald to fight the constituency under Labour Party auspices as the nominee of the I.L.P. The contest was almost a record for mud-slinging : not only was MacDonald's war record savagely attacked ; apart from this, wholly unfounded allegations were made about his private life, and no limit was set to the campaign of slander, which had the incidental effect of helping greatly to restore MacDonald's prestige in the Labour movement. He was narrowly defeated—by 13,724 votes for the Coalition Unionist, Captain Gee, V.C., who played up his war record to the full, to 13,041.

Before this, in mid-February, the Government had announced its intention of introducing at once a Bill to terminate control over the coal mines. Control had been highly profitable to the Government during the period of inflated prices ; but the collapse of the post-war boom was already turning it into a liability. The colliery owners wanted the Government to cut the miners' wages and lengthen the working week before handing the mines back to them ; but the Government preferred to leave the owners to do these things, and told them that they would have to make their own bargain with the miners. With prices falling fast, and unemployment increasing sharply, it was evident that the Miners' Federation was in a weak bargaining position. But the Miners were determined to resist with all their strength any attempt either to reduce wages or to increase hours of work. There were differences on this point, the Miners' President, Robert Smillie, in particular, despite his left-wing record, urging an attempt at compromise. When this was rejected, he resigned the Presidency, on March 10 ; and on March 24 the Coal Decontrol Bill became an Act. Control was to cease on April 1, 1921 ; and the Miners' Federation and the owners were at a complete deadlock.

At the end of March the national coal lock-out began, the owners offering employment only on terms which the miners everywhere refused to accept. Once again the Miners' Federation invoked the help of the Triple Industrial Alliance ; and on April 8 the Railwaymen and Transport Workers voted in favour of combined strike action in support of the Miners. This decision was reaffirmed on April 13, after an attempt at negotiation had broken down. On the following day a joint meeting of the Trades Union Congress Parliamentary Committee, the Labour Party Executive, and the Parliamentary Labour Party, held in the House of Commons, unanimously resolved as follows :—

That this Conference, representing the combined Labour movement in all its aspects, having heard the statements of the Triple Alliance, is convinced of the justice of the claims put forward and pledges its support to the miners, railwaymen, and transport workers, and appeals to all sections of the Labour movement, and to every citizen who cares for the well-being of the community to stand solidly against this attack on the workers' position.

This Conference condemns the action of the Government throughout, more particularly the military preparations made during the last week, as calculated to provoke public feeling and so create disorder.

The Conference then appointed a committee of nine to give effect to its recommendations " and to watch events in consultation with the Triple Alliance."

From this gathering Frank Hodges, the Secretary of the Miners' Federation, went on to address a fateful inter-party meeting of M.P.s, at which he stated the Miners' case. After he had spoken, there was a good deal of heckling ; and in the course of it he was asked whether the Miners would be prepared to accept a compromise which would ensure that wages should not " fall below the cost of living," but would leave aside the Miners' demand for a " National Pool " to be used for wage equalisation between the more and less profitable areas. To this, Hodges replied that " any such offer coming from an authoritative source would receive

very serious consideration " ; and this was generally taken as
indicating that the Miners' leaders were prepared for a compromise settlement. Lloyd George at once seized on what Hodges
had said as an offer to compromise, and invited the Miners'
Executive to meet him on that basis ; but the Executive, in effect
repudiating Frank Hodges, answered that " the only condition
upon which a temporary settlement can be arrived at is one that
must follow the concession of the two principles already made
known to you, viz., a National Wages Board and a National
Pool." Hodges thereupon tendered his resignation, but withdrew
it at the unanimous request of the Miners' Executive.

The fat, however, was in the fire. The Railwaymen and
Transport Workers, disagreeing with the Miners' repudiation of
the Hodges " offer "—for as an " offer " it was widely represented
—held stormy meetings, at which they decided to withdraw from
their promise to strike in support of the Miners unless the Miners'
Executive would modify its attitude and allow negotiations to be
resumed on the suggested basis. To this the Miners would not
agree, and the Triple Alliance's strike threat was cancelled.

The day on which this event occurred—April 15, 1921—came
to be generally known in the Labour movement as " Black
Friday." On that day, the Triple Alliance, on which high hopes
had been built, ignominiously collapsed, and there were widespread assertions that the Miners had been " betrayed " by their
partners. The truth of the matter was that the plan for the
Alliance had never been realistically thought out. As we have
seen, the original notion had been that the three groups concerned
should first arrange for all their several collective agreements
to come to an end on one and the same day, and should then all
give notice to strike when their agreements expired, each group
formulating its own programme of demands and agreeing not to
settle or to return to work until the demands of the others had
been met. In practice, this simultaneous termination of agreements proved impossible to arrange ; and each group had to face
its crisis over new conditions of employment at a different time.
Thus, instead of all being able to strike together, each group for
its own demands, what happened was that each group in turn had
either to settle or fight on its own, or to ask its partners to strike
in sympathy with it, and not on their own behalf as well.

Apart from this, it had never been made clear whether, if the
Alliance did act as a body, the control of strike policy and the
right to say what terms should be accepted or rejected would be

vested in the Alliance as a whole, or would remain in the hands
of the separate groups. The Railwaymen and Transport Workers
argued that, if they were called on to support the Miners by strike
action, they ought to share in deciding what terms the Miners
should accept. The Miners' Executive, as against this, argued that
only the miners, in delegate conference or by ballot vote, had a
right to decide on what terms they would work. The two points
of view proved to be irreconcilable, as they were to prove again
under somewhat similar circumstances in 1926.

Whatever the rights and wrongs of the matter, " Black Friday "
brought an epoch in the Labour movement's history to an end.
As we have seen, throughout 1920 the appeal to " direct action "
had been repeatedly made, on both political and industrial issues,
though it had never in fact been pushed to the point of operation.
After April, 1921 " direct action " for some time disappeared from
the scene ; and there was widespread disillusionment and anger.
The Miners, in a bitter mood, struggled on alone until June,
when they were forced back to work not only at much reduced
wages but also under district settlements without the National
Pool they had demanded or any national negotiating machinery.
The industrial left wing had suffered a serious defeat—the more
serious because the economic situation was getting all the time
very much worse. By May, 1921, partly as a consequence of the
coal dispute, the number out of work had risen above 2,000,000,
and even after the dispute was over it remained much higher than
before. In the middle of 1922 it was still above 1,500,000, or
13½ per cent of the insured population ; and not until 1924—
and then only for a few months—did it sink below 10 per cent.
This higher level of unemployment was not, of course, a consequence, except temporarily, of the coal dispute : rather was the
coal dispute due to the same cause—the collapse of the post-war
inflationary boom and the chaos in world economic affairs which
bad statesmanship and bad public finance had combined with
profit-seeking folly and speculative excess to engender over most
of the world.

The rise in unemployment and the withdrawal of the Trade
Union movement from the militant postures of 1920 were
followed, not unnaturally, by a rapid growth of agitation among
the unemployed workers, who had nothing to lose, and much to
gain, by making themselves a nuisance. The coal crisis had interrupted the campaign of the official Labour bodies for more effective measure of work-provision and of maintenance, and had in

effect finally removed the sting of the threats of ulterior measures uttered by the Labour Conference of January, 1921. When a further Emergency Joint Conference of the industrial and political wings of the movement was held in December, 1921, the earlier demands for Government measures were re-asserted, but there was no threat of direct action. Emphasis was laid at this stage largely on the international aspects of the situation, the blame being put on the mismanagement of international affairs, " particularly as regards Russia and Central Europe." Recognition of the Soviet Government was demanded, as well as a drastic revision of the economic clauses of the Treaty with Germany, a restoration of exchange stability, and an abandonment of the attempt to exact vast sums in reparations, which could " only injure the industry of the receiving nation and are indeed borne by its wage-earners in the shape of low wages and unemployment."

While the official Labour movement thus continued to protest, the unemployed, under left-wing leadership in which the Communists were already playing an active part, were attempting to act. From the unemployed marches of October, 1920, the movement continued to develop as unemployment increased. Local Unemployed Committees were formed in many areas and began to draw together, under the leadership of the Communist engineer, Wal Hannington, into the body which presently became the National Unemployed Workers' Committee Movement. A deputation, headed by Hannington, was admitted to put its case before the Labour Party Conference in June, 1921. Its members, representing the London unemployed, had marched at the head of a body of hunger marchers from London to Brighton, where the Conference was being held. The speakers, echoing the feelings of 1920, called for direct action to secure improved conditions for the unemployed and bitterly attacked the official leaders for their inaction. They were received politely ; but they had no effect on the Conference's policy. How indeed could they ? The Miners were going down to defeat : the Triple Alliance had broken down : the Trade Union leaders were in no mood to run into fresh perils by invoking strike action on anybody's behalf. The Labour Party's hopes were set on " political action " at a General Election which, they were beginning to hope, would not be long delayed. For already the foundations of the Lloyd George Coalition were beginning to rock.

Nevertheless, a year and more was still to pass before an election was held. In the interval, in the late summer of 1921, came the

dramatic protest of the Poplar Council, headed by George
Lansbury, against the unfair burdens which the localised system of
financing the relief of the unemployed who were not receiving
insurance benefits or needed supplementary help placed upon the
poorer districts. On September 1, 1921, the Mayor of Poplar and
twenty-nine other Councillors went to prison for refusing to pay
the sums due to the London County Council for purposes of local
government, on the plea that the Borough could not afford both
to relieve the distresses of its own inhabitants and to meet these
charges, which they held ought to fall upon the richer areas.
They were demanding in effect a complete pooling, over London
as a whole, of the costs of unemployment relief and the provision
of fair scales of maintenance. At this time, there were in most
areas no fixed scales of relief, most Boards of Guardians insisting
on taking each case separately, and paying out as little as possible
in cash, and as much as they could of the niggardly allowances
made in bread tickets and other grants in kind. The National
Administrative Council set up by the Unemployed Committees
was demanding regular scales for men and women, with dependants' allowances ; but this would have imposed, under the
existing system of finance, still heavier burdens on the areas least
able to bear them. In spite of this, the Poplar Guardians were
insisting on paying out at what they regarded as reasonable maintenance rates, but were also, in co-operation with the Borough
Council, demanding that the State should come to the assistance
of the areas on which the burden was falling with exceptional
severity. In October the Government introduced a system of
dependants' allowances under the Unemployment Insurance
system ; but this, though it brought relief in a large number of
cases, did nothing to help those who were out of benefit : nor
were the scales regarded as at all adequate.

The action of the Poplar Council in refusing to meet the precepts
of the London County Council was followed in October by
Stepney and Bethnal Green, which were similarly in difficulties.
Unemployed demonstrations in support of their attitude were
broken up by the police ; but on October 12 the Poplar Councillors were released from prison, with the precept still unpaid.
The Government made additional grants in aid of local relief
works and similar projects, and rushed through a Bill conferring
borrowing powers on the impoverished local relief agencies ;
but it also issued a circular to local authorities restricting wages on
relief works to 75 per cent of the standard rates. This caused

widespread indignation, and largely cancelled the effect of the accompanying measure providing for some further equalisation of poor rates in London. These were the circumstances in which the official Labour bodies refused to co-operate in the Government's investigations of the unemployment problem, and set up their own committee to make an independent report. On October 21 the Labour M.P.s, as a protest against the Government's policy, left the House in a body during the unemployment debate. The Government, however, pressed on with its policy, which included a measure designed to checkmate the Poplar policy by authorising any local authority, if its precept were not met, itself to collect through a receiver the sums required over the head of the recusant authority. This drew a strong protest from the Labour Councils in London—the stronger because the Labour Party had made considerable gains throughout the country at the November municipal elections. The Labour Mayors and Councillors forced an interview with the Prime Minister, urging that the Government's policy of easing the situation by authorising local loans was no sort of cure, and that a drastic reform of the entire system of local finance was called for. The unemployed continued to demonstrate, and to endeavour to bring pressure on the local Guardians ; but there was no general attempt to emulate the tactics of the Poplar Council, and the Government was able to persist with its policy despite the chorus of protest from official and unofficial Labour bodies alike.

CHAPTER IV

FROM SLUMP TO OFFICE

(a) Years of Depression

Further measures of decontrol—The Housing Scheme abandoned—Truce and Treaty in Ireland—The rival Internationals—The T.U.C. General Council and the National Joint Council of Labour—Foreign policy, reparations and unemployment—The " Geddes Axe "—The Cave Report on Trade Boards—The Communist Party reorganised—" Democratic Centralism "—The Local Labour Parties and the Labour Party Constitution—Eligibility of delegates at Party Conferences—No electoral alliances or arrangements—The *Daily Herald* in trouble.

(b) The General Election of 1922

The end of the Coalition—Labour's election gains—Changes in the composition and leadership of the Party—Ramsay MacDonald re-elected to the leadership—Regional distribution of Labour gains—Straight fights and three- or four-cornered contests.

(c) The Battle of the Internationals

After the Berne Conference of 1919—Foundation of the Communist International—The Split in French Socialism—Secessions from the Second International—The position of the middle Parties—The strategy of the Comintern—Lenin's advice to the I.L.P.—The Second International at Geneva, 1920—Its Headquarters transferred to London—Formation of the Vienna Working Union—The Second International appeals for unity--The I.L.P.'s international attitude—Negotiations with the Vienna Union—The Third International calls for the " United Front "—The Five Nations Conference on Reparations and Disarmament—Attempts to convene an " all-in " Conference—The Berlin " Committee of Nine "—Breakdown of negotiations with Moscow—The German Socialists re-united—The I.F.T.U. Peace Congress of 1922—The Second International and the Vienna Union come to terms—The Hamburg Congress of 1923 sets up the Labour and Socialist International—The British Labour Party and I.L.P. attitudes to International Socialist organisation—Why a unified International was impossible.

(d) The Development of the Labour Party up to 1923

The growth of the Local Labour Parties—The development of the Women's Sections—The effects of the new Labour Party on the I.L.P.—The Young Labour League and the creation of Labour Party Youth Organisation—The dispute over powers and functions of the Youth Sections—Fears of Communist infiltration—The position of the Communist Party after 1921—Further appeals for Communist affiliation rejected—The position of individual Communists in relation to the Labour Party—Communists as Labour candidates or delegates—The problem of Trade Union delegates—Communist strategy in the early stages—The Communist reorganisation of 1922—" Democratic Centralism "—The Communists and the Trade Unions—The Minority Movement—Secessions from the Communist Party—The Communists and the Miners—The Communists and the Unemployed—Trade Union weakness in handling the unemployed problem—The I.L.P. after 1918—Secession of the left wing—The Policy Reports of 1921—Sovietism, Parliamentarianism and the Bradford Plan—Workers' Control—The new I.L.P. Programme of 1922—The "Now for Socialism " Campaign—The Policy Committee of 1923—The I.L.P.'s influence increased—Relations between the I.L.P. and the Labour Party—Attitudes of MacDonald and Henderson—The *Daily Herald* under George Lansbury—The *Daily Herald* officialised—The *Workers' Weekly* and the *New Leader.*

(e)   The General Election of 1923

Baldwin becomes Prime Minister—He appeals to the country on the issue of Protection—A rushed Election—Labour's gains—Regional results of the Election —The Composition of the Parliamentary Party—Some new Members of note— Communist losses—Straight fights and three-cornered contests.

(a)   Years of Depression

Black Friday and the defeat of the Miners' Federation in the struggle of 1921 gave the signal for a general reversal of government economic policy. The decontrol of the coal mines at the beginning of April was followed in August by the decontrol of the railways, which were handed back to be operated by the four amalgamated companies created by the Railways Act of 1921. In September the Corn Production Act was allowed to lapse, bringing to an end the subsidisation of agricultural output and therewith the minimum wage granted in 1917 to the agricultural workers. Nor was this all ; for in June, 1921, the Government suddenly wound up the great housing scheme that had been launched in 1919, and announced that no further state help would be provided apart from a small amount for slum clearance.

Meanwhile, depression was spreading fast over Europe, and the Soviet Union was in the grip of sheer famine, accentuated by the continued attempts of the Western countries to boycott the Russians into submission. The only part of the world in which the state of affairs improved was Ireland, where, under increasing pressure from world opinion, the Government was at length realising the impracticability of the policy of stamping out rebellion by terror. The Home Rule Act passed at the end of 1920 proved quite unworkable, except in the six Counties of Ulster ; and in July, 1921, Lloyd George threw over the policy of violence and attempted to come to terms with Sinn Fein. The Irish truce of that month brought the fighting to an end ; but there were further breakdowns and threats to renew the war before, in December, an Irish Treaty was at last drawn up and hurriedly ratified by the British Parliament. Dail Eirann, despite De Valera's opposition, ratified the treaty in January, 1922 ; and Eire emerged as a self-governing Dominion. A most discreditable chapter in British history was thus closed ; and the Labour Party could feel that, by its steady denunciation of Lloyd George's policy of coercion, it had contributed to this result.

Nowhere else was there much cause for satisfaction. Bitter disputes over reparations were already developing between the statesmen of the victorious countries, and these disputes found an echo in the mutual recriminations of the adherents of the rival Socialist Internationals. In April, 1921, there were held in the same week three separate International Labour Conferences on the question of reparations, convened respectively by the Second International, the International Federation of Trade Unions, and the group of more left-wing Socialist Parties which had formed the so-called Vienna Union in an attempt to mediate between the Second and Third Internationals.

At home, attention turned to the question of closer unity between the political and industrial wings of Labour. The Trades Union Congress had accepted in 1920 a plan of reorganisation under which the old Parliamentary Committee was replaced by a General Council, with somewhat wider powers, chosen to represent the Unions in the principal industries and occupations. As a complement to this reorganisation the Labour Party and the Trades Union Congress together drew up a plan for a new National Joint Council, representing in equal numbers the new General Council of the T.U.C., the Labour Party's National Executive, and the Parliamentary Labour Party ; and this plan, which replaced the old Joint Board, was approved by both the Labour Party Conference and the Trades Union Congress in 1921. The T.U.C., however, rejected in 1922 a plan for closer Trade Union unity, designed to confer additional powers of co-ordination and control upon the General Council. The scheme for joint action between the national bodies included the setting up of joint departments for research, information, publicity, and international affairs under the control of the Party Executive and the General Council ; and one effect of this was to deprive the Labour Research Department of its status in relation to the national bodies, and to lay it open to capture by adherents of the Communist Party.

A great weakness of Labour Party organisation both before and after this time—indeed right up to the last few years—was understaffing and even lack of appreciation of the need for workers of first-class quality in its central and regional offices. There was no development until much later of an adequate International Department : there was hardly any research work, as distinct from the day-to-day services of information—and even these were on an inadequate scale ; and even the tasks of regional and local organisation were not tackled with any sufficient sense of what was needful. Doubtless these faults are to be explained partly by lack of funds ; for the Labour Party was continually finding that its electoral obligations outran its resources. This, however, was not the whole explanation : there was also a failure to appreciate brains and a suspicion of " cleverness " which prevented service in the party machine from offering attractions to the younger people who could have helped to provide it with the driving force that it manifestly lacked. Its propagandist literature, until quite recently, was to a great extent both dully written and most unattractively presented ; and the solid work done in these fields on the Party's behalf was written mostly by outside volunteers, who were quite often given as many kicks as thanks in return for their trouble.

The first important action of the National Joint Council was to convene, in December 1921, a fully representative Emergency Labour Conference for the discussion of the linked issues of foreign policy, reparations and unemployment. The resolutions passed on this occasion attributed both the failure to deal adequately with the relief problems presented by the famine in Russia and the prevalence of unemployment and distress over most of Europe to faulty foreign policy, including the attempt to exact fantastically large reparations, the boycott of Russian trade, and " the clauses in the Versailles and other Treaties relating to territorial distributions which have prevented peace and have kept Europe economically unsettled." The Conference demanded currency stabilisation, a removal of trade barriers, a scheme of international lending to aid European recovery, and a revision of the clauses in the treaties that were " necessitating an armed occupation of a large part of Central Europe." It called for mutual cancellation of war debts and for the reopening of commercial and political relations with the Soviet Union. But the Conference had by this time no power to implement any of its recommendations. Instead, it had to face further attacks on the home front as the Government tried to meet the depression by measures of economy and deflation and as employers pressed hard upon the Trade Unions for wage-cuts and for the withdrawal of concessions granted in the course of the post-war boom.

In February, 1922, appeared the Geddes Report, drawn up in an alarmist mood by Sir Eric Geddes, and proposing drastic cuts in public expenditure and in the social services. Housing, we have seen, had fallen victim already to the reaction from the fine promises of reconstruction ; and now the " Geddes Axe " was to be applied to education and to every branch of social service.

Public capital expenditure, including works designed to maintain employment, was also to be cut down ; and it was proposed that large economies should be achieved by amalgamating health and unemployment insurance into a single system, with the State meeting less and the contributors more of the total cost. This last project was defeated : indeed, in July, 1922, it became indispensable to make the conditions for receipt of unemployment benefit somewhat less severe by reducing the " gap " between benefit periods. But most of the Geddes proposals were carried ruthlessly into effect. A further blow came in the spring of 1922, with the publication of the Report of the Cave Committee on Trade Boards, embodying proposals to restrict the power of the boards to fix minimum wages except for the lowest grades of labour. This Report was not acted on in full ; but the creation of new Trade Boards entirely ceased, and those already in being were urged to reduce their rates in order to meet the conditions of trade depression.

Meanwhile, the unemployed were demonstrating in force ; and the Communist Party, after its rebuff at the Labour Party Conference of 1921, was setting out to organise itself as a national rival to the Labour Party. The demand for affiliation was not given up : indeed in December, 1921, the Communist International issued a manifesto—the first of many—urging the formation of a working-class United Front in every country, and the Communist Party of Great Britain duly renewed its application for affiliation. At the Labour Party Conference of 1922, Harry Pollitt, as a delegate of the Boilermakers' Union, moved the reference back of the part of the Executive's report dealing with this issue, but was overwhelmingly defeated, by 3,086,000 votes to 261,000, the Miners' Federation having changed sides since the previous year. At this time the Communist Party was in process of reorganising itself. A Committee set up in March, 1922, proposed a drastic revision designed to ensure firm central discipline in accordance with the Bolshevik doctrine of " democratic centralism " ; and in October the party conference accepted the Committee's plan and, not for the last time, reorganised the party on the Moscow model. From this time the Communists began their strategy of operating not only directly as a party, but also through a succession of special bodies which they created and controlled, destroyed and replaced as seemed fit to the central directing agency of the party. The National Unemployed Workers' Committee Movement became in effect one of these agencies ; and a parallel body, the National Minority Movement, was soon set up with the object of extending Communist influence inside the Trade Unions.

Inside the Labour Party itself, there was a good deal of discontent. In particular, many of the Local Labour Parties considered that the party was unduly dominated by the national Trade Union leaders, and that this domination was aggravated by the method of electing the National Executive adopted in 1918. At the Labour Party Conference of 1921, Herbert Morrison, on behalf of the London Labour Party, moved an amendment designed to give the Local Parties the right to elect, as well as to nominate, their own representatives to serve on the National Executive, instead of election being by the whole Conference and only nomination being in the hands of the section concerned. The amendment was defeated by a large majority—2,913,000 to 591,000—but the size of the minority shows that most of the local parties voted in favour of the change. Morrison returned to the charge at the Edinburgh Conference of 1922, but was again defeated. This time, however, he polled 954,000 votes against 2,688,000, receiving some Trade Union support. At this Conference the National Executive raised the question of the eligibility of Communists or others not favourable to the Labour Party to serve as delegates ; and by a vote of 342 to 161, on a show of hands, a new rule was adopted. This laid down, first, that every delegate should " individually accept the Constitution and principles of the Labour Party," and secondly that " no person shall be eligible as a delegate who is a member of any organisation having for one of its objects the return to Parliament or to any local governing authority of a candidate or candidates other than such as have been endorsed by the Labour Party, or have been approved as running in association with the Labour Party." The final phrase here refers to candidates of the Co-operative Party : the new rule was carefully worded so as to exclude not only Communists but also Liberals.

The Edinburgh Conference was also notable for the carrying of a resolution, moved by Robert Williams, declaring " against any alliance or electoral arrangement with any section of the Liberal or Conservative Parties." There had been some fears that a group within the Labour Party favoured some sort of electoral arrangement with the Asquithite Liberals ; but no one appeared at the Conference to uphold this point of view. The Edinburgh Conference also ratified the action of the National Executive in joining forces with the T.U.C. General Council to take over responsibility for the publication of the *Daily Herald*, which had been threatened with financial collapse. The taking over was only an interim measure, pending the drawing up of a permanent scheme ; but for the time being it involved the Labour Party in a heavy financial liability just at the time when it was endeavouring to set aside funds for a General Election that was expected in the very near future. The *Herald* had been staggering on under repeated financial difficulties ever since its return to daily publication at the end of the war. It was felt that the services of a daily newspaper were absolutely necessary to the Labour Movement ; but the *Herald* had far too little capital or resources to perform the functions required of it as long as it continued to depend on such help as could be got from time to time in response to appeals for voluntary gifts. It was plain that the *Herald* would die unless some arrangement could be made for supplying it with capital, as well as for meeting its large current deficit. Such a plan could not be made at once ; and accordingly the immediate difficulty had to be tided over by the two national bodies accepting financial responsibility for the time being.

(b) *The General Election of 1922*

In October, 1922, the Tories, meeting at the Carlton Club, decided to break up the Coalition and to make use of their majority to install a purely Conservative Government. Lloyd George was forced to resign on October 19, and on the following day Bonar Law became Prime Minister. The Labour Party had been for some time getting ready for a General Election ; and when the Tories decided to dissolve Parliament both parties had already most of their candidates in the field. In the General Election of 1922 the Labour Party fought over two-thirds of all the seats in Great Britain—414, as against 361 in 1918. At the dissolution the Party held seventy-five seats : it lost nineteen of these, but gained eighty-six others, and returned to the House of Commons 142 strong, almost doubling its numbers. Its total poll rose from 2,224,945 in 1918 to 4,236,733 in 1922—an increase roughly corresponding to its gain in seats. As against this total the Tories polled 5,383,896, the National Liberals 1,678,088, and the Independent Liberals 2,507,204 ; and 375,510 votes were given for candidates of other complexions. The Communists fought only five seats, all in Scotland, and scored a single success, J. T. Walton Newbold winning at Motherwell in a four-cornered contest against an Independent Unionist and two rival Liberals, with no Labour candidate in the field. The result of the General Election was the return of a clear Conservative majority, in the first Parliament elected without representatives from Southern Ireland.

The Parliamentary Labour Party elected in 1922 was not only larger than the Party in the 1918 Parliament but also significantly different in its composition. In 1918, out of fifty-seven M.P.s elected, only three had been nominees of the I.L.P. and five of the Divisional Labour Parties. There had been one Co-operative Party nominee ; and the remaining forty-eight had been Trade Union nominees, of whom twenty-five came from the Miners' Federation. In the new House of Commons, though the Miners had increased their representation to forty-two and the total number of Trade Union nominees had risen to eighty-five, the other groups had greatly increased their share in the total. The I.L.P. had won thirty-two seats, and the Fabians and the Social Democratic Federation each had one : the Divisional Labour Parties accounted for nineteen, and the Co-operative Party for four. Nor was the change less notable in terms of personalities. The anti-war leaders defeated in 1918 regained seats in the new House, and there was a good sprinkling of new figures destined to take a leading place in the Party. The only serious loss was that of Arthur Henderson, who was defeated at Widnes, and was out of Parliament until he was elected for East Newcastle at a by-election in January, 1923.

Thus, the Labour leaders in the previous Parliament—Clynes, Adamson, Thomas, Shaw, Walsh, Hodge, Thorne, Tillett, Sexton and William Graham—were reinforced not only by the return to the House of Ramsay MacDonald, Philip Snowden, George Lansbury, F. W. Jowett and others defeated as " pacifists " in 1918, but also by Clement Attlee, A. V. Alexander, Arthur Greenwood, David Kirkwood, James Maxton, John Wheatley, Thomas Johnston, Emanuel Shinwell, Sidney Webb, Charles Trevelyan, and H. B. Lees-Smith, who all made their first appearance as Labour M.P.s in the Parliament of 1922, though the two last had sat as Liberals in Parliaments before 1918. Of these eleven, seven sat as I.L.P. nominees, Webb as a Fabian, Greenwood as a Divisional Party nominee, and Kirkwood, who was also active in the I.L.P., as a nominee of the Amalgamated Engineering Union. The I.L.P. also counted a good many of the Divisional Labour Party representatives and some of the Trade Union group among its members ; and for the time its influence in the affairs of the Parliamentary Party was greatly increased. It promptly used its power to secure the election of Ramsay MacDonald to the party leadership which he had vacated in 1914, J. R. Clynes, his defeated rival, readily accepting the position of Deputy Leader.

The Labour Party made its greatest gains in Scotland, where the I.L.P. was very strong. As against seven Scottish seats won in 1918, the Labour Party now held twenty-nine, and most of the Scottish contingent acted closely together as a " Clyde Group." They made the mistake of thinking that MacDonald, who owed to them his re-election as leader, would favour the advanced

LABOUR AT THE GENERAL ELECTION OF 1922

	Members elected		Net gains over 1918	Total seats fought	Communist etc. Candidates
	Total	Losses			
Greater London .	16	2	12	72	—
Southern England .	—	—	—	29	—
Western England .	1	—	—	16	—
South-west England .	—	—	—	6	—
West Midlands . .	9	2	3	33	—
East Midlands . .	8	4	1	33	—
Eastern Counties .	1	1	1	22	—
Lancs. and Cheshire .	19	6	5	58	—
Yorkshire . .	21	2	15	42	—
North-west England .	3	—	2	3	—
North-east England .	17	1	12	25	—
Wales and Monmouth	18	—	8	28	—
Scotland . . .	29	1	22	43	5
Northern Ireland .	—	—	—	—	—
Universities . .	—	—	—	3	—
				413	5 (1 elected)

Socialist policy which they desired. There were also large gains in Yorkshire—another I.L.P. stronghold—and in South Wales and the North-Eastern Counties. In London too the Labour Party did something to reverse its heavy defeat in 1918 ; but outside Greater London it could muster but two seats in all the southern half of England—North Norfolk and the mining area of the Forest of Dean.

The election of 1922 was fought under very complicated conditions. With two Liberal parties in the field, there were some areas in which either Conservatives or National Liberals stood aside in order to present a united front, whereas in others Conservatives fought National Liberals. Of Labour's 142 seats, four were won without a contest, sixty-two in straight fights, and seventy-two in three- or four-cornered contests, excluding the four seats won in constituencies returning two members. The straight fights were fairly evenly divided between Conservative and National Liberal opponents, whereas in the three-cornered contests the predominant type was between Labour, Conservative and Independent Liberal. Communist candidates, as we have seen, appeared only in a few constituencies in Scotland, though in England one or two Communists managed to stand under Labour auspices. Of the major parties, the principal losers were the National Liberals, who sank from 146 to 58, whereas the Independent Liberals increased from 27 to 59. The National Democratic Party was wiped out : the Conservatives came through with a comparatively small loss.

LABOUR PARTY : BODIES SPONSORING SUCCESSFUL CANDIDATES, 1922

I.L.P. . . .	32	}		
Fabian Society .	1	} Socialist Societies .	34
S.D.F. . . .	1	}		
D.L.P.s . . .	19	Divisional Parties .	19
Miners' Federation .	42	}		
U. Textile Workers .	3	}		
General Workers .	4	}		
Transport Workers .	5	} Trade Unions .	85
A.E.U. . . .	6	}		
N.U.R. . . .	3	}		
Other T.U.s . .	22	}		
Co-op Party . .	4	Co-operative Party .	4
	142		142

LABOUR AT THE GENERAL ELECTION OF 1922

Nature of Contests

Labour M.P.s *elected*

Against Conservative only	28
Against National Liberal only . . .	32
Against Independent Liberal only . . .	1
Against Independent only	1
Total straight fights	62
Against Conservative and Independent Liberal .	41
Against Conservative and National Liberal .	12
Against Conservative and Independent . .	1
Against Independent Liberal and National Liberal	12
Against National Liberal and Communist .	1
Total three-cornered fights . . .	67
Against Conservative, National Liberal and Independent Liberal	3
Against Conservative, National Liberal and Independent	1
Against National Liberal, Independent Liberal and Communist	1
Total four-cornered fights . . .	5
Unopposed	4

In two-member constituencies :

Two Labour, one Conservative, one Independent Liberal	2
One Labour, two Conservatives, one Independent Liberal	1
One Labour, one Communist, one Conservative, two National Liberal, one Independent .	1
	4

(c) *The Battle of the Internationals*

We have seen in a previous chapter how an attempt was made at the Berne Conference of February, 1919, to reconstruct the Socialist International which had collapsed in 1914. This was immediately followed by the foundation at Moscow of the Third, or Communist, International, which was hurriedly improvised with the object of detaching as many as possible of the more advanced European Socialist Parties and groups from their allegiance to the reformist leadership of the old International. The Third International, at the outset, was hardly more than a

façade.   Only embryonic Communist parties existed outside the
Soviet Union ; and it was made up, apart from the Soviet delegates, of a haphazard collection of left-wing Socialists from various
countries, most of whom could claim no real representative
status.   Until its second Conference, held at Moscow in
July, 1920, it had no definite constitution or basis of affiliation,
and existed much more as an idea than as an established fact.
In 1919, the Russian Communists were hoping for world revolution, and felt confident that at any rate the major part of the
European working class would speedily rally, not only to the
support of the Russian Revolution, but also to the call to reorganise their own parties as movements on revolutionary lines pat-
terned on the Russian achievement.

For a time events appeared to be answering to their hopes.   At
the Tours Congress of 1919, the majority of the French Socialist
Party went over to Communism, leaving the dissident leaders to
re-form the Socialist Party in opposition.   The Swiss, the Nor-
wegians, and other parties voted in favour of the Third International.   The German Independents, the Austrians, and the
British I.L.P. (at Easter, 1920) decided to leave the Second
International and set out to work for an all-in International
broad enough to embrace both Communists and Social Democrats.   The Italians, also seeking unity, decided to keep apart for
the time being from both the rival Internationals.   The Second
International came to be dominated in practice by the British
Labour Party and the German Majority Socialists, with the
support of the Swedish, Belgian and Dutch parties and with the
embarrassing allegiance of various right-wing Socialist groups from
Russia and from other parts of the territory claimed by the
Soviet Union, but not yet under the Soviet Government's effective
control.

Before long the parties which stood poised between the Second
and Third Internationals began to draw together.   Within each
of them, there was a section which was pressing strongly for
affiliation to the Third International and for a policy of revolutionary Socialism, and another section which strongly upheld
parliamentary methods and constitutional agitation and repudiated violence as a means of achieving Socialism ; and between
these extremes was a middle group, which refused to declare
either for or against revolutionary action as a matter of principle
and maintained that the Socialists in each country must be left
to work out the strategies and policies most appropriate to their

own national conditions. In the eyes of this group, the policy of Soviet Communism might suit Russia, but might be quite inapposite under the conditions existing in Western Europe ; and accordingly they set out to work for an inclusive International which would be equally open to Communists and to Social Democrats and Labour Socialists of every complexion—or at all events would be wide enough to take in the Bolsheviks at the one end and all save the most right-wing groups at the other.

The adherents of this view felt, in 1919, very strong sympathy for the Russian Revolution, and most of them wanted to give their own parties as leftward an orientation as could be made consistent with the continued use of parliamentary methods and with the knowledge that, as far as Western Europe was concerned, there was no prospect at all of successful revolutions on the Russian model. Most of them were highly critical of the extreme constitutionalism of the leaders of the Second International, and disliked the liaison between the German Majority Socialists and the British Labour Party on which the foundations of the Second International appeared to rest. Moreover, in 1919, most Socialists who did not belong to the extreme right felt more revolutionary than they really were, and were keenly anxious to be on good terms with the Soviet Union and to help it in resisting international capitalist attacks, to the point of wishing for unity in a single International if only the leaders of the Third would meet them half way.

This, however, the Russian Communists were by no means minded to do. Failing to understand the situation in the West, and believing that there was a real prospect of universal revolution, they by no means wished for an inclusive International in which the leaders of the established Labour and Socialist Parties would be able to retain their influence. When they called for working-class unity, they meant unity of the working classes under new, revolutionary leadership and on the basis of a clear revolutionary programme ; and they regularly coupled with the demand for unity violent denunciations of the established leaders of Western Socialism (and of the non-Communist Socialist leaders among the Russians, Ukrainians, Georgians, Finns and other peoples who had been subject to the Czarist Empire). All these were lumped together as " social traitors," and no secret was made of the intention to use the cry of " Unity " as a means to destroying their influence. Therefore, when the delegates of the middle parties and groups went to the Soviet Union in the hope of building bridges between the Second and Third Internationals, or of being allowed to join the Third without committing themselves to violent revolution in their own countries, Lenin and Radek and the other Bolshevik leaders, far from coming half-way to meet them, insisted that they should first prove their good faith by committing themselves, fully and without qualification, to the Communist doctrine of revolution and to the acceptance of the leadership of the Comintern—which meant in effect the leadership of the Russians—in working out a common and centrally controlled strategy of world-wide revolution in accordance with Russian ideas. Lenin, for example, when asked for his advice by the I.L.P. delegates to the Soviet Union in the spring of 1920, simply told them that the best thing they could do was to go home and have a revolution in Great Britain—advice which it was as much beyond their power as beyond their will to carry out.

By July, 1920, when the Second International met in Conference at Geneva, it was evident that the hopes entertained at Berne of its reconstruction were not likely to be fulfilled. Only the British Labour Party, the German Majority Socialists, the Belgians, Dutch, Swedes and Danes were fully represented, together with a few groups from other countries. The British, who under the influence of Henderson and MacDonald had played the leading part in the attempt to rebuild the old International, found themselves strongly pressed to accept the transfer of the headquarters to Great Britain and to take the main responsibility for further efforts at reconstruction. The Labour Party was very reluctant to accept this charge, as it felt that the International's centre ought to be on the Continent ; but, faced with the knowledge that the only alternative was complete collapse, the National Executive finally agreed to a temporary transfer to London.

Meanwhile the I.L.P., rebuffed by Moscow, the Swiss, and the German Independent Socialists were all laying separate plans for the convening of an international conference representing the Socialist parties which belonged neither to the Second nor to the Third International, in the hope of using their combined influence to build a bridge between right and left. The outcome was a Conference held at Berne in December, 1920, and attended by delegates of the French, Swiss and Austrian Socialist parties, of the German Independent Socialists and the German-Czech Socialists, and of the American Socialist Party, as well as of the British I.L.P. This led on directly to a further Conference, held at Vienna in February, 1921, at which these parties and some others formed the Vienna Working Union of Socialist Parties, commonly known as the "Two-and-a-Half" International. The Vienna Union did not call itself an "International" : it claimed to be no more than a provisional body set up for the purpose of working for the establishment of an inclusive International as speedily as conditions allowed. The parties which formed it agreed that none of them would take separate action to join either the Second or the Third International, or to negotiate with either, without mutual consultation ; and the resolutions passed at Vienna were so drawn as to leave the door open to both reformist and revolutionary methods, and to keep neutral between parliamentarianism and sovietism as rival political systems.

Between the Berne and the Vienna meetings the British Labour Party, left in charge of the affairs of the Second International, had issued in December, 1920, a circular letter to the Socialist and Communist parties of all countries, urging unity under its auspices and replying to the attacks made on it from Moscow. The circular went on to say that " obviously every Socialist who has any international instinct at all will see that an International based upon Moscow principles can never represent more than the smallest and least influential fraction of the Socialist movement in the various countries. The Second International has, therefore, rejected Bolshevism as the basis of its existence. . . . If . . . we ask for a united International upon a more liberal basis than that demanded by Moscow, we do so because we are convinced that Moscow possesses neither the breadth nor the stability to maintain an International. We ourselves desire to keep in the closest organic touch with our comrades in every other land ; we desire to be represented at their Conferences, to consult with them, to help and be helped by them ; but we must decline Moscow conditions and Moscow methods as the price of that co-operation. We must also believe that the better militant sections of other countries hold the same view."

This letter, which bears the clear stamp of Ramsay MacDonald's literary style, was in part a counterblast to the " Twenty-one Conditions " put forward by the Third International as requisite for affiliation to it, and in part an attempt to regain the allegiance of the middle parties and to prevent them from going forward with the establishment of the Vienna Working Union. In this latter objective it was unsuccessful : the parties outside the Second

International made no reply to the British blandishments and continued to speak a language much more revolutionary than that of the Second International's letter. Indeed, the I.L.P. delegates at Berne and Vienna felt it necessary to make a special reservation to the effect that the resolutions must not be taken as committing them to any sort of advocacy of revolution by violence in Great Britain.

The I.L.P.'s attitude was further defined at its Annual Conference at Easter, 1921. At its Glasgow Conference in 1920 disaffiliation from the Second International had been voted by 529 to 144, and 205 had voted in favour of immediate affiliation to the Third, against 472 who favoured prior consultation about the conditions. The Southport I.L.P. Conference of 1921 rejected the Third International's " Twenty-one Conditions " by 521 votes to 97, and then approved joining the Vienna Union by 362 votes to 32. The Communist minority in the I.L.P. thereupon seceded and joined forces with the Communist Party, leaving the majority to continue the internal struggle between the MacDonaldite right and the centre group headed by Wallhead and Clifford Allen.

Next came a period of confused attempts at negotiation. In June, 1921, the Labour Party attempted to summon a joint meeting of the Second International and the Vienna Union, but the latter body refused unless the Third International were also invited. In October the Vienna Union agreed to meet the Labour Party without the other sections of the Second International, but persisted in its view that Communist as well as Socialist parties must be invited to attend any conference called for the purpose of re-building the International. There was a deadlock for the time being. Then in December the Third International issued, in face of the advent of world-wide depression and the obvious absence of any further prospect of world revolution, its series of theses on the policy and tactics of the United Front. The Vienna Union responded by attempting, unsuccessfully, to call an all-in international Socialist conference ; but a bridge was built between the Second and the Vienna Internationals by a more indirect method. The British Labour Party took the lead in summoning a " Five Nations " Conference, representing the Socialists of Great Britain, Germany, France, Belgium and Italy, to consider, not the question of the International, but the formulation of an agreed policy on the limited issues of Reparations and Disarmament, in relation to European recovery. At this Conference, which met at

Frankfurt-on-Main in February, 1922, the leaders of the Second and Vienna Internationals found themselves acting together in substantial agreement ; and advantage was taken of the opportunity to resume discussions informally on the wider issue. The representatives of the Second International, in order to secure the assent of the Vienna Union, agreed to the attempt to convoke an all-in International Conference, to which they had hitherto objected, on condition that they should be allowed to raise at it any issue they pleased, including such matters as the persecution of right-wing Socialists in the Soviet Union and the attempts of the Communists to split the international Trade Union movement by creating the Red International of Labour Unions as a rival to the Amsterdam-centred International Federation of Trade Unions.

These negotiations led, in April, 1921, to a joint meeting in Berlin of the Executives of all three Internationals and to the setting up of an Organising Committee of the three to promote joint action. This Committee agreed to take steps to summon an all-in conference with a view to the establishment of a unified International ; but even at this stage the representatives of the Second and Third Internationals made it plain enough that the meeting of such a conference would be more likely to serve as an occasion for mutual denunciations than for any real reconciliation of attitudes. When the " Committee of Nine " met again the following month the whole thing blew up. The Vienna Union, objecting to the intransigeance of the Communist representatives, retracted its proposal for an all-in conference ; and the Third International withdrew altogether. The net effect of the discussions had been to make thoroughly evident not only the impossibility of reconciling the two extremes, but also that the Communists were by no means prepared to mitigate their insistence on centralised control of any International to which they adhered. Such control being objected to quite as much by the Vienna Union as by the Second International, the breakdown brought these two closer together, though they still continued to manœuvre for leadership and to stand for different conceptions of Socialist policy.

In the summer of 1922 both bodies set to work to summon separate International Conferences designed to unify the Socialist parties which were outside the Third International. The situation was, however, radically altered when, in September, the two German Socialist parties were reunited ; for the unified German

Party had now a strong interest in bringing together the rival bodies to which its sections had been attached. By December the bridge was built. The International Federation of Trade Unions had summoned to meet at Amsterdam a World Peace Congress to which it invited not only the trade union centres of the various countries, but also the Socialist Parties and a number of other organisations—Peace Societies, Women's Societies, and so on. Advantage was taken of this gathering for meetings between the representatives of the Second and Vienna Internationals, which agreed to join in summoning an International Conference to meet in Hamburg in May, 1923, for the purpose of founding a new, united International. At this Conference, which met after joint action had received a further stimulus from the invasion of the Ruhr, the parties represented set up the Labour and Socialist International, as successor to both the Second International and the Vienna Union.

The attempt of the middle parties to create an all-in International thus finally broke down, as it was bound to do, and these parties were driven to ally themselves with the right-wing Socialists, rather than with the Communists, despite their desire to keep to the left. The reason for this is not far to seek. The parties of the Vienna Union, whatever their degree of " leftness," were fully determined to maintain their right to settle their own policies in accordance with their varying national conditions and traditions. The Communists, on the other hand, stood absolutely for a centralised and centrally disciplined international movement pledged to follow a common strategy with the objective of world revolution, and were entirely convinced both that the Russians were the only possible leaders for such a revolutionary movement, and that the first duty of Socialists throughout the world should be the defence of the Soviet Union as the protagonist of the revolution.

Thus, there were two interrelated impossibilities in the way of reconciliation. The right wing of Social Democracy and Labourism was equally opposed to the actual régime set up in the Soviet Union and to the notion of international centralised control for which the Bolsheviks stood ; and the left-wing Social Democrats, though they refused to denounce the Soviet " dictatorship," were no less firm than the right wing in rejecting the notion that Russian methods were everywhere applicable and the claim that the International, however constituted, should be authorised to dictate policy to its constituent parties.

In the course of the prolonged quarrel which preceded the final rupture between Communism and Social Democracy, the British Labour Party, as we have seen, acted throughout with the " right," whereas the I.L.P. associated itself with the Viennese " centre." Yet, because the I.L.P. was affiliated to the Labour Party and had no intention of severing this connection, there arose the curious spectacle of I.L.P. leaders acting as representatives of the Second International after the I.L.P. had left it. Ramsay MacDonald, in particular, was active from start to finish on behalf of the Second International, and freely denounced the Vienna Union at I.L.P. Conferences despite the I.L.P.'s association with it ; and other I.L.P. leaders, who praised rather than denounced, regarded the Vienna Union more as a means of keeping the I.L.P. out of the Third International until the chance offered of re-establishing Social Democratic unity than as a means to the creation of an International wide enough to embrace the Communists as well. After the extreme left of the I.L.P. had seceded to join the Communist Party, there remained in it no substantial section which believed in revolutionary action as the means to Socialism in Great Britain. There did remain, as we shall see, a majority which stood for a more militant Socialist policy than the Labour Party was prepared to accept—a policy that was soon to crystallise into the programme of " Socialism in Our Time." But the advocates of this policy set out to achieve it not by revolution but by constitutional and parliamentary means. They wanted to reform Parliament, so as to render possible both a swifter pace of legislative change and a larger amount of democratic control over administration. But they had no wish to sweep Parliament away, and they were strong opponents of any kind of centralised dictatorship, even if it were to be exercised in the proletariat's name.

As for the Labour Party, accident rather than intention made it during these years the protagonist of the Second International against the Vienna Union as well as against the Third. Arthur Henderson had set out in all good faith after 1918 to rebuild the International on the widest possible basis, and in his desire to re-establish good international relations in Europe had been intent on getting the Germans back at once as full partners in the International. Unhappily, his attempt broke down, mainly for two reasons—the secession of the French Socialists, whose support was indispensable, and the division between the rival German Socialist parties, which left him allied in the Second International with the German Majority Party, at a time when that party was engaged in most damaging measures against the German Socialist left wing. The secession of the French and of the German Independents left the Second International a mere right-wing rump, badly exposed to the attacks of the Communists and most unattractive even to moderate Socialist opinion.

From this awkward situation the British Labour Party was rescued by the intransigeant revolutionism of the Soviet Union, whose leaders, in pursuance of their doctrine of centralised dictatorship, gradually antagonised all the middle parties and groups which were instinctively disposed to sympathise with them as against the Social Democratic right wing. It is, however, a mistake to attribute this intransigeance merely to faults of tactics on the Communist side. The Communist attitude rested on a conviction which remained unshaken that the method of revolutionary action which had been followed in Russia was the only possible road to Socialism, and that the world revolution, even if hopes of its immediate advent were not fulfilled, must come in due course, so that the essential task of all Socialists was to prepare for it, and meantime to defend the country in which it had been actually achieved. Granted all these assumptions, the Communists were right enough in denouncing the Social Democrats as " social traitors," and in doing all they could to break up the parties and Trade Unions that were under Social Democratic control. This being so, there was no possible basis for collaboration in a unified International ; but it took many Socialists a long while to appreciate this fact, and even when it had been appreciated many were sad at heart at finding themselves at one with the " right " and in a state of antagonism to the policy of the Soviet Union, which they continued to regard with affection and respect as the one country in which the Socialist Revolution had been victoriously accomplished.

(d) *The Development of the Labour Party up to 1923*

From 1918 onwards the Labour Party, under its new Constitution, had been steadily building up its local organisation. By 1924 there were only three constituencies in Great Britain in which no sort of Local Labour Party was in existence. There were nearly 3,000 Divisional or Local Labour Parties or Trades and Labour Councils undertaking political work ; and the Trades

Councils, except in a number of boroughs in which a single body undertook both the political and the industrial work, had been replaced for political purposes by Local or Divisional Parties formed in accordance with the Model Rules approved in 1918. In 1923 the number of directly affiliated Divisional or Borough Labour Parties and Trades and Labour Councils for the first time exceeded 500, covering about 600 constituencies. Of course, these bodies differed greatly in strength, and in many of the County Divisions there was only a skeleton organisation ; but progress had been remarkable, and was maintained at a rapid rate even during the post-war depression.

Inside the local parties, nothing was more notable than the development of the special Women's Sections. Up to 1918 the organisation of women in support of the Labour Party had been in the hands of the affiliated, but independent, Women's Labour League ; but thereafter the League became an integral part of the machine and its branches were reorganised as Women's Sections of the local parties. Five full-time women organisers were appointed in 1918 and 1919, and a systematic campaign for the establishment of more Women's Sections was begun. In order to aid this movement and to replace the national work of the Women's Labour League, a National Labour Women's Annual Conference was set on foot in 1918, and has been maintained with growing success ever since. In scattered county divisions, where it seemed impracticable to set up separate Women's Sections, Central Women's Committees were constituted and County Women's Conferences were held from time to time. In addition, District Labour Women's Advisory Councils were formed in a number of areas. By the end of 1922 there were over 1,000 Women's Sections, not including Ward Sections or Groups, and the Sections had a membership of over 120,000. By the middle of 1924 the Sections numbered 1,332, and the membership had risen to 150,000. Two areas, Woolwich and Barrow-in-Furness, had each more than 1,000 women members enrolled.

This growth of organisation followed of course on the enfranchisement of the older women in 1918. But it was also largely an outcome of the greatly increased part taken by women in Labour Party and Trade Union activities during the war, as well as of the pioneering work of the Women's Co-operative Guilds and the Socialist societies. Indeed, under the scheme of individual Labour Party membership adopted in 1918, the organisation of women went ahead a good deal faster than that of men, mainly because more men were affiliated party members through their Trade Unions, to which they paid the political levy. The enrolment of women was greatest among housewives who were not in wage-earning employment ; and in the development of the new Labour Party the Women's Sections played an invaluable educational part, above all among this large and hitherto unorganised fraction of the people. The women were largely the making of the Local Labour Parties ; and the fears which had been entertained by some of the I.L.P. leaders that the lower rates of contribution for individual membership of the Labour Party would drain away support from the I.L.P. branches were by no means realised during the early years. Men who wanted to play an active part in local Labour work, as well as women who could afford the contribution, poured into the I.L.P. in increasing numbers : the individual membership of the Labour Party, where it did not overlap that of the I.L.P., was made up mainly of women whom the I.L.P. would not in any case have been able to enrol. Competition did develop at a later stage ; but there was little of it during the early years.

Indeed, the I.L.P. probably benefited from the spread of local Labour organisation to many areas in which it had hardly existed before. The I.L.P.'s membership had been rising fast during the later stages of the war. At the 1918 Conference a rise of over 50 per cent during the previous year was recorded, and further substantial increases were reported over the next two years. By 1920-1 the advent of the post-war slump had checked the rise, and had led to a fall in the revenue from subscriptions ; and in the following year, 1921-2, there was a definite drop. In 1922-3 there was a recovery, membership being reported as 31,116, with a regular paying total of between 26,000 and 27,000. Then came a further rise, and for 1924-5 the National Administrative Council was able to report that with the advent of the first Labour Government " all records in progress had been eclipsed," the number of branches having risen from 637 at the beginning of 1923 to 1,028 two years later. Even at this high point, however, the membership on which affiliation fees were paid to the Labour Party was only 30,000, as compared with 26,000 in 1922-3 and 35,000 in 1918-19. The actual membership of the I.L.P. can never be accurately ascertained. Probably they paid in 1918-19 on something like their full nominal membership, but had learnt by 1925 to restrict their payment to the Labour Party to the level of their average fully paid membership throughout the year. The difference was considerable. In 1925 the nominal " good-on-the-books " members numbered 56,000, but the paid-up members were put at only 34,000, the average paid-up membership for the full year being presumably a good deal less.

Unsatisfactory as these figures are, they serve to show that the growth of the Local Labour Parties had up to this point no adverse effect on the I.L.P., which still retained its position as the principal propagandist agency for the Labour Party as well as for Socialism in general. The Social Democratic Federation, which had replaced the British Socialist Party as an affiliated Socialist society, was numerically unimportant, paying on only 2,000 members : the Fabian Society, with 1,844, was smaller still.

From 1922, when a resolution on the matter was adopted at the Conference of Labour Women, the Labour Party began to interest itself in the organisation of youth. At this stage, there existed already a small independent body, the Young Labour League ; and some Local Labour Parties were working in with the branches of this body, whereas others wished to set up Youth Sections on the lines of the Women's Sections inside the party machine. The Young Labour League had been started in Clapham in 1920, and had its main strength in and around London : it wanted the Labour Party to give it official recognition and some financial help. But the predominant view at party headquarters was that, just as the Women's Labour League had been taken over and absorbed, so the Youth Organisation had better be definitely a part of the party machine. In 1923 the National Executive set up a sub-committee to go into the question, and in accordance with the recommendations of this body the Executive decided in favour of Youth Sections inside the Local Labour Parties, limited to members between the ages of 14 and 21. The Youth Sections were to have their own Committees of Management, including two persons appointed by the Local Parties, and they were to be allowed two representatives, with voice but without vote, on the General Committees of the Parties to which they were attached. Provision was also made for the setting up of Junior Sections for children under fourteen, for recreational purposes apart from politics, which were not to be discussed. The work of the Youth Sections was to be " mainly recreational and educational," and it was laid down that " care should be taken not to overemphasise their political side." Every encouragement was, however, to be given to participation in election work. At the Labour Party Conference of 1924 these proposals were challenged from several quarters. Those who had been associated with the Young Labour League complained that they had been ignored and rebuffed by the Executive ; and Mark Starr, of the Wimbledon Labour Party, moved that the Youth Sections to be set up within the Local Parties should be given the same rights as Men's and Women's Sections, including full freedom of political discussion and activity. The Executive opposed these claims, and secured a vote endorsing its own scheme, and by the middle of 1925 it had succeeded in getting about 150 Youth Sections into existence under the conditions laid down. The Young Labour League, unable to carry on by itself, had agreed to the conversion of its branches into Youth Sections ; and in London a Young People's Advisory Committee had been formed under the auspices of the London Labour Party. Thus, for the time being all seemed to be going well ; but we shall see later that this appearance was illusory. There was to be a great deal of trouble in subsequent years over the amount of freedom to be allowed to the Labour Party's Youth Organisation, especially in relation to its right to discuss and adopt political policies. Indeed, the problem has never been satisfactorily settled ; for again and again the Youth Organisations have been accused of harbouring, or of falling victims to, subversive tendencies and movements, and there has been hardly a year in which some sort of acrimonious dispute has not been in progress.

Even at the early stage with which we are here dealing, the main fear in the National Executive's mind was that an independent, or largely independent, League of Youth might lend itself to Communist methods of infiltration. Throughout the early 1920's, the problems presented by the rise of the Communist Party and by its attempts to push its way into the Labour Party and the Trade Unions were giving constant trouble to the Party leaders. At the outset, though the Communist Party's request for affiliation to the Labour Party was rejected, the relations of individual Communists to the Labour Party were undefined. Harry Pollitt was able to speak in favour of Communist affiliation at the Labour Party Conference in 1922, as Arthur Cook had done in 1921, both being duly accredited delegates of their respective Trade Unions—the Boilermakers and the Miners' Federation. In the 1922 General Election, S. Saklatvala, a known member of the Communist Party, ran as an endorsed Labour Party candidate and secured election, having pledged himself to abide by the Labour Party Constitution. As against this, other Communists put forward as candidates, but refusing to give similar pledges, were not endorsed ; and the Parliamentary Labour Party rejected after the Election an application to receive the Labour Party Whip from J. T. Walton Newbold, who had been elected as Communist M.P. for Motherwell.

Year after year the Labour Party Conference supported the National Executive in rejecting the Communist Party's applications for affiliation. In 1921 the matter was disposed of by the carrying of the previous question by 4,115,000 votes to 224,000. In 1922 an attempt to refer back the section of the Annual Report recording the Executive's rejection was defeated by 3,086,000 to 261,000. In 1923 a direct motion in favour of the affiliation was beaten by 2,880,000 to 366,000 ; and in 1924 an Executive motion against affiliation was carried by 3,185,000 to 193,000. The pro-Communist vote thus varied from year to year ; but there was always an overwhelming majority on the other side.

This, however, did not dispose of the more difficult question of the position of individual Communists in relation to the Party. This matter was first formally raised at the Edinburgh Conference of 1922, when, as we have seen, the Executive proposed a new Rule laying down that "every person nominated to serve as a delegate [to either a Local Labour Party or to a national Conference of the Party] shall individually accept the Constitution and principles of the Labour Party," and further that " no person shall be eligible as a delegate who is a member of any organisation having for one of its objects the return to Parliament or to any Local Governing Authority of a candidate or candidates other than such as have been endorsed by the Labour Party, or have been approved as running in association with the Labour Party."* This new Rule, after some questioning of its practicability, was endorsed by a vote of 342 to 161 ; and the National Executive proceeded to interpret it, in relation to other Conference decisions, as barring members of the Communist Party not only from serving as delegates in any capacity, but also from joining the Labour Party as individual members. The National Executive soon discovered, however, that the new Rule could not be administered as it stood without serious difficulty ; for it could be invoked to disqualify not only Communists but also, for example, members of professional associations, such as the National Union of Teachers, which adopted the policy of

*i.e., candidates of the Co-operative Party.

putting forward candidates under the auspices of any party. There were also serious difficulties in the way of preventing Trade Unions from nominating whom they pleased as delegates ; and the Executive reached the conclusion that it had best limit the rule to insisting that all persons chosen as delegates must " individually accept the Constitution and principles of the Labour Party," dropping the further excluding clause. This change was approved at the London Conference of 1923. But the whole question came up again at the 1924 Conference, when it was decided, by a vote of 2,456,000 to 654,000, that no member of the Communist Party should be eligible as a Labour Party candidate, and by the much narrower majority of 1,804,000 to 1,540,000 that no member of the Communist Party should be eligible for individual membership of the Labour Party. Even this did not finally dispose of the issue ; for at the 1925 Conference the Executive not only reported in favour of excluding Communists from individual membership, but also intimated to the delegates " that in its opinion affiliated Trade Unions can only act consistently with the decisions of the Annual Conference in its relation to the Communists by appealing to their members, when electing delegates to national or local Labour Party conferences or meetings, to refrain from nominating or electing known members of non-affiliated political parties, including the Communists."

When these declarations came up, it soon appeared that there were a number of Communist delegates in the hall. William Gallacher, representing the Paisley Labour Party, moved the reference back, and was defeated by 2,954,000 to 321,000. Harry Pollitt, as a delegate of the Boilermakers, moved the rejection of the ban on individual membership, and was beaten, after a vigorous speech by Ernest Bevin, by 2,870,000 to 321,000. Then Emanuel Shinwell, who belonged to the left wing of the I.L.P., moved the rejection of the second Executive proposal, and was in his turn defeated by 2,692,000 votes to 480,000.

The Communists, after their first application for affiliation to the Labour Party had been rejected, had decided to adopt systematically the strategy of maintaining their connection with the Local Labour Parties to the fullest possible extent, and of working inside the Labour Party and the Trade Unions for the purpose of discrediting the existing leadership. In this policy they achieved a substantial amount of success, though not nearly so much as they had hoped for. At first there were considerable differences in day-to-day Communist tactics in different areas, for the Party was but loosely knit together and included a number of warring elements. In particular, a considerable group, drawn mainly from the Workers' Committee Movement, which was the relic of the war-time Shop Stewards' organisation, had little belief in centralised political action, and concerned itself mainly with left-wing activities directed against the official machinery of the Trade Unions. This group undertook propaganda on behalf of the Red International of Labour Unions, which had been established at Moscow in opposition to the Amsterdam I.F.T.U. ; and there was a good deal of conflict between it and the more Moscow-minded section which dominated the party machine. Then, in October, 1922, the Communist Party underwent, at the orders of the Communist International, a thorough reorganisation. The loosely organised Executive made up of delegates from the districts was replaced by a Political Bureau constituted in accordance with the principle of " democratic centralism " ; and from that point the Communist Party, shedding considerable numbers of its most prominent supporters, followed a " party line " which was firmly laid down for it by its leaders in constant consultation with the Comintern.

Communist work inside the Trade Unions was also reorganised and brought under the control of the central directing group. The new strategy included the formation of the " Minority Movement" early in 1923. This was at first conceived as an agency through which the Communists could capture the support and guide the activities of all left-wing elements in the political as well as in the industrial field ; but it actually developed into an industrial off-shoot of the Communist Party, with the object of stirring up unofficial strike activity and making things as difficult as possible for the official Trade Union leaders, whom it accused of betraying the workers' cause. As the Communists were gradually driven back in the Local Labour Parties, they transferred more and more of their energies to the industrial side, with the result that the Trade Union leaders, who had at first been but lukewarm in backing up the Labour Party Executive's resistance to " infiltration," were stirred in their turn into anti-Communist activity under stress of the attacks made on them from inside their own Unions.

It has to be borne in mind that throughout this period the Communists, though they made a great display, were numerically quite insignificant. They had never more than a few thousand members scattered about the country, and they were on the average losing as many as they gained—indeed, for some time they were losing more. A great many of those who had joined them in the first flush of enthusiasm for the Russian Revolution soon found themselves alienated by the strict discipline to which, from 1922, every member was subject at the hands of the centralised Political Bureau. A good many of the best-known leaders of the Labour Party and the Trade Unions in later years served an apprenticeship in the Communist Party in its early days. As many of the leading figures began to drop off from 1922 onwards, the Communist Party was saved from insignificance mainly by two things—by the bitter feelings left behind among the Miners by " Black Friday," and by the growth of unemployment, which gave them their chance through the National Unemployed Workers' Committee Movement both to draw in embittered recruits and to keep themselves well to the fore with Hunger Marches, demonstrations, and processions of protest against the Government and the Poor Law Guardians, and with denunciations of the supineness of the Labour Party and the Trade Unions in pressing the claims of the unemployed. The Trade Unions were slow to react to these tactics, largely because there was no organic connection between the Trades Union Congress and the local Trades Councils, which were left without either lead or help from the centre and were thus easily induced to back the Communists and the National Unemployed Workers' Committee Movement, as they at any rate appeared to be doing something locally beyond the mere passing of ineffective resolutions. It is surprising that the Trade Union leaders did not see the need for more effective local action, or make any real attempt to assume the headship of the unemployed agitation. But the fact remains that they did not, and that the series of National Conferences in which the Labour Party and the Trade Unions joined forces to work out and proclaim a national unemployment policy remained barren, because so little was done to base upon them any continuous agitation or to enlist rank and file support.

While the Communists were thus developing into a small, highly disciplined party with mass contacts chiefly with the unemployed, the I.L.P. was passing through a quite different evolution. Up to the establishment of the Communist Party and to the breach with the Third International over the " Twenty-one Conditions," the I.L.P. included a substantial Communist, or semi-Communist, minority. The secession of this element to the Communist Party left the I.L.P. divided between a right wing which looked to MacDonald for leadership and a central group in which F. W. Jowett was the most prominent of the older leaders, and Clifford Allen and R. C. Wallhead were the protagonists. Snowden, who had great prestige in the party, stood between these groups, strongly antagonistic to the new ideas of the centre, but mistrustful of MacDonald and vigorous in advocacy of a Socialism which was equally hostile to ideas of Sovietism and Workers' Control on the one hand and to mere social reformism on the other. As MacDonald transferred more and more of his loyalty from the I.L.P. to the Labour Party, in which he was working closely with Henderson to make the new Constitution of 1918 a success, Snowden and the younger leaders came to terms on the basis of an uneasy compromise. The advocates of Workers' Control, among whom Attlee was a prominent figure, were allowed to have their head : Jowett was allowed to push his particular ideas of parliamentary reform—designed to convert Parliament into something rather like an expanded Town Council working on the Committee system—and there emerged the slogan " For Socialism Now." This meant in effect that the I.L.P. set out to press the Labour Party to commit itself to a much more precise and immediate programme of Socialist legislation than had been embodied in *Labour and the New Social Order*, and, with this object, began to conduct an extensive propaganda of its own inside the Local Labour Parties.

At the I.L.P.'s Southport Conference of 1921 there were prolonged debates on Socialist policy, arising out of the Reports of a series of special Policy Sub-Committees set up the previous year. These reports, which MacDonald, the Chairman of the main Committee, refused to sign, involved a sharp move to the left, though on almost every issue there were rival drafts embodying conflicting views. There were many signs of strong Guild Socialist influence, and of equally strong hostility to this influence on the part of Snowden and of other established leaders. On many critical issues the division of opinion was practically equal. The National Administrative Council, faced with the sharp divergence of views, gladly accepted a Conference motion to refer back the whole of the Reports for further consideration ; and most of them were in fact washed away so thoroughly as never to be heard of again. By 1922, when the draft Programme came up for consideration at the Nottingham Conference, the extreme left had largely vanished, and a revised version went through without a great deal of opposition after a rival Bradford draft had been easily

defeated, and after Attlee had succeeded in amending the proposed text by including a strengthened paragraph in favour of
Industrial Democracy based on Workers' Control. The Nottingham Conference then proceeded to pass a resolution declaring for
opposition to all war, even if it were said to be defensive, and
calling for a General Strike as a means of combating any threat
of war. The following year it was decided to urge the Labour Party
to vote against all military estimates ; and a resolution in favour
of this policy was brought up, and defeated, at the Labour Party
Conference.

The I.L.P. Conference of 1922 also decided to launch a national
" Now for Socialism " Campaign in support of its newly adopted
programme ; but the General Election of 1922 caused this campaign to be postponed. In 1923 a new Policy Committee was
appointed ; but its first reports—on Land and Agriculture—
were not adopted until Easter, 1924, when the Labour Government had already been for some months in office. The advent of
the Labour Government in effect caused the " Now for Socialism " crusade to be put off yet again, so that it was not really
begun until after the Government's fall. We shall return to it in a
subsequent chapter.

On the whole, from the end of the war up to 1924, the I.L.P.'s
influence in the Labour Party increased. Its resolutions were for
the most part favourably received by the Labour Party Conference ; and, as we have seen, its position in the Parliamentary
Party was greatly strengthened by the General Election of 1922.
It succeeded in writing its conception of Socialism more precisely
into the Labour Party programme ; and during these years it
did not fall into the error, of which it was guilty later, of seeming to
set itself up as a rival body pressing for a programme of its own
radically different from that of the Labour Party. This was partly
because MacDonald and Snowden still retained up to 1924 enough
influence to hold it back from attacking over too wide a front,
and partly because Arthur Henderson went as far as he could to
meet its claims and to recognise its special position and value as
a propagandist and electioneering agency. It was largely due to
Henderson's efforts that war antagonisms were so speedily
smoothed over and that the dispute over the rival Internationals
was not allowed to drive the I.L.P. out of the Labour Party. No
doubt, both MacDonald and Henderson were actuated by a
belief that the leftism of the I.L.P. rebels in the period just after
the war was only a passing phase, and that as things settled down

the I.L.P. would return to its pre-1914 moderate brand of
evolutionary Socialism. In this they were partly, but not entirely,
right. The I.L.P. was so rebuffed by the Third International and
so shorn of its extremists as a sequel to the rebuff as to move back
rapidly to a centre position. But it did not give up the idea that
the process of turning the Labour Party into a Socialist Party
had been only begun, and not completed, by the new Constitution
of 1918 and by the adoption of *Labour and the New Social Order* ;
and it did consider that its mission was to press constantly for a
further move to the left. Not until 1924 did most I.L.P.ers
understand that such pressure would find the strongest resistance
in Ramsay MacDonald—or they would not have played the part
they did in reinstating him and holding him firm in the leadership of the Labour Party.

During the years of confusion after 1917 the left wing of the
Labour and Socialist Movement had for some time the considerable advantage of being in command of the only daily newspaper
that supported Labour's claims. During the war, the official
Labour newspaper, *The Daily Citizen*, had been abandoned, and
the *Herald*, its unofficial left-wing rival, had been compelled to
become a weekly. In March, 1919, the *Herald* resumed publication as a daily, with George Lansbury continuing as editor ;
and up to 1922 the paper retained its unofficial position and took
up a consistently radical line. It was, however, always in serious
financial difficulties ; and in the spring of 1922 its funds were
exhausted and an appeal had to be made to the Labour Party and
the Trades Union Congress to save it from collapse. As we saw,
the two national bodies thereupon agreed to assume temporary
financial responsibility until some permanent arrangement for
its maintenance could be devised. Later in the year a plan was
adopted whereby the Trades Union Congress, with some aid from
the Labour Party, subscribed a substantial capital sum for the
development of the paper. The price was reduced from 2d. to
1d., and an extensive propaganda campaign to increase its circulation was set on foot. In spite of some success, heavy losses continued to be incurred ; and for some years the *Daily Herald*
continued to be a serious drain on Labour and Trade Union
resources. Under the new régime instituted when the T.U.C.
and the Labour Party took over control, George Lansbury ceased
to be editor, but remained as manager of the paper. His place
as editor was taken by Hamilton Fyfe, and there was a marked
change of tone. From 1922 the *Herald* was primarily an exponent

not of left-wing views, but of official Labour Party and Trade Union policy. One effect of this change was to give the Communists an opportunity, which they promptly seized, of capturing the position in left-wing journalism that had been left empty by the *Herald's* officialisation. The Communist Party replaced its weekly review, *The Communist*, by *The Workers' Weekly*, which was much more in form and substance a newspaper, though it appeared only once a week. The I.L.P. also reorganised its weekly, the *Labour Leader*, which was transformed in 1923 into the *New Leader*, with H. N. Brailsford as editor, and achieved a greatly increased circulation.

(e) *The General Election of 1923*

Stanley Baldwin succeeded Bonar Law as Prime Minister in May, 1923, in the midst of the Ruhr crisis. Six months later he announced his intention of dissolving Parliament and appealing to the country for a mandate to introduce a system of Tariff Protection. Thus, a Second General Election was held only a year after that of 1922, in which the Labour Party had more than doubled its strength. The dissolution caught the Party to some extent unprepared, with only 239 endorsed candidates, including sitting M.P.s, in the field. Within a fortnight nearly 200 additional adoptions were rushed through ; and in the event 428 endorsed candidates were put forward, as compared with 414 in 1922. The Election took place on December 6, and the total number of votes cast was 14,500,000—a 74 per cent poll. The Labour vote rose only slightly above the level of the previous year —from 4,236,733 to 4,348,379 ; but the results were much more favourable. Of the 144 seats held by Labour, only sixteen were lost, and sixty-three new seats were gained, raising the strength of the Party to 191. Conservative and allied candidates polled a larger total vote—5,544,540—and secured 258 seats. The Liberals, fighting this time as a single party, polled nearly as many votes as Labour—4,314,202—and secured 158 seats. The Conservatives thus remained considerably the largest party, but were outnumbered by the Labour and Liberal parties combined. It lay with the Liberals either to keep the Conservatives in power or to turn them out, and thus to offer Labour, as the second largest party, the chance, if it would, of forming a minority Government. The Liberals decided for the second course, and the Labour Party,

under Ramsay MacDonald, decided to accept office, though they
realised that they would be liable to be turned out whenever the
Liberal Party felt minded to vote against them.

In the General Election of 1923, the Labour Party made its
biggest gains in and around London. The number of Labour
M.P.s for the entire Greater London area rose from sixteen to
thirty-seven. No comparable gains were made in other parts of
the country, though in most there was some advance. The only
setback was in the North-east, where there was a net loss of three
seats. In the South and South-west as a whole, excluding Greater
London, the number of Labour M.P.s was increased from one to
five, and in the Eastern Counties from one to seven. There were

LABOUR AT THE GENERAL ELECTION OF 1923

	Members elected		Total seats fought		Communist, etc. Candidates
	1923	1922	1923	1922	
London County	22	(9)	46	(45)	1
Greater London .	15	(7)	40	(27)	
Southern England .	1	(0)	27		
South-west England .	4	(1)	21	(22)	
West Midlands . .	11	(9)	35	(33)	
East Midlands . .	14	(8)	31	(33)	1
Eastern Counties .	7	(1)	21	(22)	
Lancs. and Cheshire .	24	(19)	51	(58)	1
Yorkshire . .	23	(21)	46	(42)	
North-west England .	3	(3)	3	(3)	
North-east England .	14	(17)	27	(25)	
Wales and Monmouth	19	(18)	27	(28)	
Scotland . . .	34	(29)	50	(43)	3
Northern Ireland .	—	(—)	1	(—)	
Universities . .	—*	(—)	2	(3)	
	191	(142)	428	(413)	6

* A Labour Independent was elected for the University of Wales.

five gains in Scotland, five in Lancashire and Cheshire, and six in the East Midlands.

The unexpected hurrying on of the Election was on the whole favourable to the I.L.P. and to the Divisional Parties, which could rush through the processes of adoption more rapidly than the Trade Unions. The number of I.L.P. candidates returned to the House of Commons rose from thirty-two in 1922 to forty-six in the following year, and that of members put forward under the auspices of Divisional Parties from nineteen to thirty-five. Trade Union representation increased much less—from eighty-five to ninety-eight. The Co-operative Party rose from four to six M.P.s. The Parliamentary Labour Party of 1924 was less domi- nated by Trade Union representatives than the Party in the previous Parliament, even as that had been less Trade Unionist than its predecessor. The Miners numbered forty-four—two more than in 1922 : the Transport Workers came next, with seven representatives, followed by the General Workers, with five. The Engineers lost three out of the six seats gained the year before.

In the party leadership there was not much change. Arthur Henderson contrived once more to lose his seat—this time at Newcastle-on-Tyne—but he was returned for Burnley at a by-election in February, 1924, on the death of the veteran Social Democrat, Dan Irving, who had held the seat since 1918. The best known among the new M.P.s were Margaret Bondfield, Charles Dukes, Frank Hodges, George Isaacs, Herbert Morrison, Susan Lawrence, and F. W. Pethick Lawrence. Of these, Morrison was already making a name for himself as leader of the London Labour Party. Robert Smillie, the former leader of the Miners, held the Northumberland seat which he had won at a by-election earlier in the year.

The Communists made but a poor showing. Saklatvala and Walton Newbold, their two sitting members, both lost their seats, and Gallacher, at Dundee, was at the bottom of the poll. They fought only six seats in all, three of them in Scotland.

The pattern of the General Election of 1923 was simpler than that of its predecessors, because there was only one Liberal Party in the field. Eighty-three out of the 191 Labour M.P.s were elected in three-cornered contests with a Tory and a Liberal ; and of these eighty-three only nineteen had clear majorities. Ninety- seven were elected in straight fights, sixty-four against Conserva- tive, and thirty-two against Liberal opponents. One had only a Communist opponent ; and three were returned unopposed.

These figures omit the eight Labour M.P.s who were elected for
two-member constituencies. The clear majorities in three-
cornered fights were largely in the mining areas, which also
provided a high proportion of the straight fights. The relatively
equal appeal of the three main parties meant that an exceptionally large number of M.P.s were elected on a minority vote.

LABOUR PARTY : BODIES SPONSORING SUCCESSFUL CANDIDATES, 1923

	1923	1922		1923	1922
I.L.P. . . .	46	32	Socialist Societies .	52	34
Fabian Society . .	2	1			
S.D.F. . . .	4	1			
D.L.P. . . .	35	19	Divisional Parties .	35	19
Miner's Federation .	44	42			
Transport Workers .	7	5			
General Workers .	5	4			
N.U.R. . . .	3	3	Trade Unions .	98	85
A.E.U. . . .	3	6			
Textile Factory Workers	3	3			
Other Trade Unions .	32	22			
N.U. Teachers . .	1	—			
Co-operative Party .	6	4	Co-operative Party .	6	4
	191	142		191	142

CHAPTER V

THE FIRST LABOUR GOVERNMENT
AND THE " RED LETTER " ELECTION

(a) The First Labour Government

Resignation of the Baldwin Government and formation of the first MacDonald Government—The Choice before the Labour Party—MacDonald's attitude—The position of the Liberal Party—John Wheatley and the Poplar Guardians—The Government and the unemployed—The " Gap " abolished—Benefits raised and made a matter of right—The Government's plans for Public Works—Old Age Pensions improved—The Rent struggle and the Labour Rent Bills—The Wheatley Housing Act—The Treaty with the building operatives—The attempt to control building materials—Trevelyan at the Board of Education—Reform by administration—The Agricultural Wages Act—Philip Snowden's " Free Trade " Budget—The repeal of the McKenna Duties—The limits of the Government's home policy—No socialisation attempted—MacDonald at the Foreign Office—The Ruhr and Reparations crises—Co-operation with the Herriot Government—The Dawes Plan and the Geneva Protocol—The failure in Egypt and India—Recognition of the Soviet Government—The Anglo-Russian Treaties and the projected loan to Russia—The " Campbell Case "—The Liberals and Tories unite to defeat the Government—The dissolution of Parliament—The " Red Letter " scare and its effects—Was the letter genuine ?—An analysis of MacDonald's conduct and of that of the Foreign Office officials—Was it a " Tory plot " ?

(b) The General Election of 1924

An increased Labour vote, but a loss in seats—Straight fights and three-cornered contests—Liberal-Tory pacts—Fewer Labour M.P.s returned on a minority vote—Analysis of losses by regions—And of some regional gains—Decrease in I.L.P. and D.L.P. representation—The composition of the Labour Party in the new Parliament—Defeated leaders—The fate of the Liberal Party.

(a) The First Labour Government

CABINET

J. Ramsay MacDonald	Prime Minister and Foreign Secretary.
J. R. Clynes	Lord Privy Seal and Deputy Leader of the House.
Lord Parmoor	Lord President of the Council.
Lord Haldane	Lord Chancellor.
Philip Snowden	Chancellor of the Exchequer.
Arthur Henderson	Home Secretary.
J. H. Thomas	Colonial Secretary.
Stephen Walsh	Secretary for War.
Lord Olivier	Secretary for India.
Lord Thomson	Secretary for Air.
Lord Chelmsford	First Lord of the Admiralty.
Sidney Webb	President of the Board of Trade.
John Wheatley	Minister of Health.

Noel Buxton	Minister of Agriculture.
William Adamson	Secretary of State for Scotland.
C. P. Trevelyan	President of the Board of Education.
Thomas Shaw	Minister of Labour.
Vernon Hartshorn	Postmaster-General.
J. C. Wedgwood	Chancellor of the Duchy of Lancaster.
F. W. Jowett	First Commissioner of Works.

NOT IN THE CABINET

H. Gosling	Minister of Transport.
F. O. Roberts	Minister of Pensions.
Sir Patrick Hastings	Attorney-General.
Sir H. H. Slesser	Solicitor-General.
Ben C. Spoor	Chief Whip.

Among the Under-Secretaries were W. Graham (Treasury), C. R. Attlee (War), A. V. Alexander (Board of Trade), E. Shinwell (Mines), Margaret Bondfield (Labour), Arthur Greenwood (Health).

On January 22, 1924, the King called on Ramsay MacDonald to form a Government, and the names of the leading members of the new Cabinet were made known the next day. On December 18, 1923, when the results of the Election were known, Asquith had announced that the Liberals would not maintain the Conservative Government in power ; but Stanley Baldwin did not resign until his Government had actually met, and been defeated in, the new House of Commons. On January 21, the Liberals supported the Vote of Censure moved on behalf of the Labour Party ; but the tone of Liberal speeches both on this occasion and earlier showed that they had every intention of using their voting power to keep the Government under a very tight control. The Labour Party had in fact to choose between refusing office and taking it under conditions which made it utterly impossible to carry out any sort of Socialist policy, even of the mildest. Some valuable measures of social reform Labour could hope to be allowed to put into effect, always subject to the Liberal veto ; but it was evident that no step towards constructive Socialist achievement would be allowed.

The Labour Party had in effect to choose between three alternatives—refusal to take office, acceptance of office on conditions which the Liberal Party would impose (for the Government would require positive Liberal support for its measures—abstention would not suffice to keep it in office), and acceptance of office with the sole purpose of producing at once a challenging Socialist programme, suffering defeat on it in the House of

Commons, and appealing immediately to the country in a new General Election.

The first of these courses—refusal of office—was difficult. It would have been widely misrepresented as showing Labour's fears of its own capacity, and it would have meant leaving the unemployed to their plight and—what weighed even more with many Socialists—doing nothing to improve the state of international relations or to further European reconstruction and recovery. It would have meant either the continuance of the Tories in power with the support of the right-wing Liberals or a Tory-Liberal Coalition in the hands of the more reactionary elements. The third course had its advocates ; but the Labour Party was ill-placed financially for facing another General Election, and the leaders of the Party for the most part believed that such an election would leave matters pretty much as they were, and were fairly sure that Labour would not be able to improve its position much, if at all. Indeed, it might have lost ground seriously, if Tories and Liberals had combined against it ; for a third of all the Labour M.P.s held their seats on a minority vote.

The second course also had very serious disadvantages. If the Labour Government could do, even in the House of Commons, only what the Liberals would allow it to do and would actually vote for, and if further its measures were to be at the mercy of an overwhelmingly Conservative House of Lords, the results of Labour in office were pretty well bound to bring serious disappointment to many of its supporters, and to look like weakness and ineffectiveness even if they were not. At least, this was bound to happen to the extent to which the Government had to rely on legislation for getting results : to the extent of its power to act administratively, without fresh legislation, it might be rather more strongly placed, because the onus in challenging its administrative actions would rest on the Opposition, whereas Labour would have to ask for positive approval of its legislative projects.

As between the three alternatives MacDonald seems to have felt no doubt. He wanted to be Prime Minister : he wanted to be at the head of a Government that would follow an exceedingly moderate and cautious policy in applying Socialism, and he probably felt that the necessity of getting Liberal backing would serve him well in resisting the pressure of the Labour left wing. Moreover, he genuinely thought that he could help to bring about large and salutary changes in international relations and to build up a concert of Europe as a means of preventing war and checking

the advance of Communism. In all these matters Arthur Henderson, who was entirely ready to sink his personal pretensions for
the good of the Party, was wholeheartedly with him ; and so,
on the whole, were most of the other outstanding leaders. No
doubt, there were many among the Labour M.P.s who either
did not realise how fully a MacDonald Government would be in
the power of the Liberals, or were unaware how far MacDonald
would regard the terms of office as inconsistent with any attempt
at Socialist legislation. The Party took office with mixed, or even
confused, feelings ; but there was never really any doubt either
that it would accept the chance or that, having done so, it would
refrain from any action that would deliberately provoke parliamentary defeat and would try to make the best it could of such
measures as the Liberals could be induced to support.

The composition of the Labour Cabinet, with only two or three
exceptions, gave no cause for surprise. Snowden was a certain
choice for the Exchequer : Clynes was Lord Privy Seal and
Deputy Leader of the House. Thomas was Colonial Secretary ;
Sidney Webb was President of the Board of Trade ; Trevelyan
was at the Board of Education. The Ministry of Labour went to
Tom Shaw, of the Textile Workers, the War Office to the miner,
Stephen Walsh, the India Office to the old Fabian administrator,
Sydney Olivier, and the Scottish Office to William Adamson, a
former leader of the Parliamentary Party. Arthur Henderson
was relegated to the Home Office, as MacDonald proposed to be
Foreign Secretary as well as Prime Minister. John Wheatley,
at the Ministry of Health, and F. W. Jowett, at the Office of
Works, represented the advanced wing of the I.L.P.

More notable were the choice of the ex-Liberal, Lord Haldane,
as Lord Chancellor, and the appointment of Lord Parmoor, the
ex-Tory pacifist lawyer, as Lord President of the Council, with a
special mission to the League of Nations. The Air Ministry went
to General Thomson, as Lord Thomson, a proved friend to
Labour ; but for the Admiralty MacDonald chose Lord
Chelmsford, who made no pretence of being a Socialist, or even a
Labour Party member. The Scottish Law Offices were also
filled by persons unconnected with the Labour Party ; but these,
unlike Lord Chelmsford, were not in the Cabinet.

When Parliament met, the Liberals lost no time in showing
their teeth. The first act of John Wheatley, the Minister of Health
from Clydeside and the most left-wing member of the Cabinet,
was to revoke the regulations imposed by his predecessor on the

recalcitrant Poplar Board of Guardians. Asquith, for the Liberals, at once took strong objection ; but, when Wheatley refused to give way, the Liberal Party, unwilling to force an issue on a matter on which popular feeling was likely to be against them, swallowed its protest and voted on the Government side. The precedent was important, as showing that administrative action could be taken by the Government under favourable strategic conditions, even where legislation of a similar tendency might be impracticable.

In view of the state of opinion in the country and of the line which the Labour Party had taken in opposition, clearly the first thing the new Government had to tackle was unemployment. This had two immediate aspects—improved conditions of relief and maintenance for the unemployed, and the provision of work. On February 19, Clynes announced that a Cabinet Committee had been set up to consider schemes of public works for the relief of unemployment ; and on the same day an Act became law abolishing the hated " gap " between periods of benefit under the Unemployment Insurance scheme. On both these issues the Liberals were prepared to support the Government : indeed, there was much Liberal, as well as Labour, criticism of the inadequacy of the plans at first put forward for the development of public works, and it was not until July that Snowden announced schemes of road and railway construction and electrical development that went some way towards satisfying the critics. It was not the Labour Government's fault that many of these projects never came to fruition. In the meantime there had been further Bills for the improvement of Unemployment Insurance. Rates of benefit and children's allowances were increased, and " uncovenanted " benefit—that is to say, benefit of unlimited duration—was made a statutory right instead of a concession dependent on official discretion in each individual instance. At the same time improvements were made in the condition of Old Age pensioners, by allowing small incomes from savings to be disregarded in calculating the pension due.

Housing was another problem which the Government, in view of its pledges, was compelled to face without delay. This had three distinct aspects—the provision of more houses for letting at rents within the means of ordinary working-class tenants, the prevention of unduly high costs of construction, and the more effective control of rents for existing houses. At the time when the Government took office, rent strikes, beginning on Clydeside, had spread to London and to other big towns ; and the Communists had been quick to take up the agitation and to endeavour to put themselves at its head. But the Labour Bill for general amendment of the law relating to rent control, though it passed its second reading, encountered so much obstruction in the committee stage that it had to be abandoned. In its place, the Government put forward and successfully carried into law a small Bill modifying the landlord's right to obtain possession of a house for his own family's use, where undue hardship would be caused to the tenant ; but a more important Bill, designed to prevent evictions for non-payment of rent due to unemployment, was defeated on second reading through failure of Liberal support.

These failures were more than offset by the successful enactment of John Wheatley's Housing Act. The Chamberlain Housing Act of 1923 had done nothing towards the provision of houses for letting at reasonable rents ; but the Labour Act gave additional subsidies to local authorities which were prepared to erect standard houses for renting at controlled rents, and not for sale. In connection with this measure, which only began to show its valuable effects after the fall of the Government, Wheatley successfully negotiated a treaty with the building operatives' Trade Unions, allowing for special entry and training in the building crafts in order to ensure an adequate supply of labour. The condition of this treaty, under which the building workers withdrew their opposition to " dilution," was that housing activity should be maintained over a period of years at a high enough level to ensure full employment. This pledge was broken later, when Labour had fallen from power ; but the Wheatley Act did last long enough under its original impetus to make an exceedingly important contribution towards the solution of the housing problem in the big towns which seriously took up the scheme, including the Tory stronghold of Birmingham as well as London.

Wheatley intended to complement his Housing Act with a second measure, providing for the control of prices and the checking of monopoly in respect of building materials ; but the Bill which he introduced for this purpose met with heavy opposition, and failed to become law before the Government's fall.

In the case of education, the Government was in a favourable position. Wide statutory powers existed for the development of secondary schools, for the improvement of primary education, and for the payment of more and better scholarships and maintenance allowances. The developments contemplated in the

Fisher Education Act had been lopped off for the time being by the " Geddes Axe " ; but this had been done by administration, and the suspended legislation was still on the statute book. Charles Trevelyan, at the Board of Education, was able to relax the conditions for the payment of state grants and to encourage the more progressive local authorities to go ahead. During his term of office, approval was given to forty new secondary schools ; a survey was instituted in order to provide for the replacement of as many as possible of the more insanitary or obsolete elementary schools ; the proportion of free places in secondary schools was increased ; state scholarships, which had been in suspense, were restored, and maintenance allowances for young people in secondary schools were increased ; the adult education grant was tripled ; and local authorities were empowered, where they wished, to raise the school-leaving age to fifteen. Many of these admirable reforms were in fact cut short by the fall of the Labour Government ; but Trevelyan's tenure of the Presidency of the Board of Education, almost as much as Wheatley's of the Ministry of Health, left a lasting mark.

Because of Liberal opposition, the Government was less successful in its efforts on behalf of the agricultural workers. The Agricultural Wages Bill, designed to restore the minimum wage that had been taken away in 1921, was mutilated by depriving the new Central Wages Board of power to over-ride the decisions of the County Agricultural Wages Committees, and the Board was thus prevented from enforcing a national minimum wage. Despite this emasculation the Act did bring about a substantial improvement over most of the country ; but the Liberals' action in weakening its provisions by an amendment which removed the power of the Central Wages Board to revise the decisions of the County Committees was not soon forgotten in the countryside.   True, the Liberals claimed merit for attempting to insert in the Bill a definite minimum wage of 30s. 0d. a week, and attacked the Labour Government for opposing this. The Labour view, right or wrong, was that, in view of the uncertainty of living costs, it was better to have no definite figure laid down by statute, as any figure thus given legal sanction might easily become a standard rather than a minimum.

Apart from the Budget these, with the addition of an Act for the regulation of London traffic and an Act bringing miners' silicosis fully within the provisions for workmen's compensation; were the Labour Government's main legislative achievements.

A large-scale Factory Bill, a Bill for the ratification of the Washington International Labour Convention providing for a maximum working week of forty-eight hours, and a Bill for the setting up of a National Minimum Wage Commission were still unenacted when the Government fell from power.

Philip Snowden's Budget was the one Labour measure to secure cordial Liberal support. It was essentially a free trader's Budget. The duties on tea, coffee, cocoa and sugar were halved ; those on dried fruits were reduced, and those on mineral waters abolished. The McKenna protective duties, introduced during the war to protect the motor car and other industries, were swept away. In addition, Snowden repealed the inhabited house duty, and reduced entertainment duty on cheap seats, telephone charges, and the taxes on motor vehicles. He also swept away, much to the joy of the City, the special tax on Corporation Profits. There were, of course, loud outcries from the industries which forfeited their protective advantages ; and there were many warnings that the motor industry in particular would be ruined. Actually, it continued to prosper, and the price of cars fell as the output increased.

So much for the Labour Government's achievements on the home front. It will be seen that it attempted no single measure of socialisation, or, with the exception of building materials, of state control over industry. No such measure had indeed any chance of passing, and none could have been pressed without inviting defeat. Whether the Government ought, none the less, to have made some effort, at least to the extent of introducing a Coal Mines Nationalisation Bill, is a matter of opinion. Conceivably it would have done so, had it been allowed to continue longer in office. More probably it would have made no such attempt without a further appeal to the country. What it could and did achieve was to undo a good many of the administrative effects of the " Geddes Axe," to pass several valuable measures of social reform, and to make a somewhat faint-hearted attempt at coping with the unemployment problem by the institution of public works. Its most important legislative achievement was the Wheatley Housing Act.

Ramsay MacDonald, however, was much more deeply interested in foreign than in home affairs. Despite the huge burden of work involved, he insisted on acting as his own Foreign Minister ; and, aided by the fall of Poincaré and the advent of the Radical Herriot Government in France in May, 1924, he did succeed for the time being in altering the face of international affairs. The French were induced to evacuate the Ruhr : what seemed to many at the time a workable settlement of the Reparations problem was arrived at in the Dawes Plan (though we can see in retrospect that it could not possibly have worked for long) ; and, abandoning the proposed Pact of Mutual Assistance, MacDonald went all out, by means of the Geneva Protocol, to advance towards a general acceptance of international arbitration as a necessary step towards disarmament. The first steps were taken towards recognition of the need for a modification of the Versailles Treaty ; and for a short time it began to look as if the League of Nations might be made workable after all. As against these relative successes, the Government failed to reach an agreement in its negotiations with the Egyptians ; and in India much discontent was caused by its failure to respond to the growing demand for self-government with any clear plan of reform.

Over and above these measures in the West, the Labour Government promptly extended full diplomatic recognition to the Government of the Soviet Union, and opened discussions for a resumption of closer relations with Russia. Out of the Anglo-Russian Conference, of which Arthur Ponsonby was mainly in charge on the British side, emerged in August, 1924, two draft treaties, providing for a settlement of most of the outstanding issues between the two countries and designed to smooth the way for the granting of a British loan to the Soviet Union. This last proposal aroused ferocious opposition from Lloyd George and many other Liberals as well as from the Conservatives ; and the press raised a great anti-Bolshevik scare, with the slogan " No Money for Murderers." The proposed loan to Russia was indeed the main cause of the Government's fall ; for it was fundamentally on this issue that Tories and Liberals joined forces against it.

An occasion for compassing the Government's destruction was found in October in the " Campbell Case." The Communist paper, *The Workers' Weekly*, edited by J. R. Campbell, published an article which the Law Officers of the Government held to be seditious. A prosecution was foolishly begun, and then withdrawn in face of a growing chorus of left-wing protest. The Law Officers responsible stated that the decision to withdraw had not been taken on political grounds ; but hardly anyone believed them. The Tories then put down a vote of censure, to which the Liberals put forward an amendment calling for a Select Committee of investigation. MacDonald announced that he would regard the carrying of the Liberal amendment, equally with that of the Tory motion, as a vote of censure. The Tories, seeing their chance, voted for the Liberal amendment ; and the Government on October 8 announced the dissolution of Parliament, having been in office for less than nine months. A General Election, the third in three years, followed almost at once.

Up to the summer recess the Government, in view of the great difficulties under which it had to work in Parliament, was on the whole doing reasonably well, except in its handling of Indian and Egyptian affairs. Then came the sad bungle of the Campbell prosecution, accompanied by signs that MacDonald was suffering from a bad attack of anti-Bolshevism, which was aggravated instead of being corrected by the campaign carried on in the press and in Parliament against the Russian Treaties. If the Campbell episode was bad, that of the alleged " Red Letter," which occurred during the election campaign, was infinitely worse.

This episode is, indeed, in some of its aspects well nigh incredible ; and the most astounding parts in it were played by the Prime Minister, who was also Foreign Secretary, and by the officials of the Foreign Office. The story begins with the acquisition by somebody in England—it is not clear by whom—of what was alleged to be a copy of a letter sent on September 15 from the Communist International in Moscow to the British Communist Party, chiefly for the purpose of urging the British Communists to take all possible action to ensure the ratification of the Anglo-Soviet Treaties. The letter purported to be signed by G. Zinoviev, the President, and Kuusinen, the Finnish Secretary, of the Comintern, and also by Arthur Macmanus, a British member of its Presidium. After dealing with its main purpose, it proceeded, in a series of extravagant sentences, to advocate preparation for military insurrection in working-class areas of Great Britain, for subverting the allegiance of the army and navy, and for " paralysing the military preparations of the bourgeoisie," of which the Labour Government was treated as the instrument. A copy of this curious document reached the Foreign Office, from an unknown source, on October 10 ; but well before that its existence was the subject of a whispering campaign in Tory circles, and copies seem to have been in the possession of the *Daily Mail* or of the Conservative Head Office, or of both. Thus, the Foreign Office did not receive the letter until after the Government had been defeated over the Campbell Case and had decided on a General

Election ; and MacDonald did not receive a copy until October 16, when it was sent to him in Manchester, where he was speaking in the election campaign. MacDonald replied to the Foreign Office the same day, commenting that the greatest care would have to be taken in discovering whether the alleged letter was authentic or not, and that, if it were found to be authentic, it should be published. In the meantime a draft note to the Russian Ambassador should be prepared in the Foreign Office, for use if the letter turned out to have been really sent.

The draft note was sent from the Foreign Office to MacDonald on October 21, but owing to his movements on his election tour he did not get it until the 23rd. On the 24th he sent the draft back in an amended form, expecting it to be returned to him for further consideration if and when proof of the authenticity of the Zinoviev Letter were forthcoming. But on this same day the Foreign Office officials, without further consultation with the Prime Minister and Foreign Secretary, sent both the Zinoviev Letter and the draft note to the Russian Ambassador to the press. They were published on the following morning, Saturday, the voting in the Election being due to take place on the next Wednesday.

The Foreign Office's reason for this extraordinary action was alleged to be that the *Daily Mail* was in any case proposing to publish the letter on October 25, and that its appearance could not be allowed without any British reply to show that the Government had the matter well in hand. This explanation of course assumes that the letter was authentic, and it must be presumed that the officials concerned believed it to be so. Whether it was or not may probably never be known : it seems on the whole most likely that the greater part of it was authentic, but that some forger, in order to get a good price for disclosing it, touched it up by inserting the more lurid and nonsensical passages about a coming British insurrection. This is not certain ; for Zinoviev may have been capable of the utter misunderstanding of the British situation which the text implies. It has, however, to be taken into account that nobody—neither the Foreign Office nor the Conservative Head Office nor the *Daily Mail*—was ever said to have seen the original of the alleged letter, of which only copies were ever produced. The style undoubtedly was that of the Comintern ; but no style could well be simpler to imitate. When the affair was over, the Labour Party's own committee of investigation came to the conclusion that the letter was probably, but not certainly, a forgery, whereas MacDonald's Conservative successor at the Foreign Office, Austen Chamberlain, asserted his belief in its authenticity. There the matter must be left.

The Foreign Office note published with the " Zinoviev Letter " assumed its authentic character, and on this basis denounced it as a flagrant breach of undertakings given by the Soviet Government in the course of the negotiations for the Anglo-Soviet Treaties. It asserted the existence of close connection between the Soviet Government and the Comintern, and held the former responsible for ensuring that the latter should be bound by the engagements into which the Soviet Government had entered. It concluded, in effect, with a threat that the treaties could not be ratified unless the Soviet Government called the Comintern to order and put a firm stop to the activities within its territory of agencies " whose aim is to spread discontent or to foment rebellion in any part of the British Empire."

The publication, not so much of the letter itself as of the note presumed to have been sent and issued on Ramsay MacDonald's authority, placed Labour candidates everywhere in an appalling difficulty. The signing of the Anglo-Russian Treaties was *the* main election issue ; but now what were they to say ? They could not say nothing with every newspaper full of the affair and every opposition candidate and speaker making the most of it ; but they could not tell what to say until MacDonald explained. The most extraordinary thing of all is that MacDonald for two days did not explain at all, and, when he did offer an explanation, only contrived to make matters worse and more obscure. On the Saturday, though he spoke and the papers were full of the letter, he made no reference to it. On the Sunday he was still silent. On the Monday, two days before the polling, he merely recited the dates and facts given above, leaving it quite as obscure as ever whether the letter was authentic or not, and whether he endorsed or did not endorse the terms of the Foreign Office note.

The letter, and still more the note, settled the fate of the Election, and made every Labour candidate feel and appear a fool. The electors who voted Labour and returned over 150 Labour Members to the new Parliament did so out of loyalty, in spite of the terrible bungling. It is indeed surprising that the defeat was not worse than it was, and that MacDonald was able, in spite of his extraordinary behaviour, to retain the leadership and to wear down the demands for a real explanation of what had occurred. One notable feature of his attitude was that he steadily defended the Foreign Office officials from every charge of having worked against him. There were many who suspected a plot between the *Daily Mail*, the Tories, and some of the officials at the Foreign Office, designed to put the Government in an impossible electoral position. MacDonald gave no support to these allegations : he maintained that the officials had acted for the best, honestly believing that the letter could not be allowed to be published without a Government note to offset it. The officials might have blundered ; but he never suggested that they had done worse. Nor did he ever admit that he had blundered himself.

Yet plainly he had blundered. It seems pretty clear that what he was trying to do was to spin out the discussion of draft replies until the Election was safely over, and that he did believe in the letter's authenticity, even though he wanted to be in possession of fuller proof. But his more extraordinary blunder was his failure to realise the effect of the letter and note when they had been published, unless and until he had been able to clear the matter up. On the morning of the publication, Philip Snowden and J. H. Thomas (whose comment on seeing the documents in the paper was " We're bunkered ") actually telephoned to MacDonald in Wales, only to find that he did not attach any great urgency to it, was uncertain whether the letter was genuine or not, was making inquiries, and would in due time refer to it in a speech. This attitude, if it was not put on to conceal his embarrassment, was almost unbelievably foolish. Indeed, the story of MacDonald's connection with the episode, as far as it is known, simply does not make sense.

It would make even less sense had it not been widely rumoured, well before the " Zinoviev Letter " appeared, that MacDonald, though he was compelled to stand for the Russian Treaties and to fight the Election on them, was far from enthusiastic for them, and was already contemplating some sort of protest against the subversive propaganda against him and against Great Britain which the Comintern was carrying on. The alleged letter urged the British Communists specifically to " organise a campaign of disclosure of the foreign policy of MacDonald," and represented him as forced by working-class pressure to make the Treaties with the Soviet Union. These references, in the paragraphs least suspect of having been tampered with, probably angered him a great deal ; for to accuse him of a reactionary attitude in foreign affairs was to touch his vanity on its tenderest spot.

At all events, the letter and MacDonald and the Foreign Office between them did their work ; and there can be no doubt that the publication of the letter by the *Daily Mail* was deliberately organised well in advance as an eleventh hour election scoop ; for, even without the Foreign Office note and MacDonald's subsequent shuffling, the letter would have done much harm to the Labour cause, as there would not have been time enough to get even the best answer to it into the minds of the electors whom it had impressed.

(b) *The General Election of 1924*

At the General Election which followed the fall of the first Labour Government the Labour Party fought more seats than on any previous occasion—515 as against 428 in 1923—and increased its total vote from 4,348,379 to 5,487,620. But, with over 16,000,000 voting on an 80 per cent poll of the electorate, as against 14,500,000 on a 74 per cent poll in 1923, and with the Liberals losing votes heavily to the Tories, there was a net loss of forty seats, made up of sixty-four losses as against only twenty-two new seats gained. Of the seats gained, fifteen were won in three-cornered contests, and only seven in straight fights with either Conservative or Liberal opponents. Altogether there were 240 three-, four- or five-cornered contests, as against 265 straight fights ; the Liberals putting forward a hundred fewer candidates than the year before, mainly as a result of local pacts with the Conservatives directed against Labour.

Of the successful Labour candidates, one hundred were victorious in straight fights—seventy-four against Tories and twenty-six against Liberals. Of the twenty-nine who won in three-cornered fights, excluding the two-member constituencies, six had clear majorities over both opponents, the remaining thirty-three being elected on a minority vote. Thus a larger proportion than in 1923 had clear majorities, partly because the safer seats were held, and partly because of the increased number of straight fights. The Communists put forward only seven candidates ; and of these only Saklatvala, in North Battersea, was elected, regaining the seat which he had lost in 1923.

Regionally, the heaviest losses were in Greater London outside the L.C.C. area (eight seats), Scotland (eight seats), Lancashire and Cheshire (six seats), and the Eastern Counties (six seats). Proportionately the position was worst in the Eastern Counties,

LABOUR AT THE GENERAL ELECTION OF 1924

	Members elected		Total seats fought		Communist Candidates
	1924	1923	1924	1923	1924
London County .	19	22	54	46	2 (1 elected)
Greater London .	7	15	41	40	1
Southern England .	—	1	40	27	—
South-west England .	2	4	39	21	—
West Midlands . .	11	11	40	35	—
East Midlands . .	10	14	33	31	1
Eastern Counties .	1	7	23	21	1
Lancashire and Cheshire . .	18	24	65	51	1
Yorkshire . .	24	23	47	46	—
North-west England .	1	3	6	3	—
North-east England .	16	14	27	27	—
Wales and Monmouth	16	19	33	27	—
Scotland . . .	26	34	63	50	2
N. Ireland . .	—	—	1	1	—
Universities . .	—	—*	3	2	—
	151	191	515	428	7

*One Labour Independent.

where Labour representation fell from seven seats to one, and in Outer London, where the fall was from fifteen to seven. There were net gains of two seats in the North-east, where Labour had done badly in 1923, and of one in Yorkshire.

One effect of the setback was to reduce the relative strength of the I.L.P. and Divisional Party representation in the new Parliament. The I.L.P. contingent shrank by fourteen, from forty-six to thirty-two, and the total representation of the Socialist Societies from fifty-two to thirty-six. The D.L.P.s were down by ten—from thirty-five to twenty-five. The Trade Union representation, on the other hand, fell only from ninety-eight to eighty-six—a smaller proportionate fall. The Co-operators lost two out of their six seats in the previous House of Commons. The Miners' representatives in the new Parliament numbered forty, as against forty-four.

Most of the leading figures in the Party held their seats. The leading Members defeated were Margaret Bondfield, Susan Lawrence, George Isaacs, Charles Dukes, Frank Hodges, Emanuel Shinwell, Thomas Johnston, and Herbert Morrison—all, except the two women, the victims of Liberal-Tory pacts in constituencies where there were three-cornered fights at the previous Election.

The principal sufferers at the Election of 1924 were the Liberals, whose total poll fell by more than 1,250,000, as against·a Labour increase of well over 1,000,000 and a Conservative increase of over 2,000,000. In terms of seats, the Liberals fell from 158 to a mere rump of 42, and ceased thereafter to count as a party comparable with the other two. The Liberal losses were some consolation to Labour in its defeat, both as giving the Labour Party an unquestionable status as *the* Opposition, and because they were felt to be a meet retribution for the Liberal Party's action in compassing the fall of the MacDonald Government over the " Campbell Case."

LABOUR PARTY : BODIES SPONSORING SUCCESSFUL CANDIDATES, 1924

	1924	1923			1924	1923
I.L.P.	32	46				
Fabian Society	1	2	Socialist Societies	.	36	52
S.D.F.	3	4				
D.L.P.	25	35	Divisional Parties	.	25	35
Miners' Federation	40	44				
Transport Workers	6	7				
General Workers	4	5				
N.U.R.	3	3	Trade Unions	.	86	98
A.E.U.	3	3				
Textile Factory Workers	2	3				
Other Trade Unions	27	32				
N.U. Teachers	1	1				
Co-operative Party	4	6	Co-operative Party	.	4	6
	151	191			151	191

CHAPTER VI

THE GENERAL STRIKE AND AFTER

(a) *Reactions to Electoral Defeat*

The Labour Party's financial position—Problems of election finance—A campaign for individual members—Ward organisation—The By-elections Fund—The Party Badge—The I.L.P. is alarmed—I.L.P. Women's Sections and Guild of Youth—The Labour Party League of Youth—The I.L.P. Conference of 1925 congratulates the Labour Government—The Liverpool Labour Party Conference of 1925—Ernest Bevin's resolution against minority Government—The Conference's attitude—The Labour Party and the Communists—The *Sunday Worker*—Lansbury leaves the *Daily Herald—Lansbury's Labour Weekly*—Anglo-Soviet Trade Union relations—The attitude of the I.F.T.U.—The Anglo-Soviet Trade Union Committee—The proposed Workers' Industrial Alliance.

(b) *The General Strike of 1926*

The attack on the miners' standards—The return to the Gold Standard and its effects—The evacuation of the Ruhr and its effect on coal prices and supplies—Policy of the Miners' Federation—The colliery owners terminate the 1924 Agreement—The Miners appeal to the whole Labour Movement—The Court of Inquiry—Pledges of Trade Union support—An embargo on the movement of coal—The Government refuses a subsidy—Baldwin on the need for lower wages—The General Council threatens a General Strike—The Government gives way—The Coal Subsidy of 1925—The Government's anti-strike preparations—The O.M.S.—The Samuel Coal Commission—The proposed Workers' Industrial Alliance breaks down—The Coal Commission's Report and its reception—The Miners' Federation rejects compromise—Resumed negotiations break down—The Coal Lock-out begins—The Trade Unions and the Government—The *Daily Mail* incident—The Government breaks off negotiations—The General Strike begins—The response to the strike call—Trades Councils and Councils of Action—*The British Gazette* and *The British Worker*—The B.B.C. and the Government—The question of the strike's legality—Sir John Simon and Mr. Justice Astbury—The attitude of the T.U.C.—The Government and the Archbishop's Mediation Committee—Sir Herbert Samuel's intervention—The T.U.C. and the Miners fall out—Calling out the " second line "—The Samuel Memorandum—The General Council calls off the strike—Bewilderment among the strikers—The terms of settlement—The Miners fight on—The Government and the Guardians—The " Default " Act of 1926—The Miners again ask for help—The repeal of the Seven Hours Act—Further attempts at mediation—Resumed negotiations break down—District *versus* National Agreements—Local break-aways—The Trade Unions agree to a levy—The Trade Union Mediation Committee—The strike at length called off—Effects of the defeat—Could the General Strike have succeeded ?—Differing views of its character—Strikes and lock-outs before and after 1926.

(c) *The Trade Unions Act of 1927*

The aftermath of the General Strike—The fight against the Trade Unions Bill—" Illegal strikes "—Ambiguity of the Act's phrasing—Restrictions on picketing—" Intimidation "—The ban on the Civil Servants—Restraints on Local Authorities—The Political Levy—" Contracting-out " and " contracting-in "—The effects on Labour Party membership—and on Party finance—The financial difficulties of the Party, national and local—The Tories fail to smash the Party.

(d) *A Move to the Right*—Labour and the Nation

Trade Unionism after the General Strike—The Chinese Crisis of 1926-7—The Arcos Raid and the Rupture of Anglo-Soviet Relations—The ban on " subversive activities " in the Trades Councils and Local Labour Parties—The I.L.P.

and the Miners—The development of I.L.P. policy—The " Living Income " programme—The I.L.P. at the Labour Party Conference of 1927—The controversy over Family Allowances begins—MacDonald on " flashy futilities "—The Joint Committee of the Labour Party and the T.U.C. on Living Wage Policy—The Trade Unions and Family Allowances—Cash Allowances *versus* Social Services in kind—The Socialisation of Banking—Birth Control—The I.L.P. and war policy—The I.L.P. and Imperialism—The I.L.P. and Trade Unionism—Workers' Control—The Trade Union leaders resent I.L.P. " interference "—The " Mond-Turner " negotiations—The " Cook-Maxton " Manifesto—The I.L.P. and the Manifesto—" Mondism " at the Trades Union Congress—The position of I.L.P. Members of Parliament—Charles Buxton opposes I.L.P. policy—The Labour Party decides to produce a new Programme—Ernest Bevin on the need for a short Programme—The drafting of *Labour and the Nation*—Its contents summarised—Five Labour Party " Principles "—Social Reform and Economic Development—The Control of Industry—The Scope of Nationalisation—Taxation policy—International issues—" The Implications of Democracy "—Banking and Credit—The Bank of England to be made a Public Corporation—The problem of the joint stock banks—*Labour and the Nation* debated at the Birmingham Conference—I.L.P. opposition—Programme or Declaration of Faith ?—Is it Socialism ?—Maxton's and Wheatley's criticisms and MacDonald's defence—The " Living Income " policy rejected—Snowden on financial policy—Snowden rejects early nationalisation of the joint stock banks—Frank Wise's criticisms—*Labour and the Nation* approved—Labour's Election Programme of 1929—Its limited objectives—" Party Loyalty "—New disciplinary rules laid down—The Labour Party and the Communists—Dissensions in the Communist Party—The " United Front " and the new " Class against Class " policy—*The Daily Worker*—Relations between the Labour and Co-operative Parties from 1925 to 1929—The Labour Party League of Youth—Joint Labour Party and T.U.C. Departments wound up—The move to Transport House—The *Daily Herald* and the T.U.C.—The Labour Party leader to be on the National Executive *ex officio*.

(*e*)   *The General Election of 1929*

By-elections between 1924 and 1929—Results of the General Election of 1929—Labour the largest party—The party situation after the Election—No Tory-Liberal Coalition—The Labour and Liberal Election Programmes—The Liberals and the unemployment problem—How the parties polled—Votes and seats—The Communist Election fiasco—Members elected on a majority and a minority vote—Women M.P.s—Composition of the Labour Party in the 1929 Parliament—Great increase in Divisional Party representation—The reasons—Effects of the Trade Unions Act—Trade Union representatives and safe seats—The position of the I.L.P. in Scotland and elsewhere—Weakness of Divisional Parties in Scotland—The position in Wales—Regional gains in Lancashire and Greater London—and in other areas—Reasons for the different dispersal of votes and seats—Sir Oswald Mosley and the situation in Birmingham.

(*a*)   *Reactions to Electoral Defeat*

After the electoral defeat of 1924 the Labour Party settled down to a new period of opposition and preparation. Three General Elections in three years had placed a severe strain on the Party's finances, and the determination to fight every possible seat had meant that in a large number of constituencies the campaigns had been badly hampered by lack of funds. Where a Trade Union assumed responsibility for one of its own candidates, enough money was usually available to provide for the services of a regular agent and to maintain organisation in a good state between elections ; but many of the Divisional Labour Parties had to improvise an organisation when an election came round and were not able to have paid agents regularly at work. The I.L.P. was also under the necessity of spreading its funds thinly over the constituencies for which it was responsible, and was not in a position to put a larger number of candidates into the field. The Trade Unions were prepared to finance only a limited number of contests ; nor was it felt to be desirable that the Labour Party should become more than it was already a Trade Union party. Still more undesirable was it that wealthy supporters should be in a position to buy the right to contest seats, by promising to bear the entire expenses of organisation as well as of the actual election.

The only possible remedy, as the Executive saw the situation, lay in building up the finances of the Local Labour Parties and in inducing them to take their responsibilities more seriously. With this end in view, the Party decided in 1925 to begin a national drive to secure a much larger number of individual party members, men as well as women, and including Trade Unionists who were already contributors to the Trade Unions' Political Funds. A model scheme, based on those already in force in Barrow and in a few other areas, was drawn up and recommended for adoption wherever possible. It was to include arrangements for regular collection of small sums, in order to avoid having to demand the full annual contribution all at once ; and it included a detailed plan of ward organisation within each urban constituency, with similar arrangements for local action in scattered county areas. The real drive for individual membership among men began after 1925 : until then, except in relatively few areas, the main drive had been designed to secure members for the Women's Sections.

At the same time the Party decided to introduce a special By-elections Fund, to which a small contribution was asked for from each Local Party. In the past, a good many by-elections had gone uncontested because the Divisional Parties had no funds for fighting them and could not raise the money within the time allowed. The new scheme made provision for a central fund, which could be used to aid Divisional Parties in such cases. It was started only in a small way, but was gradually built up until it became reasonably adequate to meet the need. At the same time, the Party Badge scheme, started in 1924, was developed, in the hope of giving the members of Local Parties a keener sense of belonging to a united national movement ; and it was decided to throw more responsibility on the Local Parties by tapering off, and extinguishing within four years, the central grants previously paid in aid of the employment of full-time local agents. These grants, it was felt, had gone chiefly to the parties which were best able to stand on their own feet ; and the desire was to use the scanty central funds as far as possible for helping the weaker and poorer areas.

The plans for the development of individual membership and Local Labour Party organisation were bound to alarm the I.L.P., which realised that their success would mean keener competition with the I.L.P. branches. As we shall see, the I.L.P. was at this time engaged on a vigorous expansionist campaign of its own, with the " Living Wage " and " Socialism Now " policies as its driving force. At its 1925 Conference it had already decided to institute Women's Groups within the I.L.P., to some extent in competition with the Labour Party's Women's Sections ; and it had also organised an I.L.P. Guild of Youth in competition with the Youth Sections of the Local Labour Parties. At the 1926 Conference it was reported that there were 182 Guild branches, with about 9,000 members. To this latter move the Labour Party responded in 1926 by reorganising its own Youth Sections as the Labour Party League of Youth, allowing young people between the ages of twenty-one and twenty-five to retain membership provided that they also joined the Labour Party as individual members, and authorising the holding of an annual League of Youth conference of delegates from the local sections. The more general Labour Party drive for individual members the I.L.P. could neither oppose nor counteract by any special measures. It could only intensify its own recruiting campaign and stress its claim to be regarded as the Socialist spearhead of the Labour Party.

There had been, on the left wing of the Socialist movement, a good deal of criticism of the Labour Government during its period of office, on the ground that it had, at any rate in home affairs, shown itself much too ready to compromise with the Liberals instead of risking parliamentary defeat by standing firmly by its principles. Left-wing criticism was intensified in some quarters by the bungling of the Campbell Case and by MacDonald's extraordinary behaviour over the Zinoviev Letter ; but in other quarters this criticism led to a rallying of support to

MacDonald, whose conduct of foreign affairs up to that point had won high praise. The National Administrative Council of the I.L.P., in its Report to the 1925 Conference, was enthusiastic in praise of the Labour Government, especially on the score of its foreign policy ; and when John Scurr introduced the Report of the I.L.P. Parliamentary Group the Yorkshire Divisional Council moved a resolution of congratulation to the Labour Government, not only on its " efforts to secure peace, goodwill and co-operation between the nations," but also on its home record. The resolution went on to recognise the limitations of minority government, and to stress the importance of constructive Socialist propaganda and of the pursuance of a vigorous policy of Socialist opposition in the new Parliament. In the ensuing debate, most of the speeches followed the lines of the resolution ; but George Buchanan, of the Clyde group, made a sharp attack on some aspects of the Government's record, and when the vote was taken the resolution was carried by 398 against the substantial minority of 139.

At the Labour Party's Liverpool Conference later in the year discussion took a rather different line. Ernest Bevin, on behalf of the Transport and General Workers' Union, moved that " in view of the experiences of the recent Labour Government, it is inadvisable that the Labour Party should again accept office whilst having a minority of Members in the House of Commons." Bevin did not question the correctness of the Labour Party's decision to accept office in 1923 ; but he held that the events of 1924 had shown conclusively that it would be an error ever to do the same again. No single policy resolution of the Party Conference, he agreed, would have the smallest chance of being translated into law through a minority Government ; and he held that more compromise of the kind they had seen while Labour was in office would destroy the confidence of those whom the Labour M.P.s were supposed to represent. " If I were in Parliament and were called upon to take office and represent a great movement like ours, I would not accept it unless, when I spoke to the representatives of other nations or to our own people in the House of Commons, I were able to speak with the power that rested on the knowledge that I had a majority behind me both inside in the House and outside in the nation."

As soon as Bevin's resolution had been seconded, Herbert Smith, for the Miners, moved the Previous Question, which, if carried, would have ended the debate. After some confusion, the suspen-

sion of Standing Orders was carried, and the debate was allowed
to go on. J. H. Thomas, James Doonan of the Miners, and Ramsay
MacDonald spoke strongly against the resolution, urging the
unwisdom of the Party binding itself not to take office before it
could know under what circumstances the question might arise.
John Bromley, of the Locomotive Engineers, Neil Maclean, from
Glasgow, and Ben Tillett backed up Bevin ; and Bevin, in his
reply, delivered a strong attack on MacDonald for his failure,
when in office, to give backing to Trade Union claims and for his
" dictatorial attitude."   " MacDonald's speech," he said, " was
enough to make Keir Hardie turn in his grave," and he (Bevin)
" although he was a Labour leader, had not forgotten the doctrines he taught on the soap-box twenty years ago—when they
were preaching as young men about the independence of the
Labour Party." Despite the Transport Workers' support, Bevin's
resolution was lost by 2,587,000 votes to 512,000, most of the big
Unions voting against him.   Even many who were highly critical
of MacDonald and of the first Labour Government were not
prepared to lay down that Labour should not again take office
without a clear majority.   No such majority seemed to be in
sight ; and the prospect of an indefinite spell of Tory rule was by
no means pleasant. Already, the delegates were experiencing the
undoing of some of the Labour Government's main achievements—the stiffening up of Poor Law and of Unemployment
Insurance administration, the slowing down of educational advance and of new housing development under the Wheatley
Act, and an increasing resistance to industrial demands.   These
feelings overcame the dislike of the humiliations involved in
minority office, and helped MacDonald to regain his prestige
with the Trade Union leaders.   The Miners especially, confronted
already with the prospects of a prodigious economic struggle,
wanted a friendly Government on almost any conditions.

The question of the Communist Party, as we have seen, came
up again at the Liverpool Labour Party Conference of 1925,
when the National Executive proposed that, in addition to the
ban on Communist Party members becoming individual members
of the Labour Party, Trade Unions should be urged not to appoint
Communists or members of other political parties as delegates
either to the Party Conference or to Local Parties.   William
Gallacher, as the delegate of the Paisley Labour Party, moved to
refer back this section of the Report, and mustered 321,000 votes :
the question of the proposed Trade Union ban on Communist

delegates was voted on separately, and the Executive carried its point by 2,692,000 votes to 480,000.

At the beginning of 1925 George Lansbury, who had stayed on as manager of the *Daily Herald* after being ousted from his position as editor, resigned and proceeded to found a new left-wing journal, *Lansbury's Labour Weekly*, which reproduced the spirit of the old *Herald* and served as a rallying point for left-wing activity, especially in relation to the developing mining crisis. Lansbury also made at the Liverpool Party Conference a trenchant speech, in support of an Executive resolution on Indian self-government. Apart from the issue of minority government, the Party Conference, in reaction to its electoral defeat, was in a fairly militant mood, and the Executive gave it a lead with a series of policy resolutions, including one, moved by Sidney Webb, in favour of the socialisation of banking. The Communists, after their defeat on the issue of Communist delegates, did appreciably better on a resolution urging support for their new journalistic venture, *The Sunday Worker*, to which they were trying to give a less exclusive flavour by enlisting non-Communist Trade Union support. The resolution was beaten by 2,036,000 to 1,143,000.

Political developments in 1925 were, however, much less important than developments on the industrial side of the Labour movement. The immediate sequel to the defeat of the Anglo-Soviet Treaties was an attempt to build up closer relation between the British and Soviet Trade Union movements. This took shape in the Anglo-Russian Trade Union Agreement of April, 1925, under which the two movements formed a Joint Committee and agreed to work together in the cause of Trade Union unity. The *rapprochement* between the British and Russian Trade Unions had begun some time before this, while the MacDonald Government was still in power. A Soviet Trade Union delegation visited Great Britain in 1924, and was well received at the Trades Union Congress ; and in the early winter a British Trade Union delegation paid a return visit to the Soviet Union. In the meantime the British representatives on the International Federation of Trade Unions had been endeavouring to get that body to agree to an attempt to bring the rival Trade Union Internationals together into a single body. The Soviet Trade Unions had expressed the desire for unity, and were pressing for a World Congress attended by the bodies connected both with the I.F.T.U. and with the rival Red International of Labour Unions, which the Russians completely dominated. The

I.F.T.U., however, would have nothing to do with the R.I.L.U. ; and it also refused, despite pressure from the British delegation, to enter into any discussions with the Soviet Trade Union movement unless that body first accepted the constitution of the I.F.T.U. and agreed to affiliate to it. The continental leaders of the I.F.T.U.—especially the Germans—were violently opposed to any attempt to come to terms with the Soviet Trade Unions ; and the Bureau of the Labour and Socialist International also intervened with a strong protest against the line taken by the British Trade Unions. These attacks, however, which were re-echoed in the British press, served only to confirm the Trades Union Congress General Council in its determination, if it could not carry the I.F.T.U. along with it, to come to its own accommodation with the Soviet Trade Unions ; and at the joint meeting of the two groups in April, 1925, full agreement was reached to establish closer relations, including a standing Joint Committee, which was to meet alternately in Great Britain and in the Soviet Union.

While these international negotiations were in progress, an attempt was also being made to revive in an amended form the kind of joint Trade Union action which the ill-fated Triple Alliance had been intended to bring about. The new Workers' Industrial Alliance, which was mooted early in the year, was to include four sections—Miners, Railwaymen, Transport Workers, and Engineers ; and in June a conference of these four set up a committee to draft a detailed plan. At once, however, the project was pushed into the background by the development of an acute crisis in the coal industry—the beginning of the struggle which culminated the next year in the General Strike. To this crisis, and to its effects on Labour's fortunes, we must now turn our attention.

(b) The General Strike of 1926

This book is not the place for any full account of the mining crisis of 1925 and 1926, or of the General Strike which, in May, 1926, the Trade Unions called in the miners' support. This crisis, however, so dominated the movement of events that some account has to be taken of it in this history. The Labour movement, smarting under its political defeat, turned the more enthusiastically to industrial action against the forces which had overthrown the MacDonald Government and were busy undoing its work. The attack on the miners was generally felt to be the opening move in a general capitalist offensive ; and the new Prime Minister in effect confirmed this feeling when he declared, in July, 1925, that not only the miners, but all classes of workers, would have to be prepared to accept wage-reductions. The attempt to enforce a general fall in money-wages was indeed implicit in the return to the gold standard, which was announced by Winston Churchill, as Chancellor of the Exchequer, early in the year and was given legislative effect in May, 1925. It was clear from the outset that the old parity to which the pound sterling had been brought back could be sustained only by a forcing down of British prices, especially of export goods, and that there would be a general attempt to cut wages in order to achieve this result. The Trade Unions, however, were in no mood to accept this scheme, which they regarded as an attempt to pass on to the workers the entire burden of meeting an economic crisis that had been deliberately intensified by bad financial policy, accepted by the Government at the dictation of the bankers here and in the United States.

The coal industry stood to suffer more than most by the effects of the return to the gold standard. In 1923 and 1924 British coal-mining had been made artificially prosperous as a result of the invasion of the Ruhr, which had caused a heavy decline in German production and exports. The evacuation of the Ruhr in 1924 was followed by a rapid increase in German exports, largely as part of an attempt to secure funds for meeting the payments due under the Dawes Plan. At the same time a general world recession set in, reducing the demand for coal ; and the export price of coal slumped heavily.

In the early months of 1925 the Miners' Federation was busily preparing a programme of demands for improved conditions when the agreement negotiated in June, 1924, expired at the end of the twelve months for which it had been made. This agreement had been concluded while the coal industry was prosperous ; and the Miners' leaders seem to have been unaware of the likelihood that this prosperity would vanish before the year ran out. At all events they were planning to demand a national minimum wage of 12s. od. a shift, with provision for actual minima to be set in the districts at levels high enough to correspond to the rise in the cost of living since August, 1914. When, however, they met the colliery owners in March, in order to negotiate for a new agreement, they soon discovered that the owners, far from being prepared to consider fresh concessions, were likely to demand heavy wage reductions and probably an increase in working hours. The Miners pressed the Government to accept an amended Coal Mines Minimum Wage Bill incorporating the 12s. od. national minimum, and renewed their demand for a system of national pooling designed to enable the weaker districts to meet the cost ; but they speedily realised that the Government was acting closely with the owners. In June the negotiations between owners and miners broke down : the owners announced that on June 30 they would give one month's notice to terminate the existing conditions, and that in default of acceptance of their terms by the Miners' Federation they proposed to open discussions separately with the Miners' District Associations, and to enforce both wage-cuts and a return to a longer working day—the latter subject to the Government's agreement to legislate for the abolition of the seven hours day conceded in 1919.

Confronted with this ultimatum, the Miners' Executive at once appealed to the entire Trade Union movement for help. It was clear that the proposed Workers' Industrial Alliance, even if it would have been capable of handling the crisis, could not be brought into existence in time to be used ; and the Miners accordingly appealed at once to the Trades Union Congress General Council, and also to the Labour Party, to rally the entire Labour movement for resistance to the threat to working-class standards. On July 3 the Miners' Delegate Conference confirmed both the rejection of the owners' demands and the appeal to the whole Labour movement ; and on July 10 the T.U.C. General Council, after meetings with the Miners, issued a strong manifesto in their support.

The day before this, the Government had made its first intervention in the dispute ; and on July 14 it announced the setting up of a Court of Inquiry under the Industrial Courts Act to report upon the circumstances of the conflict. The Miners' Federation rejected the inquiry, pointing out that the Court would have no power to make any award, or to force any settlement upon the owners. Feeling was heightened when, on July 15, the fact was made public that the Government was already taking steps to organise strike-breaking services in the event of a stoppage in support of the miners. At this point, on July 17, the delegates of the Unions concerned in the Workers' Industrial Alliance plan met to consider the proposals drawn up by the committee appointed earlier in the year : they agreed to recommend the plan, and referred it for acceptance to their several governing bodies. On July 20 the Transport and General Workers' Union agreed to strike action in support of the miners, if it were called for by the Trades Union Congress ; and on July 23 the Miners' Executive agreed to give the charge of conducting its case over to the General Council as representing the entire Trade Union movement. On the following day a National Trade Union Conference, called to discuss the unemployment problem, was due to meet in London ; and the Miners' leaders addressed this gathering, and received further assurances of support. That same evening the Government called the owners and miners together for renewed discussions ; but no progress was made, and it became clear that the Government was supporting the owners and was prepared to do nothing to avert the heavy reductions demanded by them. On July 26 the railway and transport Trade Unions announced that, if the owners enforced the notices which were due to expire at the end of the month, they would place a complete embargo on the movement of coal. On the following day a Trade Union deputation met the Prime Minister and strongly urged him to take steps to get the lock-out notices postponed with a view to further negotiations. The same day the Court of Inquiry produced its Report, highly critical of the owners' proceedings, but without any definite proposals for settling the dispute. On July 29 the Government stated that it was not prepared to offer any subsidy to the coal industry for the purpose of easing the burden ; and on this occasion Baldwin made his remark, already cited, about the necessity for all workers, and not only the miners, to be prepared to accept lower wages.

In the atmosphere created by these announcements, a National Conference of Trade Union Executives, convened by the General Council, met on July 30, ordered an embargo on coal movements from the end of the month, when the notices expired, and empowered the General Council to call a strike, on any scale deemed requisite, in the event of a continuance of the deadlock.

To this threat of a General Strike the Government promptly yielded—for the time being. A subsidy, which had been declared to be out of the question, was offered for a period of nine months ; and during these months wages and conditions were to be stabilised, and a new Coal Commission was to conduct a thorough investigation into the industry and to make recommendations for the future. The lock-out notices were thereupon withdrawn ;

and the Trade Union delegates went home with the feeling that they had won a glorious victory.

So indeed they had, for the moment. They won it, because the Government was not yet ready to meet the Trade Union threat : it needed time to organise its counter-measures against a General Strike. The nine months subsidy was meant to give it time to arm itself for the task of breaking the strike should the threat be renewed when the breathing-space had been exhausted. From that moment the Government, chiefly under Winston Churchill's driving force, began to get ready to deliver a crushing blow unless the Unions gave way. The preparations went on, for the most part, in secret ; but in November a circular became public, explaining the strike-breaking measures that the Government was working out for the Local Authorities to put into effect. Throughout the ensuing months there was much activity, both official and unofficial, in organising various voluntary bodies for action against a strike—especially the O.M.S.—the Organisation for the Maintenance of Supplies—which was to collaborate with the Government and the Local Authorities in preventing a breakdown of essential services.

Meanwhile, the colliery owners in a number of areas attempted to evade the temporary settlement by cutting basic wage-rates, on the pretext that these were not protected by the letter of the agreement. On this ground, the Miners' Federation at first refused to have anything to do with the Coal Commission, which was appointed on September 3 under the chairmanship of Sir Herbert Samuel, the other members being the Liberal economist, Sir William Beveridge, and two well-known employers. There was no Labour member, and none even regarded as sympathetic to the Labour point of view.

While the Coal Commission was sitting, the proposed Workers' Industrial Alliance broke down. The Trades Union Congress General Council renewed in October its pledge to support the Miners' Federation ; and the Miners, the General Council, and the Labour Party collaborated in producing a plan for the nationalisation of the coal industry. But the National Union of Railwaymen, having failed to get certain amendments they wanted (mainly designed to secure the amalgamation of the Unions in each industry into a single body) withdrew in November from the projected Alliance, leaving to the Trades Union Congress the task of providing for co-ordinated action in any further stage of the crisis.

On March 10, 1926, the Samuel Coal Commission produced its

Report, following the Sankey Commission of 1919 in recommending the nationalisation of coal royalties, but rejecting public ownership of the coal industry itself in favour of a plan of amalgamations on a voluntary basis, with compulsion in reserve if the voluntary method were to fail. The Commission held that costs of production must be reduced by cutting wages, and advocated giving the miners the choice between severe wage-cuts without a change in working hours, and less severe cuts accompanied by some increase in the working day. The Government at once offered to act on the Report, on the condition—which they were well aware would not be met—of its acceptance by both owners and miners before May 1, when the subsidy was due to expire. Both the owners and the Miners' Federation thereupon rejected the Samuel proposals. The Miners, on April 9, 1926, declared their inability to accept any worsening of either hours or wages (" Not a penny off the pay : not a second on the day "), and appealed to the Trades Union Congress for a renewal of its support. The special Industrial Committee set up by the Trades Union Congress reaffirmed its backing of the Miners. On April 13 the owners and miners met, but reached no agreement, the owners announcing that they would refuse to negotiate further on a national scale and would seek separate settlements in the districts unless the Miners' Federation gave way. The International Miners' Federation, which had offered strong support in the crisis of 1925 by promising to place an embargo on coal movements designed to replace British supplies, met on April 16, and renewed its promises. The Miners' Federation held further meetings with the T.U.C.'s Industrial Committee, which was endeavouring to secure from the Government a continuance of the subsidy ; and on April 22 the Miners' Executive again met the owners, who produced proposals requiring a return to district settlements and involving drastic changes in wages, in default of longer working shifts. There was no approach to agreement ; and on April 30 the lock-out notices expired. On May 1 the pits stopped.

At the same time a further special Conference of Trade Union Executives approved of strike action, to any extent that might be deemed necessary in order to give the miners effective backing. The T.U.C. General Council, taking charge of the negotiations with the Government, met the Prime Minister, in the hope of repeating the success of the previous year. The situation was, however, by this time very different. The Government had made large preparations for the maintenance of essential services in the event of a strike ; and a considerable section of the Cabinet, headed by Churchill, was intent on a show-down, in the confidence that the strike movement would speedily collapse if the Government showed a firm front. The next day, May 2, this section of the Cabinet got its way and procured the breaking off of negotiations by the Government, using the pretext of a refusal by the *Daily Mail* staff to print a leading article attacking the Trade Unions. The Trade Union negotiators, attending at Downing Street for a last-moment effort at negotiation, found the Cabinet dispersed and the door banged in their faces. This was in the small hours, after midnight. On May 3, the General Strike began.

Strictly speaking, the strike of 1926 was never general. Indeed, the General Council always spoke of it, not as a " General " but as a " National " Strike. Only a limited group of industries was called out—in the first instance, only the railway and other transport workers, the iron and steel workers, the builders, and the printing trades. The aim was to stop certain key services—not to bring everybody out on strike at once. At the very end, on May 11, it was decided to call out the rest of the metal workers, including the engineers ; but the next day the entire strike was called off.

The response to the strike call in the industries affected was nearly universal. It was at once apparent that the General Council and its Industrial Committee had made quite inadequate preparations for carrying on the strike ; and the burden of organisation fell mainly on the local Trades Councils, or on improvised local Councils of Action, most of which showed a remarkable capacity for taking quick decisions and for putting them into effect. The paralysis of transport and of the Press made co-ordination of local action even more difficult for the strikers than for the Government. Regular newspapers disappeared, and were replaced by the rival organs of the Government and the Trade Unions—the *British Gazette*, produced under Churchill's control with the machinery of the Tory *Morning Post*, and the *British Worker*—a strike substitute for the *Daily Herald*. Other newspapers could issue only tiny fly-sheets ; and a host of little printed or cyclostyled sheets and news-letters appeared in every locality, presenting every conceivable point of view, but for the most part very short of real news. The Government had the great advantage of controlling the wireless, of which it made great use in denouncing the strike, and in appealing for volunteer help in breaking it.

On May 6, Sir John Simon declared in the House of Commons that the strike was unlawful, and made vague threats concerning the punishment to which the strikers and strike-leaders were exposing themselves.   A great argument went on about the legality of the movement ; and on May 11, Mr. Justice Astbury declared that it was illegal and that no Trade Union funds could lawfully be used for carrying it on.   This declaration had no legal effect, being made only as an *obiter dictum*, in a judgment on a case in which the question was not really involved.   But much use was made of these and other lawyers' declarations, though other well-known lawyers pronounced no less decidedly in a contrary sense.   It was of course beyond question that those who struck without due notice—as many were called upon to do—rendered themselves liable to civil actions for breach of contract ; but it was widely asserted that the strike was a criminal conspiracy and that those who took part in it were liable to prosecution under the criminal law.   No one can really say whether this was the case or not ; for the answer would have depended on what the judges might have decided if the question had ever come up in court.   In fact, it did not ; but the mere assertions of illegality had some effect.   The General Council asserted throughout that the strike had no political purpose, and was a " purely industrial movement," meant to aid the miners in resisting oppression.   It affirmed its determination to keep the movement entirely " constitutional," and was therefore flurried by the charges that it was engaged in a quasi-revolutionary conspiracy against the constitution and the law.   The strikers, however, were not flurried : with hardly any exceptions they stood solid from the beginning to the end of the affair.

After May 3 the Government refused to have any further negotiations with the strike leaders.   Attempts by a committee headed by the Archbishop of Canterbury to mediate were rejected : it was announced that a special force, the Civil Reserve Constabulary, was being recruited from the Territorial Army, and a statement was issued saying that " all ranks of the armed forces of the Crown are hereby notified that any action which they may find necessary to take in an honest endeavour to aid the Civil Power will receive, both now and afterwards, the full support of His Majesty's Government."

On May 9 it was widely reported that the Government had decided to arrest the General Council, to call up the army reserves, and to repeal the Trade Disputes Act in order to put the illegality of the strike beyond question. On the following day Sir Herbert Samuel approached the General Council with an offer of mediation, but without any authority from the Government to offer terms. The General Council, already much alarmed at the movement which it had called up, gladly accepted his offer, and on the following day was in conference with the Miners' Executive over the conditions on which the strike could be brought to an end. They found the Miners' Federation still determined to accept neither a reduction in wages nor an increase in working hours, and quite unprepared to give the General Council a free hand to reach a compromise settlement on their behalf, even if the Government could be brought to agree. This led to a quarrel— essentially the same quarrel as had occurred on " Black Friday " in 1921. The General Council considered that the Trade Unions which had struck in support of the Miners had thereby acquired a right to a determining voice in the terms on which the strike should be ended : the Miners' leaders counter-affirmed that it was for the Miners' delegates, in conference assembled, and for them alone, to decide on what terms they were prepared to work. Despite this disagreement, the General Council went on with its preparations for extending the strike to the " second line " ; but they also kept touch with Sir Herbert Samuel, who assured them that, as soon as they called off the strike, the Government would be prepared to resume negotiations and would conduct them in a generous and unvindictive spirit. Sir Herbert had drawn up a document, generally known as the " Samuel Memorandum," proposing terms, which he showed both to the Prime Minister and to the General Council ; and he appears to have led the General Council to believe that this Memorandum had in some sense the Government's sanction—or perhaps, rather, the wish to believe this was father to the thought. At all events, on the morning of May 12 the General Council suddenly announced that the strike was over, and ordered a general resumption of work without stating any terms of settlement—indeed, there were none to state. The strikers, in many cases believing that they had won a great victory, went back to work, though a number of them were refused employment, and a number more came out again when they realised that no settlement of the Miners' claims had been reached. Gradually, to the accompaniment of a good deal of victimisation, these groups went back again to work ; and the General Strike ended in ignominious collapse.

The Miners, however, did not go back. They fought on alone

and on May 20 their Delegate Conference again rejected compromise, and called upon the railway and transport Unions to renew the embargo on the movement of coal. There was no response. The Trade Unions in general had accepted defeat, and were in a number of cases agreeing to pay over sums to the employers in settlement of the actions for breach of contract which were threatened against many thousands of their members who had responded to the strike call without legal notice to terminate their employment. There were also many threats to deprive those who had struck of accumulated pension rights ; and these helped to induce the Unions to accept such terms as the employers in the various industries were prepared to give.

The Miners, though in hopeless case, kept up their resistance for a long six months after the collapse of the General Strike. In the end, they were driven back to work by sheer exhaustion, after the Government, by repealing the Seven Hours Act, had enabled the colliery owners to enforce longer hours as well as severe cuts in wages. The Government, moreover, maintained its emergency powers, which it used for breaking the strike and for making numerous arrests of local Miners' leaders ; and it also laid a heavy hand on those Boards of Guardians which attempted to relieve the distress in the mining areas. This policy was legalised by the Boards of Guardians (Default) Act, passed in July, 1926, which armed the Ministry of Health with power to suspend any Board which refused to carry out its orders concerning relief. On July 20 the West Ham Board of Guardians was suspended under the new Act, and its powers were transferred to three nominees of the Ministry ; and before long similar treatment was meted out to other Boards, especially in the mining areas.

In the meantime, there had been various further attempts at mediation : and the Miners' Federation had made renewed requests for help from the other Trade Unions. It had been arranged to call a further Conference of Trade Union Executives on June 25 to consider what action could be taken on behalf of the Miners ; but on June 23 the General Council and the Miners' Federation issued a notice cancelling the Conference, as the result of a further failure to agree about the terms of settlement. This was before the repeal of the Seven Hours Act. When the repealing Bill passed the House of Commons, the General Council issued a manifesto denouncing it, and calling for financial assistance for the miners and for workers victimised as a consequence of the General Strike. On July 8 the Coal Mines Eight Hours Act received the Royal Assent ; the Archibishop's Committee then made a renewed attempt at mediation, which was accepted by the Miners' Executive, but rejected by the Government. On July 29 the Parliamentary Labour Party invited the Miners' Federation to meet it in the hope of arranging a settlement ; but the Miners refused. On August 10 the Miners' Conference rejected the compromise proposed by the Archbishop's Committee ; but a week later it empowered the Executive to reopen negotiations with the Government and the owners. The negotiations at once broke down, the Miners still refusing to accept any increase in working hours. A mèeting between the Miners and the Government on August 26 produced no result, the Government refusing to intervene further in the dispute. The Miners were still insisting on a national settlement, whereas the owners were only prepared to negotiate for district settlements.   In September the International Miners' Federation issued a threat of international strike action, but this threat did not mature. The Government put forward fresh proposals for a settlement on a district basis ; but on October 7 these were rejected by the Miners' Delegate Conference, which demanded the calling of a National Trade Union Conference for the purpose of bringing all Trade Unions out in their support. By this time serious breakaways had occurred in a few districts, especially in the Midlands ; but the bulk of the miners were still standing firm, and further votes in the districts showed a continued determination to resist. In these circumstances the General Council agreed to the Miners' request, and summoned a further Conference of Trade Union Executives to meet on November 3. This Conference endorsed the proposal for a general levy, and received the report of a Trade Union Mediation Committee which had reopened negotiations with the Government. There emerged new proposals for a settlement on a district basis, but with certain guarantees limiting the wage-reductions to be enforced. On November 13 the Miners' Conference at length agreed to refer these proposals to the districts and, by a small majority, to recommend their acceptance ; but the district voting still showed a majority of 147,000 for rejection. Nevertheless, the Miners' Conference on November 19 recommended the districts to open separate negotiations and to get the best terms they could, with the proviso that no district settlement should be ratified until a further National Conference had received a report on all the negotiations and had advised acceptance. District negotiations followed, with profoundly unsatisfactory results in most areas ; but the miners' powers of resistance were almost at an end ; and finally, on November 26, the Delegate Conference called off the strike, leaving the District Associations to settle as they could.

Thus, the protracted struggle ended in disastrous defeat, which had indeed been inevitable from the moment when the General Strike broke down—if not even before then. Economic conditions were against the Miners ; and when once the Government had made up its mind firmly to resist the Trade Union claims and to treat the strike policy of the Trade Unions as a " conspiracy against the State," it was clear that no strike could succeed unless those in command of it were prepared in effect to carry it to the length of revolution—not necessarily in the sense of armed revolt, but at least to the extent of seeking definitely to compel the Government to resign, despite the large parliamentary majority at its command. Such action neither the Trade Union leaders nor the Labour Party were ever prepared to contemplate. The Trade Union leaders hoped that they would be able to repeat their success of 1925, and to intimidate the Government at least to the extent of procuring a compromise which the Miners' Federation could be induced to accept. In this, they were reckoning without Winston Churchill, who was fully determined to " call their bluff," and also without the miners, who were in no mood to compromise until they were driven by sheer starvation to submit.

In 1920 the threat of a General Strike was effective in stopping intervention in the Russo-Polish War because the Government knew that the great mass of the people were against war, that there was widespread semi-revolutionary feeling in the country, and that the game was not worth the candle. In 1925 it was effective temporarily, because the Government was not ready to meet it ; but there was never really any question of the Government giving way to the extent of either nationalising the mines or agreeing to any subsidy for an indefinite period. In 1925 and 1926 the wave of semi-revolutionary feeling had so subsided that only a small section on the left still felt any revolutionary impulse, and there was no chance of their carrying the mass of the people along with them in any movement designed to throw the Government out by unconstitutional means. There was plenty of sympathy for the miners, and of readiness for strike action in their support on the most extensive scale ; but there was no thought, except among a very few, of turning the strike into any sort of revolutionary movement. In the minds of most of the strikers, the strike was just a strike—exceptionally big no doubt, but no different in its objects from other strikes. Its purpose was to get the miners a square deal, and it was only incidental that this involved attempting to force the hands of the Government as well as of the colliery owners. From the side of the Tories and of the bulk of the middle classes, the affair looked very different. The Trade Unions, as these elements saw the matter, were endeavouring to coerce the Government by means which, whether unlawful or not, were definitely a challenge to the Constitution and to parliamentary government. Winston Churchill, and those who thought like him, saw their chance to teach Trade Unionists and Socialists a sharp lesson, and did not mean the chance to be missed. Although it was obvious that the Trade Union leaders were only too anxious to compromise and to escape by almost any means from the necessity of calling a strike in which they fully expected to be beaten if the Government stood firm, the majority of the Cabinet saw in this the best of reasons for not compromising, however far the General Council was prepared to go to meet them. Hence the use of a flimsy pretext for breaking off the negotiations as soon as the counter-strike measures were well in train.

Of course, the attitude of the Miners played into the hands of Winston Churchill and his group ; for this made it difficult for the General Council to make clear to the public how ready it had been to compromise, or how entirely the breakdown of negotiations had been deliberately engineered by the Government. At the same time, working-class sympathy for the miners was so strong that the General Council did not dare openly to throw the Miners' Federation over when it persisted in standing out against any concession in respect of either wages or hours. The General Council was in a cleft stick : it found itself committed to a strike which it had never expected to happen and for which it had made hardly any preparations.

Since 1926 no really large strike has ever occurred in Great Britain. The figures tell their own story. Over the seven years, 1919–25, the days lost by strikes averaged nearly 28,000,000 a year : over the seven years, 1927–33, they averaged rather over 4,000,000 : over the seven years, 1934–40, they averaged well under 2,000,000 ; and over the six years, 1941–6, just over 2,000,000, or less than half the average during the first World War.

STRIKES AND LOCK-OUTS 1911–1947

	Workers involved (thousands)	Duration in days	
1911	952	10,126	
1912	1,462	38,255	Coal Strike
1913	664	10,239	
1914	447	9,362	
1915	448	2,969	
1916	276	2,367	War
1917	872	5,865	
1918	1,116	5,892	
1919	2,591	36,330	
1920	1,932	28,858	
1921	1,801	82,269	Coal Dispute
1922	552	19,652	
1923	405	10,949	
1924	613	8,361	First Labour Government
1925	445	7,952	
1926	2,751	162,233	COAL DISPUTE GENERAL STRIKE
1927	108	1,174	
1928	124	1,388	
1929	533	8,287	
1930	307	4,399	Second Labour Government
1931	490	6,983	
1932	379	6,488	World Crisis
1933	136	1,072	
1934	134	959	
1935	279	1,924	
1936	321	1,830	
1937	597	3,410	
1938	275	1,330	
1939	337	1,360	
1940	299	940	
1941	360	1,080	
1942	457	1,530	War
1943	557	1,810	
1944	821	3,710	
1945	531	2,840	
1946	525	2,160	Third Labour Government
1947	620	2,430	

(c) The Trade Unions Act of 1927

The immediate aftermath of the General Strike was the Trade Disputes and Trade Unions Act of 1927—a vindictive law enacted by the Conservatives for the purpose not only of curbing strike action and Trade Union bargaining power, but also of crippling the Labour Party by hitting at the main source of its funds. The Labour Party did its best to fight the Bill in Parliament through all its stages ; and the Bill emerged with some of its more monstrous provisions modified. But no major concessions were made ; and, from the Trade Union standpoint, one of the worst features of the Act was the extreme uncertainty in which it left the legal position on a number of points.

There had been much talk before the Bill was produced of a complete sweeping away of the Trade Disputes Act of 1906, so as to put the Trade Unions back in the impossible position in which they had been placed by the Taff Vale Judgment. But even Conservative lawyers soon discovered this to be impracticable : the Act of 1906 was allowed to stand, but under the new law its scope was to be limited, and certain types of strike action were no longer to be protected under it. The Act of 1927 created a new class of " illegal strikes " ; and when a strike was held to be illegal an injunction could be issued preventing the use of any trade union funds in its support. Moreover, any person who " declares, instigates, incites others to take part in or otherwise acts in furtherance of " a strike declared to be illegal was made liable under the Act to fine or to imprisonment up to two years. The class of " illegal strikes " of course included strikes of the type of the General Strike of 1926 ; but it was much wider than this. The ban covered all strikes which *both* extended beyond a single trade or industry *and* were " designed or calculated to coerce the Government either directly or by inflicting hardship upon the community." Lock-outs were included, as well as strikes, as in other legislation ; but this made little difference, as lock-outs, in the legal sense of the term, are few. Legally, the workers are on strike even if they are only refusing to accept a change in conditions which their employers are seeking to enforce.

As the words " trade or industry " were not defined, and as the terms " coerce the Government " and " hardship upon the community " were also left to the interpretation of the courts, no one could really tell how far the category of " illegal strikes " would in practice be extended : not did the matter become any clearer during the nineteen years for which the Act remained in force. The prohibition of " illegal strikes "was in fact never invoked : the clause did its work, as far as it did anything at all, by preventing Trade Unions from involving themselves in strike action which they feared might be held to be illegal by the Courts. The deterrent was not so much the direct penalty upon those inciting to or taking part in " illegal " strikes as the fear of actions for damages against the Trade Unions, similar to the actions successfully brought against the Amalgamated Society of Railway

Servants by the Taff Vale Railway Company at the beginning of
the century.

In addition to prohibiting certain kinds of strike and enabling
the courts to interfere to protect the rights of persons refusing to
take part in such strikes, the Act of 1927 imposed very severe
restrictions on the right of " peaceful picketing." No picketing at
all of a person's home was to be allowed ; and even the picketing
of works during a trade dispute was made highly perilous by the
revival of the old offence of " intimidation." In the first draft of
the Bill, the definition of " intimidation " was pushed to ridiculous
lengths, so as to include the arousing of feelings of apprehension
in a person's mind. This particular phrasing was struck out ; but
the effect was to leave the word " intimidation " undefined, and
thus to threaten a revival of the extravagant meanings that the
courts put upon it in the earlier part of the nineteenth century,
before the law was amended by the Conspiracy and Protection
of Property Act of 1875. Much use was made of this section of the
Act in dealing with local strikes during the next twenty years.

Other sections of the 1927 Act prohibited regular Civil Servants
from joining Trade Unions which were associated with either the
Trades Union Congress or the Labour Party, and forbade Local
Authorities to make Trade Union membership a condition of
employment or to give preferential conditions to Trade Unionists
in their service. Local Authorities were also prevented from
imposing any similar conditions on contractors ; and a new clause
was introduced making breach of contract by a worker in an
essential public employment a crime punishable by fine or
imprisonment. This again was a return to the old law of master
and servant which had been swept away by the Employers and
Workmen Act of 1875.

Finally, the 1927 Act drastically restricted the political activities of the Trade Unions. Under the Trade Union Act of 1913,
which followed upon the Osborne Judgment, Trade Unions had
been authorised, subject to getting a majority vote in favour on a
ballot of their members, to undertake all lawful forms of political
action, provided that electoral and related activities were financed
out of a special Political Fund, and that any objectors were allowed
to " contract out " of contributing to this fund without being
prejudiced in their non-political Trade Union rights. This procedure was now reversed ; and the Unions' Political Funds could
be raised only from members who positively " contracted-in,"
by signing a form expressing their desire to pay. The purpose

of course was to make carelessness, lukewarmness and inertia act against contributing, instead of in its favour, and thus to reduce the funds at the disposal of the Unions for helping the Labour Party or for financing their own candidates in either parliamentary or local elections.

The effect of this change in the law was considerable. The Labour Party's affiliated membership fell sharply from 3,388,000 in 1926 to 2,077,000 two years later, whereas total Trade Union membership had fallen over the same period only from 5,218,000 to 4,804,000. A part of the Labour Party's loss was accounted for by the compulsory disaffiliation of the civil service Trade Unions ; but the major part of it was attributable to the substitution of " contracting-in " for " contracting-out."* It speaks very well for the efficiency of the Labour Party's organisation and for the loyalty of the Trade Unions to the Party that the affiliated membership did not fall much further. It did fall a little lower during the slump of the 1930's ; but this further fall was due to a decline in total Trade Union membership and not to the Act. In 1926 there was a difference of 1,000,000 between the affiliated memberships of the Trades Union Congress and the Labour Party: two years later the gap had widened to 2,750,000, though the Congress as well as the Labour Party had been deprived of its civil service affiliations.

The passing of the 1927 Act aroused widespread and justifiable resentment. It was felt that, even if there were a case for legis-lating against General Strikes, it was a piece of quite unjustifiable political sharp practice to use the occasion for a manœuvre designed to put the Labour Party in a financial quandary. Actually, between 1927 and 1929 the Labour Party lost over a quarter of its total income from affiliation fees ; and the Local Labour Parties also suffered heavy losses. Moreover, the deple-tion of Trade Union Political Funds meant that the Unions had to restrict their financing of candidates. From 1927 onwards the Labour Party was working under very serious financial handicaps, deliberately imposed on it by its political opponents. As against this, the resentment felt at the Act of 1927 tended to increase Trade Union support for the Party, within the limits set upon Trade Union political action. The Tories in effect over-reached themselves : so far from smashing the Labour Party, they compelled it to strengthen itself by building up its individual membership.

*For the effects of the Act on the Labour Party see further Appendix on page 480.

(d) *A Move to the Right*—" Labour and the Nation "

The events of 1926 and the passing of the Trade Unions Act in 1927 were followed by a sharp change in Trade Union policy. Trade continued bad : there was much unemployment, and the Unions were losing members. There were fears of a general employers' offensive to increase hours as well as reduce wages ; and the Trade Union leaders, conscious of their weak bargaining position and uncertain of the effect of the new Act, were in no mood to fight if they could avoid it. The Trades Union Congress of September, 1926, had indeed passed a resolution calling for the reorganisation of the Trade Union movement on a basis of " Union by industry," and had still shown signs of a militant spirit. But this was while the Miners' struggle was still in progress, and before the Trade Union Bill had been produced. In January, 1927, a National Conference of Trade Union Executives, called together by the General Council, held a sort of inquest on the General Strike, but rather with a view to decent burial than to any further action. By that time the attention of the more militant section had been diverted mainly to the Chinese crisis which followed upon the invasion of Central China by the Nationalist forces. Serious trouble arose over the foreign Concessions at Hankow and Shanghai ; and the use of force by the British and the dispatch of military and naval reinforcements to China led to fears of war against the Nationalists in support of British capitalist interests. The I.L.P. and the Communists both took the China agitation up with vigour ; and in January, 1927, the Labour Party issued a manifesto against British intervention in Chinese affairs, and the National Joint Council of Labour sent a message of sympathy to the Chinese Nationalist Government. Soon, however, the Chinese Nationalists fell out : Chiang Kai-Shek rebelled against the Nationalist Government, and the Kuomintang drove out its Russian advisers and overthrew its own left wing. A counter-rebellion in the South led to the setting up of a short-lived Communist Government in Canton in December, 1927 ; but this Government was speedily overthrown, and the right wing was able to consolidate its position under the leadership of Chiang Kai-Shek. This was a great setback to Communism as a world force, and had its reactions everywhere on the influence of the Communist Parties.

Meanwhile, Great Britain, under its new Conservative rulers, had carried through in May, 1927, the raid on " Arcos "—the

Soviet trading agency in London—and had taken other police measures against the Communists. These steps were followed the same month by the severance of diplomatic relations with the Soviet Union. The Trades Union Congress and the Labour Party, though they did not approve of these measures, were at the same time intensifying their own attempts to stamp out " subversive activities " in the Labour movement. In February, 1927, the General Council imposed a ban on local Trades Councils which held any relations with the Communist-dominated " Minority Movement " ; and the Labour Party Executive similarly disaffiliated a number of Local Labour Parties which persisted in maintaining Communist connections.

The Communists, being few and for the time being in a weak position, were fairly easy to deal with. The I.L.P., much bigger and not merely inside the Labour Party but very strongly represented in the Parliamentary Party, was a much tougher nut to crack. The I.L.P. had given strong support to the Miners in 1926 ; it had started a special journal, *The Miner*, which it subsequently handed over to the Miners' Federation ; it had organised collections and propaganda tours in support of the Miners' cause, and had pressed strongly for a renewal of Labour help after the collapse of the General Strike ; and it had shown itself highly critical of both the Trade Unions and the Labour Party in relation to the mining struggle. All this, however, was only one aspect of the widening cleavage between the I.L.P. and the Labour Party leadership over the main issues of Socialist policy.

We have seen already how, after the fall of the Labour Government, the I.L.P. had resumed its attempt to work out a militant, though constitutional, policy for the achievement of " Socialism Now," or, as it came to be called, " Socialism in Our Time." This policy was elaborated in a series of special Policy Reports presented to the I.L.P. Annual Conferences from 1924 onwards. These covered a wide ground—Land and Agriculture, Finance, Parliamentary Reform, Unemployment, International Trade and Import Boards (specially advocated by E. F. Wise), and a number of other issues ; but the controversy came to centre above all round a Report dealing with the question of the Living Wage, in which it was in effect argued that the provision of a minimum living income for every citizen should be made a first charge on the national product, and that Labour should make this its first and immediate objective, relating such matters as socialisation to it, and treating it as the pivot of all home policy. The

Living Wage, or Living Income, Plan was presented in a number of forms, differing one from another on secondary points, and some involving more drastic immediate action than others. There was, indeed, inside the I.L.P. itself, a continuing struggle between those who wanted to ginger the plan up and those who wanted to water it down ; but in all its forms it demanded a Labour programme a good deal more drastic than the leaders of the Labour Party were prepared willingly to accept. At the least, it called for the immediate adoption of a national minimum wage adequate to meet all needs in all public services and by all employers working on public contracts, supplemented by machinery for the legal enforcement of rising minima on industry as a whole, as well as by expanded social services financed out of taxation on the bigger incomes, and by a nationally financed system of Family Allowances.

Instalments of the I.L.P.'s new policy had been bought up in the form of resolutions at the Labour Party Conference of 1926 ; and at the 1927 Conference the Living Wage Plan was brought forward in full. Up to this point the Labour Party leaders had been clearly anxious to avoid antagonising the I.L.P. ; and a considerable number of its resolutions and amendments had been accepted, though in 1926 its proposal that the Labour Party should commit itself to Children's Allowances had been defeated by 2,242,000 to 1,143,000, mainly through the opposition of a number of Trade Unions, which feared that the Allowances might be used to justify wage-reductions, and of a section in the Party which favoured the development of social services in kind— such as school meals—in preference to cash allowances.

At the 1927 Labour Party Conference the Living Wage Plan was not met with a blank negation, though it, and the rest of the I.L.P.'s new policy, had been the subject of very strong attacks from Ramsay MacDonald and other former I.L.P. stalwarts. MacDonald had called the I.L.P.'s proposals " flashy futilities," and had dismissed the entire programme for " Socialism in Our Time " as likely to involve in practice the postponement of all advance, because it would only frighten the electorate and ensure a crushing Labour defeat. By way of retaliation, the I.L.P. had refused to re-nominate MacDonald either for the office of Treasurer of the Labour Party or as a delegate to the Labour Party Conference, and had compelled him to seek an alternative nomination from his Local Labour Party at Lossiemouth. MacDonald, at the Conference, repeated his denunciations of the

I.L.P. programme ; but the Executive, instead of attempting to get them rejected outright, proposed that a special Committee should be set up to examine them in conjunction with the Trade Unions, and the Conference ended without an actual " showdown " between the I.L.P. and its opponents. From this time, however, MacDonald ceased to have any real connection with the I.L.P. ; and Philip Snowden definitely resigned from it at the beginning of 1928.

The Living Wage policy, having been disposed of for the time being by the promise to investigate it, became bogged in a Joint Committee of the Labour Party and the Trades Union Congress, which proceeded to take a great deal of evidence from various societies and experts. By the time the Labour Party Conference met in 1928, it had become clear that there were strong Trade Union disagreements over Family Allowances. The Trades Union Congress General Council had sent out a questionnaire on the subject, and had received conflicting answers. Its representatives on the Joint Committee could therefore pronounce no verdict, and the proceedings were held up. At the Conference, Dorothy Jewson, for the I.L.P., moved the reference back of this section of the Report, but withdrew her motion after Henderson had fully explained how matters stood. When the question came up again at the 1929 Party Conference, it had to be reported that the Trade Unions were almost equally divided about Family Allowances, and that, though a majority on the Joint Committee was in favour of them, no definite recommendations could be made " owing to the inability of the General Council of the Trades Union Congress to express an opinion on behalf of the Trade Union Movement." Dorothy Jewson thereupon moved a resolution in favour of Family Allowances ; and a very long debate ensued. The Miners, through Herbert Smith, gave strong support : the General Workers, through Charles Dukes, and one or two other Trade Unions were opposed. Clynes, Ernest Bevin, and other speakers entreated the Conference not to take a decision until the Trade Union movement had made up its mind. Bevin argued that the Allowances were only one element in the general Living Wage policy put forward by the I.L.P., and that it was unreasonable to ask for a decision on them alone : he urged the Conference to send the whole matter back to the Joint Committee, in order that a comprehensive Report might be prepared, dealing with the Living Wage in all its aspects. The I.L.P. was asked to withdraw its resolution, but James Maxton refused, saying that they were always being put off. In the end the Previous Question was carried, by 1,253,000 to 866,000.

It is convenient to round off the account here, though this involves travelling beyond the period covered in this chapter. The question of Family Allowances went back to the Joint Committee, which produced rival Reports, the majority favouring their introduction. The Trades Union Congress General Council thereupon adopted the Minority Report, which advocated the extension of the social services as a preferable alternative. The Labour Party Executive, on which a majority favoured both Family Allowances and extended social services, wished the matter to be again adjourned in the hope of an agreed decision; but the reference back of the Executive's Report was again moved, and was defeated after Henderson had made plain both his and the Executive's sympathy. Assurances were given that the Living Wage inquiry as a whole would not be abandoned ; and the Joint Committee in fact went on. But the wider issues raised in the I.L.P.'s Reports and resolutions had in practice been swept aside long before, when the Labour Party set to work in 1927 to produce a new Programme to supersede *Labour and the New Social Order.*

The I.L.P.'s challenge, as we saw, was not limited to the Living Wage Plan, though most of its other proposals on home policy were grouped round that issue. It also pressed strongly for the nationalisation of banking and credit, including the joint stock banks and the " City " as well as the Bank of England. The Labour Party Executive itself had favoured, and the Annual Party Conference of 1925 had approved, such a policy ; but when the I.L.P. brought it up again in 1927, as a step necessary for the carrying out of the Living Wage, MacDonald opposed the resolution, asking the Conference to refer it back for further report, and to this the I.L.P. agreed. The result was that this question too became merged in the general discussion of the new Labour Party programme.

A further issue on which the I.L.P. fell foul of the Labour Party Executive was that of Birth Control. In 1927 the Labour Women's Conference adopted a resolution in favour of removing the Ministry of Health's ban on the giving of advice on birth control at Maternity Centres. The Party Executive, asked to act on this decision, recommended the Conference to reaffirm its resolution of 1925, when it had declared that " the subject of Birth Control is in its nature not one which should be made a political party issue, but should remain a matter upon which members of the Party should be free to hold and promote their individual convictions." The reason for this attitude was, of course, the presence in the Labour Party of strong religious (especially Roman Catholic) groups hostile to family limitation. The reference back was moved, but was defeated by 2,885,000 to 275,000.

The principal remaining issue between the I.L.P. and the Labour Party was that of Socialist policy in relation to war. In 1926 the I.L.P. succeeded in carrying at the Labour Party Conference its resolution favouring working-class resistance to all wars ; and it sought to follow up this success with a demand that the Labour Party in Parliament should be instructed to vote against all military estimates. Owing to the special conditions of the 1928 Conference, which was preoccupied with the new Labour Party programme, the proposed resolution could not be moved. The I.L.P. carried it instead to the Labour and Socialist International, which decided to circulate the I.L.P. proposals to all its affiliated parties.

All these, and many other, conflicts between the I.L.P. and the Labour Party leadership involved increasing tension. The I.L.P. also took up a strong line on the question of imperial and colonial policy. It set up in 1926 a special Committee on Imperialism, and sent delegates to the Brussels Conference of the League of Oppressed Peoples in February, 1927. It took a definite stand in favour of independence for India, of colonial emancipation, and of improvement in native conditions and rights of organisation in South Africa. In all these matters it was continually taking a line well to the left of the Labour Party's, and was seeking to impel the Labour Party to follow its lead. In particular, it criticised the Labour Party's attitude to the appointment of the Simon Commission on Indian Reforms, and pressed for a stronger policy in demanding British withdrawal from Egypt.

These disagreements were complicated by the I.L.P.'s intervention into the field of Trade Unionism. Its programme included, as we saw, a demand for " industrial democracy " and " workers' control " ; and its work in support of the Miners in 1926 stimulated its zeal to promote reorganisation of the Trade Union movement with a view both to a more militant industrial policy and to the creation of a type of Trade Unionism better adapted to play a part in the control of socialised industries. In 1927 the I.L.P. produced a Report, *The Organised Worker,* embodying its conclusions on these issues, and was able to announce that it had 146 Industrial Committees at work in connection with I.L.P. branches. The policy advocated by the I.L.P. had much to recommend it ; but it came forward at a time when the Trade Union movement's policy was shifting sharply right-wards, and this helped to fan the resentment of many Trade Union leaders at what they regarded as unwarrantable inter-ference in Trade Union domestic affairs. The I.L.P., of course, argued that as a Socialist body, not confined to political activity, it had every right to do all it could to influence the Trade Unions in a Socialist direction. The Trade Union leaders, harassed already by the Communists, were in no mood to admit this right, and carried their resentment into the political field, stiffening their hostility to the I.L.P.'s Living Wage policy and indeed to all its doings.

The conflict on the industrial side became acute in connection with the " Mond-Turner " negotiations of 1927–8. In November, 1927, Sir Alfred Mond, of I.C.I., and a group of big employers from a number of industries informally approached the Trades Union Congress General Council with a proposal that they should meet to discuss possible methods of promoting improved industrial relations. The General Council, of which Ben Turner was Chairman, accepted the invitation ; and in July, 1928, there was issued an agreed Interim Report, which included, together with proposals for dealing with unemployment, a recommenda-tion in favour of recognition of Trade Unions as bargaining agencies and the encouragement by employers of Trade Union membership, and plans for the setting up of joint consultative machinery by the Trades Union Congress, the Federation of British Industries, and the National Confederation of Employers' Organisations. The Report proposed that both in particular industries and on matters of general industrial and economic policy employers' associations and Trade Unions should in future work closely together, and should insist on being jointly consulted by the Government before it introduced legislative or other measures affecting industry. In effect, the notions under-lying the Whitley Report of 1917 and the National Industrial Conference of 1919 were revived.

The employers who took part in these discussions spoke only for themselves, and had no authority to commit the F.B.I. or the National Confederation. They were, in fact, an influential group of large-scale employers who believed in seizing the

opportunity presented by the Trade Union defeat of 1926 and by
the Trade Unions Act for the purpose, not of crushing Trade
Unionism, but of taming it, and enlisting its co-operation in the
conduct of capitalist enterprise. They held out as a bait the offer
of full recognition and encouragement of Trade Union membership, and the prospect of action to reduce unemployment by
changes in the unemployment insurance system.

The " Mond-Turner " proposals became known by instalments between April and July, 1928. In June of that year, a
counterblast, known as the " Cook-Maxton Manifesto," appeared
over the signatures of A. J. Cook, the Secretary of the Miners'
Federation, and James Maxton, the Chairman of the I.L.P. The
Manifesto vigorously denounced all forms of " class-collaboration," recorded " serious disturbance " at the direction in which
the British Labour movement was being led, called for " un-
ceasing war against capitalism," protested that " much of the
energy which should be expended in fighting capitalism is now
expended in crushing everybody who dares to remain true to the
ideals of the movement," and announced a national campaign of
conferences and meetings to recall the Labour movement to its
task of destroying the capitalist system.

The Cook-Maxton Manifesto put the cat among the pigeons,
not only in the Trade Unions, but also in the I.L.P. Maxton had
signed it without consulting his colleagues ; and when it was
brought up at the I.L.P.'s National Administrative Council there
was a lively altercation, and Maxton carried the day only by a
single vote. John Scurr, until then a faithful adherent of the
I.L.P., resigned in protest ; but the 1929 I.L.P. Conference
affirmed its confidence in Maxton by re-electing him to the
chairmanship by an overwhelming majority over Shinwell and
Patrick Dollan. Cook, on the other hand, after fighting a lone
battle against the " Mond-Turner " proposals on the General
Council, was heavily defeated at the Trades Union Congress in
September, 1928, when a motion by the Amalgamated Engineering Union to refer the proposals for consideration by the separate
Unions was beaten by 2,920,000 votes to 768,000, and the
General Council's action in approving them was endorsed by
3,075,000 to 566,000. This Trades Union Congress also instructed
the General Council to make a special investigation of the
activities of " disruptive elements " in the Trade Unions, and
adopted a resolution empowering the General Council to take
action against Trade Unions which it considered to be following

policies hostile to the general interests of the Labour movement.

The cleavage between the I.L.P. and the main body of the Labour Party leadership involved difficulties over the position of the I.L.P. Members of Parliament. More than two-thirds of the Labour M.P.s elected in 1924 belonged to the I.L.P., though only twenty-seven of them sat as I.L.P. Members for whose candidature the I.L.P. was wholly responsible. In 1925 Ben Spoor, an old I.L.P. adherent, was turned off the I.L.P. list for advocating Labour co-operation with the Liberals ; and thereafter increasing trouble arose out of allegations that even the M.P.s elected under I.L.P. auspices were not carrying out the full policy of the I.L.P., but were putting their loyalty to the Labour Party above their loyalty to the I.L.P. At the 1928 I.L.P. Conference Maxton in his Chairman's address spoke strongly of the duty of the I.L.P. to put first its loyalty to Socialism and to carry on an active campaign for left-wing Socialism inside the Labour Party. The mission of the I.L.P., he said, was to be " a Socialist Party within the Labour Party." When, however, delegates attacked the I.L.P. Members of Parliament for their failure to follow a Socialist line, Maxton made a conciliatory speech, and prevented the criticism from coming to a vote. The following year the critics returned to the attack, a section of the Conference demanding that all I.L.P. candidates should be required to give definite pledges to carry out the I.L.P.'s policy, even if it conflicted with that of a majority of the Labour Party, and that the I.L.P. Parliamentary Group, instead of being open to all I.L.P. members in Parliament, should be limited to M.P.s who were prepared to give the required pledges. This resolution was defeated, by 214 votes to 124 ; but the Conference adopted a regulation which, without restricting the membership of the Parliamentary Group, required all candidates put forward under I.L.P. auspices to give a pledge that, if elected, they would carry out the policies laid down by the I.L.P. Conference.

On this occasion Charles Buxton, a former Treasurer and leading figure in the I.L.P., delivered a frontal attack on its policy. It was impossible, he urged, for the I.L.P. to exist as a Party within a Party, putting forward a rival programme to that of the Labour Party. He wanted the I.L.P. to give up putting up candidates of its own for Parliament and to concentrate on educational and propagandist work for Socialism without setting itself up as a rival political party. Buxton's attitude found little support, for most of those who criticised Maxton's line were b no means prepared for the I.L.P. to give up its separate position as a political body nominating candidates, and saw in what he proposed only a danger of increased Trade Union domination of the Labour Party's affairs.

Meanwhile, the Labour Party, pushing the I.L.P.'s proposals aside, had been busy working out its own policy in preparation for the General Election which was due to take place in 1929. At the Labour Party Conference of 1927, MacDonald moved a resolution in favour of the preparation of a new Election Programme. In the debate, Ernest Bevin urged the Party to be careful not to put forward a programme that would be " over the heads of the people—something that they could not understand." They had to recognise that " Trade Unionists were not all Labour Party Socialists, and that there were thousands of Trade Unionists who were Tories." He criticised the I.L.P. for putting forward programmes which " entered into the realm of what was legitimate Trade Union business," and thus antagonised Trade Union branches. He wanted " a short programme of immediate objectives that Labour could really hope to accomplish " ; and then " they could go back and say ' At least we have done what we said we would : we have delivered the goods.' " Such a programme, he thought, would unite all of them ; it would " create confidence, so that they would be returned a second time with even greater power." As against this, Cook, Maxton and others argued for a full-blooded Socialist programme ; and MacDonald, in reply to the discussion, made a high-sounding speech about Socialism which, on analysis, turns out to mean absolutely nothing. It served its end, by giving the Executive a free hand to draft whatever programme it pleased for submission to the next Annual Conference.

The outcome was the new detailed statement published under the name *Labour and the Nation*, which was submitted to the 1928 Party Conference in such a way that only broad points of criticism could be made, any necessary re-drafting being left to the Executive in the light of the Conference discussions. In a preface to the draft Ramsay MacDonald wrote that " the Labour Party, unlike other Parties, is not concerned with patching the rents in a bad system, but with transforming Capitalism into Socialism " ; and the draft itself, on its opening page, declared the Labour Party to be " a Socialist party," standing for a Socialism based " on practical recognition of the familiar commonplace that ' morality is in the nature of things,' and that men are all, in very truth, members one of another." It went on to praise "the tentative, doctrineless Socialism" which had found imperfect recognition in existing social legislation, and to urge that the time had come, "by experimental methods, without violence or disturbance," for the establishment of "a social order in which the resources of the community shall be organised and administered with a single eye to securing for all its members the largest possible measure of economic welfare and personal freedom."

The draft then proceeded to a long denunciation of the home and international policies of the Conservative Government and to an attack on the Liberal Party, designed to counteract the appeal of Lloyd George's advanced proposals for handling the unemployment problem. Coming to the constructive side, the draft laid down five principles in the light of which Labour would use its power, if it were placed again in office.

(i) To secure to every member of the community the standards of life and employment which are necessary to a healthy, independent, and self-respecting existence.

(ii) To convert industry, step by step, and with due regard to the special needs and varying circumstances of different occupations, from a sordid struggle for private gain into a co-operative undertaking, carried on for the service of the community and amenable to its control.

(iii) To extend rapidly and widely those forms of social provision—education, public health, housing, pensions, the care of the sick, and maintenance during unemployment—in the absence of which the individual is the sport of economic chance and the slave of his environment.

(iv) To adjust taxation in such a way as to secure that due provision is made for the maintenance and improvement of the apparatus of industry, and that surpluses created by social effort shall be applied by society for the good of all.

(v) To establish peace, freedom and justice by removing from among the nations the root causes of international disputes, by conciliation and all-in arbitration, by renouncing war as an instrument of national policy, by disarmament, by political and economic co-operation through the League of Nations, and by mutual agreements with States which are not members of the League.*

The amplification and application of these very general principles occupied the remainder of the draft. Stress was laid on the need for a new Factory Act and for other industrial legislation, on the amendment of the Unemployment Insurance

*i.e., mainly, the Soviet Union and the U.S.A.

scheme to provide adequate maintenance for all those out of work, and to take the unfair burden off local rates, and on the establishment of permanent machinery for the prevention of unemployment by means of well-thought-out plans for the development of natural resources. It was promised that a Labour Government would set up a " National Economic Committee, acting under the directions of the Prime Minister, which will be his eyes and ears on economic questions . . . and would ensure that economic policy was accurately adjusted to the needs of the moment." With this was to go an Employment and Development Board, with the duty " to bring development schemes to the point of execution in readiness for the time when they should be pushed ahead in the interests of employment and trade."

Under the heading " The Democratic Control of Industry," the draft then went on to declare that " the Labour Party, which believes in democracy in industry as well as in government, intends that the great foundation industries, on which the welfare of all depends, shall be owned and administered for the common advantage of the whole community." It stated that " without haste, but without rest," the Labour Party would vest in the nation the ownership of land, both agricultural and urban, of coal and power, of transport and communication services, and of life insurance. About other industries it made no precise proposals, beyond promising " stringent control over monopolies and combines," enlarged powers for the Food Council, and measures of " bulk importation of foodstuffs and raw materials by a public authority." It advocated extension of municipal trading enterprise, and the granting of large enabling powers to Local Authorities ; and it announced that the Labour Party regarded the Co-operative movement " as an indispensable element in the Socialist Commonwealth," and would work in the fullest alliance with it. For agriculture there was to be a guarantee of assured markets and a development of capital values made possible by public ownership of the land.

Next came the sections dealing with Public Health, Housing, Education, and the development of the social services, with proposals for a shift from indirect to direct taxation, for the higher taxation of inheritance, and for a special surtax on unearned incomes of more than £500 a year. Urban land values were to be subject to special taxation ; and the proceeds of more equitable national taxation were to be used to relieve the burdens on local rates.

The draft then turned to international issues, laying great stress on the need for all-in arbitration, radical disarmament, and the complete renunciation of war, which were to be coupled with the development of closer international co-operation, both economic and political, including the re-opening and development of trading relations with Russia. Closer contact between the Governments of Great Britain and the Dominions was strongly urged, including a full survey of Empire resources and the promotion of schemes of empire migration designed to ensure their better use. The economic exploitation of colonial peoples was denounced ; and promises were made of a colonial policy that would combine economic advancement with protection of the colonial peoples " in the occupation and enjoyment of their land," and would prevent forced labour and unfair labour contracts.

Finally, there were some pages on " The Implications of Democracy," both political and economic. On the economic side, the Labour Party's object was said to be " to secure for the nation the control of its economic destinies, and for the workers a position in which they will be free to manage their own lives, to take part in the government of their own professions, and to serve the great body of their own countrymen, not a handful of property-owners." This was the only reference to the vexed issue of " workers' control." It was followed by an assertion that the Labour Party stood " for the unquestioned supremacy of the House of Commons, and for uncompromising resistance to any attempt to establish a Second Chamber representative of special classes or interests, designed to thwart the duly registered decisions of the democracy and with power to interfere with financial measures." This, of course, was a reference to the Conservative plans for a reformed Upper Chamber, with extended powers, and for a reversal of the Parliament Act.

To this draft of *Labour and the Nation* was added a Supplement, dealing with Currency, Banking and Credit. This document proposed that the Bank of England should be reorganised as a Public Corporation " containing representatives of such essential factors in the community as the Treasury, Board of Trade, Industry, Labour and the Co-operative Movement." It further proposed an extension of Municipal and Co-operative Banking, international regulation of the value of gold designed to secure both exchange stability and stable prices in accordance with the proposals of the Geneva Conference of 1922 ; and " control of

investment and the allocation of credit " by methods to be decided upon after further inquiry. It is obvious that the part of the
proposals relating to Banking and Finance had been by no means
adequately thought out. The probable incompatibility of stable
prices and stable exchanges was not recognised ; and there was
in effect no policy at all for dealing with the joint stock banks, to
the nationalisation of which Snowden, Labour's destined Chancellor of the Exchequer, was opposed, despite the Party resolutions carried in earlier years. Indeed, Snowden's rigid financial
orthodoxy was in sharp conflict with the proposals of the I.L.P.
and of other financial radicals ; and most of the Party's leaders
did not at all know where they stood—an ignorance which was to
cost them dear in the economic crisis of 1931.

The Birmingham Labour Party Conference of 1928 spent a
large part of its time debating *Labour and the Nation,* first in general
terms and then in a series of discussions on the particular sections.
In the general debate, the draft was challenged from two distinct
points of view. It was urged, especially by the I.L.P. speakers,
including Maxton and Wheatley, that even if the whole of the
proposals embodied in it could be carried out, the result would be,
not Socialism, but a form of controlled Capitalism that could
never be made to work. It was also argued, in some instances by
the same speakers, that *Labour and the Nation* was not a programme
for the next General Election, such as the Executive was understood to have promised to produce, but a general statement of
aims, covering immensely more ground than any Government,
even with a clear majority behind it, could possibly hope to put
into effect during a single period, or for that matter during several
successive periods of office. It was argued that the draft fell
between two stools, being neither a declaration of fully Socialist
objectives nor an immediate programme. That it was neither,
but something betwixt and between, was undeniable ; and in
defending the draft, MacDonald, who presented it, did not deny
this, giving it to be understood that it was definitely meant not
as a programme for an incoming Socialist Government, but rather
as a statement of the aims and principles by which such a Government would be guided. Wheatley, making the double criticism,
said that it would take at least half a century to carry through by
parliamentary methods, and at the end would have achieved no
real change in the basis of the social and economic system. Its
defenders, including some who were regarded as having " left "
tendencies, contended either that it was a clear statement of

Socialist objectives (though not of all the steps needed to reach them), or that, if it was not, it was at any rate all the electorate could reasonably be expected to assimilate of Socialism at its present stage of enlightenment.

It was clear throughout that MacDonald and those who followed his lead did not want the Conference to have before it any programme that would bind a Labour Government in respect of the measures to which it would give priority if it came to office. They argued that an Election Programme ought to be formulated just before a General Election, when the circumstances were known, and that in any case a large delegate assembly was unfitted to draft such a programme, because it would, under pressure of a host of special claims, tend to put in far too much and also to pay inadequate attention to the interests of the electors as a whole and to parliamentary practicabilities. MacDonald wanted a statement of long-term policy that would leave him and his immediate colleagues a free choice both in selecting the election issues and in framing a Labour Government's positive programme.

As against this the I.L.P. and its sympathisers wanted to commit the Labour Party as decisively as possible to Socialism, not merely as an ideal, but as a practical immediate objective, and further to commit it to their particular notion of the way to achieve " Socialism in Our Time." Maxton, in his speech, prophesied that the next General Election would make Labour the largest party, but would fail to give it a clear majority. He wanted to make sure that, if a second minority Government took office, it would produce a challenging policy on which it could court defeat in Parliament in order to make a further appeal to the electors. This was, of course, exactly what MacDonald did not wish to have forced on him. When Maxton complained that *Labour and the Nation* gave the Socialist M.P.s and propagandists no guidance at all upon the immediate policy of the Labour Party, the sponsors of the draft replied that this was not what it was meant for, and that its purpose was to enlighten public opinion concerning the Labour Party's " conception of society " and, in MacDonald's words, " to draw the minds of the electors from mere patchwork and direct them to fine, creative, and constructive work." The critics retorted that what MacDonald regarded as " fine, creative and constructive " appeared to them to be no better than a cloud of words, through which nothing definite could be seen. Maxton attacked the draft on the ground that " the whole formation of it, the utterances of those who have been most strongly defending it, lead one to the conclusion that they are looking at their responsibilities as if the approach to Socialism was to be a long slow process of gradualistic, peaceful, parliamentary change "—as of course they were. " A Labour Government," he went on to say, " cannot run Capitalism any more successfully than Baldwin and the others. A Labour Government can only redeem its pledges and promises, made for fifty years to the workers of this country, if it recognises that nationalisation—public ownership—has got to be done on large-scale operations at tremendous speed . . . we are past the propagandist stage."

On the other side, Herbert Morrison strongly defended the draft ; and Shinwell, who criticised it because it was not the immediate limited and definite programme that he thought was needed, defended it as a good statement of the Socialist case. MacDonald in his reply made play with the critics' differences among themselves. No vote was taken at this stage, an attempt to refer the whole document back being ruled out of order.

The Conference then proceeded to discuss the separate sections, and at once the I.L.P. renewed its challenge with a demand for the insertion of the " Living Income " policy into the draft. It was made clear that what the I.L.P. wanted was that an incoming Labour Government should immediately introduce the legislation necessary to establish a minimum living income and social security, and should then use the inability of capitalism to bear the strain of such measures as a signal to go straight ahead with socialisation and with whatever else might prove necessary in order to make the " Living Income " policy workable. John Paton and Fenner Brockway put this point of view to the Conference ; but nobody deemed it worth while to answer them, as the same ground had been gone over so largely in the previous debate. The reference back on the " Living Income " issue was defeated by 2,780,000 to 143,000. After a number of less important issues had been dealt with, Snowden moved the Finance and Banking section of the draft in a long speech, in which, after laying down his taxation policy, he went on to admit that on the question of banking and currency none of them had yet any well-considered views. This was why the Report on the subject was so tentative. He then defended the proposal to convert the Bank of England into a public corporation, but said that, though he favoured in principle the nationalisation of the joint stock

banks, he did not believe the time to be ripe for it while most of
the trade and industry of the country remained in private hands.
This led to a sharp attack from Frank Wise, of the I.L.P., who
argued that unless the banks in general were taken over, it would
be found impracticable to carry through the proposed measures
for industrial development and the prevention of unemployment.
If the Labour Party were not ready at once to take over the
commercial banks, when would it be ready ? How long were they
to wait ? Other critics of the draft attacked the proposal to turn
the Bank of England into a public corporation, and argued in
favour of " straight " nationalisation in order to ensure effective
government control.   Pethick Lawrence replied that the public
corporation proposal amounted to nationalisation, and that it was
necessary to avoid " monkeying " with the currency for political
purposes. He contended that it was quite unnecessary to take over
the joint stock banks, because a publicly owned Bank of England
would be fully able to ensure their compliance with the requirements of public policy.   In the end, all this section of the draft
was accepted without a division.

There was much more debate ; and on a number of points
MacDonald agreed to make changes in the draft, mainly by
inserting or making more precise things which had been omitted
or left vague.   For example, new sections were put in dealing
with seamen, strengthening the section on unemployment benefits, reinforcing the provisions about disarmament, and making
clear the commitment to " equal pay for equal work." Then the
draft as a whole was approved without opposition.

Thus the Labour Party adopted a new statement of its general
aims and objectives, replacing *Labour and the New Social Order*,
but in essentials not much different from it. This left the Party
still without anything that could be called an Election Programme ; and the formulation of such a programme was left over
until the Election actually came, and was then done by the
Executive and the Party leader without any further consultation
of the Party as a whole. In this shorter programme, pride of place
was given to the problem of unemployment. " The Labour
Party gives an unqualified pledge to deal immediately and
practically with this problem."   The Programme then outlined
the schemes of " National Development " that it would set on
foot—Housing and Slum Clearance, Land Drainage and Reclamation, Electrification, the Reorganisation of Railways and
Transport, New Roads and Road and Bridge Improvements,

Afforestation associated with Small Holdings, and Assisted Migration to the Dominions. It insisted on the need to restore the depressed industries, and to develop the home market " by increasing the purchasing power of the working classes " at home, and of the impoverished masses in India and the Colonies. It announced the intention to develop export credits and trade facilities guarantees. Almost the same proposals appeared in the election programme of the Liberal Party, which, under the inspiration of Lloyd George and on the advice of J. M. Keynes, based its main appeal to the people on large-scale measures for increasing the level of employment.

For the rest, the Election Programme dealt mainly with social reform and with foreign affairs. On the issue of nationalisation it was careful, promising to nationalise the mines if the Labour Party received a clear majority, but promising only " public control," and not nationalisation of the land, and making no reference to public ownership of any other industry, or even to the proposal to convert the Bank of England into a Public Corporation. Committees of Inquiry were promised to consider the " reorganisation " of the cotton and steel industries ; but no mention was made of nationalising either of them. The Programme was in fact essentially a moderate, social reform programme, in which Socialism found neither place nor mention. It was evidently drafted in contemplation of a result to the Election which, at best, might enable Labour to take minority office with a stronger backing than in 1924.

Such a Programme was, of course, highly displeasing to those who followed the I.L.P. lead. It was a further stage in the move to the right which MacDonald had been steadily engineering in the Party, and which had been accentuated by the changes in Trade Union policy, as well as by the strong resentments aroused by the I.L.P.'s attempts to influence the Trade Unions, by the Cook-Maxton Manifesto, and by Maxton's " flirting " with the Communists—a point that was brought up to discredit him during the discussions on *Labour and the Nation*.

At the Birmingham Conference, where *Labour and the Nation* was adopted, the Labour Party Executive also brought up a special declaration on " Party Loyalty," which it asked the delegates to endorse. This laid down that " affiliation to the Labour Party implies general loyalty to the decisions of the Party Conference and debars affiliated organisations and their branches from promoting or associating in the promotion of

candidates for Public Authorities in opposition to those of the
Labour Party." It went on to declare ineligible as delegates to
National or Local Labour Party Conferences or meetings persons,
no matter by whom appointed [i.e., including Trade Union
delegates] who opposed Labour Party candidates or were
" members of Political Parties declared by the Annual Conference or by the National Executive Committee in pursuance of
Conference decisions to be ineligible for affiliation to the Labour
Party." Thirdly, it was laid down that Local Parties and other
affiliated organisations should not invite or permit on their
platforms Communist Party members or members of other parties
ineligible for affiliation to the Labour Party. This was the
beginning of the formal black list of banned organisations which
the Party operated on an increasing scale in later years. It
involved a very great tightening up against the Communists in
particular, though in fact the Labour Party Executive could not
enforce it against the Trade Unions or, completely, even in the
case of its own Local Parties. At the Birmingham Conference,
Alexander Gossip, of the Furnishing Trades Association, moved
the reference back of these directives, but was beaten overwhelmingly on a show of hands, and did not challenge a card vote.

At this time, bitterness between the Labour Party and the
Communists was steadily growing. The Communist Party,
which had had only about 5,000 members at the beginning of
1926, had doubled its membership during the mining struggle ;
but many of the new recruits had soon been lost, and by the end of
1927 the Communist Party was in a very weak condition. Internal
dissensions then developed, between those who still believed in
the tactics of the " United Front " and those who advocated
giving up the demand for affiliation to the Labour Party and
embarking on outright opposition. Some of these latter favoured
an attempt to build up a new " Left Wing " Party round the
elements which were being driven into opposition by the Labour
Party's rightward trend, and especially round the Local Labour
Parties and Trades Councils which were being disaffiliated or
disowned by the national Labour bodies ; whereas others
regarded such a " Left Wing " Party as a potentially dangerous
rival to the Communist Party, and wished the Communist Party
to act more openly on its own, and less under the disguise of
" United Front " agencies. Controversy developed in particular
over the tactics to be followed in the Trade Unions, over the
question of the Trade Union Political Levy, and over the attitude

to be adopted towards the " Maxton-Cook " movement of 1928.
On the first of these issues there were disputes over the expediency
of forming " split " left-wing Trade Unions where the existing
Unions suppressed Communist activity or took disciplinary
action against Communist-led branches or sections. On the second
issue, some were for paying and others for refusing to pay the
Political Levy ; and some who advocated payment wanted a
campaign to persuade Trade Union branches to refuse to pay the
money over to the Unions' Political Funds, and to keep it instead
for local financing of Communist or other left-wing candidates.
On the third issue, some favoured giving full support to Cook
and Maxton, whereas others held that this would only serve to
weaken the Communist Party and to play into the hands of the I.L.P.

At this point the Communist International intervened by
ordering a sharp change in Communist policy, not only in Great
Britain but in all countries where the Social Democratic or Labour
political movements were strong. The Communist Parties were
told to give up United Front tactics and to take up a line of
forthright attack on the Social Democratic Parties. These instructions gave rise to a sharp cleavage in the ranks of the British
Communist Party, the majority of whose Central Committee
believed in the policy of boring from within the Labour Party and
the Trade Unions. Only in 1929 was the struggle resolved by the
victory of the minority executive group, led by Harry Pollitt
and Palme Dutt. There was a purge of the leadership ; and the
new " class against class " policy proposed by the Comintern was
endorsed. This included the establishment of a daily newspaper,
for which Moscow had long been pressing. The *Daily Worker*
was launched in January, 1930, after the second Labour Government had been some months in office.

On the opposite wing of the working-class movement, the
Co-operators were being attracted into closer relations with the
Labour Party as it emphasised the moderation of its claims. The
Co-operative Congress of 1925 had carried a resolution in favour
of a working arrangement with the Labour Party over candidates
and elections ; and an agreement drawn up by a Joint Committee
of the Labour and Co-operative Parties was accepted at the
Co-operative Congress of 1927 by a very narrow majority—
1,960,000 to 1,843,000. This agreement provided for a joint
committee to arrange electoral matters and prevent Labour-
Co-operative contests, and also for the conduct of joint campaigns. Under it, Local Co-operative Parties were to be eligible

for affiliation, where they so desired, to Divisional Labour Parties, with voting rights corresponding to the affiliation fees which they agreed to pay. Within the Divisional Parties, affiliated Co-operative Parties and Co-operative Political Councils were to have the same rights as other affiliated bodies in nominating and voting on candidates, and in other respects. There was to be no obligation on Co-operative Local Parties to affiliate to the D.L.P.s ; and where other arrangements were in being they were to stand unless they were altered by agreement. These arrangements did not work smoothly in all cases ; and there was a good deal of opposition to them in some Co-operative quarters because it was feared that they might prove a first step towards the absorption of the Co-operative Party into the Labour Party. On the whole however, relations between the Co-operators and the Labour Party improved, and the two allies entered into the Election of 1929 on the basis of a successful plan of mutual support. From 1925 the Co-operative Party, which had at the outset been kept in strict subordination to the Co-operative Union, was allowed to hold its own Annual Conference and to achieve a growing amount of autonomy, though it remained subject in the last resort to the Co-operative Congress. One great Co-operative Society—the Royal Arsenal—decided in 1927, instead of belonging to the Co-operative Party, to join the Labour Party direct as a national affiliated society ; and the Co-operative Congress was induced to accept the terms of the agreement with the Labour Party partly by fears of other Co-operative Societies following this lead. It was not, however, followed : the Co-operative Party retained its nominal independence and separateness, though there was obviously no room for two really separate Parties appealing to the same sections of the electorate with programmes that were largely the same. *Labour and the Nation*, as we have seen, pledged the Labour Party to strong support for Co-operative enterprise ; and the Co-operative Party had to rest content with the somewhat ambiguous status given to it by the agreement. On the other hand, the Labour Party Executive was not wholly satisfied. It would have liked to swallow the Co-operative Party whole ; but there was plainly no chance of getting any such policy accepted by the Co-operative Congress.

At this same Conference, there was trouble over the Labour Party League of Youth, of which the progress had been reported on with high hopes the previous year. The Executive was now refusing the request of a number of the Youth Sections that it should set up a national organisation of the League. The refusal was put on financial grounds ; but it was clear that there were also fears in the Executive's mind that a national youth organisation might wish to take matters too much into its own hands. In the discussion, after Ernest Bevin had spoken in support of the League's demands, Henderson promised to see what could be done to hold League rallies in London and perhaps elsewhere, and held out the hope of more definite action after the General Election was out of the way.

It remains to be mentioned that in 1926 the Joint Departments which had been set up in 1922 by the Labour Party and the Trades Union Congress for research, information, publicity, and various other services were wound up ; and thereafter each body established its own separate departments for these purposes. In 1928 the headquarters of both bodies were transferred from Eccleston Square to Transport House—the big new block of offices built in Smith Square, Westminster, by the Transport and General Workers' Union, which agreed to build them large enough to provide the requisite accommodation. In 1928–9 the Labour Party's share in responsibility for the *Daily Herald* was transferred to the Trades Union Congress, in order to facilitate the new arrangements for developing the paper which will be described in due course. Finally, in 1927, after the refusal of the I.L.P. to re-nominate Ramsay MacDonald, the Party leader, for the office of Treasurer had threatened to create an awkward situation by depriving him of his seat on the National Executive, it was decided that the Party leader should have a seat on the Executive *ex officio*, without the need for any special nomination.

(e) The General Election of 1929

The General Election of 1929 was the first to be fought on a basis of virtual Adult Suffrage, partly vitiated by the continuance of plural voting in respect of business and University qualifications. The Franchise Act of 1928 had extended the parliamentary vote to women on the same terms as men, thus enfranchising the younger women who had been left voteless in 1918—the so-called " flapper vote." The result of this, coupled with the rise in population, was an increase of the total electorate from 21,729,385 in 1924 to 28,943,566 in 1929, and of the numbers actually voting from 16,384,629 to 22,639,297. The electorate of

1929 was made up of 13,665,938 men and 15,277,628 women—a female majority of over 1,500,000.

Between 1924 and 1929 by-elections brought the Labour Party a net gain of ten seats, raising the number of Labour M.P.s from 152 to 162. This total takes account of two losses not due to by-elections—the expulsion of G. A. Spencer, the leader of the breakaway among the Nottinghamshire Miners, and the resignation from the party of Dr. Haden Guest, whose seat was lost in the ensuing by-election. The twelve by-election gains were spread fairly evenly over the years—one in 1925, four in 1926, one in 1927, three in 1928, and three again in 1929. In comparison with 1924 the General Election brought a gain of 138 seats ; and the Labour Party had nearly one hundred more seats than in the Parliament of 1923. For the first time Labour was the largest party, with twenty-nine more seats than the Conservatives ; but the fifty-eight Liberals and the eight M.P.s of other shades left it in a minority of thirty-eight in the House of Commons, and, of course, with an immense majority against it in the House of Lords. In these circumstances, there was no hesitation at all about taking office. There was no question of a coalition between the Liberals, now under Lloyd George's leadership, and the Tories : indeed, the Liberals, though there had been bitter warfare between them and the Labour candidates, had fought the election on a programme which, in respect of home affairs, was not so very different from that of Labour, and included fully as trenchant proposals for dealing with the unemployment problem. The Labour Programme, as we have seen, had put socialisation in the background (promising only to nationalise the mines if the Party were given a clear majority), and had concentrated mainly on social reform and foreign affairs, and on the unemployment issue. On this last the Liberals, with their " Yellow Book " proposals for economic development and their very energetic propaganda on the question of public action to expand employment, had largely stolen the Labour Party's thunder ; and only at the last moment did Labour put forward a pamphlet of its own, *How to Conquer Unemployment*, (which I wrote) explaining its employment proposals in any detail. The high quality and excellent presentation of the Liberal propaganda on this question did not greatly help the Liberal candidates in the Election ; but the tone they had taken put any coalition between them and the Tories quite out of the question for the time being.

Labour's total poll rose from 5,500,000 in 1924 to 8,365,000 in 1929. The Labour Party contested fifty-five more seats, and this time there were no unopposed returns. The Conservatives actually polled more votes than Labour—8,664,000—though they got fewer seats. The Liberals, with 512 candidates as against 343 in 1924, polled 5,301,000, and with only fifty-seven seats fared very badly in relation to their total vote. This was bound to happen to them, as the weakest of the three main parties, under the single-member constituency system of voting. Even so, they had sixteen more seats than in 1924, and, of course, were in a position to hold the balance of power.

The Communists, in pursuance of their new policy of all-out opposition to Labour, fought twenty-five seats, choosing particularly those held by Labour leaders who were specially obnoxious to them. Among those whom they opposed were MacDonald, Herbert Morrison, Attlee, Clynes, and Margaret Bondfield. No fewer than ten of their candidates were in Scotland : the rest were widely scattered. They did very badly, and their intervention cost the Labour Party at most two seats—Greenock, and possibly South-west Bethnal Green. Most of them forfeited their deposits, and a good many polled only a derisory vote. Thirty-five Labour candidates, fighting in backward areas, forfeited their deposits, as against twenty-eight in 1924, when fewer seats were fought.

In an Election in which all three main parties were fighting the great majority of the seats, a large number of members of all of them were naturally elected on a minority vote. The Labour Party published an analysis of the voting in 471 single-member constituencies in which more than two candidates went to the poll. This gave the following result :—

GENERAL ELECTION OF 1929 : ANALYSIS OF VOTING IN 471 SINGLE-MEMBER CONSTITUENCIES WHERE THERE WERE MORE THAN TWO CANDIDATES

	(a) Seats won by a Clear Majority	(b) Seats won on a Minority Vote	(c) Percentage of (a) to Total
Labour . . .	98	118	45.5
Conservative . .	60	150	28.6
Liberal . .	4	40	9.1
Independents . .	—	1	—

The Labour Party victors included nine women, out of fourteen in all returned to the new House of Commons.

The composition of the Labour Party was considerably changed, in respect of the balance between Trade Union, Socialist,and Divisional Labour Party representation. The representation of the Socialist Societies rose from thirty-three to thirty-seven, that of the Co-operative Party from four to nine, and that of the Trade Unions from 88 to 114. But the main increase was in Divisional Labour Party representation, which increased from 25 to 128. This increase was largely due to the Trade Unions Act of 1927, which forced some Unions (the Civil Servants) to run their candidates under D.L.P. auspices and many others to cut down their lists because of the depletion of their Political Funds. It was also partly due to secessions from the I.L.P. by candidates who disagreed with its new policy. MacDonald. Snowden and Attlee were among those who ceased to be I.L.P. candidates, and stood under the auspices of Divisional Parties, Over and above these factors, however, the increase in the share of the Divisional Parties was a natural result of electoral success, as they had always been given most of the more difficult seats to fight. The Trade Union candidates tended to get, if not safe, at any rate promising constituencies, because they were in a position to put up the money for organisation ; and therefore Trade Union representation tended to be more stable than that of the D.L.P.s. The Trade Unions Act, however, did a good deal to shift the balance in the Party. In particular, after 1929, the Miners' M.P.s were a much smaller fraction of the total than ever before.

Of the I.L.P.'s fifty-two candidates, no fewer than twenty-nine were in Scotland ; and of the thirty-seven who were elected seventeen sat for Scottish seats. The Divisional Labour Parties had only twenty Scottish candidates, of whom only seven secured election. To a considerable extent the I.L.P. still retained in Scotland, and especially on Clydeside, its old position of acting as the local constituency organisation of the Labour Party ; and the Divisional Labour Parties and the Labour Party's individual membership were comparatively little developed north of the Border. In 1928 the Labour Party had in all only about 215,000 individual members ; and very few of these were in Scotland. The I.L.P. and " the Clydesiders" were already coming to be used as to some extent interchangeable terms : I.L.P. influence was already waning in England. It remained considerable in Wales, though there was only one I.L.P. Member of Parliament for the whole Principality. This was largely because in Wales the Miners dominated the situation ; but it was also because the Welsh I.L.P. branches worked through the Divisional Labour Parties, whereas in Scotland the I.L.P. did its best to prevent the development of D.L.P. organisation that might endanger its influence.

Regionally, the greatest gains in 1929 were in Lancashire and in Greater London. Labour's representation in Lancashire and Cheshire rose by twenty-six to forty-four ; and in Greater London the increase was twenty-eight, to a total of fifty-four. Yorkshire recorded sixteen gains over 1924, the West Midlands fourteen (including six in Birmingham, against one loss), the East Midlands twelve, Scotland eleven and Wales nine. The North-east, where Labour had done well in 1924, had only six : the rest were widely dispersed. The whole of the South, South-west and West (excluding Greater London) showed eleven gains ; but over this great area Labour still held only thirteen seats out of ninety-four.

In general, the Election was more successful in terms of seats than many Labour supporters had ventured to hope. This was mainly because there were fewer Liberal victories than had been expected. Labour had been fairly confident of emerging as the largest party, but had expected the Conservatives to do worse than they did and the Liberals better. As it was, the weakness of the Liberals allowed a number of Labour candidates to get in on a minority vote. Conservative majorities remained very big in many of the residential and country areas, including the dormitory suburbs with their swollen electorates. Already the depression of the basic industries was beginning to depopulate some of the Labour strongholds ; and this partly accounts for the different distribution of total votes and total seats between Labour and Tory.

Among the Labour victors of 1929 was Sir Oswald Mosley, who, after sitting for Harrow from 1918 to 1924, first as a Conservative and then as an Independent, had been elected as Labour M.P. for Smethwick in 1926, and had set to work in hope of leading a movement to break the power of the Tory caucus in Birmingham. Mosley sat as an I.L.P. nominee, and was fairly closely associated at this stage with the I.L.P. Undoubtedly he and his group, which then included John Strachey, had a good deal to do with the Labour successes in the West Midlands at the 1929 Election. Mosley, however, did not succeed in establishing any lasting leadership, such as he aimed at, in Joseph

Chamberlain's old Radical stronghold. The West Midland Labour Members were a mixed bag, and by no means all endorsed his leadership.

LABOUR PROGRESS AT BY-ELECTIONS BETWEEN THE GENERAL ELECTIONS OF 1924 AND 1929

	Held	Won	Lost	2nd in three-corner	3rd in three-corner	2nd in straight fight	Not fought
1924	1						
1925	1	1		1	3	1	
1926	3	4	–	–	4	2	4
1927	–	1	1*	3	2	1	1
1928	3	3	–	7	6	–	–
1929	2	3	–	2	1	–	1
	10	12	2†	13	16	4	6

*A second seat was lost by the withdrawal of the Labour Party Whip from G. A. Spencer.

†Dr. Haden Guest resigned from the Labour Party in 1927 and fought a by-election as an Independent. Both he and the Labour candidate were beaten.

LABOUR AT THE GENERAL ELECTION OF 1929

	Won	Lost	Not fought	Communist etc. Candidates	Gains over 1924
Scotland . .	37*	31	3	10	11
North-east .	22	6	—	2	6
North-west .	3	3	—	—	2
Lancs. and Cheshire .	44†	32	4	2	26
Yorkshire .	40	14	3	2	16
East Midlands .	22	16	1	1	12
West Midlands .	25	21	1	2	14
Eastern Counties	4	24	2	—	3
London County and City .	36	22	4	4	17
Greater London	18	21	1	1	11
South . .	5	51	1	—	5
South-west .	1	15	—	—	1
West . .	7	13	1	—	5
Wales . .	25	8	2	3	9
N. Ireland .	—	—	12	—	—
Universities .	—	3	9	—	—
	289	280	44	27	138

*Including Neil Maclean, who fought as Independent Labour.

†Including Sir W. Jowitt, who was elected as a Liberal, but joined the Labour Party The Labour Party lost only four Labour seats (N. Midlothian [won in a by-election] E. Newcastle, King's Norton and N.E. Bethnal Green).

LABOUR PARTY : BODIES SPONSORING CANDIDATES, 1929

	Candidates	Elected	Increases over 1924
I.L.P. . . .	52	37	8
Other Socialist Societies	—	—	—·4
D.L.P. . . .	361	128	103
Co-op Party . .	12	9	5
M.F.G.B. . . .	43	42	1
N.U.R. . . .	10	8	5
R.C.A. . . .	7	7	7
T. & G.W.U. . .	11	7	1
W.U.	6	6	3
N.U.G.M.W. . .	8	6	2
A.S.W. . . .	6	5	3
N.U.D.A.W. . .	5	4	—
U.T.F.W.A. . .	6	4	2
B.I.S.A.K.T.A. . .	5	4	1
N.U.B.S.O. . .	5	2	2
U.B.M.S. . . .	3	2	—
L.S.C. . . .	2	2	—
A.E.U. . . .	3	2	—2
Other Unions . .	16	13	1
Total T.U.s . .	136	114	26
Total	561	288	138

CHAPTER VII

THE SECOND LABOUR GOVERNMENT
AND THE CRISIS OF 1931

(a)   *The Second Labour Government*

Composition of the Government—The process of Cabinet-making—Jowett and Wheatley dropped—The position of George Lansbury—Old and new blood—The ex-Liberals—Wheatley's death—MacDonald's policy—The Government's first session—A moderate programme—The quesion of the rebel Guardians—The Government and the Parliamentary Party—Pensions and Unemployment Benefits—The Economic Advisory Council—Relations resumed with the Soviet Union—The Five-Power Naval Conference—Public Works projects—The Coal Mines Bill—The Education Bill—Trouble over the non-provided schools—The Consumers' Council Bill—The Forty-eight Hours Bill—Snowden's Budget of 1930—The Housing Bill—Private Members' Bills—Indian affairs—The question of " Dominion status "—Reparations : the Young Plan and the Hague Conferences—Trade development—The Optional Clause signed—Mounting figures of unemployment—The Wall Street crisis of 1929—The Government's employment policy—I.L.P. criticism—Snowden's fiscal and free trade policy—The gold standard—The decline of world trade—Snowden's position in the Government—Revolt in the Labour Party—The " Mosley Memorandum " of 1930—What Mosley proposed—His resignation from the Government—MacDonald takes over employment policy—Lansbury's position—Trevelyan resigns—The employment issue at the Labour Party Conference of 1930—The debate on " Mosley "—The " Mosley Manifesto " and the New Party—The Ashton by-election—The Labour Government's second year—The legislative programme and its fortunes—The Education Bill—The Trade Union Bill—The Electoral Reform Bill—The London Passenger Transport Bill—The Agricultural Marketing Bill and the Land Utilisation Bill—The Taxation of Land Values—India : the Round Table Conference—The End of Civil Disobedience—Ratification of the General Act—The Liberals and the unemployed—The Royal Commission on Unemployment Insurance reports—The " Anomalies " Act—The Labour Party and the I.L.P.—The position of the I.L.P. Parliamentary Group—An unresolved conflict—The Parliamentary Labour Party's Standing Orders—The Labour Party and the Communists—The " Black Circular "—Activities of the Comintern—The Labour Party's individual membership—Reorganisation of the *Daily Herald*.

(b)   *The Crisis of 1931*

The burden of unemployment—Reactions on the national finances—Borrowing for the Unemployment Fund—Proposals of the Royal Commission on Unemployment Insurance—Philip Snowden's financial policy—His alarmist speech of February 1931—His second Budget evades the problem—The appointment of the May Committee—The May Committee reports—Cuts proposed in unemployment benefit, social services, and teachers' pay—The Cabinet Economy Committee—Consultations with Tories and Liberals—The drain on sterling begins—Snowden insists on the maintenance of the gold standard—Borrowing from New York and Paris—Attitude of the American bankers—Pressure on the Cabinet to accept the May proposals—MacDonald asks for the resignation of the Cabinet—Formation of the " National " Government—MacDonald's attitude discussed—Snowden's attitude compared with it—The Labour Cabinet and the crisis—The part played by the American and French bankers—and by the Bank of England—Snowden's account of the crisis—Judgment on Snowden and MacDonald—and on the Labour Government as a whole.

(c) *The General Election of 1931*

The "National" Government and its mandate—Composition of the new Cabinet—The position of Lloyd George—Snowden's emergency Budget—The run on the pound continues—The Gold Standard suspended—Continuance of the economic crisis—The Tories raise the tariff question—and force a General Election—The "doctor's mandate"—Henderson elected as leader of the Labour Party—Labour in the House of Commons under the new régime—Snowden's vendetta—The General Election campaign—Election *canards*—Snowden's election campaign—Voting in the General Election—Distribution of votes and seats—The Coalition against Labour—Analysis of Labour contests—The Liberal split—Simonites, Samuelites, and Lloyd Georgites—The fate of the "New Party"—Mosley's defeat—Failure of the Communists—The I.L.P. fights as a separate party—The split in the I.L.P.—The changed composition of the Parliamentary Labour Party—Regional analysis of Labour's fortunes—How "National Labour" fared—The Labour Party bereft of its leaders, except Lansbury—Its weakness in the new Parliament.

THE LABOUR GOVERNMENT OF 1929

The Cabinet		Office in 1924 Government
Prime Minister	*J. Ramsay MacDonald	Prime Minister and Foreign Secretary
Foreign Secretary	*Arthur Henderson	Home Secretary
Lord President of the Council	*Lord Parmoor	Lord President
Lord Chancellor	Lord Sankey	
Lord Privy Seal	*J. H. Thomas	Colonial Secretary
Chancellor of the Exchequer	*Philip Snowden	Chancellor of the Exchequer
Home Secretary	*J. R. Clynes	Lord Privy Seal
Dominions and Colonial Secretary	*Lord Passfield (Sidney Webb)	President of the Board of Trade
Secretary for War	*Thomas Shaw	Minister of Labour
Secretary for India	W. Wedgwood Benn	
Secretary for Scotland	*W. Adamson	Secretary for Scotland
Secretary for Air	*Lord Thomson	Secretary for Air
Minister of Health	Arthur Greenwood	Parliamentary Secretary, Ministry of Health
Minister of Labour	Margaret Bondfield	Parliamentary Secretary, Ministry of Labour
Minister of Agriculture	*Noel Buxton	Minister of Agriculture
President of the Board of Education	*Sir Charles Trevelyan	President of the Board of Education
President of the Board of Trade	William Graham	Financial Secretary to the Treasury
First Lord of the Admiralty	A. V. Alexander	Parliamentary Secretary, Board of Trade
First Commissioner of Works	George Lansbury	

*Members of the 1924 Cabinet.

Not in the Cabinet (selected names)

Chancellor of the Duchy of Lancaster	Sir Oswald Mosley	
Minister of Transport	Herbert Morrison	
Minister of Pensions	F. O. Roberts	Minister of Pensions

Postmaster-General	H. B. Lees-Smith	
Paymaster-General	Lord Arnold	Under-Secretary, Colonial Office
Attorney-General	Sir William Jowitt	
Solicitor-General	Sir J. B. Melville	
Financial Secretary to the Treasury	F. W. Pethick-Lawrence	
Under-Secretary for Foreign Affairs	Hugh Dalton	
Under-Secretary for Scotland	Thomas Johnston	
Secretary for Mines	Ben Turner	
Parliamentary Secretary to the Ministry of Agriculture	Christopher Addison	
Parliamentary Secretary to the Ministry of Health	Susan Lawrence	
Under-Secretary, Dominions Office	Arthur Ponsonby	Under-Secretary, Foreign Office

John Wheatley, F. W. Jowett and J. C. Wedgwood, who served in the Cabinet in 1924, were dropped. So were Clement Attlee, who was busy with the Simon Commission on Indian Reform, and E. Shinwell, among those who had occupied minor posts in 1924. Attlee became Chancellor of the Duchy of Lancaster in 1930 in succession to Oswald Mosley. Sir Stafford Cripps succeeded Sir James Melville as Solicitor-General in 1930 ; and Christopher Addison succeeded Noel-Buxton as Minister of Agriculture the same year. Vernon Hartshorn, who had been in the 1924 Cabinet as Post-master-General, became Lord Privy Seal, with a seat in the Cabinet, in 1930, when J. H. Thomas became Dominions Secretary on the separation of that office from that of Colonial Secretary. On Lord Thomson's death in the air disaster of 1930, Lord Amulree took his place as Secretary for Air. E. Shinwell again became Secretary for Mines in 1930, in succession to Ben Turner.

(a) *The Second Labour Government*

The Labour Government which took office in June, 1929, consisted largely of the same persons as had held leading positions in its predecessor of 1924. Of the nineteen members of the Cabinet, twelve had been in the previous Cabinet, and four others had held minor office in the first Labour Government. The newcomers were Lord Sankey, as Lord Chancellor, in place of Lord Haldane, who had died ; Wedgwood Benn, a convert from Liberalism, at the India Office ; and George Lansbury, who had been left out in 1924, at the Office of Works. The four who were brought into the Cabinet, having previously held minor posts, were Arthur Greenwood, Margaret Bondfield, A. V. Alexander, and William Graham. Herbert Morrison, as Minister of Transport, was not in the Cabinet : Clement Attlee was busy with the Indian Commission : Vernon Hartshorn was ill ; John Wheatley and F. W. Jowett and Colonel Wedgwood, who had been in the Cabinet in 1924, were dropped—Wheatley and Jowett because of their strong support of the I.L.P.'s " Socialism Now " programme.

Other newcomers who had not held office in 1924 included Hugh Dalton, as Under-Secretary for Foreign Affairs, and Sir Oswald Mosley, as Chancellor of the Duchy of Lancaster, who was specially associated with J. H. Thomas and George Lansbury in a Cabinet Committee on the employment problem. Sir William Jowitt, who had been elected as a Liberal, crossed the floor of the House to join the Government as Attorney-General. Christopher Addison, another ex-Liberal, took for the time the modest office of Parliamentary Secretary to the Ministry of Agriculture under Noel Buxton, but presently succeeded to Buxton's office.

There was considerable trouble behind the scenes over Cabinet-making, which was conducted by MacDonald in consultation with J. H. Thomas, Snowden, and Henderson. MacDonald was determined not to have Wheatley, and overbore the others, who were inclined to think he might be less trouble inside the Cabinet than outside. MacDonald wished to have J. H. Thomas at the Foreign Office, which Henderson very much wanted ; and he attempted to persuade Henderson to become Lord Privy Seal, in charge of employment policy. Henderson refused this ; and MacDonald then said he would take the Foreign Office himself. Henderson thereupon threatened to refuse office altogether ; and he finally won his point and became Foreign Secretary, Thomas taking the position of Lord Privy Seal. MacDonald wanted Lansbury in the Government, as a sop to the left wing, in view of Wheatley's exclusion. Snowden, in his *Autobiography*, characteristically remarks that he and MacDonald agreed that Lansbury could not be put in charge of any important department, because " the stigma of ' Poplarism ' still clung to him." Snowden added, " I suggested that he might be given the Office of Works . . . He would not have much opportunity of squandering money, but he would be able to do a good many small things which would improve the amenities of government buildings and the public parks." So Lansbury was offered the Office of Works, but consented only on condition of a seat in the Cabinet and a share in shaping the Government's employment policy.

Ramsay MacDonald in the end did not attempt again to double the parts of Prime Minister and Foreign Secretary. Arthur Henderson, at the Foreign Office, soon made a great international reputation. Snowden was again at the Exchequer ; and others who resumed their former offices included Charles Trevelyan at the Board of Education, Lord Thomson at the Air Ministry, William Adamson at the Scottish Office, and Lord Parmoor, as Lord President, as well as Noel Buxton. The other leaders were shuffled round—Clynes to the Home Office, Sidney Webb (as Lord Passfield) to the Colonial Office, Tom Shaw to the War Office, A. V. Alexander to the Admiralty, J. H. Thomas to be Lord Privy Seal, but to deal mainly with employment. Arthur Greenwood was promoted to the Ministry of Health, and William Graham to the Board of Trade ; and Margaret Bondfield, at the Ministry of Labour, became the first woman to hold Cabinet office.

The team, then, was not very different from that of 1924, though it was differently grouped. But this time no one from outside the Party was given a seat in the Cabinet, as Lord Chelmsford had been in the first Labour Government. Wedgwood Benn, indeed, was almost a newcomer, and Lord Sankey was an ex-Tory, but had been regarded as a Labour supporter since his Chairmanship of the Coal Commission in 1919. Charles Trevelyan had come over soon after the war, and Addison, an ex-Liberal and Coalition Cabinet Minister, had joined the Labour Party soon after the fall of the Coalition in 1922 : Mosley, after a period as an Independent, had become a Labour M.P. in 1926. Other ex-Liberals in minor offices included H. B. Lees-Smith and Lord Arnold.

If there was a difference between the first and second Labour Governments, it lay mainly in the exclusion of the I.L.P. leaders, Wheatley and Fred Jowett ; for Wheatley had been a leading figure in the 1924 Cabinet and had been responsible for its out-standing legislative success. The only known " left winger " in the 1929 Cabinet was George Lansbury, though Trevelyan was soon to acquire a reputation for " leftism." On the whole, the second Labour Cabinet was to the right of its predecessor, in correspondence with the rightward trend of the Party, under MacDonald's leadership, during the intervening years. Wheatley's exclusion might have led to much trouble had he not fallen ill and died in 1930. His loss left a serious void, and was particularly disastrous to the I.L.P., in which he had been the outstanding parliamentary figure since 1924. Maxton with Wheatley to advise him and Maxton without Wheatley were two very different propositions.

MacDonald, in forming his second Government, was determined to have no arrangement with the Liberals, such as had existed informally in 1924. According to Snowden's *Autobiography*, he even coquetted with the idea of coming to some arrangement with the Tories to promise the Government a sufficient lease of power to make the taking of office worth while. If he did have such an idea, nothing came of it ; and his immediate confidants were as much against it as the Party as a whole would certainly have been. The second Labour Government took office without any understanding with either of the other parties, but of course in dependence on some Liberal or Tory votes to maintain it in power.

The new Parliament met for the swearing-in of Members on June 25, and the session was formally opened on July 2. The King's Speech began with references to the new (Young) Reparations Plan, which was meant to supersede the Dawes Plan of 1924, to naval disarmament, to international arbitration and the signing of the Optional Clause of the League Covenant, and to the resumption of relations with the Soviet Union. It then went on to refer to the Government's intention to " deal effectively " with unemployment, and to undertake large schemes of economic development with this end in view. It announced that proposals would be made for the reorganisation of the coal industry, including public ownership of the minerals (but not of the mines). Inquiries would be set on foot into the iron and steel and cotton industries " in order to discover means for co-operating with them to improve their position in the markets of the world." A new Factory Bill would be introduced, and also a Bill to ratify the Washington Forty-eight Hours Convention. Fresh provision would be made for slum clearance, and for urban and rural housing. There was to be a Royal Commission on the Drink Traffic. The Widows' and Old Age Pensions Act passed by the Tories in 1925 was to be amended : a measure was to be introduced " to remedy the situation caused by the Trade Disputes and Trade Unions Act of 1927 " ; and there was to be an inquiry into Electoral Law, with a view to further reforms.

This was an essentially moderate programme, with no hint in it of any sort of " Socialism Now." The Tories moved a protectionist amendment dealing with safeguarding and the McKenna duties, and were beaten by 340 to 220. The Liberals limited themselves to an amendment dealing with Scottish local government, which the Tories did not support. The Government had decided to restrict itself to a short sitting of Parliament before the summer recess, taking only a few very urgent matters and giving the Ministers time for departmental preparation for an autumn session. These immediate measures included a temporary amendment of the Unemployment Insurance Acts, increasing the State contribution to the Fund ; a Development Act authorising grants up to £25,000,000 and a further £25,000,000 in guarantees for schemes of public works designed to increase employment ; a parallel Colonial Development Act authorising grants up to £1,000,000 a year for schemes in the Colonies ; a measure continuing at the existing levels the subsidies under the Housing Acts, which the Tories had threatened to reduce ; and a removal of the appointed Guardians whom the Tories had put in office in place of the elected Boards in West Ham, Chester-le-Street and Bedwellty. It was also announced that Thomas, aided by Lansbury and Mosley, would have charge of employment policy ; that the school-leaving age would be raised to 15 in 1931 ; and that the naval building programme would be at once reduced. Moreover, MacDonald would visit the United States in order to discuss further naval disarmament with the President. All these things were done without much parliamentary difficulty, though not without strong Tory protests over the naval reductions and over the removal of the appointed Boards of Guardians.

An important issue arose over the position of the Parliamentary Labour Party in relation to the Government. In opposition, the Party had its own Executive Committee, which reported to a full weekly meeting of Members. It was persuaded to suspend its weekly meeting in order to give the Government a freer hand ; and the Executive was replaced by a Consultative Committee of M.P.s on which a number of members of the Government were to serve.

In the autumn session, for a time all appeared to be going well. The Widows' and Old Age Pensions Act was successfully amended to cover some hundreds of thousands of additional pensioners, under improved conditions. A further Unemployment Insurance Act re-drafted the terms of benefit, so as to remove the major part of the grievance relating to the disqualification of persons alleged to be " not genuinely seeking work." Other measures successfuly carried through in 1929–30 included the Road Traffic

Act, the Land Drainage Act, and the Public Works Facilities Act (conferring easier borrowing powers). An informal group, which developed in 1930 into an Economic Advisory Council, composed of leading economists, accountants, employers, and Trade Unionists, with members of the Cabinet, was set up under the Prime Minister to advise him confidentially on general economic policy, but was left entirely unrelated to the organisation of the departments, and was given practically no staff. Diplomatic relations with the Soviet Union were resumed in November, 1929. The Prime Minister's *démarche* in the United States was followed by the Five-Power Naval Conference of January, 1930, and by the agreements of April, involving agreed naval reductions by Great Britain, the United States and Japan, but not by France or Italy, which stood out against the ratios proposed. A number of projects were put forward for the development of public works programmes, up to the imposing total of £135,000,000 in loans and guarantees, including £50,000,000 for road works, £47,000,000 to be spent through the Unemployment Grants Committee, which was strengthened and given statutory powers, £28,000,000 for other home development schemes, £8,000,000 for Colonial Development, and £2,000,000 to be spent in other ways. The home schemes were related mainly to railways, docks, water, gas and electricity. This expenditure, however, even if it all matured, was meant to be spread over a considerable number of years. Owing to the long time taken in getting plans to the point of actual execution, the immediate effect on employment was negligible ; and even the longer-run effect could not be very great. As we shall see, the plans proved to be quite inadequate in face of the rapid spread of world depression during the Government's two years of office.

These were, or seemed at the time, the Government's relative successes. It was soon in trouble over other measures—especially over its Coal Mines Bill. A promise had been given to repeal the Eight Hours Act passed after the General Strike, and to restore the Seven Hours Act of 1919. But it at once appeared that the colliery owners would meet any such measure with drastic wage-reductions, which the Miners' Federation would not be strong enough to resist ; and the Government persuaded the Miners' Federation to agree to a seven-and-a-half hours compromise, on condition that it was coupled with the establishment of a National Wages Board. To such a Board the owners, set on district agreements, offered strong opposition. The Government wished to include in its Bill provision for joint marketing schemes in the various coalfields, in order to eliminate price-cutting ; and these were to be accompanied by quota arrangements, assigning limits to the output of each district and of each pit, and by a system of levies designed to assist exports and to enable the worse-situated districts to pay a tolerable minimum wage.   The Liberals wanted provision for amalgamations, to be carried through, in default of voluntary action by the owners, under a Coal Mines Reorganisation Commission.   This had been left out of the first draft of the Bill ; but new clauses covering amalgamations were inserted to meet the Liberal criticism.

The Coal Bill was throughout a compromise, meant to give the owners as well as the miners a part of what they wanted.   In effect, it set up a national coal cartel, and conferred on the owners large powers to regulate output and prices at the consumers' expense. The owners were ready enough, in most areas, to avail themselves of the Bill's advantages, though in some areas there was at first hot individualist hostility to the proposals ; but they were by no means prepared in return to swallow either the National Wages Board, or the proposed levy, or compulsory amalgamations.   In the House of Commons, the Bill met with heavy opposition.   The second reading was carried only by 281 votes to 273.   In com-mittee, the proposal for a central levy to subsidise the weaker areas was defeated by 282 to 274 ; and a number of other changes were made.   The third reading was carried by 277 to 234 ; but when the Bill went to the House of Lords it was badly mutilated, the Lords striking out the remaining levy proposals and introducing what proved to be crippling changes in the amalgamation provisions.   The Government accepted these alterations in order to save the Bill ; but, in face of the owners' determined refusal, the National Wages Board never operated.

In the course of the 1930 session other serious troubles developed in the Commons.   The Government's Education Bill, bogged in controversy over the position of Catholic and Church schools and over maintenance allowances, had to be withdrawn ; and the same fate overtook the Bill for the setting up of a Consumers' Council with power to collect evidence about costs and prices, in order to check monopolistic exploitation.   The Bill for rati-fication of the Washington Forty-eight Hours Convention was also withdrawn.

Meanwhile, Snowden's Budget of 1930 had to provide for substantially increased expenditure, due largely, not to the

Labour Government's measures, which had not yet matured, but to the deficit and commitments left over by its predecessor. Snowden raised the standard rate of income tax from 4s. od. to 4s. 6d. and increased the surtax, while making concessions to the smaller taxpayers ; but he made no major changes in the tax system this year. The Tories strongly attacked his measures for the avoidance of tax evasion, and indeed bitterly criticised the entire Budget ; but it went through with Liberal support. The Government's major measure of the session was its Housing Act, which set on foot a large scheme of state-aided slum clearance with valuable long-term effects, but without any great immediate contribution to solving the unemployment problem.

Meanwhile, Labour M.P.s were pressing for other reforms, by means of Private Members' Bills. Of these one, providing for holidays with pay, was put off with a promise of official inquiry with a view to legislation ; and the same fate befell a Bill providing for the regulation of hours of work in shops. The Labour Party's old standby, the Local Authorities Enabling Bill, designed to give wide powers of municipal trading without the need for *ad hoc* legislation in every case, was refused facilities on the ground that the matter involved many complications, which could be dealt with only in a fully considered Government Bill. The intention to proceed with important measures of agricultural development was announced ; but the required Bills needed much preparation.

In June, 1930, the Reports of the Indian Statutory Commission were published, and disappointed a good many Labour people, especially in view of Attlee's participation in them. Before this, in March, the Indians had launched their campaign of Civil Disobedience, in view of continued repression ; and the Indian situation was going from bad to worse. The Parliamentary Party, in its Report to the Party Conference of 1930, recorded its " disappointment " with the Commission, and its " anxiety " over the whole situation, but pinned its hopes on the Round Table Conference, which was to meet in the autumn with the participation of the Indian leaders. Even so, the Parliamentary Party, though critical of the Commission, only went so far as to state that " the Party's aim is to see India take its full place in the British Commonwealth of Nations." This fitted in with the Viceroy's declaration, made at the Labour Government's instance, that British policy for India had " Dominion status " as its objective. At the Conference the I.L.P. moved a resolution calling, *inter alia*, for the recognition of India's right to independence and for the immediate ending of repression and the transfer of political power to Indian hands ; but the Previous Question was carried on the resolution and on an amendment less critical of the Government. This was done on the motion of the Miners' Federation, presumably in order to leave MacDonald a free hand at the Round Table Conference. At any rate, that was the effect.

In May, 1930, the Young Plan for a revision of Germany's obligations in respect of Reparations came into force, after Snowden, at the Hague Conferences of August, 1929, and January, 1930, had secured much praise in unexpected quarters for his success in getting Great Britain an improved share in the revised payments—a success achieved only at the expense of Great Britain's war allies. In April a commercial treaty was concluded with the Soviet Union, and the establishment of an Overseas Trade Development Council was announced. Export Credits had already been extended to cover dealings with the Soviet Union ; and there were high hopes of an expansion of international trade. William Graham, as President of the Board of Trade, was busy negotiating through the League of Nations for a Tariff Truce. At Geneva the Disarmament negotiations, which had come to a standstill, were taken up again, and in November, 1930, the Preparatory Commission for the proposed Disarmament Conference resumed work. The Labour Government, in 1929, had already signed the Optional Clause of the League Covenant, together with the other members of the British Commonwealth ; and the British Government took the lead in advocating measures to harmonise the Covenant with the Kellogg Pact for the renunciation of war. Despite its difficulties with Parliament and in India, the Labour Party head office felt itself able to issue, under the title *What the Labour Government Has Done*, a very self-congratulatory account of the first year's work.

Through 1930, however, the figures of unemployment were persistently rising ; and it was becoming evident that the schemes which had been set on foot would be quite ineffective in bringing them down, even when there had been time for them to produce their full effect. In June, 1929, when the Labour Government took office, the registered unemployed in Great Britain and Northern Ireland numbered 1,163,000, or 9.6 per cent of the insured population. A year later they numbered 1,912,000 or 15.4 per cent ; and by December the total was up to 2,500,000, or practically 20 per cent. This was a much larger figure than had been recorded at the height of the troubles in 1926, or indeed at any time since the insurance scheme was instituted. Since January, 1922, the total had been always below 2,000,000 ; and since 1927 it had not exceeded 1,500,000, and had been often below 1,250,000. Unemployment, under a Labour Government which had promised drastic action to deal with it, had more than doubled in eighteen months.

Of course, this increase was not due to the Labour Government, and in some countries the situation was a good deal worse. The rise in unemployment was due to world causes, and was the advance sign of the world-wide crisis which was to break the following year. The first great Wall Street crash had occurred well before the end of 1929, and the withdrawal of American finance from Europe and the shortage of dollars which accompanied it were already threatening to bring the whole structure of world economy crashing in ruins. Nevertheless, for a Government which had vied with the Liberals in loud assertion of its ability to solve the unemployment problem, the mounting figures of enforced idleness were serious in the extreme ; and the efforts of J. H. Thomas to put the best face on what the Government was doing served only to make its achievement look the more pitiful.

From the first, the Labour Government was between two fires over its handling of the unemployment problem. On the one hand it had to face the criticisms of its own left wing, which regarded unemployment as a by-product of capitalism, incurable within the capitalist system, and demanded a frontal attack on capitalism, either in the form of extensive socialisation of industry or in the I.L.P. form of bankrupting capitalist industries by insistence on a Living Wage, and then taking over every section that defaulted on this obligation ; and on the other hand it was continually pressed by the Liberals, who believed that the problem could be solved under capitalism by a combination of reformed credit and banking policy, public control and stimulation of investment, and public works on a scale which Snowden, who would have had to raise the money, regarded as prohibitively expensive. In facing these critics the Government had to take account of the gold standard, to which Churchill had brought Great Britain back in 1925, and of the fact that Snowden believed fanatically in the gold standard and would sanction nothing that might endanger its maintenance. With the gold standard in force, any fall in world prices or demand meant reducing the prices of British exports in terms of pounds, shillings and pence ; and this meant not only that wages could not be raised, but also pressure to reduce them steadily as the world situation got worse. Moreover, as long as Great Britain adhered to Free Trade and put practically no restriction on imports, every contraction in world demand set other industrial countries competing more keenly in the British home market as well as in other export markets, and involved an attempt to dump surplus goods in Great Britain, at the same time as other countries were putting additional restrictions on their imports either by raising tariffs or by direct or financial controls. Snowden, however, believed as fanatically in Free Trade as in the gold standard, and would agree to nothing that would interfere with either.

In these circumstances, it was utterly impossible to check the rise in unemployment, which followed partly on export dumping in the British home and export markets and partly on the necessity of internal deflation in order to maintain the rates of exchange in face of falling world prices. Either going off the gold standard or a drastic policy of restrictions on imports might have made some contribution to dealing with the problem, though neither could have prevented Great Britain from feeling some of the effects of the developing world crisis. When Snowden would have no truck with either expedient, there was no alternative left to allowing unemployment to go on rising until the arrival of the inevitable financial crisis that would force the country to act in sheer self-preservation.

Why, it may be asked, was the situation not dealt with by overriding, and if necessary replacing, Philip Snowden ? The answer is, first, that Snowden held a very strong position in the Party as its one recognised financial expert, as well as on the strength of his reputation for Socialist inflexibility. Neither MacDonald nor most of the other members of the Cabinet had any understanding of finance, or even thought they had. Graham, who had and saw the problem, was too weak to stand up to Snowden. Thomas wanted a tariff, which was anathema to most of the Labour Party as well as to the Liberals, but had no grasp of the financial problem. Henderson was too busy on foreign affairs to pay much attention to economic problems, and was, in any case, never consulted by MacDonald about such matters. The Economic Advisory Council, of which I was a member, discussed the situation again and again ; and some of us, including Keynes, tried to get MacDonald to understand the sheer necessity of adopting some definite policy for stopping the rot. Snowden was inflexible ; and MacDonald could not make up his mind, with the consequence that Great Britain drifted steadily towards a disaster of whose imminence the main body of Labour M.P.s and of the Labour movement were wholly unaware. All these troubles came to a head only in 1931 ; but they were there in 1930, plainly to be seen by those who were prepared to look facts in the face.

The mounting total of unemployment began to provoke revolt inside the Labour Party ; and for a time the leadership in the revolt was taken by Sir Oswald Mosley, who, as Chancellor of the Duchy of Lancaster, was Thomas's second in command in handling the Government's employment policy. Mosley, who was then on the left wing of the Labour Party, soon fell out with Thomas, and, early in 1930, produced a Memorandum proposing an ambitious policy for combating unemployment. His principal recommendations centred round the expansion of purchasing power in the home market in order to increase demand, and the " insulation " of the British economy necessary for the carrying out of this policy. He wanted control of imports, either by tariffs or by direct limitation, bulk purchase agreements with overseas suppliers, especially in the Dominions and Colonies, and active development of home agriculture in order to reduce dependence on imports ; and he proposed the use of a liberal credit policy, to be ensured by public control of banking, a development of the social services and a more generous policy of pensions on retirement and of benefits and allowances, and a rationalisation of industry under public control in order both to increase exports and to make more goods available in the home market. Mosley's policy resembled at many points the " Socialism Now " programme of the I.L.P.—with which indeed he was actively associated at the time. It was, however, different in emphasis, being put forward not as a general Socialist programme, but as a set of measures designed to cope with unemployment. Right or wrong—and I feel sure it was largely right—it stood no chance of acceptance as long as Snowden was at the Exchequer. Snowden rejected it on at least three main grounds. It was far too expensive, and the estimates given in it were much too optimistic about the effects on production of an expansion of purchasing power. Secondly, its banking policy was inconsistent with gold standard economics—to which indeed Mosley and his supporters were strongly opposed. Thirdly—and this was in Snowden's eyes the worst offence of all—it involved giving up Free Trade and resorting to a regulated economy either for Great

Britain alone or for the British Empire, if the Empire countries could be brought in. On all these grounds Snowden fought the " Mosley Memorandum " tooth and nail.

I call it the " Mosley Memorandum," because that was the name by which it came to be universally known. In fact, however, it was written by Mosley in close conjunction with George Lansbury and with Thomas Johnston, who had been brought in to join the Government's employment policy team in order to represent Scottish interests. The Memorandum went to the Cabinet with Lansbury's (and I think with Johnston's) approval; and it took rank automatically as a Cabinet document, and therefore secret. It was speedily rejected by the Cabinet.

Thereupon Mosley resigned from the Government, in May, 1930, and made a forcible defence of his policy in the House of Commons. This was in effect a direct and powerful attack on the Government for its failure to tackle unemployment ; and it made a considerable impression. There was widespread feeling in the Party that the Government was making a poor showing over employment ; and, quite apart from Mosley's activities, criticism was already widespread both in the Local Labour Parties and in the Trade Unions. MacDonald had to recognise the force of the attack : indeed, he was himself seriously disturbed. J. H. Thomas was removed from his position in charge of employment policy, and became Dominions Secretary with the task of playing the main part in the forthcoming Imperial Conference. Attlee succeeded Mosley as Chancellor of the Duchy of Lancaster : Vernon Hartshorn was made Lord Privy Seal ; and MacDonald announced that he himself would undertake general supervision of the Government's employment policy, while leaving each department concerned to answer in the House on matters affecting its own activities. The Government also departed from its earlier attitude of making no arrangements with the other parties. MacDonald made a gesture in the hope of getting agreement to treat unemployment as a non-party issue. He invited both Tories and Liberals to confer with him on the measures that could be taken to meet the crisis. The Tories refused. The Liberals accepted, and were thereafter associated with an informal committee for discussion of employment and unemployment policies. This created much confusion ; for the talks with the Liberals overlapped both the Government's own discussions and the work of the Economic Advisory Council. All the proceedings were secret, and no committee knew what the others were doing. The handling of the problem, which was growing more serious every day, went from bad to worse.

The " Mosley Memorandum," being a Cabinet document, remained unpublished. But most of its contents leaked out and became a matter of lively debate throughout the Labour movement. Mosley, still inside the Labour Party though out of the Government, was energetically mobilising support ; and his backers were calling for publication of the Memorandum and for a full inquiry into it by the Labour Party Executive and the Trade Unions. Lansbury did not resign from the Government, but was known to be strongly in favour of a more vigorous policy. He ceased to have any special responsibility for employment policy after the Mosley crisis, and devoted himself to his job as First Commissioner of Works, making a great success of his efforts to improve amenities in the public parks and to humanise his hitherto lethargic department. " Lansbury's Lido," in Hyde Park, was a popular innovation ; and the Government was only too well pleased to have its leading left-wing member so harm-lessly occupied. The other left-wing member of the Cabinet, Sir Charles Trevelyan, stayed on for the time being, but resigned from the Government after its defeat, in January, 1931, on a Labour amendment to its Education Bill moved by the defenders of the Catholic schools, and the throwing out of the whole Bill by the House of Lords in March. Trevelyan, in resigning, emphasised his disagreement with the whole trend of the Government's policy, not only on education, but on other matters as well.

Long before this, the question of the " Mosley Memorandum " and of the Government's employment policy had come up at the Labour Party's Llandudno Conference of October, 1930. The General Workers there moved a resolution which, while careful to avoid censuring the Government and to recognise its difficulties, called for a more active policy, including " schemes of nationalisation " and " the vigorous application of all other proposals embodied in *Labour and the Nation.*" Andrew Naesmith, of the Weavers, seconded ; and then Maxton moved an I.L.P. amendment directly attacking the Government for its " timidity and vacillation in refusing to apply Socialist remedies." The amendment called for measures to increase the workers' purchasing power, to reduce working hours, to initiate a national housing programme, to extend credits to Russia and other countries, " and above all to socialise the basic industries and services, using the provision of work or adequate maintenance as its first basic principle." Finally, it urged that, "if necessary," an appeal should be made to the people—that is, an election on a clear and immediate Socialist programme of action. MacDonald replied in a cloudy speech, denying Maxton's antithesis between "Socialist" and "Capitalist" policies for dealing with the crisis, and asserting that "we never said you could draw a line between Socialism and Capitalism." Frank Wise followed with a detailed attack on the Government's failure to carry out even the moderate policy set forth in *Labour and the Nation*, with special stress on the failure to establish any control over the Bank of England or over financial policy. He accused the Bank of working in with the American bankers to defeat the policy of expansion, and arraigned the Government for leaving industrial reorganisation in the hands of the bankers instead of attempting to apply a Socialist policy. Clynes defended the Government, and counter-attacked the I.L.P. ; and then Ernest Bevin made a curious speech in which he first defended the "Mond-Turner" policy on the ground that it had enabled the Trade Unions to prove that industrial peace was no cure for unemployment, and then went on to insist that the Government "must accept the absolute principle of responsibility for unemployment" and to express his disappointment with J. H. Thomas and with what had been done. He wanted the Labour Party to "go out to the country and say, not merely that capitalism had broken down, but that . . . the employer could no longer find work : therefore send us back in order that the State may find it—not by Tariffs, not by Free Trade, but by a regulated industry, producing the things we need and exchanging them with other nations for the things they produce." More speeches followed ; and then the Conference rejected the I.L.P. amendment by 1,803,000 to 334,000 and carried the General Workers' resolution without a division—thus, if not censuring the Government, at all events calling upon it to follow a much more active policy.

This debate was immediately succeeded by a resolution calling for a full report on the Mosley proposals. This was moved by the Doncaster Labour Party, and gave Mosley the opportunity for a speech in defence of his projects. Strongly criticising the Government's "ambulance work" of relief, he said that its plans could not absorb more than 100,000 men, or one out of every ten who had been added to the unemployed since the Government took office. Mosley then described his own policy, stressing the point that it was " in direct conflict " with that of the Chancellor of the Exchequer. He argued that the Government would get very little public sympathy as long as it confined itself to mere relief works, but that if Labour would come out with " a great policy of permanent national reconstruction," their difficulties would be less and their support much greater. Mosley spoke for the most part with careful moderation, not claiming any finality for his plans, but urging that the Party as a whole should examine and improve upon them.

Lansbury, speaking uncomfortably for the Executive, explained why the " Mosley Memorandum " could not be published, said that he and Thomas Johnston had been parties to it, and urged Mosley to write and publish a fresh document covering the same ground. He questioned Mosley's figures about the amount of employment provided by the Government's measures, stressing indirect as well as direct effects on the demand for labour ; but he admitted that the Government could do no more for the main body of the unemployed than give them fair maintenance. He was too old a Socialist, he explained, to believe that they could cure unemployment under capitalism. Lansbury's heart was clearly not in his defence of the Government : his peroration was a plea for a campaign to get a Socialist public opinion that would make it practicable to attempt more radical methods.

The division on the Doncaster resolution was close. 1,046,000 voted for it, and 1,251,000 against. This was plain evidence of a very wide measure of support, if not for Mosley, at any rate for many of the ideas of which he had made himself spokesman. The results of the election for the new Party Executive drove home the lesson. Thomas was defeated : Sir Oswald Mosley secured election as a representative of the Local Parties in company with Lansbury, Herbert Morrison, Hugh Dalton, and George Dallas.

Sir Oswald Mosley continued his campaign, calling upon the Labour Party to adopt his proposals or at any rate to investigate them. After his resignation he had got the Parliamentary Labour Party to call a special meeting to discuss his plans and had made a highly effective speech criticising the Government's and the Party's inaction. Henderson, intent as usual on preserving unity in the Party, had made a sympathetic speech, evidently acknowledging the strength of Mosley's attack. He then appealed to Mosley to withdraw his motion, on the ground that he had made his point and would achieve more by not pressing it to a vote which could only be regarded as a censure on the Government by its own supporters. Mosley, however, insisted on a vote, and was decisively beaten, as he was almost bound to be ; for his success would have meant the break-up of the Party.

At this stage, Mosley was still affirming his loyalty to the Labour Party, and was endeavouring to build up his following within it, in the hope of winning over a majority and becoming the recognised leader of the left wing and in due course of the Party, when he had persuaded the majority to run the risk of overturning the Government by insisting on their point of view. During the ensuing months he continued his intrigues in the Party ; and by December he managed to get seventeen Labour M.P.s and Arthur Cook, the Miners' Secretary, to join in issuing the " Mosley Manifesto "—a demand for action on the lines of his earlier memorandum. Further Manifestoes followed, culminating in February, 1931, with a substantial pamphlet, under the title *A National Policy*, in which the policy of the " Memorandum " was for the first time presented in full to the public. It was announced as having been prepared to express the view of seventeen Labour M.P.s and to have been drafted, in collaboration with Mosley, by John Strachey, W. J. Brown, Aneurin Bevan, and Mosley's secretary, Allen Young.

It seems fairly clear that Mosley, though most of the Labour M.P.s who were working with him did not realise the fact, had by this time decided on a break with the Labour Party, having realised that he had no chance of winning more than a small fraction of the Parliamentary Party over to full support, as distinct from sympathy with many of his ideas. He overestimated greatly the number of the minority who would follow him in a breakaway party ; and he managed to convince himself that a new left-wing party under his leadership would sweep the country, or at the least would secure the allegiance of the main body of rank-and-file workers. At all events, he followed up his Manifestoes, after a further defeat at a meeting of the Parliamentary Party, by announcing that he was forming a New Party, under that name, on the basis of the programme outlined in the pamphlet on *A National Policy*.

Only four Labour M.P.s (and one Irish Unionist) followed him. These were his wife, Lady Cynthia Mosley, daughter of Lord Curzon, Oliver Baldwin, son of the Tory leader, Robert Forgan, and John Strachey. W. J. Brown, who had just been expelled from the Trade Union Group of M.P.s, refused to join the New Party; and so did Aneurin Bevan and most of the others who had supported the earlier Manifestoes. Strachey, who did join, resigned within a few weeks, when he discovered the nature of Mosley's real ambitions and the purposes which the New Party was meant to serve. Nor did Mosley's Labour support come to much in the country : his hopes of breaking the Labour Party and becoming the new Socialist leader were utterly disappointed ; and he soon began to change his tune and to develop openly dictatorial propensities. Before long he was to become the leader of British Fascism, the devout admirer of Mussolini and of Hitler, the " general " of a Blackshirt army in bitter opposition to the left-wing forces which he had hoped to lead.

For the time being, however, the New Party still preserved something of a left-wing façade. Mosley announced a great national campaign, with a view to putting 400 candidates in the field at the next General Election. Meantime, he proposed to fight by-elections against all comers. His first chance came in April, 1931, at Ashton-under-Lyne, a Labour seat vacated by the death of Albert Bellamy, the railwaymen's President. Allen Young fought the seat as a New Party candidate and, polling 4,472 votes, secured the election of a Conservative by a majority of 1,415 over the Labour candidate—the Liberals standing aside.

The establishment of the New Party of course involved the expulsion of Mosley and of those who had followed him from the Labour Party. It is indeed astonishing that the National Executive, of which he was a member, did not expel him at once, but first summoned him to attend and explain his conduct, and expelled him only when he had failed either to attend or to send any reply. This may have been partly because Mosley was ill ; but it was probably due even more to Henderson's desire to heal the breach with the minimum of defections, in the knowledge that disapproval of Mosley's tactics was accompanied by widespread sympathy for many elements in the policy he had put forward. The success of these tactics was marked. Even the Divisional Parties represented by the seceders did not support the New Party. Mosley, instead of leading a formidable breakaway, passed right out of the Labour Movement with singularly little disturbance.

The disappearance of the Mosley faction, however, did not in any way ease the Government's parliamentary difficulties, or help it to deal more effectively with the unemployment problem, The King's Speech of October, 1930, had announced a legislative programme for the Government's second year which included the taxation of land values, the amendment of the Trade Unions Act, the raising of the school-leaving age and other educational reforms, the Forty-eight Hours Bill, the Consumers' Council Bill, a measure of Electoral Reform, and two large-scale Agricultural Bills, dealing respectively with land utilisation and with agricultural marketing. This was a formidable list; but it included nothing specific for dealing with unemployment, except the announcement of a Royal Commission to report on Unemployment Insurance. The Tories moved an amendment calling attention to this omission, and were beaten by 281 to 250: the Liberals mostly abstained, but a few voted for the Tory motion and a few with the Government.

The programme was soon in difficulties. The Education Bill, as we have seen, became bogged in the controversy over Catholic and Church schools, and, after mutilation in the Commons, was defeated in the Lords. The Trade Unions Bill passed its second reading by the narrow majority of twenty-seven, and was so hacked about by Liberals and Tories in committee that the Government had to abandon it. The Representation of the People Bill, which included provision for the Alternative Vote, as well as for the abolition of plural voting, for the reduction of permitted election expenses, and for a number of other reforms, was severely mauled, first in the Commons and then in the Lords, and was still under discussion when the Government fell. The Consumers' Council Bill was forced through committee against heavy opposition, but was still awaiting report when the crisis killed it. The London Passenger Transport Bill, based on private Bills brought forward before 1929, went to a Joint Select Committee of Lords and Commons, and was similarly left unfinished. The Agricultural Marketing Bill, providing for the establishment of Marketing Boards under the control of the farmers, became law; but the Land Utilisation Bill was heavily amended in the House of Lords, which struck out most of the essential clauses, including those dealing with the formation of a public Farming Corporation, with the establishment of Demonstration Farms, and with land reclamation, besides crippling the part of the Bill providing for a national Small Holdings policy. Most of these clauses were eventually put back, and accepted by the Lords in a revised form; but the State Farming Corporation had to be jettisoned in order to save the Bill. The Land Tax proposals, which were included in the Finance Bill, were carried after a severe struggle, but never became operative owing to the Government's fall.

The Round Table Conference on India, which had begun in the autumn of 1930 without the participation of the National Congress, was adjourned in January, 1931 ; and a fresh attempt was made to secure a reopening of negotiations with the Congress and a suspension of the Civil Disobedience movement, which had continued throughout its sittings. This was achieved in April, 1931, and it was announced that the Round Table Conference would be resumed in the autumn, with good hope of Gandhi and the other Congress leaders taking part. In March, against Conservative opposition, the Government secured a vote for the ratification of the General Act, accepting arbitration in non-justiciable international disputes.

The Government, in addition to its troubles over legislation, had to face during 1931 growingly severe attacks from both Tories and Liberals on its failure to deal with unemployment. While the Mosley secession was in train, the Liberals, in February, 1931, put down a reasoned motion in favour of a more active policy for the provision of work ; and the Government escaped the risk of defeat only by accepting the motion. The Tories followed in April with a vote of censure, accusing the Government of failure " to carry out their election pledges with regard to unemployment," and were beaten by fifty-four, ten Liberals voting with them and thirty-seven against. Government spokesmen did their best to put a good face on the measures which had been taken—measures which might have made a good showing against an ordinary recession of trade, but were quite inadequate to make any impression on the spreading paralysis of industry brought about by the developing world crisis.

Much more serious than these open motions was the behind-the-scenes activity of the Liberals on the question of retrenchments in public expenditure for the maintenance of the unemployed. Ever since MacDonald, in the first " Mosley " crisis of 1930, had taken the Liberals into consultation over unemployment, there had been constant pressure from them to force the Government to introduce legislation for the prevention of alleged " anomalies " and abuses in connection with the administration of unemployment benefit and relief. At the same time the Tories in the House of Commons pressed openly for the removal of " abuses " in the working of the Unemployment Insurance Acts, and the Government, compelled to seek parliamentary approval for increased borrowing powers for the Insurance Fund and to legislate for the extension of the system of transitional benefit, found itself in danger unless it could make sure of Liberal support. The Liberals, for their part, made full use of their position of vantage ; and the recently appointed Royal Commission submitted in June, 1931, an Interim Report in which it proposed increased contributions, lower benefits, and the alteration of the law to exclude some real and some fancied abuses. The Government, hard pressed by the Liberals, introduced an " Anomalies " Bill which, in attempting to correct the real abuses, opened the door wide to wholesale deprivation of benefit of considerable classes of unemployed workers, especially married women who " could not reasonably expect to obtain employment " in their home areas. The I.L.P. and the New Party both opposed the Bill ; but the Tories and Liberals were for it, and it was allowed to pass by very large majorities on the very eve of the Government's fall.

The " Anomalies " Act brought to a head the trouble between the Government and the I.L.P., which had been acute ever since the assumption of office with a programme to which the I.L.P. took strong objection. The I.L.P.'s Birmingham Conference of 1930 had adopted a statement put forward by the National Administrative Council declaring the I.L.P. to be " an independent Socialist organisation, making its distinctive contribution to Labour Party policy and having its distinctive position within the Party." The statement had gone on to emphasise that the I.L.P. had always cherished liberty of action and that " it is unreasonable to ask members of the Party to accept without question all the proposals of the Government when those proposals are not themselves subject to the decisions of the Parliamentary Party, and in many instances do not comply with the programmes authorised by the Labour Party Conference." Finally, the hope was expressed that the Labour Party Executive would refrain from exercising rigid discipline " preventing liberty of action on matters of deep conviction " ; and the statement ended with the affirmation that " the I.L.P. considers it desirable to make clear that it cannot accept new limitations of its rights and of the obligations of Members of Parliament to their constituents and to Socialism."

Having made these declarations, the Conference proceeded to reconstruct the I.L.P. Parliamentary Group in such a way as to make membership of it conditional on full acceptance of I.L.P.

policy. The Labour Party Executive responded to this challenge by inviting the I.L.P. to meet it for the discussion of future relations ; and at a meeting in July, 1930, the differences seemed to have been narrowed down, and Henderson and Maxton were left to continue the discussions with a view to an agreement. At this point, however, the I.L.P. sent out' a letter to all M.P.s associated with it, announcing the Easter Conference decisions and asking as many of them as wished to belong to the I.L.P. Group in the House to give the required pledges of loyalty to I.L.P. policy decisions. The letter required that I.L.P. Members and candidates should pledge themselves to accept the " Socialism in Our Time " and " Internationalism in Our Time " Programmes passed by the I.L.P. in Conference. It was laid down that I.L.P. members, though they would normally press for these policies " through the Parliamentary Labour Party," would be required to go against the Labour Party where it was a question of carrying out a positive decision of the I.L.P. Conference or, in emergency, of the National Administrative Council. Further negotiations followed, and at one point Henderson and Maxton appeared almost to have reached agreement. But neither Executive was as ready as its appointed negotiator to slur over the differences. The I.L.P. continued to press M.P.s for pledges to obey its policy decisions ; and the Labour Party Executive retaliated by deciding to hold up all endorsements of I.L.P. candidates until a settlement had been arrived at. The I.L.P. claimed that the Labour Party was seeking to alter a long-established practice under which the I.L.P. representatives had been allowed freedom to act up to their Socialist principles : the Labour Party Executive maintained that the I.L.P. was the innovator and was attempting to impose pledges which were in conflict with the Labour Party Constitution.

In November, 1930, the Labour Party Executive refused to endorse the I.L.P. candidate at the East Renfrew by-election, and he had to fight without endorsement or central support. This followed on an earlier trouble, in June 1930, over John McGovern's candidature at Shettleston, Glasgow, on the death of John Wheatley ; but in this case the Executive had given way.

While these discussions were proceeding, the question of " Party Discipline " had also been under consideration by the Parliamentary Party in special connection with the " Mosley " revolt ; and in April, 1931, a Joint Committee of the Consultative Committee of the Parliamentary Party and the National

Executive presented a Report on this question. This Joint Committee, after making an appeal for " a fuller measure of loyalty in the future," recommended the setting up of a Standing Joint Committee on Party Discipline, with the duty of examining all alleged breaches and of reporting offenders to the bodies responsible for their nomination as candidates. It was further proposed that the Joint Committee should be empowered to recommend withdrawal of the Party Whip. Meanwhile the negotiations with the I.L.P. were continued and dragged on until the fall of the Government interrupted them. The General Election of 1931 was fought under an uneasy truce between the contestants ; and then the whole issue came up again at the Labour Party Conference in October, 1931, when the I.L.P. attempted to refer back the Executive's Report on the discussions and was defeated by 2,117,000 to 193,000. The Parliamentary Party in the new Parliament set to work to re-draft its Standing Orders ; and the quarrel between the National Executive and the I.L.P. was resumed, ending as we shall see in the I.L.P.'s secession from the Party which it had taken the lead in creating.

The " Mosley " revolt and the dispute with the I.L.P. overshadowed during the second Labour Government's period of office the perennial problem of the Communist Party. But the problem remained alive ; and in February, 1930, the Labour Party Executive issued the first of its " Black Circulars," declaring ineligible for affiliation to the Labour Party a number of organisations stated to be under Communist control. These included the League against Imperialism, the Left Wing Movement, the Minority Movement, the Workers' International Relief, the National Unemployed Workers' Committee Movement, the Friends of Soviet Russia, and the International Class War Prisoners' Aid. Members of these bodies were declared to be ineligible as individual members of, or as delegates to, the Labour Party, or as candidates of the Party in national or local elections : and Local Parties were warned not to affiliate to or support them or other organisations or parties declared to be ineligible for affiliation to the Labour Party. Members were requested to cease all connections with the bodies named "as a condition of their continued membership of the Labour Party." The Executive, in advocating this policy, quoted extensively from instructions issued by the Communist International to its affiliated Parties advocating the establishment of " sympathising mass organisation for definite special purposes " as a valuable

method of Communist propaganda.   At the Labour Party
Conference of 1930 the Executive's policy was passed practically
without discussion, the motion to refer back being beaten on a
show of hands after George Lansbury had been put up to defend
the ban, and had done so mainly on the ground that there was an
unbridgeable gap between the Labour Party and the Communists on the issue of parliamentary action *versus* " violent,
bloody revolution."

It was announced at this Conference that the Labour Party's
individual membership had reached 350,000 in August, 1930 ;
but the following year the figure for paid-up membership in
1930 was given as only 277,000.

The Conference of 1930 had also before it as an accomplished
fact an agreement between Messrs. Odhams and the Trades
Union Congress General Council concerning the *Daily Herald.*
Under this agreement Messrs. Odhams, as printers and pub-
lishers, took over full financial responsibility for the paper, putting
adequate capital for the first time behind it and converting it
into an all-round daily newspaper able to compete on commercial
terms with other popular newspapers and to emulate them in the
then fashionable practice of lavish offers of free insurance for
registered readers.   The arrangement safeguarded the responsibility of the Trades Union Congress for control over general
policy, including the appointment of the editor. A new Board of
Directors, composed of nominees of Odhams and of the Trades
Union Congress, was installed in office ; and the new paper,
launched in March, 1930, at once achieved a circulation of more
than a million, or about four times that of the old *Daily Herald*
before its transformation.   Within the next year or so the circulation rose to over 1,500,000. A northern edition was printed and
published in Manchester ; and as part of the understanding with
Messrs. Odhams the machinery of the Labour Party was used
for an active campaign to push the circulation.

(b) The Crisis of 1931

Throughout the first half of 1931 the percentage of workers
resgistered as out of work stood at over twenty, and in July the
number so registered rose well above 2,750,000.   The rate of
increase in unemployment was no longer rapid ; but there were
great stagnant pools of idle workers, and the cost of maintenance
was at a high level. This cost, as far as it exceeded the income

of the Unemployment Insurance Fund, was met partly by the State, which had taken over the cost of transitional benefits, and partly by borrowing for the Fund—a process for which fresh parliamentary sanction had to be sought again and again. The sums thus borrowed did not figure in the recorded total of state expenditure : indeed the interest on them, being payable to the Treasury, appeared on the revenue side of the national accounts. But even so the State's share in the cost of maintaining the unemployed was high and rising ; and a cry set in that retrenchment was indispensable. As we have seen, the Royal Commission on Unemployment Insurance produced in June, 1931, an Interim Report recommending higher contributions and reduced benefits. Over this proposal there was much debate in the Labour Cabinet, which was being threatened with a Tory-Liberal combination to turn it out unless it agreed to act on the Commission's proposals.

The mounting cost of unemployment benefits in face of falling revenue due to the depression of industry and trade was, however, only one factor in the situation. At any rate by the beginning of 1931 Philip Snowden had made up his own mind that the " state of the nation " called for a policy of drastic retrenchment in public expenditure, which could in practice be brought about only by cuts in the social services. Snowden was determined to balance his Budget for 1931–2, and was also determined not to impose any additional taxes on trade or industry, wishing rather to reduce taxes which he regarded as falling on the cost of production, and therefore as hindering overseas trade and tending to reduce employment. If the Budget was to be balanced without additional taxation, the only course was to reduce expenditure heavily—or rather, this was the only course on the assumption that the Sinking Fund for the repayment of the National Debt must be left intact. Snowden insisted that the Sinking Fund must be kept up, partly because he was looking for a chance to convert a large mass of maturing debt to a lower rate of interest, but also partly because he regarded it as almost inviolable on grounds of financial integrity, and believed that any suspension of it would shake international confidence in Great Britain's economic position. The problem, as Snowden saw it, was to persuade the Labour Party to accept a policy of retrenchment at the expense of the social services and, above all, of the unemployed, and at the same time to keep up debt repayments and to refrain from further taxes falling on profits.

Snowden was, of course, well aware that to present any such set of proposals to the Labour Party would be to invite over-whelming defeat. He therefore took a devious course towards what he had in mind to do. In February, 1931, he took advantage of a Tory motion and a Liberal amendment both calling for reductions in national expenditure to make a vaguely alarmist speech, without going into details or putting forward any positive proposals. The Liberal amendment proposed the appointment of " a small and independent Committee to make representations to Mr. Chancellor of the Exchequer for effecting forthwith all practical and legitimate reductions in the national expenditure consistent with the efficiency of the services." To this amendment Snowden persuaded the Government to give its support ; and when it was carried he proceeded to appoint the notorious " May Committee," under the chairmanship of Sir George May, the retiring Chairman of the Prudential Insurance Company. There were only two Labour representatives on the Committee, to which Snowden evidently looked for a swingeing Report that would compel his own Party to yield.

Having done this, Snowden proceeded to introduce a very mild Budget, which, he was well aware, would leave the deficit un-covered and would make no contribution towards a solution of the financial crisis. He as good as admits this in his *Autobiography*, and as good as says that his idea was to get the May Committee's Report first, and then introduce a second " Economy " Budget in the autumn. In fact, he was planning to force his colleagues' hands, with the aid of the reactionaries whom he had appointed to sound the alarm.

Snowden got what he wanted. In July, 1931, the May Com-mittee produced (with the two Labour representatives dissenting) its intentionally sensational Report. By adding the deficit on the Unemployment Insurance Fund to the deficit on the Budget proper, by making the gloomiest possible forecasts of future deficits, and by treating the sums to be applied to repayment of debt as necessary parts of the national expenditure, the May Committee managed to present a picture of Great Britain as on the verge of sheer financial disaster. On this basis it went on to propose cutting £96,000,000 off the national expenditure. Of this total £66,500,000 was to be " saved " by cutting unemployment benefits by 20 per cent, by raising contributions to the Fund, and by imposing a means test on applicants for transitional benefit. Another £13,000,000 was to be " saved " by cutting teachers' salaries and grants in aid of them, another £3,500,000 by cutting service and police pay, another £8,000,000 by reducing public works expenditure for the maintenance of employment. Apart from the direct effects of these proposed cuts, they would of course have given the signal for a general campaign to reduce wages ; and this was doubtless a part of the Committee's intention.

Immediately upon the receipt of the May Report, the Labour Cabinet set up an " Economy Committee," consisting of MacDonald, Snowden, Henderson, Thomas and William Graham ; and Snowden began through this body to press his policy hard. The Labour Government had already involved itself in constant consultation with the leading members of the Liberal and Tory Parties ; and from this time on there was also constant consultation between Snowden and MacDonald and the bankers—not only the Bank of England but also the representatives of the " City " and of the joint stock banks. The May Report had been intended for home consumption, as a weapon against the main body of the Labour M.P.s and against Labour opinion in the country. What it did in fact was to create abroad a belief in the insolvency of Great Britain and in the insecurity of the British currency, and thus to start a run on sterling, vast amounts of which were held by foreigners who had exchanged their own currencies for it in the belief that it was " as good as gold." This foreign-owned sterling now began to be withdrawn at an increasing pace, and exchanged into gold or dollars ; and the withdrawals involved a drain on the exchanges, and soon began to threaten the stability of the pound. The simple immediate counter to this danger would have been to stop the export of gold, and to go off the gold standard. But this Snowden was not prepared even to consider ; and the bankers agreed with him in regarding the gold standard as the ark of the financial covenant. I, for one, took a different view, and urged the Government, both in private and in public, to control the exchanges at once, instead of waiting to be driven off gold by forces too strong to be resisted. No such solution was considered at all : instead the Bank of England took the futile step of borrowing £50,000,000 from the Bank of France and the New York Federal Reserve Bank in the hope of checking the drain. The May Report, however, had done its work all too well. The drain continued ; and the £50,000,000 was soon drawn away.

The Bank of England, with the Government's assent, then set

to work to negotiate further loans of £80,000,000 from Paris and New York, only to find that the New York Federal Reserve Bank, with which the main negotiations took place, was insisting that, as a condition of further help, the Government should balance its Budget by accepting the proposals of the May Committee, or at least by endorsing retrenchments on a scale which involved severe cuts in unemployment benefits, in other social services, and in expenditure on the maintenance of employment. The representatives of the Tory and Liberal Parties, with whom the Government had hopelessly entangled itself, similarly pressed for drastic " economies," threatening to turn the Government out unless it obeyed. Soon the leading figures in the Government— MacDonald, Snowden and Thomas—had reached the ignominious position of going to and fro between the Tories and Liberals and the bankers on the one hand, asking with how small cuts in expenditure they would put up, and their Cabinet colleagues on the other, asking how large cuts they would endorse under the influence of these pressures. The Cabinet was pushed reluctantly by its own Economy Committee into accepting one cut after another at the expense of the salaried classes, the unemployed, and the social services, always to be told that what it had accepted was not enough to placate either the American bankers and the Bank of England or the Opposition leaders. The Cabinet was driven to toying with the idea of cuts in benefit rates and to positive acceptance of the means test ; but from the former of these surrenders it finally recoiled, to the extent of making it clear that acceptance of the proposed cuts would involve resignations and probably a split in the Labour Party.

These were the circumstances under which Ramsay MacDonald announced to his colleagues his intention to hand in his resignation to the King, and demanded from them the surrender of their portfolios. Thus armed, he went to the King, leaving them to suppose that either a purely Tory Government, or possibly a Tory-Liberal Coalition under Baldwin, would succeed them ; but he returned to announce that he himself had been entrusted with the task of forming a " National " Government, in which Baldwin and the other Tory leaders and also the Liberals had agreed to serve under his leadership. He invited Snowden, Thomas, and the Lord Chancellor, Sankey, to remain with him and to join the new Government, and, with the minimum of ceremony, kicked his other colleagues out. He made no attempt to explain his conduct to the Labour M.P.s, or to the Labour Party

Executive, and did not attend the meetings at which the bewildered Labour Party received the news of what he had done. He simply left his Party in the lurch, saying blithely to Snowden that " tomorrow every duchess in London will be wanting to kiss me."

MacDonald's attitude in the crisis of 1931 largely explains itself. Ever since his troubles began, he had been getting more and more out of sympathy and patience with his own followers and had been spending more and more of his time, both socially and politically, with the opponents of his party. He could see clearly that the Labour Government was drifting upon the rocks ; but he had no policy for averting the shipwreck except by calling upon the Liberals and Tories to help him against the people he was supposed to command. As Labour Party leader, he could not make up his mind upon anything. He abetted Snowden in his projects of retrenchment at the expense of the unemployed and the social services ; but, though he personally was much more than half in favour of a revenue tariff, which would have served the double purpose of reducing the deficit and of keeping out imports, he would not stand up to Snowden on this issue—and Snowden remained an implacable Free Trader and was even considering the launching of a joint campaign with the orthodox Liberals in defence of Free Trade against those, such as Keynes, who were ready to abandon it in order to redress the trade balance.

MacDonald, in fact, had been coquetting, ever since his Government took office, with the idea of some sort of government with the aid of a " Council of State," pledged to collaborate in handling the unemployment problem on non-party lines. Such a Council, he believed, would enable him to keep his own party well in subordination ; and, the longer he held office, the more he held his own followers in contempt. Snowden's attitude, if no less equivocal, was entirely different. Even if he hated the Labour left wing, he hated the Liberals and Tories too. His idea was not to make any coalition with them, but to make use of them for coercing his own party into accepting the drastic " economies " which he believed to be indispensable. If the Labour Party refused to yield under all the pressure which he set out to apply, he was fully prepared to see the Labour Government fall, and even to help in accelerating its fall by resignation. But he expected MacDonald to fall with him, and Baldwin to come to power. He had no idea at all that MacDonald would persuade the Tories and Liberals to act under him as Prime Minister, or that he himself would have to face the question of accepting or refusing office in an allegedly " National " Government. When this issue did arise, he was taken entirely by surprise. It arose, however, at a moment when he had been utterly exasperated by the refusal of the Labour Cabinet to fall unitedly into the pit which he had digged to hold it, by accepting the ultimatum which he, the bankers, and the Opposition had united to present ; and in angry reaction he joined the " National " Government, on the promise, speedily to be dishonoured, that it would limit itself strictly to emergency measures, and that there would be no " coupon " election such as had taken place in 1918.

Snowden, however, having joined the " National " coalition, allowed his venom against his late colleagues full scope, and played his evil part in it without scruple, by lending himself to the propaganda which was put up to induce the electors to believe that a Labour victory would mean gross inflation and the confiscation of the people's savings. He behaved about as badly as man could behave, and did all he could to wipe out the memory of his own integrity and of his long service to the Socialist cause. Equally with MacDonald he must bear the blame for the events of 1931 ; for he first made the crisis inevitable by rejecting all the possible remedies, then did his best to aggravate it by inciting the May Committee to spread panic, and then turned and rent his late colleagues with the most unctuous self-righteousness.

These colleagues, to be sure, had for the most part very little to be proud about, except their last-minute decision to be loyal to those whom they were supposed to represent. Henderson had indeed been doing excellent work at the Foreign Office, and, apart from Snowden's unfortunate achievements over Reparations, the Government had every reason to feel proud of its record in international affairs. But on the home front the Cabinet —as distinct from the main body of Labour supporters, whose faith stood firm in face of all discouragements—made a sorry showing. Most of the Cabinet never came near to understanding the crisis, or to having any notion of how to deal with it ; and a majority of them were prepared, almost up to the last moment, to endorse concessions to the bankers and to the Opposition which would have involved nothing short of an abdication from the principles on which they had been raised to office. That enough of them drew back at the last moment to induce MacDonald to throw his party over instead of leading it into surrender was due more to the extravagance of the demands made upon them by the bankers and by the other parties than to any sagacity on their part. There was no doubt a minority in the Cabinet that would have preferred throughout to stand firm against concessions which ran directly counter to Labour Party policy ; but the majority allowed themselves to be led on by MacDonald and Snowden from one concession to another, until it was almost too late to draw back. Even Henderson, doubtless in his anxiety to keep the Government in office for the pursuance of the international policy on which he had set his heart, as well as in his abhorrence of the idea of a split in the Party which it had been his life's work to build, went a very long way in accepting MacDonald's and Snowden's demands, before he finally recoiled from the acceptance of the heavy cuts in unemployment benefit which were insisted upon as the price of the bankers' aid and of the maintenance of the Government's majority in Parliament.

There was much dispute at the time, and there has been much since, about the part which the financiers, and especially the Bank of England and the New York Federal Reserve Bank, played in bringing the Government down. It was categorically denied that either of these bodies had insisted on unemployment benefits being reduced, or had interfered with the Government's freedom to handle the crisis as it deemed best. What in fact occurred is, however, sufficiently clear. Snowden and MacDonald received the advice of the Bank of England that further international credits were indispensable for stopping the drain of gold, and used the Bank of England as go-between in negotiating for advances from the Federal Reserve Bank and the Bank of France. The American and French bankers, alarmed by the May Report, refused advances (beyond the original £50,000,000) unless the British Government took the steps necessary to balance the Budget and to stop the borrowing on behalf of the Unemployment Fund. The alternative course of stopping the drain by going off the gold standard was simply ruled out of court, and Snowden flatly rejected the course of balancing the Budget by means of additional taxation. This left no means open of meeting the bankers' demands except by drastic cutting of both unemployment benefits and other social services, including teachers' and other public salaries ; and, this being so, the American and French bankers, as interpreted by the Bank of England, were demanding these cuts, even though their formal demand was only that the Budget should be fully balanced in the sense recommended by the May Committee. The Bank of England disclaimed that it had any part in this insistence : it claimed to be acting merely as a go-between. But in effect it was backing up the foreign bankers and the City and the Opposition in denying that there was any alternative way of avoiding the crisis. Probably it was not realised that, whatever " economies " were made, the panic that had been started by the May Committee was far too serious to be averted by a loan of £80,000,000, or indeed by any loan that could possibly be raised. Probably the bankers and the Opposition leaders believed that the drain on sterling could be stopped if the Labour Government were either driven from office or compelled to give in entirely to their claims. At all events, they fully intended either to force the Government to surrender or to bring it down.

Snowden, who has given in his *Autobiography* the fullest inside story of the crisis that has been made public, unintentionally confirms this view of the events. According to him, the bankers and the Opposition leaders were throughout entirely helpful and friendly ; but for what ? They helped him to engineer the crisis, and to force his own colleagues into surrender to his demands. That the outcome was not what he expected was no excuse for his conduct. He had planned to use the Tories and the Liberals and the bankers to compel the submission of his own party, or to break it. In the event, the Labour Party did not submit, and was not broken ; but, owing to his manœuvres and to MacDonald's vacillations and final betrayal, it went down for the time in disastrous electoral defeat.

In the case of both Snowden and MacDonald, vanity played an outstanding part. Their vanities, however, were widely different. Snowden was utterly sure of being always and entirely both right and righteous, and had no scruples over his methods of handling colleagues whom he regarded as fools. MacDonald was equally self-righteous, but had no similar confidence that he knew the right answer to every question. He loved playing with ideas and policies, and fancying how he could put them across ; but he hated making up his mind. He was always seeing the force in the policies put up by his opponents—provided only that they were not to the left of him. But, as soon as he met the counter-arguments, he was reduced to a sheer incapacity to decide. Thus, whereas Snowden knew precisely what he wanted (though what he wanted was in fact sheerly impracticable, for he wanted to preserve both Free Trade and the gold standard in a world situation which rendered them quite incompatible), MacDonald knew only that he wanted to remain in office, because he regarded himself as the indispensable man. In deciding what to do, he allowed Snowden to drag him along, rejecting, after playing with it, every policy to which Snowden said " No." MacDonald had no policy, except a rejection of the programme which he had been elected to carry out. Up to the last moment he allowed Snowden to dictate his line ; and then, in the final *volte-face*, he dragged Snowden along with him into a " National " Government which he valued chiefly because it enabled him to preserve his vanity intact.

In describing the development of the crisis of 1931 I have been compelled to use strong words. It seems, indeed, in retrospect fully as miserable an affair as it seemed at the time, when I collaborated with Ernest Bevin in describing it in a pamphlet. We then wrote :

Labour has decisively rejected the policy of wage-cutting, unemployed-baiting, and putting back economic and social progress that is advocated by the self-styled " National " Government and the financial interests behind it. But it cannot successfully defeat that policy unless it is prepared to advance at once to the determined enforcement of a constructive Socialist policy of its own.*

The Labour Government of 1929–31 had never attempted to apply a constructive Socialist policy, or even to follow the mild precepts of the sections of *Labour and the Nation* which dealt with social reform and with employment policy. Caught in entanglements with the other parties, which were in a position at any moment to turn it out, led by a Prime Minister who was set on retaining office at any price and by a Chancellor of the Exchequer who was utterly determined to resist the only measures which could have enabled it to confront the crisis without surrendering its principles, and consisting mainly of men who had no understanding of the nature of the crisis or of the forces that were arrayed to defeat them, the second Labour Government floundered from mistake to mistake, and allowed itself to be deluded into the belief that in defeating Mosley it was winning its own battle. It is a sorry story ; and there is nothing to be gained by attempting to make it out as better than it actually was.

* *The Crisis*, by Ernest Bevin and G. D. H. Cole. *New Statesman and Nation*, 1931.

(c) The General Election of 1931

The " National " Government which took office in August,
1931, was formed as a temporary Coalition, which was to balance
the Budget and to deal with the immediate emergency only, and
was not to attempt any legislation not necessary for this purpose
on which the parties forming the Coalition were not agreed. It
had thus no mandate to introduce a tariff, which was what the
Tories wanted ; for both Snowden and the Liberal leaders were
against a tariff, even for revenue purposes. It was, in effect, a
stopgap Ministry, which the Tories intended to use for compassing
the destruction of the Labour Party, and then to throw aside as
soon as they could in favour of a Ministry that would put their
own policy into operation.

The new Cabinet consisted of ten members, of whom four were
ex-Labour Ministers—MacDonald, Snowden, Thomas and
Sankey—four Tories—Baldwin, Neville Chamberlain, Hoare,
and Cunliffe-Lister (later Lord Swinton)—and two Liberals—
Samuel and Lord Reading. Lloyd George was not a member :
he was ill at the time, and in fact never supported the " National "
Coalition. The four ex-Labour Ministers kept their previous
offices ; and it therefore fell to Snowden to introduce the emergency Budget which, as we have seen, he had been planning for
long before the political crisis arose. This included a cut of
10 per cent in Unemployment Benefits, besides the economies
which had been reluctantly accepted by the Labour Cabinet.
It also included increased duties on beer and spirits, petrol and
entertainments, and higher income tax and surtax, and thus
achieved a balance partly by means of cuts in expenditure and
partly by increases in taxation. It had no tariff provisions ; and
at this stage nothing was done to regulate imports in any way.
Snowden hoped that the balancing of the Budget and the driving
of the Labour Party from office would suffice to restore capitalist
"confidence" in Great Britain, and to stop the run on the pound.

The loan of £80,000,000 from New York and Paris to the Bank
of England was at once forthcoming under the new political
régime. But the run on the pound continued. The " National "
Government had taken office pledged to defend the gold standard.
Indeed, that had been given as the principal reason for its existence. But by the middle of September it had become evident
that the gold standard simply could not be defended ; and the
Bank of England was asking the Government to relieve it of its

responsibility for paying out gold under the Gold Standard Act of 1925. On September 21, Snowden, that arch-devotee of orthodox finance, had to introduce into Parliament a Bill suspending the gold standard ; and this measure was passed practically without opposition. This Act, so far from ruining the country, as the orthodox had maintained that it would, immediately solved the balance of payments problem. I well remember a leading banker telling me the week before the Act that Great Britain would be ruined if the gold standard were given up, and the week after, at the same Committee, what a relief it was to be off it, and what a calamity it would be if it were put back.

Thus before the end of September the financial crisis was over, and the " National " Government had carried out its mandate. The economic crisis, of course, remained ; but that was quite another matter. The Tories at once began to press for a tariff and to demand a General Election which, they were convinced, would give them a clear majority and enable them to put their own policy into effect. On September 22—the day after the Gold Standard Bill was introduced—a meeting of Tory M.P.s presented Baldwin with an ultimatum demanding an Election on the tariff issue, but offering to support MacDonald as Prime Minister if he would adopt the Tory policy. To this Snowden and the Liberals of course objected ; and in the ensuing negotiations they were induced to remain in the Government only by a promise that the Election, which they did not want but had to accept, would be fought on a platform leaving the tariff an open question. Finally, it was agreed that the " National " Coalition should go to the country and ask, not for a tariff, but for a " doctor's mandate," as MacDonald termed it, to introduce such measures as the new Government might think fit, including a tariff and other restrictions on imports, should it decide that they were needed. The Free Traders had obviously very much the worst of the bargain ; for it enabled the Tories to appeal to the country as " Nationals," with a practical certainty of getting a clear majority of their own and of being in a position, by virtue of the " doctor's mandate," thereafter to do just what they pleased. It is not surprising that MacDonald, who had for some time been more than half in favour of a tariff, lent himself to this manœuvre, as it promised to allow him to remain Prime Minister. It is at first sight more surprising that Snowden and the Liberals agreed ; but the event showed that they allowed their venom against Labour to override their free trade principles.

On MacDonald's desertion, the Labour Party had elected Arthur Henderson as its leader, with Clynes and William Graham as his deputies. The Party opposed the new Government's economy measures in Parliament, but was at a disadvantage because it could be twitted with the fact that most of them had been accepted—or at any rate half accepted—by the Labour Cabinet before its fall. On the whole, the Party put up only a somewhat perfunctory opposition, being still disorganised and bewildered by the recent events. Henderson, busy with preparations for the expected General Election, attended the House of Commons but little : angry exchanges between Snowden and the Labour back benchers were of daily occurrence. Snowden, indeed, pursued his recent colleagues with neurotic fury, losing no chance of discrediting them or of making the most of their past yielding to his demands.

At the beginning of October an Election was finally decided on ; and Parliament was dissolved on October 7. In the ensuing campaign the wildest misrepresentations were made. The Labour Party was represented as a squandermaniac Party bent not only on ruining the country, but also on confiscating the savings of the poor, on using the deposits in the Post Office Savings Bank to meet the budget deficit, and on leading the country by way of economic collapse into revolution. It was the Liberal, Runciman, who started the scare about the Post Office Savings Bank—the worst of all the election *canards* ; but Snowden, who did not stick at backing him up even in this outrageous suggestion, outdid all others in the rancour of his attacks. He was not well enough to stump the country ; but he assailed the Labour Party in broadcast speech, in circular letters, and in communications to the Press. He himself says in his *Autobiography* " Every day from the first day of the election campaign to the eve of the poll I launched attacks upon my late Labour colleagues." He said that the Labour policy " would destroy our national credit, the currency would collapse, and your incomes and wages and pensions and unemployment pay would have their purchasing value reduced enormously." He described the Labour Party programme as " Bolshevism run mad " and said that " the issue of this Election is between prosperity and ruin." Presumably he had got into such a state as to believe all this : at all events he said it, though he must have known that the more he succeeded in frightening the electorate the more certain was it that Free Trade, the second of the cherished institutions he had upheld all through the

Labour Government, would go the way the first—the gold standard—had gone already, at his own hands.

Snowden was more responsible than any other man for the immensity of the Labour defeat. He was not himself a candidate, having made up his mind to retire even before the Labour Government's fall. But he came back after the Election as Viscount Snowden, Lord Privy Seal in the reconstructed " National " Ministry.

In the extraordinary Election of 1931 the Labour Party's poll fell by 2,000,000, whereas the Tory poll rose by more than 3,000,000 and the Liberal, including all brands of Liberalism, fell by nearly 3,000,000. " National Labour," the MacDonaldites, polled 342,000 votes. The total poll was smaller by nearly 1,000,000 than in 1929. The change in terms of seats was sensational. The Labour Party fell from 289 M.P.s in 1929 to forty-six in 1931, *plus* five I.L.P. Members and Colonel Wedgwood, who stood as an Independent. The Liberals on the other hand rose from fifty-nine to seventy-two, despite their greatly reduced vote, and the Tories, with 471 M.P.s as against 260 in 1929, had a clear majority of about 330 over all other parties. The reason for the big difference between the shift in votes and the shift in seats was of course mainly that, in most constituencies, Tory, Liberal and National Labour were fighting in alliance against the Labour Party. Under these circumstances, the Liberals were over-represented, and not under-represented as they had been in 1929, when they had fought almost everywhere as a third party. With hardly more than one-third of the Labour votes, the Liberals had twenty more seats than Labour and Independent Labour combined.

An analysis of the seats fought by Labour shows that, in 474 constituencies returning a single Member, there were 361 straight fights with single candidates carrying the Coalition label, and another fifty in which there was only one Coalition candidate in the field, though Independent or New Party or Communist candidates intervened. Add the sixteen seats in which independent Labour candidates had only one Coalitionist against them and eighteen seats in two-member constituencies where there were only two Coalition nominees. This gives a total of 445 seats in which Labour candidates, official or unofficial, had to fight a united Coalition. There were in all only sixty cases in which two Coalition candidates fought each other in single-member constituencies, *plus* one in which there were three Coalition candidates for two seats ; and in some of these cases the second candidate was of derisory standing. In seven cases, all in mining areas, there was no Coalition candidate, and Labour M.P.s were returned, either unopposed or with only Communist or New Party opposition. Colonel Wedgwood, as an Independent, was also unopposed. In effect, the Election was a struggle between Labour and a united Coalition of the other established parties.

This was so, even though the Liberals were already split. Sir John Simon had started the Liberal-National secession before the fall of the Labour Government ; and in the new Parliament the Liberals were almost equally divided between the Simonites on the one hand and the Samuelites *plus* the Lloyd George Group on the other. Only in a few cases did the rival Liberal factions fight each other in 1931 ; but they were soon to split wide apart when the reorganised " National " Government proceeded to raise the issue of general protectionist policy.

The New Party under Sir Oswald Mosley, who earlier in the year had been promising to put 400 candidates in the field, could muster in the event only twenty-four, who were all beaten—most of them getting only an insignificant number of votes. Mosley himself was driven out of Smethwick before the Election, and stood for his wife's seat at Stoke-on-Trent, where he was bottom of the poll against a victorious Tory and a Labour candidate. John Strachey, who had left the New Party soon after its formation, lost his seat at Aston as an Independent : he too was at the bottom of the poll, against a Tory, who won, and a Labour man. Forgan, the other ex-Labour M.P. who fought under New Party auspices, met with a similar defeat, and so did the couple of M.P.s who had joined the New Party from other parties. The New Party was simply wiped out.

The Communists also fared very badly, with twenty-six candidates and not a single success. Even Gallacher, in West Fife, was at the bottom of the poll ; and Pollitt and Horner were both heavily beaten. For the most part, the Communist Party attacked seats held by Labour or " National Labour " men ; but their intervention had practically no effect.

The Independent Labour Party, owing to the dispute described in a previous section, fought the General Election as a separate party. This, however, involved a split in its ranks. Out of forty-two candidates adopted under I.L.P. auspices, only nineteen fought in the Election as I.L.P. candidates, the other twenty-three accepting the Labour Party terms and giving the pledges required of them. Of the nineteen I.L.P. candidates only three—

LABOUR AT THE GENERAL ELECTION OF 1931

	M.P.s Elected 1931	M.P.s Elected 1929	Net losses	Total seats fought 1931	Total seats fought 1929	I.L.P. 1931 M.P.s Elected	I.L.P. 1931 Total Seats fought	Other Labour Independents 1931 Elected	Other Labour Independents Seats fought	National Labour 1931 Elected	National Labour 1931 Seats fought	Communists Seats fought	New Party Seats fought
London County	5	36	31	56	58	—	2	—	—	1	2	8	5
Greater London	4	18	14	36	39	—	1	—	—	1	1	—	—
Southern England	—	5	5	51	56	—	—	—	—	—	—	—	2
Western England	1	7	6	17	20	—	1	—	—	1	1	—	—
South-west England	—	1	1	9	16	—	—	—	—	—	—	—	—
West Midlands	—	25	25	40	46	—	—	1	4	1	1	1	3
East Midlands	3	22	19	29	38	—	—	—	—	4	4	—	1
Eastern Counties	—	4	4	31	28	—	1	—	—	1	1	—	—
Lancs. and Cheshire	5	44	39	68	76	—	2	—	—	1	2	3	2
Yorkshire	7	40	33	51	54	—	1	—	—	1	1	2	2
North-west England	1	3	2	3	6	—	—	—	—	—	—	—	—
North-east England	2	22	20	24	28	—	—	—	1	1	3	1	1
Wales and Monmouth	15	25	10	29	33	1	1	—	1	1	1	3	2
Scotland	3	37	34	44	68	2	10	2	2	—	2	8	5
Northern Ireland	—	—	—	1	—	—	—	—	—	—	—	—	—
Universities	—	—	—	—	3	—	—	—	—	—	1	—	1
TOTALS	46	289	243	489*	569	3†	19	3‡	8	13§	20	26	24

* Including twenty-three I.L.P. candidates who fought under Labour Party auspices.
† Maxton, McGovern, Wallhead.
‡ Kirkwood, Buchanan, Wedgwood.
§ Including MacDonald, Thomas, and Malcolm MacDonald.

LABOUR PARTY : BODIES SPONSORING SUCCESSFUL CANDIDATES, 1931

Labour		Others	
D.L.P.	13	I.L.P.	3
Co-op. Party	1	Trade Unions	2
Miners' Federation	23	Other	1
T. & G.W.U.	2		
N.U.G.M.W.	2		
Other Trade Unions	5		
	46		6

Wallhead, Maxton and McGovern—were elected ; but two other successful candidates—David Kirkwood and George Buchanan—who stood under Trade Union auspices, refused to give the required pledges to the Labour Party, and remained in the I.L.P. Parliamentary Group. They are not included in the total of forty-six official Labour Party candidates returned.

The heavy Labour defeat and the partial secession of the I.L.P. naturally involved a substantial change in the composition of the Parliamentary Labour Party, which, in the new House of Commons, was half composed of Miners' representatives. The Divisional Labour Parties returned thirteen Members, other Trade Unions nine, and the Co-operative Party a solitary Member.

Regionally, the Labour losses were everywhere severe. Wales and Monmouthshire did best, with fifteen Labour Party and one I.L.P. Member in the new Parliament as against twenty-five Labour Members in 1929. The Labour Party did worst in Scotland and in the Midlands. In Scotland its representation fell from thirty-seven in 1929 to three, not counting four belonging to the I.L.P. group. In the Midlands Labour Party representation fell from forty-seven to three, not counting Colonel Wedgwood. Thirty-nine seats were lost in Lancashire and Cheshire, forty-five in Greater London, and thirty-three in Yorkshire. The Labour Party was left without a single seat in the South, outside Greater London, and with only one M.P.—Sir Stafford Cripps— in the West.

" National Labour " was a party of leaders without followers and owed its successes—thirteen M.P.s out of twenty candidates— to the Coalition label. MacDonald, Snowden and Thomas carried with them almost nobody of any account in the Labour world, and had practically no following among the Labour rank and file. A few middle-class Labour men—Sir William Jowitt, Norman Angell, and Clifford Allen among them—and Lords

GENERAL ELECTION OF 1931
NATURE OF CONTESTS IN SEATS FOUGHT BY LABOUR CANDIDATES
(*Single-member Constituencies*)

	LABOUR PARTY		I.L.P. AND OTHERS	
	Seats fought	Seats won	Seats fought	Seats won
A. *No Coalition candidate* Unopposed . . .	5	5	1	1
Communist only . .	2	2	—	—
New Party only . .	—	—	1	—
TOTAL . . .	7	7	2	1
B. *Straight Fights with Coalition* Conservative only . .	304	24	11	2
Liberal National only .	25	3	—	—
Liberal only . . .	20	5	—	—
National Labour only .	11	—	1	—
National only . . .	1	—	—	—
TOTAL . . .	361	32	12	2
C. *Other Contests with only one Coalition Candidate* Conservatives and other .	38	5	4	—
Liberal National and other	3	—	—	—
Liberal and other . .	7	1	—	—
National Labour and other	1	—	—	—
National and other . .	1	—	—	—
TOTAL . . .	50	6	4	—
D. *Coalition Vote Split* Conservative and Liberal .	50	1	3	—
Conservative, Liberal and other	2	—	—	—
Other Contests . .	4	—	1	—
TOTAL . . .	56	1	4	—

Double-member constituencies are not included above. In nine out of ten of these there were two Coalition candidates against two Labour candidates (including two unendorsed). In the remaining case one Labour candidate and an Independent of Labour sympathies fought two Conservatives and a Liberal.

Sankey and Amulree followed MacDonald into the camp of reaction ; but " National Labour " never for a moment looked like becoming a real party, and after 1931 it faded gradually away.

Among the leaders of the Labour Party who remained " loyal," the election losses were very severe. Of Cabinet Ministers only George Lansbury held his seat, to become Chairman of the Labour Party in the new Parliament. His principal lieutenants were Attlee and Stafford Cripps. The defeated included Arthur Henderson (Burnley), Clynes (Miles Platting, Manchester), Greenwood, Dalton, Susan Lawrence, Tom Shaw, Dukes, Sexton, Tillett, Pethick-Lawrence, Bowerman, Herbert Morrison, Isaacs, Shinwell, Margaret Bondfield, F. O. Roberts, Noel-Baker, Addison, Ben Turner, Ellen Wilkinson, Alexander, Lees-Smith, Wedgwood Benn, Adamson, Joseph Westwood, William Graham and Tom Johnston, besides F. W. Jowett and Fenner Brockway, of the I.L.P. Group. Sidney Webb, who had gone to the Lords in 1929, and Noel-Buxton, who had followed him in 1930, were not involved. The Labour Party in the new Parliament, apart from its small numbers, was very weak in parliamentary knowledge and debating strength.

CHAPTER VIII

AFTER THE DELUGE

(a) Exit the I.L.P.

The development of the world crisis—Political repercussions—The Japanese in Manchuria—India and the Simon Commission—Henderson and the Disarmament Conference—The Sino-Japanese conflict—Germany : the fall of Bruening and the von Papen Government—The " National " Government in Great Britain and the Tariff issue—Snowden leaves the Government—The Liberal Nationals, the Samuelites, and the Lloyd Georgites—The Labour Party in defeat—George Lansbury elected Chairman—The Party's weakness in the House of Commons— Its policy in the new Parliament—Unrest in the country—The Means Test—The Communists and the Unemployed—The Hunger Marchers of 1932–3—The Trades Union Congress and the Unemployed Movement—The dispute between the Labour Party and the I.L.P.—The Labour Party's Standing Orders—The I.L.P. and " conditional affiliation "—Lansbury tries for reconciliation—The I.L.P. leaves the Labour Party—The conflict of views in the I.L.P.—The effects of the secession—The Labour Party sets up a Policy Committee—Its first Reports— The Leicester Labour Party Conference of 1932—The dispute about the joint stock banks—Conflicting views on Workers' Control—Trevelyan's resolution on Socialist policy—Henderson resigns the Party leadership—Did the left win at the Leicester Conference ?—Foundation of the Socialist League—Its antecedents— The Society for Socialist Inquiry and Propaganda—The New Fabian Research Bureau—Fusion of the S.S.I.P. and the ex-I.L.P. Group—The Scottish Socialist Party—the policy of the Socialist League.

(b) In Face of Nazism

The events of 1933—The Nazis come to power in Germany—A fresh Japanese offensive in China—The American banking crisis—Roosevelt becomes President of the United States—America leaves the gold standard—The World Economic Conference fails—Germany withdraws from tne League—The demand for a United Front—The policy of the Comintern—The I.L.P. and Unity—The attitude of the Labour and Socialist International—British reactions—The *Democracy versus Dictatorship* Manifesto—British protests against Nazism—Measures against " disruptive agencies "—*The Communist Solar System*—United Front demonstrations—British Fascism begins—Further demonstrations against the Government's unemployment policy—The Meerut Trial—Tom Mann's imprisonment—The development of the Labour Programme—Housing—Colonial Development—*Socialism and the Condition of the People*—A Banking Corporation proposed— The Hastings Labour Party Conference—The policy of the Socialist League— International Socialist co-operation—Marking time—The " Ayles " resolution and the Report on the position of any future Labour Government—Position of the Prime Minister and the Cabinet in relation to the Party and the Trade Unions— The Workers' Control issue again—Discussions on the United Front—Conflicting views on the morals to be drawn from the events in Germany.

(c) " For Socialism and Peace "

The world situation in 1934—Manchuria—The Nazi Purge—The Overthrow of Socialism in Austria—The United Front in France—The rise of British Fascism —The United Front campaign in Great Britain—Labour's Municipal successes : capture of the London County Council—Changes in the Labour Party's leadership—Work of the Policy Committee—*For Socialism and Peace*—The new Labour Party policy outlined—The Reform of Parliament—The rival views of the Socialist League—The Southport Labour Party Conference of 1934—Defeat of the Socialist League—The Labour statement on *War and Peace*—Collective security— The General Strike discarded—The " War and Peace " debate at Southport—

268

The improvement in employment—The Means Test and the Unemployment
Assistance Board—The Reports on the Distressed Areas—The Special Areas Bill—
The mass protests against the U.A.B. scales—The Communists and the unemployed—*For Soviet Britain*—Lloyd George's " New Deal "—The Liberals and the
next Election—Resignation of Ramsay MacDonald—The Peace Ballot—The
Abyssinian Crisis—The Stresa Conference and the Franco-Soviet Pact—Labour
action in the Abyssinian conflict—The League and " Sanctions "—The question
of re-armament—The Tories and the League of Nations—Choosing the Election
issue.

(*d*)   *Death of Arthur Henderson—The Sanctions Issue*

Death of Arthur Henderson—His service to the Labour Party—His policy and
character—George Lansbury's illness—Lansbury and pacifism—The Sanctions
issue—Cripps resigns from the Executive—" Sanctions " at the Brighton Labour
Party Conference—Cripps's attitude—Lansbury's speech—and Bevin's—The
decision—Lansbury resigns the leadership and Attlee succeeds him.

(*e*)   *The General Election of 1935*

A confusing Election—Tory and Labour policies on sanctions and collective
security—The Re-armament question—Conservative differences of attitude—The
Conservatives and the Nazis—Labour differences—The pacifists—The Cripps
group—Labour policy on armaments—The Election : numbers voting—Labour
votes and seats compared with 1929 and 1931—The Liberals—The personnel of
the Labour Party after 1935—The old leaders return—Regional distribution of
Labour gains and seats fought—The I.L.P. and the Communist Party in the Election
—Nature of contests analysed—Composition of the Labour Party : Trade Union
candidates and others—Defeat of the younger Labour candidates—The decline of
National Labour—Death of Ramsay MacDonald.

(*a*)   *Exit the I.L.P.*

The British crisis of 1931 had run its course to the accompaniment of crises all over the world. It was indeed a part of the
world crisis ; for the British financial and economic difficulties,
though they had existed before, had been immensely aggravated
by the worldwide economic collapse, which was itself due mainly
to the withdrawal of support for the European economy from the
United States. The Americans, plunging into a domestic crisis of
their own, brought on by speculative excesses superimposed on a
gross maldistribution of purchasing power, had stopped lending to
Europe—and especially to Germany—the capital sums which
alone had enabled Reparations to be paid and the European
States to maintain an illusory economic stability. As soon as this
support was withdrawn, unemployment began to spread everywhere, and one country after another, alarmed by this and by the
growing unbalance of its international accounts, set out to restore
balance by shutting out imports and endeavouring to push exports in every market into which they could be forced. These
conditions reacted seriously both on British exports and on the
open British market for imports, and produced the financial

crisis which was wrongly attributed in capitalist quarters to the
" spendthrift " policy of the British Labour Government ;
whereas in truth their fault was not spending too much, but
failing to take measures to stop the drain either by giving up the
gold standard or by restricting imports, and to initiate international measures for dealing with the crisis before it had gone
too far.   On the latter point, it may be said that international
measures at this stage, with the Republicans in power in the
United States, would have had no chance of success ; but even
so it was folly to let months drift without taking any step to redress
the British balance of payments.   Snowden's obstinacy and
MacDonald's vacillations prevented this from being done ; and
it was left to the " National " Government to take under duress
the step, which ought to have been taken long before, of suspending the gold standard.

The crisis had at once its political repercussions. The Japanese,
at the moment when the Labour Government was staggering to
its fall, had seized the occasion presented by the preoccupation
of the rest of the world with economic difficulties to invade
Manchuria, to occupy Mukden, and to make preparations for the
establishment of a puppet State in Manchuria and Northern
China.   In India the onset of depression had caused immense
suffering by its disastrous effects on agricultural prices ; but the
political consequences of agrarian suffering and unrest had been
for the time diverted by the Irwin-Gandhi conversations of
February, 1931, which had led to the cessation of Civil Disobedience.   After the accession of Lord Willingdon as Viceroy,
in succession to Lord Irwin, in April, 1931, relations had rapidly
worsened, and a policy of repression had set in. At the moment of
the Labour Government's fall a Round Table Conference on
India was about to open in London to work out a new Constitution.   This Conference was being boycotted by the Indian
Nationalists, who were acutely disappointed with the Report
of the Simon Commission (which Attlee signed) ; but MacDonald
seems to have been building large hopes upon it, and it was
doubtless one factor which made him most unwilling to give up
his position as Prime Minister.

The state of affairs in the League of Nations was another
reason for the Labour Government's reluctance to leave office,
or to risk challenging in Parliament a vote that might drive it
from power. Preparations were in train for the great Disarmament Conference on which Arthur Henderson had set his heart ;

and it was plain that a return of the Tories to power in Great Britain would wreck the chances of the Conference. The Disarmament Conference met in February, 1932 ; but, in fact, it had no chance. This, however, was not yet appreciated, and Henderson, as well as MacDonald, had been exceedingly unwilling to give the League's cause up as lost. In the event, Henderson was left in his position as Chairman of the Disarmament Conference, despite the Labour Government's fall, and spent his last years in a fruitless effort to save it from shipwreck. This kept him practically out of British politics after 1931 ; and, at Geneva, he had to work in the knowledge that he could look for no effective support from his own country. MacDonald, a prisoner in the hands of the Tories, could have given him no adequate backing, even if he had wished to. Henderson stuck grimly to his hopeless task ; and in his absence the Labour Party was left without effective leadership either in Parliament or in the country.

The year 1932 was one of disaster and reaction all over the world. In the Far East, Manchuria, re-named Manchukuo, was proclaimed an independent State under Japanese protection ; and the Japanese began the invasion of Northern China, in addition to attacking Shanghai. The long-drawn-out Sino-Japanese conflict was already well under way ; and the Japanese were turning to a more aggressive militarism in face of economic depression and the reduced chances of anyone stopping their expansionist schemes. The League of Nations met to consider the Manchurian problem, set up the Lytton Committee of Investigation, and failed to take any action, largely because the new British Government, with Simon as Foreign Secretary, would do nothing to support the League Covenant. In America the slump grew worse and worse ; and President Hoover, the pillar of the business interests, did nothing effective to deal with it. In Europe, Ivar Kreuger, the Swedish " match king," committed suicide in March, 1932, amid the collapse of his grandiose international financial swindles ; and panic spread far and wide. The Bruening Government in Germany, which had been attempting vainly to stem the crisis by one yielding after another to the reactionary forces, fell from office. Hindenburg was re-elected as President in the spring, and appointed the reactionary von Papen as Chancellor. The Weimar Republic was collapsing : the Nazis were increasing in influence and in intransigeance : unemployment was far worse than in Great Britain, and was rapidly preparing the way for Hitler's accession to power. Reparations

were being abandoned : default on international debts was
spreading rapidly from country to country.

This was the background against which the new " National "
Government formed after the General Election of 1931 conducted
its operations. At the Election, the Coalition had asked for a
" doctor's mandate," but had given it to be understood that no
tariff would be introduced until there had been a thorough study
of alternative remedies for the unbalanced state of the international accounts. Nevertheless, Runciman, the new Chancellor
of the Exchequer (Snowden had gone to the Lords after proposing
Runciman, a reputed Free Trader, as his successor) immediately
introduced the Abnormal Importations Bill for imposing a
temporary tariff on goods of which imports had increased. The
Bill was rushed through and became an Act in November, 1931 ;
and the power given by it was at once used to impose a 50 per
cent tariff on a wide range of imports. Snowden and some of the
Liberal Ministers at once protested to the Prime Minister at the
tone of the speeches made by Runciman and others in defence
of the Bill and at the scale of the duties imposed. MacDonald
made evasive answers : it was of course perfectly clear that the
Tories meant to enact a permanent tariff, and that if MacDonald
opposed them they would at once throw him out, now that he
had served his purpose in getting them their immense majority.

Nevertheless, Snowden and the Free Trade Liberals with
whom he was now acting did not leave the Government. They
merely recorded their dissent from the Majority Report of the
Cabinet Committee which proceeded to recommend a permanent
general tariff of 10 per cent, *plus* further duties to be imposed on
the advice of a specially appointed Import Duties Advisory Committee. Their threat to resign was met by an extraordinary
decision to allow them to remain in the Government with a free
hand to oppose its tariff proposals. The Import Duties Bill
was then rushed through Parliament in face of their opposition,
which they must have known to be futile ; and the Tories, having
got their tariff, proceeded to make preparations for the Ottawa
Conference, which was intended to bring about closer economic
union with the countries of the Empire.

It was Ottawa, and not the tariff, that finally drove Snowden
and the Samuelite Liberals out of the " National " Government
in September, 1932, after the negotiations had resulted in an
extension of imperial preference mainly by increasing tariffs on
non-empire goods, and had made it plain beyond the smallest

doubt that Protection had come, not merely as an emergency measure, but as a permanent policy. Before this, in July, the Simonites had completed their organisation as a separate party, the Liberal Nationals ; and the Lloyd George family had come to form what was virtually a separate little party on its own. Meanwhile the Labour Party was licking its wounds after its electoral defeat. In the new Parliament, Arthur Henderson was re-elected as leader ; but he was out of the House, and George Lansbury was re-elected as Chairman of the Party, with Attlee as Vice-Chairman. These two and Sir Stafford Cripps were the only outstanding parliamentary figures who had kept their seats ; for Aneurin Bevan was not yet recognised as a leader, and Maxton was now outside the Party, though he had held his seat. Arthur Greenwood got back as M.P. for Wakefield in April, 1932, on a very narrow majority : Arthur Henderson did not come back until September, 1933, when, on Charles Duncan's death, he was elected for Clay Cross—a safe Labour seat. He did not resume the leadership, being fully engaged with his efforts at Geneva. In November, 1931, the Labour Party moved a Socialist amendment to the King's Speech, calling for public ownership or control of the principal industries and of the banks, as well as protesting against the economies at the expense of the unemployed and of the social services. The Party opposed the Abnormal Importations Bill of 1931 and the Tariff Bill of the following year ; and it tried in vain to prevent the whittling down of the Town and Country Planning Bill, originally a Labour measure, which was now spoilt by limiting planning powers to land already developed or actually in course of development. It successfully insisted, when the Exchange Equalisation Fund was set up in 1932, that control should be in the hands of the Treasury and not of the Bank of England ; and it opposed the Bill to continue the seven-and-a-half hours shift in the coal mines. It moved repeated motions against the Means Test : it opposed the continuance of coercion in India ; and it pressed for support from Great Britain for Henderson's efforts at the Disarmament Conference. But these were all, of course, empty gestures ; and the Labour Party's weakness in debate could not be hidden. In the House of Commons, the Conservatives had matters all their own way.

This was not equally the case in the country. The cuts in unemployment pay, the imposition of the Means Test in respect of transitional benefits in November, 1931, and the other

" economy " measures, including the salary reductions and
lengthening of hours in the public services, created widespread
unrest and gave rise to intense local agitations, in which there
was a renewed willingness on the part of rank-and-file workers to
accept left-wing leadership. The mood of the unemployed was
defiant, and many of the employed joined hands with them in the
local movements of protest. The Communists were of course
active in stirring up these revolts, especially among the unemployed, among whom their strength mainly lay. The agitation
took time to gather force. It became much more intensive in the
autumn of 1931, after the Naval Mutiny at Invergordon in
September, when a section of the fleet successfully revolted against
pay cuts levied with extreme unfairness. The Admiralty, compelled to give way, retorted a little later by discharging the
leaders of the revolt from the service ; but the victory remained,
and had an immense effect on working-class opinion. In October,
1932, a fresh national Hunger March was organised, mainly
under Communist leadership, but with much non-Communist
support ; and all over the country mass demonstrations besieged
Local Authorities and Public Assistance Committees. There were
many clashes with the police, especially in London, in Manchester,
in Glasgow, and in South Wales ; and loud calls were made for
the Trades Union Congress and the Labour Party to assume the
national leadership of the agitation.

Unfortunately, the Communist leadership of the movement
caused the national leaders to set their faces against it. In
January, 1933, the Trades Union Congress General Council at
last made a half-hearted attempt to organise the unemployed
through local Unemployed Organisations attached to the Trades
Councils and accepting T.U.C. control. But the National
Unemployed Workers' Movement, led by the Communist, Wal
Hannington, and mainly controlled by Communist " cells,"
was much too strongly entrenched to be displaced unless the
Trade Unions had been prepared to throw all their weight into
the struggle on behalf of the unemployed ; and this, conscious
of their weakness in face of the depression, they were not prepared
to risk, even if their fears of concessions to the left wing had not
held them back.

The Labour Party, for its part, was engaged all through 1932 in
a battle on two fronts. On the one hand it was seeking to reorganise its forces in face of the MacDonaldite secessions ; and on
the other it was continuing the dispute with the I.L.P. which had

begun during the Labour Government's term of office and had led to the I.L.P.'s appearance in the 1931 Election as a separate party, though it was still nominally affiliated to the Labour Party.

The position, as we have seen, was that the Labour Party Executive from 1930 had been refusing to endorse any candidate who would not pledge himself to accept the discipline of the Party, in the form of Standing Orders which controlled his voting rights in the House of Commons. It was recognised that an M.P. could not fairly be forced to vote against his conscience ; and a right to abstain from voting on conscientious grounds was recognised, but did not include a right to vote against the Party when it had decided to take a particular line. This right to abstain had been meant mainly to cover the scruples of pacifists, of rigid teetotallers, and of the advocates of denominational education. The I.L.P. had wanted much more than this, and had claimed the right to instruct the I.L.P. Members of Parliament to vote in accordance with I.L.P. policy decisions, even against their Labour colleagues. In the discussions the I.L.P. had seemed at one stage to be pre- pared to modify its position, by agreeing that its members should not be called on to vote against Labour Party decisions except when they were in violation of the policy laid down by the Labour Party Conference. This, the I.L.P. claimed, was the case with many of the proceedings of the Labour Government, which the Parliamentary Labour Party was called upon to support ; and the I.L.P.'s claim was that it must be judge in such matters, at all events against the Labour Party Executive, even if it agreed that the Labour Party Conference had a final right to override either.

The *casus belli* had for the most part disappeared with the fall of the Labour Government ; for in the new Parliament occasion was seldom likely to arise for the two wings of Labour to vote on opposite sides. Nevertheless, the quarrel continued. The Labour Party Conference in October, 1931, had given the National Executive power to enforce the Standing Orders to which the I.L.P. objected, Brockway's motion for the reference back being defeated by 2,117,000 to 193,000. This had involved the non- endorsement at the General Election of the nineteen I.L.P. and the few Trade Union candidates of I.L.P. sympathies who had refused to give the required pledge, though a majority of the candidates already endorsed under I.L.P. auspices and nearly all the I.L.P. members who were standing under other auspices had accepted the Labour Party's terms. After the Election, further discussions between Maxton and Henderson having failed to break the deadlock, the National Administrative Council of the I.L.P. decided to report the entire matter to the I L.P. Conference at Easter, 1932, and to leave the delegates to decide between continued affiliation to the Labour Party and disaffiliation, which would involve continuance as an entirely separate party. At first, it had been intended to call a Special Conference for an earlier date ; but this had to be given up because too few branches were in a position to send delegates.

The I.L.P. Conference at Easter, 1932, revealed a sharp difference of opinion. Three rival policies were put forward. James Maxton and most of the leaders of the Clyde Group were in favour of immediate disaffiliation from the Labour Party ; a section headed by Frank Wise and Patrick Dollan favoured unconditional affiliation, involving the acceptance of the disputed Standing Orders. A third section, of which David Kirkwood was the best-known spokesman, wanted the Conference to vote for " conditional " affiliation—that is, for affiliation on condition of an amendment in the Labour Party's Standing Orders. This third policy in the end carried the day, though there was practically no chance of anything coming of it ; for the Labour Party was not at all likely to give way, especially as the I.L.P. was itself so sharply divided. The third policy won, not on its merits, but because there was a majority against both the others. Maxton mustered, in favour of disaffiliation, 144 votes against 183 ; the Wise section got 98 against 214 in favour of unconditional affiliation ; the middle party then carried the day by 250 to 53. At the same Conference the I.L.P. adopted a new left-wing Statement of Policy, in which it announced the impending downfall of capitalism, proclaimed the class-struggle as " the dynamic force in a social change nearing its decisive moment," called for a new class militancy in support of an immediately Socialist objective, affirmed the inadequacy of purely parliamentary methods and demanded " mass industrial action " " as an additional means," reasserted its faith in internationalism, and affirmed its mission as the endeavour " to prepare the workers for the critical struggle which lies immediately ahead to replace capitalism by the Socialist Commonwealth."

Further negotiations with the Labour Party followed. Lansbury, as Chairman of the Parliamentary Party, tried to persuade the I.L.P. to rejoin the Labour Party and then seek to get the Standing Orders amended ; but the I.L.P. refused. The Labour Party then decided to consider whether the Standing

Orders needed revision, but in June, 1932, the Parliamentary Party decided to reaffirm them unchanged, with the proviso that they might need re-draftng in the event of a Labour Government coming again to office. The reason for the proviso was that the I.L.P. had stressed the difficulties in which it had been put by the MacDonald Cabinet's policy of compromise and concession, in relation to which it was now recognised that there was a real case. The Parliamentary Party's view was that such difficulties were unlikely to arise with Labour in opposition, and that therefore no case had been made out for altering the Standing Orders at once. The I.L.P. made one more attempt at negotiation ; but when the Labour Party would make no concession, the National Administrative Council determined to call a Special Conference of the I.L.P. and to recommend disaffiliation.

This Conference was held at Bradford at the end of July, 1932. The advocates of continued affiliation to the Labour Party were defeated by 255 votes to 120, and after a great confusion of amendments disaffiliation was carried by 241 to 142. The Conference then proceeded to order the withdrawal of I.L.P. members from Local Labour Parties and from Labour Groups on Local Authorities and similar bodies, on which they were in future to sit as I.L.P. representatives only. The Statement of Policy adopted at Easter was amplified and made more challenging, and it was decided to organise an I.L.P. campaign throughout the country on the basis of it. Frank Wise promptly resigned from the National Administrative Council ; and the split in the I.L.P.'s ranks became final.

Thus ended the long association of the I.L.P. with the Labour Party. It is at first thought surprising that the parting took place as it did. With the Labour Government's fall, the conditions that had led to the rupture of relations had disappeared, and the Labour Party itself, as we shall see, was moving leftwards in reaction to its defeat in the General Election and in a desire to wash itself clean of MacDonaldism. In these circumstances, it would have been natural for some attempt to be made to bring the contending parties together. It has, however, to be borne in mind that the leaders who remained loyal to the Labour Party in the crisis of 1931 had previously gone a very long way in concessions to MacDonald and Snowden, and that many of them by no means attributed the Government's fall to anything wrong with its fundamental policy of gradualism and moderation. Maxton and his followers, on the other hand, had become convinced that this entire policy was wrong, and felt hardly less hostile to Henderson and to the " loyal " Labour Party leaders than to those who had gone out with MacDonald. In Maxton's view it was necessary for the I.L.P. to insist all the more on its policy of " Socialism Now " because the rival policy of gradualism had been so thoroughly discredited. Maxton, coming from Clydeside and conscious of the rising temper of the workers there and in other depressed areas as they felt the weight of the Means Test and of other measures of economy and repression, probably took the Labour Party's election defeat to mean much more than it turned out to mean, and had hopes of building up the I.L.P. into a mass party standing for a left-wing policy. He might have taken warning from the heavy defection of I.L.P. candidates to the Labour Party at the General Election and from the manifestly weakened state of the I.L.P. in the early months of 1932. He did not ; or, if he did, he regarded the issue as one of principle, on which no compromise was allowable—and he carried the majority of those who were left in the I.L.P. with him. It must, however, be remembered that a good many who would have voted against him had already dropped out.

Disaffiliation brought about a sharp fall in I.L.P. membership. From 653 branches (250 of them in Scotland) at the beginning of 1932 the I.L.P. shrank to 452 branches a year later. Branch affiliation fees fell from £1,258 to £832. The next year no figures were given in the Report.

In the meantime the Labour Party, shorn of the I.L.P. left wing, had been busy with its own tasks of reorganisation and re-statement of policy. In December, 1931, the Party Executive appointed a Policy Committee, under George Lathan, its Chairman, to begin working out a complete new policy for the Party. Among the leading members of this Committee were Herbert Morrison and Hugh Dalton : Clynes was also a member, and Lansbury had a seat ex officio, as Chairman of the Parliamentary Party. The Committee set up a number of sub-committees on particular aspects of policy, with the task of preparing comprehensive Reports setting out the Party Programme. Four of these Reports, on " Currency, Banking and Finance," on " The Land and the Planning of Agriculture," on " The National Planning of Transport," and on " The Reorganisation of the Electricity Supply Industry," were ready in time to be considered by the Annual Conference in October, 1932 ; and further Reports were to be presented the following year, " so that by the 1933 Annual

Conference the Party will be in possession of a body of Reports covering a considerable range of policy."

In a previous volume* I have made a careful study of these and of other Reports that went to the remaking of the Labour Party's policy between 1932 and 1939 ; and I do not propose to attempt any full account of them here, though I shall have something to say later about their general drift. The relevant point here is that the Labour Party, fresh from its experience of the second MacDonald Government, realised the need for much more careful preparation for office than it had attempted hitherto. Both *Labour and the New Social Order* and *Labour and the Nation* had been broad and inclusive statements of objects which neither committed a Labour Government to anything precise nor gave it any clear guidance for the drafting of such measures as it might decide to introduce. The Party Executive had made up its mind that such vagueness would not do, and that the coming years of opposition must be devoted to working out a clear and precise policy which the Party would be pledged and able to translate into legislation when its chance came. This was unquestionably wise ; and in fact the Policy Reports which were put forward at every Conference from 1932 onwards did serve as the foundation for the third Labour Government's legislative and administrative programme in 1945 : so that the main difficulties over policy then arose in fields which had been surveyed inadequately, or not at all, or where the situation had changed so greatly as to make the programmes devised before 1939 no longer workable in the post-war world.

At the Leicester Conference of 1932 the four Reports presented by the Executive were adopted, but only after sharp differences of view on certain key issues had been revealed. The controversy which occupied the central field of attention arose over the Report on Currency and Banking. The resolution embodying the main conclusions of the Report was moved by Hugh Dalton. After a preamble referring to the financiers' part in the crisis of 1931 it went on to advocate price stabilisation as an alternative to the gold standard and to demand the public ownership and control of the Bank of England and the establishment of a National Investment Board " with the object of preventing waste and misdirection in the use of long-term capital " and with power to recommend government guarantees of desirable capital projects " subject to the acceptance of public control by the industries

A Plan for Democratic Britain (Odhams, 1939).

concerned." The most noticeable thing about this resolution was that it made no mention of the joint stock banks, other than the Bank of England. These were presumably included among the matters on which, Dalton said in his speech, the Executive had not yet reached any conclusion.

Frank Wise, now out of the I.L.P. and busy organising his followers in the new Socialist League, to which I shall come later, moved an amendment in favour of nationalising the other banks as well as the Bank of England, on the ground that control over short-term credit, as well as over long-term capital, would be essential for the carrying out of any real programme of Socialist planning. Ernest Bevin, Pethick-Lawrence, and John Wilmot opposed the amendment : Stafford Cripps supported it ; and the Conference finally carried it by the narrow majority of 1,141,000 to 984,000. The closeness of the division was all the more remarkable in that, the previous year, the Conference, on Pethick-Lawrence's motion, and with Ernest Bevin's support, had demanded that " the banking and credit system " should " be brought under public ownership." The difference was that the 1931 resolution was a general resolution, moved in the heat of the crisis, whereas the resolution of 1932 was part of the process of drafting a programme for the next Labour Government. The opponents of Wise's amendment did not deny that it might be necessary at some time to nationalise the joint stock banks ; but they did not want to commit a Labour Government to doing it during its first term of office. This was what the sponsors of the amendment—who, to Ernest Bevin's particular fury, carried the day with the Miners' and Railwaymen's backing—did want the Conference to insist on.

The second issue on which dispute arose was that of Workers' Control. The Reports on socialisation of transport and electricity made no reference to this question. Harold Clay, on behalf of the Transport Workers, moved an amendment providing that certain of the members of the proposed Transport Board should be appointed by the responsible Minister " only after consultation with the Trade Unions having members employed in the industry." The same issue had been under discussion at the Trades Union Congress the previous.month, and had been remitted for further consideration by the separate Trade Unions. After A. G. Walkden, of the Railway Clerks, and C. T. Cramp, of the National Union of Railwaymen, had spoken against Clay and after Shinwell and also John Bromley, of the Locomotive Engineers, had supported him, Herbert Morrison, who had moved the Report, and Bevin agreed that the whole question should be referred for consultation between the Labour Party and the Trades Union Congress, without commitment either way. The Clay section stressed the need for according to the workers a new status in nationalised industry, whereas their opponents were afraid that, if Trade Union representation on public Boards were conceded, it would be difficult to exclude the representatives of other interests—including capital. The entire discussion was affected by recent events in connection with the setting up of the London Passenger Transport Board. The Labour Government's Bill setting up the Board had been left unenacted at the Government's fall ; and the " National " Government had thereafter mauled the Bill about, particularly in respect of the composition of the Board, which it had caused to be appointed by a curious body of " Appointing Trustees " designed to exclude Government control over its affairs. This had reinforced Herbert Morrison's already strong convictions in favour of direct Government appointment to the exclusion of all " interests," including the workers. But a good many Trade Unionists disliked the " bureaucratic " solution which Morrison preferred. On this issue the Leicester Conference agreed to postpone decision.

The general question of future policy came up at Leicester on a resolution moved by Sir Charles Trevelyan, who as we saw had resigned in disgust from the MacDonald Government before the final collapse. Trevelyan's resolution laid down " that the leaders of the next Labour Government and the Parliamentary Labour Party be instructed by the National Conference that, on assuming office, either with or without power, definite Socialist legislation must be immediately promulgated, and that the Party shall stand or fall in the House of Commons on the principles in which it has faith." Henderson opposed the resolution, on the ground that it was unwise for the Conference to tie its own hands. Attlee, on the other hand, strongly supported Trevelyan, and so clear was it that the sentiment of the delegates was with them that the resolution was carried without a card vote being challenged.

At this point, in October, 1932, Arthur Henderson had formally resigned the leadership of the Labour Party, and George Lansbury had succeeded him as fully recognised leader, having been up to that point only Chairman of the Parliamentary Party in view of Henderson's absence from the House of Commons.

The Leicester Conference was generally regarded as a move of the Labour Party to the left, in reaction against MacDonaldism and the unduly compromising attitude of the second Labour Government. Up to a point, this was the case ; but it was by no means true that there had been a leftward movement among the leaders at all corresponding to the temporary leftward swing of the delegates, including those of the Trade Unions as well as of the Local Parties. The Party leadership remained " gradualist," though not so gradualist as MacDonald ; and the new programme which it set to work to elaborate was still to be a gradualist programme very different from the " Socialism Now " which was desired not only by the I.L.P.ers who had left the Party, but also by those who had remained within it and were already reorganising their forces in the newly founded Socialist League. To the history of this body's origin and early development we must now turn.

The Socialist League was founded at Leicester in 1932 immediately before the meeting of the Labour Party Conference. It was an amalgamation of two bodies—the part of the I.L.P. which had broken away when the I.L.P. Conference decided to leave the Labour Party, and a purely propagandist body of Labour Party supporters which had been formed while the Labour Government was still in office in an endeavour to secure the adoption of a well-considered Socialist policy. This latter body, the Society for Socialist Inquiry and Propaganda, had Ernest Bevin as its Chairman, and I was Vice-Chairman. It had been formed in close association with yet another body, the New Fabian Research Bureau, of which Attlee was Chairman and I was Honorary Secretary, on the understanding that the N.F.R.B. would undertake research for the development of a constructive Socialist programme, while the S.S.I.P. would devote itself to the diffusion of the results of this research and would establish small but active local branches to undertake educational work in the wider Labour movement, to help Labour Groups on Local Councils, and generally to organise the key workers inside the Labour Party in support of a constructive Socialist programme. All this was planned and begun before the fall of the Labour Government, and before the Labour Party had set up any policy-making organisation of its own. N.F.R.B. in particular was planned in close consultation with Arthur Henderson, the Webbs, and others who saw the fatal drift of the Government and the need for a clearer formulation of policy. It was an essential part

of the plan on which both S.S.I.P. and N.F.R.B. were founded
that neither should take any direct part in parliamentary politics,
or seek formal affiliation to the Labour Party. They were designed
to work as independent auxiliaries, free to discuss and advance
policies without committing the Party, and thus able to plan ahead
with less regard for immediate expediency or the current state of
Party or Trade Union sentiment.

The New Fabian Research Bureau was entirely independent
of the Fabian Society, though it had its blessing. The Fabian
Society had at this time sunk into a condition of lethargy ; and
its younger and more active adherents saw better hopes in
founding a new body allied to it than in trying to work through it
as it was. Besides, the Fabian Society was an affiliated body of the
Labour Party, and was therefore less free than N.F.R.B. was meant
to be. The group which founded both S.S.I.P. and N.F.R.B.
was determined to avoid a repetition of the disaster which had
brought the I.L.P. into head-on conflict with the Labour Party,
and believed this would best be done if the new bodies remained
without official contacts and without power to move resolutions
at Party Conferences, seeking simply to influence Labour opinion
without pressing their ideas on the movement in any organised
way.

All began well. But when the I.L.P. split a very difficult
situation arose. The section of the I.L.P. which desired to remain
inside the Labour Party called on S.S.I.P. and N.F.R.B. to join
them in making a new inclusive Socialist Society, affiliated to the
Party, to replace the I.L.P. The Scottish ex-I.L.P.ers, though
they were associated with the approach, decided to form a separate
Scottish Socialist Party, in loose connection with any Society
that might emerge in England and Wales. This was done in
September, 1932. The N.F.R.B., holding to its purpose as an
objective research agency and refusing to become involved in
" politics " outside the sphere of research, maintained its separate
existence and went on with its work until it was able in 1939
virtually to take over the Fabian Society on its own terms and to
rejuvenate it for a new and lively existence. S.S.I.P., on the other
hand, being a propagandist body with branches, was placed in a
difficulty ; for it had either to come to terms with the ex-I.L.P.
group or to enter into rivalry with them in a field in which there
could hardly be room for both to do good work. S.S.I.P. accordingly agreed to negotiate ; but difficulties at once arose. The ex-
I.L.P. group was determined on having a body which would be

affiliated to the Labour Party and free to engage in parliamentary activities ; and it was also determined not to accept Ernest Bevin as Chairman of any combined body, and to insist on Frank Wise. On this personal issue the negotiations very nearly broke down—and I heartily wish they had. I regarded it as indispensable to carry Bevin into the new body, as the outstanding Trade Union figure capable of rallying Trade Union opinion behind it. I accordingly voted against the fusion of S.S.I.P. with the Wise group ; but I was outvoted and agreed to go with the majority— a yielding of which I was soon to repent. Had I not been seriously ill at the time, I do not think I should have agreed. I was heartily glad when, in my absence through illness, N.F.R.B. decided to maintain its separate existence.

At the time, however, I tried to make the best of a bad business by giving full support to the Socialist League. I spoke hopefully at its Inaugural Conference at Leicester, and for a year served on its Executive. By the end of the year a number of us had become convinced that it was heading for a disaster very like that which had befallen the I.L.P., by putting forward a programme of its own in opposition to that of the Labour Party, instead of trying to work for improving the official Labour programme. I resigned, and thereafter devoted my attention to the New Fabian Research Bureau : I had no part in the unfortunate later history of the Socialist League, in which, after Frank Wise's lamented death in 1933, the ascendancy passed to Sir Stafford Cripps.

(b) In Face of Nazism

In January, 1933, Adolf Hitler became Chancellor of Germany. The episode of the Reichstag Fire followed in February ; and at the beginning of March came the election which gave the Nazis and their Nationalist supporters a clear majority in the Reichstag. Labour and Socialism all the world over had to face the immense consequences of the new German Revolution. Simultaneously with the Nazi conquest of power the Japanese launched a new offensive in Northern China, and the United States was laid low by a banking crisis which caused a widespread suspension of payments. In the midst of this crisis Roosevelt came into office as President and began his emergency measures : in April the United States suspended the gold standard and depreciated the gold value of the dollar. In June, came the World Economic

Conference, which broke down the following month. In October the Germans withdrew from the Disarmament Conference and gave notice of withdrawal from the League of Nations. The same month there were serious troubles between Jews and Arabs in Palestine. Finally, in December the Stavisky scandal broke in France, bringing discredit on many leading politicians, and leading on to the fall of Daladier in February, 1934.

Such was the world background of the year 1933, in which, of course, the Nazi conquest of Germany overshadowed all other events. Socialists everywhere had to consider what were the appropriate measures for countering the new danger and arresting the spread of Fascism ; and the Communists naturally responded to the situation with a renewed demand for the United Front. In February, the Executive of the Labour and Socialist International met at Zurich and took the initiative in declaring the need for united working-class resistance and its readiness to negotiate with the Comintern for common action. Moscow, in reply, issued a Manifesto calling on the Communist Party in each separate country to seek to convene a Conference to form a United Front. The British Communist Party thereupon approached the Labour Party, the Trades Union Congress, and the Co-operative Party on the question. The I.L.P. also issued an appeal for the United Front, and in March arrived at a general agreement with the Communist Party for a common effort to bring it about. The Labour and Socialist International, meeting again at Zurich on March 6, rejected the Comintern's method of promoting unity and called on its affiliated parties not to respond to the separate national approaches until it had defined its attitude to the Comintern's new programme. Following this lead, the Labour National Joint Council in Great Britain declined the proposals of the Communist Party and the I.L.P., and issued a Manifesto, *Democracy versus Dictatorship*, in which it coupled a denunciation of the Nazi dictatorship in Germany with an attack on Communist dictatorship in the Soviet Union and elsewhere, treated the Nazi victory as a reaction to the dictatorial " reaction of the left," declared that the " historic task " of British Labour was " to uphold the principles of Social Democracy " against dictatorship of every kind, and prided itself on having " successfully resisted attempts at disruption both from the Right and from the Left—from ' National Labour ' on the one hand and from ' Independent Labour ' on the other." The Manifesto ended tamely enough by calling on the British workers to strengthen the Trade Unions, the Co-operative Societies, and the Labour Party " against dictators, Fascist or Communist."

This curious document, as the Labour Party's National Executive admitted in its Report later in the year, aroused not only violent opposition on the part of the Communists and the I.L.P. but also " a certain amount of criticism from sections of the Party." Its equation of Nazism with Soviet Communism was widely resented ; and its failure to give any lead in the extremely critical situation was felt to be lamentably weak. " Nevertheless," the Labour Party Executive Report went on, " it was clearly evident that the Manifesto broadly expressed the prevailing opinion of the Industrial and Political Movements and in the Parliamentary Party." If it did, so much the worse for all these bodies.

Having said in effect that Nazism and Communism were much the same, the National Joint Council proceeded on April 12 to hold at the Albert Hall a Mass Demonstration of Protest against the Nazi régime, and also set up a fund to help the Germans who were fleeing already from the Nazi terror. Some months later, in July, the N.J.C. also attempted to institute a ban on the purchase of German goods ; but this had little effect. Over the same period, the United Front agitation led the Labour Party Executive to intensify its measures against bodies supposed to be acting under Communist influence. The Executive sent out a general circular urging its affiliated societies to have no dealings with such bodies, and also " to refrain from assisting to establish special organisations for any political or industrial purposes which could be pursued through the Trade Union Movement or the Labour Party." It also published a pamphlet, *The Communist Solar System*, designed to expose the tactics of the Communist Party in working through a number of crypto-Communist agencies in the hope of attracting Labour support.

Many local Labour bodies, however, stirred by the events in Germany, were ready to join in the demand for a United Front. In April the left-wing bodies held a big United Front Demonstration in Hyde Park ; and in May the Communist Party and the I.L.P. came to a working agreement for joint action against Fascism. Mosley had by this time liquidated his New Party and appeared openly as the leader of a British Fascist movement ; and the first Fascist demonstrations began to be held in London. Meanwhile, the agitation against the Means Test continued ; and from February onwards the National Joint Council organised a series of meetings and demonstrations to protest against the Government's policy on the employment question and on the treatment of the unemployed. The N.J.C. also joined in the protest movement against the treatment of the prisoners involved in the Meerut Trial, and protested against the sentences passed at the end of 1932 on Tom Mann and Emrhys Llewellyn under the obsolete Seditious Meetings Act of 1817. Protests were also made against the embargo on Russian trade imposed after the trial of the Metropolitan-Vickers engineers in the Soviet Union in April, 1933.

But the main activity of the Labour Party in 1933 was concerned, not with the new international menace, but with the development of its own new programme. During the summer it produced two further special Reports from its Policy Committee, one on Housing and the other embodying a plan of Colonial Development. Of wider scope than these was the Report on *Socialism and the Condition of the People*, which dealt largely with employment policy and the problems of the standard of living, but also included a proposal, designed to carry out the decision of the 1932 Conference, to amalgamate the joint stock banks into a single publicly owned and controlled Banking Corporation, to act in close conjunction with the socialised Bank of England in regulating the supply of short-term credit. This Report also embodied proposals for the planned development of national resources, and for the public " ownership or control " of steel and other vital industries not covered by previous proposals for socialisation.

At the Hastings Conference of 1933 the Report on *Socialism and the Condition of the People* was met with an amendment by Sir Stafford Cripps, as delegate from the East Bristol Labour Party but speaking in effect for the Socialist League. What Cripps wanted was an assurance that the next Labour Government would proceed immediately to abolish the House of Lords and would then pass into law an Emergency Powers Act " giving the Government authority to take over or regulate the financial machine, and to put into force any measure that the situation may require for the immediate control or socialisation of industry and for safeguarding the supply of food and other necessaries." Therewith the resolution demanded the revision of parliamentary procedure " so that a rapid transition to Socialism may be carried through constitutionally, and dictatorship avoided," and " an Economic Plan for Industry, Finance, and Foreign Trade designed rapidly to end the present system and thus to abolish unemployment and poverty." After speeches from Shinwell, Bevin, Attlee and others these proposals were referred to the Executive for consideration—it is a notable fact that they were not rejected out of hand—and the Conference went on to write into the Report a demand for close collaboration " with Russia and other Socialist Governments in order to form a nucleus for international Socialist co-operation," and to lay down that " in the event of a parliamentary Labour majority, the Government shall immediately proceed to bring into operation the Socialist programme on which it had been elected." It was then agreed that the National Executive should prepare and issue for the next General Election " a concise declaration of the measures which a Labour Government will endeavour to place on the Statute Book," and that it should also " produce at once a short and readable publication for popular use outlining the definite Party Policy in plain and unmistakable terms." This last proposal meant in effect that the Executive was told to produce a substitute for the verbose equivocations of *Labour and the Nation*.

The 1933 Conference was in the main marking time in respect of the controversy between the right and left wings. There were echoes of the temper of the Leicester Conference ; but there were also signs that the Executive, though unwilling to challenge the left wing outright, was disinclined to accept its proposals, and was playing for time. In particular, the Executive had to report on a resolution that had been passed by the Parliamentary Labour Party in 1931, immediately after the fall of the Labour Government, dealing with " the procedure to be followed when the Party is asked to form a Government after any future Election." This resolution, known as the " Ayles " resolution (it had been moved by Walter Ayles of Bristol) called for a report " with regard to the choice of the Premier and Members of the Government," and also on " the policy to be outlined in the King's Speech, and generally to be followed by the Party in applying National Conference decisions and handling questions on which no decisions exist." The report was also to cover the revision of the Party's Standing Orders " and the relation of the Cabinet to the Parliamentary Party."

In reporting on these matters to the 1933 Conference the Executive recommended that " after a General Election which has resulted in the possibility of a Labour Government, the final decision as to the steps to be taken would rest with the meeting

of the Parliamentary Party," but that this body " should have
before it the considered views of the most representative body in
the Labour Movement "—i.e., the National Joint Council—
which should consult the bodies represented in it, so that "their
joint recommendations would be communicated to the Parliamentary Party." If, however, the Labour Party were in a
position to form only a Minority Government, it was recommended that a special Labour Party Conference should be called
to consider the situation. In the choice of Ministers, the Executive
said that " it is realised that final responsibility . . . must rest
with the Prime Minister " ; but it proposed that three members
of the Parliamentary Party should be elected to advise the Party
leader, and that the Secretary of the Party should be associated
with them in this task. The Government's policy in office should
be based on Conference resolutions and on the Party's Election
Manifesto ; and the King's Speech should " from year to year,
announce the instalments of the Party's policy with which the
Government proposed to deal." The Prime Minister " should be
subject to majority decisions of the Cabinet " and " should only
recommend the dissolution of Parliament on the decision of the
Cabinet confirmed by a Parliamentary Party meeting." Financial
policy should be determined by the Cabinet, and " the Party
should put an end to the practice by which excessive authority
in this field has in the past been exercised by the Chancellor of the
Exchequer." There should be " closer contact among Ministers,
and also between the Government and the Parliamentary Party
and between both and the National Joint Council as standing
for the Labour Movement as a whole. A particular Minister
should be appointed to keep regular liaison with the Parliamentary Party, and three Cabinet Ministers should be appointed to
maintain close touch with the National Joint Council. Finally, it
was proposed that " in order to make fuller use of the services
of private Members, Ministers should keep in touch with groups
of Members interested in, and having special knowledge of, " the
problems of particular departments."

The Conference, on Clynes's motion, carried this far-reaching
report, rejecting an amendment designed to place the actual
choice of Ministers in the hands of the National Joint Council,
with representatives of the Co-operative Party.

Another issue which came up at Hastings was that of Workers'
Control in relation to socialised industries and services. After
the discussions on the question at Leicester the matter was taken

up again between the Party Executive and the T.U.C. General Council, and the Executive came to the Hastings Conference with an agreed Memorandum which had already been approved by a small majority at the Trades Union Congress. This recognised in somewhat guarded terms the right of the Trade Unions to be represented on the " Boards of Management and Control " of socialised industries, but was obviously drafted for the purpose of concealing rather than resolving real differences of view. It did not satisfy the delegates ; and an addendum moved by Charles Dukes of the General Workers was carried by a fairly narrow majority after keen discussion. This laid down that Trade Union representation must be not merely accepted in principle, but laid down as a statutory right in any Bill embodying a Labour socialisation scheme. It was then announced that the question would be taken up again with the General Council, with a view to the working out of an agreed formula.

On the United Front issue, the Executive carried the day. An attempt to refer back the paragraphs in its Report dealing with the *Democracy versus Dictatorship* manifesto was defeated after a speech by Herbert Morrison, who said the Labour Party could not " hunt with the hounds and also run with the hare," and that " if we are opposed to dictatorship, we must be open and say so." Association with the Communists, who advocated dictatorship, would be " only asking for trouble," and, as for the I.L.P., it did not know where it stood. The Conference then went on to defeat by show of hands a resolution calling directly for the United Front. It also carried the Previous Question on a resolution declaring that no member of the Labour Party should accept " honours " for political services.

In short, the Hastings Conference was in no mood to accept the Communist demand for unity at its face value, regarding it merely as another manœuvre meant to give the Communist leaders a chance of getting inside the Labour Party and the Trade Unions with the object of discrediting their leaders and of disrupting the existing machine. The two sides in the controversy which followed the Nazi victory in Germany put directly opposite interpretations on what had occurred. The left wing denounced the pusillanimity of the German Social Democratic leaders, and saw in their collapse the justification for an attack on the entire policy of gradualism and Social Democracy ; whereas the Labour moderates blamed the defeat upon the Communists, whose tactics had weakened and divided the German working class,

and had thus cleared the road for Hitler's revolution. In retrospect it is clear enough that there was a good deal of justification
for both views, and that gross errors had been committed on both
sides. But in the heat of the controversy few could see more
than one aspect ; and accordingly nothing was done to foster the
united working-class action which each side professed to want, but
wanted in practice only under its own exclusive leadership and
on the basis of its own policy.

I do not suggest that unity could have been easy to achieve,
in face of the deep differences of principle and policy between
the rival leaderships. I do suggest that the conditions were such
as to make a real effort to achieve it, in face of the dangerous
international situation, necessary and worth every possible concession. Even a strictly limited unity for the purpose of the
common struggle against Fascism might have made a vital difference to the course of events.

(c) " For Socialism and Peace "

Nineteen hundred and thirty-four was a year in which the
economic situation, thanks largely to President Roosevelt's
" New Deal " policy, grew markedly better, and the political
situation markedly worse. Abroad it opened with the Stavisky
scandal bringing down the French Government and putting
a more reactionary Ministry under Doumergue in its place. On
top of this came the Viennese Civil War, in which in a few days of
February the Austrian Socialists were overwhelmed and Dollfuss
established his fragile Christian dictatorship. In the Far East the
Japanese installed a puppet Emperor in Manchuria, and went on
in April to repudiate the Nine-Power Treaty regulating intervention in China. In May dictatorship was installed in Bulgaria
by a *coup de main*. In June came the Nazi Purge, in which Hitler
got rid of Schleicher, Strasser, Roehm and others who stood in
the way of his absolute authority. Three months later, on
Hindenburg's death, he installed himself as President of the
Reich. Before that, in July, Dollfuss had been assassinated and
Schuschnigg had replaced him and had attempted a deal with
Mussolini to protect him against Hitler. In France, Socialists
and Communists had agreed in July to form a United Front ;
and a Spanish United Front followed in September, leading on
to the Spanish General Strike of October, with its forewarnings

of Civil War. In October the rival French Trade Union move-
ments—the *C.G.T.* and the Communist-controlled *C.G.T.
Unitaire*—agreed to unite, almost at the moment when King
Alexander of Yugoslavia was being assassinated on French soil.
In November the Democrats won a Congressional Election in the
United States, thus helping to consolidate Roosevelt's power.
Finally, in December came the assassination of Kirov in the
Soviet Union, and later Japan's repudiation of the Washington
Naval Treaty.

From the standpoint of international Labour, the outstanding
events were the consolidation of Nazi power in Germany and the
complete liquidation of all open opposition, and the overthrow
of the Viennese Socialists—the best of the continental Social
Democratic Parties. In Great Britain Mosley's Fascist movement
began to take an uglier shape, with marches and counter-marches
leading up to the scenes of violence in connection with the
Olympia Fascist demonstration in June. There were many
Communist and other left-wing clashes with the police, who were
accused of showing, under orders, favour to the Fascists and
marked disfavour to working-class counter-demonstrations. Anti-
Semitism began to be preached openly in London's East End. In
September there was a big Fascist demonstration, met by a much
bigger counter-demonstration, in Hyde Park. In November the
Government placed on the statute book the Incitement to Dis-
affection Act, which was used mainly against the Communists.

Throughout the year the Communist Party went on actively
with its campaign for the United Front. This, after the rejection
of its overtures the previous year, had become more openly an
attempt to rally left-wing elements under Communist leadership against the Trade Union and Labour Party leaders. Big
Hunger Marches were organised at the beginning of the year ;
and in connection with these a National Unity Congress was held
in Bermondsey Town Hall in February, 1934. Inside the I.L.P.
a Revolutionary Policy Committee was set up under Communist
inspiration to bring the I.L.P.—what was left of it—over to the
Third International ; but the Easter Conference of the I.L.P.
rejected a proposal that it should join that body " as a sympathising party." The Labour Party Executive issued in January,
1934, a pronouncement reaffirming its definitive opposition " to
Individual or Group Dictatorship, whether from the Right or
from the Left," and its unshaken faith in " Democratic Government, with a free electoral system and an active and efficient

Parliamentary machine for reaching effective decisions, after reasonable opportunities for discussion and criticism." This was mainly directed against the Socialist League, which was calling for a drastic reform of parliamentary procedure in order to make possible a rapid enactment of Socialist measures, and was being accused by Government spokesmen of advocating a policy of " dictatorship."

In February, in view of the events in Austria, the Communist Party and the I.L.P. again made approaches to the Labour Party on the question of the United Front. The Labour Party Executive replied that it was well aware of the need for unity and was seeking to achieve it by united action on Austria and on other matters with the Trade Union and Co-operative Movements. This, it said, was " the real united front for common purposes." The I.L.P. and the Communists were told that this was " unity based upon common agreement as to aims, policies and methods, without which ' united ' action would be fictitious and superficial, and, in the long run, would gravely injure the effective power of the organised working class." Consultations had nevertheless taken place between the Labour Party and the I.L.P., but had led to no agreement : with the Communist Party the Labour Party Executive refused to consult at all, asserting that it did not believe in Parliamentary Democracy, was controlled by the Comintern, and was pursuing towards the Labour and Trade Union Movements an attitude of " misrepresentation, denunciation and disruption." An attempt to refer back the Executive's Report on these issues was overwhelmingly defeated at the Labour Party's Southport Conference in October, 1934

The Labour Party's hostility to any compromise with the Communists or the I.L.P. was strengthened by the London Labour Party's success in the March elections, at which it captured for the first time a clear majority of seats on the London County Council. There were also considerable provincial successes on the County and District Councils at this time, followed in November by large gains at the annual municipal elections. To these were added encouraging by-election victories in London—East Fulham, in October, 1933, North Hammersmith in April, 1934, and the Upton Division of West Ham in the following month ; but these were not paralleled by successes in the rest of the country, though everywhere the " National " majorities were considerably reduced.

The course of events in the Labour Party during 1934 was also affected by changes in its leadership. In December, 1933, George Lansbury, the Parliamentary leader, fell seriously ill, and Clement Attlee took his place pending his recovery, which was not until the autumn of 1934. In May, Arthur Henderson, who had also been seriously ill and was still devoting such strength as was left him to the Disarmament Conference, resigned from the position of Secretary to the Party, which he had held since 1911. Henderson agreed to stay on as Treasurer ; but from this point he ceased to be in constant charge of Party affairs. J. S. Middleton, who had been Assistant Secretary from the very early years, replaced him first as Acting Secretary and then as full Secretary, after it had been decided that the holder of the position should be debarred from sitting in the House of Commons. R. C. Wallhead, who had rejoined the Labour Party in 1933 after seceding with the I.L.P. in 1931, died in April, 1934 ; and Frank Wise, the leader of the ex-I.L.P. group in the Socialist League, also died in November, 1933. William Graham, Snowden's successor as the Labour Party's chief expert on public finance, had died the previous year. These losses left Attlee, Greenwood and Cripps to bear the main brunt of leadership in the House of Commons, with Morrison and Dalton still outside, but active on the Party Executive.

Largely in their hands, the special Policy Committee actively continued its work. The Party Conference in 1934 found itself called on to deal with special Policy Reports on housing (held over from 1933), rent control, education, compensation on the taking over of industries and services into public hands, water supply, a State Health Service, welfare of the blind, import boards, and Parliamentary problems and procedure, as well as with a more general statement, entitled *For Socialism and Peace*, which was intended to embody a broad and popular account of the Labour Party's objects and programme, in both home and international affairs. In view of this new technique of special Executive Reports on main issues of policy, the Conference Standing Orders Committee had recommended in 1933 and the Executive had endorsed important changes in Conference procedure, under which much more time was to be allotted to resolutions and amendments based on or arising out of these Policy Reports, and much less to general resolutions. The effect of this was to give the Executive more control over the agenda, and to reduce the power of the affiliated bodies. There were some complaints on this score ; but it was fairly generally recognised that the Reports needed careful discussion, and, as no suggestion was made that the Conference should break up into commissions on the continental model, something had to be jettisoned in order to spare more time for the main debates.

At the Southport Conference the special Policy Reports mostly went through with very little discussion, only a few amendments being moved. The main debates centred round the more general document, *For Socialism and Peace*, which bore the sub-title " The Labour Party's Programme of Action," and was described by the Executive, in issuing it, as " a comprehensive and concise statement of policy." In effect, it was designed to replace *Labour and the Nation* as the authoritative exposition of Labour Party policy as a whole. It summed up Labour's aims in the following propositions :—

(a) To establish peace, freedom and justice by removing from among the nations the root causes of international disputes, by conciliation and arbitration, by renouncing war as an instrument of national policy, by disarmament, by political and economic co-operation through the League of Nations, and by agreements with States which are not yet members of the League.*

(b) To secure to every member of the community the standards of life and employment necessary to a healthy, independent and self-respecting existence, and to give equality of opportunity, both political and economic, to men and women alike.

(c) To convert industry, with due regard to the varying needs and circumstances of different sections, from a haphazard struggle for private gain to a planned national economy owned and carried on for the service of the community.

(d) To extend rapidly and widely those forms of social provision— education, public health, housing, pensions, and maintenance during unemployment—in the absence of which the individual is the sport of economic chance and the slave of his environment.

(e) To adjust taxation in such a way that due provision is made for the maintenance and improvement of the material apparatus of industry, and that surpluses created by social effort shall be applied for the good of all.

The draft began with international policy. It took a strong " League of Nations " line and proposed the enactment of a " Peace Act " embodying a full statement of international obligations, including those in being or contemplated under the League Covenant. It announced a " Peace Crusade," national and world-wide, for the purpose of raising up " a great mass movement

*This draft was issued in July, 1934. The Soviet Union decided to join the League of Nations in September.

against war." It asserted the need for " full co-operation " with both the United States and the Soviet Union, and called for " a treaty of non-aggression and conciliation " with the latter and also for a development of commercial relations.

The draft then turned to home affairs, beginning with the statement " The electors are entitled to know what the establishment of Socialism means in terms of concrete domestic measures." It declared for a double policy of " great fundamental measures of economic reconstruction " and of the building up of " many forms of social provision." These two, it said, would have to go together . . . " The whole basis must be the recognition that what the nation now requires is not mere social reform, but Socialism. That is the end for which Labour asks the mandate of the electors."

In the economic field, " banking and credit, transport, electricity, water, iron and steel, coal, gas, agriculture, textiles, shipping, ship-building, engineering—in all these the time has come for drastic reorganisation, and for the most part nothing short of public ownership and control will be effective . . . The employees in a socialised industry have a right, which should be acknowledged by law, to an effective share in the control and direction of the industry." The draft then declared for " fair compensation " to dispossessed owners, in the case of transport on a basis of " net maintainable revenue " and on " a corresponding basis " for other industries and services. The need for measures to increase efficiency in production and to set up effective buying and selling agencies was then asserted, and therewith the dependence of good wages and conditions on more efficient conduct of industry and trade. The banking proposals already approved were next summarised ; and so were the special Reports already issued or about to be issued on Transport, Electricity Supply, Land and Agriculture, Water Supply, Housing, Rents, a State Health Service, Welfare of the Blind, and Education. On the coal question, the draft declared for " unification under public ownership " ; on iron and steel, it proposed the setting up of an Iron and Steel Corporation, to be appointed by the President of the Board of Trade, " to take over all undertakings manufacturing iron and steel products, from pig iron to finished goods," with Sectional Boards for the various branches.

The draft then went on to outline measures of industrial legislation, including an attempt to secure an International Forty-hour Week Convention, and in the meantime help to the Trade

Unions in negotiating forty-hour week agreements, and the introduction of the forty-hour week into the public services. Under
the social service provisions, the draft promised abolition of the
Means Test and maintenance of the unemployed " as a national
charge." It promised to raise the school-leaving age, to take the
older workers out of industry by means of an improved pensions
scheme, and to improve conditions of rural living. It then
recapitulated the policy for the development of full employment
laid down in *Socialism and the Condition of the People*, and promised
large changes in the distribution of tax burdens and for the
prevention of tax evasion by the rich.

In the concluding sections the draft turned to the question of
Parliamentary Government. It declared that " the Labour
Party, given a majority, would interpret the mandate as conferring
upon it the right, particularly if the House of Lords seeks to wreck
its essential measures, forthwith to proceed to the abolition of that
chamber," and added that " in any event," the Party was committed to abolishing the House of Lords. The draft then declared
that " the reform of the procedure of the House of Commons
brooks no delay," and that the Labour Party, if returned to power,
would ask the House to set up a " Time-table " Committee to
arrange for the adequate handling of Government Bills, which
would " after their second reading, be sent to Standing Committees." This part of the draft was elaborated in one of the
Special Reports submitted to the 1934 Conference.

Finally, the draft affirmed the Labour Party's faith in parliamentary democracy. " Its whole faith reposes in the achievement of change by the process of consent." Changes in democratic
procedure were needed in view of twentieth-century conditions
and the necessities of rapid, all-round reconstruction of the social
and economic system ; but the Labour Party " sees no reason why
a people who, first in the world, achieved through Parliamentary
institutions their political and religious freedom should not, by
the same means, achieve their economic emancipation."

For Socialism and Peace was a very much more incisive and
definite statement of the Labour Party's Socialist intentions than
Labour and the Nation had been ; but it was also a challenge to
those who were claiming that Socialism could not be brought
about by the established methods of Parliamentarism, on the
ground that the attempt to do this would provoke in the first place
obstruction by vested interests and abuse of parliamentary
procedure to delay action to an intolerable extent, and then, if

this were not enough, a " Fascist " appeal to force against the institutions of parliamentary democracy. The Socialist League, in particular, was taking this line, and was demanding that the Labour Party should accept the need for a Socialist Government to make drastic use of emergency powers both for getting its legislation through and for enforcing administrative action against capitalist attempts to engineer an economic crisis or to secure a boycott of a Socialist Britain by capitalist States—especially the U.S.A. The Labour Party Executive wished to dissociate itself from these views of the " left," which were being vehemently attacked in the Press as revealing the " real mind " of the Socialists.

Naturally, then, *For Socialism and Peace* did not go unchallenged. At the Southport Labour Party Conference the Socialist League put down no fewer than seventy-five amendments to the draft, beginning with a proposal to delete the whole of the five " Aims " which I have cited, and to substitute a five-point " Programme of Action " involving " a decisive advance within five years towards a Socialist Britain." Labour in office was " at once to proceed," not only " to make Parliament effective," but also " to secure at once for the Government Economic Power sufficient to enable it to proceed unhampered with the Socialist reorganisation of our industrial and social system." It was " to change the whole basis of production and distribution so that productive power may be used to satisfy the needs of the people in accordance with a Planned Economy." This amendment was moved at the Conference by Stafford Cripps. Hugh Dalton, for the Executive, asked for its withdrawal, promising to follow up *For Socialism and Peace* with a short statement of Labour's immediate programme. The Socialist League refused to withdraw. Herbert Morrison attacked the amendment for its dangerous generality and for the Communist notions which he held to underlie it. The vote showed 2,146,000 for the Executive, and only 206,000 for the Socialist League. The League renewed its attack on a number of specific issues, including compensation. It wished to reject the right of compensation at full value and to substitute a system of terminable annuities designed only to prevent hardship to dispossessed owners over a limited time. On this issue only 149,000, against 2,118,000, voted with the Socialist League. The League tried again, with an amendment to stiffen up the section dealing with iron and steel by inserting a definite provision for workers' control ; but on almost every issue it was left in a very small minority. Finally, *For Socialism and Peace* was adopted as a whole without substantial amendment.

Together with this general re-statement of policy, the Executive put before the 1934 Conference a separate document on " War and Peace," arising out of a resolution adopted at Hastings the year before. This document was put forward in the joint names of the three national bodies : it was designed to fill a gap left by the Hastings resolution, which had dealt only with war resistance and propaganda against war, by making proposals " for preventing war by organising peace." Its main sections dealt with the development of a system of collective security and economic co-operation within the framework of the League of Nations and the International Labour Organisation ; and it proposed a stiffening of the League Covenant and measures " to abolish all national armed forces maintained for the purpose of self-defence against other nations, and to substitute an International Police Force under the League's authority." The abolition of national air forces was advocated as a first step, to be accompanied by the internationalisation of civil aviation. The need for bringing the Soviet Union into the League and for advancing step by step in agreement with the United States was emphasised ; and it was urged that each country should have national legislation designed to strengthen the peace system and to accept the obligation never to resort to force as an instrument of national policy. Full support was given to an all-in system of arbitration ; and under the heading of " Sanctions " the memorandum affirmed " the duty unflinchingly to support our Government in all the risks and consequences of fulfilling its duty to take part in collective action against a peace-breaker." ' War resistance ' to service in any war undertaken in violation of these principles was advocated.

The document then turned to the question of a General Strike to stop a war. It was pointed out that such action had become an impossibility in Germany, Italy and other countries which might engage in aggression ; and the conclusion was drawn that " the responsibility for stopping war ought not to be placed upon the Trade Union Movement alone." Refusal to handle munitions might easily develop into a General Strike, and it would be unwise for the Labour Movement to commit itself further than under the Trades Union Congress's Standing Orders it had done already. These provided for the calling of a Special Congress in the event of there being a danger of war, and beyond this it was undesirable to go. There was no alternative to " the collective peace system " except " a relapse into international anarchy." In other words, the Labour Movement was not prepared to take the responsibility for stopping war by its own action : it called for " collective security " through the League of Nations.

On this question also the Socialist League joined issue with the Executive, putting forward an amendment which involved a practically complete re-draft. The Socialist League regarded the League of Nations as " indissolubly bound up with " the Treaty of Versailles, and as built on unsound foundations and capable only of upholding the *status quo*. " The League of Nations inevitably reflects the economic conflicts of the capitalist system . . . The League of Nations cannot end war." Instead of relying on the League, a Labour Government should " seek to establish the closest political and economic relations with the Soviet Union and with all other countries where Socialist Governments are in control." The amendment ended by calling on the workers throughout the capitalist countries " to prepare resistance to war declared by their own Governments," and to demand that the Labour Party should undertake " to resist a war entered into by this Government by every means in its power, including a General Strike." On this issue too the Socialist League was summarily voted down, and the Report was adopted by 1,519,000 votes to 673,000—a large minority which for once united nearly all the opposition groups at the Conference.

During 1934, as we saw, the employment situation had been improving, as the worst of the world depression passed away. The cuts in the standard rates of unemployment benefit were restored in April ; but the hated Means Test remained. Under the new Unemployment Insurance Act of 1934, based on the Final Report of the Royal Commission set up in 1931, the unemployed were split up into three categories—those eligible for insurance benefit proper, those who on exhausting their strict insurance claim were to be transferred to the new service of Unemployment Assistance, administered by a " non-political " Unemployment Assistance Board, and those who either were not covered by insurance or were regarded as having exhausted their claims to help from the U.A.B. For this third group, Public Assistance—i.e., the old Poor Law—was the sole resort. In December, 1934, the U.A.B. issued its draft Regulations for Unemployment Assistance, and large numbers of unemployed workers found that the Means Test in the revised form proposed, meant heavy reductions below the sums which they had been receiving under the transitional system which had been in operation since 1931. Some workers would gain under the new scales ; but in the most heavily depressed areas—above all in the coalfields—the cuts would be severe.

Just before the U.A.B. published its draft scales, there had been published, in November, 1934, a series of Reports on conditions in the Distressed Areas, showing that despite the improvement in trade there remained in these parts of the country great stagnant pools of long-term unemployment, and that whole towns were practically derelict. The Government introduced a Special Areas Bill providing for the appointment of Commissioners with very limited powers to aid in the provision of employment, mainly through public works ; and the Labour Party did what it could to improve this grossly inadequate Bill. Meanwhile, a storm was blowing up against the Regulations put forward by the U.A.B. Once more, the local Unemployed Committees became active and secured widespread support from Trades Councils and local Trade Union branches. The T.U.C. General Council refused to have any dealings with the Communist-controlled National Unemployed Workers' Movement ; but the demonstrations against the U.A.B. spread like wildfire, and early in February the Government was forced to suspend the proposed new scales and to provide for a temporary system maintaining the old rates wherever they were threatened until the U.A.B. had had time to " think again." During this struggle the Communists and the I.L.P. again applied to the national Labour bodies to agree to " united action " ; but the National Joint Council of Labour preferred to take its own line in a manifesto protesting against the U.A.B. proposals under the title " An Appeal to the National Conscience." The Communist Party Congress in February, 1935, on the other hand, launched a new policy of its own, with the slogan " For Soviet Britain," setting out for the first time in detail its own plans for the achievement of the British Socialist Revolution.

About this time Lloyd George also attempted a " come-back," with a plan under the slogan " Organising Prosperity." This was at first put forward without the endorsement of the other Liberal leaders ; and there was a good deal of controversy over it in the Liberal Party, which had announced its intention of putting up 400 candidates at the next General Election and was looking hard for a programme on which it could fight both Labour and the " Nationals." Lloyd George wanted a Supreme Economic

Council, directed by a small inner Cabinet, to carry through a thorough reorganisation of the staple industries and to undertake a large programme of economic and social development on a basis of " national unity " and of forthright action such as had been achieved during the war. He was prepared for some nationalisation, but appeared to contemplate mainly state financial assistance to private industry combined with some measure of public control. He outlined his programme first in a series of speeches and then in a book, offering to collaborate with the " National " Government if it would carry out his scheme. But of course nothing came of this. The " National " Government was in fact on the point of jettisoning its nominal leader and becoming a purely Tory Government backed by the Simonite Liberal-Nationals, who were Tories in all but name. In June, 1935, Ramsay MacDonald was forced into resignation, and Stanley Baldwin again became Prime Minister.

This month of June was notable also for the publication of the final results of the Peace Ballot which had been organised by the League of Nations Union and a number of other bodies in the latter part of 1934, mainly for the purpose of mobilising British opinion behind an attempt to strengthen the League as an instrument of collective security. In this ballot, over 11,500,000 persons voted, answering a series of questions about their attitude to international policy. Over 11,000,000 voted in favour of Great Britain remaining a member of the League : nearly 10,500,000 favoured " an all-round reduction of armaments by international agreement " ; over 9,500,000 wanted " the all-round abolition of national military and naval aircraft by international agreement " ; nearly 10,500,000 wanted the private manufacture and sale of arms abolished on the same terms ; and, on the two final questions, relating to collective sanctions against an aggressor, 10,000,000 voted for " economic and non-military sanctions," and over 6,750,000 (against 2,350,000 adverse votes and nearly 2,500,000 abstentions or " doubtfuls ") for " military sanctions " as well.

The Peace Ballot immediately preceded the outbreak of the Abyssinian crisis. The Italians had already for some time been threatening Abyssinian independence ; and the Abyssinians had already in January expressed their desire to lay their case before the League of Nations. In February the Italians began open mobilisation for the Abyssinian campaign ; but as late as April, when, faced by the reintroduction of conscription in Germany, the delegates of the British, French and Italian Governments met at Stresa to discuss this new threat to peace, neither the British nor the French, as the Labour Party Executive remarked, " appear to have warned Mussolini that his military expedition was a strange commentary upon the foreign policy of a Power, ' the object of whose policy is the collective maintenance of peace within the framework of the League of Nations.' " Abyssinia was not even mentioned at the Stresa Conference : Laval, for France, had already made an agreement with Mussolini in January ; and Great Britain and France were engaged in complicated discussions of possible regional pacts in Europe, and by no means wished to have a quarrel with Italy on their hands. The British Government even concluded a Naval Agreement with Germany in June, in face of the flat violation of the disarmament provisions of the Versailles Treaty.

In May the Franco-Soviet Pact was signed ; and in June the French Radicals agreed to join a Popular Front with the Socialist and Communist Parties. In May, the Labour and Socialist International protested against the tendency for Governments, in return for giving nominal adhesion to the League system, to require the complaisance of other League States in their own acts of imperialist aggression. The Fascists continued, with the advantage of this complaisance, to assemble their forces on the Abyssinian frontier. The International and the National Council of Labour demanded a meeting of the League to deal with the Abyssinian problem, and the former urged its affiliated Parties to do all they could to stop the dispatch of war supplies to Italy, and to organise demonstrations against the threatened imperialist war. At the beginning of September the Trades Union Congress passed a resolution strongly condemning the Italian aggression, and pledging " its firm support of any action consistent with the principles and statutes of the League to restrain the Italian Government and to uphold the authority of the League in enforcing peace." None of these activities in any way deterred the Italian Fascists, who were confident that nothing effective would be done against them by the League Powers. In the autumn the Italians began bombing and fighting their way into Abyssinia, undeterred by the League's protests or by the threat of sanctions. In September, Sir Samual Hoare, as Foreign Secretary, made a pro-League speech at Geneva, influenced thereto by the Peace Ballot voting and by the unmistakable strength of League sentiment in Great Britain ; and in October the majority of the League countries were driven to endorse a policy of " economic sanctions " against Italy. But the action resolved on was half-hearted, and even so was not fully applied : in effect nothing was done thoroughly to cut off Italian war supplies, such as petrol—much less to stop the invasion by more drastic means.

In the meantime, the British Government had published, in September, a White Paper on Armaments, recommending substantial increases. But, even in face of the threatening attitude of Germany, as well as of the Italian war on Abyssinia, peace feeling in Great Britain was strong, and there was a deep reluctance to accept the need for larger armaments at any rate until a real attempt had been made to achieve a system of collective security, based on pooled armaments, through the League. In these circumstances the Tories, who had no real belief in the League and regarded re-armament as necessary, not so much with a view to fighting Hitler or overawing Mussolini as to doing a series of deals with both, decided to double-cross the Labour Party by coming out in a General Election as strong supporters of the League, with every intention, when they had won the Election by this device, of carrying out a policy diametrically opposed to that on which they meant to appeal to the electorate. The Labour Party and the Trade Unions had given strong support to the Peace Ballot ; and it was clear to Baldwin, in the light of its results, that if he asked for British re-armament except as a contribution to a League system of collective security, he would be likely to fare but ill at the polls. If, on the other hand, he could get a clear Tory majority in a new House of Commons by deceiving the electors into a belief that he would stand by the League, he would be free after the Election to go his own way without the League, and to combine a purely British re-armament policy with an attempt to come to terms with the European dictators. Baldwin practically admitted all this after the Election was over, in the famous speech in which he explained to the Conservative Party that he would never have been able to put his policy of re-armament across to the electors, and had therefore been compelled to posture before them as the friend of the League and the apostle of a peace policy which he had borrowed whole from the Labour Party and the League of Nations Union.

(d) *Death of Arthur Henderson—The Sanctions Issue*

The whole problem of Labour's international policy came to a head at the Brighton Conference in the early days of October, 1935. Henderson was away ill : he died three weeks later, on October 20, after an operation from which he failed to rally. He had fought on, against discouragement and severe illness, in his attempt to make the Disarmament Conference a success ; and he had been for the most part out of the Labour leadership, because of this, for some years. His influence, however, on Labour's international policy had remained very strong ; and no one had been more responsible for the intensity of the Labour Party's clinging to the League and to the hope of agreed disarmament when in truth the cause was lost. For most of his life Henderson had served the Labour Party with incomparable loyalty, building up its organisation and always putting his devotion to it far ahead of his personal interests, and even on occasion of his own opinions. He had worked loyally under MacDonald, even though he distrusted him and was sick at heart at the second Labour Government's dismal failure to stand up to its responsibilities in the crisis of 1931. In that crisis, he had made many—too many—concessions in the hope of holding the Party together ; and when in the end the break had come, he had been very unhappy at it—the more so because, as a lifelong moderate and constitutionalist, he feared that the effect would be to drive it much further to the left than he had any wish to go. Nevertheless, he did his best to reach an accommodation with the I.L.P. and thereafter to prevent a new cleavage from developing with the Socialist League. He encouraged the new move which centred round the New Fabian Research Bureau and its ally, the Society for Socialist Inquiry and Propaganda ; and he was bitterly disappointed when he saw a further head-on conflict developing between the right and the left. Belonging to the right, he saw the need to carry the left along with it in a united Party, if that could possibly be done consistently with his belief in Parliamentarism at home and in the League of Nations and collective security in the world as a whole.

Arthur Henderson was not a particularly clever man, or an inspiring speaker. He had neither the glamour of MacDonald, nor the incisiveness of Snowden, nor the human warmth of George Lansbury. But he had great qualities—honesty, absence of self-seeking, doggedness and patience in action, and an unshakable faith in the ethical ideals of justice and freedom. I worked with him closely for a number of years, and respected him not least when I differed from him, as I often did. He never let a colleague down, or attempted to shift on to other men's shoulders the burden of his own mistakes. " Uncle Arthur," as he was commonly called, much more than any other man, made the Labour Party what it was—both what was good in it, and some that I think was bad. Whatever he made it, he made it for the common people, and not for himself.

George Lansbury had come back to the Party leadership after his severe illness. But, as leader, he was profoundly unhappy. He saw the drift to war, hated the rising forces of dictatorship and violence in Europe, but was inhibited by his personal pacifism and his abhorrence of war and warlike gestures under all conditions from believing whole-heartedly in a collective security resting on armed force, or in any sort of re-armament directed against the threat of Nazi aggression. Up to 1935, it was possible to leave these doubts in the background and to concentrate on working for Disarmament and for the strengthening of the League system by developing the provisions for arbitration and for international co-operation in the economic and political fields. But Hitler's open measures of re-armament and the Abyssinian crisis together compelled everyone to re-examine his fundamental position. No responsible Labour leader could any longer avoid taking a line on the question of British re-armament or answering the question whether he was prepared, if need arose, for Great Britain to go to war in order to stop Italian aggression. The same question, no doubt, had been raised earlier over Japan's action in Manchuria and China ; but the scene of conflict was a long way off, and the course of events made it possible to evade the issue. By the summer of 1935 it could be evaded no longer. For Lansbury the question was between his pacifism and his hatred of Fascism and aggression ; but it was also complicated by his utter lack of faith in the Government to which would have to be entrusted both the carrying into effect of sanctions against Italy and the control of any additional [armed forces that might be demanded in the name of defence against Fascist and Nazi aggression.

Most of the Left in the Labour movement did not share Lansbury's pacifist convictions. But they were moved, as he was, by deep mistrust of the Government, and were exceedingly reluctant to agree to a re-armament policy which they felt sure would be used not to support the League but to do without it and to betray it. This was Stafford Cripps's feeling when, on the eve of the Labour Party's Brighton Conference, he resigned from the Party Executive and decided to challenge the resolution which the Executive had drafted for submission to the Conference on the Abyssinian affair. This resolution, which was moved by Hugh Dalton, called upon the Government " in co-operation with other nations represented at the Council and Assembly of the League, to use all the necessary measures provided by the Covenant to prevent Italy's unjust and rapacious attack upon the territory of a fellow-member of the League." It further called upon the Labour Conference to pledge its firm support of any action consistent with League principles. Cripps, in opposing the resolution, argued that sanctions might lead to war, and that, if they did, Labour would find itself " without power of control or recall," committed to supporting a war which the Government would wage, not for Socialism or democracy, but in pursuance of imperialist aims. If Great Britain had a Socialist Government, he argued, the situation would be different ; for in that case " there would be no risk of capitalist and imperialist aims being pursued." As matters stood, the risks were too great : it was tragic, but also inescapably true, that the British workers, not being in control of the Government, could not be effective in the international political field. To arm the Government for war would merely wreck the chance of getting a Socialist Government, and might result " in the sacrifice of our whole Movement." If they felt they must do something, let them fall back on " working-class sanctions." Cripps ended by begging the delegates " not to ordain that the Labour Movement shall join without power in the responsibility for capitalist and imperialist war that sanctions may entail," but, instead, to devote the Movement's entire energies "to the defeat of that very capitalism and imperialism which is represented in this country by our class-enemies masquerading under the title of a ' National ' Government."

Then followed the longest debate ever heard at a Labour Party Conference. Lord Ponsonby, William Mellor, and one or two others supported Sir Stafford Cripps ; but from the first the great weight of opinion was on the other side. Trevelyan was among those who strongly supported the Executive's policy. Dr. Alfred Salter stated the absolute pacifist position ; but other leading pacifists, such as Rhys Davies, were against him. The leaders of the big Trade Unions came in heavily on the Executive's side. Attlee spoke in the same sense ; and then George Lansbury rose to state his own position, and, as a believer in pacifism, to oppose the Executive's policy. He spoke under stress of great emotion, realising fully that if the resolution were carried he would have to place an offer of resignation in the hands of the Parliamentary Party, which had elected him as leader. This he said he would do, and abide by their verdict. Lansbury took his stand on his Christian pacifist conviction, which forbade him to counsel or to countenance force as the means of attaining his ends. It was a moving speech, because of its deep sincerity of feeling ; but no one who was not an absolute pacifist could have been convinced by it.

Ernest Bevin rose as Lansbury sat down, and delivered a violent personal attack. He accused Lansbury of " taking his conscience round from body to body asking to be told what he ought to do with it." Bevin's speech was unnecessarily offensive, and was widely resented by delegates who did not at all agree with Lansbury's attitude. Then, after a good many more speeches, Herbert Morrison wound up for the Executive, and the vote was taken. 2,168,000 voted for the resolution ; a mere 102,000 voted against. When it was all over, Lansbury took the first opportunity of placing his resignation as leader in the hands of the Parliamentary Party. It was accepted, and Attlee took his place—to be confirmed in the leadership when the Party re-assembled after the General Election.

(e) The General Election of 1935

The General Election of November, 1935, was a thoroughly confusing affair. The Labour Party was calling loudly for sanctions against Italy and for an endeavour to carry out a policy of collective security through the League of Nations in resistance to Fascist and Nazi threats of aggression. The Conservatives also appeared to have committed themselves to sanctions, though in a more qualified way, and they also fought the Election on the cry that they were the true friends of the League and were determined to make collective security work. To the uninstructed elector, both parties appeared, in respect of international war and peace policy, to be saying the same thing ; and many electors were in fact bewildered by the hostility between rival candidates who both used the same slogans. In truth, however, the policies of the two parties were widely different ; and within each party there were also very important differences of view. There were some Conservatives who did believe in collective security and were prepared to take advantage of the Soviet Union's adhesion to the League of Nations to attempt to build up a system of resistance to German aggression ; whereas others—probably the great majority—had no faith at all in the League or in any pooling of armed power behind it, and were all out for unilateral British rearmament as a means either to holding off Hitler, if need arose, or to doing a deal with him if he would let Western Europe alone and confine his acts of aggression to the East. Conservatives of this school had of course no faith in the Soviet Union as a partner in the League : they did not understand how greatly the fear of the Nazis had strengthened in the Soviet Union the elements favourable to a *rapprochement* with the West, or that Litvinov's chance of bringing this about depended on a real willingness in the West to join in building up a common system of collective security. The main body of Tory opinion was very much more hostile to the Soviet Union than to Hitler or to Mussolini : even those who feared Hitler and stressed the need for re-armament in face of Germany's new militarist policy mostly hoped to be able to come to terms with him and were not at all inclined to line up in any " Anti-Fascist Front " in which they would find themselves the allies of the Communists and the defenders of the working-class Parties and Trade Unions which the Nazis were suppressing. They might not approve of concentration camps, Jew-baiting, and sheer brutality such as the Nazis glorified ; but they were still disposed to argue that Nazi atrocities were directed mainly against persons who thoroughly deserved to be put down, and they were not at all inclined to regard the atrocities as a reason for not coming to a deal with Hitler if he would agree to let Western Europe—or at least Great Britain—alone.

The Tories fought the Election, with these differences in the background, on a profession of belief in the League and in collective security, keeping the issue of rearmament well out of the limelight, except as far as they could treat it as Great Britain's contribution to collective security. Labour was in a much more serious difficulty, not only because its leader had just resigned on the issue of pacifism and a considerable and vocal pacifist or near-pacifist group remained in its ranks, but even more because it had been opposing rearmament even after the Nazi victory and included another section—Cripps and his group—who were still opposed to putting additional arms into the hands of a

Government which they could not trust to use them in the right way, either in war or in diplomacy. The main body of the delegates had indeed come over to accepting the necessity of giving even a Tory Government the arms required in order to make it possible to follow a policy of sanctions that might lead to war. But this conversion was recent, and the earlier utterances of many Labour leaders could be quoted tellingly against them. This was not because these leaders had previously been opposed to armaments adequate to make an effective League policy workable : it was because, with the advent of Hitler to power and the unimpeded throwing-over by Germany of the disarmament imposed by the Versailles Treaty, it was already becoming plain that much larger forces would be needed to enforce the League's authority and to check aggression. Labour had been pressing hard for agreed disarmament, on terms which would leave the League with adequate forces until such forces could be rendered unnecessary by the consolidation of international peace. But now their insistence on disarmament could be cited against them as if it had been inconsistent with their support of the League, and they could be twitted with calling for strong action against the aggressor while refusing to will the means. These taunts were unfair, and for the most part undeserved ; but there was enough in them to make them effective as election points, and the Tories made the most of them.

In the Election, 22,000,000 voted, out of an electorate of 31,373,223. Fewer voted than in 1929, when the electorate was 2,500,000 smaller : rather more voted than in 1931, when it was smaller by nearly 1,500,000. The Labour Party polled 8,326,000 votes, as against 6,648,000 in 1931, and 8,380,000 in 1929. It won 154 seats, as against 52 (including the I.L.Pers) in 1931 and 288 in 1929. Labour had been lucky in the matter of seats in 1929, and unlucky in 1931 : the luck was still against it, though not so heavily, in 1935.

The Liberals again did badly. In 1931 both wings—Samuelite and Simonite—had fought as supporters of the " National " Government, getting between them 2,320,000 votes and seventy-two seats. In 1935 the Liberal-Nationals were still a Government party, in full co-operation with the Tories ; whereas the Liberals proper were a third-party Opposition, trying to slip in between Labour and the " Nationals." The Liberal-Nationals, by grace of the Tories, got thirty-three seats with their 867,000 (mainly Tory) votes. The Independent Liberals got only twenty-one seats, with a voting strength of 1,443,000 in the 161 seats which they managed to contest. They had been promising to put up 400 candidates ; but that was talk. Nevertheless, the Liberal vote showed that there were a great many Liberals left up and down the country, though there were few places where they were numerous enough to win the seat. Lloyd George's " New Deal," however, had fallen flat, and not much was heard of it in the Election.

Naturally, even in spite of its difficulties, the Labour Party did much better than in the sheer disaster of 1931. But, though the Party in the new Parliament was three times the size of the Party after the 1931 Election, it was not much more than half as big as the Party which had formed the Minority Government of 1929. The Tories and Liberal-Nationals, with 420 Members, had still an overwhelming majority in the House of Commons : indeed, the Tories alone had 387, as against 228 of all other parties, including their allies. Labour was still under a heavy handicap in the new House, though it was a good deal better off for leaders and debaters. In addition to Attlee, Greenwood, and Aneurin Bevan, it had now Herbert Morrison, Hugh Dalton, Clynes, Alexander, Shinwell, Lees-Smith, Tom Johnston, Pethick-Lawrence, Grenfell, Creech Jones, Chuter Ede, and other leaders who were already well-known. Lansbury was re-elected, but took little part after 1935. There was once more a team that could reasonably cover the field, though the Party was weak on foreign affairs and none too strong in incisive debating power.

Regionally, the Labour Party made its largest gains in Greater London, Yorkshire and Scotland. In Greater London, including the L.C.C. area, it gained twenty-five seats over its representation in 1931, but was still short of its 1929 total. In Yorkshire it gained twenty, but was thirteen short : in Scotland, where it had been nearly wiped out in 1931, it gained seventeen, leaving it still twenty short of 1929. Sixteen seats were gained in the Midlands, thirteen in Lancashire and Cheshire, eleven on the North-east Coast ; but in all these areas the gains failed nearly to equal the losses of 1931. In all the South and West, outside Greater London, Labour won even in 1935 only three seats, as against a single seat in 1931.

More seats were fought—552 as against 489 in 1931, when in the confusion a number were left without Labour candidates at the last moment. These totals compare with 569 seats fought in 1929, when the I.L.P. was still part of the Party. In 1935 the number of I.L.P. candidates had shrunk to seventeen, of whom eleven were in Scotland. Its four wins were all in Glasgow. The Communists fought only two seats, withdrawing all their other candidates—or so they claimed—as a gesture in support of the United Front. The two who went to the poll were William Gallacher and Harry Pollitt. Gallacher, in Western Fife, won against the sitting Tory, who was at the bottom of the poll, and the Miners' leader, William Adamson, with whom the Communists had a long-standing feud. Pollitt, in East Rhondda, was beaten by another Miners' leader, W. H. Mainwaring, in a straight fight, polling 13,655 to Mainwaring's 22,088.

Of Labour's 154 seats, 110 were won in straight fights with a single Coalition candidate, and nineteen others in constituencies where there was no Coalition candidate in the field—including four against a Liberal and thirteen unopposed. Only twenty-five were won in three-or-more-cornered contests. Not a single seat was won in any of the double-member constituencies or in the Universities. The I.L.P. won all its four seats against both Tory and Labour opponents.

The Labour Party M.P.s of 1945 were made up of seventy-nine Trade Union candidates, including thirty-four sponsored by the Miners, sixty-six Divisional Labour Party candidates, and nine Co-operators. The Trade Union representatives thus still had more than half the seats ; but the D.L.P. Group recovered part of the ground lost in 1931, and the Miners formed a much smaller fraction of the total Party. One unfortunate feature of the Election was that, although most of the leaders defeated in 1931 recovered their seats, very few indeed of the younger Party candidates were elected. An exception was John Parker, the Secretary of the New Fabian Research Bureau, and later of the Fabian Society, who was elected for Romford.

The National Labour Party sank to eight, with J. H. Thomas as the only survivor of the Labour Cabinet seceders of 1931. Ramsay MacDonald was overwhelmingly defeated at Seaham by Emanuel Shinwell, who beat him by 38,380 votes to 17,882. MacDonald got back as M.P. for the Scottish Universities at a by-election in 1936, but died the following year. Thomas resigned in 1936, after a scandal connected with a leakage of Budget information. Thereafter, the National Labour Party quietly vanished away, and few observed the manner of its going.

THE LABOUR PARTY AND BY-ELECTIONS, 1931–5

	1932	1933	1934	1935	Total
Labour seats held :					
(*a*) Unopposed . .	—	2	1	—	3
(*b*) Contested . .	—	2	—	—	2
Seats won by Labour . .	2	2	4	2	10
Seats contested unsuccessfully .	6	10	10	6	32
Seats not fought . . .	7	—	—	6	13
Totals . . .	15	16	15	14	60

In addition, one I.L.P. seat and one held by an unendorsed candidate in 1931 became Labour Party seats ; and one M.P. elected as a Liberal joined the Labour Party. This brought the Labour Party total from forty-six in 1931 to fifty-nine in 1935.

LABOUR PARTY : BODIES SPONSORING SUCCESSFUL CANDIDATES, 1935

	Total	Elected
D.L.P.	395	66
Univ. L.P. . . .	4	—
Scottish Socialist Party . .	4	—
Co-operative Party . .	21	9
M.F.G.B.	39	34
N.U.R. . . .	12	4
T. & G.W.U. . . .	11	7
N.U.G.M.W. . . .	11	6
R.C.A.	10	6
N.U.D.A.W. . . .	7	5
U.T.F.W.A. . . .	6	—
Other Trade Unions . .	32	17
Total T.U.s . .	128	79
TOTAL	552	154

LABOUR AT THE GENERAL ELECTION OF 1935

	Labour Party						I.L.P.		Communist Candidates		National Labour	
	M.P.s elected			Net gains over 1931	Total seats fought		M.P.s Elected	Total seats Fought	Elected	Fought	Elected	Fought
	1935	1931	1929		1935	1931						
London County	22	5	36	17	60	56	—	—	—	—	—	2
Greater London	12	4	18	8	41	36	—	—	—	—	—	1
Southern England	—	1	5	—	50	51	—	—	—	—	—	—
Western England	3	—	7	2	17	17	—	—	—	—	—	2
South-west England	—	—	1	—	12	9	—	1	—	—	—	—
West Midlands	10	—	25	10	44	40	—	—	—	—	1	3
East Midlands	9	3	22	6	39	29	—	—	—	—	3	4
Eastern Counties	—	—	4	—	26	31	—	1	—	—	—	1
Lancs. and Cheshire	18	5	44	13	76	68	—	1	—	—	1	3
Yorkshire	27	7	40	20	55	51	—	1	—	—	—	2
North-west England	2	1	3	1	5	3	—	—	—	—	1	1
North-east England	13	2	22	11	27	24	—	1	—	—	—	1
Wales and Monmouth	18	15	25	3	33	29	—	1	—	1	1	—
Scotland	20	3	37	17	63	44	4	11	1	1	1	—
Northern Ireland	—	—	—	—	—	1	—	—	—	—	—	—
Universities	—	—	—	—	4	3	—	—	—	—	—	—
TOTALS	154	46	289	108	552	489	4	17	1	2	8	20

The General Election of 1935 : Nature of Contests in Seats Fought by Labour Candidates

	Labour Party			I.L.P.	
	Seats fought	Seats won		Seats fought	Seats won
A. No National Candidate					
Unopposed . . .	13	13	Labour only . .	1	—
Liberal only . .	5	4			
I.L.P. only . . .	1	1			
Communist only . .	1	1			
Liberal and Independent	1	—			
	21	19		1	—
B. Straight Fights with National Candidates					
Conservative only . .	300	88	Conservative and Labour	11	4
Liberal National only .	31	10	Conservative, Liberal and Labour . .	3	—
National Labour only .	12	9	National Labour, Liberal and Independent .	1	—
National only . .	5	3			
	348	110		15	4
C. Other Contests with only One National Candidate					
Conservative and Liberal	112	12			
Conservative, Liberal and I.L.P. . . .	3	1			
Conservative, Liberal and Independent . .	3	2			
Conservative, Independent and I.L.P. . .	1	—			
Conservative and Independent . . .	12	2			
Conservative and I.L.P. . .	11	4			
Conservative and Communist . . .	1	—			
Conservative and Social Credit . . .	1	1			
Liberal National and Independent . .	3	1			
Liberal National and Liberal . . .	1	—			
National Labour and Liberal . . .	5	2			
	153	25			

	Labour Party			I.L.P.	
	Seats fought	Seats won		Seats fought	Seats won
D. *Two-member Constituencies (2 Labour Candidates in each case)*					
Two Conservatives only (6) . . .	12	—	Two Labour, 1 Conservative, 1 Liberal National . . .	1	—
One Conservative and 1 Liberal-National (2)	4	—			
One Conservative and 1 National Labour (1) .	2	—			
One Conservative and 1 Liberal (1) . .	2	—			
One Conservative, 1 Liberal National and 1 Liberal (1) . .	2	—			
(11)	22	—		1	—
E. *University Constituencies*					
One Labour, 2 Conservative . . .	1	—		—	—
One Labour, 2 Conservative, 1 Independent	1	—		—	—
One Labour, 1 National	1	—		—	—
One Labour, 1 Liberal .	1	—		—	—
	4	—		—	—

CHAPTER IX

YEARS OF AGGRESSION

(a) Labour's Foreign Policy, 1935-8

Crisis upon crisis—The Hoare-Laval Agreement—Treason Trials in Russia—Spain and China—Austria and Czechoslovakia—Litvinov's rise and fall—The Second World War—The policy of "appeasement"—Churchill's attitude—Conservative differences—The attitude of the Labour Party and its supporters—The strength of pacifist feeling—Types of pacifism—Arthur Henderson's legacy—The changing Labour Party attitude—The local Labour Parties and the Trade Unions—Anti-Fascism—Hitler's attempts to exploit peace feeling—Re-armament and "appeasement"—Labour's foreign policy—The League and pooled security—Sanctions and the League—*For Socialism and Peace—Labour and the Defence of Peace*—The emphasis on League action—Attitude of the Parliamentary Party on armaments—The Edinburgh Conference of 1936—An ambiguous resolution and an inconclusive debate—"Unilateral non-rearmament"—"Passing the buck"—Labour's dilemma—The Spanish conflict—Labour and the Non-Intervention Pact—The French attitude—The debates on non-intervention—The Spanish delegates' speeches—A change of tone—Non-Intervention continued—The Government attitude to Spain—The *Front Populaire* and non-intervention—Labour abandons non-intervention—The Communists and the International Brigade—Piracy and the blockade—Guernica—The Parliamentary Labour Party's policy after 1936—The situation in 1937—*International Policy and Defence*—The Labour Party Conference of 1937—Lansbury returns to the charge—Aneurin Bevan's opposition—The Sino-Japanese War—Labour support for China—The boycott of Japanese goods—Eden's resignation—Germany annexes Austria—The Czechoslovak crisis—Labour attitude on the crisis—*Labour and the International Situation*—Labour's indecision ends—Munich, 1938.

(b) Labour Party Organisation, 1935-6—Labour's Immediate Programme

Further Policy Reports—Broadcasting—Cotton and Workers' Control—Social Credit—Local Government and the Depressed Areas—Sugar Beet—Tithes—The growth of individual membership—Labour and the Co-operative movement—Position of the I.L.P.—The growth of the League of Youth—The United Front and the Popular Front—The Next Five Years Group—The *Front Populaire* in France—The Communists again ask for affiliation—*British Labour and Communism* Affiliation and the United Front rejected at Edinburgh—*Reynolds'* newspaper—The Left Book Club—The U.A.B. regulations revised—Anti-Fascist demonstrations and Hunger Marches—The position in the depressed areas—A Committee of Inquiry appointed—Revision of the Labour Party Constitution deferred—A controversy with the Co-operative Party—The League of Youth reorganised—The readmission of National Labour supporters—Action against Fascism—Political uniforms—The Report on Ceremonies and Honours rejected—*Coal, The Labour Plan*—A Local Government Department set up at Transport House—*Labour's Immediate Programme* of 1937 analysed.

(c) Unity and the Popular Front—After Munich

The Unity Manifesto of the Communists, the I.L.P., and the Socialist League—*Party Loyalty*—The Socialist League and the United Front—The League dissolved—The Bournemouth Labour Party Conference—The Party Constitution revised—Fascist troubles in London—Anti-Fascism and the Popular Front—The United Peace Alliance—Co-operators and the Popular Front—The Labour Party Executive denounces the Popular Front—Differing conceptions of the Popular Front—The Co-operative Congress repudiates the Peace Alliance—The Oxford and Bridgwater by-elections—*Labour's Claim to Government*—A.R.P. and National

(a) Labour's Foreign Policy, 1935–8

The four years between the late summer of 1935 and the outbreak of the second World War in September, 1939, were filled
with disaster and panic as the full implications of Fascism were
made plain in open action. Crisis followed crisis in relentless
succession : indeed, the crises came so thick and fast as to overlap.
The Italians invaded Abyssinia in October, 1935, bringing the
issue of sanctions to a head at the League of Nations. Then came
in December the discreditable Hoare-Laval Agreement, which
caused so great a wave of indignation that the Cabinet had to
throw its Foreign Secretary overboard. In March, 1936, came
Hitler's march into the Rhineland and a fresh European crisis
over the breach of the Locarno Treaties. In June, 1936, the
Spanish Civil War began, and became at once the central issue
facing the working-class movement in both France and Great
Britain. The contest over intervention and " non-intervention "
in Spain was still at its height when in December, 1936, Great
Britain's private crisis over the Abdication of Edward VIII was
settled with singularly little fuss ; and, earlier in the year, the
establishment of a right-wing dictatorship in Greece seemed too
small an affair to call for much attention.

Meanwhile, in the Soviet Union the long series of treason trials
had begun with the conviction of Zinoviev and Kamenev in
August, 1936, and it continued with the " Trotskyist " Trials of
January, 1937, in which Radek was the most prominent among
the accused. In April, the bombing of Guernica by German
aircraft raised the anger of the friends of Republican Spain to a
new pitch. In May, Baldwin gave place to Neville Chamberlain
as Prime Minister ; and in July the long-smouldering Sino-
Japanese struggle flared up into a new full-dress war, bringing on
yet another crisis in the unhappy League of Nations. In September
came the Nyon Conference, called to deal with the acts of piracy
in the Mediterranean and Atlantic against vessels plying to and

from Republican Spain. In November, Germany, Italy and Austria proclaimed the " Anti-Comintern Pact " and the threats of war in Europe became more vocal and insistent than ever. Eden resigned in protest against the Government's bad policy in February, 1938 ; and in the next month came the Nazi invasion of Austria, leading to the proclamation of the *Anschluss* in April. Almost at the same moment the Sudeten Germans in Czechoslovakia launched their demands ; and the great Czech crisis began. While it was in progress, there was fighting between the Soviet Union and the Japanese on the Manchurian frontier ; but Hitler persuaded the Japanese to wait. The ignominious Munich settlement followed in September and early October ; and the Czech State was dismembered and made helpless.

Meanwhile, with German and Italian aid, Franco was winning in Spain, despite the long and heroic defence of Madrid, which fell only in March, 1939, when the struggle ended in an orgy of reprisals against the Republicans. In the same month, the Germans marched into Prague, and Czechoslovakia ceased to exist as an independent State. Chamberlain, who had refused to aid the Czechs when he could have had Soviet help, gave reckless pledges to half-Fascist Poland and to dictator-ridden Greece and Rumania. In the Soviet Union Litvinov, who had tried hard for anti-Fascist unity, fell from office in May ; and in August, 1939, came the terrible news of the German-Soviet Pact. In the meantime, in April, the Italians had overrun Albania. At the beginning of September the Nazis invaded Poland ; and the second World War began.

This shattering series of events rocked every party in both Great Britain and France, the two Western countries on which depended the possibility of successful resistance to Fascist aggression. It divided the Tories, with Eden desiring at any rate some attempt to stand by the League of Nations and some limits to the policy of " appeasement " pursued by Chamberlain and the big business interests, and with Winston Churchill emerging as the leader of a war party which stood for firm resistance to German aggression, not out of any love for democracy, but because he well understood that Britain's very existence as a great power was at stake. It was, however, difficult for these elements in the Conservative Party, and especially for the Churchill group, to form any sort of alliance with the left. Churchill remained an intransigeant imperialist, who had been fighting in the last ditch against Indian self-government : he had been the principal engineer of the Labour defeat in the General Strike of 1926 and was a vehement upholder of the Trade Unions Act of 1927; and no one had been more unsparing in denunciation of the Soviet Union. Many Labour leaders could share his hostility to Communism and yet mistrust him greatly as an ally because they regarded him as standing not for an anti-Fascist or democratic, but for an imperialist, opposition to the Nazis, and were afraid of being dragged into a policy of rearmament designed not to support the League or collective security but to establish a new imperialist balance of power, or, what was even worse in their eyes, to draw the country into war instead of taking steps to prevent war from breaking out. Almost as much as Chamberlain and his followers, the main body of the Labour Party clung to the hope of peace, although they sought it by a different method. They wanted, not to " appease " Hitler and Mussolini, but to strengthen the League against aggression ; and they continued to cherish the hope that, if the anti-Fascist powers would but rally round the League, Germany and Italy could be kept in check without such large-scale rearmament as the Churchillian policy appeared certain to involve.

Moreover, pacifism, of a sort, was strong in the Labour Party. It was not for the most part George Lansbury's pacifism, involving an absolute repudiation of the appeal to force. It was rather a strong, instinctive revulsion against contemplating the idea of war. This sentiment was strongest among the older members of the Party, who remembered the disillusionments of the first World War, had guilty consciences about the Versailles settlement, and were disposed to argue that nothing except evil ever came out of war, and to believe that the wish to avoid war would somehow make avoidance possible without surrender to the dictators if only it were strongly enough felt. This kind of pacifism was particularly strong in the Women's Sections of the Local Labour Parties ; but it was not found there only. It was a pervasive sentiment, both in Great Britain and in France, not perhaps in a majority of the people, but among enough to make solid support even for a pro-League policy involving the risk of war very difficult, and for any rearmament programme not based definitely on the League quite out of the question until the Nazis had dotted the " i's " and crossed the " t's " of their aggressive intentions a great many times. The Labour Party had been standing solidly behind Arthur Henderson in his struggle to make disarmament a reality : it could not easily cross over to rearmament on any terms, and it was hardest of all when support for rearmament meant arming a Government which had shown its lack of faith in the League and was seeking to combine rearmament with " appeasement " of the dictators and could by no means be trusted not to turn the arms it was asking for against, say, India instead of against Germany or Italy or Japan.

The ambiguity of Labour foreign policy which arose out of these difficulties persisted to some extent right up to the Munich crisis of 1938, though continuously from 1935 those who saw the sheer necessity of getting the arms with which to fight the Fascists if necessity arose were gaining ground against those who would on no account agree to back the rearmament policy of the reactionary Conservative Government. In this matter the Trade Unions shifted over more quickly and with less opposition than the Local Labour Parties, largely because they were less affected by the ethical sentiment against war. On the other hand, the Local Labour Parties responded more readily than the Trade Unions to the call for an Anti-Fascist crusade, precisely because they were more ethically minded and therefore more shocked by Fascist atrocities. Thus arose the curious situation in which the same bodies were sending out anguished cries for peace and calling for sanctions and for other forms of action against Fascist aggression that plainly involved the risk of war. A great many people, both in and outside the Labour movement, managed to satisfy themselves that an attitude of full loyalty to the League could generate forces powerful enough to preserve the peace, and thus were able at the same time to support collective security and to avoid really facing the implications of resistance to Fascism. Some on the Labour side contrived to persuade themselves, as Lansbury did, that it might avail to appeal to the German and Italian peoples—and even to their rulers—in the name of God and the common principles of Western morality : many more, even without this faith, went on hoping that somehow the peril would pass, and the dictators draw back, even at the last, from a conflict that boded ruin to victors and vanquished alike.

The dictators, naturally, did their best to foster these confusions. Hitler, who represented the real danger—for Mussolini could do little with Italy's unaided strength—was continually reiterating his desire for peace, and representing himself as having no quarrel with the West, but only with the Eastern menace of Communism. If only he were granted this one thing, he kept saying—that is, the thing which he was making his next particular objective—

he would be satisfied and would be thereafter no menace to the peace of the West, but on the contrary its defender against Bolshevist aggression. Even those who did not take what he said at its face value were in many cases influenced—the Conservatives to hope that he might exhaust himself in fighting the Soviet Union, the more progressive to believe that he might be stalled off by an opposition that stopped short of any considerable measure of war preparation. In the Labour movement many salved their consciences for opposing increased war expenditure by saying that they were opposing, not rearmament itself, but the Tory form of it, and that their task was to put a better Government into power and then, and then only, to take such steps as were necessary. Let the Tories do the rearming, many of them said, without Labour taking any of the responsibility for it—as if the responsibility for either supporting or opposing it could really be evaded.

For the Tories this attitude was a godsend. It enabled them to defend their own policy of half-hearted rearmament combined with " appeasement " on the ground that Labour opposition and its effects on public opinion did not allow them to do anything else. This was a highly disingenuous argument ; for the big Tory majority in Parliament in fact gave the Government full power to do what it pleased and the plain duty of doing what it considered to be necessary. But the divided mind of Labour enabled the Government again and again to cover up its own deficiencies by dwelling on those of the Opposition. The British Labour movement was, moreover, hampered by the very great strength of pacifism in the French Socialist Party, with which it desired to act in close co-operation.

The Labour Party, indeed, spoke from the first brave words in favour of the full enforcement of the principles of the League Covenant and of the building up of a system of " pooled security " as the basis of the indivisibility of world peace. It called for sanctions against Japan in Manchuria and against Italy in the Abyssinian conflict, as well as later against successive acts of Fascist aggression. But it combined its appeal for sanctions and for a strong " League " policy with insistence on disarmament as the means to peace, persisting in this attitude long after all real hope of agreed disarmament had disappeared. Thus, the Party Executive in its 1935 Report in dealing with the Far Eastern and Abyssinian crises put the main stress on the argument, advanced in *For Socialism and Peace,* that " a feeble and disingenuous policy on Disarmament and Security has helped to frustrate the attempts to achieve a reduction in armaments, and has stimulated the arms race to which Far Eastern events gave the initial impulse." This was only too true ; but it was not very helpful in the situation of 1935. It might have been possible at an earlier stage to base a strong League policy on disarmament : by 1935 only a strongly armed system of pooled security stood any chance of holding the dictators in check.

The Manifesto issued in May, 1935, by the Labour and Socialist International, in which the Labour Party concurred, appeared to recognise this when it laid down that " the danger of war in Europe will be averted only when it is fully realised that any act of aggression will be confronted by collective strength powerful enough to overcome it and promptly to restore peace " ; but the Party Executive, after quoting these words in its Report, promptly went back to the theme of disarmament and to denunciation of the " National " Government for having failed to support a policy of pooled security resting on agreed disarmament. Its arguments *for* sanctions and *against* rearmament were woven so closely together as to be inseparable. The Parliamentary Party, in its Report to the same Conference (1935) recorded its actions in urging continued support for the Disarmament Conference and in opposing the Government's Defence White Paper and the increased Air Estimates presented in August.

By May, 1936, when Italy's conquest of Abyssinia had been followed by Hitler's march into the Rhineland and open repudiation of Germany's Locarno obligations, the tune had somewhat changed. The National Council of Labour's Manifesto on *Labour and the Defence of Peace*, issued in that month, embodied a strongly worded plea for an effective system of collective security, and declared that " Labour must be prepared to accept the consequences of its policy. A man who joins a Trade Union accepts the obligation of collective action in defence of its principles. A man who enjoys the collective security of a Trade Union must be prepared to take the risks of loyalty to his principles when a strike or lock-out is threatened. Similarly, a Movement which supports the League system cannot desert it in a crisis." But the whole emphasis was still put on collective, League action ; and the Manifesto came back in its conclusion to the demand that " an effort must be made now to frame a general agreement for mutual aid and security and for disarmament, to cover at least the whole of Europe, in which Germany must be invited to participate on an equal footing with other States." Meanwhile the Parliamentary Party, while pressing strongly for an effective policy of pooled security and for a resolute stand against Italian and German aggression, continued to oppose all the Government's proposals for increased expenditure on armaments, arguing that " no case had yet been made out for the vast commitments into which the Government were entering," and pressing for a renewed attempt to secure agreed disarmament and for a World Economic Conference to remove causes of international dispute based on the inequality of access to materials and markets, the obstacles in the way of migration, and other " economic factors " of a like kind.

At the Labour Party's Edinburgh Conference in October, 1936, the difficulty in which the Party felt itself to be placed came out very clearly indeed. In previous years, the National Council of Labour had produced an agreed statement which had been submitted first to the Trades Union Congress in September and then to the Labour Party Conference in October ; but in 1936 this was not done, and the Trades Union Congress made no general pronouncement. The Party Executive put forward at Edinburgh a resolution of its own, and there was a very long debate, wound up by a speech from Attlee, as leader of the Party. Both the resolution and the discussion upon it brought out the Labour Party's quandary. The resolution began with a sharp dissociation of the Labour Party from the international policy of the Government, which was accused of having " betrayed the League of Nations and Abyssinia " and of having broken its pledges to the electors to follow a " League " line. It then went on to say that " another World War would destroy European civilisation," and that " the piling up of competitive armaments cannot bring peace and security." It contrasted with the Government's attitude the Labour Party's " belief in the League of Nations, in disarmament by international agreement, and in the principle of Collective Security." It called for a strengthening of the League Covenant to make sanctions automatic against an aggressor ; and it declared that " the armed strength of the countries loyal to the League of Nations must be conditioned by the armed strength of the potential aggressors." It then proceeded to state that " the Labour Party refuses to accept responsibility for a purely competitive armament policy," and ended with an appeal for the return of a Labour Government to power.

This resolution was excellent as far as it went ; but it entirely failed to tell the delegates what they really wanted to know—

whether the Parliamentary Labour Party meant to go on opposing the Government's estimates for rearmament or not. On that issue, the members of the Executive itself appeared to speak with different voices ; and even Attlee, who came nearest to attempting an answer, did not really give one. He only emphasised what the resolution had said—that the Party, while favouring adequate total armaments in the hands of the powers loyal to the League, could give no endorsement to the policy of unco-ordinated rearmament which the Government was actually following. Bevin and others pressed for a clearer answer ; but they did not get one. Lansbury and others opposed the resolution on pacifist grounds : Cripps and others opposed it because it did not take a clear line against putting arms into the hands of a capitalist Government. Herbert Morrison urged strongly that the Party could not go beyond voting for enough armaments to make an adequate contribution to a totality of international force available against aggressors ; whereas Dalton, who moved the resolution, conveyed a different impression when he said that he found it difficult in logic to believe that the Labour Party Conference could support " unilateral non-rearmament in a world where all are increasing their armaments." It was a most unsatisfactory discussion ; for, however right the Labour Party's attack on the Government's policy was, they had in Parliament to vote either for increased armaments or against them ; and the Conference wanted to know which it was supposed to be instructing the Parliamentary Party to do. That, however, was what it was never told, by any of the official speakers.

When the vote was taken, the resolution was carried by 1,713,000 to 652,000 ; but the voting meant nothing, for those who supported and those who opposed the Executive's proposals were alike in putting different meanings on them. In effect, the delegates were well aware that, as Bevin had said in the debate, the resolution was merely " passing the buck " to the Parliamentary Party. The Executive, the delegates, and the Parliamentary Party were all in a quandary ; and unfortunately the quandary extended to their followers throughout the country, who were left uncertain what to say and even what to think. No one who wanted to resist Fascist aggression could really be in doubt any longer that more armaments were necessary, even if the policy behind rearmament were to be one of " pooled security " with such other powers as were prepared to come in. On paper, it might be possible to show a plain superiority of League forces

(including the Russians) against any likely combination of aggressors ; but the pooled security system was not in existence, and the
events in Abyssinia and in Spain, as well as in Germany, had
already shown that there would have been serious obstacles to
its working even if the British Government had been whole-
heartedly behind it. It remained possible to advocate and to
labour for collective security ; but it was no longer possible, if it
had ever been, to calculate the British contribution to the task
of resisting aggression on the basis of assuming that all the other
possible contributors would supply their quotas. However
loyal Labour might remain to the League, it had in some degree
to do exactly what its leaders were protesting they could not do—
approve of some measure of unilateral rearmament to be carried
through as a purely British act, and not as part of an agreed
League plan.

On the other hand, the moment Labour admitted this necessity, it would in effect be handing the " National " Government
a blank cheque and forfeiting at least to some extent such power
as it had to urge the Government towards a real attempt to turn
pooled security into a practical proposition. The Government,
assured of Labour's vote for its rearmament programme, would
be in a position simply to ignore Labour pressure for a better
foreign policy. At any rate, that was what many of the Labour
leaders feared : the answer, I think, was that they were just as
impotent whether they voted for or against the armament estimates, and would therefore have done better to say openly that
they would vote for them, while continuing to attack the Government's policy ; for, in that case, they would have been clearly
understood by the people, instead of conveying an impression of
confusedness, undecidedness, and even self-contradiction. The
decision, however, was hard to make because of the strength of
pacifist sentiment within the Local Labour Parties and also
among others who remembered the first World War and its effects.

The Edinburgh Conference, before it came to the resolution
with which I have been dealing, had been discussing the even more
urgent issue of its policy in relation to the rebellion in Spain. The
British Government, in association with other leading powers,
had adopted in the Spanish conflict the policy known as " non-
intervention," which was supposed to mean an agreement among
them not to supply arms or other assistance to either side. This
decision ran counter to the undoubted right of the Spanish
Government under international law to buy arms abroad for the

purpose of suppressing the rebels : the only justification advanced in support of it was that it was the only way of preventing Germany and Italy from intervening actively on the rebel side and perhaps of legalising their action under international law by recognising the rebels as the legitimate Government of Spain. It was feared that if Great Britain, France and the Soviet Union were to supply arms to the Republican Government, whereas Germany and Italy were to do the same to Franco, the outcome might easily be a general European War. This fear was especially lively in France, where a *Front Populaire* Government was somewhat precariously in power ; and it was no less lively in the Soviet Union, which had also the fear that if it gave open support to the Republicans, France and Great Britain would let it down and leave it to face Germany and Italy alone.

The Germans and Italians, for their part, accepted " non-intervention " without any intention of abiding by it. They fully intended to use it as a means of blockading the Spanish Republicans while they sent in 'planes and supplies to help the rebels, and even made preparations for sending armed forces. During the early stages of " non-intervention " they did this with some attempt at secrecy, and accompanied it with denials, though later both Mussolini and the Nazis boasted of what they had done and the Italians in particular openly sent whole armies to fight in the Spanish War. At the time of the Labour Party Conference this later stage had not been reached. Only supplies were being sent, secretly, in violation of the Non-Intervention Agreement ; and the Fascist powers were still denying that even this was being done.

Before the Conference the National Council of Labour, in consultation with the Labour and Socialist International, the I.F.T.U., and the French Socialists, had accepted the non-intervention policy. They had done so, reluctantly, because they did not see what else to do. The Blum Government in France, in a weak internal position and faced with acute fears of a quarrel with Germany among a large section of the French people—including many of its own supporters—was not prepared to back the Spanish Government unless it could be assured that the British and Soviet Governments would stand by it. The British Government under Baldwin and Chamberlain would give no such assurance ; and the Soviet Government would give none either, unless it could be sure of both the British and the French. In this situation, each could put the blame on the others for its failure

to take a stronger line ; and all three fell back on " non-intervention," though they must have known that there was no chance
of the Germans and Italians observing it unless they saw that the
rebels could win without their further aid. What they did not
realise was the scale on which the pledge against intervention
would be flouted, or the open derision with which the Nazis
and Fascists would soon be treating the Non-Intervention Pact
to which they nominally adhered.

At Edinburgh it was still possible to argue that breaches of the
Pact were unproven, though everybody really knew that they
were already occurring. The official resolution, put forward with
the backing of the National Council of Labour and moved,
apologetically, by Arthur Greenwood, was therefore so drafted
as to assume that non-intervention could be made a reality, and
to support it on condition that it was. The assumption underlying
the resolution, and the entire policy represented by it, were
vigorously attacked by Charles Trevelyan, Christopher Addison,
William Dobbie of the N.U.R., Aneurin Bevan, and Noel-Baker :
the defenders of the official policy included, besides Greenwood,
Ernest Bevin, Charles Dukes, George Hicks, Dai Grenfell, and
Clement Attlee, who wound up the debate. The resolution
was carried by 1,836,000 to 519,000 ; but it left the Conference
with an uneasy conscience. Then, the next day, came the
speeches of the Spanish fraternal delegates, de Asua and Senore
de Palencia—who received an ovation. These profoundly
moved the delegates, and simply swept away the pretence
that the Non-Intervention Pact was not proved to have been
broken. The National Council, impressed by the feeling of the
Conference, met at once and decided to send Attlee and Greenwood to interview the Prime Minister and to demand that the
charges of breach of the Pact should be fully investigated without
delay. When they came back, Attlee moved a new resolution
demanding that, if the Non-Intervention Pact were found to be
ineffective or to have been definitely violated, the French and
British Governments, which had been responsible for initiating
it, should forthwith restore to the Spanish Government its right
to buy arms. The resolution further called on the National Council
of Labour to meet " with the object of carrying out the policy
involved in this statement." This resolution, strengthened on
Cripps's motion with a phrase placing on record the Conference's view that the Fascist powers had already violated the
Pact, was carried unanimously.

This second debate took place after the Conference had passed its ambiguous general resolution about rearmament. It represented a perfectly definite change of feeling on the Spanish issue, to which the leaders gave way. But it did not persuade the Governments concerned to give up the policy of non-intervention, even when it had come to be an open farce. The Labour Party continued to protest ; but it did not go beyond protests. The French Socialists were hesitant, and the French Government would not act without assured British support. The Labour and Socialist International did not see its way to recommend decisive action. The official Labour bodies did their best to salve the Labour Movement's conscience by organising much needed relief measures and Red Cross services for the Spanish Republicans ; but, though the Italians and Germans poured in military help more and more openly and were plainly using the Spanish conflict as a dress-rehearsal for the coming European War, nothing was done on the other side to aid the Republican cause. On the left, this situation called very strong feelings into play : it became, as we shall see, the main driving force behind the various United Front and Popular Front movements of the years 1937 to 1939.

The truth of course was that the British Government did not want to help the Spanish Republicans, who had against them the whole weight of the Roman Catholic Church as well as most upper-class sentiment and considerable capitalist interests in Spanish industry. Even the Labour Movement could not make up its mind to press really hard for intervention on the side of the Spanish Government, to match the Fascist intervention, because it was felt that this involved a real prospect of bringing on a general European War. Therefore, the Labour leaders, while they tried to bring pressure on the Government to insist on a better observance of the Non-Intervention Pact—a vain hope—found themselves strongly resisting pressure from the left to give up all hope of making non-intervention work and to insist on the Spanish Government being at least accorded the right to purchase arms and British subjects the full freedom to take privately any steps they chose to help the Republicans. Even when, in November, 1936, a delegation from the *Front Populaire*, headed by Jean Longuet, came to London with Léon Blum's approval to seek British support if the French were to denounce the Non-Intervention Pact, the British Labour leaders held off, because they could not assure the French of British Government support, and were hesitant about invoking the war danger which stronger pressure, if it had been successful, would have involved. By this time, indeed, the National Council of Labour had abandoned its support of non-intervention ; but it refused to inaugurate any national campaign in the Spanish cause, apart from collecting funds for the relief of the victims of the war, and thus left the field to unofficial bodies—and of course to the Communist Party, which from July had been campaigning actively for positive aid to the Spanish workers, and was mainly responsible later for organising the British part of the International Brigade which went to fight in Spain against the Fascist forces. After the *impasse* of November, the Communists found in these efforts a growing number of allies from the Labour left wing and even from progressives outside the Labour and Socialist movement. But they could achieve but little. The civil war went increasingly against the Republicans as more and more German and Italian help was poured in ; and soon, by piracy on the open seas, Italian and German war vessels were sinking British ships which attempted to run the blockade imposed in Franco's interests by his " non-interventionist " allies. The Republicans got some help from the Soviet Union ; but the Russians could not do much without help in the west. Right up to the fall of Madrid, after an heroic defence, early in 1939, the Civil War continued on its tragic course. Guernica was wiped out by German planes practising " frightfulness " in April, 1937 ; horror was piled on horror, and a sense of shame spread among decent people, who tried to make up for their helplessness by receiving Spanish refugee children, organising ambulance units, and contributing liberally to official and unofficial Labour funds for Spain. The chance of saving the situation without war, though not without the risk of it, had gone by : the Fascists were scoring their first great European military success.

In Parliament, the Labour Party after the 1936 Party Conference made repeated motions and amendments protesting against the maintenance of the non-intervention farce and supporting the sending of arms to Spain. It also protested against the Government's ban on British volunteers for service in the Republican forces ; but of course it was voted down. On the wider question of armaments it continued for some time to vote against the increased estimates, moving reasoned amendments calling attention to the absence of any policy of collective security or promotion of agreed disarmament. This went on until July,

1937, when the Parliamentary Party reconsidered its line and decided that " bearing in mind that its position had already been made abundantly clear," it would " in view of the international situation . . . abstain from any further division against the Estimates for the Fighting Services, but vote as usual against all the other Estimates involving policy." The difficulty, of course, had been partly that the regular parliamentary way of indicating disapproval of Government policy was to move for a reduction in the Estimate of the department concerned. This involved appearing to oppose rearmament, and was open to misunderstanding by the public. But the fear of misunderstanding was not the main reason for the Party's change of front. The need for large-scale rearmament, even if it was largely attributable to failure to stop the Fascists sooner, had become too obvious not to be recognised.

As the appointed dates for the Trades Union Congress and the Labour Party Conference of 1937 drew near, it became evident that a new agreed statement of British Labour policy on international issues would have to be presented to them ; and the National Council of Labour drew up a document entitled *International Policy and Defence*, which was issued in July. This traversed the whole field of international developments since the Treaty of Versailles, of which it was strongly critical. It emphasised the special vulnerability of Great Britain and of the British Commonwealth in the event of war, and recognised that the League of Nations " for the time being, has been rendered ineffective." It recognised by implication some reality in the economic grievances of the Fascist powers, and affirmed its readiness for a generous international economic settlement based on equal access for all to colonial resources ; and it also asked for a revision of the League Covenant to authorise the League to tackle frontier questions. Its policy was restated in terms of reinvigorating the League and of making it an effective instrument of pooled security, agreed disarmament, and economic co-operation, with an International Air Force in substitution for national forces ; and it put on the British Government a large, if not the main, share in the blame for the League's failure. It insisted that the proffered advantages of economic co-operation could be open only to countries which were prepared loyally to accept the League system and all-in arbitration ; and, after referring to the strength of isolationism in America, it went on to urge the importance of " improving Anglo-American relations." As against this, it made no mention from beginning to end of the Soviet Union, except to say that the Soviet Union, then in the League, as well as France and Britain, had been a party to non-intervention in Spain.

The document then proceeded to record the abandonment by British Labour of the non-intervention policy, and to reaffirm the demand for aid to Republican Spain, at any rate to the extent of recognising its right to buy arms and of protecting British vessels plying to Spanish ports. It dwelt on the grave dangers certain to arise out of a rebel victory in Spain ; and then it ended, not by laying down any clear immediate policy, but by calling for the return of a Labour Government to power and stating the policy such a Government would follow. This included reinvigorating the League of Nations, stopping the arms race, and promoting a General Disarmament Treaty. It was insisted that "such a Government, in the present state of the world, must be strongly equipped to defend this country, to play its full part in Collective Security, and to meet any intimidation by the Fascist Powers," and that " until the change in the international situation caused by its advent had had its effect, it would be unable to reverse the present programme of rearmament."

With this most inadequate guidance the Trades Union Congress in September and the Labour Party Conference in October met to consider the situation ; and at both meetings the National Council of Labour's Report was debated mainly as if it had been a declaration in favour of supporting the Government's rearmament programme, though as far as words went it certainly was nothing of the sort. On both occasions the Report was approved on this basis, of course with the qualification that voting for rearmament did not in any way detract from Labour's opposition to the Government's foreign policy, or alter the Labour demand for a further attempt to achieve a system of collective security. At the Labour Party Conference, held at Bournemouth, Clynes moved the acceptance of the National Council's Report. After Sydney Silverman had moved an amendment on the lines of Cripps's speech the year before, demanding Socialist opposition to any rearmament in the hands of a capitalist Government that could not be trusted to use its weapons in the right cause, the debate went off on the issue of absolute pacifism. George Lansbury, who had been on a peace pilgrimage in Europe and had made personal appeals to Hitler and to Mussolini, opposed the Report with an appeal for unilateral disarmament as an example to the world ; and the morning was spent mainly in speeches for rearmament in order to resist the Fascists or against it on non-resistance grounds.   In the afternoon Aneurin Bevan made a powerful speech against the Report, urging that if they gave the Government a free hand over armaments on plea of the international danger the next thing would be a demand for a complete political and industrial truce in the name of " national unity," with the effect of leaving Labour totally disarmed and the reactionaries secure in power.   He found little support.   Clynes's resolution endorsing the Report was carried by 2,169,000, against 262,000 for the reference back.   The result was generally taken as implying Labour support for an active rearmament policy.   The Conference also adopted, on Charles Trevelyan's motion, a strong resolution demanding the end of non-intervention in Spain and the restoration to the Spanish Government of its right to purchase arms to maintain its authority.

By this time there was a fresh international crisis to be faced. The Japanese had launched a general offensive against Northern China and had occupied the entire Pekin-Tientsin area, employing the methods of " frightfulness," including air bombardment, which the Fascists had been successfully trying out in Spain. On August 12 a number of Japan's co-signatories to the Nine-Power Treaty guaranteeing Chinese independence had addressed a note to Japan ; but on the following day the Japanese had launched a further attack on Shanghai, directly menacing foreign interests in Central China as well as the integrity of the main centres of Chinese authority.   On August 24 the National Council of Labour issued a strong protest, and called on the Government to concert measures with other Governments, including the Americans, " to secure respect by Japan for international law and treaty rights " ; and at the Party Conference in October Attlee moved and Morrison seconded a forcibly worded resolution calling upon the Government, in conjunction with the League and the United States, to " impose measures of economic and financial pressure designed to bring Japanese aggression to an end."   The resolution also demanded an early meeting of Parliament to consider the situation.   The National Council of Labour had already endorsed these proposals and had called for a boycott of Japanese goods ; and in October it organised a Mass Demonstration in London and a number of other meetings throughout the country in support of its policy.   Plans were drawn up for sanctions, to be operated both by Governments and by Labour in default of Government action ; and the backing of the Co-operative Movement for the boycott was secured.   The matter was taken up with the Labour and Socialist International and with the I.F.T.U. ; and an unsuccessful attempt was made to get the American Federation of Labor to join in the boycott. Deputations were sent to the Government to urge action both directly and through the League of Nations ; but though the League met at Brussels in November to consider the question, nothing effective was done. While the meeting was in progress Germany, Italy and Japan were signing the " Anti-Comintern " Pact, and were further concerting their plans of world aggression.

In this atmosphere 1937 ended, with a record that was black enough. 1938 was to be very much worse. Neville Chamberlain had succeeded Baldwin as Prime Minister in May, 1937, and the trend towards " appeasement " had become more pronounced. In February, 1938, Eden resigned his office as Foreign Secretary, and Halifax took his place. In March and April came the Nazi conquest and annexation of Austria ; and in April the Sudeten German leader, Henlein, issued his programme of demands upon the Czechoslovak Republic. The British Government at once counselled the Czechs to adopt a policy of concession ; and in May it became evident that Hitler was set on annexation of the German districts and on settling a new frontier that would utterly destroy Czechoslovakia's defences. The crisis dragged on through the summer. In July Runciman was sent to advise the Czechs to give way on almost everything : in August the British Government told them that it could give them no military guarantee in the event of a German attack : in September and early October came the visits of Chamberlain and Daladier to Hitler and the ignominious surrender at Munich.

In May, 1938, the Labour and Socialist International, on the motion of the British delegation, had recorded its sympathy with the Czechs, but had also expressed its appreciation of the conciliatory attitude which their Government was adopting towards the Sudeten demands. As it became evident to what lengths of concession the British and French Governments were uniting to impel the unfortunate Czechs, Labour sentiment was more and more aroused, and an endeavour was made to get united action with the L.S.I. and the I.F.T.U., and especially between the British and French Labour Movements. The French, however, were too sharply divided by the fear of war to give effective support. Though the Radical, Daladier, had become Prime Minister and there was no longer a Blum Government to be saved, the imminent threat of war set the French Socialists all at sixes and sevens. The British Labour Movement, however, was now undeterred by French divisions. There was no Labour Party Conference in 1938, owing to a change in the annual date of meeting which had meant holding no Conference between October, 1937, and May, 1939 ; but the National Council of Labour prepared and submitted to the Trades Union Congress at the beginning of September a statement under the heading *Labour and the International Situation : On the Brink of War.* In this statement it was urged that the Nazi demands on Czechoslovakia were " incompatible with the integrity and independence of that country," and it was laid down that " British Labour emphatically repudiates the right of the British or any other Government to use diplomatic or other pressure to compel an acceptance of such a humiliation." The declaration went on to say that " the time has come for a positive and unmistakable lead for collective defence against aggression and to safeguard peace. The British Government must leave no doubt in the mind of the German Government that they will unite with the French and Soviet Governments to resist any attack upon Czechoslovakia. The Labour Movement urges the British Government to give this lead, confident that such a policy would have the solid support of the British people . . . Labour cannot acquiesce in the destruction of the rule of law by savage aggression."

Thus, at length, in the Czech crisis, the British Labour Movement came out quite unequivocally in favour of resistance to the Nazis, facing the prospect of immediate world war. The Soviet Union had indicated its preparedness to join with Great Britain and France against the Nazis : the last chance for applying the policy of collective security, in support of which the Soviet Union had entered the League of Nations in 1934, had definitely come. It was not taken : the appeasers, Chamberlain and Daladier, without any appeal to the Soviet Union, surrendered to Hitler and compelled the Czechs to accept the destruction of their State. For the British people, in an appalling situation there was one redeeming feature : British Labour had at last thrown off its ambiguities and indecisions and had taken a firm stand, facing the threat of immediate war.

(b) Labour Party Organisation, 1935-6 — Labour's Immediate Programme

The course of events described in the preceding section naturally kept political feeling at a high pitch and had its reactions on the internal condition of the Labour Party and on its relations with other bodies, affiliated and unaffiliated. At the Brighton Conference of 1935, held just before the General Election, the Party continued its work of policy-making by dealing with a very mixed collection of further Reports from the Executive's Policy Committee or from other committees to which certain parts of the work of policy-making had been assigned. These included a Report on "Broadcasting Policy," drawn up by the National Council of Labour ; a brief Interim Report on the "Socialisation of Coal and Allied Industries," announcing that a full plan for the socialisation of fuel and power was being worked out in conjunction with the Trades Union Congress ; a plan for the "Socialisation of the Cotton Industry," worked out by the T.U.C. and submitted to the Party Conference for adoption ; a Report on "Socialism and Social Credit," dealing *inter alia* with the Douglas Credit scheme ; a Report on "Local Government and Depressed Areas," embodying a proposal for the constitution of Regional Authorities, at any rate for the depressed areas, and for special financial assistance, but not going into any detail ; and Reports on "Tithes" and on "The Sugar Beet Industry"—the latter proposing direct Exchequer subsidies to growers and the national ownership of the sugar factories, with management by a publicly appointed Corporation working under a representative Sugar Commission also appointed by the Government

On the Broadcasting issue, the National Council of Labour wished to maintain the B.B.C.'s monopoly, but to transfer responsibility for the appointment of Governors from the Postmaster-General to the Prime Minister. Accepting the need for the B.B.C. to be at the Government's disposal for broadcasting such matter as it might require, the Report urged that "the Corporation should not become the mere instrument of the Government for the time being, to be exploited for political party purposes." This was largely a reaction to the use made of the B.B.C. by the Government during the General Strike of 1926.

On the Cotton Report, William Mellor, speaking for the Socialist League, secured an assurance that the provisions relating to Workers' Control would be brought into line with the general policy laid down by the Party and the Trades Union Congress on this issue. In connection with the Report on "Social Credit" a resolution was carried to the effect that "no scheme of Monetary Reform, whether in the guise of a National Dividend or otherwise, must be allowed to deflect the Labour Movement from the pursuit of its declared financial policy in respect of the Bank of England, the Joint Stock Banks, and the formation of a National Investment Board." On Local Government it was made clear that a fuller plan of reform was under consideration. The Report on Tithes—a vexed question in the rural areas, in which Labour was carrying on a special campaign—proposed extinction over a period of years, and in the meantime a sliding scale based on price movements.

Besides these special Reports, the 1935 Conference dealt with a number of matters of organisation. It was reported that the campaign for Individual Members was going well, the total for 1934 being over 480,000, of whom 158,000 were women. One Divisional Party—Romford—had over 5,000 Individual Members, and twenty-two others had more than 2,000. Proposals for revising the Party Constitution were deferred owing to the imminence of the General Election. J. S. Middleton was formally elected as Secretary in succession to Arthur Henderson : he had been Acting Secretary for a long time past. A number of questions were raised about the relations between the Labour and Co-operative Parties and about Labour and Co-operative policy on the subject of agricultural marketing boards, to which the Co-operative Movement took objection as inconsistent with the consumers' claims to final control. There had been some local troubles with the Co-operative Party over the choice of candidates in elections ; and in one or two cases Co-operative candidates had been put forward in opposition to Labour candidates in municipal elections. The Executive reported that it was in the middle of negotiations with the Co-operative Party for a revised general agreement dealing with electoral collaboration and other matters; and the Labour Party Conference contented itself with a resolution asking the Executive " to negotiate immediately with the Co-operative Party with the object of closer agreement and the avoidance of overlapping or disputes in matters of candidates, propaganda, and the political field generally." It was reported that an unsuccessful attempt had been made to persuade the Co-operative Movement to join the National Council of Labour.

The problem of the I.L.P. also came up at Brighton. The Executive in its Report laid down that, in view of the I.L.P.'s secession from the Labour Party, members of the I.L.P. were not eligible either for Individual Membership of the Party or to serve as delegates of affiliated bodies or Local Parties. The Birmingham Party moved the reference back, but was defeated, after G. R.

Shepherd, the National Agent, had explained that the Executive had carefully refrained from blacklisting the I.L.P. itself as a body ineligible for affiliation, and had given a broad hint that it would be welcomed back if it saw its way to rejoin and to " abide by the Constitution." Several speakers stressed the good local work that was being done by I.L.P. Members for the Party, despite the breach, and Shepherd went out of his way to be conciliatory, representing the Executive's decision as merely an unavoidable consequence of the disaffiliation, which had been the I.L.P.'s doing.

The perennial question of the League of Youth also came up again at Brighton. Organisation of the League had been going well : 110 new branches had been formed during the year, making 373 since the Youth Campaign started two years earlier. There were now 526 branches, mostly federated regionally, with regional Advisory Committees. A Socialist Youth Day had been arranged, with demonstrations all over the country, and a " Youth Organisation Bulletin " was to be started, in addition to *The New Nation*, which was the magazine of Labour Party Youth. There had been a very successful Youth Conference in London, and the League had been informed of the decision to give it direct representation at the Party Conference and on the National Executive. The Youth Conference, however, had also asked for the right to discuss policy matters at League of Youth Conferences and to adopt resolutions on Party policy. To this the National Executive was unable to agree. " The League," said the Executive, " was not established to make policy but to recruit and educate young people for the Party." On this issue the reference back was moved at Brighton, but was lost, after Shepherd had explained that the League was free to *discuss* policy, but not to pass resolutions about it. There was to be more trouble over this matter in the near future.

The year 1936 opened with the main attention concentrated on foreign affairs in connection with the Abyssinian crisis : by its end the outstanding interest had shifted to the Spanish struggle. As we saw, one effect of these developments was to cause a renewal in various forms of the demand for some sort of united action by all who were opposed to the Government's foreign policy. This demand stirred up a good many different groups, including at the one end the Communists and at the other many Liberals and even some Conservative supporters of the League of Nations. The Communists and a number of left-wing Socialists, including the

I.L.P. and the Socialist League, came forward with demands for a " United Working-class Front." or sometimes for a wider " Popular Front," to include Liberals and other " Progressives " who could be rallied behind the agitation for a stronger international policy to counter Fascist aggression, coupled with a " progressive " home policy in such matters as the treatment of the unemployed, the promotion of employment by " public works " or the stimulation of investment, and the further development of the social services. A few Labour supporters had associated themselves with Lloyd George's " New Deal," and others came forward in 1936 in support of the programme of the " Next Five Years Group," formed to follow up the ideas of a collaborative volume, *The Next Five Years : an Essay in Political Agreement*, which had been published in 1935, under the auspices of a group including the Tory, Harold Macmillan, Sir Arthur Salter and a number of Liberals, Clifford Allen (now Lord Allen of Hurtwood), and others of the " National Labour " persuasion, Sir Arthur Pugh, of the Trades Union Congress, and John Bromley, of the Locomotive Engineers, as well as H. G. Wells and a number of leading intellectuals. These movements did not in themselves amount to much ; but the idea of some sort of " Popular Front " received very powerful reinforcement when in the spring of 1936 the French *Front Populaire*, embracing Communists, Socialists and Radicals, won a sweeping election victory and brought Léon Blum into power at the head of a coalition Government of Socialists and Radicals, with the Communists supporting though not taking part. In France, the serious troubles of 1934, when the French Fascists had nearly captured the Chamber of Deputies in a riot and had forced Daladier to resign, had led to the creation of the *Front Populaire* as a means of rallying French democratic opinion against the Fascist danger ; and the electoral victory which followed naturally set a good many opponents of the " National " Government in Great Britain wondering whether the same strategy might not be effective here. There arose a number of new movements, some mainly Communist in inspiration, some mainly Socialist, and others mainly Liberal or vaguely " Progressive," but all calling for some sort of common action to evict the Government and secure a stronger policy against Fascism and for " democracy," first and foremost in foreign affairs, but also at home.

The first to take the field were the Communist Party, who in November, 1935, renewed their appeal for affiliation to the Labour

Party, basing their claim on the need for united working-class action in face of the rising Fascist danger, and referring to their work for Labour candidates in the General Election, at which they had withdrawn in the interests of unity all save two of their nominees. The Communist Party now declared its preparedness " to work loyally within the Labour Party on all current electoral and other campaigns," and to do this " not as a manœuvre or for any concealed aims, but because it believes that this would unite the working class and make it better able to face the immediate fight against the National Government, against Fascism and imperialist war."

The Labour Party Executive, in January, 1936, rejected this appeal, on the ground that " the fundamental difference between the democratic policy and practice of the Labour Party and the policy of dictatorship which the Communist Party had been created to promote was irreconcilable." The Executive expressed the view that the advances of Fascism in Europe had been " in part facilitated by the campaigns for Communist dictatorship that preceded them—campaigns which effectively split the Working-class Movements and rendered their overthrow possible." The Executive continued that they were " as firmly convinced as were their predecessors that any weakening in the Labour Party's defence of political democracy, such as the affiliation of the Communist Party would imply, would inevitably assist the forces of reaction, would endanger our existing liberties, and would retard the achievement of Socialism in this country."

Not content with rejecting the application, the Executive proceeded to issue a scathing report, under the title *British Labour and Communism*. This document, while paying tribute to the achievements of the Russian Revolution, attacked the Communist International for its attempts to establish revolutionary Communist Parties in other countries, and accused the British Communists of having used large subventions from Russia for the purpose of " one long stream of invective and vilification " of the British Labour Movement and its leaders. The Communist Party, it pointed out, had only about 7,000 members in 1935, and " it is this abject failure to secure a substantial membership that has dictated the more subtle tactic of the ' United Front '." The comparability of French and British political conditions was denied, and it was asserted that in France " the ' Popular Front ' has served Communist purposes." The Communist Party was accused of taking its orders from its paymaster, the Comintern ;

and it was denied that Communist affiliation or any sort of United Front in Great Britain would be anything but damaging to the Labour Party's electoral prospects.

At the Party Conference at Edinburgh in October, 1936, the Edinburgh Trades and Labour Council moved that, in view of the need for working-class unity, the Communist Party's application should be accepted " on the conditions laid down in the Party Constitution " ; and the resolution mustered 592,000 votes, including that of the Miners' Federation, against 1,728,000 for rejection. At a subsequent session the Amalgamated Engineering Union moved a resolution in favour of a meeting of " representatives of all working-class bodies to bring about a United Front," but was defeated by 1,805,000 to 435,000. The Conference then went on to pass without a division a resolution in which it declared itself " irrevocably opposed to any attempts to ' liberalise ' the Labour Party by watering down its policy in order to increase its membership." This was a hit at those who were alleged to be working for a programme designed to ensure Liberal support, but nobody rose to defend any such attempt.

Meanwhile, the movement for some sort of United or Popular Front had received powerful reinforcement from the transformation of *Reynolds' Newspaper* under Co-operative ownership into a really good popular Sunday paper and from the foundation of the Left Book Club by Victor Gollancz in May, 1936. *Reynolds'* soon turned to the advocacy of democratic unity on the broadest possible basis ; while the Left Book Club, in support of which the Communists as well as left-wing Socialists of every shade were active, soon began to set up Left Book Club Groups all over the country and to attract into them a large number of unattached persons, mostly young, who were thereafter fed steadily with a diet of propagandist books, issued at an astonishingly low price, and representing a variety of left-wing opinions with a bias towards the discussion of international affairs.

In July, 1936, a new set of Regulations was issued by the Unemployment Assistance Board to replace those which it had been compelled to withdraw early in the previous year. The new Regulations, though they fell a long way short of meeting Labour demands, took the edge off the Means Test and were a considerable concession to the strength of working-class feeling. Both the unemployed organisations and the Labour Movement as a whole continued to demand the complete abolition of the Means Test ; but the unemployed agitation lost some of its force in view of the changes, and was also put into the background by the diversion of the main efforts of the Communists and their sympathisers to the struggle over foreign policy and Fascism. In the summer there were big Anti-Fascist and Spanish demonstrations in London and in other centres. In the autumn Hunger Marches were resumed ; but they came now mainly from the depressed areas and were concerned more with appeals for larger measures to revive employment in South Wales, Scotland, and the North-east than with general unemployed grievances. The Parliamentary Labour Party moved in July a vote of censure on the Government for its failure to produce any constructive employment policy ; and at the Edinburgh Party Conference the Executive was instructed, in view of the failure of the Government to take adequate steps, to set up an Inquiry Committee of its own to visit the Special Areas with a view to working out a Socialist programme for their restoration and to laying proposals before the public.

The Edinburgh Conference also took up again the problems of the League of Youth and of relations with the Co-operative Party, as well as the question of revision of the Party Constitution held over from the previous year. This latter question had again to be deferred for lack of time, after Dalton had stated on behalf of the Executive that they recognised the strength of feeling among the Divisional Labour Parties in favour of revision, and said that " we are all of us very deeply troubled in all sections of the Conference at the apparent divergences which show themselves, and the evidence that certain sections feel that they are not having fair treatment." This was a reference to the movement which was in progress among the Divisional Parties to secure both greater representation on the Executive and the right to elect their own representatives instead of having them elected by the whole Conference—i.e., mainly by the Trade Unions—from nominations made by the Divisional Parties. Individual Membership of the Party showed a rise of 38,000 on the year ; and there were now thirty-one parties with more than 2,000 such members.

On the question of the Co-operative Party considerable differences were now reported. The Labour Party Executive had been pressing for the affiliation of the Co-operative Party " in some form " ; but the Co-operative Party was not in a position to agree to this, even if it had been willing, for it was well aware that the Co-operative Congress, to which it was subject, would reject any such proposal and would insist on the continued independence of the Party. The Labour Party Executive, I think unreasonably, was taking the line that the continuance of a separate Co-operative Party, associated with it but not affiliated, was unacceptable because it " placed Co-operative nominees in a preferential position compared with those put forward by affiliated organisations." The Co-operators of course retorted that they were not prepared to have their great movement treated simply on a par with the numerous affiliated Trade Unions and other bodies inside the Labour Party. The Edinburgh Conference, while recording its general endorsement of the Executive's attitude, left the negotiations to be completed before making any decision on the points at issue.

The Edinburgh Conference was presented by the Executive with a report strongly attacking the conduct of the Labour Party League of Youth, which as we saw had been pressing for the right to discuss and adopt resolutions dealing with Party policy and had actually been taking a line highly critical of the Party leadership. The Executive proposed to take the drastic steps of disbanding the National Advisory Committee of the League, of suspending publication of its journal, *The New Nation*, and of not convening its Annual Conference in 1937. The Executive asked the Party Conference to give it full authority to reorganise the League as a " Youth Section of the Party, based upon loyalty to the Party and its Conference decisions," to restrict membership to persons under twenty-one (instead of twenty-five) and to ensure that the new organisation should not meddle with policy, but should confine itself to recreational, educational and election work, and to discussions not leading to policy resolutions. For this purpose the Executive put forward a new Constitution for the League, defining its functions and confining its National Advisory Committee strictly to the types of work which the Executive wished it to carry on. There was to be an Annual Conference of the League, but resolutions on policy were to be out of order. These proposals were challenged at Edinburgh ; but the Executive got its way by very large majorities.

The question came up of readmitting as members persons who had left the Labour Party, or had been expelled, in the 1931 crisis. It was decided that they could be readmitted only with the consent of the local Parties concerned and with the endorsement of the National Executive. Under this provision, the " National Labour " contingent, except for a few, who had gone finally over, soon began to dribble back.

Fascist disturbances in London, including outbursts of Anti-Semitism in the East End, had been giving trouble ; and Herbert Morrison moved at Edinburgh an Executive resolution calling for the prohibition of the use of political uniforms and for an immediate official inquiry into the activities and finances of the Fascist organisations. This was approved unanimously.

Another interesting discussion at Edinburgh turned on the acceptance of " honours " and titles by Party members. This had been discussed in 1935, when the Executive had been instructed by the Conference to bring up a report. This it now did, in a document divided into two parts. On the question of " ceremonial functions " it was held that no rules could be laid down in relation to Local Government, and that nationally " there are official funcions from which it would be impossible for members of the Labour Party to divorce themselves." The Report held that " pageantry is not in itself objectionable. There is a great deal to be said for encouraging it on the right lines." On the question of " honours," the Report began by laying down that " so long as the House of Lords continues to exist, the Labour case must be competently presented there." It was legally necessary for some members of any Government to sit in the House of Lords. " Further, the creation of Peers in large numbers may prove to be the only possible way to abolish the House of Lords." Membership of the Privy Council must be accepted by Labour Ministers : in the Civil Service, " honours " were a recognised way of conferring status. Some " honours," such as the Order of Merit and honorary degrees at Universities, were " a recognition of merit and service." In these circumstances, no binding rules could be laid down. So thought the National Executive ; but the Edinburgh Conference, on a show of hands, referred the whole Report back by 185 votes to 174, and nothing more was done about it.

The Edinburgh Conference also approved *Coal : the Labour Plan,* a full report on the socialisation of the coal industry mainly prepared by the T.U.C. General Council and approved by the Trades Union Congress the previous month. It also approved the establishment of a Local Government Department at Party headquarters and a memorandum dealing with the selection of candidates for local elections, the organisation of Labour Party Groups on local Councils, and a number of other questions relating to Local Government administration. By this time the Policy Committee had nearly finished its work of elaborating the revised Party programme ; and the Executive was preparing to produce a shortened Immediate Programme on which it could appeal to the country for electoral support. *Labour's Immediate Programme* actually appeared in March, 1937 : it was put forward as "a programme of measures of Socialism and Social Amelioration, which a Labour Government would carry out during a full term of office when returned to power by the electors "—i.e., if it were in a majority. It concentrated upon " Four Vital Measures of Reconstruction . . . Four Great Benefits . . . Revival of the Distressed Areas . . . and Positive Policy for Peace." The financial section promised that the Bank of England would become a Public Corporation under the general direction of the Government, and would be used to control credit in the interests of trade and employment. There would be no return to the gold standard. A National Investment Board would be set up to mobilise and guide financial resources, and large schemes of public development would be carried out. Taxation would be used to secure a better distribution of wealth. Scientific research and development would be encouraged and, if necessary "where scientific discovery creates the possibility of a new industry," Labour would finance and develop it as a public enterprise. No mention was made of the Joint Stock Banks.

The land *should* belong to the people : a Bill would be promoted to enable the Government and other public bodies to acquire land for any purpose without delay and at a reasonable price. A National Transport Board would be set up to co-ordinate all transport agencies except overseas shipping, and " to operate the Railways and such other Transport Services as are suitable for transfer to Public Ownership." The Coal Industry, including treatment and marketing, would be unified under public ownership, and public ownership would also be extended to the whole of the industries of Gas and Electricity Supply. These were the " four vital measures of reconstruction " : the " four great benefits " included the reorganisation of agriculture and food supply to ensure a plentiful supply at fair prices and a living wage for the rural workers. On wages generally, a Labour Government would co-operate with the Trade Unions in raising standards and with the I.L.O. in improving world conditions. Holidays with pay would be made compulsory; the working week would be shortened, " taking as a standard a 40-Hour Working Week," with modifications. Labour would launch " a determined attack on insecurity due to loss of livelihood " and would take vigorous measures to increase employment and to promote retirement of the old on adequate pensions. The school-leaving age would be raised to fifteen, and as soon as possible to sixteen, with maintenance allowances. A new Workmen's Compensation Act would be passed, and Health Services extended. The Means Test would be abolished.

With regard to the state of the Distressed Areas, " the State must accept responsibility for the location of industry." New industries would be brought into these areas, and the " crushing burden of local rates " would be relieved. " Drastic and immediate action " would be taken " to raise the shockingly low standards of life."

Finally, on " Foreign Policy and Defence " the Immediate Programme reiterated the policy described in the preceding chapter—reinvigoration of the League " as an instrument of international co-operation and Collective Security," an effort to stop the arms race, the substitution of an " International Air Police Force " for national Air Forces, and the establishment of an " International Service of Civil Aviation." It was added that " A Labour Government will unhesitatingly maintain such armed forces as are necessary to defend our country and to fulfil our obligations as a member of the British Commonwealth and of the League of Nations." A Defence Ministry was promised to co-ordinate the defence services, and also a Bill " enabling the Government to take over any undertakings manufacturing munitions of war."

This Programme had, on most points, the great merit of precision. The features most criticised were the absence of reference to the Joint Stock Banks and the brevity of the section on international policy, which made no mention of Fascism or of the Soviet Union or of Spain or of any other immediately current issue. The answer given was that such matters were being adequately dealt with elsewhere. The Programme at any rate gave, in respect of home affairs, a clear indication of what a majority Labour Government would set out to do. But the General Election in expectation of which it was drawn up never happened ; and the Labour Party had no chance of presenting its Immediate Programme to the electors for another eight years.

(c) Unity and the Popular Front—After Munich

In January, 1937, the Communist Party, the I.L.P., and the Socialist League, having reached agreement for common action, issued a jointly signed " Unity Manifesto " calling for " Unity in the struggle against Fascism, Reaction and War, and against the National Government." The Manifesto called for " unity of all sections of the working class . . . in the struggle for immediate demands and the return of a Labour Government, as the next stage in the advance to working-class power." It advocated " the adoption of a fighting programme of mass-struggle, through the democratisation of the Labour Party and the Trade Union Movement " : it repudiated " class-collaboration," denounced the Government as " the agent of British Capitalism and Imperialism," and recorded its " implacable opposition to the rearmament and recruiting programme of the National Government," which it accused of using armaments " only in support of Fascism, of Imperialist War, of Reaction, and of Colonial Suppression." The workers were summoned to " mobilise for the maintenance of peace, for the defence of the Soviet Union and its fight for peace, and for a pact between Great Britain, the Soviet Union, France, and all other states in which the working class have political freedom." The Manifesto went on to demand the nationalisation of the Arms Industry and " the abolition of the caste and class system within the armed forces." It emphasised the need to struggle against Imperialism in India and in the Colonies ; and it urged the workers " to wage incessant struggle, political and industrial alike, for simple things the workers need," not waiting for General Elections, but at once " by active demonstrations." Then followed a list of these " simple demands " —abolition of the Means Test, Trade Union scales of Unemployment Benefit, national work of social value for the Distressed Areas, the Forty-hour Week and Paid Holidays for all workers, non-contributory pensions at sixty, co-ordinated Trade Union action for higher wages, power to get back the land for the people, nationalisation of the mines, effective control of banks and stock markets, making the rich pay for social amelioration.

The content of these demands was at many points the same as that of the Labour Party Programme ; but the tone was vastly different. Among the signatories to the Manifesto were Cripps, Mellor, Pollitt, Gallacher, Maxton, Jowett, Fenner Brockway, Harold Laski, Brailsford, Aneurin Bevan, John Strachey, Tom

Mann, Jack Tanner of the A.E.U., Arthur Horner, Palme Dutt, G. R. Mitchison and Frank Horrabin.

The Labour Party Executive reacted at once with a circular headed " Party Loyalty," in which it recited Conference decisions making united action with the Communist Party " incompatible with membership of the Labour Party," and went on to declare that association with any organisations " clearly formed to pursue ' United Front ' or ' Popular Front ' activities or to promote association with other parties " should not be given support by any member of the Labour Party. This was before the *Unity Manifesto* had been formally issued, though after its substance was known.

The Socialist League, the only constituent of the new United Front that was affiliated to the Labour Party, did not endorse participation without a serious internal conflict. At the Special Conference called to endorse the campaign, the Unity proposals were carried only by fifty-six votes to thirty-eight, with twenty-three abstentions ; and there was at once a substantial secession from the Socialist League. On January 27, the Labour Party Executive expelled the Socialist League from the Party and appealed to its branches to secede from it. A further circular on " The Labour Party and the So-called ' Unity Campaign ' " was at once issued, reciting the misdemeanours of the Socialist League and declaring membership of it inconsistent with membership of the Labour Party. The circular added " The Labour Party has never exercised an iron discipline nor does it demand unthinking loyalty. It encourages free discussion and it has been tolerant in its fellowship. It seeks a loyalty to its general principles, based on understanding and democratic consent. In this particular case, the National Executive Committee has not acted hastily, but only after its appeal for loyalty has been completely disregarded . . . It calls for a real, and not a sham unity. The real United Front is that of the Socialist, Trade Union, and Co-operative Movements."

The Socialist League soon realised that it was placed in a very awkward position. The majority of its members did not at all wish to be flung out of the Labour Party and thus to lose their chance of pursuing their policy through the Local Labour Parties and of playing their part in the general work of the Labour Movement. The League, in fact, began at once to fall to pieces ; and when the Party Executive reiterated in March its determination to expel all Party members who continued to belong to it, the League attempted to meet the situation by dissolving, at the same time announcing that its adherents would continue in their individual capacities to support the Unity Movement. To this the Labour Party Executive retorted in May with a further circular, in which it laid down that " while individual members may advocate within the Party proposals for a ' United Front ' and endeavour to get them accepted by Conference, it is not open to loyal members of the Party to act in contravention of existing decisions." Party members were accordingly called upon " to refrain from any further joint activities with the Communist Party and the I.L.P. and to concentrate on Labour's constructive proposals "—that is, on *Labour's Immediate Programme*, which had recently been issued.

In the meantime, the Unity Campaign Committee had been carrying on an active propaganda of meetings throughout the country, first under the auspices of the three bodies and then of two only, with the participation of some of the Socialist Leaguers as individuals. In addition, the Leaguers formed a " Committee of Party Members sympathetic to Unity," which carried on a separate campaign of its own. The Party Executive proceeded in July to ban this Committee and to prohibit any public campaign by Party members to prosecute the cause of Unity with the Communists and the I.L.P. A number of affiliated organisations sent in resolutions for the Annual Conference on the United Front and the position of the Socialist League ; but the Executive used its power to ban them all under the " three years' rule," which did not allow any question that had been voted upon at the Party Conference to be brought up again for another three years without special permission. The Executive held that the entire question had in effect been settled at the 1936 Conference. This left moving the reference back of the Executive's Report as the only way of challenging the expulsions or of raising the " United Front " issue in any form.

At the Bournemouth Party Conference in October, Sir Stafford Cripps accordingly moved the reference back of the Report. His views, he said, were unchanged ; and he pointed out that the ban imposed on association with the Communist Party and the I.L.P. was " not extended to those who associated themselves with members of opposing capitalist parties "—a reference mainly to the Next Five Years Group and to such bodies as the National Peace Council. He urged that, in response to the Executive's objections, the Labour Unity Committee had been set up entirely within the Party, and argued that the ban upon this body was quite unconstitutional. Why was only the Left denied a right of association which passed unchallenged when indulged in by the Right ? Harold Laski seconded Cripps, saying that if he had to choose between appearing on the same platform with Winston Churchill or with Harry Pollitt, he had no doubt at all that his proper place was with Pollitt. Both speakers pleaded for a wide measure of toleration within the Party, for right and left alike. Clynes replied, for the Executive, saying that it had only acted on decisions made by previous Conferences, which " constituted its instructions." G. R. Strauss, who had been sacked by Herbert Morrison from his official position on the London County Council for associating himself with the Unity Campaign, spoke next, and was immediately followed by Morrison, who argued that the Executive had been very tolerant and had given the rebels much more rope than they would have got in the Communist Party. That, he said, was why they did not join it outright, instead of merely working with it. Morrison then appealed to the rebels, as having " had a good run for their money," to " drop it, and to come into the Party as comrades helping us in the job and thereby assisting us to stop the processes of discipline that we do not want to carry further, but which they will force us to carry further if this goes on." Two votes were then taken, one on the issue of the Socialist League and the other directly on the Executive's action over the United Front. In both cases, the reference back was heavily defeated—on the issue of the Socialist League by 1,730,000 to 373,000, and on that of the United Front by 2,116,000 to 331,000.

This, as we shall see, did not end the matter ; but it did leave the ex-Socialist Leaguers still members of the Labour Party, if they were prepared to abide by the decision of the Conference— as, for the time, they did. The Conference then turned its attention to other matters. It approved *Labour's Pension Plan*, drawn up by the National Council of Labour, providing for a pension of £1 a week for single persons and 35s. 0d. for married couples at sixty-five, or at sixty if unemployed and " unlikely to regain normal employment." Wives were to qualify at fifty-five, and the increased pensions were to be conditional on retirement from employment. Other provisions related to widows and their children. The Conference also approved the Reports on the Distressed Areas drawn up in accordance with the instructions of its predecessor, and decided to launch a National Campaign based on *Labour's Immediate Programme* and to raise a Special Campaign Fund for this purpose.

One of the most important matters before the 1937 Conference was the revision of the Labour Party Constitution, which, as we saw, had been deferred for two years running. There had been an accumulating discontent among the Divisional Labour Parties at the meagre representation allowed to them on the Party Executive and at the system under which all the members of the Executive, though nominated by sections, were voted on by the entire Conference, so that the big Trade Unions could, if they wished, determine the entire composition of the Executive. There had been several unofficial joint movements among the Constituency Parties to get this system altered and their representation increased ; and the Executive now brought forward a series of proposals which went a long way towards meeting their claims. Trade Union opinion was sharply divided, some Trade Unions resenting any attempt to lessen their preponderance ; and it was doubtful to the last how the voting would go, especially because Stafford Cripps and other advocates of the United Front had been active on the side of the Constituency Parties, and there were fears on the Right that to give them more powers would strengthen the Left within the Party. The Executive, however, wisely took the view that the best course was to do everything possible to allay discontent within the Constituency Parties, in the hope of making them more amenable to party discipline.

After a long debate, the proposal to increase Constituency Party representation on the Executive from five to seven was carried by 1,408,000 to 1,134,000 ; and the right of these Parties to elect their representatives separately had an easy passage, by 1,814,000 to 658,000.* A further proposal, to allow Local Parties which could not afford to send delegates to the Annual Conference to vote by proxy, was heavily defeated. The representative of the League of Youth was dismissed from the Executive by 2,056,000 to 423,000 : it was decided to take amendments to the Constitution and to Standing Orders only every third year ; and the date of the Conference was shifted from October to Whitsuntide, largely in order that it might not follow closely on the meeting of the Trades Union Congress in September. The Conference also carried a plan for the reorganisation of the League of Youth under the control of the Head Office and of the Local Labour Parties, after the Executive had accepted

*Despite the change, all the old members were re-elected.

an amendment to its original scheme providing that a Conference of the League's branches should be called to elect representatives to serve on a new Advisory Committee and to " consider proposals for the future development of the League." Relations with the Co-operative Party had improved ; and the Executive was able to report an agreement on the arrangements to be made in constituencies to be contested by Co-operative candidates. On other matters the negotiations were still in progress.

Meanwhile, especially in London, the troubles arising out of the development of Mosley's Fascist movement continued unabated. There were many fracas between Fascist and Communist demonstrations and processions, and in the East End a regular warfare developed between the Fascists and the Labour organisations. The Fascists organised big marches with the deliberate object of provoking disturbances in working-class areas ; and in June, 1937, the Government used its powers under the recently enacted Public Order Act to prohibit all political processions in London for six weeks—a prohibition which was renewed in August and again in September. The Fascists nevertheless staged a march through Bermondsey in October, and a serious fracas occurred, with police charges and numerous arrests.

In 1937 the demand for an " Anti-Fascist Front " had chiefly taken, under Communist influence and with the support of the Socialist League and the I.L.P., the form of a proposal for " working-class unity." The slogans used had been sometimes " United Front " and sometimes " Popular Front "—the latter by way of reference to the French *Front Populaire* and the Spanish *Frente Popular*—but, although both these combinations rested on a basis broader than that of the working class, including Radicals as well as Socialists, the British propaganda of 1937 had been mainly a demand for joint action between the Labour Party and the Communists to meet the Fascist danger both abroad and at home. From the later months of 1937, however, there began to appear, side by side with this agitation for working-class unity, a growing demand for the widest possible coalition of anti-Government, anti-Fascist forces, with the object of evicting Chamberlain from office and installing by pressure of public opinion a Government that would definitely drop appeasement and stand up to the aggressor nations. Anthony Eden's resignation in February, 1938, followed by the talks of Halifax, his successor at the Foreign Office, with Ribbentrop in March, and by the annexation of

Austria, considerably strengthened this movement, in which a growing number of Liberals joined. It was, however, unlike the United Front movement of the previous year, an agitation without either a definite organising centre or a single focus. From the working-class end it was taken up actively by *Reynolds' News* under the editorship of S. R. Elliott, who made his appeal first and foremost to the Co-operative Movement. *Reynolds'* advocated a " United Peace Alliance," with the Labour and Co-operative Movements as its mass support, but wide enough to include the Liberals, or such of them as were prepared to come in, and even such Tories as were critical of Chamberlain and believed in the League and in Collective Security. The *News-Chronicle* also took up the demand for some sort of Popular Front on much the same basis ; and a number of local " Popular Fronts " made their appearance, composed mainly of Labour intellectuals, Liberals of the more progressive types, and active supporters of the League of Nations Union, the National Peace Council, and other non-party bodies.

At Easter, this movement, in the form in which it was advocated by *Reynolds' News*, secured the support of the Conference of the Co-operative Party. At the same time, the Popular Front was repudiated by the I.L.P., which reiterated its demand for a United Front broad enough to include all the working-class bodies, but nobody besides. In April the Labour Party Executive issued a Manifesto against the proposed United Peace Alliance, which it regarded as tending to the " weakening of Party policy to accommodate other political demands " and as having been condemned in advance by the decisions of the 1937 Party Conference. Instead, the Local Parties were urged to concentrate their efforts on winning support for the Labour Party in order to secure a Labour majority in Parliament : the Executive said that it " emphasised its belief that with the exercise of disciplined loyalty, thorough organisation, and widespread propaganda, the capture of power can be achieved." Perhaps, but when ? the advocates of the Popular Front retorted, as they watched to see when Hitler would make his next *coup*, and no one stop him. A number of Local Parties disregarded this appeal and, in the words of the displeased Party Executive, " initiated action in their areas to form Local Councils of Action, based on ' Popular Front ' principles." The Executive not merely expressed its displeasure in a second and longer Manifesto, *The Labour Party and the Popular Front*, but also put strong pressure on the Local Parties concerned

" to liquidate the new organisations," and " where occasion warranted, the Parties were disaffiliated and new Parties created upon the lines laid down in the Party Constitution."

In the May Manifesto, the Executive did not offer absolutely unqualified hostility to " Popular Front " movements under all possible circumstances. It argued that the case might be altered " were there any evidence of an internal crisis in the Conservative Party," but that there was no evidence of any substantial Conservative revolt. " A new situation might arise, of course, if any considerable number of Members of Parliament now supporting the Government were to rebel against the Prime Minister's authority." As for the Liberals, it was argued that the " Popular Front " movement

. . . fails to take account of the diminishing force of the Liberal Party. [now divided between supporters and opponents of the Government.] We have no direct evidence that the latter would join the proposed combination as a body ; and there is some evidence to the contrary. There is, further, profound uncertainty whether the Liberal electorate would follow the advice of the Liberal Opposition leaders. In many parts of the country Liberals and Conservatives have long formed a " United Front " against Labour both in Municipal and Parliamentary elections. In many constituencies the absence of a Liberal assists the Conservative rather than the Labour candidate.

Still envisaging the whole problem in electoral terms—which the advocates of the " Popular Front " did not—the Labour Party Executive went on to argue that such a front

. . . would have less electoral appeal than a united and independent Labour Party . . . It would create more controversy in our own ranks than it would remove. It would take the heart out of large numbers of our most loyal supporters . . . The membership of the Labour Party deeply values its unity and independence . . . They would not sacrifice that independence even temporarily, unless they were satisfied that such sacrifice was the sole condition for the preservation of peace and democracy . . . We do not believe that condition exists. On the contrary, we believe that there is an increasing probability of a Labour Party victory *at the next Election* . . . (italics mine).

Of course, this quite missed the point of the " Popular Front " movement, which was designed to stop the policy of appeasement at once, and not to wait until the Conservatives saw fit to dissolve Parliament. The Popular Front was never mainly an electoral movement, save to the extent that it sought to use by-elections as a means of exercising pressure and showing the strength of feeling

against Fascism and against the Chamberlain policy of appease-
ment. It was, however, part of the policy of the Labour Party
Executive to represent it as primarily related to a coming General
Election.

Following up this line, the Executive proceeded to argue that,
even if a Popular Front could win an election victory, it could
never govern effectively. To hold that it could do so was to
" disregard the serious fact that the Liberal Members of Parliament would hold the balance of power," and that they would be
in a position at any moment to " defeat the Government and put
the Conservatives in." This, of course, harked back to evil memo-
ries of 1924 and of 1931. The Manifesto went on to discuss the
Liberal record in these years ; and then it ended up with an
appeal to " all men and women who desire Great Britain to take
the lead for democracy and peace, whatever their political attach-
ment," to help the Labour Party to defeat the " National "
Government *at the next General Election*. But, in the meantime,
what ?—or rather, what beyond preparing for an Election that
might not occur till 1940, and meantime watching Hitler commit
one successful aggression after another? On this issue, the Labour
Party's Manifesto offered no sort of guidance.

In June, 1938, the movement for a " Popular Front " suffered
a serious blow when the resolution in favour of the United Peace
Alliance, though sponsored by the Co-operative Party, was de-
feated by 4,492,000 votes to 2,382,000 at the Annual Co-operative
Congress, the majority including the opponents of Co-operative
political action as well as the Co-operators who followed the
Labour Party Executive's policy. The Conference of the National
Union of Railwaymen, held the same month, also voted down the
Popular Front by sixty-two votes to eighteen. This did not end
the movement ; but it was reduced, despite the attempts of a
National People's Front Propaganda Committee, to a series of
local actions, on which the Labour Party Executive stamped as
hard as it dared in the particular circumstances of each area.
At Oxford City, in October, the Constituency Labour Party was
induced to withdraw its candidate in favour of the Master of
Balliol, A. D. Lindsay, a member of the Labour Party, who stood
as an " Independent Progressive " on a Popular Front programme.
Lindsay was beaten by a Tory ; but he reduced the majority
from 6,645 to 3,434. The Labour Party Executive took no
disciplinary action in this case. The following month the Liberal,
Vernon Bartlett of the *News-Chronicle*, standing in the same way

as an " Independent Progressive," won in a straight fight at
Bridgwater, which had gone to the Tories at the General Election
in a three-cornered contest. But, despite this isolated success,
the Popular Front movement of 1938 petered out. It had become
after the defeats at the Co-operative Congress and at the Railwaymen's Conference mainly a rank and file movement for Liberal-
Labour co-operation, with no backing from the leaders of either
party, and supported only embarrassingly by the Labour and
Communist left, where they backed it at all—for they, for the most
part, were still combining the demand for a vigorous anti-Fascist
policy with opposition to rearmament as long as the Chamber-
lainites were in power, whereas the Popular Front leaders insisted
on the need for rearmament, well knowing that it would be of
no avail to turn the Government out and find themselves helpless
to carry out their own policy for lack of arms.

Both the Oxford and the Bridgwater by-elections occurred
after the Munich ignominy, and were essentially reactions to it.
In 1938, as we have seen, there was no Labour Party Conference
to express the Labour Party's reaction to the betrayal of Czechoslovakia. The Trades Union Congress, held early in September,
was over long before the decisive phase of the crisis was reached ;
but it went on record by a very large majority in favour not only
of the Memorandum drafted by the National Council of Labour
urging the summoning of Parliament, but also of a resolution
demanding that Great Britain should stand firmly with France
and the Soviet Union in the defence of Czechoslovakia against the
Nazis. The Amalgamated Engineering Union attempted to
censure the General Council for entering into discussions with the
Government on the industrial measures needed to speed up rearmament, but was heavily beaten. In a private session a proposal for industrial action designed to secure a change of foreign
policy by forcing the Government's resignation was defeated ;
but the Congress's attitude in favour of strong action against
Nazi aggression was unmistakably expressed.

Shortly after the Munich crisis, the Labour Party issued a
Manifesto, under the title *Labour's Claim to Government*, calling for
the replacement of the " National " Government by a Labour
Government as an urgent necessity if the country's resources were
to be mobilised in the democratic cause. " The voluntary effort
of a free people," it was declared, " can far surpass those of a
regimented dictatorship. But these efforts can only be made if
our nation is led by a Government whose policy it can trust and

by men and women who truly represent the nation and command its respect. Such a Government can yet save peace." No indication, however, was given of the means of getting such a Government in time to avert disaster. Apart from denunciations of the Chamberlain policy the Manifesto concentrated its attention largely on the demand for a strengthening of the national defences, mainly insisting on better security against air attack. " Air Raid Precautions must be regarded as of equal importance with the other three Defence Departments and made thoroughly efficient." Anti-aircraft guns and a balloon barrage were called for, and also a rapid increase in the strength of the Air Force, especially in fighter planes. Of the wider military aspects of defence but little was said, except in insisting on the rejection of compulsory service. Right to the end the Labour Party and the Trade Unions maintained this attitude of intense suspicion of conscription and denial of its necessity. Right up to 1940 there was a widespread belief, by no means confined to Labour, that war would not call for large armed forces nearly so much as for intensive mechanisation and the employment of great numbers on the industrial front.

The year which intervened between the Czech crisis and the outbreak of war in 1939 saw a revival of the Popular Front agitation in a new form, this time under the leadership of Sir Stafford Cripps. In January, 1939, Cripps, who had kept his seat on the Labour Party Executive despite his United Front activities of 1937, sent to the Secretary a Memorandum urging the creation of a Popular Front open to every Opposition group, and demanding a special meeting of the Executive to consider his proposals. The meeting was held ; and the Executive defeated Cripps's proposals by seventeen votes to three. Cripps thereupon circulated his Memorandum widely, under the auspices of an *ad hoc* National Petition Committee. The Executive took strong objection to this action, and demanded that Cripps should both reaffirm his loyalty to the Labour Party Constitution and policy and withdraw his Memorandum by circular to the bodies to which it had been sent. Cripps refused both demands, the first on the ground that his work for the Labour Party should be sufficient evidence of his loyalty, and the second because he held that he had acted entirely within his rights as a member of the Party. The Executive thereupon expelled him from membership of the Labour Party, and issued two further manifestos directed against the Popular Front and against Cripps in particular. These were called respectively *Socialism or Surrender ?* and *Unity, True or Sham ?* and in both the

Executive sought to show not only that Cripps had behaved disloyally, but also that his purpose had been to give up Socialism in order to secure Liberal adherence to the Popular Front. He was accused of proposing to drop the Labour Party's demand for public ownership of industry and to substitute a vague formula referring only to public control, and of wishing in general to water down *Labour's Immediate Programme*. Cripps was also accused, not without justice, of having radically changed his line. " Yesterday," said the Executive in *Socialism or Surrender ?* " he wanted a ' United Front ' with the Communists. Today he wants a ' Popular Front ' with the Liberals. Tomorrow ? . . . who knows ? "

In order to understand the controversy between Cripps and the Party Executive, it is necessary to understand clearly what he and his group were demanding. The Cripps Memorandum of January, 1939, followed upon an earlier document which he had submitted to the Executive in May, 1938, in conjunction with three other members of that body—Laski, Ellen Wilkinson, and D. N. Pritt—and was connected with his opposition to the line taken by the Executive in refusing to allow the Labour Party League of Youth to collaborate with Youth Organisations outside the Party, while allowing the leaders of the Labour Party to join with members of the " National " Government in addressing meetings on behalf of the Government's " National Fitness Campaign." The 1939 Memorandum, however, was presented by Cripps alone, and travelled far beyond this field. It was essentially a plea for a common programme wide enough to be supported by " progressives " of many shades of opinion, including non-Socialists, for the purpose of turning out the " National " Government and putting in its place a Government that would follow a radically different international policy. The Executive was quite correct in saying that, in such a programme, Cripps was prepared to suppress all mention of socialisation, and to substitute vague references to "control," provided that he could get a strong policy both of resistance to Fascism and of measures for the expansion of employment and the development of social security at home.

Cripps laid himself open to attack by arguing with the Labour Party Executive, on the ground which it had chosen, as if the Popular Front were mainly a device for winning the next General Election, when it came, rather than for mobilising public opinion at once against the Government's foreign policy. He entered into elaborate calculations of the unlikelihood of Labour alone getting a clear majority at the next Election, and made the Popular Front appear to be primarily an electoral manœuvre involving the temporary sacrifice of a large part of the Labour programme. This enabled the Executive to retort effectively upon him with the charge of " surrendering Socialism." It was also able to retort upon him that his opposition to rearmament was inconsistent with his demand for effective resistance to the aggressors ; for even if the Government were turned out, what would be the use if years must pass before its successor could be adequately armed ? Cripps's reply that he could be no party to arming a Government which would only use the weapons placed in its hands for the purpose of waging " imperialist war " furnished no answer to this dilemma, which continued to stultify the propaganda of the left. This aspect of the Cripps policy was, however, pushed into the background by most of his supporters, who were no longer in doubt that arms had to be provided quickly if there were to be any chance of stopping the Nazis from overrunning the greater part of Europe.

The National Petition Campaign was continued in spite of the expulsion of Cripps ; but it was seriously weakened because every Labour Party member who supported it ran the risk of sharing the same treatment, and most were not prepared to face the prospect. Of those who did persist in the campaign, Sir Charles Trevelyan, Aneurin Bevan, and G. R. Strauss were also presently expelled from the Labour Party, and a number of " disloyal " Labour Parties were disaffiliated and, where possible, replaced. Cripps, on receiving news of his expulsion, announced his intention of appealing to the Labour Party Conference against the Executive's decision, but was informed that, being no longer a member of the Party, he had no such right. There was, however, a widespread demand in the Movement that he should be heard ; and the Executive decided to leave it to the Conference itself to settle whether he should be heard or not.

The Conference, in accordance with the change made in 1937, was held at Whitsuntide. It decided, by a vote of 1,227,000 to 1,083,000, to suspend the Constitution and Standing Orders, and allow Cripps to speak against his expulsion. This he did ; but instead of attempting to argue the case in favour of his Popular Front policy, he made a legalistic speech turning almost entirely on the question of the Executive's constitutional right to expel him. He argued that he had a perfect right to attempt to get his views accepted by the Party, and to campaign publicly with this object : he did not, except inferentially, put his views before the Conference. The result would probably have been the same whatever he had done ; but the form of his speech was not such as to appeal to the audience to which it was made. He disappointed the delegates, and gave his supporters in the Conference a poor lead for their attempt to get the Executive's Report on its action referred back. On this issue, the Executive won by 2,100,000 votes to 402,000, thus putting the final seal of the Party's displeasure on the entire movement for any sort of Popular Front. The movement for it was, indeed, dead well before that. Even the Co-operative Party, in April, reversed its vote of the previous year, and, in obedience to the Co-operative Congress, rejected the United Peace Alliance plan.

By the time the 1939 Labour Party Conference met, Fascism had marched on a long way. The Spanish Civil War had ended in March with the surrender of Madrid. Before that, in February, the " National " Government had recognised Franco. The Germans had occupied Prague in March, and had annihilated the Czechoslovak State. In April the Italians had seized Albania. Chamberlain in March had changed his tune, and had given his extraordinary guarantee to Poland—extraordinary because it was entirely unconcerted with the Soviet Union and was manifestly beyond Great Britain's power to implement without Soviet help. Early in May Litvinov had been driven from office, because the Soviet Government had become convinced of the impossibility of coming to satisfactory terms with the Western Powers. A new Pact between Germany and Italy had been signed. Although negotiations between Great Britain, France and the Soviet Union still dragged on through May in Moscow, the stage was in fact fully set for a war in which Hitler could overrun Poland without fear that any other country could come to its assistance. The German-Soviet Pact, though not signed until August, was already in the making. Hitler was seizing his chance of dealing with the West before turning his forces against the East. Chamberlain's appeasement policy had finally wrecked the chance of building up the League, with Soviet participation, into an instrument of collective security. The thing itself was all settled : only the timing was still unknown.

The Labour Party, however, had not yet accepted, even if many of its members had recognised, the inevitable outcome. The official resolution submitted by the Executive to the Southport

Conference at the end of May, and moved by Philip Noel-Baker, the most devoted friend of the League of Nations, was still cast in terms which implied the possibility of preserving the peace. It called for " a return to the spirit and the principles which animated the foreign policy of the Labour Government from 1929 to 1931 " as the only hope of restoring " Britain's moral influence and power of international leadership," and of rebuilding a real League of Nations. It deplored " the prolonged delay in concluding a definite and unequivocal pact with France and the Soviet Union for mutual defence." It welcomed Roosevelt's proposal to Germany and Italy that they should give pledges against further aggression, and called for " the closest contact with the Government of the United States and with other Governments willing to join in carrying out " a programme of agreed limitation of armaments and of collective handling of world economic problems ; and it ended with a "selah" in praise of "the rule of law among nations " and of " organised international co-operation to eliminate the fundamental causes of war and to raise the standard of living in all lands." After a discussion which rambled over a great many issues and included the moving by K. Zilliacus of a left-wing amendment demanding that Great Britain should join the Franco-Soviet Pact and that the Conference should make a strong declaration against participation in any imperialist war aims, the delegates voted almost unanimously for the Executive's resolution. Zilliacus's amendment got 286,000 votes against 1,670,000.

The Executive also laid before the Southport Conference a long document subsequently issued as a pamphlet under the title *Labour and Defence*. This dealt mainly with two sets of issues democratisation of the armed forces by improvements in pay and conditions and assimilation of the rights of soldiers to those of civilians and also by changes in the systems of recruitment and promotion of both officers and " other ranks " ; and the better organisation of supply services through a properly constituted Ministry of Supply with wide industrial functions and powers. This statement of policy also made reference to Labour's opposition to conscription, which, in the form of compulsory military training, the Government was then pushing through the House of Commons. The National Council of Labour, on April 25, had reaffirmed " its uncompromising opposition to Conscription," and had demanded " that the Government shall apply itself with energy, confidence, and practical determination to the task of developing the organisation of our national resources through the system of voluntary service." The Labour Party was still under the belief that all that needed to be done in peace-time could be done through voluntary recruitment, if only the conditions of service in the armed forces were thoroughly reformed ; but, having been defeated in Parliament on the conscription issue, it was not prepared to go beyond protests. The official resolution, moved by Herbert Morrison, declared " that the voluntary system has not failed," and called " for every effort to ensure its increasing success." It asked the Conference to endorse the Memorandum on *Labour and Defence* and the National Council of Labour's demand for " the proper protection of the civilian population in time of war " (the much-disputed issue of A.R.P.). To this resolution an amendment was moved calling, in view of the advent of conscription, " for the complete cessation of all further support for all National Service Schemes (with the exception of A.R.P.) initiated by the National Government." This amendment, even at this stage of the war peril, mustered 729,000 votes against 1,767,000—so strong was the hostility to conscription and the fear of its spread from the armed forces to industrial services. The amendment having been lost, the Executive's resolution was carried by 1,967,000 to 574,000.

In Parliament the Labour Party fought the Military Training Bill in accordance with the official policy ; but, when the Bill became an Act, no further attempt was made to oppose its operation. In the Labour Party's view, the Bill was unnecessary and was a breach of undertakings which had been given by the Government only a month or two before, as well as earlier, in connection with its requests to the Trade Unions and to the Party to take part in the National Voluntary Service Scheme near the beginning of the year. One main purpose of this scheme had been to secure sufficient recruits for the essential services, including civil defence, in the event of the outbreak of war ; and another had been to compile a register of essential occupations, showing which types of men would have to be left in their own trades and which could be made available for more essential work. There had been considerable fears that this plan would serve as the thin end of the wedge of conscription, industrial as well as military ; and a good many Labour bodies were reluctant to take part in it. The Trades Union Congress and the Labour Party were, however, induced to participate and to urge participation on the local Labour bodies, partly in the hope of making the success of the scheme a means of defending the voluntary system, but also largely because they recognised the absolute need for it if Great Britain were to be put in a position to stand up to Nazi aggression. Indeed, the National Council of Labour, in its circular of March, 1939, urging all Labour organisations to do their best to help the scheme, went further than in any other statement in recognising the paramount necessity of rearmament, even under a Government of whose policy it thoroughly disapproved.

Thus, the circular asserted that " whatever democratic Government is in office, rearmament is necessary, and indeed unavoidable in the interests of self-defence alone." It could be argued that this was question begging, on the ground that the " National " Government was not " democratic " ; but the context made it clear that what was meant was " non-totalitarian," and that the " National " Government was meant to be covered by it. " In the present state of the world," said the circular, " Great Britain must be strongly equipped to defend herself, to play her full part in collective security, and to resist any intimidation by the Fascist Powers designed to frustrate the fulfilment of her obligations . . . Although the Government, in carrying out rearmament, has displayed gross indecision and ineptitude, that in itself is not a reason for opposing rearmament." The circular then went on to say that on the special questions of " deep shelters, evacuation arrangements, school camps, anti-aircraft defence, aircraft production, and Ministries of Defence and Supply " many sections of the Labour Movement had been pressing hard for greater speed and efficiency, that Labour Groups on Local Authorities had been active in carrying out A.R.P. measures, and that the attitude taken by the Movement in these respects was inconsistent with refusal to take part in shaping the National Voluntary Service scheme as a whole, in order to bring it into harmony as far as possible with Labour policy. As early as 1935 Local Authority Labour Groups had been advised by the Party to participate in A.R.P., and in January, 1939, a comprehensive statement on *A.R.P. Labour's Policy* had been issued. Most Trade Unions and Local Labour bodies followed this lead, though some dissented to the last. The Labour Movement was especially active in pressing for the development of A.R.P. and for the careful advance planning of schemes for evacuation of crowded areas in the event of war ; and in these matters the left wing, including the Communists, had been particularly vocal. Participation in the whole National Service Scheme was represented as no more than the logical development of this attitude in face of the nearer and nearer threat of war.

Labour's participation in the scheme was secured by assurances of its voluntary nature. " Categorical assurances," said the circular, " were given by the Ministers that it was the Government's intention to preserve the voluntary system." There was, accordingly, a sense of having been tricked when the Military Training Bill was introduced, just as there had been over the " Derby Scheme " during the first World War.

In relation to the Labour Party's internal development, 1939 was not a particularly significant year. Negotiations with the Co-operative Party over joint constituency arrangements dragged on, agreement being reached on some points, but hard to arrive at on others. The Labour Party was induced to sign an agreement defining conditions of joint action where the Co-operators refused locally to affiliate to a Constituency Labour Party, and arrangements were also made to cover the selection of Co-operative candidates in local elections. But the discussions were still slowly proceeding when war broke out in 1939 ; and it was then decided to let the outstanding issues rest for the time being, in view of the suspension of contested elections during the war and the necessary scaling-down of the organising activities of both Parties.

In the case of the League of Youth, 1938 had been a year of attempted revival after the quarrel recorded earlier in this chapter. In 1938 a Youth Organiser was appointed on the central Party staff ; a National League of Youth Conference was allowed to meet in March, and a new statement of Policy and Objectives for the League was accepted at the Conference. The Youth Advisory Committee was allowed to function with the aid of Executive representatives, who included Sir Stafford Cripps ; and a Youth Week was arranged for September, 1939. *Advance* was recognised as the League's organ. But by 1939 trouble had started all over again. The Executive alleged that the National Advisory Committee was again exceeding its functions, and in particular it was said that the League was supporting Cripps in his conflict with the Executive. In March, 1939, that body swooped again, cancelling the appointment of both the National and the Local Advisory Committees of the League and refusing to allow its Annual Conference to be convened. The Executive's actions were challenged at the Southport Conference later in the year ; but an attempt to secure the reference back was lost.

On the other hand, the Executive suffered defeat when it attempted, not for the first time, to introduce into the Party Constitution a provision for Associate Members. This was intended to attract " men and women occupying professional or administrative posts, either nationally, locally, or abroad, who are debarred from active participation in political work . . . but who would like to express their sympathy with the Party in some tangible manner." A majority at the Conference did not like the look of this proposal to make special provision for the " intelligentsia," and it was rejected in private session by 1,331,000 to 1,007,000, on the motion of the Mineworkers' Federation. The Mineworkers also secured the defeat of the Executive's proposal to increase affiliation fees to 6d. a member (from 4½d.). The Annual Conference closed, however, on a note of solidarity, by giving unanimous approval to *Labour's Immediate Programme*, which was still expected to be needed for an impending General Election ; for even in June, 1939, the imminence of war was not generally felt as necessitating a departure from normal plans.

THE LABOUR PARTY'S FORTUNES AT BY-ELECTIONS, 1936–9

	1936	1937	1938	1939 to August	Total
Seats held in straight fights	2	2	4	3	11
Seats held in other contests	—	—	—	1	1
Seats won in straight fights	3	2	4	3	12
Seats won in other contests	1	—	—	—	1
Seats contested but not won Straight fights . .	4	10	5	5	24
Other contests . .	3	6	2	1	12
Seats not fought . .	—	6	5	5	16
TOTALS . .	13	26	20	18	77

CHAPTER X

LABOUR IN THE SECOND WORLD WAR

(a) *The First Phase—to May, 1940*

The invasion of Poland—Great Britain, the Soviet Union, and the Nazis—Hitler's expectations—The Labour Party and the Polish crisis—The Soviet Union's proposals for a Peace Pact—The National Council of Labour's attitude—The military mission to Moscow, and why it failed—The German-Soviet Pact and the Soviet attitude—Effects of the Pact on Western Socialist opinion—British Labour's appeals to the German people—The declaration of war—Labour and the Conscription Bill—Labour supports the war effort—Refusal to join a Coalition under Chamberlain—The Trades Union Congress and the War—The I.L.P. and the " imperialist " war—The Communist Party's first reaction—Its speedy change of front—Harry Pollitt's pamphlet and his removal from office—Molotov attacks the " imperialists "—The " phoney " war—The Soviet-Finnish War and the reaction to it in the West—The League expels the Soviet Union—The Labour delegation to Finland—The Home Front—Evacuation—Price-control and war finance—Social Services in war-time—The mobilisation of economic resources—Unemployment—The Electoral Truce—The Local Government Truce—Labour organisation under war conditions—Labour and the Co-operative Party—The Co-operators and the National Council of Labour—War Aims—Attlee defines Labour's War Aims—*Labour, the War, and the Peace*—Labour's *Home Policy*—War controls as the basis of a permanent new order—" Socialism within our time "—Bevan and Strauss reinstated—Cripps rejects the conditions—Pritt expelled —" Chamberlain Must Go "—The fall of the Chamberlain Government—Death of George Lansbury.

(b) *Labour in the Churchill Coalition*

Fall of the Chamberlain Government—Chamberlain and the Labour Party—Churchill's anti-Labour record—Labour's part in the new Government—The state of affairs in May, 1940—The fall of France—The Party Conference approves Labour's entry into the Government—The terms of coalition—The new Emergency Powers Act of 1940—The control and " direction " of labour—The Trade Unions and the man-power problem—Bevin and Morrison, and their tasks—The Battle for Britain—The National Arbitration Tribunal—Joint Consultative Committees—The division of functions in the Churchill Government—Man-power and industrial organisation—War aims and domestic reconstruction—Changes in the Government—and in the Parliamentary Labour Party—The Means Test—Public Assistance—Service pay and other war-time problems—The question of Family Allowances—Industrial organisation and the " Controls "—The coal problem during the war—War-time transport—Demands for war-time socialisation—The continuance of the " Controls "—The Co-operative movement and the " Control " system—Rationing and allocation of supplies—Fuel rationing—Labour Manifesto on *The Peace* : its claims of war-time achievement—The dispute over the Trade Unions Act—Churchill and the Conservatives refuse amendments—The industrial side of the war effort—Joint Production Committees and Shop Stewards' Committees—The increase in Trade Union power—The Communists in the workshops before and after 1941—The " Trotskyist " faction—The " People's Convention " of 1941.

(c) *Party Affairs during the Electoral Truce*

The Electoral Truce—The question of " Coupon " Candidates—By-elections in war-time—The rise of splinter groups and parties—By-elections up to 1941—By-elections after the Soviet entry into the War—" Progressive " and Common Wealth contests—The Local Labour Parties and the Truce—The Truce in Local Government—The Truce issue at the Labour Party Conference—The official

attitude to the Truce—The emergence of the Common Wealth Party—Registration of electors and re-distribution of seats—Effects of the war on Party organisation—The fall in individual membership—The suspension and renewal of the selection of Party candidates—Relations with the Communist Party—The Communist Party after the Nazi attack on the Soviet Union—Co-operation with the Communists rejected—The suppression of *The Daily Worker*—The Communist Party's renewed request for affiliation—Dissolution of the Communist International—The Communist application again refused—The position of Communists in Trades and Labour Councils—The Labour Party and the Socialist Societies—Relations with the Co-operative Party—The Co-operators join the National Council of Labour—The League of Youth in war-time—The University Labour Federation and the National Association of Labour Students—The Labour Research Department banned—Sir Richard Acland and the rise of Common Wealth—Common Wealth's war-time appeal—Common Wealth banned—*Labour and the General Election*—The future of the Coalition Government—Demands for the ending of the Coalition—Renewed Appeals for " Progressive Unity " rejected—Labour's Election proposals—Retirement of J. S. Middleton.

(*d*)   *Facing the Future*

Problems of Reconstruction—*The Old World and the New Society*—The essential ideas behind the new Labour statement—National Sovereignty and International Organisation—The " Four Freedoms " and the Atlantic Charter—Total and final victory over the dictators—The need for a Planned Society—Four objectives in home policy—Labour's educational policy—Great Britain's place in the post-war world—The outstanding factors of democracy—Democratic Government and the doctrine of " Consent "—Commonwealth Affairs—Colonial Policy—India—Disarming the aggressors—Allied unity in war and peace—Further Policy Reports—The gaps in Labour policy—Reception of the Reports—A dispute about Local Government—Housing and Planning—Land Acquisition and the Uthwatt Report—The British Commonwealth Labour Conference of 1944—*Let Us Face the Future*—International issues—The gaps in *Let Us Face the Future*—Labour's Home Programme—An appeal to " All Progressives."

(*e*)   *The General Election of 1945*

The Churchill Coalition before and after Japan's entry into the War—The Labour Party's attitude to the Coalition—Churchill's Four Year Plan proposal—No agreement on reconstruction policy—Labour and the " Beveridge " White Paper—No " Coupon " Election—The Coalition after the German surrender—Churchill's alternatives—Should the Coalition go on to the end of the Far Eastern War ?—Was the General Election of 1945 unfairly " rushed " ?—The state of the register and the question of the service vote—The Tories fight the Election on Churchill's prestige—The effects of Churchill's behaviour during the campaign—The Election—Numbers voting—The strength of the leading Party votes—The division between Right and Left—Votes and seats : reasons for differences in distribution—Comparison with previous Elections—The balance of Parties in the new House of Commons—Clear majorities and split votes—Small and large constituencies—Voting by Regions—Regional distribution of seats compared with 1935 and 1929—Where Labour gained most and least—Class-distribution of voting in 1945—The position in Greater London and in the Home Counties—Seaside resorts and spas—Great cities—The service voters—A comparison of 1945 with the Liberal victory of 1906—What happened in 1910—Labour's electoral prospects—Tables illustrating the 1945 Election.

(*a*)   *The First Phase—to May, 1940*

The Nazis invaded Poland on September 1, 1939, and two days later Great Britain and France declared war on Germany. The ensuing eight months, up to the fall of Neville Chamberlain on May 10, 1940, brought out with extreme clarity the folly of the Government's pre-war policies, as well as its sheer inability to undertake the task of mobilising the nation for war. Even if the French made an even worse showing, that is no credit to Chamberlain or to the British Conservative Party. The guarantee given to Poland earlier in the year was utterly futile without the support of the Soviet Union ; but the British Government, instead of coming to terms with the Soviet Union while it could, had allowed its fears of Bolshevism and its support for reactionary forces in Poland to stand in the way of military and political agreement. The Soviet Union, unable to get from Britain and France the free hand which it demanded in the East, had turned instead to the Nazis, who were very ready to buy it off with an agreement to partition Poland between them. Hitler was thus enabled, by means of a promise which he had no intention of keeping longer than it suited him, first to overrun most of Poland and then swiftly to turn on the Western Allies without the necessity of fighting a war on two fronts. The Nazis, as soon as they were assured of Soviet neutrality, were entirely confident of their ability to crush Poland in a brief campaign, without any risk of effective interference from the West. They could then, with their rear secured, strike hard and swiftly at France, over-running in the process as many other West European countries as they chose. Having done this, they felt sure of their ability to destroy Great Britain by cutting off food supplies, with invasion as a further practicable measure should starvation fail to bring about surrender. Thereafter, having crushed resistance in the West, they would be in a position to choose their time for tearing up the Soviet-German Pact and for turning their arms against the Soviet Union, probably timing their attack to coincide with a Japanese onslaught in the Far East. The world, or at any rate Europe and the colonial empires of the European powers, seemed to be well within the grasp of Nazi imperialism. Anglo-French folly had played into Hitler's hands : the French and British would either fight half-heartedly and be defeated, or not fight at all, but give way again over Poland as they had over Czecho-slovakia the year before. Hitler seems to have been doubtful whether they would fight. The two weak men—Chamberlain and Daladier—who had given in to him at Munich were still in office : he knew pacifism to be strong in France, and believed it to be so in Great Britain as well. He had been appeased so often that it was quite on the cards that these statesmen would be ready to appease him again. If so, all the better : if not, well enough. Germany was ready for war, on the assumption of a quick victory, whereas, even a year after Munich, Great Britain and France were not. If they chose to give in, Hitler was ready for peace—until the time came for his next *coup*. If they fought, he felt sure of crushing them, aided by the pacifists and the fifth columnists behind their lines. France, at any rate, would be an easy prey, and, with France fallen, Great Britain would be soon at his mercy.

That all this did not happen, right to the bitter end, according to plan was no doing of the Governments of Great Britain and France. Much of it did happen : all of it nearly happened—how nearly, it is important not to forget. It happened, moreover, or nearly happened, to the accompaniment of Soviet denunciations of Franco-British imperialism and of the best efforts of the Communist Parties in all countries to aid a Nazi victory.

In face of the Polish crisis, there was no hesitation at all about the attitude of the Labour Party or the Trade Unions. The National Council of Labour had been struggling up to the moment of the Soviet-German Pact to bring pressure on the British Government to enter into a mutual defence pact with the Soviet Union. On May 31, Molotov had outlined the Soviet Union's proposed terms for such a pact, to embrace France, Great Britain, and the Soviet Union. The pact was to be purely defensive : it was to give a guarantee of help in the event of attack to all the States of Central and Eastern Europe without exception ; and it was to include a concrete agreement about the forms and extent of the military assistance which each country was to supply. In June the National Council of Labour put pressure on the Government to send a first-class negotiator to Moscow to speed up the negotiations, which were hanging fire ; but nothing effective was done. In Parliament the Labour Party kept up a stream of questions and at length at the end of July made a frontal attack on the Government for its " diplomatic dawdling " over the negotiations and urged that the Foreign Secretary should go to Moscow himself. They were then told that a military mission was leaving at once for the Soviet Union ; and the mission did actually go. The root trouble, however, was political rather than military. The Government had given guarantees to Poland, Rumania and Greece, but was not prepared for the general guarantee demanded by the Soviet Union. Nor was the reluctance of the Poles to allow Soviet forces to operate on their soil overcome, though manifestly, without this, the guarantee to Poland could not be made to work. Before the military mission arrived, the Soviet leaders had in effect made up their minds that they would get nothing out of Chamberlain and Daladier and that, in self-defence, they had better respond to the counter-offers that the Nazis were making to them for a Mutual Non-Aggression Pact. On August 23 the Soviet-German Pact was signed.

This is not the place for a discussion of the justification of the Soviet Union's action in concluding this Pact. I have discussed the question elsewhere ; and I stand by what I said about it in 1939.* The Pact, in my view, was not justified ; but I can well understand how it came to be made. The Soviet leaders cannot be supposed to have seriously believed that Hitler meant to keep it any longer than suited his plans. What the Soviet Union stood to gain was, first, a further period for preparation for war ; secondly, a weakening both of the Nazis and of their antagonists, which would mean a relative strengthening of the Soviet Union (for I think the Soviet leaders expected the war between the Nazis and the Western Powers to end in stalemate, with both sides exhausted) ; and thirdly, the reincorporation in the Soviet Union of those parts of the Polish State, east of the Curzon Line, which had been unjustifiably taken away in the war of 1920. Over and above this, a war between the Nazis and the West would give the Soviet Union, if it stood aloof, a clear field in Bessarabia and Bukovina, in the Baltic States, and very likely in the Middle East, as well as in Eastern Poland. The advantages were great and obvious, provided that Hitler did not win in the West, but only exhausted both Germany and his enemies in an indecisive conflict. Of course, the Pact meant that Western Poland would go the way Czechoslovakia had already gone, and that in future the Soviet Union and Germany would have a common land frontier ; but the countries which had thrown Czechoslovakia to the wolves could not say much about the Soviet Union's readiness to throw Poland as well ; and, from the Soviet standpoint, Poland was a centre of dangerous reaction, for which, under its aristocratic dictators, there was nothing to be said. Nevertheless I thought, and think, the Soviet leaders were wrong in making their pact with Germany, however rightly they felt that Chamberlain and Daladier were ready at any moment to betray them to the Nazis. They were wrong because the Nazis were their principal enemies, and because they were gambling on the unlikelihood of a Nazi victory that would make Hitler stronger instead of weaker, and

*In *War Aims*, published by the *New Statesman and Nation*, in November, 1939.

would thus prepare the way for an onslaught on the Soviet Union
as soon as the West had been overwhelmed.

Whatever the rights and wrongs of the Soviet Union's turn-
round, the effects were disastrous on Socialist opinion in both
France and Great Britain, where it was widely regarded as a
betrayal of the cause of peace and collective security and as making war inevitable by giving the Nazis a free hand in Poland and
thus forcing Great Britain and France into war in fulfilment of
the promises that had been made.   Labour opinion in Great
Britain, which had been becoming more favourable to the Soviet
Union (though not to Communism in the West), at once swung
back, and Labour leaders who had been accustomed to denouncing Nazism and Communism in the same breath as twin dic-
tatorships regained their influence.   The bottom was knocked right
out of the agitation for a real system of collective security, which
had always rested on the assumption of common action between
Great Britain, France, and the Soviet Union, and became
meaningless when the Soviet Union dropped out.   A great many
people could not help feeling that the Soviet Union had betrayed
the cause of peace and made war inevitable ; and the counter-
contention that the Soviet Union had acted only when it had been
driven to abandon all hope of getting a satisfactory agreement
with Chamberlain and Daladier, whatever its real force, did not
have much appeal to those who saw themselves faced with the
need to fight the Nazis without Soviet help.   Even those who had
been denouncing Chamberlain most vigorously for his imperialism and his anti-democratic sympathies felt " let down " by the
Soviet-German Pact.

Before the Pact was made, the National Council of Labour had
been combining its pressure for agreement with the Soviet Union
with attempts to appeal over the heads of the Nazi Government
directly to the German people.   A Manifesto to the German People
was issued at the end of June, under the title *Why Kill Each Other ?*
It was an attempt to answer the argument that Germany was
being " encircled " and to make clear that the aggressive tactics
of the Fascist dictators would force peace-loving nations to take
up arms unless they were checked from within the Fascist countries.   " The British people have come to feel that their own
security requires them to join with as many other countries as
possible to keep the Peace and resist aggression . . .   Far from
wishing to encircle your country with a view to crushing it, we
invite you to come into the circle yourselves, to join up with a

world-wide combination of nations so that the great abilities of the German people may make their contribution to the establishment of a friendly world in which mankind can prosper." After the German-Soviet Pact the National Council of Labour issued, on August 25, a further *Message to the German People*, making plain that, if Hitler attacked Poland, Great Britain and France would stand by the pledges that had been given and that in this matter the German-Soviet Pact had made no difference. " We have no wish," the Message went on, " to destroy the German people . . . The workers of Germany and the world can share fully in a new epoch of prosperity through Peace." The Message further asserted, somewhat too assuredly, that " If war comes . . . the British and French will command the seas," and implied that the danger of starvation and privation would fall mainly on the Germans. The Nazis were erring the other way—assuring the German people that they would be able with their U-boats to starve Great Britain out. Both views were wrong : neither was without arguments of some force to back it up.

The hope that the German people could or would act to stop the war was of course futile. Even as the *Message* was being sent out, an Emergency Powers Act was being rushed through a hastily reconvened British Parliament, and Chamberlain was facing the collapse of his policies and reluctantly making ready for war. During the two days—September 1–3—which intervened between the invasion of Poland and the declaration of war against Germany by Great Britain and France, the Labour Party, having thrown all doubts aside, protested only at the delay. Attlee was away ill, and it fell to Arthur Greenwood, as Deputy Leader of the Party in Parliament, to speak for Labour at this critical time. He made it clear that the Labour Party was wholly committed to the struggle against Nazism and, deeply suspicious though it remained of the Chamberlain Government, would do nothing to stand in the way of the full mobilisation of British resources that the situation required. The Labour Party even gave its support to the Military Service Bill which extended conscription for men to the age of forty-one, proposing only to raise the starting age for compulsory service from eighteen to twenty. Earlier the same day, the Party Executive and the Parliamentary Party had jointly resolved to give full support to the war effort, but to refuse to take part in a Coalition Government under Chamberlain's leadership. It had been impracticable to consult with the Trades Union Congress General Council at this stage, as its members were meeting at Bridlington, where the full Congress was due to open the following day. The General Council, however, adopted a resolution of its own on similar lines ; and on September 4 the full Trades Union Congress carried, with only two dissentients, a resolution denouncing Nazi aggression and pledging Trade Union support. Having done this, the Congress hurried through the more urgent items on its agenda and then adjourned. Meanwhile, the House of Commons, having carried the Military Service Act, was passing rapidly through its stages the Control of Employment Bill—the first of many measures which gave the Government a large power to direct the use of man-power in industry—and was enacting other emergency measures about which the remarkable thing is, not that they were made law, but that almost no use was made of them during the ensuing eight months of increasing disaster.

The Labour Party and the Trade Unions thus assumed unhesitatingly, when the crisis came, the responsibility for sustaining the war effort, despite their utter lack of confidence in the Government by which the war machine was to be directed. The leaders of both bodies felt—and most of their followers agreed—that no other course was open to them after their protests at the Munich surrender and in view of their repeated demands for a collective stand against Fascist aggression. There were, however, small minorities that took a different view. The I.L.P. at once issued an anti-war manifesto, and proceeded to organise a series of " War and the Workers " Conferences, in which, while denouncing the Nazis, they also denounced the Chamberlain and Daladier Governments as the upholders of imperialist exploitation, and called upon the workers to refuse support to any war not waged under the auspices of a " Workers' Government." In their Annual Report for 1939–40 the I.L.P. Council expressed their " uncompromising opposition " both to war preparation and to the prosecution of war under the auspices of capitalist Governments. Earlier in 1939 the I.L.P. had taken the lead in organising a No Conscription League ; and this body maintained its activity. The I.L.P. also attempted to carry on its connection with the International Workers' Front against War, which had been organised in conjunction with a number of left-wing continental groups. This line adopted by the I.L.P. brought to an abrupt end the negotiations which had been proceeding for some time with the Labour Party. In the summer of 1939 the National Administrative Council had gone to the length of advocating reaffiliation to the Labour Party and of summoning a Special Conference for this purpose to meet in September. Owing to the outbreak of war the Conference was never held ; and when the Annual Conference did meet at Easter in the following year the Council had changed its view and, because of the sharp difference on the war issue, no longer favoured affiliation.

The I.L.P.'s policy on the war was at least consistent : the Communist Party's was not. The Communists, as we saw, had been combining strong demands for resistance to Fascism with equally strong denunciations of Anglo-French imperialism, and had been in one and the same breath calling on Great Britain to fight the Nazis and refusing to place arms in the hands of a reactionary Government. The German-Soviet Pact bewildered them, and for a time they hardly knew what to say. Then, hard upon it, came the actual outbreak of war ; and they had to take a positive line either for helping the Government to fight Fascism or against doing so because of the Government's reactionary policy. So far from choosing, as the I.L.P. did, the second of these lines, the Communist Party came out, both through its Secretary, Harry Pollitt, and collectively, with a thoroughgoing pronouncement in favour of the war. " Now that the war has come," proclaimed the Communist Party's Manifesto of September, 1939, " we have no hesitation in stating the policy of the Communist Party. We are in full support of all necessary measures to secure the victory of democracy over Fascism . . . The essence of the present situation is that the people have now to wage a struggle on two fronts : first, to secure the military victory over Fascism ; and second, in order to achieve this, the political victory over Chamberlain and the enemies of democracy in this country. These two aims are inseparable, and the harder the efforts to win one, the more sustained must be the activity to win the other." The Manifesto went on to demand measures for organising the war effort in such a way as to safeguard the workers' interests and to call for the replacement of the " National" Government by a " People's" Government purged of appeasers and reactionaries—that is, by a " Popular Front " Government such as the Communists had been demanding earlier in association with other groups.

In support of this Manifesto Pollitt published his pamphlet, *How to Win the War*, and the Communist Party appeared, despite the German-Soviet Pact, to have committed itself whole-heartedly to backing the war as a logical development of the struggle against Fascism in which it had been attempting for years past to take the lead. But within a very few weeks all this was changed. On October 6 the Communist Party came out with a second manifesto, flatly contradicting the first. The war, it appeared, was after all not a war of " Democracy against Fascism " but an " imperialist war " which it was the workers' task to oppose. When the British and French Governments rejected the proposal of peace negotiations put forward by the monarchs of Holland and Belgium, the Communists denounced them—and the Labour Party—as imperialist warmongers. When Hitler blandly proposed a peace that would allow him to keep Poland and prepare for his next aggression, the anti-Fascists were again denounced as warmongers for rejecting his overtures. Molotov, from the Soviet Union, took up the same story ; and somewhat bewildered Communists everywhere had to " switch " in response to the new Party call. Pollitt, on October 10, was removed from the secretaryship of the Communist Party, but switched with the rest, agreeing loyally to follow the new marching orders from Moscow. It was all, in a way, highly comic ; but it was also a remarkable illustration of the fervency of the Communists' faith in the Soviet Union—their one fixed star of hope in a world run mad. I think they were badly wrong ; and certainly for the time their *volte-face* lost them most of their support among the British workers. What is notable is that they survived, and were able presently, when the situation changed in 1941, to recover their influence with so little memory, either on their own part or on that of the workers to whom they appealed, of the strange figure they had cut in the early months of the war.

They were helped in this by the curious course which the war itself took during the next few months—the " phoney " war, as it came not at all inappositely to be called. For it speedily became plain that neither Great Britain nor France was waging war except in the most half-hearted way against the Nazis ; and then, in November, came the altogether astonishing episode of the Soviet-Finnish War—or rather of the British and French action in relation to it. It seemed as if the French and British Governments thought they had not enough on their hands in fighting Germany—though they were soon to discover they had more than enough—but were eager to take on the Soviet Union as well. There may be two opinions about the justifiability of the Soviet claims on Finland, which led on November 30, 1939, to the actual outbreak of war. Looking back now, it is easy to see how greatly the concessions exacted from the Finns strengthened the defences of Leningrad when the Nazis did launch their attack on the Soviet Union, and to understand the motives that lay behind the Soviet Union's actions. At the time, so far from making any attempt to understand, the Western Powers leapt to the defence of Finland, seized the chance to expel the Soviet Union from the League of Nations, and made plans—fortunately frustrated by the better sense of the Scandinavians—for sending an expeditionary force across Norway and Sweden to join the Finns in fighting against the Soviet Union.

The most astonishing thing of all is that the Labour Party and the Trades Union Congress, which did seriously mean to fight the Nazis and should have realised fully what they were up against, joined in the call for action against the Soviet Union and gave complete and enthusiastic support to the Finnish Government. A week after the outbreak of war between the Finns and the Soviet Union the National Council of Labour issued a Manifesto recording " profound horror and indignation at the Soviet Government's unprovoked attack upon a small State with whom it had made a Pact of Non-Aggression . . . Soviet Imperialism has thus revealed itself as using the same methods as the Nazi power against which the British working class is united in the war now raging . . . Therefore, on the eve of the meeting of the League Council, it calls upon the free nations of the world to give every practicable aid to the Finnish nation in its struggle to preserve its own institutions of Civilisation and Democracy."

Even if the Soviet Union's action had deserved the abuse heaped on it at this time, it should have been plain to the leaders of British Labour that they could not fight the Soviet Union and the Nazis both at once, and that the reactionaries who did not want a fight to the bitter end against Hitler received with glee the prospect of embroilment with the Soviet Union. Yet the National Council of Labour proceeded to organise an " Aid to Finland " Fund and to send to that country a delegation which came back enthusiastic in the Finnish cause and violent in denunciation of the Soviet Union. Only the collapse of Finnish military resistance and the conclusion of a Peace Treaty in March, 1940, on terms which revealed the limited character of the Soviet Union's objectives, saved the British Labour Movement from diverting the energies which were sorely needed for the strengthening of the war effort against the Nazis into a futile conflict with the Soviet Union. Allowance has of course to be made for

the strong feelings that had been aroused by the German-Soviet
Pact and for a total failure to understand the Russian motives
for the ultimatum to Finland ; but even so the episode was
revealing. It showed how deeply-seated was the antipathy of
many of the British and other West European Socialist and Trade
Union leaders, not only to the Communist Parties in their own
countries, but to the Soviet Union as well. These strong feelings
blinded them for the moment to the necessity for letting nothing
get in the way of the vital struggle with the Nazi power—a
struggle that did not begin to be really waged until they had
played their part first in ousting Chamberlain and then in
organising a truly national resistance in the heroic days of the
French disaster and the successful evacuation from Dunkirk.
Fortunately, before then, the Finnish complication was out of the
way, on terms which left Finland its independence and indeed
released it from the reactionary influences that had dominated it
up to its military defeat.

During the opening months of the second World War the
Labour Party, out of office and without direct responsibility for
its conduct, played the part of co-operative critic of the Chamberlain Government. It pressed for more thorough measures of
evacuation of children and mothers from the great towns and the
threatened areas : it demanded effective control over prices and
the equitable sharing of war burdens : it raised many issues
connected with service pay and allowances, the hardships
attendant on the call-up for the armed forces, the effective maintenance and supplementation of the social services to meet the
needs of war, the improvement of air-raid precautions, and many
similar matters. It pressed for more effective mobilisation of the
nation's economic resources, and especially for the setting up of
proper machinery for economic co-ordination under an Economic
General Staff ; and, as the months passed, it drew attention with
increasing urgency to the continuance of unemployment in the
distressed areas, despite the evident need for the full use of the
services of every available worker. Politically, the Labour Party
agreed, as soon as war had broken out, to an Electoral Truce,
under which the Conservative, Labour and Liberal Parties were
" not to nominate candidates for any parliamentary vacancies
that now exist, or may occur, against the candidate nominated
by the Party holding the seat at the time of the vacancy occurring."
This agreement was to hold good for the duration of the war,
subject to the right of any of the three Parties to terminate it at

any time. It was also agreed that municipal vacancies should be filled by co-option and that no municipal elections should be held until the end of 1940, when the question was to come up for review.   This Electoral Truce, it should be noted, was not a " Political Truce " in any fuller sense.   It did nothing to limit the right of the Parties to carry on such propagandist activities as they thought fit ; and the Labour Party undertook in October, 1939, a special review of its local organisation designed to ensure that it should be kept as far as possible in good working order during the war.   For the time being, negotiations for a closer working arrangement with the Co-operative Party were suspended ; but the Co-operative Movement was induced, in 1939, to send representatives to sit as observers on the National Council of Labour, though not yet to serve as full members.

The war had not been long in progress before there arose an anxious demand for a clear statement of British " War Aims." This demand was addressed primarily to the Government, which remained carefully vague about its intentions.   If, however, Labour was to press the Government effectively to disclose what it was fighting for, it was obviously necessary for the Labour Party to define as clearly as possible its own war objectives.   This was attempted by Attlee on November 8, 1939, in a speech which was widely circulated in pamphlet form, as defining the Party's point of view.

Today, Attlee's speech makes in a good many respects curious reading.   A good deal of it was simply a justification of Labour's past policy—especially of the stand which the Labour Party had made for an effective system of collective security under the auspices of a strengthened League of Nations.   These ideas still guided the Labour Party in laying its plans for the peace.   Attlee demanded a new international authority, with wide economic as well as political powers, and with an armed force of its own strong enough to outlaw and defeat any future aggressor State. He demanded that this authority should be democratic, in the sense that it should not be dominated by a few Great Powers, but should give a real place to the small nations.   An authority controlled by the Great Powers, he said, " might be merely an Imperialism in commission."   He denounced Imperialism roundly, and declared that a mere redistribution of colonial territories between rival Imperialisms would be a disaster.   As for Germany, he repudiated all idea of dismemberment.   " We have no desire to humiliate, to crush, or to divide the German nation . . . We wish the German people to know that they can now secure, if they will, an honourable peace." But there must be in Germany " a Government which can be trusted, a Government which has abandoned Hitlerism and is prepared to enter into negotiations for peace on the basis of the repudiation of a policy of aggression." " Anyone who urges that the war should be ended at any price is no real friend of peace." There would have to be " restitution " —to the Czechs, to the Poles, to the Austrians, and to the other victims of Nazi aggression. But Attlee was careful—he made the point twice—not to assert that the pre-Nazi frontiers of the European States should be put back. There would have to be a new settlement, made under the auspices of the new international authority, and particularly of a united European body. " Europe," he said, " must federate or perish."

Attlee was also careful to disclaim all proposals for a military occupation of Germany by the Allies. He proposed that, pending a final settlement, the territories in dispute at the end of the war should be occupied by " an administration and forces drawn from neutral States." He repudiated a " dictated peace," and took his stand on the " rule of law " in international affairs.

This speech stood as the recognised declaration of Labour's " War Aims " until, in February, 1940, the Party Executive issued an official declaration of policy, *Labour, the War, and the Peace*. In the main, this declaration echoed what Attlee had said some months before. It called on the British people " to contribute their utmost effort to the overthrow of the Hitler system in Germany," and declared against any peace negotiations " except with a German Government which has not merely promised, but actually performed, certain acts of restitution." It demanded " undertakings to the German people " that their " just and real interests," equally with those of other peoples, would be respected in the settlement. It recognised, in phrases clearly related to meetings which were being held with the representatives of the French Labour movement, the French right to " security," which it bracketed with the " German claim to equality." It said to the French " Henceforth, in resistance to any German aggression, our two peoples must be not merely allies for a season, but brothers for all time." It laid down that " the present close co-operation between the British Commonwealth, France, and their Allies in the political and economic spheres should be the nucleus " of the proposed new international authority, which should rest " on social justice *within* States, no less than on political

justice between States." It reiterated Attlee's promise that
Germany should not be dismembered, but went further than he
had done in calling for a German democratic Revolution as a
necessary step to peace. Finally, it included a sharp attack on the
Soviet Union, not only for signing the German-Soviet Pact, but
also " for its unprovoked attack on Finland in shameless imitation
of the Nazi technique in foreign policy."

In March, 1940, the Labour Party followed up this manifesto
with a parallel pronouncement on *Labour's Home Policy*. This was
for the most part a restatement of the Labour programme as it
had been put forward in previous manifestos and reports ; but it
sought to relate these previous declarations to the war situation.
After denouncing the half-heartedness of the mobilisation of
national resources by the Chamberlain Government and declaring
the need for much more forthright measures of control, it went on
to say that the war-time controls should be regarded not as temporary expedients to be removed when the war ended but as
foundations for a permanent new social order. It demanded that
mining and other key industries should be transferred to public
operation on this basis, and that war-time planning should be
treated as the precursor of a post-war planned economy based on
the conception of social justice. It called for a great expansion of
the social security services, and declared that " for the Labour
Party, a Socialist Britain is not some far-off Utopia, but an ideal
that can be realised within our time." At the same time it affirmed
that the Labour Party's Socialism " is built upon a profound faith
in the people of Britain and a determination to press for necessary
social changes upon the basis of Democracy and Justice." " We
reject," the Manifesto reiterated, " all demands for Dictatorship,
whether from the Left or from the Right. We take our stand upon
that faith in reason which looks to the declared will of the people
as the only valid source of power." Reforms were needed in the
machinery of government ; but " these can be undertaken without infringing at any point a full respect for the spirit of Parliamentary Democracy."

Well before this Manifesto appeared, Aneurin Bevan, sponsored
by the Mineworkers' Federation, and G. R. Strauss had returned
to the Labour Party fold, having given undertakings of " loyalty "
which satisfied the Party Executive. Cripps on the other hand had
not returned, as he refused to accept the Executive's conditions.
In March, 1940, another well-known Socialist lawyer, D. N.
Pritt, followed him into exile, being expelled for taking a strong

line against the Party policy in connection with the Soviet-Finnish War. Pritt also took an anti-war line close to that of the Communist Party, but kept his position in Parliament as an Independent and did not join the Communists, though, as we shall see, he collaborated with them. At the time of his expulsion, the Labour Party Executive also took action against a number of Local Parties which were following an anti-war line and were working with the Communists in their policy of opposition to the war effort. But as disaster succeeded disaster in Western Europe from April, 1940, when the Nazis invaded Denmark and Norway, to May, when they swept over Belgium and Holland and the fall of France was seen to be an imminent danger, the evident peril not only of the British Expeditionary Force in France and Belgium but of Great Britain itself almost silenced the expression of anti-war feeling and reduced to a very low point the influence of the anti-war groups, including the Communists. Before the crisis reached its height, the cry that Chamberlain must go had grown louder ; but it was taken out of the mouth of those who had used his presence in power as an argument for opposing the " imperialist " war and was heard more and more loudly from those who demanded his supersession in order that the war might be more energetically and sincerely carried on.

The Chamberlain Government, overthrown by a Conservative revolt under Winston Churchill's leadership, with Labour's active support, fell on May 10, 1940 ; and the Churchill Government, with full Labour participation, succeeded it on May 12. Three days before Chamberlain's resignation, George Lansbury died. He had been for some time seriously ill, and had taken but little part in the Labour Party's affairs since his resignation from the leadership in 1935. But despite the aberrations into which his heartfelt pacifism had led him in his last years, he had remained a very great human figure—the best-loved man by far in the Labour Movement and a symbol of the simple ethical feelings which, however often thwarted, were still the foundation of its mass appeal. George Lansbury was an intensely lovable man, with a great wealth of love and sincerity and humane feeling. He had fought in his day many battles with the other leaders of the Party —over Women's Suffrage, over Poplarism, and over a host of other human causes, as well as over Pacifism. Even among those who did not at all share his attitude, there were few who knew him and failed to love him. Ernest Bevin was one ; but he was exceptional in this, as in much besides. I loved him dearly : I have

said more than once that he was the only man who could induce
me to do things I believed to be mistaken. There was an empti-
ness when he was gone, though his place had been vacant, to the
Movement's human loss, for some time before his final passing.

(b) Labour in the Churchill Coalition

It had, of course, been quite beyond the Labour Party's power
to turn the Chamberlain Government out of office. In view of
the composition of the House of Commons, only a split in the
ranks of the Conservatives could do that ; and no such split
occurred until sheer disaster was plainly imminent. Even then
the Chamberlain Government was not beaten in an open vote :
in the critical division of May 10, 1940, it still mustered a majority
of eighty-one. But Chamberlain recognised that the discontent
was too deep for him to carry on : perhaps he even felt that, in
the crisis that was upon Great Britain, a leadership different from
his was required. After the Munich affair, and after his handling
of relations with the Soviet Union during the months that
followed Munich, he was an impossible leader for the rally of all
the forces of the nation that was needed to retrieve the disasters that
had occurred and the further disasters he knew were coming.
Labour could never have rallied to any Government under
Chamberlain—neither the Labour Party nor the workers in mine
and factory on whom, in the critical months ahead, everything
was bound to depend. Chamberlain had to go ; and, though
most Conservative politicians would have preferred to keep him
as their leader, enough realised his hopelessness as a war organiser
and as an inspirer of the people, and saw Churchill's unquestionable superiority in both these capacities, to force the hands of the
rest. Chamberlain stayed on in the new Cabinet, a concession
to orthodox Conservative sentiment ; but Churchill, long his
critic, replaced him as Prime Minister, to face the direst extremity
of the war.

Labour, in and out of Parliament, played its part in putting
Churchill into power ; and Churchill, old and inveterate enemy
of the Labour Party and the Trade Unions though he was, knew
well that he could not do without Labour's help. It was going to
be a workmen's battle, even more than a soldiers' ; and the last
ounce of the workmen's energy was going to be needed to see it
through. The Trade Union and Labour Party leaders, for their

part, were equally aware that they could not do without Churchill; and they swallowed their old resentments and accepted his leadership, even though he was the man who in 1926 had called their bluff, broken the General Strike, and then set to work to fasten the Trade Unions Act upon them with the object of weakening them both industrially and politically. They were well aware that these old scores had to be put aside ; for unless they could beat back the Nazis everything that they stood for would be lost.

So Churchill made his Government, with Attlee and Greenwood, leader and deputy leader of the Parliamentary Labour Party, as members of his small War Cabinet, and with Ernest Bevin in the key position of Minister of Labour and National Service and Herbert Morrison as Minister of Supply. These two were not in the War Cabinet ; but upon them was bound to fall the main brunt of the organisation of man-power and of industry, first to cope with the immediate emergency, which was tremendous, and secondly, to face the long-term tasks that had been so neglected under Chamberlain's nerveless guidance. Besides these four front-rank Ministers, A. V. Alexander went to the Admiralty, Hugh Dalton was Minister of Economic Warfare, and Sir William Jowitt was Solicitor-General. Labour held but a small proportion of the offices in the Churchill Government ; but three of its representatives—Attlee as Deputy Leader under Churchill, Bevin and Morrison—held posts of prime importance.

As the new Government took over, the German armies were advancing fast through Holland and Belgium, and the entire defensive system of the Maginot Line was being outflanked. The Dutch surrendered two days after Churchill announced his Cabinet : Brussels fell three days after that. The British Expeditionary Force was in dire peril : the fall of France was already looming ahead. The Labour Party, which had so long been calling for Chamberlain's displacement, could entertain no doubts about the necessity of entering the new Government under Churchill, who was fully committed to a vigorous prosecution of the war against the Nazis ; but though, in entering it, they knew the situation to be serious, they can hardly have realised how nearly desperate it would look in less than a month's time. Within their first month of office the British army had been almost miraculously extracted from Dunkirk with the loss of all its equipment, and Italy had seized the moment to declare war. Four days after that Paris fell ; and two days later Pétain was Prime Minister of a defeated France that had surrendered its

honour to the conqueror. Churchill had made his abortive offer
of common citizenship to the French people : Hitler's " new
order " seemed on the point of establishing itself over all Western
Europe.

At the time when the Churchill Government was being formed,
the Labour Party Conference was assembling at Bournemouth
for its annual session. The Party Executive at once approved
Labour's participation ; and the Conference, on Attlee's motion,
passed by 2,413,000 to 170,000 a resolution endorsing this action
and pledging its full support. A few Local Labour Party delegates
spoke against the resolution on I.L.P. or Communist lines,
declaring that the war was an " imperialist war " and that no
support should be given unless a Socialist Government were
placed in power ; but they were lonely voices. When the vote
was taken in the House of Commons on a motion of confidence in
the new Government, only two I.L.P. members—Maxton and
Campbell Stephen—opposed.

The Labour Party had no hesitations about entering the
Churchill Coalition Government ; but there were conditions,
both explicit and implied. One explicit condition was that the
rate of Excess Profits Tax should be raised to 100 per cent, and
another, closely related to it, was that the Government should arm
itself with full powers over property as well as over human beings,
in order to mobilise the entire resources of the nation for the
supreme struggle. The new Emergency Powers Bill introduced by
Attlee and passed through all its stages on a single day gave the
Government authority to direct any person to perform any
services that might be required of him or her in the national
interest, to take control of any property, and to take over any
industrial establishment and direct its operation. A Special
Conference of Trade Union Executives, held immediately after
this measure became law, pledged full support, while affirming
a determination " to preserve the powers and functions of the
Trade Unions and to ensure the maintenance of the hard-won
rights and liberties of the workers." Direction of labour was used
only where it became sheerly necessary ; but effective use was
made of the power to " control engagements," which, conferred
on the Government by the Control of Employment Act in September, 1939, had not been used at all.

The Government at once set to work upon its immense and
urgent task, of which not the least part was the rapid redistribution of the national man-power. This responsibility fell mainly

upon Ernest Bevin and the Ministry of Labour ; and the task was, on the whole, astonishingly well done, with surprisingly little friction despite the great uprooting of habits and cherished customs which it involved. At the same time, Herbert Morrison, at the Ministry of Supply, was doing his best to introduce some sort of order into the chaos of independent " Controls " of which the Ministry was made up, as well as to speed up the construction of the new war factories, which were far behind schedule, and to rush through to completion in the shortest possible time equipment to replace the heavy losses sustained in the evacuation of the British Expeditionary Force. The next few weeks were a time of prodigious individual effort, sustained by real enthusiasm and by the consciousness that the very existence of British democracy was at stake. A great deal was sheer improvisation—such was the chaos inherited from the Chamberlain régime ; but gradually order began to emerge and, when the intense effort of the summer could plainly no longer be kept up because of sheer physical exhaustion, enough had been achieved towards better organisation of the factories and towards increased womanpower to fill the gaps in the labour force, to make it possible to " let up " a little without disaster.

The new régime of controlled factories, directed or controlled labour, controlled prices and profits, and controlled wages and conditions involved the provision of special machinery. In July the National Arbitration Tribunal was set up by order to deal with all industrial disputes that could not be otherwise settled. Compulsory arbitration in this form was accepted by the Trades Union Congress and by the British Employers' Confederation ; but it was agreed with these bodies that the existing machinery of negotiation in each trade or industry should continue to be used, and that there should be no attempt by the Government to impose an over-all wages policy. The agreement was made in the first instance only for a short period ; but it continued in force for the rest of the war.

The new Government also strengthened greatly the joint consultative machinery which had been set up to advise its predecessor on industrial matters. Soon each department concerned with such questions had its own joint consultative committee, side by side with the general Joint Consultative Committee of Employers and Trade Unionists which had been set up in October, 1939 ; and the next step was to establish regional machinery of a similar type. A demand began for the setting up of a co-ordinating Ministry of Production to unify the policies of the various industrial departments and to put into force a clear system of priorities in the supply both of scarce materials and equipment, and of labour. This demand was not met until much later ; but Arthur Greenwood was made Chairman of a Joint Production Council which was at least a first step towards more effective prevention of inter-departmental scrambling for factories, supplies and man-power, though at the outset it was given far too little authority.

It would take me much too far afield from my subject were I to attempt to describe or assess the work done by the Labour Ministers in the Churchill Government. That work could not be described apart from its relation to the activities of the Government as a whole ; and to attempt any such account would involve writing a complete history of the war effort. I cannot do more than offer a few very broad generalisations.

In effect, the basis of the Coalition was that Churchill should run the military side of the war while the Labour Ministers looked after the " home front," including the mobilisation of man-power and the maintenance of essential social services. The Tories kept the Exchequer, but under firm understandings with Labour about the equitable distribution of tax burdens. The control of industry on the capitalist side was a disputed terrain : it fell more into the hands of capitalist Ministers after Herbert Morrison had been shifted in October, 1940, from the Ministry of Supply to that of Home Security ; but Bevin's position at the Ministry of Labour, in control of man-power, gave him a continuing influence over the entire field of industrial policy.

This broad distribution of functions left two main spheres of action under indeterminate control. These were foreign policy— that is to say, broadly, war aims—and domestic reconstruction. In the first of these fields Churchill was, of course, a very powerful influence, working almost alone at first but subsequently in consultation with President Roosevelt and with Stalin. Labour could proclaim its war aims, but what it said could not for the time have much effect. Indeed, in 1940 and 1941 there was to all intents and purposes only one war aim that counted—beating back the Nazis—and nobody was paying much attention to the terms of a post-war settlement the conditions of which it was impossible to foresee. Nor was anyone giving much attention at that stage of the war to the problems of domestic reconstruction. When, in January, 1941, Arthur Greenwood was transferred

from his work as Chairman of the Production Council and was
set to preside over a committee of Ministers which was to study
post-war internal problems, the change was generally regarded
as relegating him to a position of minor importance.

At first, as we saw, only two Labour men—Attlee and Greenwood—were in the small War Cabinet of five set up by Churchill
on taking office. Bevin became a member of the War Cabinet in
October, 1940 : Herbert Morrison not until November, 1942.
In the meantime Greenwood had been ousted ; and Cripps, who,
though not a member of the Labour Party, counted in effect with
it, had served as a member and as leader of the House of Commons
for the greater part of 1942. As Morrison joined the War Cabinet,
Cripps left it, to become Minister of Aircraft Production.

These were the leaders of the Party in the Coalition Government. The entry of Labour into the Government made it necessary for the Parliamentary Labour Party to appoint a Chairman
to act as leader in the absence of the Ministers. H. B. Lees-Smith
was chosen, aided by an Administrative Committee which had to
be largely reconstituted because so many members had been
translated to government posts. When Greenwood was evicted
from the Government in February, 1942, he resumed his position
as Deputy Leader of the Parliamentary Party. At the same time,
in the Government, Attlee was given the new title of Deputy
Prime Minister.

One of the demands made by the Labour leaders on joining the
Coalition had been that steps should be taken to do away with
the family Means Test, against which the Labour Party had been
fighting ever since its imposition after the crisis of 1931. Accordingly, in November, 1940, the Prime Minister announced that
the Government would introduce legislation to substitute for the
" family " test a " personal " Means Test which would involve
no aggregation of household resources for the purpose of assessing
needs. Husband and wives were still to be treated as recipients
of joint income; but the earnings of other residents in the household were no longer normally to be taken into account. The
change was embodied in the Determination of Needs Bill, which,
after the Labour Party had secured a number of improvements
in detail, became law early in 1941. The Act by no means met
the whole of Labour's objections to the Means Test ; but it was
generally regarded as a great advance, and, at the Party Conference in June, Ernest Bevin in particular received many con-
gratulations on his part in getting it passed into law. The fol-

lowing year a resolution demanding that the Party and the
Labour Ministers in the Government "should have no compromise whatsoever with the Means Test" was defeated after an
appeal had been made for its withdrawal and after James
Griffiths had explained for the Executive that, though they were
against the Means Test as a whole, a refusal to compromise was
impracticable as matters stood. The Labour Movement continued to press for improvements, particularly for the extension
of the principles of the new Act, which applied only to the
Assistance Board, to cover Public Assistance and other services
as well. In 1943 this too was secured by further legislation, which
also improved the conditions relating to supplementary Pensions.
Throughout the war period, the Labour Movement, in and out
of Parliament, pressed successfully for a good many changes
liberalising the administration of the social services, though of
course many grievances were left unremedied, and it was often
argued that the whole problem ought to be held up until post-
war "reconstruction" came to be considered on comprehensive
lines. The Labour Party was also continuously active, with some
success, in pressing for improvements in service pay and allowances, for more effective control of prices, for fair systems of food
rationing and distribution, and for better arrangements of housing
and billeting both of evacuees and of the workers transferred for
war services to already congested industrial areas. It also pressed
hard for war-time nurseries for the children of women workers,
for more and better civic and industrial restaurants and canteens,
and for better provision for the victims of air warfare.

One large question which the war forced to the front was that
of Family Allowances, about which, as we saw, the Labour movement had been disputing for a long time. The Labour Party
Executive, by a large majority, had favoured the reform . the
Trade Unions had been sharply divided, and their divisions had
in practice paralysed all action by the Party. In 1941 the National
Executive had to report to the Party Conference that, though it
had drawn up a memorandum in favour of Family Allowances,
stressing the increased need for them under war conditions as
well as their permanent value as a means of reducing malnutrition
and strengthening family security, the T.U.C. General Council
had failed to agree and had adjourned *sine die* further discussion
of the issue. At the Party Conference Charles Dukes, for the
General Workers, moved the reference back of the relevant
section of the Report and made a strong speech against Family

Allowances, which he feared would be used to reduce wages and would react on Trade Union bargaining powers. He was induced to withdraw his motion only when Hugh Dalton had said, on behalf of the Executive, that its memorandum in no way committed the Labour movement, though it indicated the Executive's favour for Family Allowances, not in substitution for, but over and above, a development of the social services. At the 1943 Conference the issue came up again. James Griffiths moved for the Executive a general resolution on Social Security, including a recommendation in favour of Family Allowances. The Locomotive Engineers moved an amendment to delete this recommendation, and were supported by the Transport Workers. The Miners, the Distributive Workers, and the Iron and Steel Trades Confederation came in on the opposite side ; and the hostile amendment was defeated by 1,718,000 votes to 690,000. Thus at last the Party went formally on record in favour of Family Allowances, which had long been advocated by the majority of its leading supporters. The Trades Union Congress accepted the position ; and, two years later, the Family Allowances Bill became law, but with the restriction that no payment was made except where there was more than one dependent child.

On the general question of war-time industrial organisation there were somewhat divergent views. There was strong criticism at the beginning of the war of the system of " Controls " introduced by the Chamberlain Government, which meant in one case after another that to all intents and purposes the leading capitalist agencies, such as the Iron and Steel Federation and the petroleum combine, became the " Controls " and were authorised to act as the Government's agents, or that the persons put in control of trades and commodities were persons associated with the leading firms in the trades concerned. In many instances, the staffs of the " Controls," or a good number of them, were simply lent to the Government by their firms, which continued to pay their salaries. This, it was alleged, meant both that the " Controls" would be unduly favourable to capitalist interests and that the big concerns which dominated them would get an unfair advantage over their smaller competitors. When, however, Labour entered the Government this system was not in fact much altered, except by the gradual strengthening of the central machinery of co-ordination. It was argued in its defence that it was necessary to have control in the hands of those who knew most about the industries and commodities concerned, and to continue to use normal trade channels as much as possible. Morrison, during his period at the Ministry of Supply, failed to shake the system ; and to a great extent it remained in operation right to the end of the war. It was modified here and there ; and in some cases, where the capitalist interests were relatively weak, control became vested largely in the Civil Service, in fact as well as in name. In general, however, the Labour Ministers acquiesced in the system, and directed their efforts to ensuring better control of co-ordinating policy at the centre rather than to its replacement. The keenest struggle developed in the mining industry, in which after long-sustained pressure greatly enlarged authority was placed nominally in the hands of the Ministry of Fuel and Power. But, despite changes on paper, the effective power continued largely to rest with the colliery companies, or at any rate to be so divided, under a system of " dual control," as to remain in a highly unsatisfactory state. The Government had given a public pledge that the mines would not be handed back after the war to private operation except as the result of a considered decision to that effect, to be made, or not made, by the Government in office when the question had to be settled. A large body of Labour opinion pressed continually that " dual control " should be put an end to by outright nationalisation of the mining industry during the war. The National Council of Labour, however, in conjunction with the Mineworkers' Federation, demanded in its memorandum of February, 1942, only the establishment of a National Coal Board, representing miners, mineowners, and the Government, with full power to conduct the industry as a war service ; and this plan, put forward as a compromise, was endorsed by the Labour Party Conference later in the year. At subsequent Conferences, attention was turned mainly to post-war plans of reorganisation, on a basis of public ownership. Despite much unofficial advocacy of immediate nationalisation outright, the official Labour demand remained, in respect of the war period, no more than that the coal industry should be effectively unified under public control.

In relation to transport the attitude was the same. At the 1942 Party Conference Arthur Deakin, of the Transport and General Workers, moved, and a Railwaymen's delegate seconded, a resolution urging upon the Government " the necessity for co-ordinating all forms of transport—road, rail, and inland waterways—under national ownership, with special emphasis on the need to take immediate steps to meet the war-time requirement for an effective transport system." This might, as far as the words went, have been taken as a demand for immediate national ownership ; but Deakin went out of his way to explain that this was not what was meant. His Union, he said, was not asking to go even as far as the Miners during the war : they would be content with effective co-ordination under public control until the war was over. Then, they wanted full public ownership ; but they recognised the difficulties in the way of a quick change of system, especially under war conditions. The Conference passed Deakin's resolution without challenge, and proceeded to a resolution from the Chislehurst Labour Party declaring that " in order to achieve maximum output, which is . . . essential to victory, the whole economy of war production should be put, progressively, on a socialistic basis, with workers sharing control." This, rather surprisingly, the Executive accepted, rejecting an amendment which required that the Labour Party should " resume freedom of action in Parliament and in the country " if it were not carried out. The Conference endorsed the Executive's attitude ; but the ambiguous wording of the resolution robbed it of any really binding effect.

Thus, in general, the Labour Party, in relation to war-time policy, refrained from pressing for outright nationalisation, which the Tory majority in the Coalition would certainly have refused to accept, and limited itself to demanding more complete and effective control, under stronger co-ordinating agencies directly responsible to the Government. Its spokesmen also insisted, with many references to what had been done in 1919, that the war-time " Controls " must not again be hastily liquidated when the fighting ceased, and that the question whether and when industries and services should be handed back to private ownership must be settled as part of the general issue of post-war " reconstruction." This, we shall see, meant in effect that the issue could not be decided at all while the war lasted ; for about " reconstruction " there was, on such matters, no basis for agreement between the parties forming the Coalition, and it had been one of the conditions of the Churchill Government that, with a very few specified exceptions, controversial issues should be left over for settlement after the war had been won.

Protests against the system of entrusting war-time Controls to interested capitalist agencies came especially from the Co-operative Movement, which saw in the powers conferred on its capitalist competitors a serious danger to itself as well as to the consuming public. Soon after the formation of the Churchill Government

the Co-operators, in June, 1940, put forward a memorandum
expressing their hostility to the system thitherto adopted, and
their sense of the danger that it would tend to enlarge the powers
of cartels and monopolies not only during the war but also
permanently. Co-operative criticism was directed especially at
the Ministry of Food, which worked very largely through the
various Trade Associations. The criticisms were met, not by
changing the system, but by the giving of more attention and
representation to Co-operative interests. The Co-operators, in
common with the Labour Party and the Trade Unions, pressed
hard from the beginning of the war for the extension of the food
rationing system to cover all essential supplies, on the ground that
the existence of an unrationed " sector " tended to create class
injustices and to cause an undue expenditure of time in seeking
supplies from shop to shop. The Labour Party, following Co-
operative demands on these issues in March, 1941, set up a Food
Deputation Committee of its own to work for more effective
control and rationing of food supplies and for the institution of an
effective Consumers' Council. The Parliamentary Labour Party
also supported proposals for fuel rationing on the lines proposed
by Sir William Beveridge in 1941 ; but Conservative opposition,
in this as in many other matters, was too strong to be overborne.

The general attitude of the Labour Party towards the problems
of war-time organisation was summed up in a Manifesto on *The
Peace*, which was adopted by the Annual Conference in 1941, a
year after the Party had joined the Churchill Coalition. It was
therein claimed that since the change of Government the war had
been fought, not only with much greater efficiency, but also with
a high regard for considerations of social equity.

The area of the social services has been increased. Largely through
the care and determination of the Trade Unions, the standard of life
has been well safeguarded. The health of the workers has been protected by the maintenance of the factory codes, and by the institution
of factory doctors, canteens, and nurseries. Labour, national and local,
has taken its share in civil defence ; and in every sphere its activities
have done much to improve the provision for the safety and comfort of
citizens. The social protection of our people has been facilitated by the
alert and continuous watch which has been kept over financial policy.
Interest rates have been kept down. The Treasury has assumed powers
over the Banks which assure their full co-operation in the policy upon
which Parliament decides. The dangers of inflation, ever present in
war-time, have been kept to a minimum.

These claims were on the whole justified, at any rate to the extent that in most respects the record of the second World War on the home front compared very favourably indeed with that of the first. Profiteering was kept down : there was much greater equity both in taxation and in the allocation of supplies : social services were not merely kept up, but expanded to meet war-time needs.

In some other respects the Labour Party met with very much less success. It had been hoped that, as an earnest of the will to co-operate, Churchill and the Conservatives would agree, if not to the repeal, at all events to the modification of the vindictive Trade Unions Act of 1927. Early in 1940 the Trades Union Congress General Council had approached Chamberlain in vain ; and after the formation of the Churchill Government a combined approach was made to the new Prime Minister by the Labour Ministers and the National Council of Labour, in the hope that he would agree to amendment as a gesture of " national unity." Churchill, however, replied that the subject was too " controversial " to be dealt with, and that any attempt to deal with it would prejudice, rather than consolidate, unity. At the 1942 Conference it had to be reported that no progress had been made, even on a modified request for amendment only of the clauses in the Act dealing with the position of Civil Servants and local government employees. The following year the position was still the same ; and the Party Conference passed a strong resolution of protest at the attitude taken up by the Conservatives. By this time the Union of Post Office Workers, losing patience, had announced that, if the Act were not speedily amended, it would defy the law by applying for affiliation to the Trades Union Congress and, through its branches, to local Trades Councils ; and the General Council had stated that, if the application were made, it would feel unable to reject it, whatever the legal position might be. Churchill retorted to this threat with a counter-threat to meet any such action by disestablishing and thus depriving of pension rights any members of Civil Service Unions who continued their membership of Unions defying the law ; and the bodies concerned did not, in face of this, carry out their defiance. Instead there were further abortive negotiations ; and the matter dragged on until, in March, 1945, Churchill stated, in a letter to the Trades Union Congress that, in face of the hostility of " the overwhelming mass of Conservatives," it would have to be left to be settled by the outcome of the then approaching General Election.

With the more purely industrial aspects of war-time organisation the Labour Party, as a party, naturally had comparatively
little to do, though the Labour Ministers had a great deal. Such
questions were left to the Trades Union Congress and to the
Trade Unions chiefly concerned. Thus, it falls outside the scope
of this book to discuss either the development of wage-policy and
the steps taken to ensure the effective mobilisation of the labour
force, or the struggle to secure workers' participation in the
factory effort through the establishment of Joint Production
Committees and other special agencies for consultation and
control. In such matters the Parliamentary Party could only
second the activities of the industrial side of the movement and
see that the right questions were put to Ministers about grievances and problems as they arose. That employers were in most
cases very tardy in responding to the claim that labour should
be given a new status in industry corresponding to its place in
the control of the nation's political affairs was not by any means
surprising ; but the struggle to secure changes had to be carried
on partly by Labour Ministers with their Cabinet colleagues and
with the employers, and partly by the Trade Unions and the actual
workers applying pressure from outside the government machine.
War conditions, by making labour scarce, necessarily enhanced
its power ; and this remained the case even when labour, like
other factors of production, came under " direction " by the
State. The Labour Ministers had to see to it that the powers of
direction and control were not unfairly exercised at the workers'
expense ; and on the whole they were successful. Trade Union
membership rose, despite the absorption of vast numbers into
the armed forces ; and in the factories the activities of Shop
Stewards' Committees and similar bodies greatly increased. The
Communists, who had largely forfeited their influence by their
volte-face of 1939, regained a good deal of what they had lost when
in face of the Nazi attack on the Soviet Union, they were suddenly
transformed in 1941 into enthusiastic promoters of the war effort.
They then endeavoured to acquire key positions in the Shop
Stewards' Committees and Joint Production Committees wherever
they could, and did much excellent work on these bodies in co-
operation with other Trade Unionists who shared their will to
victory, though not their Communist convictions. When the
enforced entry of the Soviet Union into the war had created a
community of purpose among practically all sections of the
workers there was not a great deal of scope for trouble in the

industrial field between the official Trade Union leaders and the Communist and other " left " groups inside the Trade Unions. There remained a small minority, usually dubbed " Trotskyist," which kept up its opposition to the war effort; but it hardly counted. For the time being, the industrial ranks were kept closed by a common will to defeat the Nazi power.

In this respect, the second World War presented a marked contrast to the first. Whereas during the first World War the strength of the anti-war opposition—or at any rate of the demand for " peace by negotiation "—steadily increased after the early days, in the second War there was after 1940 no real question of a negotiated peace, and after the extension of the war in 1941 almost nobody thought there was. The demand for a settlement that would leave the Nazis still in power in Germany died out as it became evident that there was no real possibility of containing their power within limits, and that it must either be allowed to dominate the world or be utterly overthrown. Thus, from 1940 onwards, the small minority which had been attempting to evade the issue by treating the war as an " imperialist war," and therefore none of the workers' concern, had less and less to say that was even plausibly relevant to the real situation. As long as Chamberlain remained in power, their contentions had some force ; for it was at any rate doubtful whether Chamberlain was trying to do more than contain the Nazi power. As soon as the Churchill Coalition took office, though it remained possible to denounce Churchill as a rabid imperialist, who would seek to drag his Labour colleagues after him into a struggle for the furtherance of imperialist aims, the actual war situation was so different as to rob any such argument of most of its practical force. The war, whatever the ambitions of the Government or of its leader, had become so plainly a war for sheer survival of Great Britain as a self-governing country that this factor was all-important in most working people's minds and directed their sympathies and actions to the exclusion of everything else. In such a situation, there was no room for any considerable unofficial movement hostile to the war effort.

The nearest thing to such a movement was the so-called " People's Convention," led by D. N. Pritt, with the support of a few not very prominent Trade Unionists and with a mainly Communist or near-Communist following. At the Convention held in London in January, 1941, a scratch collection of nearly 2,000 delegates, mainly from unofficial factory groups and local branches of Trade Unions or of the Communist Party and its associated bodies, approved an eight-point programme to be carried out by a " People's Government " which was somehow to replace the Churchill-Labour Coalition. The demands were mainly for economic and social changes—higher wages, service pay, pensions and social services generally ; better air-raid precautions and provision for air-raid victims ; restoration of Trade Union liberties ; democratisation of the armed forces ; and the use of emergency powers " to take over the banks, land, transport, armaments, and other large industries in order to organise our economic life in the interests of the people." With these demands, which naturally commanded a good deal of support, were coupled " National Independence for India, the right of all Colonial peoples to determine their own destiny, and the ending of enforced partition of Ireland." Next came the demand for friendship with the Soviet Union—then of course still outside the war and under pact with Nazi Germany. The last two demands were for " A People's Government truly representative of the working people," and for " A People's Peace, won by the working people of all countries, and based on the right of all peoples to determine their own destiny."

The sting of this movement, of course, was in the tail. It was an attempt, by putting forward a programme of economic and social demands that would divide the Government against itself, to secure working-class support for a specious advocacy of a " People's Peace " for which there was no possible basis in reality. The National Council of Labour issued in February, 1941, a circular describing the " People's Convention " movement as " another Innocents' Club," another manœuvre of the Communist Party and its associates " for the purpose of distracting our mass membership, disrupting our nation-wide organisation, and deluding the general public with their reiterated claim to represent the British Working Class." It was said that " The Communist object is to convert the present international struggle into a civil war : the Communist contention being that it is the duty of the Working Class in each country to work for the military defeat of its own Government by the rival Governments, in the hope and expectation that in the general demoralisation associated with defeat the Communists could seize power and dictate peace." This was, of course, the well-known policy called " Revolutionary Defeatism " : in the situation which existed in 1941 it was fantastically inapposite, in face of the complete suppression of

the working-class movement in Germany and of the certainty
that its effect would be to make a Nazi victory secure. The
National Council of Labour proceeded to advise the workers
" that support for the so-called " People's Convention " (or for
any other body having similar objects) is inconsistent with loyalty
to our organised Labour movement." In face of this declaration
most of the Local Labour Parties which had sent delegates to the
Convention withdrew. Two Local Parties were disaffiliated, and
a few others reorganised ; but the movement obtained but little
hold, and was presently swept away when the Nazi attack on the
Soviet Union led to a further abrupt change of front by the
Communist Party.

(c) Party Affairs during the Electoral Truce

The electoral truce arranged at the outbreak of war in 1939,
though it had been concluded at the outset only subject to the
right of any of the parties to terminate it at will, in fact remained in
force right up to the end of the war. This meant both that there
was no General Election until 1945 and that the main parties
did not contest by-elections against one another's candidates,
each Party being left to nominate unopposed a candidate to
succeed any sitting Member of Parliament who died or retired.
In Local Government the truce operated somewhat differently,
but with much the same effect. Nationally there was no attempt
to suspend by-elections or to give the truce any foundation in
law ; but municipal elections were formally suspended by Act
of Parliament, each Local Authority being left to recruit itself
by co-option, with an understanding that, when party members
died or retired, their successors would be chosen from the same
party—usually on the nomination of the local party machine.
Thus, parliamentary by-elections continued to take place under
the truce, whereas municipal contests did not. There was nothing
to prevent anyone who chose from standing as a parliamentary
candidate ; but there was never in any contest more than one
candidate officially representing the parties included in the
Government. Contests, where they did occur, were due to the
intervention of individuals or groups or parties not bound by the
truce.

After the formation of the Churchill Coalition the question at
once arose whether there was to be any sort of " coupon " giving

the candidate of the party which had previously held the seat the joint endorsement of all the Coalition parties. Churchill approached Attlee on this point (and presumably also the Liberals) ; and Attlee laid the matter before the Labour Party Executive, which authorised him to join with Churchill and Sinclair, the Liberal leader, in signed statements giving support to Coalition candidates. At the same time the Executive decided that, beyond this, the Party should give no support to any candidates except its own, and should ask for no support from the other parties for its own candidates. The Executive stated that it " was influenced in this decision by its anxiety to maintain Party unity in the Constituencies, and to secure a common policy to which all Party members could give their adherence."

Independent and smaller party candidates had already made their appearance during the lifetime of the Chamberlain Government. Out of twenty-four by-elections held between the outbreak of war and May, 1940, no fewer than eleven were contested, the seat going in all cases to the party which had held it previously. The opposition candidates appeared under a variety of labels—two Communist Party, two I.L.P., three " Stop-the-War," one Pacifist, one Progressive, two Fascists, a " National Independent," and a Scottish Nationalist. Their polls were mostly very small. Eleven Conservatives and two Labour candidates were returned unopposed. During the latter part of 1940 (from May) there were twenty-three by-elections. Fifteen Conservatives, one Liberal, and two Labour men were returned unopposed. For one seat two Conservatives fought each other ; one Communist opposed a Labour candidate ; and the rest of the opposition comprised one " Stop-the-War " man, one Fascist, and one Independent. In 1941 there were twenty-five by-elections. Eight Conservatives, one Liberal and six Labour men were returned unopposed. One Communist fought a Labour candidate, and two I.L.P. candidates fought Conservatives, the rest of the opposition being made up of various Independents, including two " Bomb-Berlin " candidates and one Pacifist.

From the summer of 1941 Communist opposition disappeared with the entry of the Soviet Union into the war. In 1942, out of twenty-five by-elections, twelve (one Conservative and eleven Labour) were unopposed. In the contested campaigns, one definitely and one reputedly " leftish " Independent got in for previously Conservative seats. Otherwise, all the seats went to the Government candidates. The opposition was made up of two

I.L.P., one Labour Independent, one Christian Socialist, one Scottish Nationalist, and five miscellaneous " Independents."

In 1943 a fresh challenger appeared in Sir Richard Acland's Common Wealth Party, with its idealistic Socialist programme. Common Wealth fought nine seats, and won one of them—the only victory against the Government. There were three I.L.P. and three Independent Socialist candidates, four Liberal Independents, and a considerable number of other " Independents " of various shades. Out of twenty-two by-elections, only one—a Labour seat—was uncontested ; and a number of the opposition candidates polled substantially. It was already evident that the Electoral Truce was threatening to break down. A similar situation, with a smaller number of by-elections, occurred in 1944, when out of a dozen elections only two—one Labour and one Conservative seat—went uncontested. Common Wealth won a second seat at the expense of a Conservative, and fought one other without success. One I.L.P. and one Christian Socialist, one Scottish Nationalist, one Independent Liberal, and a scatter of " Independents " accounted for the remaining contests.

The Electoral Truce was from the first widely disliked by Local Parties which saw themselves deprived of the chance of seats they hoped to win. Its effect was inevitably unfavourable to Labour, which had been the attacking party and was still seriously under-represented in the Parliament elected in 1935. The Party Executive, in reporting upon the matter to the Conference of 1940, stressed the point that the Truce could be ended at any moment, and also that it was not a " Political " but only an " Electoral " Truce, in the sense that it left the parties entirely free to carry on the work of organisation and propaganda as they thought fit. None the less, there were on the Conference agenda a large number of resolutions from Constituency Parties in favour of ending the Truce ; but when the delegates met the situation had just been transformed by the formation of the Churchill Government. A long discussion took place on the question of the Truce ; but it was recognised that the time was not opportune for moving resolutions about it. A good deal of discontent, however, was expressed at the working of the Truce in Local Government ; and the Executive promised that, in accordance with the terms originally agreed on between the parties, that aspect of the Truce should be reviewed at the end of the year. The decision was that the municipal as well as the national Truce should continue in force ; and a further Act suspending local government elections was duly passed. At the 1941 Labour Party Conference the Electoral Truce was allowed to pass unchallenged ; but by 1942 the issue had again become " live." The Executive then asked the Conference to endorse the policy, on which it had already embarked, of giving positive support to Government candidates of any party at by-elections " subject to special circumstances and consideration of the views of the Constituency Party concerned." Herbert Morrison, who moved the Executive's resolution, said that there was no question of forcing Local Parties to support non-Labour candidates against their will, but only of preventing them from supporting opposition candidates and of supplying in suitable cases Labour speakers to appear on the platforms of Government candidates of other parties. Aneurin Bevan led the opposition to the Executive proposal, which, after a long debate, was endorsed by the very narrow margin of 1,275,000 votes to 1,209,000.

By the time the 1943 Conference met there was still more sense of frustration in many of the Constituency Parties, which had been compelled by the Truce to stand aside and allow by-elections to be contested by a variety of independent and splinter party candidates. The Executive in its Report came out strongly in favour of the continuance of the Truce, arguing on the double ground of the need for maintaining national unity until the war was won and of the importance that Labour Ministers should have a share in preparing for the peace and in determining post-war policy in both home and international affairs. Attlee, in moving the official resolution, took the line that ending the Truce would mean ending the Coalition Government, and, though some of the speakers denied this, the fear that it might be true undoubtedly had a great influence on the vote. 2,243,000 votes were cast in favour of maintaining the Truce, and only 374,000 for ending it ; and a resolution in favour of terminating the Local Government Truce was declared lost on a show of hands. The difference between the narrow majority of 1942 and the large majority of 1943 was due mainly to the difference between the issues on which the two votes were recorded. In 1942 the delegates were being asked to endorse the very distasteful proposal that positive support should be given by the Labour Party to Tory and Liberal candidates : in 1943 the question was whether the Truce itself—and by inference the Coalition Government—should be maintained or not. There were very few who wanted to bring the Government to an end until the war was over : had this been directly at issue, the minority would have been a good deal smaller than it was. Many who cordially disliked the Truce voted for it for fear of endangering the Government ; and the speakers for the Truce naturally made the most of the argument that the two issues were really one. Some left-wing speakers were on one side and some on the other.

One factor which made some of the delegates wish strongly to end the Truce was the emergence of the Common Wealth Party, led by the former Liberal, Sir Richard Acland, who had become a convert to a thorough-going Socialism based on Christianity, and was for the time being winning many converts, especially among the marginal middle-class electors. Acland's party, unrestricted by the Truce, could nominate candidates where it pleased, and local Labour people were under a strong temptation to support them against reactionaries labelled as Government candidates. This, however, cut both ways ; for some Local Labour Parties resented the instrusion of Common Wealth, and were made by it more determined to maintain the Truce in the interests of war unity.

The factor that might most have tended to swing votes against the Truce was the fear, present in many delegates' minds, that some of the Labour Party's leaders might be planning to maintain the Coalition not only for the duration of the war but also for a period afterwards, during which an attempt would be made to put into force a reconstruction programme based on compromise between conflicting views. There was an overwhelming preponderance of feeling in the Labour Party against any such notion ; and both George Ridley in winding up the debate on the " Truce " resolution and other Executive speakers were at pains to disclaim it. " For us," said the Chairman, A. J. Dobbs, " a Coupon Election is not in the picture, and never will be in the picture." George Ridley said " There is not the slightest truth in the rumour that any leader . . . has said that the Electoral Truce will continue after the war." The Party's post-war attitude, he declared, would be determined by a full Party Conference. The Executive admitted that there was a widespread feeling of frustration in the Local Parties as a consequence of the Truce ; but everything had to be subordinated to the supreme necessity of winning the war.

In 1944 the Electoral Truce again went unchallenged. Attention had by that time shifted to the arrangements that were being made for compiling a special register of electors, for enabling service electors to record their votes, and for certain measures of redistribution of seats, on a limited scale, to break up the more unwieldy constituencies. It was recognised that any full scheme of redistribution would have to be left over, as the post-war movements of population could not be adequately foreseen ; but a few very big constituencies obviously needed breaking up at once. The question of service voters gave much trouble, partly owing to the slackness of the army authorities in getting forms filled up ; but in the end a fairly large proportion of those in the services were enabled to vote. The question of the Local Government Truce was again raised in 1944 ; but a further Act, prolonging the suspension of municipal elections, was passed in the end without challenge, on the understanding that arrangements would be made to resume elections immediately hostilities ended.

Although the Electoral Truce was not a " Political Truce " in any fuller sense, war conditions necessarily involved a great diminution of local Party activity, which had been largely focused in time of peace upon electoral matters. For one thing there were no elections to keep the Local Parties up to scratch. For another, a high proportion of full-time Party agents and of active Party workers in the constituencies were called away to more urgent work, and a number were killed in the blitz, and there were extensive movements of population out of the evacuation areas and into the chief centres of war-time industrial activity, besides the call-up for the armed forces and the women's services. The reactions on Party organisation were especially serious in 1940 ; and at the 1941 Conference the Executive reported that it was making a special effort to restore the position, particularly in a number of large towns which had been very adversely affected. This brought to their feet a number of delegates who complained that Party organisation had been going from bad to worse in the rural areas ; and the Executive promised to give all the help it could, and pointed to what it was doing to organise Policy Conferences all over the country with the object of re-animating the Local Parties. In 1942 it was reported that great efforts had been made to maintain organisation, both by means of regional Policy Conferences on " Democracy and Reconstruction " and by holding special Conferences on " Party Organisation in Wartime " in a number of areas. The following year it was recorded that the organising machinery had been overhauled and the number of Organising Districts increased, and also that a special campaign had been set on foot for increasing individual membership. Policy Conferences had been held in the main centres on " Local Government in the Post-War World " and on the issues raised by the Beveridge Report on the Social Services, and demonstrations on the Party's attitude to the war and to the post-war settlement had been a success.

Despite these efforts, which in the opinion of many Local Parties were inadequate in relation to the need, the war brought with it a sharp fall in the Labour Party's individual membership. The individual membership of the Local Parties had reached a peak in 1937, when there were 258,000 men and 189,000 women members enrolled. By 1942 the numbers had fallen to 123,000 men and 95,000 women, as a result partly of call-ups and partly of extensive migration, but also because the machinery for the collection of contributions had in many places fallen into disrepair for lack of voluntary workers. After 1942 there was a slow improvement ; but even in 1944 the numbers were only 153,000 men and 113,000 women—a long way below the pre-war level. The end of the war brought a rapid increase ; and in 1945 membership rose to 487,000 as against 447,000 in 1937. The 1945 figure was made up of 291,000 men and nearly 196,000 women, and the rise was of course closely connected with the General Election campaign.

One factor in the decline of local Party organisation was the decision, reported to the 1942 Conference, to hold the selection of candidates for Parliament in abeyance for the time being. This decision was put on the ground of " the depleted state of organisation in many constituencies, the unavailability of many suitable men and women as candidates, and a probable redistribution of seats before a General Election." It was left open to endorse candidates in special circumstances ; but the Executive hinted that it might prove desirable, if an Election were long deferred, to cancel all existing endorsements in order to secure a complete review. The purpose, of course, was to give a chance to young, and especially to service, candidates, and to prevent older men and women, who were available in war-time, from getting adopted for most of the more promising constituencies. In 1943–4 the Executive to some extent altered its policy and allowed a number of candidatures to be approved, taking care to get the claims of the younger people considered. At the same time, in 1943, the Executive took steps to stiffen up the procedure for the adoption of candidates, in such a way as to give the central organisation

more influence in the selection and to limit the financial inducements that a candidate or his Trade Union could hold out with
the object of securing adoption.

The perennial question of relations with the Communist Party
naturally cropped up again during the war, especially after the
Nazi attack on the Soviet Union had converted the Communists
from opponents into ardent supporters of the war effort. In July,
1941, the National Council of Labour issued a statement in which,
while it welcomed the entry of the Soviet Union into the war and
the co-operation which had been established between the Soviet
Union and Great Britain, it denied that the new situation called
for any common action with the British Communist Party. The
statement strongly assailed the war record of the Communist
Party, which it accused of irresponsibility and instability. The
Communist Party, it declared, had " taken every opportunity to
obstruct and weaken the national effort." " No vestige of
sympathy for the British people, or for the cause for which Britain
fights, has appeared in Communist declarations. Unlike the
British Labour Movement, its policy is not, and has never been,
determined by democratic methods, nor by reference to the needs
and purposes of the British people." Later in the year the Labour
Party Executive delivered a further broadside at the new " subversive movements " which had been launched by the Communists in pursuance of their new pro-war line. The Anglo-
Soviet Unity Committee, the National Conference for Anglo-
Soviet Unity, and the Anglo-Soviet Youth Friendship Alliance
were denounced as bodies designed to " confuse the minds of the
British workers " ; and even a non-party Anglo-Russian Public
Relations Committee, which did not include Communists,
received but a cold welcome. " Although the National Executive
Committee did not feel it could offer objection to this organisation, it took the line that if the Labour Party desires to secure
better relations with Russia, it could do so much more effectively
through its own machinery than through that of any other *ad
hoc* body." Members of the Labour Party who were public
speakers were advised, except after consulting the Head Office,
to address no meetings not held under official Labour auspices,
except civic meetings convened by the civic authorities or meetings
held under the auspices of the Ministry of Information. Needless
to say, this drastic advice was very imperfectly observed : indeed,
it can hardly have been meant to be taken in a fully literal sense.

The Party Conference of 1942, following the Executive's

advice, rejected by 1,899,000 votes to 132,000 a resolution which
would have allowed members of the Labour Party to co-operate
with Communists on specific issues. As against this, it passed, by
1,244,000 votes to 1,231,000, a resolution moved by Percy Collick,
of the Locomotive Engineers, calling for the removal of the ban
which the Government had put on the publication of the Communist Party's newspaper, *The Daily Worker*. This paper had been
suppressed in January, 1941, when the Communists were at the
height of their opposition to the war. Many who keenly disliked
its attitude were nevertheless extremely reluctant to acquiesce
in any such curtailment of the freedom of the press ; and the vote
reflected both the strength of this feeling and the sense that the
situation had changed since the ban was imposed. Actually, the
paper was allowed to reappear in September, 1942, four months
after the Conference had voted against continuance of the ban.

In December, 1942, the Communist Party renewed its application for affiliation to the Labour Party, on the ground that " the
experience gained in the struggle against Fascism has shown the
tremendous part that a united working-class movement can play,
not only in the winning of the war, but also in what will be needed
from the workers in helping to solve the serious problems of
reconstruction when the peace has been achieved." The Labour
Party Executive rejected this application, arguing that the
Communist Party was neither a free agent, being " subject to
overriding commitments " to the Communist International, nor
reconciliable with the Labour Party in terms of their respective
Constitutions and objects. The Communist Party replied with a
categorical assertion that its policy was determined " on the
basis of its democratically elected Congresses and through its
democratically elected Central Committee," and not by any
outside body, and that it was prepared fully to accept the Constitution of the Labour Party " and the obligations and loyalty
involved in such acceptance." It stated that its viewpoint " on
all questions " was " based on conditions prevailing here in
Great Britain and on the interests of the British Labour Movement," and that, if differences arose over policy, it would consult
the Labour Party Executive and would " not claim any special
privileges . . . other than those enjoyed by other sections
already affiliated to the Labour Party." To this the Labour
Party Executive retorted that it could not accept as true the
statement that the Communist Party determined its own policy
democratically, and quoted the Constitution of the Comintern

as showing that this body had authority to give binding instructions on policy to its affiliated parties. " The Communist Party,"
the Labour Executive summed up, " is neither independent,
self-governing, nor self-supporting, and the National Executive
Committee is convinced that the Labour Party's efforts either in
war or peace will not be enhanced or strengthened by any
association with the Communist Party." The correspondence
between Harry Pollitt and J. S. Middleton, on behalf of their
respective parties, dragged on for months, without any advance
being made. Then came, in May, 1943, the dissolution in Moscow
of the Communist International, followed by a renewed proposal
from the British Communist Party for a meeting with the Labour
Party Executive to discuss the changed situation. The Executive
refused this meeting and issued a fresh declaration asserting that
the dissolution of the Comintern " does not imply the repudiation
of ' Revolutionary Dictatorship ' and the acceptance of Parliamentary Democracy as a guiding principle." " It is common
knowledge," said the Executive, " that the philosophies and
methods of the two parties are incompatible. The Labour Party
has developed, to the great benefit of its people, under the
influence of the British tradition of democratic consent. Its
belief in Parliamentary Government is fundamental to its conception of orderly social change." Accordingly, the Executive asked
the Annual Conference, despite the disappearance of the Comintern, to reject the Communist Party's application.

At the 1943 Conference Will Lawther, for the Mineworkers'
Federation, moved an amendment in favour of accepting the
Communist Party into affiliation " provided that it agrees to
accept and abide by the Constitution of the Labour Party."
Despite the Miners' support this propsoal was defeated, after a
long debate, by 1,951,000 votes to 712,000 ; and a proposal to
remove the ban on local co-operation with Communists was also
rejected. The Executive, while it took a strong line on this issue,
was at pains to assert in special circulars and manifestos its desire
to dissociate itself from any antagonism to the Soviet Union, and
to affirm that " the Labour Party has always stood firmly for a
policy of friendship between the U.S.S.R. and Great Britain . . .
Its admiration for the heroism of the forces of the Soviet Union is
profound." The Executive emphatically denied that the two issues
were in any way connected : it asserted its belief that association
with the Communist Party would " defer, if not destroy," the
accomplishment of its hopes of social change in the post-war world.

In accordance with this attitude the Labour Party maintained throughout the war its ban on members of the Communist Party serving as delegates to Local Labour Parties or to Trades and Labour Councils acting as Local Parties for their areas. Up to 1943 this ban was operated in conjunction with the Trades Union Congress, which imposed a similar restriction on Trades Councils recognised by it for industrial purposes. Then, however, the Trades Union Congress withdrew this particular prohibition, while maintaining the parallel ban on any local co-operation with the Communist Party or any body associated with it. This change created some awkward problems for the Labour Party, which wished to maintain the ban entire. The Party Executive decided that no change made by the Trades Union Congress could alter the position of bodies affiliated to the Labour Party, and sent out a circular instructing its affiliated bodies to maintain the embargo in full force. The Executive even proposed in 1942 to extend a similar control to the Socialist Societies affiliated to it, so as both to compel them to restrict their membership to supporters of the Labour Party and ban supporters of parties or groups declared ineligible for affiliation to the Labour Party, and also to devote their activities to promoting the aims and objects of the Labour Party, and not to support or associate with any " banned " organisations. To this proposal the Fabian Society rightly took objection, on the ground that it was not a part of the Labour Party in the same sense as a Local Party, but had its own work to do as a Socialist society, much of it outside the parliamentary or electoral sphere, and must insist on its independence to do this work in its own way, fully as much as an affiliated Trade Union would insist on not being fettered in its industrial work. In face of these objections the Labour Party Executive wisely withdrew its proposal, and thus allowed the Fabian Society to remain affiliated on self-respecting terms to the party which it had helped to found. The Fabian Society does not in practice admit members who are ineligible for Labour Party membership ; but it imposes this limitation upon itself, under its own Rules, and not at the dictation of any other body.

Relations between the Labour and Co-operative Parties remained unchanged throughout the war period. The Co-operative Movement, however, moved into closer relations with the Labour Party and the Trade Unions when the Co-operative Congress of 1941 agreed to convert to a basis of formal membership the informal arrangement by which, since the outbreak of war,

Co-operative representatives had attended the meetings of the National Council of Labour. The Labour Party Executive continued to cherish the hope that in due course the Co-operative Party would be induced to affiliate to the Labour Party and to urge its local Parties and Political Councils to affiliate to the Constituency Labour Parties ; but this issue remained in abeyance, though at the end of the war more Co-operative bodies did link up with the Labour Party locally and amicable arrangements were made in the constituencies which were to be contested by Co-operative candidates at the expected General Election.

The troubles over the League of Youth also for the most part died down during the war years—mainly because the call-up and the heavy claims of industry on juvenile labour led to a great diminution in the League's activities. Attempts were made to secure recognition of the League by the Government as an agency eligible for help under the terms of the National Youth Campaign ; but it was excluded in common with other Youth organisations attached to political parties. Student Youth, on the other hand, gave the Executive plenty of trouble. The Party Executive in 1940 disaffiliated the University Labour Federation, in which the Communists had a considerable influence, and helped to organise a rival National Association of Labour Students ; but the new body was unable to establish itself under war conditions, and was not in fact got into practical operation until after 1945. Another victim of the " ban " in 1942 was the Labour Research Department, which was outlawed by the Party Executive at the request of the Trades Union Congress on account of its " interference in Trade Union policy," as well as on account of the influential part played by Communists in its control. Nevertheless a good many Trade Unions continued to support the L.R.D., which they found useful as an information agency and had to thank for many valuable services in its earlier days.*

By 1943 the Labour Party had a fresh problem to face—the rise

*The Labour Research Department was originally founded in 1912 as the Fabian Research Department, mainly by the Webbs. In 1915–16 it broke away from the Fabian Society and became an independent body, based on Trade Union, Labour, and Co-operative affiliations. For some time it acted closely with the Trades Union Congress and the Labour Party, serving these bodies with many types of research. I was Honorary Secretary of it during most of this period, as well as of the official " Advisory Committees Department " of the Labour Party. When the T.U.C. and the Labour Party decided to set up their own joint Research and Information Departments in 1921, official support was withdrawn from the L.R.D., and it passed largely, though never exclusively, under Communist influence. It continued, however, to do valuable work, especially for Trades Councils and Trade Union District Committees and branches, and a number of well-known Trade Unionists continued to give it support.

of Sir Richard Acland's Common Wealth Party. Common Wealth, as we have seen, began to contest by-elections early in that year, choosing constituencies in which, because of the Electoral Truce, there was no Labour candidate in the field. The Common Wealth movement was essentially the creation of one man—Acland—a Liberal Member of Parliament and of a family traditionally associated with Liberalism in its most progressive aspects. Realising the inadequacy of the Liberal creed in face of the need for a radically new way of living, Acland became a convert to Socialism, and from 1939 onwards issued a series of pamphlets and small books calling for a programme of immediate Socialism, based on a thoroughgoing attempt to apply the principles of Christianity to the contemporary world. Out of his efforts Common Wealth came into formal being in the middle of 1942, and at once exercised a wide appeal with its call for a more socialistic organisation of the nation for facing the tasks of war, as well as in preparation for the peace. Many local Labour supporters felt frustrated by an Electoral Truce under which they were called on to support—or at the very least to refrain from opposing—reactionary candidates at by-elections. Common Wealth demanded an immediate ending of the Electoral Truce, and declared its intention in the meantime to fight elections with its own candidates wherever a reactionary Government candidate was in the field without Labour opposition or that of some other candidate of progressive views. Its slogans were " Vital Democracy," to win the war and to secure the peace ; " Common Ownership " of all essential industries and services, with delegated and non-bureaucratic administration ; " Beveridge Now "—that is, a full and immediate application of the principles of Social Security proclaimed in the Beveridge Report ; " Social Equality " between men and women, as well as to override class differences ; " Colonial Freedom " ; " European Federation " and " World Unity " : in other words a programme much like the Labour Party's own, but proclaimed as applicable immediately, and not by gradualist stages, and stated in terms of Christian morality with an evangelical fervour that was absent from most of the Labour Party's official pronouncements. In 1943–4, as we have seen, Common Wealth won two by-elections and was instrumental in winning a third for an unofficial " Progressive " of Socialist views. It appealed most to young people, including many whom the Labour Party's propaganda was entirely failing to reach ; and in the ethical quality of its appeal it was at the opposite pole from Communism, making Christian morality and not Marxian " Scientific Socialism " the foundation of its doctrine.

The Labour Party had to make up its mind what attitude to take up towards this new movement, which was free to fight by-elections when the Local Labour Parties were not. From the outset the Executive's attitude was hostile. It reported to the 1943 Labour Party Conference that it had " deemed Common Wealth to be an organisation ineligible for affiliation to the Labour Party," with the result of making "membership of, or association with, Common Wealth incompatible with membership of the Labour Party." The ground given was that Common Wealth was " an electoral organisation, the interests of which will clash with those of the Labour Party in the constituencies." It was also complained that Common Wealth was interfering with the business of the Constituency Parties in connection with by-elections— as it obviously was.

At the Labour Party Conference of 1943 Emil Davies, of the Fabian Society, moved the reference back of the section of the Executive's Report embodying these views. He stressed the point that, in speaking up and down the country, he had found many branches of Common Wealth doing excellent work in converting the doubtful voters to Socialism. He appealed against a " heresy-hunt " that would ban all association with Common Wealth. George Ridley, answering for the Executive, accused Common Wealth of splitting the progressive forces in the name of Unity but threw doubts on the importance of the movement. Davies's motion was defeated on a show of hands ; and Common Wealth joined the lengthening list of " banned organisations." The ban was not, however, in practice at all rigidly enforced ; and, as soon as the war ended and the Labour Party was no longer tied by the Electoral Truce, the basis of Common Wealth's support began to be knocked away. Acland himself, after defeat in the General Election, and a number of his leading supporters presently joined the Labour Party ; and though the movement continued it ceased to have any real significance after the Labour election victory of 1945.

Meanwhile, in October, 1944, the Labour Party Executive had issued a Manifesto under the title *Labour and the General Election*. The purpose of this statement was two-fold—to insist on the need for the Labour Ministers to remain in the Coalition Government until the war had been finally won, and to define the conditions under which the war-time partnership would be thereafter dissolved.

When that time comes, as come it must, to dissolve what has been a great partnership, the dissolution should be accomplished with the dignity and good feeling that is fitting for those who have together encountered and overcome the greatest danger that our nation has ever had to face . . . We cannot tell when will be the appropriate time, but . . . as soon as possible, having regard to the international situation and to the need for giving the electors, especially those who are in the fighting Services, a full and fair opportunity not only of voting, but of appreciating the issues involved, a General Election must take place . . . It is in our view vital that the Election should afford a real choice to the electors between candidates supporting definite policies.

Then followed an account of the " Coupon Election " of 1918, and a statement that " no responsible leader of Labour has ever toyed with the idea of a ' Coupon Election ' "—despite malicious whisperings to the contrary. When the time came, the Labour Party would go before the country " with a practical programme based upon the Socialist principles in which it believes," and would ask for a clear Labour majority. Some preparation for the coming Election must be made at once, and could be made " without detracting from the war effort." Finally, the Manifesto urged the Constituency Parties to select as Labour candidates " men and women who are fitted by character and ability to contribute effectively to the solution of the tremendous problems which will face a Government in the period after the war."

At the Party Conference in December, 1944, Arthur Greenwood, moving the endorsement of this Manifesto, replied to Winston Churchill's proposal for a post-war Coalition on a Four Years Programme of reconstruction. He made it clear that the Manifesto had been issued as a reply to this proposal. He stressed the point that it would be for a Party Conference, and not for the Executive, to decide how long the Coalition should last. In the discussion, Dr. Haden Guest and others tried to get the terms of the statement strengthened in order to put it beyond doubt that the Coalition would be ended at the earliest possible moment after victory ; while another group wished to amend it in such a way as to open the door to arrangements for " Progressive Unity," in order to make sure of turning the Conservatives out. The Conference rejected both motions by show of hands, and passed the Manifesto as it stood. Again, Executive speakers pooh-poohed the significance of Common Wealth and of other splinter movements, and expressed their confidence in the Labour Party's ability to win an independent majority without any electoral arrangements or accommodations.

At this Conference there had been on the agenda a number of resolutions on " Progressive Unity " in various forms ; but they were not discussed, the general question being debated instead by way of discussion on the Executive's Manifesto. Similar resolutions, put down for the 1945 Conference, which was held in May with the General Election well in sight, were ruled out of order under the " three-years' rule," which forbade the rediscussion of matters already settled at Conferences until three years had elapsed. Jack Tanner, for the A.E.U., and Joseph Hallsworth, for the Distributive Workers, protested that the rule should not apply, as the resolutions had not been actually moved in 1944. Tanner moved the reference back of the relevant section of the Standing Orders Committee's Report in a speech in which he clearly indicated his doubts of a Labour victory at the Election unless some sort of arrangement were made. " If we are going to develop the power that is so necessary to win this General Election and to carry, after it has taken place, a Government which is going to represent Labour and the Progressive Parties, then it seems to me that we have got to make some arrangement." The vote, which was taken without further debate, showed 1,219,000 in favour of Tanner's motion and 1,314,000 against it. Evidently the feeling in favour of some sort of " Progressive Front " was a good deal stronger, at the eleventh hour, than the decisions of the 1944 Annual Conference had made it appear.

In 1944 James Smith Middleton retired from the position of Secretary to the Labour Party and was succeeded by Morgan Phillips. Jim Middleton had served the Party for forty-one years without a break, almost from its inception. He had been Assistant Secretary, and for a considerable period Acting Secretary in Arthur Henderson's absence, up to 1935, and thereafter full Secretary. In his later years he had been criticised increasingly by the left wing of the Party ; but everyone recognised the high quality of his lifelong service. The defection of Ramsay MacDonald, with whom he had been closely associated in the Party's years of struggle, had been a sore blow to him, and he had never fully recovered from it. But he had held on his way with the Party, and the good wishes of all sections went with him in his retirement.

THE COURSE OF BY-ELECTIONS, 1939–44

	Seats fought and won by						Seats fought by						
	Conservative or Liberal-National		Labour		Liberal		I.L.P.	Communist	Common Wealth	Ind. Soc. or Ind. Lab.	Anti-War	British Union	Ind. elected
	Un-opposed	Opposed	Un-opposed	Opposed	Un-opposed	Opposed							
1939	6	1	1	1	—	—	1	1	—	—	1	—	—
1940 (to May)	5	5	1	3	—	—	1	1	—	—	3	2	—
1940 (from May)	15	4	2	1	1	—	—	1	—	—	1	1	—
1941	8	8	6	1	1	—	2	1	—	—	1	—	—
1942	1	5	11	2	—	—	2	—	—	2	—	—	1
1943	3	11	1	1	—	1	3	—	1*	2	—	—	—
1944	1	5	1	2	—	1	1	—	2†	1	—	—	—
Totals	39	39	23	11	2	2	10	4	3	5	6	3	1

*Elected.   †One elected.

(d) *Facing the Future*

At the height of the struggle for sheer national survival, in 1940 and the early months of 1941, there were few who had much time to spare for planning what should be done when the war was over. But by the time the Annual Labour Party Conference met, in June, 1941, the problems of " reconstruction " were coming again to take some place in men's minds. The Government, in January, had assigned to Arthur Greenwood, as Minister without Portfolio, a somewhat vague commission to study reconstruction problems and to co-ordinate departmental action in relation to them ; and the Nuffield College Social Reconstruction Survey, under my direction, had been given a mandate to make a number of preliminary investigations on the Government's behalf— though of course without any power to commit it in matters of policy. It was felt at the Labour Conference that the Labour Party too should be setting to work defining its post-war intentions ; and a promise was made that the Executive would set up a " Reconstruction Committee " and submit a Report to the Conference the following year. Out of this promise came, early in 1942, what was described as an " Interim Report on the Problems of War and Peace Reconstruction," under the title, *The Old World and the New Society*. This document which was lengthy, was not itself debated at the Conference. Harold Laski, for the Executive, moved a single brief resolution on post-war policy ; and the brief discussion which followed was taken as sufficiently covering the ground, and the vote carrying the resolution as a sufficient endorsement of the Report.

The Old World and the New Society was essentially a pamphlet rather than a programme. It travelled over a very wide field, without either laying down any order of priorities or indicating at all precisely what a post-war Labour Government would actually do. It was much more nearly a rewriting of *For Socialism and Peace*, the last previous full statement of Labour Party aims, which had appeared in 1934, than a substitute for *Labour's Immediate Programme*, which had been issued in 1937. That was what some delegates complained of : they wanted a precise programme committing the Party to definite lines of action and indicating some order of priorities for a Labour Government. For this the Executive was not ready in 1942 : it offered *The Old World and the New Society* only as an interim statement that was to be filled out by further work of the Reconstruction Committee, elaborating its various sections. Only when this had been done would the time be ripe, in the Executive's opinion, for replacing the *Immediate Programme* of 1937 by a more up-to-date and equally positive declaration. The Interim Report was challenged on other grounds also—by speakers who wanted to get the Labour Ministers out of the Government even during the war, or at least to force them to take up within it a more aggressively Socialist line. The Conference swept both groups of critics aside, and endorsed Laski's resolution by an overwhelming majority.

As a broad statement of Labour aims, *The Old World and the New Society* was at once challenging in its general standpoint and too much the product of immediate circumstances to stand good for long. There was too much recent history in it for it not to get quite rapidly out of date—not in its essential ideas, but in its way of presenting them.

The essential ideas of the Report were simple. The " old world " of 1939 was dead : its ideas were " already obsolete." The war had swept it away ; for " totalitarian war, under modern techno-logical conditions, is revolutionary in its impact." The " new society " would have to be based on radically different founda-tions. In the sphere of international relations, national sovereignty would have to be given up : its " parochialism " was inconsistent with the requirements of democratic civilisation. Small nations could no longer hope to defend themselves unaided against aggression : the control of armed forces would have to pass into the hands of an international authority. National rights of " security and independence " would have to be recognised ; but the Report denied " that this recognition can imply any nation's right to sovereignty in the sense that this was claimed and exercised by states in the inter-war years." " All the authority the nations, great and small alike, require for their self-respect and freedom is fully compatible with their full participation in, and acceptance of, the making of international standards in matters of common concern." The Labour Party stood, then, internationally, for a much stronger substitute for the League of Nations ; and, preparing its Report at the beginning of 1942, it expressed what it wanted in the language of the day, by asserting its adherence to the principles enunciated in President Roose-velt's Message on " The Four Freedoms " (January, 1941) and in the Atlantic Charter (August, 1941). Freedom of speech and expression, freedom of religion, freedom from want, and freedom from fear—these were adopted as slogans of Labour ;

and the vague phrases of the Atlantic Charter were used as a foundation on which to build a superstructure of aspirations towards a new World Society founded upon democratic Socialist ideas.

The Old World and the New Society opened with an unequivocal assertion of the need for total and final victory over the dictators— "victory complete, victory unmistakable, victory upon which there can be no going back." Not only must there be no peace with the dictators : "the *peoples* of Germany, Italy and Japan must be brought finally to realise that the power which the peace-loving nations can mobilise against aggression is overwhelming in its strength and absolute in its assurance of success." Next came a review of "the appeasement period," in which appeasement was traced to the shortcomings of an unplanned capitalist society, dominated by powerful vested interests and therefore unable to devote itself to the full use of its resources for improving production and enhancing the quality of life. Nazism and Fascism themselves were traced to this cause, as the product of vested interests intent on maintaining a system of privilege and exploitation. The British Government's failure to stand up to Fascism was denounced as a consequence of the same supremacy of vested interest. "All the major evils of the appeasement period are directly traceable to the unregulated operation of our economic system. Its failure at home to discover the conditions of expanding welfare bred lack of confidence in democracy : its fear of dealing firmly with aggressors abroad took it straight into the war which its timidity made possible."

In place of the old, unplanned society the Report demanded "planned production for community consumption" as "the condition on which the essential freedoms become effective in the lives of ordinary citizens." It demanded planned production based on full employment, and argued that for this to be secured "the nation must own and operate the essential instruments of production." In the transition from war to peace, the war controls must be maintained, in order to avert a repetition of the disasters of 1920–1. There must be also "the organised import of staple commodities and their orderly marketing." "If the nation begins now the task of permeating the war economy with the principles here affirmed, as peace comes, the minds of men will become accustomed to their acceptance and enlargement."

In home policy the Report laid down four essential objectives, the pursuit of which must be begun as an integral part of the war effort itself. " We have to provide full employment : we have to rebuild a Britain to standards worthy of the men and women who have preserved it ; we have to organise social services at a level which secures adequate health, nutrition, and care in old age, for all citizens, and we have to provide educational opportunities for all which ensure that our cultural heritage is denied to none." The Report put heavy stress on education as an instrument for the making of a democratic community, demanding that the school-leaving age should be raised to fifteen as soon as the war ended, and to sixteen within three years. Indeed, it was more specific on this issue than on most others. It called also for a thorough overhaul of the long-untouched machinery of justice and of the treatment of crime and of the criminal ; for factory reform and more democratic management of industry, with greater provision for workers' participation ; and for a great, all-round development of the social services, together with the institution of " a minimum living wage for every employed person."

On all these matters, except education, the Report limited itself to quite general statements of objective. In effect, it largely took for granted the plans which had been laid down in previous statements of Labour Party policy and endeavoured to strike out on new lines directly related to the war situation. It was much more internationalist in balance of content than previous general pronouncements, setting its economic policy more in a framework of world-wide economic development. It recognised explicitly that " the future economic and social well-being of British citizens is bound up with the prosperity of all other peoples." It was, moreover, based on a keen consciousness of the key position held by Great Britain in determining the course of affairs in other countries. The Labour Party " is fully aware that the choice we now make will largely determine the future of democracy upon the Continent of Europe. For only the proof that the outstanding fortress of democracy can use its political institutions to solve its economic and social problems by the methods of democracy will maintain faith and hope in its creative power." Great Britain was thus marked out for a rôle of democratic leadership in Europe, or even in the world as a whole—for, the Report went on, " All over the world the evidence is abundant that this revolution [i.e., the social revolution already being effected by the war] has deeply affected men's minds ; our central problem is to discover its appropriate institutions, above all, if we can, to discover them by consent."

This theme of " consent," as the characteristic implication of British democracy, recurred in the Report. *The Old World and the New Society*, though it proclaimed, in Laski's phraseology, " the revolution of our time," was still emphatically not a revolutionary document, in the usual sense of the term. It remained gradualist, even if the pace was to be speeded up. " The Labour Party does not ask for some sudden and overnight transformation of our society. It proposes here only the basis upon which the nation can proceed forthwith to build." This, however, it was argued, involved getting the right foundations at once, by extensive socialisation of the essential instruments of production.

From home affairs and general principles the Report proceeded to the affairs of the British Commonwealth. It declared emphatically against the " colour bar " in all its forms and in favour of the doctrine of trusteeship in colonial areas. It demanded public ownership and exploitation of colonial mineral resources, the abolition of forced labour, and the prohibition of alienation of native lands to white settlers. But it had little to say about colonial self-government, and it " admitted " that effective control must remain for a long time with the Colonial Office, demanding only that " the whole process of government be geared to the supreme purpose of fitting the native races to determine their own destiny." This had much less of an anti-imperialist ring than Attlee's speech on War Aims, which I cited earlier.*

About India, too, the Report was carefully vague, half-supporting the view that self-government, in any full sense, must wait on agreement between the rival parties in India, though it added that " it is also the duty of the British Government to take every possible step to promote that agreement." There was no endorsement of the Indian claim to full *independence* or to that of any other country falling within the British Empire. It was, however, demanded that "both at the centre and in the Provinces, Indians must be given full responsibility now, and Indians must take their full place alongside Dominion statesmen in the direction of the war effort."

As for the peace, " aggressor nations, after military defeat, must be disarmed and kept disarmed. This involves the destruction of the social and economic relationships which make possible the alliance between military castes and economic privilege." Later on it was added that " the power of democracy in the future

*See page 378.

to maintain international peace is, in the long run, inseparable from the growth, in each country, of the common ownership of the main instruments of production and their co-ordinated planning for common ends." Finally, the Report stressed the need for reaching a clear understanding " before victory " with allied countries, " and, above all, with the Soviet Union and the United States."

This is by no means a complete summary of *The Old World and the New Society :* I have attempted only to indicate its salient features. It was followed up during the next two years with a good deal of more detailed planning, which found expression in a series of Reports on particular aspects of policy. These included *The Colonies* (1943) ; *National Service for Health* (1943) ; *Housing and Planning* (1943) ; *Our Land, The Future of Britain's Agriculture* (1943) ; *The Nation's Food* (1943), drafted by Sir John Orr ; *The Future of Local Government* (1943) ; *Post-war Organisation of British Transport* (1944) ; *Full Employment and Financial Policy* (1944) ; *The International Post-war Settlement* (1944) ; Interim Report on *Organisation and Finance* (1944) ; *Wings for Peace : Labour's Post-war Policy for Civil Flying* (1944) ; *Coal and Power* (1944) ; *Water Supply* (1944) and *Social Insurance, Workmen's Compensation and a National Health Service* (1944). The Party's Reconstruction Committee had been very industrious : it had filled in the gaps in the considerable series of Policy Reports prepared during the 1930's, and, where it felt the situation to have changed enough to warrant complete restatement of policies, had prepared entirely new Reports.

With these materials at command, the Labour Party was well equipped for facing the tasks of policy-making in practice over a large part of the field when it came to office in 1945. There were, however, very serious gaps. In general, home policy had been planned very much more thoroughly than international policy, either political or economic. Foreign trade, which was to show itself a matter of absolutely vital importance, had not been tackled at all ;* nor was there any realistic appraisal of specific international problems—or, indeed, any apparent recognition of the possibility that the great international issues might not, after all, get settled by the talismanic co-operation of Great Britain, the Soviet Union, and the United States in a new Society of

*The Fabian Society, however, issued in 1942, under the title *A Word on the Future to British Socialists*, a pamphlet in which it did attempt to take full account of such post-war problems as the balance of payments and the control of international trade. Unfortunately, this initiative was not followed up by the Labour Party.

Nations armed with " real teeth." Labour's international world remained a dream world of harmoniously co-operating Great Powers basing their policies on the " Four Freedoms " and the Atlantic Charter.

Most of the Policy Reports prepared by the Executive in 1943 and 1944 went through the Party Conference without much discussion and without any amendment at all. It was practically impossible, under the procedure adopted, to discuss specific points ; for the Reports were moved not directly but in the form of summarising resolutions, so that they could be effectively challenged only on very broad grounds. The Reports on a National Health Service, on Housing, on Coal, and on Colonial Policy, among others, were passed practically without challenge ; and most of the others were not seriously contested. The only Report which aroused serious disagreement was that which dealt with the future of Local Government. There, the Executive's endorsement of a form of Regionalism based on large elective authorities was challenged by delegates who argued that Local Government could not be democratically conducted except within reasonably small and homogeneous areas, and that nothing must be done to undermine the independence of the existing local authorities in town and country, even if regional arrangements were needed for the co-ordination of particular services over wider areas. An attempt to refer back the Executive's Report on *The Future of Local Government*, which did in truth suffer from serious weaknesses and ambiguities, gathered 966,000 votes against 1,542,000 ; but this was the only instance in which the Executive's policy met with really serious opposition. An attempt to challenge the Report on *Housing and Planning*, mainly on the ground that it did not take its stand more firmly on the need for public ownership of land, was defeated because, though a good many delegates considered the Report too unprecise on this issue, it did in fact urge public ownership as a remedy. The problem was complicated because, at that stage, the Uthwatt Committee had recently put forward its proposals for nationalising the " development value " of land, without nationalising the land itself, and a good many delegates were more anxious to get the Government to endorse the Uthwatt proposals as a compromise solution than to press for land nationalisation, which they knew there was no chance of persuading the existing House of Commons —much less the House of Lords—to accept. The Policy Committee in 1944 urged the Party to " accept as a matter of immediate

urgency the recommendations of the Uthwatt Committee which
empower Local Authorities to acquire the whole of the reconstruction areas " . . . to " approve the principle that any
undeveloped land required for development should be first pur-
chased by the State," and to accept the principle that " ' betterment ' conferred upon private property by communal action
should be collected from the owners by the appropriate Authorities."

In the summary of *The Old World and the New Society* brief
reference has been made to the section dealing with " Commonwealth Affairs." Co-operation with the Labour Parties in the
British Dominions was carried a good deal further at the Conference of British and Dominion Labour Parties which met in
London in September, 1944, and was attended by representatives
of the Labour Parties in Great Britain, Australia, New Zealand,
Canada (Co-operative Commonwealth Federation), and South
Africa. The Conference, which lasted for a fortnight, drew up an
important Manifesto, under the title *From a People's War to a
People's Peace*. Meeting with victory well in sight, the delegates
pointed to the great opportunities lying ahead of the Labour
Movements in the countries already liberated, or in process of
liberation, from Fascist oppression, as well as for the Movements
in the British Commonwealth. The new world, it proclaimed,
" must be built through unremitting struggle and International
Labour and Socialist Unity." " Full employment and the
raising of standards of living are the first condition of an increase
in production and purchasing power . . . Full employment and
a full standard of life require full trade." On this basis the
Manifesto urged that " the principal war-time financial controls
should be maintained until more permanent and satisfactory
arrangements can be made." It advocated the organisation of
banking as a public service, the national and international
control of investment, and the continuance of war-time arrangements for bulk purchase of foodstuffs and raw materials. There
should be " as much stability as possible in foreign exchange
rates, subject to the need for full employment in the countries
concerned."

The Manifesto then turned to international affairs. Japan
must be completely defeated and disarmed ; in Germany, Japan
and elsewhere " the social and political institutions which permitted the emergence of Nazism and Fascism must be destroyed " ; the Labour Movements in the defeated countries

must be rebuilt ; a new World Organisation must be established
on a basis of agreement among the participant nations to renounce
war and to settle all disputes by peaceful means. The " principle
of majority rule " should obtain in this new organisation ; and
there should be within it Regional Organisations to " perform
the functions appropriate to the interests of nations whose
relationship is specially close by reason of geographical situation
or other causes." All such regional arrangements, however,
should be subject to the paramount claims of loyalty to the World
Organisation.

The Manifesto next recognised " the right of India to full
self-government," and expressed the hope " that a free India will
decide to remain a partner in the British Commonwealth of
Nations." It asserted that " the inhabitants of Dependent
Territories in the British Empire must be recognised to have
paramount interests in the areas where they dwell," and demanded a cessation of colonial exploitation, and measures both
to develop the standard of life among the native races and " to
quicken the pace of their advance to self-government." This
last was declared to be " not merely the concern of Great Britain
alone but a factor of importance in the general relations of the
British Commonwealth of Nations."

Next, the Manifesto asserted the need for fuller consultation
in future between Great Britain and the Dominions and also
between the British and Dominion Labour Parties. It looked
forward to the speedy revival of " a Socialist International in
which it recommends that both the British Labour Party and the
Dominion Labour Parties shall seek to play their full part " ;
and finally it recognised that a special responsibility lay on the
Dominion Labour Parties to take their share in building the new
democratic and Socialist order, and " to ensure that the unity
which has been achieved during the war between the British
Commonwealth, the United States, China, and the Soviet
Union is carried unbroken and strengthened into the Peace."

This Conference was meant to be the first of a regular series ;
and it was later arranged that a further meeting should be held
in Canada in 1947.

Having prepared the ground by this Conference as well as by
its series of special Reports, supplementing both the Policy
Reports of the 1930's and the broader statement embodied in
The Old World and the New Society, the Party Executive was in a
position to " get down to brass tacks " and to formulate a state-

ment of policy which would define more clearly what a Labour Government would attempt to do during its tenure of office if it were given a working majority. In April, 1945, appeared *Let Us Face the Future : A Declaration of Labour Policy for the Consideration of the Nation*—in effect an Election Manifesto, though it was not yet known when it was drawn up how soon an Election would occur.

Let Us Face the Future had the great merit of precision, the lack of which had been a cause of (not necessarily merited) criticism in *The Old World and the New Society*. No one who studied *Let Us Face the Future* was left, in respect of home policy, in any doubt about what a Labour Government would set out to do if it were returned to power. In respect of international policy, on the other hand, the lack of precision remained—not altogether surprisingly, in view of the extreme difficulty of looking ahead on the immediate morrow of the assurance of military victory, but most unfortunately, in view of the vital importance of getting a correct start in international action with the purpose of rallying the forces of Socialist democracy in Europe and throughout the world. *Let Us Face the Future* did indeed begin with a section entitled " Victory in War Must be Followed by a Prosperous Peace " and end, apart from the peroration, with a section calling for " A World of Progress and Peace " ; but internationally it had no very clear message. " We cannot," it declared, " cut ourselves off from the rest of the world—and we ought not to try." It went on to urge that " we must consolidate in peace the great war-time association of the British Commonwealth with the U.S.A. and the U.S.S.R." and to insist that " we must join with France and China and all others who have contributed to the common victory in forming an International Organisation capable of keeping the peace in years to come." But it did not discuss either the question whether the association with the United States and the U.S.S.R. could in fact be maintained or the basis on which a Socialist Government should seek to conduct its relations with countries as divergent in ideas and " ways of life " as these two. Nor did it say anything about the problems of common action between the Socialist and Labour movements of Western Europe, or about the " iron curtain " which was already descending between East and West. These issues were in fact set aside in favour of a general hopefulness about the prospects of international co-operation ; nor was there any recognition of the extremely difficult international economic position in which

Great Britain was bound to find itself as soon as Lease-Lend supplies were no longer available and the country, having sacrificed most of its export trade and its foreign investments to the needs of war, had to face the task of paying for the imported foodstuffs and materials required for keeping its people fed and its industries at work.

Nevertheless, within its limitations, *Let Us Face the Future* was a highly effective manifesto. It told the electors what they wanted to know—which was not quite the same as what they would have wanted to know if they had more fully appreciated the realities of Great Britain's exceedingly difficult international position.*

Let Us Face the Future was mainly a manifesto about home policy. Under the heading " What the Election will be about " it put in the forefront the statement—quite true as far as it went—that " the nation wants food, work and homes." These, it said, were aims on which all parties would nominally agree ; but " the test of a political programme is whether it is sufficiently in earnest about the objectives to adopt the means needed to realise them . . . All parties say so—the Labour Party means it." On this basis, the Party proceeded to state, in forthright terms, the actual steps which a Labour Government would take to give effect to its immediate aims. It would ensure full employment and high production by maintaining purchasing power " through good wages, social services and insurance, and taxation which bears less heavily on the lower income groups." It would control rents and prices. It would plan investment through a National Investment Board, would use war factories to meet the needs of peace, would regulate the location of industry, and would make an end of the depressed areas, if necessary building new Government factories. It would bring the Bank of England under public ownership, and would " harmonise " the operations of the other banks with public needs. At the same time it would set on foot thorough-going measures designed to increase industrial efficiency. It would socialise the fuel and power industries, inland transport, and iron and steel. It would prohibit restrictive trade practices and bring monopolies and cartels under public control. It would enforce priorities in the use of scarce materials, hold

---

*I feel entitled to make this point because I had done my best to draw attention to these difficulties both in my book, *Great Britain in the Post-war World* (1942) and in the pamphlet already mentioned which I drafted for the Fabian Society in May, 1942, under the title *A Word on the Future to British Socialists*. What I had to say in these writings was, however, too unpalatable to be given serious attention.

food prices against inflationary forces, put houses before mansions and necessities before luxuries over the entire field of production. It would plan agriculture for increased production of foodstuffs of high quality, and would see that capital was applied to agricultural improvement and the small farmer given a square deal. It would stabilise agricultural marketing and maintain civic restaurants, canteens, free and cheap milk for mothers and children, and other new food services established under the stress of war.

Housing was put high up on the list of priorities which a Labour Government would apply. " Housing," it was said (and at the time almost everyone would have echoed the sentiment) " will be one of the greatest and one of the earliest tests of a Government's real determination to put the nation first. Labour's pledge is firm and direct—it will proceed with a housing programme with the maximum practical speed until every family in this island has a good standard of accommodation." The establishment of a Ministry of Housing and Planning was urged—one of the few points of home policy on which Labour in power did not carry out its declared intentions.

On the land question, belief in land nationalisation was affirmed but no immediate promise was made to achieve it. The programme limited itself to " wider and speedier powers to acquire land for public purposes wherever the public interest so requires," with fair compensation but subject to a " betterment " charge. In respect of education, the Butler Act having been already made law, the Labour Party's pledge was to carry the Act " not merely into legal force but into practical effect." A National Health Service was promised, available to all, with health centres, " more and better hospitals, and proper conditions for doctors and nurses." " Money must no longer be the passport to the best treatment." Comprehensive legislation was promised on Social Insurance—" social provision against rainy days, with economic policies designed to reduce rainy days to a minimum." Finally, a paragraph headed " Labour's Call to All Progressives " appealed to " all men and women of progressive outlook " to rally behind the Labour Party as the only force powerful enough to carry a democratic policy into effect. If there were no clear majority, the result of the General Election " might well mean parliamentary instability and confusion, or another Election."

On this programme the Labour Party, a few months later, fought and won the General Election of 1945.

(e) The General Election of 1945

THE THIRD LABOUR GOVERNMENT, 1945

The Cabinet consisted of :

C. R. Attlee	Prime Minister and Minister of Defence
Herbert Morrison	Lord President and Leader of the House of Commons
Ernest Bevin	Foreign Secretary
Arthur Greenwood	Lord Privy Seal (retired September, 1947)
Hugh Dalton	Chancellor of the Exchequer (resigned November, 1947)
Sir Stafford Cripps	President of the Board of Trade
Lord Jowitt	Lord Chancellor
A. V. Alexander	First Lord of the Admiralty
J. Chuter Ede	Home Secretary
Viscount Addison	Dominions Secretary and Leader of the House of Lords
Lord Pethick Lawrence	Secretary of State for India and Burma
G. H. Hall	Colonial Secretary
J. J. Lawson	Secretary for War (retired October, 1946)
Viscount Stansgate	Secretary for Air (retired October, 1946)
J. Westwood	Secretary for Scotland (retired October, 1947)
G. A. Isaacs	Minister of Labour
E. Shinwell	Minister of Fuel and Power
Ellen Wilkinson	Minister of Education (died February, 1947)
Aneurin Bevan	Minister of Health
T. Williams	Minister of Agriculture and Fisheries

Ministers not in the Cabinet included :

Alfred Barnes	Minister of Transport
J. Griffiths	Minister of National Insurance
J. B. Hynd	Chancellor of the Duchy of Lancaster (resigned, October, 1947)
Lord Listowel	Postmaster-General
P. J. Noel-Baker	Minister of State
W. Paling	Minister of Pensions
Sir Hartley Shawcross	Attorney-General
L. Silkin	Minister of Town and Country Planning
Sir Ben Smith	Minister of Food
Sir Frank Soskice	Solicitor-General
G. R. Thomson	Lord Advocate
George Tomlinson	Minister of Works
E. J. Williams	Minister of Information
J. Wilmot	Minister of Supply (resigned October, 1947)
Lord Winster	Minister for Civil Aviation

Among the Under-Secretaries were :

George Buchanan (Scotland), A. Creech Jones (Colonies), W. G. Hall (Treasury), A. Henderson (India and Burma), C. W. Key (Health), Hector McNeil (Foreign Affairs), H. A. Marquand (Overseas Trade), Lord Nathan (War Office), John Strachey (Air), G. R. Strauss (Transport), Harold Wilson (Works).

In November, 1947, the Cabinet was constituted as follows :

C. R. Attlee	Prime Minister
Herbert Morrison	Lord President and Leader of the House of Commons
Ernest Bevin	Foreign Secretary
Sir Stafford Cripps	Chancellor of the Exchequer
A. V. Alexander	Minister of Defence
Lord Addison	Lord Privy Seal and Leader of the House of Lords
Lord Jowitt	Lord Chancellor
J. Chuter Ede	Home Secretary
A. Creech Jones	Colonial Secretary
Lord Listowel	Secretary of State for Burma
P. J. Noel-Baker	Secretary of State for Commonwealth Relations
Arthur Woodburn	Secretary of State for Scotland
G. A. Isaacs	Minister of Labour
Aneurin Bevan	Minister of Health
T. Williams	Minister of Agriculture and Fisheries
G. Tomlinson	Minister of Education
Harold Wilson	President of the Board of Trade

Members not in the Cabinet included :

Alfred Barnes	Minister of Transport
George Buchanan	Minister of Pensions
Hugh Gaitskell	Minister of Fuel and Power
James Griffiths	Minister of National Insurance
Viscount Hall	First Lord of the Admiralty
Arthur Henderson	Secretary of State for Air
C. W. Key	Minister of Works
Hector McNeil	Minister of State
H. A. Marquand	Paymaster-General
Lord Nathan	Minister of Civil Aviation
Lord Pakenham	Chancellor of the Duchy of Lancaster
W. Paling	Postmaster-General
Sir Hartley Shawcross	Attorney-General
E. Shinwell	Secretary of State for War
Lewis Silkin	Minister of Town and Country Planning
Sir Frank Soskice	Solicitor-General
John Strachey	Minister of Food
G. R. Strauss	Minister of Supply
John Wheatley	Lord Advocate

The Members of the Cabinet were at this time aged as follows :
Addison (78), Bevin (66), Ede (65), Attlee (64), Isaacs (64),
Alexander (62), Jowitt (62), Morrison (59), Williams (59), Cripps (58),
Noel-Baker (58), Tomlinson (57), Woodburn (57), Creech Jones (56),
Bevan (49), Listowel (41), Wilson (31).

The Coalition Government of 1940 had been formed for a
single plain purpose—to beat the Nazis. On that issue it had from
first to last the great majority of the people behind it, and,
despite alarums and excursions from time to time, there was never
any real question of ending it before its task was done. From
the moment, however, when Japan entered the war, the position
became unclear. It was part of the deliberate war strategy of the
Allies to dispose finally of Hitler before turning their attention to
the Japanese ; and it was generally expected that the war in the
East would go on for a considerable time after hostilities in Europe
had come to an end. So probably it would have done, but for the
atomic bomb ; and it remains unknown how far Churchill and
the other national leaders took their foreknowledge of the new
weapon into account in making their private estimates of the
probable duration of the Eastern war. The public and most of
the politicians, not being in the secret, could take no account of
this factor ; and Churchill, sincerely or not, behaved throughout
as if it did not exist—as indeed he had to do if the secret was to
be kept. Accordingly, all the arguments which accompanied the
break-up of the war-time Coalition were conducted on the
assumption that the war would probably go on for a long time
after the Nazis had been forced to surrender.

The Labour Party, as we have seen, had been behind the
Labour Ministers in wishing to keep the Coalition in full strength
up to the end of the European War, but had been throughout
eager to resume its freedom and to fight a General Election as
soon as possible after the Coalition's original purpose had been
fulfilled. When, in 1944, Churchill threw out his proposal for a
Four Years Plan of reconstruction, to be agreed on between the
parties and carried out by a post-war Coalition Government, the
Labour Party unequivocally rejected the notion; and its leaders
took care to make the Party Conference understand that they
were in no way responsible for it. Indeed, from the moment
when the Government began seriously to turn its attention to
post-war problems, and to produce—or fail to produce—White
Papers outlining a projected reconstruction policy, it became
evident that there was no possible basis for agreement, even upon

such relatively unprovocative issues as Social Security and full employment policy. Much less could there be any agreement about nationalisation of key industries and services, the nature of post-war " controls," or the post-war structure of taxation. The one occasion during the war in Europe when the Labour Party rank and file went solidly into the lobby against the Government and their own Ministers was in 1943, when the Coalition produced its White Paper on the Beveridge Report. There were, however, a good many other occasions on which the existence of wide differences of view about post-war policy was quite clear—the future of coal and of transport, the action to be taken on the Uthwatt Report dealing with land development rights, and the measures necessary for the effective maintenance of full employment, for example.

It was abundantly plain that, as soon as the war situation allowed, Parliament needed to be renewed by a General Election, and that the Labour Party would not stand for any sort of " coupon " election based on an agreement to continue the Coalition. Any agreement for such an Election would necessarily have meant a continuance of Conservative predominance in the House of Commons, irrespective of the state of opinion in the country ; for it would have involved reproducing in the main the composition of the Parliament elected in 1935, when the Labour Party had not half recovered from its overwhelming defeat in 1931. Even if there had been no such sharp difference of party opinion about reconstruction policies as did in fact exist, it would have been out of the question to expect the Labour Party to condemn itself for a further period of years to a continuance of its position of parliamentary inferiority, which had already lasted far beyond the normal life of a Parliament. There had to be a General Election as soon as possible, and it had to be fought as a contest for power between the Labour and Conservative Parties.

This being the position, there was obviously a strong case for holding an Election as soon as it could be reasonably arranged after the Nazi surrender of May, 1945. Had it been known that the war in the East would be ended within a very few months there might have been powerful reasons for keeping the Coalition in being until it too was over ; but even if this was in Churchill's mind he could not say so, and, when he offered the Labour Party the choice between facing an immediate General Election and staying in the Coalition until the Japanese war was over, everyone understood the second alternative as involving in all probability the continuance of the Churchill Government as it was for at least a year, and possibly for two or three years. This being so, there was for the Labour Party only one possible answer—unless indeed they had been prepared to entertain the curious suggestion, thrown out by Churchill, of a referendum to decide whether the Coalition should continue or not. To such a question the electors would quite possibly have answered " yes," voting under the influence of Churchill's personal prestige. But the answer, if given, would not have made it practicable to create a new Coalition capable of carrying on with an agreed policy. The Labour Party rejected both the proposal that the Labour Ministers should stay in the Government up to the end of the war with Japan, and the proposal for a referendum ; and it is not easy to see how it could have been expected to do anything else.

The Labour Party, however, objected strongly to Churchill's wish to rush the General Election on, so as to hold it within a few weeks of the German surrender. The Party wanted an autumn election, which could be held on a new and greatly improved register, and would give the service electors adequate time to consider the issues and to get and return their voting papers, and the service candidates a fair chance to meet their constituents and get themselves known. The Labour Ministers, with the support of their party, were quite willing to stay in the Government until the autumn, in order to get the Election fairly fought, but to this Churchill would not consent. Either they must agree to serve till the Eastern war was over, or they must get out at once, leaving him to form a " caretaker " Government, composed mainly of Conservatives, which would have a free hand to liquidate such " controls " as it dared dispense with and would be able to appeal to the electors as the Government, headed by Churchill, the great leader who had " won the war."

The defence offered for rushing the Election was that, if the country was to be appealed to by rival parties, the sooner the better, because it was desirable for the party that was to govern the country during the period of peace-making and reconstruction to be given a clear mandate as soon as possible, in order that it might be free to get on with the job. This argument would have been valid against any long delay ; but it hardly excused the haste that was actually used, in view of the known badness of the electoral register and of the certainty that, despite arrangements for proxies and for postal voting, the early date would seriously reduce the size of the service vote. (Actually, many more soldiers voted than had been expected to do so ; but even so more than 40 per cent of the service vote was not cast).

The Labour Party, then, went into the General Election on the one hand elated at the regaining of their independence, but on the other hand sore at having been rushed, and convinced that the Tories and Churchill with them were seeking party advantage both from a register and voting conditions which would exclude many working-class and service voters and from holding the polls before there had been time for the " Victory " atmosphere to clear. This view was confirmed when it became plain that the Tories meant to fight, not on any programme, but almost exclusively on Churchill's personality—a technique which failed largely because Churchill himself so signally failed to keep his temper or to make himself sound in the least like the leader the people wanted for facing the tasks of peace. Churchill's war record no doubt gained the Conservatives many votes ; but he did his best to lose an even greater number by abusing his late colleagues instead of attempting to state a policy or a programme. His attacks on Labour as a " totalitarian " party were supremely ridiculous to anyone who knew its record, and not at all convincing to anyone who was not already eager to be convinced. Nor did Churchill's attempt to erect Professor Laski into a sinister revolutionary plotter, standing behind the Labour Party ready to use it to overturn the Constitution, impress anyone except the Americans, who like and are used to that sort of thing. Professor Laski is not universally loved, and would, one supposes, not wish to be ; but assuredly he is neither Lenin nor Mephistopheles, and the attempt to make him double the parts produced mainly laughter.

The General Election, rushed to suit Conservative interests, but rushed, as soon appeared, to small purpose, was held in July, 1945. Out of a total electorate (on a very defective register) of nearly 33,000,000, practically 76 per cent voted, despite the large loss of service votes. Most of those who could vote did vote ; and in the result the two main parties—Labour and Conservative— were only 2,000,000 votes apart, counting the Liberal Nationals and a few Nationals who were really Conservatives as part of the Conservative total. In all, the Churchillites polled nearly 10,000,000 votes, the Labour Party nearly 12,000,000, the Liberals 2,250,000, and all other candidates rather more than 750,000. The Labour Party was thus in a minority of about 1,000,000 as against all other parties, excluding the University

seats ; but as between " Right " and " Left " there was very little
in it, if the Liberals are counted in with the " Right " and the
Communists, I.L.P. and Common Wealth with the "Left," and
if the " Independents " are divided roughly between the two.
Of course, such a calculation shows little ; for no one can say
how the Liberals would have voted if they had had to choose
between Churchillites and Labour at a second ballot. Under such
a system, the Labour Party would clearly have won the Election,
but with a much smaller majority than it actually secured.

Undoubtedly, the voting in the 1945 General Election worked
out favourably for the Labour Party, whereas in 1931 and in 1935
the luck had gone all the other way.   It has, however, to be
borne in mind that it is one of the virtues of the British parliamentary system that it tends to favour the strongest party and
thus to yield the basis for a Government with a majority of the
House of Commons behind it.   There is, of course, no guarantee
that this result will be achieved : it was not achieved either in
1910 or in 1924 or in 1929.   There is, however, a tendency that
way ; for the single-member constituency system tends to eliminate the lesser parties, or at all events to reduce their representation.   This, indeed, can be expected to help one party to gain
a clear majority only where there are not more than two main
parties contending for power.   As long as the Liberals were still
a party with a national following not far short of the others', the
need for minority Governments or Coalitions was bound to
arise.   As soon, however, as Liberalism fell to a markedly inferior
position, its quota of seats naturally tended to fall much below
its share in the voting.   In 1931 the Labour Party, bereft of its
best-known leaders, had been overwhelmed by a coalition of
Tories and Liberals, including both the Liberal factions.   In
1935 the decline of Liberalism had given the Tories a very great
preponderance : in 1945 it had the opposite effect of helping to
put the Labour Party, with its excess of about 2,000,000 votes
over the Churchillian parties, into power with a large majority
over all other parties.

In all, the Labour Party won 394 seats out of 640 ; and seven
more went to parties unquestionably on the left—three I.L.Pers,
two Communists, one Labour Independent (Pritt) and one
Common Wealth.   Of the dozen Independents, seven, of widely
varying views, were elected for University seats, two were Irish
Nationalists, and the remaining three belonged broadly to the
left.   As against a left numbering well over 400, the Conservatives,

Ulster Unionists, Nationals and Liberal Nationals, *plus* a few University Independents, mustered fewer than 220 : the Liberals, apart from the rest of the University Independents, won only a dozen seats. Labour had a secure majority of nearly 150, even if every other party and every Independent voted on the other side. Out of 394 Labour M.P.s elected, 321 (including a very few returned unopposed) won their seats by clear majorities—216 in straight fights, and 105 in three- or more- cornered contests. As against this the Churchill candidates had only eighty-five clear majorities—twenty-nine in straight fights with Labour, and the rest either in the absence of Labour candidates or in contests with three or more candidates in the field. The Liberals had five clear majorities—all in straight fights, three against Labour and two against Churchillites. Thus, only seventy-three Labour M.P.s were elected on a minority vote, as compared with 130 Conservatives, Nationals, and Liberal Nationals. Seventy-one Labour M.P.s were either unopposed or had majorities of more than 15,000, as against only eleven such majorities on the other side. On the other hand there were twenty-five Labour majorities of less than 1,000, as against seventeen for Churchillite and three for Liberal candidates.

The difference between votes cast and seats won over the country as a whole was to a certain extent affected by Labour's proportionately stronger position in a good many constituencies with very small electorates—especially in war-damaged East and Central London, Out of fifty-two constituencies with electorates of under 30,000, the Labour Party won forty-two, the Churchillites eight, and the Liberals and Communists one each ; whereas in the eighty-seven vast constituencies with electorates of over 70,000 there was a nearer balance, the Labour Party winning fifty-three, Common Wealth one, and the Churchillites thirty-three. Even so, the Labour Party won a large clear majority in the swollen " dormitory " areas.

The Labour Party polled a clear majority of all the votes cast in London County, in the English Boroughs, and in Wales. If the I.L.P. is reckoned in, it polled a clear majority in the Scottish Burghs also : without the I.L.P. it was just short of half the total vote. In the English County Divisions it polled 44½ per cent : in the Scottish Counties just over 46 per cent. Only in Northern Ireland and in the Universities did it do badly : in every other type of constituency it was ahead of the combined vote of the Churchillites.

By Regions, Labour representation was increased everywhere. In comparison with 1935 the Regions showing the greatest gain were Lancashire and Cheshire (38), Greater London (29), London County (26), the West Midlands (24), and the East Midlands and the Eastern Counties (20 each).   A more instructive comparison, however, is with 1929, when the Labour Party had come within striking distance of a clear majority. In 1945, on that comparison, it had twenty-three more members in Greater London, sixteen more in the Eastern Counties, twelve more in Lancashire and Cheshire, and also in London County, eleven more in Southern England apart from Greater London and the South-west, and nine more in the West Midlands. It had only the same number as in 1929 in Scotland and in Wales, only three more in the North-east, and only four more in Yorkshire.

These comparisons show how large a part London, including Greater London, played in the victory. Next to them Lancashire and Cheshire, the West Midlands, and the Eastern Counties had the largest share in the turnover of seats. Scotland, Wales, and most of Northern England contributed little more than in 1929, when they were already the chief centres of Labour's strength. It proved a much harder task to convert rural Wales than to win a good many dormitory areas which had been regarded as safe Tory strongholds. In Scotland progress was disappointing outside the definitely industrial districts : the Scottish Liberals, who had always been inveterate enemies of Labour, went over to Toryism in considerably higher proportions than Liberals in most parts of England.

There has been much argument about the class-distribution of the voting in the General Election of 1945. For my part, I have no doubt about what generally happened. The wealthy, and also the well-to-do voted against the Labour candidates in fully as high proportions as in previous elections ; but there was a big turnover of voting both among the poor and among the groups standing in social estimation just above the working-class level. To anyone who knows the social characteristics of the spread of London and the dispersal of population in recent years, the following Table, showing the distribution of seats in seven " round-London " counties, speaks for itself, not only in the sharp contrast between Essex and Surrey, but also in the relative strength of the two main parties in Middlesex and in Kent.

Of the new constituencies created in these counties, mainly in areas of extensive inter-war development as housing estates,

REPRESENTATION OF " GREATER LONDON " COUNTIES IN THE PARLIAMENT
OF 1945
(Including all seats in each county—Boroughs as well as County Divisions)

	Labour	Conservative or Allied	Others
Bedfordshire . .	2	1	—
Buckinghamshire . .	3	1	—
Hertfordshire . .	4	2	—
Essex . . .	21	3	1*
Middlesex . . .	17	7	—
Kent . . .	6	8	—
Surrey . . .	3	11	—
	56	33	1

*Common Wealth

the Labour Party won thirteen, and the Churchillites four—
including Churchill's own election for Woodford, with no Labour
candidate in the field. Anyone who will go through the list of
seats won by the two sides will soon see for himself how closely
the dividing line runs between essentially middle-class and
essentially working-class-cum-blackcoat areas. Thus, the Conservatives won North Croydon, and Labour South Croydon ;
and there was a similar sharing in the case of South and North
Hendon, West and East Harrow, and East and West Ealing. The
closest contests, with majorities of less than 1,500, were in
Wimbledon, Epping, Barnet, Hitchin, Uxbridge and North
Wembley, won by Labour, and in North Croydon and Carshalton,
won by Conservatives. The largest Labour majorities were in
Dagenham, Dartford, Edmonton, Southall, West Willesden,
West Ealing, North Tottenham, and Barking—all over 15,000 :
the largest Conservative majorities were in Woodford (Churchill,
17,200), Hornsey (12,669) and Chertsey (12,262), all the rest
being under 10,000.

Labour's failure to win over the wealthier classes can also be
illustrated by the course of the Election in the principal seaside
resorts and inland spas. Out of twelve Borough seats in England
belonging to this type, the Conservatives won eleven, the only
Labour victory being in Great Yarmouth, which is a fishing port
fully as much as a seaside resort. Out of eleven County Divisions
of a similar type the Conservatives won ten, Lowestoft being the
only Labour victory. In most of these resorts there were Liberal
candidates, who polled relatively well, in two cases relegating the
Labour candidate to the third place. In Bournemouth the

Conservative majority was more than 20,000 over the Liberal, with Labour a little way further behind. In Worthing it was nearly 20,000 over Labour, with the Liberal a long way behind. The smallest majority over Labour in this group of seats was 2,000 at Bath. Most of the majorities were fairly large, and might have been larger still had there been no Liberals in the field.

The position is not so easy to bring out in other areas, where for the most part constituencies are necessarily more mixed in a social sense. But no one who looks with knowledge at the distribution of victories in the great cities will be in any doubt. The Labour Party, more than at any previous election, won the votes of the poorer urban workers and also those of a considerable stratum of the population that lives on small salaries and not on weekly wages. It also received a large majority of the votes cast by "other ranks" in the armed forces, but, I believe, despite the large number of officer Labour candidates, only a small proportion of those of the holders of commissions.

It is interesting to compare what took place in 1945 with the great Liberal landslide of 1906, when of course Labour was only a fourth party, fighting a small number of seats and outnumbered

ROUGH REGIONAL COMPARISON BETWEEN THE LIBERAL VICTORY OF 1906 AND THE LABOUR VICTORY OF 1945

	Liberals		Liberal & Labour		Labour	
	1906	1911	1906	1911	1945 after Election	1945 before Election
London County .	38	26	40	29	48	27
Greater London .	10	5	11	6	45*	13
Lancashire and Cheshire . .	41	28	54	38	56	26
Yorkshire . .	38	34	41	40	44	28
North . .	23	20	27	25	28	15
West Midlands .	28	10	29	13	34†	14
East Midlands .	31	18	32	23	33‡	11
Eastern . .	35	21	36	22	18	2
Southern . .	28	7	29	7	10	—
South Western .	34	18	34	18	15	4
Wales . .	33	26	34	31	25	19
Scotland . .	58	58	60	61	37	23

*Including thirteen New Constituencies.
†Including two New Constituencies.
‡Including one New Constituency.

NOTE.—Regional distribution in this Table does not quite tally with the Regions used in other Tables in this book. The reason is that the figures for this Table are taken from my wife's *The General Election, 1945, and After* (Fabian Society, 1945).

by the Irish Nationalists as well as by Liberals and Conservatives. Leaving out all Ireland, including the North, we have, in a smaller total, 397 Liberals in 1906, as compared with 393 Labour M.P.s in 1945. The Conservatives had 132, as compared with 193 in 1945—or, including the Liberal Nationals, 206. Where Labour in 1906 had thirty, the Liberals in 1945 had only twelve. After the two General Elections of 1910, the Liberals had shrunk by 126 to 271, whereas the Tories had increased by 114 to 246. Labour had risen to forty-two, not by winning new seats but because the Miners' M.P.s, who had previously sat as Liberals, had mostly joined the Labour Party. It would be, of course, dangerous to argue from this one instance how big a swing is well within the limits of possibility under the British electoral system. Since 1910 the electorate has been enormously enlarged by woman suffrage as well as by other changes. There has been redistribution of seats, and further redistribution is now to come. Nevertheless, the pattern of the Liberal victory of 1906 has a considerable regional resemblance to that of Labour's victory in 1945, except in a few areas—Greater London, where Labour is much stronger than Liberalism was in 1906, even after allowance has been made for the increase in the number of seats ; the Eastern, Southern, and South-western regions, where Labour has not yet approached the Liberal strength of forty years ago ; and Scotland, where also Labour is a long way short of Liberalism's former predominance. It will be seen that the regions which showed the greatest instability between 1906 and 1911 were the West Midlands and the South, and after them Greater London, Lancashire and Cheshire, the East Midlands, the Eastern Counties and the South-west. These are largely the regions in which the Labour Party in 1945 made the most sweeping gains. I leave it to my readers to draw their own conclusions, or to draw none, about future electoral possibilities should the situation turn against Labour. It is, however, necessary to point out, on the other side, that there is no valid reason why Labour should not win, especially in Scotland and in the South and South-west, a good many constituencies in which it came nowhere near victory in 1945.

A General Election in which so many victories were won naturally increased the proportion of Divisional Labour Party candidates among the elected M.P.s. Out of 603 Labour candidates, no fewer than 439 stood under the auspices of Divisional Parties, including two put forward by University Parties. Only 126 candidates were put forward under Trade Union auspices, including thirty-five Miners.   The Co-operative Party, with thirty-three candidates, and the North of Ireland Labour Party, with six, completed the total.   Of the 393 who were elected, 248 stood under Divisional Party auspices, twenty-three under Co-operative auspices, and 121 under Trade Union auspices.   Thus, only five out of 126 Trade Union candidates were defeated (two in agricultural areas), as against 189 out of 439 Divisional and University Party candidates, and ten out of thirty-three Co-opera-tors.   Obviously the Trade Union candidates, with adequate finance behind them, and usually with plenty of time before the Election, had been able to secure adoption for the safer seats—and had also been able to make them the safer by proper prepara-tion and organisation.   As against this, a good many Divisional candidates were adopted late in the day, and a good many went into the battle short of funds.   The Co-operative candidates, though they shared the advantage of the Trade Union nominees, fared much less well—mainly because there was a reluctance on the part of the Divisional Labour Parties to accept them in more than a few areas in which the Labour cause had strong support.

The Divisional Party representatives had thus a large clear majority in the Parliamentary Labour Party of 1945.   Of course, they included many Trade Unionists, among them many who received substantial support from their Trade Unions.   Out of sixty-nine Trade Union bodies affiliated to the Labour Party, only twenty-three put candidates of their own into the field under Trade Union auspices :   the rest took action through their branches, as affiliated bodies of the Divisional Parties.   It is not possible—nor would the figures have any meaning—to say how many of the Labour M.P.s were members of Trade Unions or of Co-operative Societies, or of both.   What can be said is that the Parliamentary Labour Party of 1945, although it included a greatly enlarged group of, mainly young, middle-class men and women—professional men and women, such as lawyers, journa-lists, doctors and teachers, and also ex-officers who had had no chance of settling down to a profession—still consisted in a large majority of men and women of working-class, or near-working-class, origin and outlook.   Of the Labour candidates nominated, forty-one were women and twenty-one of these were returned.   Only a single Labour candidate lost his deposit in the Election, and this was in North Hammersmith, where he was standing against a strongly supported Labour Independent, D. N. Pritt, who had held the seat in the previous Parliament.

LABOUR AT THE GENERAL ELECTION OF 1945

	1945	1935	1929	Net gains over 1935	Net gains over 1929	Seats not fought 1945
London County . . .	48*	22	36	26	12	3
Greater London . . .	41	12	18	29	23	1
Southern England . .	16	—	5	16	11	3
Western England . .	11	3	7	8	4	—
South-west England . .	4	—	1	4	3	1
West Midlands . . .	34	10	25	24	9	3
East Midlands . . .	30	9	22	21	8	—
Eastern Counties . .	19†	—	4	19	15	2
Lancashire and Cheshire .	56	18	44	38	12	—
Yorkshire	44	27	40	17	4	3
North-west England . .	3	2	3	1	—	1
North-east England . .	25	13	22	12	3	—
Wales and Monmouth . .	25	18	25	7	—	1
Scotland	37‡	20	37	17	—	3
Northern Ireland . .	1	—	—	1	1	4
Universities. . . .	—	—	—	—	—	10

*Also one Labour Independent, and one Communist.
†Also one Common Wealth.
‡Also three I.L.P. and one Communist.

THE GENERAL ELECTION OF 1945 : SUCCESSFUL CANDIDATES

	Labour	Ind. Labour Common Wealth and Communist	Conserva- tive and Nationalist	Liberal National	Liberal	Others	Total
London County . .	48	2	12	—	—	—	62
Greater London . .	41	—	17	—	—	—	58
Southern England . .	16	—	42	—	1	—	59
Western England . .	11	—	10	—	—	1	22
South-west England . .	4	—	9	2	1	—	16
West Midlands. . .	34	—	15	—	—	1	50
East Midlands . . .	30	—	8	1	—	1	40
Eastern Counties . .	19	1	6	3	1	—	30
Lancashire and Cheshire .	56	—	25	1	—	—	82
Yorkshire . . .	44	—	12	—	1	—	57
North-west England . .	3	—	2	—	1	—	6
North-east England . .	25	—	3	—	—	—	28
Wales and Monmouth .	25	—	3	1	6	—	35
Scotland	37	4	25	5	—	—	71
Northern Ireland . .	1	—	9	—	—	2	12
Universities . . .	—	—	4	—	1	7	12
TOTALS . . .	394	7	202	13	12	12	640

(thousands)

THE VOTING IN THE GENERAL ELECTION OF 1945

(excluding Universities and three Unopposed Returns)

	Electors	Conservative and National	Liberal National	Labour	I.L.P., Communist Party and Common Wealth	Liberals	Others	Total
London County	2,005	480.0	16.5	770.1	21.9	51.9	28.0	1,368.4
English Boroughs	10,987	3,356.2	320.7	4,595.4	64.7	757.3	67.9	9,162.2
English Counties	13,978	4,161.9	250.5	4,606.9	79.4	1,099.0	125.0	10,322.8
Welsh Boroughs*	452	67.4	19.2	198.0	15.9	26.1	9.4	335.9
Welsh Counties*	1,305	185.2	44.9	581.2	—	172.5	11.1	994.8
Scottish Burghs	1,536	392.3	36.1	562.7	57.3	59.3	22.8	1,130.6
Scottish Counties	1,797	486.1	72.0	581.7	20.9	73.5	25.2	1,259.4
Northern Ireland	777	392.5	—	96.2	—	—	231.1	719.8
TOTALS	32,836.4	9,521.6	759.9	11,992.2	260.1	2,239.6	520.5	25,293.9

PERCENTAGE DISTRIBUTION OF VOTES

(per cent)

	Churchill	Labour	Liberal	Others
London County	36.25	56.25	3.8	3.7
English Boroughs	38.0	52.0	8.5	1.5
English Counties	42.8	44.6	10.6	2.0
Welsh Boroughs*	25.8	59.0	7.8	7.4
Welsh Counties*	23.1	58.5	17.3	1.1
Scottish Burghs	37.9	49.8	5.2	7.1
Scottish Counties	44.3	46.2	5.8	3.7
Northern Ireland	54.5	13.3	—	32.2
TOTALS	39.9	48.0	9.0	3.1

*Including Monmouthshire.

LABOUR CANDIDATES AND M.P.s IN THE GENERAL ELECTION OF 1945
ARRANGED ACCORDING TO THE AUSPICES UNDER WHICH THEY STOOD

	Candidates	Elected
Divisional Parties	437	248
University Parties	2	—
Co-operative Party	33	23
Miners	35	35
National Union of Railwaymen . .	13	12
Railway Clerks	9	9
Locomotive Engineers	1	1
Transport and General Workers . .	18	17
General and Municipal Workers . .	10	10
Distributive and Allied Workers . .	7	7
Shop Assistants	1	1
Clerical and Administrative Workers .	1	1
Life Assurance Workers	1	1
Builders	1	1
Woodworkers	4	4
Patternmakers	2	2
Engineers	4	3
Electricians	1	1
Iron and Steel Trades	2	2
Textile Factory Workers . . .	3	3
Boot and Shoe Operatives . . .	4	4
Typographical Association . . .	2	2
London Compositors	2	2
Operative Printers	1	1
Agricultural Workers	3	1
Post Office Workers	1	1
North of Ireland Labour Party . .	6	1
	604	393

CHAPTER XI

LABOUR IN LOCAL GOVERNMENT

Early efforts for Labour representation—School Boards, Vestries, and Boards of Guardians—Effects of the Local Government Acts of 1888 and 1894—The Borough franchise—The I.L.P. and local Labour representation—The Fabian Society and the London County Council—The "Progressive Party"—Fabian propaganda and municipal enterprise—The Labour Representation Committee's small effect on Local Government—The variety of Labour candidatures—The position of Labour in local Councils up to 1914—The local elections of 1913—General state of municipal politics in 1914—The position on the London County Council and on the Metropolitan Borough Councils—The disappearance of the School Boards in England and Wales—Labour's local government policy up to 1914—Labour's sweeping local electoral victories after the first World War—The Labour reverse of 1922—The subsequent recovery up to 1929—Further reverses in 1930 and 1931—Renewed advances in the 1930's—The capture of the L.C.C. in 1934—Further successes in London and the provinces—The position of Labour in Local Government in 1939—The growth of party contests—The decline of the Liberals—Labour's weakness on the County Councils—Labour's local government policy between the wars—Municipalisation less a dominant issue—The importance of housing—Effects of the growth of national social services—The question of "enabling" powers—The increased dependence of Local Authorities on national finance and central government policy—The lack of co-ordination of local Labour policies—The Work of the Fabian Society and the I.L.P. in the field of local government information—The Fabian Society's Local Government Bureau—The Labour Party at length sets up a Local Government Department in 1936—Its previous work in this field—Model Standing Orders for Labour Council Groups—The problems of local government areas and finance—Labour Party differences about Local Government—The Advisory Committee's Report of 1918-19—The 1936 Report on *Local Government Administration*—The 1942-3 Report on *The Future of Local Government*—Regionalism advocated—The reception of the Report at the Labour Party Conference—The resumption of local elections in 1945—Sweeping Labour victories—The trend sharply reversed in 1947—Reasons for the 1947 defeat.

There is one vitally important aspect of the Labour Party's history about which, in the foregoing chapters of this book, hardly anything has been said. I mean, the Labour Party's activities, considerable from the very outset, in the field of Local Government. At one stage I tried to incorporate the record of this development in my general narrative ; but I soon found that, presented in that way, the story both impaired the clarity of the general exposition and failed to give any clear picture of the local side of Labour Party life and growth. I therefore decided to deal with the whole question, as far as I have space to deal with it at all, in a separate chapter ; and this involved placing the chapter at the end of the narrative part of my book—for, as narrative, this history must be considered as ending at 1945, though I am including a final chapter of comment on the events of the years

442

which followed immediately upon Labour's resounding electoral successes in that year.

Labour efforts to secure representation on local governing authorities go back almost, if not quite, as far as movements for Labour representation in Parliament. If we look back only to 1867—the year of the Second Reform Act—and thus leave the Chartists out of account, we find the first Labour candidates for Parliament taking the field at the General Election of 1868— to be followed speedily by Labour candidates for the new School Boards set up under Forster's Education Act of 1870. From that point, School Board elections were steadily contested in a number of areas by working-class candidates, usually connected with Trade Unions or with local Radical Working Men's Associations. There were particularly hot contests for the London School Board ; and, in London and elsewhere, Labour candidates appeared from time to time in other local government contests— for London Vestries, for example, and for Boards of Guardians, despite the deterrent effect of the extremely undemocratic basis of election. Probably for Borough Councils too, here and there, though I cannot recall an instance ; and here too the narrowness of the franchise offered little hope of success and the way was barred in any event to actual workmen, so that only a few who had become small masters or reached some other coign of vantage could even stand.

In effect, except in the case of the School Boards, there was little opening for Labour activity in Local Government until after 1888. Then came, within six years, the establishment of elected County Councils, including the London County Council, the creation of Parish Councils and Urban District Councils— the latter replacing a variety of earlier authorities—and the sweeping away of the cumulative property vote in the election of Boards of Guardians. The Borough franchise, still based on assess-ment of local rates in such a way as to exclude those tenants who paid rates indirectly through their landlords, remained heavily weighted against the working classes ; but an increasing number of workmen who owned their own houses or paid direct rates acquired the municipal vote, and it thus became possible for a sprinkling of Labour or working-class candidates to appear. They were still few ; but at least it was possible for a start to be made.

Indeed, the local government reforms of 1888 and 1894 aroused high hopes, and were among the factors which led to the

rapid growth first of local Labour Electoral Associations and
Labour Councils, and, then, largely on the foundations thus
laid, of Keir Hardie's Independent Labour Party of 1893. From
the first, the I.L.P. aimed at fighting local as well as national
elections where it saw a chance of either success or useful Labour
and Socialist propaganda ; and the Fabian Society, above all in
London but also locally through the provincial Fabian Societies
(which were mostly absorbed by the I.L.P. after 1894), set out
deliberately to foster Labour interest in Local Government and to
produce programmes of action for Labour and " Progressive "
representatives on every type of local authority.   The Fabian
Society's interest was focused mainly upon the new London
County Council and was directed, unlike that of the I.L.P. in the
provinces but like that of a good many of the local Trade Unionists, to securing the victory of a " Progressive Party " based on a
combination of Liberal and Labour forces.   Its activities thus
ran to some extent counter to the endeavour of the I.L.P. to
promote a breach between Labour and Liberalism and to establish a fully independent working-class party ; and this prevented
the Fabian propaganda in favour of advanced municipal programmes of sanitary, housing, and educational development and
of socialisation of public utility services from having as much
effect on the Labour movement as might have been the case
had there been no conflict over the question of Liberal-Labour
co-operation.   In London, the Fabians were largely successful in
shaping the policy of the Progressives on the London County
Council, especially in the educational field.   Elsewhere, their
tracts, setting forth clearly the possibilities open to local Councils
of all types that were prepared to make full use of their statutory
powers, had a considerable effect, by no means limited to Labour
representatives or local Labour Associations.   But, because the
Fabians as a body stood aloof from the attempt to create a separate
Labour Party in Local Government, advocates of strictly independent Labour representation, both nationally and locally,
were apt to be suspicious of them and to borrow less from the
schemes which were poured out for their use than they might
have done had the Fabians been prepared to throw over their
hopes of converting the Liberals, if not to national, at least to a
measure of Municipal Socialism.

The establishment of the Labour Representation Committee
in 1900 had little effect on Labour's participation in local politics.
The L.R.C. had no local electoral machinery of its own : it

worked mainly through local Trades and Labour Councils or Trades Councils which existed, or came into existence, quite apart from its efforts. Indeed, this situation, as we have seen, continued to exist in most areas right up to 1918. This meant that local electoral activity in connection with Local Government remained in most places largely in the hands of the I.L.P., which supplied and financed a high proportion of all the Labour candidates who stood in municipal or other local government contests. In some areas the Trades Councils, or Trades and Labour Councils, took an active part, putting forward candidates sometimes as " Labour " or " Trade Union and Labour," but also sometimes as merely " Trade Union," or even as Progressives or Independents with Trade Union support, or as nominees of a particular Trade Union. This last was particularly common in the mining districts, in which a good many candidates for local, and later for County, Councils came forward under the auspices of the Miners' Lodges or Local or District Associations. The Social Democratic Federation also put forward its own " Socialist and Labour " candidates in areas where its branches were active.

The materials for any comprehensive picture of Labour activity and participation in Local Government before the World War of 1914–18 would be difficult to gather together ; and as far as I know the task has never been attempted except for a very few areas, such as Bristol, Bradford and Aberdeen.* In any case, it cannot be attempted here. All I can do is to give a very rough idea of the general position as it was before local elections were suspended for the duration of the war—as they were to be again in 1939. In 1913, according to inevitably incomplete figures compiled by the I.L.P., 494 Labour and Socialist candidates were put forward under various auspices at the November municipal elections. Of these, 196 were elected, giving a gain of 106 new seats as against twenty-one seats lost—a net gain of eighty-five seats. Of these candidates nearly half—228—stood under the auspices of the I.L.P. ; and of the successful candidates 109 out of 196 were I.L.P. nominees—a net I.L.P. gain of forty-four seats. In the same year 353 Labour candidates appeared at the District and Parish Council elections, and of these 196 were successful—a net gain of sixty-eight seats. For the Boards of Guardians the number of Labour candidates is unknown ; but

*See *An Account of the Labour and Socialist Movement in Bristol.* Recorded by Samson Bryher, 1929. Also *History of the Trades Council and the Trade Union Movement in Aberdeen*, by William Diack, 1939. And, for Bradford, see *Socialism over Sixty Years*, by A. Fenner Brockway, 1946.

the I.L.P. reported a net " Labour " gain of forty-seven seats. This was the most successful year in local government contests that Labour had ever experienced : it was the culminating point in a development that had been proceeding, though not without interruption, since the General Election of 1906. In 1912, in the municipal elections only, there had been, according to the I.L.P., a net " Labour " gain of thirty-six seats. The Labour Party, in a later compilation of the figures, put the net Labour gains at the municipal elections at seventy-eight for 1911, forty-two for 1912, and eighty-five for 1913.

Of course, 494 candidates, spread over all the Boroughs, were not a very large total ; but it compared reasonably well with the fifty-eight candidates for Parliament whom the Labour Party had put into the field at the General Election of December, 1910. In a great many Boroughs there were still no party candidates at all, at any rate nominally, contests being fought, where there were any, ostensibly on non-party lines, with Ratepayers' Associations dominating the position in some places and various types of " Independents " in others.   Except in a very few mining areas Labour had made no bid to secure representation on the County Councils outside London ; and in London most of the Trade Unionists and Socialists still fought as " Progressives." A few pioneers, such as George Lansbury, who sat from 1909 to 1912, had won seats as Socialists, but in 1913 the independent Labour strength on the London County Council was one—Susan Lawrence—who had been elected as a Municipal Reformer, but had changed sides. There were, however, quite a number of Trade Unionists and Fabians in the ranks of the Progressives— though the Liberal-Labour alliance in London politics was already beginning to break down. Harry Gosling, for example, a leading figure in the Transport Workers' Federation, had sat for a number of years as a Progressive alderman ; and so had W. Stephen Sanders, the Organising Secretary of the Fabian Society, until he transferred his allegiance to the Labour Party some time after 1900. The London Labour Party, which signalised the advent of real Labour independence in metropolitan affairs, was founded only in 1914.

Well before 1914, however, Labour candidates had begun to make some impact on a number of the Metropolitan Borough Councils, which had been set up in 1899 to replace the medley of vestries and district boards within the London County area. After the 1912 elections Labour was represented on at least seven of these Councils. It had fifteen seats at Woolwich (out of thirty-six), ten at Poplar (out of forty-two), eight at Deptford (out of thirty-six), and smaller contingents in Kensington (six), Shoreditch (four) Lambeth (two) and Islington (one). Nowhere except in Woolwich was it within striking distance of a majority ; and this, it should be remembered, was the one district in which there was a well-organised local Labour League based on individual membership.

In all, there must have been by 1914 about 420 Labour representatives sitting on municipal Councils of various types, not including a few County Councillors in the mining areas, or a much larger number on District Councils, Parish Councils, and Boards of Guardians. The School Boards, except in Scotland, had disappeared in 1902, when their functions were transferred to Local Education Authorities made up mainly of elected County or Borough Councillors. This transfer had given Labour an added interest in municipal and County Council affairs ; for education was one of the main concerns of local Labour organisations in the local government field. The Education Act of 1902 had given considerable scope for development of schools above the ordinary elementary standard under public auspices ; and in some areas, notably Bradford, the I.L.P. had made full use of these powers the main plank in its municipal platform. Bradford, largely under F. W. Jowett's influence, had also been foremost in urging the feeding of school children, and had taken prompt advantage of the powers conferred by Jowett's own Act of 1906—the Labour Party's first legislative success in the new Parliament. Apart from education and the feeding and medical inspection and treatment of school children, the issues which Labour pressed most urgently in Local Government were fair wages and conditions for the employees of local authorities, the adoption and enforcement of the Fair Wages Clause in public contracts, the eight hours day, and the local provision of work for the unemployed. In some areas—notably Glasgow and Birmingham—there was also active pressure in support of municipal housing and slum clearance schemes ; and there was also, of course, in relation to the Boards of Guardians continuous agitation for improved treatment both of the unemployed and of other classes of paupers, especially the aged and the disabled.

The local elections of 1919, held after a suspension of four or five years, made an immense difference to Labour's position in Local Government. At the municipal elections, with about

900 candidates, Labour, including the Co-operators, who for the first time appeared in the field on a considerable scale, made a net gain of 412 seats, and for the first time captured control of a considerable city—Bradford.   Fifteen seats were gained in Manchester, eleven in Liverpool, ten at Swindon ; and there were also big gains at Derby, Birmingham, Coventry, Nottingham, Leeds, Sheffield, Preston, Burnley, Bristol, Blackburn, Bolton, Stockport, Norwich, and a number of other places, as well as in industrial Scotland.   In the London Metropolitan Borough elections still more sweeping victories were won.   Labour had a net gain of no fewer than 526 seats and captured control, in several cases with sweeping majorities, of no fewer than twelve Councils. In addition majorities were won on three County Councils— Durham, Glamorgan and Monmouthshire ; and on the London County Council the Labour Party's strength rose from one to fifteen elected councillors, *plus* two aldermen.

So sweeping a victory was too good to last.   The municipal elections of 1920 showed an almost even balance, with a net Labour gain of nineteen seats.   1921 was better, with a net gain of eighty ; but then, in 1922, in the midst of the post-war slump, the councillors who had been elected in 1919 came up for re-election, and the Labour Party found itself defending a very large number of seats won in 1919 on a small poll and in many cases by narrow majorities.   It suffered a net loss in the municipal elections outside London of 153 seats—rather more than one-third of the number gained in 1919.   On the Metropolitan Borough Councils it fared much worse, losing 320 net out of its 526 gains of three years before, and keeping its majority in only four Boroughs.   On the London County Council, on the other hand, it had one net gain, and secured an additional alderman as well ; but it lost control of two out of the three County Councils on which it had won a majority in 1919, holding only Glamorgan. Its majority on the Bradford City Council had already been lost in 1920, after only a single year.

This setback was followed by a recovery, albeit not on the scale of 1919.   In every year from 1923 to 1929 the municipal elections showed on balance substantial gains.   By 1925 the losses of 1922 had been more than wiped out, except on the Metropolitan Borough Councils.   There the triennial elections of 1925 brought a net gain of 105 seats, and raised the number of Labour-controlled Boroughs to eight.   In the London County Council elections the Labour Party fared much better, more than doubling its strength in Councillors—from sixteen to thirty-five—and securing another alderman. Labour also held its majority on the Glamorgan County Council, and won back Durham.

During the next four years Labour continued to gain ground, at an increasing rate, rising to a peak of 219 gains in the provincial municipal elections of 1929—the year of Labour's outstanding parliamentary success. Meanwhile, in 1928 Labour's strength on the London County Council had been raised to forty-two, *plus* six aldermen, and there had been ninety-five net gains at the Metropolitan Borough Council elections, without any increase in the number of Boroughs under Labour control. This number remained at eight* ; but by this time Labour had also majority control in twenty-one provincial Boroughs.

1930, with the Second Labour Government beginning to encounter difficulties over unemployment, brought the first set-back since 1922. It was not serious, the net loss being only seventy-three seats on all the provincial Borough Councils. 1931, following on the fall of the Government and the secession of Ramsay MacDonald, had much bigger results. Labour lost 238 provincial Borough seats ; the number of County Boroughs under Labour control fell from eleven to eight, and of other Boroughs from nine to eight. Labour also lost seven seats on the L.C.C., bringing its strength back to where it had been in 1925, and 210 seats on the Metropolitan Borough Councils, with the loss of control in five Boroughs. There was also a net loss of nine seats in the County Council elections.

These disasters were not surprising : they were as nothing in comparison with Labour's parliamentary defeat the same year. After a year, 1932, which showed small Labour gains, the losses of 1931 were completely wiped out in the provinces in 1933, where Labour gained net 250 municipal seats. This was followed by a gain of 305 in 1934, when the number of County Boroughs under Labour control rose to twenty-one, and that of non-County Boroughs to eighteen. In this year, moreover, the Labour Party, with thirty-four net gains, won a clear majority on the London County Council ; and in the Metropolitan Borough elections its victory was almost as sweeping as in 1919. It had a net gain of 472 seats, and after the election, fifteen—a clear majority—of the Metropolitan Councils were under Labour control. There were also large gains—117—in the County Council elections outside

*Battersea, Bermondsey, Bethnal Green, Deptford, Poplar, Shoreditch, Stepney and Woolwich.

London. Comparatively, the results of the parliamentary General Election of 1935 were disappointing ; and in that year Labour's net municipal gains were also slight at a total of thirty. In 1936 the tide turned mildly against Labour, and there was a net loss of forty-eight seats, followed in 1937 and 1938 by a mild recovery, with net Labour gains of forty-one and eleven. In London, however, Labour's advance continued without interruption. The L.C.C. elections of 1937 brought a net gain of six seats, leaving the Labour Party in power with a large majority ; and fifty-one further gains on the Metropolitan Borough Councils raised the number of Labour-controlled Boroughs to seventeen. On the provincial County Councils seventy more seats were gained ; but the number of Councils under Labour control was still only three.

At the outbreak of war in 1939, the Labour Party had majorities on the L.C.C., on the County Councils of Durham, Glamorgan, and Monmouthshire, on eighteen out of seventy-nine County Boroughs, on twenty-four non-county Boroughs in England and Wales, and on fourteen Burghs, large and small, in Scotland. It also controlled seventy-six Urban Districts, and seventeen out of the twenty-nine Metropolitan Boroughs. Since it had made its challenge to the interests previously in control, there had been a rapid increase in the number of areas in which local elections were fought on party lines. This had long been the case in most towns in the North of England, where Conservatives and Liberals had contended for control before Labour entered the field as a third party. In areas of this type, the effect of Labour's growing strength made for the most part against the Liberals, who were gradually pushed, on one Council after another, into a position of numerical inferiority. This, however, left them in many areas holding the balance of power. In the South of England there had been many more instances of elections fought nominally along non-party lines, by Independents or under the auspices of Ratepayers' Associations or similar bodies. Where this had been the case, Labour candidates had often in practice to meet a united anti-Socialist opposition, which made it difficult for them to get a foothold. When they did succeed in winning a few seats, the effect was sometimes to bring the Conservatives into the field openly against them, and sometimes to cause the Liberals to break away and nominate candidates of their own. On the whole, there was an increasing tendency over the whole country for contests to be fought on party lines in all the considerable towns. This was much less the case in the country areas, including the majority of the Counties—partly because the conditions of service on a County Council, involving both heavy travelling expenses and absence from work, made it very difficult to secure Labour candidates outside the areas where the Miners' Associations were very strong. Parish Council and Rural District Council elections remained mainly personal, with little political organisation of contests. London elections were throughout hotly political, first between " Progressives " (Liberal and Labour), and " Municipal Reformers " (Conservatives), with a sprinkling of independent Labour candidates, and then, after the break-up of the " Progressives " in 1919, more and more between Labour and the Municipal Reformers, with the rump of the Progressives as a dwindling Liberal group. Liberalism for a long time held its municipal strength high, despite Labour's advances, in some of the Northern cities, such as Manchester ; and the Tories who had fallen heirs to Chamberlain's Radical Party kept their hold on Birmingham. Labour had won Sheffield in 1926, to lose it in 1932, and regain it in 1933. Leeds and Leicester were won in 1928. Stoke-on-Trent and Hull were won about the same time, only to be lost in 1930–1. Glasgow was won for the first time only in 1933.

In the earlier stages of Labour's campaign for control of Local Government, municipalisation of public utilities played a large part in the Labour programme. This was an essential element in the Fabian policy, which was based more than most Fabians cared to acknowledge on Joseph Chamberlain's. In Chamberlain's Radical days and for some time afterwards proposals for municipal ownership, though they always roused hot local controversy, were not for the most part regarded as raising the issue of " Socialism." It was largely the work of the Fabians in giving " municipal enterprise " a high place in the Socialist programme that rallied the Anti-Socialists against it and caused every proposal for its extension to be fought vehemently on party lines. This new attitude largely blocked the road for local Acts designed to give the municipalities extended trading powers ; and local Labour groups, without ceasing to advocate municipalisation, were forced to direct their practical attention mainly to other issues. Up to 1918, education had pride of place : after the first World War, the question of housing leapt right to the front. Governments were compelled to subsidise house-building and, however reluctantly, to give the Local Authorities a large place in the task of meeting the acute shortage of houses for letting at rents which working-class tenants could afford to pay. Slum-clearance, always financially unattractive to private enterprise, fell almost wholly to the Local Authorities. Thus, house-building, midway between a public health service and a trading enterprise, became one of the main planks in the Labour municipal platform, and largely elbowed out other projects of municipal trading, except in the development of local electricity services.

Over the same period, the development of health and unemployment insurance, following on the initiation of Old Age Pensions, removed a good deal of the work that had fallen to the Boards of Guardians, with the result that controversy in connection with them came to turn more and more on the single question of the treatment of the long-term unemployed who had exhausted their claims to insurance benefits or, having heavy obligations for dependants, could not subsist without additional help. This meant that interest in Guardians' elections (up to their abolition in 1929) fluctuated much more between periods of good and bad trade, and also varied much more between areas of light and heavy unemployment. Over the same period, pressure on Local Authorities to provide work for the unemployed became stronger as unemployment became endemic on a large scale ; but provision of work also came to be much more a question of national as against local policy, because the power of the Local Authorities to take action depended more and more on government grants, which were a matter of central policy.

Nationally, the Labour Party continued to press for the granting of wider powers to the Local Authorities by means of some sort of Enabling Act that would allow them, without special parliamentary sanction, to embark on a wide range of trading and other enterprises. But neither Labour Government did anything to give these extended powers ; and outside the trading field the opportunities for municipal development were increasingly governed by national legislation and by the availability of grants in aid from the national exchequer. The areas in which Labour gained power were on the whole those most burdened by heavy local rates, most weakened by unemployment, and least able to undertake projects which involved spending money, unless most of it could be got from national sources. Consequently, the Labour-controlled Local Authorities, and also those in which Labour was the strongest single party, had in practice to concentrate mainly on making the most of the opportunities offered to them by national legislation—especially in the fields of housing, education, public health services, and, after 1929, the services transferred to them from the Boards of Guardians. In all these fields, Labour had a notably good local government record.

Up to a quite late stage, there was little attempt at the centre either to co-ordinate the Labour policies on the various local Councils or even to prescribe any common form of organisation for the Labour Groups. The Fabian Society, as early as 1900, formed a Local Government Information Bureau, and attempted to answer questions about Local Government, especially from Councillors and from local Labour Groups and organisations ; and the I.L.P. later followed suit. In 1911, after negotiations for Socialist Unity had broken down, the I.L.P. and the Fabian Society formed a Joint Committee, to which they both trans-ferred their work in the field of local government information ; and in 1913 this Joint Committee convened at Manchester a National Conference of Elected Persons on Local Authorities of all types—the first attempt to bring Labour Councillors together from different areas for the consideration of their common pro-blems. This initiative, however, was not followed up. The Joint Committee went out of existence during the war ; and in 1919 the Fabian Society set up a new Local Government Inquiry Bureau of its own, while the I.L.P. set out to supply local govern-ment information through its newly established Information Committee, which was chiefly concerned with other things. The new Fabian body had to be suspended in 1922, when W. A. Robson, who had been in charge of it, resigned ; but it was restarted in 1923, under an agreement with the Labour Party providing for the Fabian Society to finance it for the time being, but for the Labour Party to take it over later, when it had become firmly established. In 1924 the Bureau began to issue its own journal, *Local Government News*, and for some years very valuable work was done. But the donations which had been collected to finance the Bureau began to give out, and attempts to induce the Labour Party to accept financial responsibility were unavailing. In 1928 the Fabian Society reconstituted the Bureau as a Bureau of Local Government Information and Research, open to sub-scribing members ; but the number of subscribers proved all too small to carry the burden. At the end of 1931 *Local Government News* had to be given up. Robson resigned, and the Bureau was reduced in scale under the direction of H. Samuels. Three years later even the reduced burden proved too heavy. Samuels left, though he and others kept on a skeleton service with purely voluntary help. Only two years later, in 1936, was the Labour Party at length induced to set up its own Local Government Department at Transport House.

This, of course, does not mean that up to this date the Labour Party head office did nothing at all. As early as 1920 there appeared the first issue of a *Handbook of Local Government* for England and Wales prepared under the auspices of the Labour Party by its own Advisory Committee on Local Government in collaboration with the Labour Research Department, the Fabian Society, and the I.L.P. Information Committee. This *Handbook* was largely based on the sections dealing with Local Government that had been included in the Labour Year Books of 1916 and 1918. The Labour Party office had, however, no great share in the actual work, which was done mostly by the Labour Research Department and the Fabian Society. By 1924, when a revised version of the *Handbook* appeared, covering Scotland as well as England and Wales, the responsibility had been transferred to the Joint Publications Department of the Trades Union Congress and the Labour Party, and the other bodies had been dropped. The official Joint Research and Information Departments of the two main organisations were by this time paying some regular attention to local government work ; but the section of the *Handbook* dealing with " Labour Policy on Local Government " was noticeably jejune, and even then no attempt was being made either to work out a common national policy on local government problems or to keep the Labour representatives on different local bodies in regular touch with one another's work. After 1924 the Labour Party Head Office issued from time to time special publications relating to Local Government—for example, the *Local Government Speakers' Handbook*, published in 1925-6—and some local government information was also included in the *Labour Year Book* until publication was suspended in 1932-3. There was, however, little attempt to keep regular touch with those engaged in local government activities throughout the country.

Thus, right up to 1936, the Labour Groups on the local Councils were left to carry on with very little help from the Party headquarters. Nevertheless, from time to time, some tentative steps had been taken. The Labour Party Conferences of 1930 and 1931 debated and adopted Model Standing Orders which were recommended for adoption by local Council Groups ; and the establishment of County and Regional Federations and

Councils of the Labour Party in one area after another helped to promote consultation between Labour representatives on neighbouring authorities, though this was never the main purpose in view. There was in fact a good deal of informal consultation, but it was largely fortuitous and unorganised.

One reason for this casualness may have been that the Labour Party had no clear Local Government policy on the central issues of areas and finance, though it had of course clear enough policies on many more specific local government matters. In the years after 1918 there had been much debate on the Labour Party's Local Government Advisory Committee about these central issues ; but the effect had been to bring out sharp disagreements. On the Committee a majority favoured some sort of Regionalism, such as the Fabian Society had advocated earlier (in 1905) in its " New Heptarchy " plan ; but this was strongly opposed by a number of Labour people active in Local Government who hoped speedily to capture the control of their own industrial towns and saw in it a threat to snatch power away from them just as it was coming within their grasp. I remember that F. W. Jowett, in particular, met every regionalist project with the conclusive comment " That'd be a drag on Bradford." Consequently, though the Committee issued a plan of Local Government Reorganisation, including a form of Regionalism based on large Regions and tentative proposals for new sources of local finance in the proceeds of land-values taxation (or land nationalisation) and in receipts from a supplementary regional income tax, nothing was done to press forward its recommendations, and in effect the Labour Party remained without any clearly defined general policy until it issued in 1942 its Reconstruction Committee's provisional Report on *The Future of Local Government*, which was thereafter considered by numerous regional and local conferences and was debated and adopted, in face of strong opposition, at the Labour Party Conference of 1943. The Policy Committee which was busy restating the various aspects of the Labour Party programme during the 1930's had indeed produced, in 1936, a Report dealing with *Local Government Administration* ; but this Report touched none of the larger issues. It was concerned mainly with local election policy and with the organisation of Labour Council Groups and their relations with the Local Labour Parties, with which rested the formulation of the policies they were mandated to carry into effect.

The Report of 1942–3, on the other hand, did attempt to face the essential problems of Local Government structure. It emphasised that " there are too many Local Authorities, the majority of which are too small to tackle the problems of post-war reorganisation speedily and effectively." It drew attention to " the wide variations of the financial resources of authorities of the same status, with resulting inequalities in the standards of service." It held that " the present administration maintains an undesirable and artificial distinction between town and country," and that the movements of population " necessitate an extension of the Local Authority areas." It drew attention to the need for larger areas for the replanning of blitzed districts, and for town and country planning as a whole, in order " to ensure unity of plan over suitable geographical and industrial areas." It argued in favour of large areas for a National Health Service and for both elementary and higher education.

On this basis, the Report favoured the establishment of directly elected " Major Authorities " for large areas, with lesser Authorities within them for the carrying on of essentially local services. Its plans involved including the existing County Boroughs within the areas of the new Major Authorities, whose areas would be " an adaptation of the existing County areas, with amalgamations and absorptions of existing authorities, where necessary, to achieve a satisfactory unit."

At the Party Conference in 1943 these proposals were supported and opposed from a variety of standpoints ; but the opponents' main arguments seemed to be that Local Government could not be kept really democratic except within areas which were either fairly small or, where that was out of the question, fairly homogeneous. All the speakers agreed that there was need for drastic reform of local areas ; but they could not agree upon the form that reorganisation ought to take. In the end the resolution based on the Report was adopted by 1,542,000 against 966,000 ; but the size of the opposition did not give much hope of Local Government reform receiving a high priority in the programme of a Labour Government.

The resumption of Local Government elections in 1945, after an interval of six years, brought a repetition of the Labour victories of 1919. Indeed, the successes were on an even greater scale. In the provincial Borough Council elections of 1945, Labour followed up its General Election victory by scoring a net gain of 1,348 seats, as compared with 412 in 1919. In London there was no room, because of past gains, for so sensational an advance ; but the net gain in seats on the Metropolitan Borough Councils was 257, and the number of Boroughs under Labour control rose from seventeen to twenty-three, leaving only six still unwon. On the London County Council the number of Labour councillors rose from seventy-five to ninety, with fourteen aldermen instead of twelve. At the beginning of 1946 the Labour Party controlled forty-seven County Boroughs, as compared with eighteen in 1938, seventy-three non-county Boroughs as compared with twenty-four, and ten County Councils outside London, as compared with three. It had a net gain of 310 at the County Council elections. It controlled also 135 Urban Districts as against seventy-six in 1938, and was beginning to get a real foothold in the rural areas, where it controlled fifteen Rural Districts. In Scotland the number of Labour-controlled Boroughs rose from fourteen to thirty-seven ; and four County Councils, as against none before the war, had Labour majorities. In 1946 Labour slightly improved its position, with 196 further gains at the provincial Borough elections in England and Wales, and a rise to fifty-two County Boroughs under Labour control. In Scotland also there were further gains.

This trend was sensationally reversed in 1947, when the Labour Party had a net loss of 652 seats in England and Wales and sixty-eight in Scotland at the November municipal elections, which followed close upon the cuts in foods and other supplies made as a result of the dollar crisis. The remarkable feature of these elections was the high poll recorded almost everywhere. The Labour vote did not fall : the Labour candidates owed their defeat to the greatly increased success of their opponents in bringing voters to the poll. The reasons were complex. In the first place, the Conservative Central Office took a much bigger part in the elections than ever before. A considerable number of erstwhile " Independents " or " Ratepayers' " candidates stood as Conservatives, and the Conservative Party threw its full weight into the struggle, which was fought by the Conservative candidates almost entirely on national, rather than local, issues. The abolition of the basic petrol ration, the cuts in food supplies, the reduction in available supplies of other consumers' goods due to the export drive—all these were used as means of bringing voters to the poll to protest against the " austerities " imposed by the Labour Government. The Conservatives also exploited without scruple the housing shortage and the controls imposed on the entry of workers into non-essential occupations. In effect, they

(For footnotes see opposite)

LABOUR IN LOCAL GOVERNMENT, 1907–47

Year	Provincial Boroughs, England and Wales — Net Gains	Net Losses	Boroughs controlled by Labour‡	London County Council — Labour strength in: Councillors	Aldermen	Metropolitan Boroughs — Net Gains	Net Losses	Boroughs controlled by Labour	County Councils, England and Wales — Net Gains	Net Losses	County Councils controlled by Labour
1907	10	—		1	—						
1908	—	33									
1909	23	—									
1910	33	—		3	—						
1911	78	—									
1912	42	—				46 (Total seats held)					
1913	85	—		1							
1914–18	ELECTIONS SUSPENDED			ELECTIONS SUSPENDED		ELECTIONS SUSPENDED					
1919	412	—		15	2	526	—	12			3
1920	19	—									
1921	80	—									
1922	—	153		16	3	—	320	4			1
1923	69	—									
1924	53	—									
1925	75	—		35	4	105	—	8			2
1926	148	—	7								
1927	114	—	14								
1928	127	—	21	42	6	95	—	8			
1929	219	—	8 (Others 9)								
1930	—	73	8 (C.B.s 11)								
1931	—	238		35	3	—	210	3		9	
1932	22	—	20								
1933	250	—	25								
1934	305	—	18	69	11	472	—	15	117	—	3
1935	30	—	20								
1936	—	48	19								
1937	41	—	20	75	12	51	—	17	70	—	3
1938	11	—	24								
1939–44	ELECTIONS SUSPENDED			ELECTIONS SUSPENDED		ELECTIONS SUSPENDED					
1945	1,348	—	47			257	—	23			
1946	196	—	52	90	14				310	—	10
1947	—	652	42*								

*Not including five C.B.s in which Labour held exactly half the seats.

†Not including three in which Labour held exactly half the seats.

‡In addition, the Labour Party controlled seventy-six Urban District Councils in 1938, rising to 135 in 1945 and 139 in 1946, when it also controlled at least sixteen Rural District Councils. Earlier figures for Urban and Rural Districts are not available. In many areas, especially in Rural Districts, elections are not fought under party labels.

NOTE A.—These figures are subject to many omissions. In many cases widely different estimates are given by different newspapers. I have followed the Labour Party's estimates wherever they are available and have filled in further figures from a variety of sources. The general impression is reasonably reliable, though the actual figures are not.

NOTE B.—It is not possible to present any comparable figures for Scotland, where the Local Government system is different, especially in that the County Councils include representatives of the Burghs chosen not by direct election but by the Burgh Councils. The number of Scottish Burghs controlled by Labour has been computed by the Labour Party as follows :

1934	..	11	1938	..	14
1935	..	19	1945	..	37
1936	..	14	1946	..	41
1937	..	15	1947	..	36§

§ Not including four on which Labour held half the seats.

In 1946 the Labour Party also controlled five County Councils in Scotland, but control is always liable to be upset by changes in the Burgh representatives, who are chosen annually and not, like the " landward," or rural, representatives, directly elected for three years. The five Councils controlled in 1946 were Ayrshire, Lanarkshire, Stirlingshire, West Lothian and Midlothian—that is, the mining districts. Of the four Scottish Cities, Labour in 1947 controlled two—Glasgow (won in 1933) and Aberdeen (won in 1945). It also controlled Dundee in 1945–6, but was in a minority of one in 1947. Labour also won control in many of the large Burghs before the war, and improved its position in 1945–6, suffering a setback in 1947. In the majority of the small Burghs elections are not fought under party labels.

---

cashed in to the full on the mood of disillusionment and depression which became common after the tardy realisation of the unbalanced state of the British economy in the post-war world. The Conservatives, profiting by this mood, chose to turn the municipal elections of November, 1947, into a sort of referendum for or against the Labour Government ; and it was not at all surprising that the Labour Party, having to defend a high proportion of its huge gains of 1945, suffered very heavy losses. Had the London elections occurred at the same time, the losses would doubtless have been still more severe. As it was, they were widely spread and were especially serious in Lancashire and in the dormitory areas of Greater London. Among the great towns in which Labour lost its majority in 1947 were Manchester, Lincoln, Reading, and Dundee ; and among those in which it was reduced to exactly half the representation were Birmingham, Ipswich and York. Further losses, on a smaller scale, followed in the District Council elections early in 1947. Nevertheless the losses of 1947–8 were less than half the gains of 1945 ; and the Labour Party was left much stronger than it had been in 1939.

EPILOGUE, 1945–7

The time has not come for attempting to write the history of the Third Labour Government, which entered into office as an outcome of the General Election of 1945. I am writing this final chapter in November, 1947, with the work of two parliamentary sessions to look back on, but in the midst of a crisis which has already compelled the Government to make considerable changes in its immediate programme and, as far as the municipal elections of 1947 can be taken as evidence, has for the time being at least had a large influence on the Government's popularity with the doubtful elements in the electorate, which gave it the thumping parliamentary majority of two years ago.

In this recession of popularity and in the very great difficulties of the British economy which mainly account for it I see no cause for surprise. It should have been plainly evident in 1945, even at the time of the General Election and when the Attlee Government assumed office, that very great economic difficulties were lying ahead and that only by extreme good fortune could Great Britain hope to escape their impact. The lessons of the first World War should have been enough to show that, for all the war-devastated countries, the recovery of productive power was bound to be a slow business, and that severe shortages of both agricultural and industrial goods were certain to persist for a number of years. It was all too plain that, in all the branches of production that were less essential for war needs, the wearing out and obsolescence of capital goods that were not replaced was bound to lower efficiency, and that there would be serious problems involved in securing the redistribution of man-power to serve the needs of peace.

On Great Britain, because of its high dependence on imports of both foodstuffs and raw materials, this world situation was bound to react very seriously indeed. During the war, Great Britain had lived largely on Lease-Lend supplies and on imports paid for only in blocked sterling, to cover which no adequate quantities of British goods were available for export. British overseas investments, which had helped to pay for pre-war imports, had been largely sold off or mortgaged to purchase war supplies before Lease-Lend began. It was plain that, even if markets could be found at high prices for all the goods Great Britain could produce for export, there was likely to be for a good time to come a considerable deficit in the British balance of payments and a much larger deficit in terms of dollars. For, with production badly down in Europe and the Far East, it would be necessary to look to the Western Hemisphere and above all to the United States, Canada, and the Argentine for a high proportion of the needed supplies ; but it was not likely that these countries would be willing to take anything like an equivalent quantity of British goods, even if the goods could be made available for them.

When I went round speaking in the General Election of 1945 I made these points again and again, stressing the very great formidableness of the tasks which a Labour Government—or of course any incoming Government—would have to take in hand, and saying that, if I had not regarded it as supremely important for international reasons to have a Labour Government in Great Britain, nothing would have so much pleased me as to see the Tories left to confront the immense difficulties that lay ahead. As far as my small voice carried, I wanted the electors to be aware of these difficulties, and to be prepared to find themselves in for something much more in the nature of " blood and tears and sweat " than of " a new heaven and a new earth."

I do not think that most electors, or most candidates, whatever their party, did appreciate how serious the outlook was. Certainly, if they did, the sense of coming *economic* crisis was not adequately reflected either in their speeches and addresses or in the programmes on which they fought the Election. There was almost everywhere an assumption that, with the war over in Europe and soon to end in the Far East, things would speedily become easier and better. There were, indeed, on the Labour side, fears of what might happen to the world economy in the event of an American slump ; and it was fully understood that controls must be kept on and priorities observed until world shortages of necessary primary products had been overcome. But what was discussed in connection with a possible American slump was mainly the need for a home policy of full employment designed to insulate the British economy from its effects : there was not enough appreciation either of the danger that an American boom, leading to a sharp rise in the prices of American and other supplies, might be as disastrous as a slump, or of the fact that world-wide shortage of productivity outside America might make it impossible for Great Britain to get the supplies it needed from non-American sources, even if British industries were in a position to supply enough exports in exchange. The extent of the deterioration of British productive power outside the war industries, and the time needed for restoration, were gravely underestimated by almost everybody. Accordingly election speeches, on behalf of all parties, were quite unduly optimistic about the *near* future.

Of course, had the situation been better understood, the rival parties would have been no nearer agreement about the policy to be followed. The Conservatives, or most of them, would have argued none the less in favour of the restoration of private enterprise and of the speediest practicable relaxation and removal of controls ; and the Labour Party's supporters would have argued just as much in favour of socialisation of key industries as a means to greater efficiency and of retaining controls and rationing for as long as they were needed to ensure a tolerably fair distribution of scarce supplies. The unappreciated realities of the post-war situation did not much affect the validity of either side's programme : what they did affect were the vital issues that either were not argued about at all, or were brushed lightly aside as irrelevant to the contest for political power.

The termination of Lease-Lend and the issues that arose in connection with the negotiation of the American Loan in the latter months of 1945 should have opened everyone's eyes to these realities. Unfortunately they did not. Even when it became plain that the Loan would be on too small a scale to enable Great Britain to restore its international position before it was used up—unless indeed the Government had resorted at once to " austerity " measures much more drastic than any that had been imposed under stress of war—the hope was cherished that something would turn up to ease the situation when it ran out, or even that the pace of world recovery might after all be so rapid as to leave only a manageably small gap still to be bridged. Even when it became plain that the conditions attached to the Loan would tie Great Britain down to terms of sterling convertibility and trading " non-discrimination " that it would be a sheer impossibility to oberve when the time came—and that it would hamper Britain greatly in its search for necessary imports to be bound by—most people, including the Government, still met the plain facts with a shrug of the shoulders rather than with any will to deal with them promptly. Even when the sharp rise in American prices and the removal of price controls in the United States caused the real value of the Loan to fall continually while it was being spent, no action was taken to cope with the positive and immediate crisis that was certain to arise the moment it ran out, or was seen to be approaching exhaustion.

Why did these things happen? Why were they allowed to happen by a Government certainly much better equipped with economic knowledge than its critics? The answer, I think, is twofold. In the first place the Government, not having stressed the extreme and urgent nature of Great Britain's international economic difficulties during the Election, felt that it was quite out of the question to impose a more-than-war-time austerity on an electorate which had undoubtedly voted for it in hope of better times. Secondly, and more fundamentally, the Labour Government was working on the basis of a programme which it had been elaborating for a great many years, which it had taught its followers to understand and to believe in, and that did, in its belief (and in mine) rest on thoroughly sound long-term foundations. Nothing in the world difficulties to which Great Britain lay exposed in 1945 rendered any essential part of this programme less expedient or desirable : it was, as far as it went, a thoroughly good programme. But, having been worked out over many years and resting largely on foundations laid long before 1939, it neither did nor could cover what was needed to cope with the vital *short-run* problems arising out of the deterioration in Great Britain's international economic and financial situation as a result of the war.

The mistake the Third Labour Government made at the outset lay, not, as its anti-socialist opponents suggested, in carrying on with its programme of socialisation and social service, but in failing to realise the danger of coming to shipwreck unless it also tackled boldly the short-run problem of the international balance of payments. I believe—I said so at the time—that it ought, whatever the immediate political consequences, to have refused the American Loan *on the highly restrictive conditions on which it was offered*, in the hope of securing a Loan on less hampering conditions, but with the determination, should this hope fail, of facing the austerities involved in doing without it, and with a firm resolution, Loan or no Loan, to tackle at once the problems, however unpleasant, involved in attempting to get the British economy back into a state of ability to pay its own way.

This, I was told at the time, was " politically impossible." I can only answer that the unpopularity involved in it would have been very much easier to face, and to overcome, in 1945 than it could be in 1947, and that, if the problem had been tackled then, we might by now have been well on the way to solving it, instead of only at the beginning of realising what we have to face. I doubt whether this was in fact the main reason why so little attempt was made to confront economic realities until sheer necessity forced the Government's hand with the exhaustion of the American Loan. I think the main reason was that nothing had been thought out, and that most members of the Government were so busy handling the parts of the programme that had been prepared in advance or in facing the immediate day-to-day problems of their departments that the impending economic crisis simply failed to get the attention that it urgently required. Herbert Morrison's illness in 1946–7 may well have been an important contributory factor ; but it is not easy to acquit Hugh Dalton of failure to live up to his responsibility for the international financial aspects of the Government's policy.*

*This chapter was written before Dalton's resignation on November 13, 1947. I have let it stand, as I wrote it a week or so before that event.

Apart from this grave error, which may still be remediable though the remedies are now bound to be harder than they need have been, the Government's economic record from 1945 to 1947 was, I think, remarkably good. I can see no substance at all in the argument that measures of socialisation ought to have been postponed on account of the difficult international economic situation—unless, indeed, it is contended that Great Britain ought to submit to being governed by the United States Congress rather than by its own Parliament in the hope of being permanently supported by American charity. The greater the economic difficulties to be faced, the greater the need for getting British essential industries into the best possible shape for facing them ; and I think few people really believe that the coal industry can be satisfactorily reorganised except under public ownership or deny the need for effective co-ordination of road and rail services, or for the reshaping of the electricity supply services under unified central control, or for public operation of civil aviation services along the main routes. I also believe that the socialisation, in some form, of the key sections of the steel industry is indispensable in order to ensure the required expansion of low-cost (and low-priced) steel production. At all events, there is no reason at all why those who do believe that the socialisation of these industries is a necessary step towards greater efficiency in the national service should think so any the less on account of Great Britain's international difficulties.

In the matter of socialisation the Government, up to 1947, had been doing precisely what it had told the electors it would do if it were returned to power. Its mandate was as clear as such a mandate can be ; but this must not be misunderstood as meaning that it was for the sake of getting the basic industries and services nationalised that the majority of those who voted Labour in 1945 cast their votes. The thing that brought the electors to the poll in 1945 to vote Labour was above all else the desire for Social Security and for Social Justice. The Labour voters wanted a Government which would carry out in full the Beveridge plans of Social Security, including both the Social Insurance projects and the promised schemes of children's endowment and a National Health Service open to all. They wanted houses, at rents which they could afford to pay : they wanted an assurance that supplies, as long as they remained scarce, would be equitably shared out and would not be handed back to a black market open only to the well-to-do (even if that market were to be labelled

" white " by the removal of controls). They wanted a " full employment " policy that would be an assurance of regular incomes and would prevent the reappearance of the " distressed areas " of the inter-war years. These, above all else, were the *domestic* issues on which they voted ; and, to the extent that they voted on international considerations they cast their suffrages for the party they thought most likely to act for the prevention of further wars. Socialisation, of the kind advocated in the Labour Programme, they were prepared to vote for, not for its own sake, but as a means to these other things. On this point I should perhaps except the Miners, who voted positively *for* socialisation of the coal mines, as a reaction to their evil experience of the industry under private control.

Now, there is no good reason, arising out of Great Britain's international difficulties, why the Labour Government should not carry out the spirit of what its supporters voted for in 1945. If there has to be " austerity " because only limited imports can be afforded, that is all the more reason for sharing out what is available as equitably as it can be shared. If real incomes, in terms of the goods they can buy, must be restricted, that is all the more reason for seeing to it that they shall be secure. If as a nation we are poorer for the time being than we hoped to be, that is all the more reason for maintaining the best possible system of Social Services, in order to minimise the suffering which this national poverty involves. Everything that has come to light since 1945 about Great Britain's difficulties emphasises the need to have in power a Government which will care first and foremost for Social Security and for Social Justice. The less politically educated electors, however, or rather a considerable section of them, may easily fail to see this. Disappointed at the continuance—nay, the intensification—of " austerity," they may easily fail to realise how much worse things would be if unavoidably short supplies were less fairly shared.

The Government, between 1945 and 1947, has accomplished most of the work of legislation needed to implement its Social Security pledges. It has passed the National Insurance Act and the Industrial Injuries Act, and also the National Health Act laying the foundations for the National Health Service. It is engaged, as I write, on the final demolition of the old Poor Law and the substitution for what is left of it of a nationally financed Public Assistance system. It is attempting to humanise the criminal law and the prison system. Children's allowances in cash are an accomplished fact ; and allowances in kind are being provided as fast as the situation allows.

Housing is giving rise to much more serious difficulties, because of the shortages of man-power and materials and of the strength of rival claims on the building industry. There has been a clamour—which the Government has rightly resisted—for an almost complete liquidation of the housing programme, in some quarters on the ground that factory-building is more urgent than house-building, but in others on the quite different ground that Great Britain cannot afford at present to spend energy on making *capital* goods, and should use all its resources for increasing supplies of immediately consumable goods in order to avoid " austerity." I must say that this latter argument seems to me the most pernicious nonsense. If such advice were followed, so far from recovering our productive power, we should be allowing it to run down still further, and should find ourselves each year in an increasingly evil economic plight. Capital-construction on a large scale is indispensable to economic recovery ; and the capital goods that we produce must include both factories and houses—factories in order to increase productivity, and houses because those who work in them—or on the land for increased agricultural output—must be given decent homes. It is, however, quite true that the more we spend on capital goods, and on materials for making them, the less we shall be able *immediately* to consume ; but that is not a reason for cutting out capital-construction in order to reduce austerity, for the more we spend now on the right kinds of capital goods, the sooner can we reasonably hope that the need for austerity will end.

For the maintenance of full employment the Government has so far been under no necessity of taking any action ; for the problem, except here and there, has been one of shortage of workers and not of jobs. It would, however, be a great mistake to suppose that no need for action will arise, even in the very near future. Full employment could be upset either by inability to purchase sufficient materials from abroad to keep our industries at work or by the collapse of the export markets which we are now seeking so energetically to expand—or, of course, by these two factors operating together. This is a test which the Government may still have to face before its first period of office is over ; and I hope it is prepared to meet it if it comes.

It is much more difficult to pass any judgment on the Government's record in international affairs generally, as distinct from specifically economic affairs. My own view has been from the first that Ernest Bevin's foreign policy has put much too heavy a strain on scarce British resources both of man-power and of foreign exchange, and that the Government should, whatever its reluctance on specific matters, have limited its external commitments much more strictly than it has done in fact. Placed as we are, we can no more afford to be the policemen of the Near and Middle East than we could have afforded to hold India and Burma by force, even had we so desired. Secondly, I think the British Labour Government failed, in 1945 when the chance was greatest, to give the lead to the forces of democratic Socialism in Europe that might have made all the difference both to the speed and certainty of economic recovery and to the breaking down of national barriers and the development, at least in embryo, of a common European economico-political plan. These issues, however, I have argued elsewhere* ; and it would take me much too far afield to repeat the arguments now. I can only repeat my belief that the Labour Party, by its failure to plan its international policy, both political and economic, with anything like the care that it devoted, over many years, to its purely domestic plans, laid up for itself a peck of troubles that could have been made at any rate much less troublesome had more thought been given to them in advance.

The Labour Party's internal organisation was not greatly altered as a consequence of its election victory. In the main, as soon as the war in Europe was over, Transport House set to work to build the party machine up again on the same foundations as before. Thus, a drive was begun to revive the individual membership of the Local Labour Parties, which had shrunk from 429,000 in 1938 to 219,000 at the end of the war. This campaign was markedly successful. Individual membership rose to 487,000 by the end of 1945 and to 645,000 by the end of 1946.† It was then made up of 384,000 men and 261,000 women, as against 251,000 men and 178,000 women in 1938. There was a vigorous revival of local party activity ; and headquarters made a praiseworthy attempt, by the issue of a " Labour Discussion Series " of booklets and in other ways, to stimulate the political education of its adherents. The quality and presentation of the party literature improved : the monthly *Labour Party Bulletin* was cheered up and

---

*In *Labour's Foreign Policy* (*New Statesman and Nation*, 1946) and in *The Intelligent Man's Guide to the Post-war World* (Gollancz, 1947).
†It fell, however, by nearly 37,000 in 1947.

made more informative and was enlarged to include a special section dealing with Local Government. A new venture, *Labour Forum*, was started for open discussion of controversial issues. So far, good. Excellent work was also done in revivifying the local Women's Sections, many of which had fallen into abeyance during the war. Four hundred and seventy-three Women's Sections were formed, or re-formed, between the General Election and the end of 1946. I am not so sure that the National Executive was equally well advised in the steps which it took in reviving the League of Youth. Of this body, only a very few branches were still in existence at the end of the war. After the General Election, Transport House began actively furthering the establishment of new ones, and by the end of 1946 there were 250 branches in being. The Party Conference of 1946 accepted a new model constitution for League of Youth branches, which were to be limited to members between sixteen and twenty-one and were to be given one or two representatives on the Executives of the Local Parties sponsoring them. The League's branches were to be free to discuss questions of party policy ; but there was to be no national committee or federal unity linking them together, and all regional and national correspondence on League of Youth matters was to be conducted with the regular officials of the Labour Party. The Party Executive thus attempted to prevent the re-growth of any national Youth Movement within the Party that might formulate a policy or programme of its own. At the same time, it took powers itself to convene regional or national Youth Conferences of the League's branches, so that it could control their agenda. Later, in 1946, the Executive sanctioned the setting up of Regional Advisory Youth Councils under the auspices of the Party's own Regional Councils and in some cases of Federation Advisory Committees operating over smaller areas. An attempt was made at the 1946 Party Conference to refer back the Executive's proposals on the ground that they gave the League of Youth inadequate scope ; but, though nearly all the speaking was for the reference back, the Executive carried its policy on a show of hands, and no card vote was challenged.

The Executive also helped in 1945 to get established afresh the National Association of Labour Students, which, as we have seen, had been stillborn before the war. The position had now become much easier for the Labour Party because in most of the Universities there had been decisive splits between Communists and Labour Party supporters among the students. In most places,

there were now two rival bodies—one usually calling itself
" Socialist," affiliated to the Communist-dominated Student
Labour Federation, and including the student Communists and
such other Socialists as had stayed with them in face of the split,
and the other usually calling itself " Labour," and seeking to
establish the closest possible relations with the Labour Party.
The Societies belonging to this second group were now gathered
together in the National Association of Labour Students. This
reproduced almost exactly the situation which developed after
the first World War, when the Communist-dominated University
Socialist Federation was challenged by the new University
Labour Federation—then actively sponsored by the Labour Party,
though it fell later into disgrace when it came in turn largely
under Communist influence. It should be observed that, in
general, Labour's increased strength in the country was not
reflected in and after 1945 among the student population. The
University Labour and Socialist bodies, taken as a whole, were
relatively somewhat weaker than they had been in the 1930's.
This was, I think, in part a consequence of the higher average
age of undergraduates and of the fact that many of them had
served as officers in the forces and were thinking a good deal about
their personal economic prospects—a good many being married—
and consequently more disposed to take a political line that would
square with their pretensions to privilege. But it was also in part
a result of the marked decline of the Communist appeal ; for the
Communists had supplied, before the war, a high proportion of
the most active propagandists among the students.

At the Labour Party Conference of 1946 the Party Executive
announced that it had received and rejected a fresh application
for affiliation from the Communist Party, and that it had also
refused to accept a similar application from the I.L.P.   Not
content with rejecting these specific demands, the Executive put
forward a new draft rule designed to debar from affiliation all
" political organisations not affiliated to or associated under a
National Agreement with the Party on 1st January, 1946, having
their own programmes, principles and policy for distinctive and
separate propaganda, or possessing branches in the Constituencies,
or engaged in the promotion of Parliamentary or Local Government candidatures, or owing allegiance to any political organisation situated abroad."   At the Conference, Herbert Morrison
was put forward to defend both the Executive's specific decisions
and its proposed new rule. On the issue of Communist affiliation,

he was opposed by Jack Tanner of the Amalgamated Engineering Union, who moved an amendment in favour of admitting the Communist Party in the interests of working-class unity behind the Labour Programme. With but little debate, the amendment was voted down by 2,678,000 to 468,000 ; and the delegates then, without any discussion at all, adopted the Executive's new rule by a vote of 2,413,000 to 667,000. The case of the I.L.P. was not even raised at the Conference ; nor, in relation to the Communists, were any new arguments adduced. The bulk of the delegates still felt on this issue precisely as they had felt on the many occasions on which it had been debated before.

The reference in the preceding paragraph to " parties associated under a National Agreement " with the Labour Party is of course to the Co-operative Party, with which a new and improved national agreement was negotiated in 1946. This provided for the setting up of two joint committees—one between the Labour Party and the National Co-operative Authority, representing all sides of the Co-operative Movement, to deal with all questions of policy in National or Local Government arising between the two Movements, and the other between the Labour Party and the Co-operative Party, to deal with questions of organisation, especially in connection with national and local elections. Under the new agreement it was provided that, except where special local arrangements were in force, local Co-operative Societies should be eligible for affiliation to Constituency Labour Parties and should, where they were putting forward parliamentary candidates for adoption, have, in common with other affiliated bodies doing the like, special rights of representation and discussion on the Labour Parties concerned. The agreement also covered candidates for Local Government elections, and allowed such candidates, subject to local agreements, to be designated as " Labour and Co-operative." It was explicitly laid down that the parties to the agreement remained subject, in matters of policy, to the decisions of their respective Annual Congresses or Conferences, and that the entire arrangement was subject to this proviso. The general effect was to encourage local Co-operative Societies, while retaining their connection with the Co-operative Party, to become integral parts of the Constituency Labour Parties, and thus to bring the two Movements very much closer together in their constituency organisation and in respect of Local Government activities, as well as in Parliament.

In the organisation of the Parliamentary Labour Party, the

accession to power of a Labour Government and the very great
increase in the number of Labour Members necessarily involved
considerable developments. A small Liaison Committee was set
up to keep contact between the Parliamentary Party and the
Government, with two members of the Government—the Leader
of the House and the Chief Whip—serving upon it, together with
Neil Maclean and Maurice Webb, who were elected as Chairman
and Vice-Chairman of the Parliamentary Party, a representative
of the Labour peers, and the Secretary of the Parliamentary
Party. At the same time a large number of subject groups of
back-bench M.P.s were set up, each with its own chairman, and
arrangements were made for the Ministers to meet these groups
for discussion and for the groups to be able to bring to the attention of Ministers any questions relating to their several departments that they desired to raise. An even more important step,
made practicable by the size of the Government's majority, was
the suspension of the Standing Orders regulating party discipline. This gave back-bench members a wide freedom to express
dissent and even to vote against the Government if they thought
fit. The suspension was announced as an experiment " subject
to review if circumstances require," and was " not to prejudice
the right of the Party to withdraw the Whip from Members,
should occasion require." There have been one or two occasions
on which proposals have been put forward to reimpose the
Standing Orders; but they have not in fact been re-
imposed.

There have, indeed, been very few occasions up to the end of
1947 on which any substantial section of the Party has felt called
upon to challenge the Government's policy, though there have
been individuals, such as Rhys Davies and Richard Stokes,
Raymond Blackburn and Alfred Edwards, who from various
points of view have made large use of their freedom. The main
organised challenge has come over questions of foreign policy and,
in close relation to it, of the numbers of men whom it is necessary
to keep under arms. The " Keep Left Group," so called after a
pamphlet *Keep Left*, which a number of its members issued in
1947, has been the principal organiser of these " revolts," but
has been careful not to press them too far, or to risk a crisis in the
Party. The likeliest result, indeed, of a policy crisis would be a
successful attempt to reimpose " party discipline " ; and this
would not at all suit the " Keep Left " Group, which has no
desire to endanger the Government's position, and wishes only

to exert such pressure as is compatible with the maintenance of unity both in the Government and in the party organisation throughout the country. R. H. S. Crossman and Ian Mikardo have been the principal spokesmen of this Group, the former mainly on international and the latter on industrial questions.

In the team which made up the Government of 1945 the Cabinet consisted of twenty members. Of these, nine were active Trade Unionists, with considerable experience of Trade Union administration. One, A. V. Alexander, was a Co-operator ; and the remaining ten belonged to the " intellectual " wing of the Party. This last group held the key positions, except that of Foreign Secretary, which went to Ernest Bevin. Herbert Morrison, as Lord President of the Council, had charge of the co-ordination of economic policy until, in the crisis of 1947, Sir Stafford Cripps took over this function, with considerably enlarged powers over the various economic departments and with a skeleton planning staff directly under his control.* Hugh Dalton, a professional economist, was Chancellor of the Exchequer, and set to work to operate a " cheap money " policy, much to the annoyance of the financial interests. Cripps was at the Board of Trade, in charge of industrial " conversion " and of export policy until he moved up to a wider sphere of action in 1947. Chuter Ede was at the Home Office ; the veterans, Pethick Lawrence and Addison, were at the India Office and the Dominions Office ; Arthur Greenwood was Lord Privy Seal, with a mandate to co-ordinate Social Security measures. Lord Jowitt, as Lord Chancellor, and Lord Stansgate (Wedgwood Benn) as Secretary of State for Air, completed the " intellectual " wing. The Trade Unionists included, besides Bevin, Ellen Wilkinson at the Ministry of Education, Aneurin Bevan at the Ministry of Health, George Isaacs at the Ministry of Labour, Tom Williams at the Ministry of Agriculture, Emanuel Shinwell at the Ministry of Fuel and Power, Jack Lawson at the War Office, Joseph Westwood as Secretary of State for Scotland, and G. H. Hall at the Colonial Office. Alexander, the Co-operator, was at the Admiralty, as he had been during the war. It was not an adventurous Cabinet : the only

*Only to be transferred almost immediately to the Exchequer, in succession to Dalton—thus reuniting financial and economic policy under a single control. This was, in many people's view, a desirable development ; but, in my own view, most undesirable, not only as involving an almost intolerably heavy burden, but also as tending to re-establish that Treasury domination over policy which has shown itself capable again and again of most seriously crippling effects. See my *Machinery of Socialist Planning* (1938) for my views of this question.

reputedly "left wing" members were Aneurin Bevan and Ellen Wilkinson, and the average age was high.

Ministers outside the Cabinet included Noel-Baker (Minister of State), James Griffiths (National Insurance), Lewis Silkin (Town and Country Planning), John Wilmot (Supply), Alfred Barnes, of the Co-operative Party (Transport), George Tomlinson (Works), and J. B. Hynd who, as Chancellor of the Duchy, was put in charge of the British Zone in Germany. Hector McNeil, put at the Foreign Office under Bevin, and Harold Wilson, as Parliamentary Secretary to the Ministry of Works, were among the most interesting of the junior appointments. Other Under-Secretaries who soon obtained promotion were John Strachey (Air), who became Minister of Food, and Arthur Creech Jones (Colonies), who became Colonial Secretary when G. H. Hall was moved to the Admiralty on Alexander's translation to a co-ordinating Ministry of Defence.

The principal surprise in the structure of the new Government was that no steps were taken to establish a separate Ministry of Housing, which had figured in the Labour programme. This left Aneurin Bevan, at the Ministry of Health, to wrestle simultaneously with the doctors over the new National Health Service and with the builders and the Local Authorities over housing—an almost insupportable double burden, one might have supposed. In subsequent reshuffles the most important changes not already mentioned included the promotion of Harold Wilson, at a remarkably early age, to be President of the Board of Trade, with a seat in the Cabinet, and the promotion of another " academic," Hugh Gaitskell, to be Minister of Fuel and Power when Shinwell was transferred to the War Office in 1947. Ellen Wilkinson, alas, died in 1947 and was succeeded at the Ministry of Education by George Tomlinson, who had long experience of educational work on the Lancashire County Council. Despite these changes, the structure of the Government remained at the end of 1947 broadly what it had been at the start, with the two exceptions that Alexander had been put to co-ordinate the Defence departments and that, in the 1947 crisis, Stafford Cripps had been given wide overriding economic powers. This last was the really significant development, involving as it did a much greater measure of concerted economic planning than had been attempted during the Government's first two years of office.

Both in the programme on which the Labour Government

embarked in 1945 and in the composition of the Government itself, especially among its younger members, a good deal was due to the work done by the New Fabian Research Bureau, and subsequently (after the amalgamation) by the Fabian Society. These bodies not only prepared the way for the Government's measures by careful working out in advance of plans for dealing with many of the more complex issues : they also trained not a few of the men and women who were to undertake essential tasks in translating the programme into action. A high proportion of the Labour M.P.s elected in 1945 were Fabians and had been active either on the Society's research projects or in the propagandist and educational work of the local Fabian Societies. The New Fabian Research Bureau had devoted itself particularly to enlisting the co-operation of the younger Socialist intellectuals and to encouraging them to take part in the work of the Labour Party. Thus a new generation of Fabians set to work to carry out for Socialism, under the changed conditions, a task not unlike that which the first generation of Fabians had undertaken before the Labour Party was born ; the evidence of their usefulness is to be discovered both in the long list of Fabian research books and pamphlets published in the 'thirties and 'forties and in the day-to-day activities of the Labour Party in Parliament since 1945.

How, during the years up to the last months of 1947, did Labour's " stock " stand among the electorate ? It is a remarkable fact that up to the autumn of 1947, the Labour Party did not lose a single by-election, though it was called upon to defend no fewer than twenty-two seats which it had won at the General Election. That it gained none of the seven Opposition seats for which it put forward candidates is much less remarkable ; for it had won so many seats in 1945 as to leave its opponents mainly with constituencies in which for the time being it stood little chance. Labour General Election majorities were no doubt substantially reduced, and in some cases there was an absolute rise in the opposition vote ; but up to November, 1947, nothing had occurred to indicate any substantial change of mind on the part of the electors. Then came the sensational Labour losses at the municipal elections, due, as we have seen, not to a fall in the Labour vote but rather to a very great increase in that of the Conservatives, who managed to bring an unprecedented number of local electors to the poll. How far this indicated a change of mind in relation to national politics may be disputed ; in some quarters much stress was laid on the fact that the Gallup Public Opinion Polls, which had put the Labour Party well ahead of the Conservatives ever since 1943, but had shown the gap narrowing through the latter half of 1946, put the two parties level by mid-1947, and thereafter showed the Conservatives forging well ahead, though even in September they were accorded a lead of only a few per cent.

Personally I do not doubt that these estimates, narrow as their statistical basis may be, did broadly reflect the first reactions of public opinion in face of the " dollar crisis" of the latter months of 1947. This, however, is by no means to say that the results of a General Election held at that period would necessarily have followed the same course ; for a General Election, which would have settled the composition of a new Government, would have caused a good many electors to think twice, instead of responding to their immediate reactions of disillusionment and discontent.

Indeed, the results of the by-elections held in the course of November, 1947, immediately after the municipal elections showed fairly clearly that Labour's setback in Local Government by no means implied a change of mind on the part of the electorate in national affairs. It was significant enough that John Wheatley, the new Solicitor-General for Scotland, managed to hold East Edinburgh without any difficulty ; it was far more remarkable that at Gravesend, where the Labour Member, Garry Allighan, had been expelled from the House of Commons for highly discreditable conduct, Sir Richard Acland, making his début as a Labour candidate, was able to retain the seat by a substantial though considerably reduced majority. Gravesend was one of the areas in which Labour had suffered heavily in the municipal elections ; and, though something must be attributed to the personalities of the Labour candidate and of his opponent, who made the singular mistake of fighting the election principally on the issue of an immediate removal of controls, the result was hardly the less striking an illustration of the danger of drawing conclusions directly from municipal to national electoral moods.

As there is not much likelihood of a General Election until 1950, in all probability a great deal has still to happen before the main body of the electors will be called upon to act in such a way as to determine the national tenure of political power ; and there is room for a great many swings and changes of electoral opinion before that opportunity is likely to occur. The record of the Third Labour Government, as it stood at the end of 1947, was still essentially incomplete. It had shown its capacity to act energetically up to its election promises: it had so far neither proved nor disproved its ability to stand up to the acute economic difficulties which faced Great Britain in the international field. Nor, I should add, had it either proved, or decisively disproved, its capacity in foreign affairs ; for, if the course of international events since 1945 had been about as unsatisfactory as it could have been short of actual war, it would be absurd even for those who dislike Ernest Bevin's foreign policy to lay the blame for this situation *mainly* at his door.

There I must leave this History. This " Epilogue," I hope I have made clear, is meant to be entirely provisional. It is not really part of the book, but a pendant to it, which I intend to replace by a more considered judgment in a subsequent edition, should the opportunity occur. The note on which I should wish to end is one of unquenchable admiration for the good, decent men and women all over the country who have built up the movement by their devoted service, asking and getting few thanks, but finding their reward in the spirit of goodwill which has

THE COURSE OF BY-ELECTIONS, 1945-7

Seats gained*	1945	1946	1947
Labour seats held in straight fights . .	3	6	—
Labour seats held by clear majority in three- or more- cornered contests	1	5	4
Labour returned unopposed	—	1	—
Opposition seats not won in straight fights .	1	1	—
Opposition seats not won in other contests .	2	3†	—
Seats not fought by Labour	2	1	—
Labour seats lost	—	—	—‡
TOTALS	9	17	4

*Not including seats gained without by-elections by the readmission of two I.L.P. Members to the Party.

†One of theses seats was held by an I.L.P. nominee who subsequently joined the Labour Party.

‡Not including two seats lost to Labour, one by the expulsion of G. Allighan and one by the secession of E. Walkden from the Party.

underlain all their striving to build a Party strong enough to make a Government bold enough to attempt the transformation of this dear land of ours into a home of security and justice for the common man. They must not be disappointed, even if at times the stress of events may beat hard upon their hopes. The world of 1947 may seem a chilly place ; but there is promise in it. Even now, amid crisis and shortage, the poor and the weak in Great Britain are getting a fairer deal than ever before.

APPENDICES

THE STATE OF PARTIES AT EACH GENERAL ELECTION FROM 1906 TO 1945

	Labour	Ind. Labour	Com- munist	Ind. Liberal	Liberal	Liberal National	Conser- vative Unionist and National	Coali- tion Labour	Irish National	Sinn Fein	Others
1906	30	—	—	—	397	—	132	—	83	—	—
1910 (Jan.)	40	—	—	—	275	—	273	—	82	—	—
1910 (Dec.)	42	—	—	—	270	—	273	—	84	—	1
1918	60	—	—	34	—	137	374	15	7	73	7
1922	142	—	1	59	—	59	347	1	2	1	3
1923	191	—	—	—	158	—	258	—	—	—	8
1924	152	—	1	—	42	—	415	—	—	—	6
1929	288	—	—	—	59	—	260	—	—	—	8
1931	46	6	—	—	72	—	475	13	—	—	3
1935	154	4	1	21	—	33	390	8	—	2	2
1945	394	5*	2	12	—	13	202	—	—	2	10

*Including one Common Wealth.

VOTING AT GENERAL ELECTIONS, 1900–45. MAIN PARTIES ONLY

(millions)	Electorate	Labour vote	Liberal vote		Tory vote
			Liberal	Lib-Nat. or Coalition	
1900 . .	6.6	0.06	2.1	—	2.6
1906 . .	7.3	0.3	2.7	—	2.6
1910 (Jan.) .	7.7	0.5	2.8	—	2.9
1910 (Dec.*) .	7.7	0.4	2.3	—	2.5
1918 . .	21.4	2.2	1.4	1.4	4.2
1922 . .	21.1	4.2	2.6	1.5	5.5
1923 . .	21.3	4.3	4.2	—	5.4
1924 . .	21.7	5.5	3.0	—	7.4
1929 . .	28.9	8.4	5.3	—	8.7
1931 . .	30.0	6.6	1.5	0.8	11.9
1935 . .	31.4	8.5	1.4	0.9	10.5
1945 . .	33.7	12.0	2.2	0.8	9.2

*Fewer seats fought.

These figures are only approximately correct, as the parties return discrepant figures. Ulster Unionists and Nationals have been included as Tories. The Irish Nationalists have been omitted.

APPENDIX III

LABOUR PARTY MEMBERSHIP, 1900-46

Constituency and Central Parties No.	Total individual Membership Men	Women	Trade Unions No.	Membership	Socialist and Co-operative Societies, etc. No.	Membership	*Total Membership
1900 . 7	—	—	41	353,070	3	22,861	375,931
1901 . 21	—	—	65	455,450	2	13,861	469,311
1902 . 49	—	—	127	847,315	2	13,835	861,150
1903 . 76	—	—	165	956,025	2	13,775	969,800
1904 . 73	—	—	158	855,270	2	14,730	900,000
1905 . 73	—	—	158	904,496	2	16,784	921,280
1906 . 83	—	—	176	975,182	2	20,885	998,338
1907 . 92	—	—	181	1,049,673	2	22,267	1,072,413
1908 . 133	—	—	176	1,127,035	2	27,465	1,158,565
1909 . 155	—	—	172	1,450,648	2	30,982	1,486,308
1910 . 148	—	—	151	1,394,402	2	31,377	1,430,539
1911 . 149	—	—	141	1,501,783	2	31,404	1,539,092
1912 . 146	—	—	130	1,858,178	2	31,237	1,895,498
1913 . 158	—	—	†	†	2	33,304	†
1914 . 179	—	—	101	1,572,391	2	33,230	1,612,147
1915 . 177	—	—	111	2,053,735	2	32,828	2,093,365
1916 . 199	—	—	119	2,170,782	3	42,190	2,219,764
1917 . 239	—	—	123	2,415,383	3	47,140	2,465,131
1918 . 389	—	—	131	2,960,409	4	52,720	3,013,129
1919 . 418	—	—	126	3,464,020	7	47,270	3,511,290
1920 . 492	—	—	122	4,317,537	5	42,270	4,359,807
1921 . 456	—	—	116	3,973,558	5	31,760	4,010,361
1922 . 482	—	—	102	3,279,276	5	31,760	3,311,036
1923 . 503	—	—	106	3,120,149	6	35,762	3,155,911
1924 . 529	—	—	108	3,158,002	7	36,397	3,194,399
1925 . 549	—	—	106	3,337,635	8	36,235	3,373,870
1926 . 551	—	—	104	3,352,347	8	35,939	3,388,286
1927 . 532	—	—	97	3,238,939	6	54,676	3,293,615
1928 . 535	214,970		91	2,025,139	7	52,060‡	2,292,169
1929 . 578	227,897		91	2,044,279	6	58,669‡	2,330,845
1930 . 607	277,211		89	2,011,484	7	58,213‡	2,346,908
1931 . 608	297,003		80	2,024,216	7	36,847‡	2,358,066
1932 . 608	371,607		75	1,960,269	9	39,911‡	2,371,787
1933 . 612	211,223	154,790	75	1,899,007	9	40,010‡	2,305,030
1934 . 614	222,777	158,482	72	1,857,524	8	39,707‡	2,278,490
1935 . 614	246,401	172,910	72	1,912,924	9	45,280‡	2,377,515
1936 . 614	250,761	179,933	73	1,968,538	9	45,125‡	2,444,357
1937 . 614	258,060	189,090	70	2,037,071	8	43,451‡	2,527,672
1938 . 614	250,705	178,121	70	2,158,076	9	43,384‡	2,630,286
1939 . 614	239,978	168,866	72	2,214,070	6	40,153‡	2,663,067
1940 . 614	175,606	128,518	73	2,226,575	6	40,464‡	2,571,163
1941 . 585	129,909	96,713	68	2,230,728	6	28,108‡	2,485,458
1942 . 581	123,101	95,682	69	2,206,209	6	28,940‡	2,453,932
1943 . 586	134,697	100,804	69	2,237,307	6	30,432‡	2,503,240
1944 . 598	153,132	112,631	68	2,373,381	6	31,701‡	2,672,845
1945 . 649	291,435	195,612	69	2,510,369	6	41,281‡	3,038,697
1946 . 649	384,023	261,322	71	2,635,346	6	41,667‡	3,322,358
1947 . —	608,487			4,031,434		45,738	4,685,659

*The totals to 1917 in this column include the membership of the Co-operative and Women's Labour League affiliations, in addition to those of the Trade Unions and Socialist Societies.
†Owing to the operation of the Osborne Judgment, it was made impossible to compile membership statistics for 1913.
‡The Royal Arsenal Co-operative Society, through its Political Purposes Committee, continues its affiliations with the Party, and its membership is included in these totals.

APPENDIX IV

A NOTE ON THE TRADE UNION POLITICAL LEVY

Up to the Osborne Judgment there were no special legal conditions applying to Trade Union affiliations to the Labour Party. Between 1900 and 1912 the number of Trade Unions affiliated had risen from 41 to 130, and the affiliated Trade Union membership from 353,000 to 1,858,000. Actually, the number of affiliated Unions had reached its peak in 1907, at 181 ; but affiliated membership was then only 1,050,000. The subsequent fall in the number of Unions was due largely to amalgamations. Trades Union Congress affiliated membership was 1,250,000 in 1900 and 2,002,000 in 1912. Thus, before the effect of the Osborne Judgment was felt the Labour Party had nearly as many affiliated Trade Union members as the T.U.C.

After 1913, Trade Union affiliation to the Labour Party was regulated by law under the Act of that year, which allowed objectors to contract out of paying the Political Levy and sanctioned the collection of the Levy only by Unions which had secured authorisation by a ballot vote of their members. The Act of 1913 remained in force until 1927. The following figures illustrate the comparative movements of Trades Union Congress and Labour Party affiliated Trade Union membership over this period :—

COMPARATIVE MOVEMENTS OF TRADES UNION CONGRESS AND LABOUR PARTY AFFILIATED TRADE UNION MEMBERSHIP, 1914–27

	Trades Union Congress	Labour Party
	(Thousands)	(Thousands)
1914 . . .	2,232 (1913)	1,572
1918 . . .	4,532	2,960
1921 . . .	6,418	3,974
1926 . . .	4,366	3,352
1927 . . .	4,164	3,239

After the enactment of the Trade Unions and Trade Disputes Act of 1927, which substituted " contracting-in " for " contracting-out " and enforced the disaffiliation of the Civil Servants' Unions, Labour Party membership fell sharply. Trades Union Congress membership also fell, but to a much smaller extent. The following figures illustrate the movements :—

COMPARATIVE MOVEMENTS OF TRADES UNION CONGRESS AND LABOUR PARTY AFFILIATED TRADE UNION MEMBERSHIP, 1928–47

	Trades Union Congress	Labour Party
	(Thousands)	(Thousands)
1928 . . .	3,875	2,025
1930 . . .	3,744	2,011
1934 . . .	3,295	1,858
1937 . . .	4,009	2,037
1939 . . .	4,669	2,214
1942 . . .	5,433	2,206
1944 . . .	6,642	2,375
1945 . . .	6,576	2,510
1946 . . .	6,671	2,635
1947 . . .	7,540	

Figures measuring the effect on the Labour Party of the repeal of the 1927 Act were not available at the time of writing, but *total* Labour Party membership rose to 4,685,659 in 1947.

There are large variations between Unions in the proportion of members contributing to the Political Levy. The figures for the sixty largest Trade Unions for 1946 are set out in the Table on this page Some Unions, of course, do not belong to the Labour Party at all, and others collect the Political Levy from only a small fraction of their members. Rapidly rising membership usually means a decline in the proportion of members paying to the Political Levy—or at any rate this was the case under the Act of 1927. Here are comparative figures for a few of the largest Unions for 1937 and 1946. The comparisons, both here and in the larger Table, are between the memberships on which affiliation fees were paid to the Trades Union Congress and to the Labour Party. The T.U.C. figure is in many cases smaller than the figure of total membership reported to the Ministry of Labour, as it includes only paid-up members. It affords a fairer basis for comparison than the total figure.

PERCENTAGE OF MEMBERS IN TWELVE LARGE UNIONS ON WHICH AFFILIATION FEES WERE PAID TO THE LABOUR PARTY IN 1937 AND 1946

	1937	1946
Railway Clerks' Association . . .	80	83
National Union of Mineworkers . .	77	77
Shop, Distributive and Allied Workers . .	87	67
National Union of Railwaymen . . .	64	53
Transport and General Workers . . .	57	37
Associated Society of Locomotive Engineers .	24	36
Amalgamated Engineering Union . .	28	32
General and Municipal Workers . . .	71	30
Amalgamated Society of Woodworkers . .	35	22
Amalgamated Union of Building Trade Workers	25	17
Electrical Trades Union	23	15
National Society of Painters . . .	8	4

It will be seen that the range is very wide, and that the percentages have tended to fall with increasing Trade Union membership.

THE SIXTY LARGEST TRADE UNIONS, 1946–7

showing the membership on which affiliation fees were paid to (a) the Trades Union Congress and (b) the Labour Party and the proportion of (b) to (a).

	T.U.C.	L.P.	per cent
	(Thousands)		
Transport and General Workers .	1,230	450	37
General and Municipal Workers .	795	242	30
Amalgamated Engineering Union .	723	235	32
National Union of Mineworkers .	538	415	77
National Union of Railwaymen .	453	241	53
Shop, Distributive and Allied Workers	374	249	67
Amalgamated Society of Woodworkers	195	43	22
Electrical Trades Union . .	162	25	15
Union of Post Office Workers . .	152	—	—

	T.U.C.	L.P.	per cent
	(Thousands)		
10 Civil Service Clerical Association .	138	—	—
National Union of Tailors and Garment Workers . . .	133	41	31
National Union of Agricultural Workers	124	71	57
National Union of Public Employees	123	21	17
Iron and Steel Trades Confederation	93	41	43
Amalgamated Union of Building Trade Workers	89	15	17
National Union of Boot and Shoe Operatives	88	54	62
Railway Clerks' Association . .	87	73	83
National Union of Printing, Book-binding and Paper Workers .	84	—	—
United Boilermakers and Iron and Steel Shipbuilders . . .	82	26	31
20 National Union of Dyers, Bleachers and Textile Workers . . .	74	29	39
Associated Society of Locomotive Engineers and Firemen . .	72	26	36
Amalgamated Weavers' Association	72	*	*
National Society of Painters . .	68	3	4
Amalgamated Union of Foundry Workers	63	26	41
National Union of Furnishing Trades Operatives	55	2	4
National Union of Seamen . .	55	7	13
Post Office Engineering Union .	53	—	—
Plumbing Trades Union. . .	49	—	—
Confederation of Health Service Employees	45	5	12
30 Typographical Association . .	43	14	33
Association of Engineering and Ship-building Draughtsmen . .	42	16	39
Amalgamated Association of Card, Blowing and Ring Room Opera-tives	41	*	*
National Federation of Insurance Workers	41	—	—
National Union of Sheet Metal Workers	38	11	28
National Union of Vehicle Builders .	37	16	44
Inland Revenue Staff Federation .	35	—	—
National Union of Enginemen and Firemen	33	—	—
Clerical and Administrative Workers' Union	32	25	8
National Amalgamated Trade Society of Operative Printers and Assistants	29	22	76
40 National Society of Metal Mechanics	29	12	40
Shipconstructors' and Shipwrights' Association	28	1	3
National Union of Hosiery Workers .	28	—	—

	T.U.C.	L.P.	per cent
	(Thousands)		
Amalgamated Society of Woodcutting Machinists	28	—	—
Amalgamated Union of Bakers and Confectioners	28	105	38
National Association of Theatrical and Kine Employees . . .	26	—	—
National Union of Bank Employees .	25	—	—
National Society of Pottery Workers	23	12	53
Tobacco Workers' Union . .	23	—	—
Chemical Workers' Union . .	22	—	—
50 Fire Brigades Union . . .	21	4	20
National Union of Blastfurnacemen .	19	10.6	56
Scottish Horse and Motormen . .	19	2.5	13
Guild of Insurance Officials . .	19	—	—
Amalgamated Association of Operative Cotton Spinners . . .	19	*	*
Musicians' Union . . .	17	—	—
Ministry of Labour Staff Association .	17	—	—
Association of Scientific Workers .	17	—	—
Constructional Engineering Union .	16	5.5	34
National Association of Colliery Overmen	16	—	—
60 National Association of Operative Plasterers	16	8.7	55

*Affiliated to Labour Party via United Textile Factory Workers' Association (101,000).

BIBLIOGRAPHY

For the general history of the Labour Movement during the period covered by this volume see :—

G. D. H. Cole and Raymond Postgate	*The Common People, 1746–1946.*
G. D. H. Cole	*A Short History of the British Working-class Movement* (revised 1948).
M. Beer	*A History of British Socialism* (2 vols., 1920–21).
Margaret Cole	*Makers of the Labour Movement* (1948).

For the earlier history of the Labour Party and of previous movements for Labour representation see :—

G. D. H. Cole	*British Working-class Politics, 1832–1914.*
A. W. Humphrey	*History of Labour Representation.*
K. Hutchison	*Labour in Politics*
Joseph Clayton	*The Rise and Decline of Socialism in Great Britain.*
W. Stewart	*Life of Keir Hardie.*
G. D. H. Cole	*Keir Hardie* (Fabian booklet).
G. D. H. Cole	*John Burns* (Fabian booklet).

For the Labour Party in the period covered by this volume see :—

M. A. Hamilton	*Life of Arthur Henderson.*
M. A. Hamilton	*Sidney and Beatrice Webb.*
Margaret Cole	*Beatrice Webb.*
Philip Snowden	*Autobiography* (2 vols.).
J. R. Clynes	*Memoirs* (2 vols.).
Lord Elton	*Life of Ramsay MacDonald* (to 1919).
H. H. Tiltman	*James Ramsay MacDonald* (to 1929).
L. MacNeill Weir	*The Tragedy of Ramsay MacDonald* (to 1931).
A. Fenner Brockway	*Socialism over Sixty Years* (Life of F. W. Jowett).
A. Fenner Brockway	*Inside the Left.*
Various Authors	*The Book of the Labour Party* (1925).
E. Wertheimer	*Portrait of the Labour Party* (1929).
C. R. Attlee	*The Labour Party in Perspective* (1937).
D. E. McHenry	*The Labour Party in Transition, 1931–1938* (1938).
W. P. Maddox	*Foreign Relations in British Labour Politics* (1934).
Hugh Dalton	*Practical Socialism for Britain* (1935).
G. D. H. Cole	*The Simple Case for Socialism* (1935).
Douglas Jay	*The Socialist Case* (Revised 1947).
G. D. H. Cole	*The People's Front* (1937).
G. D. H. Cole	*A Plan for Democratic Britain* (1939).
M. A. Hamilton	*The Labour Party Today* (about 1939).

John Price	*Labour and the War* (1940).
Populus (G. D. H. Cole)	*My Dear Churchill* (1941).
Ernest Bevin	*The Job to be Done* (1942).
E. Shinwell	*The Britain I Want* (1943).
Herbert Morrison	*Prospects and Policies* (1943).
Herbert Morrison	*Looking Forward* (1943).
G. D. H. Cole	*Fabian Socialism* (1943).
Brian Barker	*Labour in London* (1946).
J. E. D. Hall	*Labour's First Year* (1947).
Michael Young	*Labour's Plan for Plenty* (1947).
John Parker	*Labour Marches On* (1947).

For the Communist point of view see :—

A. Hutt	*Post-war History of the British Working-class* (1937).
T. Bell	*Short History of the British Communist Party* (1937).
Harry Pollitt	*Serving my Time* (1940).

For other hostile criticism see :—

J. Scanlon	*The Decline and Fall of the Labour Party.*
J. Scanlon	*Pillars of Cloud* (1936).

For the contemporary history of Trade Unionism and Co-operation see :—

S. and B. Webb	*History of Trade Unionism* (revised 1920).
G. D. H. Cole and others	*British Trade Unionism Today* (1939).
N. Barou	*British Trade Unions* (1947).
G. D. H. Cole	*A Century of Co-operation* (1945).
G. D. H. Cole	*The Co-ops and Labour* (London Co-operative Society, 1945).

Many of the publications of the New Fabian Research Bureau 1931–9) and of the Fabian Society (especially after 1939) are also important for the study of Labour policy and its development. Here are a few of the most important :—

New Fabian Research Bureau Research Series.—15 *Socialist Credit Policy*, by E. F. M. Durbin ; 18 *Marketing Boards*, by M. Philips Price ; 22 *A Socialist Budget*, by Colin Clark ; 31 *Nutrition*, by Barbara Drake ; 33 *How Much Compensation?* by Ernest Davies ; 34 *The Forty-hour Week*, by Michael Stewart ; 38 *The City Today*, by A Citizen ; 42 *Living Wages*, by G. D. H. Cole.

Fabian Society Research Series.—45 *Planned Investment*, by C. P. Mayhew ; 49 *The Health Services*, by R. B. Thomas ; 51 *The State and the Railways*, by Ernest Davies ; 59 *The Hospital Services*, by Somerville Hastings ; 61 *Labour in the Colonies* ; 68 *Management in Transition*, by Austen Albu ; 70 *The Nation's Land*, by L. Silkin ; 74 *Full Employment,* by Barbara Wootton ; 75 *International Action and the Colonies* ; 77 *Export Policy and Full Employment*, by E. F. Schumacher ; 79 *The Prevention of General Unemployment* ; 80 *Hunger and Health in the Colonies* ; 83 *Government and Industry* ; 85 *The International Post-war Settlement* ; 89 *Nurseries and Nursery Schools*, by Violet Creech-Jones ; 90 *The Education Act, 1944* ; 92 *Colonies and International Conscience* ; 93 *Fuel and Power* ; 94 *Reparations and the Future of German Industry*, by G. D. H. Cole ; 95 *British Transport*, by Ernest Davies ; 96 *The Farming Front* ; 101 *Palestine Controversy* ; 102 *The General Election, 1945, and After*, by Margaret Cole ; 103 *The British Gas Industry*, by Joan Mitchell ; 104 *Cotton—A Working Policy* ; 106 *Labour Control and De-control* ; 110 *The Rate for the Job*, by Margaret Cole ; 111 *The Reform of Local Government Finance*, by Michael Fogarty ; 118 *Secondary Education for All*, by Joan Thompson ; 120 *The Universities and the Future*.

Also the following, which are not numbered : *Socialists and the Empire*, by Rita Hinden ; *Labour's Colonial Policy*, by A. Creech-Jones ; *The Arts under Socialism*, by J. B. Priestley.

Fabian Society Tract Series.—62 *Parish and District Councils* ; 189 *Urban District Councils*, by C. M. Lloyd ; 191 *Borough Councils*, by C. R. Attlee ; 218 *The County Council*, by H. Samuels ; 256 *A Word on the Future to British Socialists* ; 257 *The Raw Material Controls*, by G. D. N. Worswick ; 258 *The Fabian Society Past and Present*, by G. D. H. Cole ; 260 *Small Savings* ; 261 *Dumbarton Oaks, A Fabian Commentary* ; 262 *The Future of Germany*, by Anne Whyte.

Fabian Society Discussion Series.—1 *Socialist Economic Planning*, by C. P. Mayhew ; 2 *Trade Unions in a Labour Britain*, by J. B. Jefferys ; 3 *Towards a Classless Society*, by H. D. Hughes.

Also the following among other books issued by the Fabian Society :—

Fabian Socialism, by G. D. H. Cole (1943).
The Socialisation of Iron and Steel (N.F.R.B., 1936).
Parliamentary Reform, by W. Ivor Jennings (N.F.R.B., 1934).
Plan for Africa, by Rita Hinden (1941).
Fabian Colonial Essays (1945).
Co-operation in the Colonies (1945).
Commodity Control by F. Lamartine Yates (1943).
Towards a Socialist Agriculture, ed. F. W. Bateson (1946).
Social Security, ed. W. A. Robson (1943).
Public Enterprise, ed. W. A. Robson (1937).

A CHRONOLOGICAL LIST OF LABOUR PARTY
PROGRAMMES, REPORTS, PAMPHLETS, etc., 1914–47

*Party Reports on Policy.
†Party Programmes and General Manifestos.
The main Party Programmes are given in capitals.

As the Labour Party's publications are in many cases undated, it has not been easy in all instances to assign them to the correct year. I have dated them as far as possible to correspond to the periods covered by the National Executive Committee's Annual Reports.

Up to 1918 the Labour Party issued but few publications of its own. Its Press and Publications Department was started, on a small scale, only at the end of 1917. During the first World War, most of the important pronouncements on Labour policy were issued either by the War Emergency Workers' National Committee, which dealt with current economic and social questions, or by the Joint Committee on Labour Problems after the War, which prepared the Labour plans for domestic reconstruction. The Labour Party did, however, itself issue the series of pronouncements on War Aims in which Labour's international policy was defined.

Shortly before the outbreak of war the Party issued two policy documents.

*The Labour Party and Electoral Reform (1913).
*The Labour Party and the Agricultural Problem (1914).

The more important publications of the Joint Committee on Labour Problems after the War included the following :—

*The Problem of Demobilisation.
*The Munitions Acts and the Restoration of Trade Union Customs.
*The Restoration of Trade Union Customs in Cases not Covered by the Munitions Acts.
*The Restoration of Trade Union Customs after the War.
*The Position of Women after the War.
*The Problem of Unemployment after the War.
*A Million New Houses after the War.
These were issued between 1916 and 1918.

In 1917 the Labour Party itself issued the following :—

*Labour Problems after the War.
*Memorandum on War Aims (various versions).
*Memorandum on the Issues of the War.
Report of the Special Committee to Inquire into the Clyde Deportations.

In 1917–18 Arthur Henderson wrote a series of pamphlets and booklets for the Party. These included the following :—

The Aims of Labour.
The Outlook for Labour.
Labour and an After-War Economic Policy.
A World Safe for Democracy.

In 1916 appeared the first issue of the *Labour Year Book*, under the joint auspices of the Labour Party, the Trades Union Congress, and the Fabian (subsequently Labour) Research Department—the third body doing most of the work. A second issue appeared in 1919, under the same auspices.

From 1918 onwards the Labour Party published on a much larger scale. It began in that year to issue a regular *Labour Party Bulletin* from its Information Department (founded in 1915). This *Bulletin* contained a number of important Reports on policy.

In January, 1918, appeared the first version of the Labour Party's first comprehensive statement of policy.

LABOUR AND THE NEW SOCIAL ORDER : A REPORT ON RECON-STRUCTION.—A revised version was issued in June, 1918, after approval of the statement by the Party Conference.

During 1918 and 1919 there appeared a number of Reports drawn up by the newly constituted Advisory Committees of the Party. These included :

Memoranda on International Labour Legislation.

Memoranda on Public Health. (The Ministry of Health, The Organisation of Preventative and Curative Medical Services and Hospitals, The Position of the General Practitioner in a Reorganised System of Public Health.)

Memoranda on Trade Policy and Finance. (Key Industries, the Capitalisation of Reserves, Labour Policy in relation to Bank Amalgamations and the Nationalisation of Banking.)

Memoranda on Agriculture. (Immediate Steps in Agricultural Reconstruction.)

Memoranda on the Machinery of Government. (The Civil and Political Status of Civil Servants.)

Memoranda on International Affairs. (The Problem of Austria–Hungary, India, Colonies, Freedom of the Seas, A League of Nations, Economic War after the War.)

Memoranda on Local Government. (Housing, Local Government Areas.)

Memoranda on Education. (Nursery Schools, Continued Education, The Juvenile Worker at the End of the War.)

From this point the publications of the Party can best be arranged under " Conference " years, i.e., the period between the Executive Committee's Annual Reports.

1918–19

The New Party Constitution.
The Principles of the Labour Party. By S. and B. Webb.
International Economic Policy. By Leonard Woolf.
The Peace Terms. By Arthur Henderson.
The Labour Party and the Peace Treaty : A Handbook for Speakers.
Labour and the Peace Treaty.
Labour Policy and the Famine.
Labour Women on International Legislation.

Women and the Labour Party.
The Organisation of Women within the Labour Party.
The Working Woman's House.

1919–20

*Control of Foreign Policy : Labour's Programme.
Memoranda on Industrial Legislation.
Handbook of Local Government for England and Wales.
*Labour's Russian Policy : Peace with Soviet Russia.
The White Terror in Hungary.
Report of the Labour Commission of Inquiry on Conditions in Ireland.
An Appeal to the British Nation : An Indictment of the Coalition Government.
* The Empire in Africa : Labour's Policy.
*Labour and the Milk Supply.
The Mines for the Nation.
The Nationalisation of the Coal Industry. By R. H. Tawney.
Workers' Control in the Coal-mining Industry. By Frank Hodges.
Irish Nationalism and Labour Internationalism. By Bernard Shaw.
The Capital Levy : How the Labour Party would Settle the War Debt.
By F. W. Pethick-Lawrence.
The Present State of the Poor Law. By C. M. Lloyd.
Trusts and the Public. By A.L.B.
Taxation. By J. A. Hobson.
Tariffs and the Worker. By Brougham Villiers.
Profit-sharing and Co-partnership. By E. R. Pease.

1920–1

Wages and Prices : A Reply to the Federation of British Industries. (Joint Committee on the Cost of Living, Trades Union Congress and Labour Party.)
*Unemployment : A Labour Policy. (Jointly with T.U.C.)
Labour and National " Economy." (Jointly with T.U.C.)
Labour and the Unemployment Crisis. (Jointly with T.U.C.)
Local Education Schemes.
* Unemployment, the Peace, and the Indemnity.
* The Labour Party and the Countryside.
The Government of the British Commonwealth of Nations. By H. D. Hall.
Labour and Afforestation. By A. H. Unwin.
The War for Coal and Iron. By D. F. Buxton.
Why a Tory Joined the Labour Party. By J. A. Lovat Fraser.
Labour and Ireland. By Arthur Henderson.
The Citizen's Charter. By Herbert Morrison.
The Two-shift System for Women and Young Persons.
Report of British Labour Delegation to Russia.

1921–2

The Labour Speaker's Handbook.
The Government of Greater London.
Unemployment Relief : the Government's Record and Labour Policy.

The Education and Training of Teachers.
Secondary Education for All. By R. H. Tawney.
*_Motherhood and Child Endowment._ (Jointly with T.U.C.)
*_The Labour Movement and the Hospital Crisis._ (Jointly with T.U.C.)
*_The Blind Persons Act._ (Jointly with T.U.C.)
*_Trade Boards and the Cave Report._ (Jointly with T.U.C.)

1922–3
Women's Work in the Labour Party.
Labour and the Ruhr.
*_Labour and the Liquor Trade._
Capitalism in the Pillory. (Jointly with T.U.C.)
National Health Insurance Medical Benefit. (Jointly with T.U.C.)
Sword-blades or Ploughshares ? By F. H. Rose. (Jointly with T.U.C.)
The Engineering Trades Dispute. (National Joint Council.)
Labour and the War Debt. (Jointly with T.U.C.)
The Labour Party. By F. W. Pethick-Lawrence.
Widowed Mothers' Pensions. By Rhys J. Davies.
The Woman's Burden. By F. W. Pethick-Lawrence.
The Labour Party and Agriculture. By Arthur Henderson.
Labour and Foreign Affairs. By Arthur Henderson.
How to Get Houses. By George Hicks.
Labour as the Children's Champion. By Somerville Hastings.

1923–4
†*Labour's Appeal to the Nation.*
Can Labour Rule ? Series.—1 *Labour Looking after Agriculture ;*
    2 *The New Spirit in Education ;* 3 *Labour and War Pensions ;* 4 *Labour
    and Industrial Peace ;* 5 *Housing ;* 6 *The Anglo-Soviet Treaties ;*
    7 *Towards a European Settlement ;* 8 *Legislation for the Worker ;*
    9 *Work for the Workless ;* 10 *Pensions for the Aged and the Mothers ;*
    11 *The Labour Government and the League of Nations Assembly.*
Labour's Great Record : The First Six Months of the Labour Government.
The Labour Year Book, 1924.

1924–5
Protocol or Pact ?
Labour and the Geneva Protocol.
The Land Question.
The Rich Man's Budget. By Philip Snowden.
Why Food is Dear.
Sweated Imports and International Labour Standards.
Local Government Handbook, 1924.
The Labour Year Book, 1925.

1925–6
*_Labour's Policy on Agriculture._
*_From Nursery School to University._
*_Guide to Widows', Orphans', and Old Age Pensions._
*_Education of Children over Eleven._ (Jointly with T.U.C.)
The Waste of Capitalism. (Jointly with T.U.C.)

Canada's Experiments in Public Ownership.
A Year of Tory Misgovernment.
The Tory Government's Pitiful Confession of Incapacity.
Mr. Baldwin Attacks Miners' Hours and Wages.
Coal and Commonsense (with T.U.C.).
What the Coal Commission Proposes (with T.U.C.).
Unemployment Insurance ; Principles of Labour Policy (with T.U.C.).
The Labour Year Book, 1926.
The Local Government Speaker's Handbook.

1926–7

*Labour and the Empire—Africa.
*On the Dole or Off.
Two Years of Tory Government.
What to Do with Britain's Workless Workers.
Education when Labour Rules Again.
Arbitrate! Arbitrate! Arbitrate !
The Origin of Chinese Hostility to Great Britain.
The Labour Party and the Nursing Profession.
The Tories and the House of Lords.
The Labour Year Book, 1927.

1927–8

†Labour and the Nation.
†*Labour and the Nation : Supplement on Banking and Currency Policy.*
The Latest Conservative Attack on the Unemployed.
How the Tory Government has Disappointed the Old Folk and the Widows.
The Surtax.
The Distress in South Wales.
* The Mining Situation : an Immediate Programme.
* Interim Report on Family Allowances and Child Welfare (with T.U.C.).
The Labour Year Book, 1928.

1928–9

†Labour and the Nation. Revised Edition.
Arbitration.
Safeguarding.
Wealth and Commonwealth. By Philip Snowden.
Women and the General Election.
*How to Conquer Unemployment.
The Freedom of the Seas.
Children First !
The Higher Rates Scheme Exposed.
Nationalisation : Some Facts.
The Party Constitution and Standing Orders.
Speakers' Handbook, 1929.

1929–30

Labour's Plan to Abolish the Slums. By Arthur Greenwood.
International Regulation of Women's Work.

The Open Door and the Protection of Women Workers.
The Widows', Orphans', and Old Age Pensions Act, 1929.
Guide to the Unemployment Insurance Act, 1930.
What is this " Empire Free Trade " ?
The Truth about Protection—the Worker Pays.
The Labour Year Book, 1930.

1930–1

What the Labour Government Has Done.
The Labour Government's Education Policy.
Mr. Snowden at the Exchequer. By John Wilmot.
The Menace of Protection. By Philip Snowden.
The Labour Year Book, 1931.

1931–2

Two Years of Labour Rule.
Labour and the Crisis.
Why a Labour Party ?
The League of Youth.
A New Appeal to the Young. By Herbert Morrison.
Smashing the Unemployed.
The Bread Tax. By Alfred Salter.
The Labour Speech and How to Make It. By F. Montague.
The People's Savings.
Socialism or Smash ! By R. B. Suthers.
Simple Simon. By R. B. Suthers.
The Socialist Goal. By Fred Henderson.
The People's Health. By Somerville Hastings.
The World Muddle. By W. N. Ewer and F. Williams.
Democracy and Finance. By Francis Williams.
Disarm !
Party Organisation.
The Labour Year Book, 1932.

1932–3

*Currency, Banking and Finance.
* The National Planning of Transport.
* The Reorganisation of the Electricity Supply Industry.
* The Land and the National Planning of Agriculture.
*Labour's Foreign Policy. By Arthur Henderson.
Labour in Action. By Arthur Henderson.
War and Socialism.
The Parable of the Water Tank.
The Communist Solar System.
The Labour Party and the I.L.P.
An Easy Outline of Modern Socialism. By Herbert Morrison.
Slums. By H. V. Morton.
A New Deal for the Farm Worker. By John Dugdale.
Labour's Call to Youth. By Maurice Webb.
Hitlerism (with T.U.C.).

Meerut—Release the Prisoners (with T.U.C.).
Workless (with T.U.C.).
Study-Guides Series.—1 *Banking and Finance ;* 2 *The Economic Situation ;* 3 *The Socialisation of Industry ;* 4 *Land and Agriculture ;* 5 *The Worker's Status in Industry.*
[*Labour Year Book* suspended.]

1933-4

* *The Colonial Empire.*
* *Socialism and the Condition of the People.*
* *Public Ownership and Compensation* (in Annual Report).
* *Import Boards* (in Annual Report).
* *Water Supply* (in Annual Report).
* *A State Health Service* (in Annual Report).
* *The Welfare of the Blind* (in Annual Report).
* *Parliament Procedure* (in Annual Report).
The Case for Socialism. By Fred Henderson.
Everyday Songs for Labour Singers.
Labour Outlaws War. By Arthur Henderson.
The Fatality of the National Government. By George Lansbury.
Immediate Steps Towards the New Order. By Arthur Greenwood.
The Ultimate Aims of the Labour Party. By Stafford Cripps.
Are You a Worker? By Stafford Cripps.
The Britain I Want to See. By Ernest Bevin.
Are We Heading for War? By Bernard Shaw.
Youth for Socialism. By Maurice Webb.
Hawkers of Death. By Philip Noel-Baker.
How Labour Will Save Agriculture.
County Council Fighting Points.
What is this Fascism ? (with T.U.C.).
Fascism the Enemy of the People (with T.U.C.).
Austrian Democracy under Fire. By Otto Bauer (with T.U.C.).
Peace and Freedom (with T.U.C.).
Labour and the Unemployment Bill (with T.U.C.).

1934-5

† FOR SOCIALISM AND PEACE.
* *Labour and Education.*
* *Currency, Banking and Finance* (revised).
* *Up with the Houses ! Down with the Slums !*
* *Fair Rents and No Profiteering.*
* *Water Supply* (revised).
* *Beet Sugar* (in Annual Report).
* *Tithes* (in Annual Report).
* *The Coal and Allied Industries* (in Annual Report).
* *Unemployment* (in Annual Report).
* *Local Government and Depressed Areas* (in Annual Report).
* *Broadcasting* (in Annual Report).
* *Air Raid Precautions* (in Annual Report).
* *Coal : the Labour Plan* (National Council of Labour).

*Cotton : the T.U.C. Plan of Socialisation (Trades Union Congress).
*Iron and Steel : The T.U.C. Plan of Socialisation (Trades Union Congress).
Labour's Financial Policy.
Labour and the Land.
A Nation Without Poverty.
The Case Against the " National " Government.
Nazis, Nazism, Nazidom.
Labour's Peace Policy. By Arthur Henderson.
Whither India ? By Morgan Jones.
What Labour Has Done for Agriculture. By George Dallas.
The Economic Planning of Agriculture. By Stafford Cripps.
London Under Socialist Rule. By Herbert Morrison.
Unemployment and the Distressed Areas. By Arthur Greenwood.
Trickery and Treachery of the " National " Government. By F. R. West.
The Position of the Middle-class Worker in the Transition to Socialism. By L. A. Benjamin.
Women in Industry.

1935-6

*The Demand for Colonial Territories and Equality of Economic Opportunity.
*The Blind Persons' Charter.
*Tithes (in Annual Report).
*Honours (in Annual Report).
*Local Government Administration (in Annual Report).
Labour and the Defence of Peace (National Council of Labour).
British Labour and Communism (National Council of Labour).
Socialism and Social Credit.
Protect the Nation's Mothers.
The Power of the Press.
The New Power in Politics.
Why the Banks should be Nationalised.
Malnutrition.
Women in Offices.
The Betrayal of Collective Security. By C. R. Attlee.
The Record of the Second Labour Government.
The " National " Government's Disarmament Record.
Labour and Sanctions. By Herbert Morrison.
Raw Materials and the Prevention of War. By Francis Williams.
The Sky's the Limit. By Francis Williams.
Fifty Points Against the " National " Government.
Fifty Reasons Why You Should Vote Labour.
What Socialism Will Really Mean to You. By L. A. Benjamin.

1936-7

†Labour's Immediate Programme.
*Labour's Plan for Pensions.
Labour's Policy for Coal and Power. By George Ridley.
Labour's Policy for Our Countryside. By Lord Addison.

Labour's Policy of Food for All. By T. Johnston.
Labour's Aims. By C. R. Attlee.
Your Britain.
*Interim Report on Distressed Areas.
Reports on Distressed Areas.—1 *West Cumberland ;* 2 *Durham and the North-east Coast ;* 3 *South Wales ;* 4 *Central Scotland ;* 5 *Lancashire.*
Nutrition and Food Supplies.
The Agony of Spain.
A Catholic Looks at Spain.
Madrid : Military Atrocities of the Rebels.
The Drama in Spain. By A. R. Oliveira (National Council of Labour).
Catholics and the Civil War in Spain (National Council of Labour).
The Witchcraft Trial in Moscow (National Council of Labour).
The Employment Assistance Regulations (National Council of Labour).
New Socialist Millions.
New Zealand's Progress under Socialism.
Unemployment Assistance Guide.
County Council Guide, 1936–7.
Party Loyalty : An Appeal to the Movement.
The Labour Party and the So-called " Unity " Campaign.

1937–8

†*International Policy and Defence* (National Joint Council).
*Labour's Fair Rent Policy (National Joint Council).
Labour and the Popular Front.
The Children's Charter.
Juvenile Employment and Unemployment.
Labour's National Peace Campaign.
Bread and Butter Politics.
A Trade Unionist's View of Politics.
Nazi Germany and Fascist Italy Have Invaded Spain.
The Conduct of Local Elections.
Unemployment Assistance Guide (revised).
Planning or Chaos. By Fred Henderson.
An Easy Outline of Modern Socialism.
Help Us to Build a Better Future (League of Youth).
Your Biggest Job (League of Youth).
We Say It Can be Done (League of Youth).
Your Peace (Your Britain, No. 2).
Farming and Food (Your Britain, No. 3).
We Saw in Spain.
Labour and the Crisis in Foreign Policy.
The Government's Air Muddle Exposed. By Hugh Dalton.
Socialism and Our Standard of Living.

1938–9

†*Labour's Claim to Government.*
Labour and the International Situation (September, 1938, Trades Union Congress).

This Dishonour Will Not Bring Us Peace.
Labour and Defence : the Truth.
The Menace to Peace and Democracy.
Labour's Claim to Power.
Labour and the International Situation (December, 1938. National Council of Labour).
*Labour's Plan for Oil from Coal.
The Nation's Wealth at the Nation's Service. By Douglas Jay.
Britain's Transport at Britain's Service. By Herbert Morrison.
Labour's Policy for the Schools.
Labour's Policy for A.R.P.
Unity—True or Sham ?
Socialism or Surrender : Britain Rejects the Popular Front.
Franco Bombs British Seamen. By Philip Noel-Baker.
Hitler's Threat to Czech Democracy.
Deal with the Real Causes of War. By C. R. Attlee.
Peace for Whose Time ? By Herbert Morrison.
Out of Their Own Mouths.
The Full Facts of the Czech Crisis.
Commonsense about Colonies. By Philip Noel-Baker.
Labour's Work for Youth.
Your Britain, No. 4, Municipal.
What the Spanish Government is Fighting For.
We Can Have Peace and Strength.
Conduct of Scottish Elections.
Labour Party Diary, 1939.
Pensions and You.

1939–40

*Labour and Defence : A Statement of Policy.
The Postponement of Elections.
The Electoral Truce.
Pensions and You.
Socialism for the Villages.
Labour Fights for Workmen's Compensation. By Jack Lawson.
An Emergency Tax on Wealth. By F. W. Pethick-Lawrence.
Arthur Greenwood Speaks for Labour.
Labour's Peace Aims. By C. R. Attlee.
The Labour Party, the War, and the Future. By H. J. Laski.
What are we Fighting For? By Herbert Morrison.
The Future of International Government. By Leonard Woolf.
The Children's Welfare in War-time. By Susan Lawrence.
Is This an Imperialist War?
Labour's War-time Work at Westminster.
The Shopping Basket in War-time.
*Labour, the War and the Peace : A Declaration of Policy.
Finland : the Criminal Conspiracy of Hitler and Stalin.
Finnish Facts.
Stalin's Men—About Turn !
Paying for the War. By Douglas Jay.

Commentary on " Labour's Peace Aims."
Socialist Singers and Socialist Songs.
The Labour Party Diary, 1940.

1940–1

Labour in the Government : Social Legislation in War-time.
Labour's Home Policy.
Your Labour Party.
The War and the Workers. By Ernest Bevin.
The Truth about the Means Test. By Ernest Bevin.
France at War. By Léon Blum.
Communist Activity in France.
Slavery under Hitler's New Order.
Rent Acts Guide. By G. Grant Mackenzie.
The People's Convention (National Council of Labour).
The Labour Party Diary, 1941 (and subsquent years).

1941–2

†THE OLD WORLD AND THE NEW SOCIETY.
The War and the Peace.
Civilian War Injuries.
These Things Shall Be ! Notes on the Restoration of Britain after the War.
Labour Looks Ahead.
The Social Services. By George Ridley.
The Railways : Restrospect and Prospect. By George Ridley.
Coal Between Two Wars. By James Griffiths.

1942–3

* *The Colonies.*
* *The Future of Local Government.*
* *Housing and Planning after the War.*
* *A National Service for Health.*
Labour's Fight for the Old Folks.
The Communist Party and the War.
The Communist Party and Subversive Movements.
The Labour Party and the Communist Party.
The Electoral Truce.
Labour on the March. By George Ridley.
India : What Now and What Next ? By George Ridley.
Never Again ! By Arthur Greenwood.
Spearhead of Humanity. By Herbert Morrison.
Square Meals and Square Deals. By Ernest Bevin.

1943–4

* *Our Land : The Future of Britain's Agriculture.*
* *The Nation's Food.* By Sir John Orr.
Wings for Peace : Labour's Policy for Post-war Flying.
Your Home, Planned by Labour.
Your Future.
Build Your Own Future.
Léon Blum before his Judges.

1944-5
† LET US FACE THE FUTURE.
*Coal and Power.
*The Public Operation of Transport (Trades Union Congress).
*Post-war Organisation of British Transport.
*Full Employment and Financial Policy.
*The International Post-war Settlement.
What is this Labour Party? By Morgan Phillips.
Party Organisation (revised).
Conduct of Parliamentary Elections (revised).
Interim Report on Party Organisation and Finance.
Observations on the Government's "White Papers" on Social Insurance, etc.
Herbert Morrison's Work in the War Government.
Ernest Bevin's Work in War-time.
Plan for Peace. By Ellen Wilkinson.
Village Life and the Labour Party. By Cicely McCall.
What Labour Has Done for London.

1945-6
Labour Keeps Its Word. By C. R. Attlee.
The Labour Party's Policy on Foreign Affairs. By Ernest Bevin.
National Insurance.
The Secret Battalion. By Harold Laski.
The Communist Party and Affiliation.
Labour's League of Youth.
The Difference.
What Labour Has Done. By C. R. Attlee.
Financing Labour's Plan. By Hugh Dalton.
Labour Discussion Series : Do's and Don't's for a Labour Discussion
    Group.—1 The Rise of the Labour Party; 2 Fair Shares of Scarce
    Goods; 3 The Bank of England and the Nation; 4 Local Government
    Reform; 5 Repeal of the Trade Disputes Act; 6 National Health
    Service, by Stephen Taylor; 7 Nationalisation of Coal.

1946-7
Labour's First Year : the Facts.
Britain's Foreign Policy. By C. R. Attlee and Ernest Bevin.
Foreign Affairs. By Ernest Bevin.
Labour's Economic Plan. By Herbert Morrison.
Food Shortage : the Facts.
Bread Rationing. By John Strachey.
The Government's Plans for 1946-7
How the Labour Party Works. By Sara Barker.
You Voted Left : You Did Right.
A Guide to Public Speaking. By Harold Croft.
The United Nations Charter Examined. By W. Arnold-Forster.
A Guide to the National Insurance Act, 1946. By Alban Gordon.
A Guide to the National Health Service Act, 1946. By H. Fitzgerald.
Labour Discussion Series.—8 The Labour Party and the Colonies, by
    Rita Hinden; 9 Is Woman's Place the Home?; 10 Nationalisation

of Transport, by Ernest Davies ;   11 *Approach to Foreign Policy ;*
12 *Town and Country Planning ;*   13 *Labour's Plan for 1947*, by
Douglas Jay ;   14 *How Russia Gets Output*, by R. B. Suthers ;
15 *Advance in Education*, by H. D. Hughes and G. D. Miller.

1947
   Fuel Crisis : the Facts.
   Cards on the Table : an Interpretation of Labour's Foreign Policy.
   Tell Britain the Facts.
   If the Tories Had Won. By Michael Foot.
   Some Questions for Country People.
   Electricity Transformed.
   ABC of the Crisis.
   Team Work for the Nation. By Herbert Morrison.
   A Guide to the Elements of Socialism. By G. D. H. Cole.
   Local Government Handbook Supplement, 1947–8.
   Guide to War Pensions.

INDEX

Abdication, the, 318
Aberdeen, 12, 445
Abnormal Importations Act, 272, 273
Abyssinia, 302, 306, 307, 318, 322, 323, 324, 326, 338
Acland, Sir Richard, 399, 401, 409 f., 410, 476
Adamson, William, 37, 85, 114, 128, 157, 159, 225, 228, 267, 313
Addison, Christopher, 226, 227, 228, 267, 328, 426, 427, 428, 472
Adler, Friedrich, 99, 100, 101
Advance, 364
Afforestation, 213
Agricultural Marketing Acts, 244, 337, 425
Agriculture, Labour Policy on, 56, 70, 150, 162, 207, 233, 244, 278, 296, 345, 419, 425
Air Force, International, proposed, 331, 346
— Raid Precautions, 357, 362, 363, 377, 396
— — Victims, Provision for, 388, 396
Albania, 319, 360
Alexander, A. V., 128, 157, 225, 226, 228, 267, 311, 383, 426, 427, 428, 473, 474
— of Yugoslavia, 292
Allen, Clifford, 136, 149, 265, 339
Allied Socialist Conferences, 22, 37 f., 42, 48, 97
Allighan, Garry, 476, 477
America. *See* United States
American Federation of Labor, 42, 98, 334
— Socialist Party, 134
Amritsar Massacre, 89
Amulree, Lord, 226, 267
Anarchism, 102
Anderson, W. C., 19, 20, 84
Angell, Norman, 265
Anglo-Soviet Organisations, 404
— — Trade Union Agreement, 178 f.
Anomalies Act, 245 f.
Anschluss, 319, 334, 353
Anti-Aircraft Defence, 357
Anti-Comintern Pact, 319, 334
Anti-Semitism, 309
Anti-Sweating Campaign, 60
Appeasement, 319 f., 320 ff., 334, 335, 360, 368 f., 416
Arbitration, Compulsory, 24, 385
—, International. *See* League of Nations *and* Geneva Protocol *and* Optional Clause.
Arcos Raid, 196 f.

Armaments Manufacture, Nationalisation of, 59, 346, 347
Armed Forces, Democratisation of, 347, 361, 396
Arnold, Lord, 226, 228
Asquith, H. H., 24, 25, 26, 27, 28, 30, 31, 157, 160
Assistance Board, 388. *See also* Unemployment Insurance
Astbury, Justice, 186
Atlantic Charter, 415 f., 420
Attlee, Clement R., 128, 149, 150, 157, 219, 220, 226 f., 233, 238, 267, 270, 273, 281, 288, 294, 307, 308, 311, 324, 325, 328, 333, 372, 378 f., 380, 383, 384, 387, 397, 418, 426, 427, 428, 461
Austerity, 463, 466, 467
Australian Labour Party, 421
Austria and Nazis, 319, 334, 353, 379
Austria-Hungary, 7, 17, 43
Austrian Civil War, 291
— Revolution, 43
— Socialist Party, 100, 132, 135, 291, 292
Ayles Resolution, 288
Ayles, Walter H., 288

Back-benchers, Relation to Government, 289, 472
Balance of Payments, 270, 272, 419, 461, 464, 466
Baldwin, Oliver, 242
—, Stanley, 152, 157, 180, 182, 184, 211, 253, 259, 260, 302, 304, 318, 327, 334
Balfour, A. J., 107
Baltic States, 370
Bank of England, 208, 211 ff., 213, 250, 252, 253, 256, 259, 273, 279, 280, 287, 337, 345, 424
— of France, 252, 253, 256, 259
Banking, Co-operative, 208
—, Municipal, 208
—, Socialisation of, 178, 200, 208 f., 211 f., 237, 278, 279 f., 287, 296, 347, 421, 424
Banks, Joint Stock, 252 ff., 280, 287, 337, 345, 346, 424
—, War-time Control of, 392
Barnard Castle, 5, 9, 11
Barnes, Alfred, 426, 427, 474
—, G. N., 4, 31, 36, 44, 87
Barrow-in-Furness, 10, 141
Bartlett, Vernon, 355
Bavarian Republic, 43, 89
Bedwellty, 230
Belgian Labour Party, 132, 134
— Refugees, 22

501